Title 6, United States Code

Domestic Security

Iron Press Publishing

TITLE 6—DOMESTIC SECURITY

PRIOR PROVISIONS

A prior Title 6, Surety Bonds, was enacted by act July 30, 1947, ch. 390, §1, 61 Stat. 646, and was repealed by act Sept. 13, 1982, Pub. L. 97–258, §5(b), 96 Stat. 1068, 1085.

Sections 1 to 5 were repealed by Pub. L. 92–310, title II, §203(1), June 6, 1972, 86 Stat. 202.

Section 1, acts July 30, 1947, ch. 390, 61 Stat. 646; Oct. 31, 1951, ch. 655, §13, 65 Stat. 715, related to custody of official bonds.

Section 2, act July 30, 1947, ch. 390, 61 Stat. 647, directed examination at least once every two years of sufficiency of sureties on official bonds.

Section 3, acts July 30, 1947, ch. 390, 61 Stat. 647; Sept. 3, 1954, ch. 1263, §15, 68 Stat. 1231, related to renewal of bonds and continuance of liability.

Section 4, act July 30, 1947, ch. 390, 61 Stat. 647, related to notice of delinquency of principal. The provisions of the section were reenacted by section 260 of Pub. L. 92–310, which was classified to section 497a of former Title 31. See section 3532 of Title 31, Money and Finance.

Section 5, act July 30, 1947, ch. 390, 61 Stat. 648, related to limitation of actions against sureties.

Sections 6 to 13 were repealed by Pub. L. 97–258, §5(b), Sept. 13, 1982, 96 Stat. 1068, 1085.

Section 6, acts July 30, 1947, ch. 390, 61 Stat. 648; Aug. 9, 1955, ch. 683, §2, 69 Stat. 620; June 6, 1972, Pub. L. 92–310, title II, §203(2), 86 Stat. 202, related to surety companies as sureties. See section 9304 of Title 31, Money and Finance.

Section 7, act July 30, 1947, ch. 390, 61 Stat. 648, related to appointment of agents and service of process with regards to surety companies as sureties. See section 9306 of Title 31.

Section 8, act July 30, 1947, ch. 390, 61 Stat. 649, related to deposit of copy of charter of surety company before transacting business under sections 6 to 13 of this title. See section 9305 of Title 31.

Section 9, act July 30, 1947, ch. 390, 61 Stat. 649, related to quarterly statements of surety companies filed with Secretary of the Treasury. See section 9305 of Title 31.

Section 10, act July 30, 1947, ch. 390, 61 Stat. 649, related to jurisdiction over surety companies with regards to suits on bonds. See section 9307 of Title 31.

Section 11, act July 30, 1947, ch. 390, 61 Stat. 649, provided sanctions for nonpayment of a judgment by surety company. See section 9305 of Title 31.

Section 12, act July 30, 1947, ch. 390, 61 Stat. 649, estopped a surety company to deny its corporate powers, etc. See section 9307 of Title 31.

Section 13, act July 30, 1947, ch. 390, 61 Stat. 650, provided for fining of surety companies for their failure to comply with law. See section 9308 of Title 31.

Section 14, acts July 30, 1947, ch. 390, 61 Stat. 650; Aug. 9, 1955, ch. 683, §1, 69 Stat. 618, which related to purchase of bonds to cover officers and employees of Federal Government, was repealed by Pub. L. 92–310, title II, §203(1), June 6, 1972, 86 Stat. 202.

Section 15, act July 30, 1947, ch. 390, 61 Stat. 650, which related to bonds and notes of United States in lieu of recognizance, stipulation, bond, guarantee, or undertaking and contractors' bonds, was repealed by Pub. L. 97–258, §5(b), Sept. 13, 1982, 96 Stat. 1068, 1085. See sections 9301 and 9303 of Title 31, Money and Finance.

CHAPTER 1—HOMELAND SECURITY ORGANIZATION

§ 101. Definitions

In this chapter, the following definitions apply:

(1) Each of the terms "American homeland" and "homeland" means the United States.

(2) The term "appropriate congressional committee" means any committee of the House of Representatives or the Senate having legislative or oversight jurisdiction under the Rules of the House of Representatives or the Senate, respectively, over the matter concerned.

(3) The term "assets" includes contracts, facilities, property, records, unobligated or unexpended balances of appropriations, and other funds or resources (other than personnel).

(4) The term "critical infrastructure" has the meaning given that term in section 5195c(e) of title 42.

(5) The term "Department" means the Department of Homeland Security.

(6) The term "emergency response providers" includes Federal, State, and local governmental and nongovernmental emergency public safety, fire, law enforcement, emergency response, emergency medical (including hospital emergency facilities), and related personnel, agencies, and authorities.

(7) The term "executive agency" means an executive agency and a military department, as defined, respectively, in sections 105 and 102 of title 5.

(8) The term "functions" includes authorities, powers, rights, privileges, immunities, programs, projects, activities, duties, and responsibilities.

(9) The term "intelligence component of the Department" means any element or entity of the Department that collects, gathers, processes, analyzes, produces, or disseminates intelligence information within the scope of the information sharing environment, including homeland security information, terrorism information, and weapons of mass destruction information, or national intelligence, as defined under section 401a(5) of title 50, except—

(A) the United States Secret Service; and

(B) the Coast Guard, when operating under the direct authority of the Secretary of Defense or Secretary of the Navy pursuant to section 3 of title 14, except that nothing in this paragraph shall affect or diminish the authority and responsibilities of the Commandant of the Coast Guard to command or control the Coast Guard as an armed force or the authority of the Director of National Intelligence with respect to the Coast Guard as an element of the intelligence community (as defined under section 401a(4) of title 50.[1]

(10) The term "key resources" means publicly or privately controlled resources essential to the minimal operations of the economy and government.

(11) The term "local government" means—

(A) a county, municipality, city, town, township, local public authority, school district, special district, intrastate district, council of governments (regardless of whether the council of governments is incorporated as a nonprofit corporation under State law), regional or interstate government entity, or agency or instrumentality of a local government;

(B) an Indian tribe or authorized tribal organization, or in Alaska a Native village or Alaska Regional Native Corporation; and

(C) a rural community, unincorporated town or village, or other public entity.

(12) The term "major disaster" has the meaning given in section 5122(2) of title 42.

(13) The term "personnel" means officers and employees.

(14) The term "Secretary" means the Secretary of Homeland Security.

(15) The term "State" means any State of the United States, the District of Columbia, the Commonwealth of Puerto Rico, the Virgin Islands, Guam, American Samoa, the Commonwealth of the Northern Mariana Islands, and any possession of the United States.

(16) The term "terrorism" means any activity that—

(A) involves an act that—

(i) is dangerous to human life or potentially destructive of critical infrastructure or key resources; and

(ii) is a violation of the criminal laws of the United States or of any State or other subdivision of the United States; and

(B) appears to be intended—

(i) to intimidate or coerce a civilian population;

(ii) to influence the policy of a government by intimidation or coercion; or

(iii) to affect the conduct of a government by mass destruction, assassination, or kidnapping.

(17)(A) The term "United States", when used in a geographic sense, means any State of the United States, the District of Columbia, the Commonwealth of Puerto Rico, the Virgin Islands, Guam, American Samoa, the Commonwealth of the Northern Mariana Islands, any possession of the United States, and any waters within the jurisdiction of the United States.

(B) Nothing in this paragraph or any other provision of this chapter shall be construed to modify the definition of "United States" for the purposes of the Immigration and Nationality Act [8 U.S.C. 1101 et seq.] or any other immigration or nationality law.

(18) The term "voluntary preparedness standards" means a common set of criteria for preparedness, disaster management, emergency management, and business continuity programs, such as the American National Standards Institute's National Fire Protection Association Standard on Disaster/Emergency Management and Business Continuity Programs (ANSI/NFPA 1600).

[1] So in original. A closing parenthesis probably should precede the period.

(Pub. L. 107–296, § 2, Nov. 25, 2002, 116 Stat. 2140; Pub. L. 109–295, title VI, § 612(d), Oct. 4, 2006, 120 Stat. 1410; Pub. L. 109–347, title VI, § 613, Oct. 13, 2006, 120 Stat. 1943; Pub. L. 110–53, title V, § 502(a), title IX, § 901(d), Aug. 3, 2007, 121 Stat. 310, 371.)

REFERENCES IN TEXT

This chapter, referred to in text, was in the original "this Act", meaning Pub. L. 107–296, Nov. 25, 2002, 116 Stat. 2135, known as the Homeland Security Act of 2002, which is classified principally to this chapter. For complete classification of this Act to the Code, see Short Title note set out below and Tables.

The Immigration and Nationality Act, referred to in par. (17)(B), is act June 27, 1952, ch. 477, 66 Stat. 163, as amended, which is classified principally to chapter 12 (§ 1101 et seq.) of Title 8, Aliens and Nationality. For complete classification of this Act to the Code, see Short Title note set out under section 1101 of Title 8 and Tables.

AMENDMENTS

2007—Pars. (9) to (17). Pub. L. 110–53, § 502(a), added par. (9) and redesignated former pars. (9) to (16) as (10) to (17), respectively.

Par. (18). Pub. L. 110–53, § 901(d), added par. (18).

2006—Par. (6). Pub. L. 109–347 inserted "governmental and nongovernmental" after "local".

Pub. L. 109–295 inserted "fire," after "safety,".

EFFECTIVE DATE

Pub. L. 107–296, § 4, Nov. 25, 2002, 116 Stat. 2142, provided that: "This Act [see Tables for classification] shall take effect 60 days after the date of enactment [Nov. 25, 2002]."

SHORT TITLE OF 2008 AMENDMENT

Pub. L. 110–412, § 1, Oct. 14, 2008, 122 Stat. 4336, provided that: "This Act [amending section 609 of this title] may be cited as the 'Personnel Reimbursement for Intelligence Cooperation and Enhancement of Homeland Security Act of 2008' or the 'PRICE of Homeland Security Act'."

SHORT TITLE OF 2007 AMENDMENT

Pub. L. 110–53, § 1(a), Aug. 3, 2007, 121 Stat. 266, provided that: "This Act [see Tables for classification] may be cited as the 'Implementing Recommendations of the 9/11 Commission Act of 2007'."

SHORT TITLE OF 2006 AMENDMENT

Pub. L. 109–295, title VI, § 671(a), Oct. 4, 2006, 120 Stat. 1433, provided that: "This section [enacting subchapter XIII of this chapter] may be cited as the '21st Century Emergency Communications Act of 2006'."

SHORT TITLE OF 2004 AMENDMENTS

Pub. L. 108–458, title VII, § 7001, Dec. 17, 2004, 118 Stat. 3775, provided that: "This title [see Tables for classification] may be cited as the '9/11 Commission Implementation Act of 2004'."

Pub. L. 108–458, title VIII, § 8301, Dec. 17, 2004, 118 Stat. 3867, provided that: "This subtitle [subtitle C

(§§ 8301–8306) of title VIII of Pub. L. 108–458, amending sections 111, 142, and 345 of this title and section 8I of the Inspector General Act of 1978, Pub. L. 95–452, set out in the Appendix to Title 5, Government Organization and Employees, and enacting provisions set out as a note under section 112 of this title] may be cited as the 'Homeland Security Civil Rights and Civil Liberties Protection Act of 2004'."

Pub. L. 108–330, § 1, Oct. 16, 2004, 118 Stat. 1275, provided that: "This Act [amending sections 113, 342, and 454 of this title and sections 901 and 3516 of Title 31, Money and Finance, and enacting provisions set out as notes under section 342 of this title and sections 901 and 3516 of Title 31] may be cited as 'Department of Homeland Security Financial Accountability Act'."

SHORT TITLE OF 2003 AMENDMENT

Pub. L. 108–7, div. L, Feb. 20, 2003, 117 Stat. 532, provided in part that: "This division [enacting sections 103 and 552a of this title and section 8I of the Inspector General Act of 1978, Pub. L. 95–452, set out in the Appendix to Title 5, Government Organization and Employees, amending sections 113, 162, 164, 188, 395, 453, and 551 of this title, section 8D of the Inspector General Act of 1978, sections 1103 and 1356 of Title 8, Aliens and Nationality, and section 300aa–33 of Title 42, The Public Health and Welfare, redesignating section 8I of the Inspector General Act of 1978 as section 8J, repealing section 371 of this title and former section 8J of the Inspector General Act of 1978, enacting provisions set out as notes under section 521 of this title, section 1356 of Title 8, and section 300aa–33 of Title 42, and repealing provisions set out as a note under section 300aa–33 of Title 42] may be cited as the 'Homeland Security Act Amendments of 2003'."

SHORT TITLE

Pub. L. 107–296, § 1(a), Nov. 25, 2002, 116 Stat. 2135, provided that: "This Act [see Tables for classification] may be cited as the 'Homeland Security Act of 2002'."

Pub. L. 107–296, title II, § 211, Nov. 25, 2002, 116 Stat. 2150, provided that: "This subtitle [subtitle B (§§ 211–215) of title II of Pub. L. 107–296, enacting part B of subchapter II of this chapter] may be cited as the 'Critical Infrastructure Information Act of 2002'."

Pub. L. 107–296, title VIII, § 861, Nov. 25, 2002, 116 Stat. 2238, provided that: "This subtitle [subtitle G (§§ 861–865) of title VIII of Pub. L. 107–296, enacting part G of subchapter VIII of this chapter] may be cited as the 'Support Anti-terrorism by Fostering Effective Technologies Act of 2002' or the 'SAFETY Act'."

For short title of part I of subchapter VIII of this chapter as the "Homeland Security Information Sharing Act", see section 481(a) of this title.

Pub. L. 107–296, title X, § 1001(a), Nov. 25, 2002, 116 Stat. 2259, provided that: "This title [enacting subchapter X of this chapter and sections 3531 to 3537 and 3538 of Title 44, Public Printing and Documents, amending section 2224 of Title 10, Armed Forces, sections 278g–3 and 278g–4 of Title 15, Commerce and Trade, section 11331 of Title 40, Public Buildings, Property, and Works, and sections 3504 to 3506 of Title 44, and repealing section 11332 of Title 40 and provisions set out as notes under section 3531 of Title 44] may be cited as the 'Federal Information Security Management Act of 2002'."

[For another Federal Information Security Management Act of 2002, see section 301(a) of Pub. L. 107–347, title III, Dec. 17, 2002, 116 Stat. 2946, set out as a note under section 101 of Title 44, Public Printing and Documents.]

NATIONAL COMMISSION ON TERRORIST ATTACKS UPON THE UNITED STATES

Pub. L. 107–306, title VI, Nov. 27, 2002, 116 Stat. 2408, as amended by Pub. L. 108–207, § 1, Mar. 16, 2004, 118 Stat. 556, provided that:

"SEC. 601. ESTABLISHMENT OF COMMISSION.

"There is established in the legislative branch the National Commission on Terrorist Attacks Upon the United States (in this title referred to as the 'Commission').

"SEC. 602. PURPOSES.

"The purposes of the Commission are to—

"(1) examine and report upon the facts and causes relating to the terrorist attacks of September 11, 2001, occurring at the World Trade Center in New York, New York, in Somerset County, Pennsylvania, and at the Pentagon in Virginia;

"(2) ascertain, evaluate, and report on the evidence developed by all relevant governmental agencies regarding the facts and circumstances surrounding the attacks;

"(3) build upon the investigations of other entities, and avoid unnecessary duplication, by reviewing the findings, conclusions, and recommendations of—

"(A) the Joint Inquiry of the Select Committee on Intelligence of the Senate and the Permanent Select Committee on Intelligence of the House of Representatives regarding the terrorist attacks of September 11, 2001, (hereinafter in this title referred to as the 'Joint Inquiry'); and

"(B) other executive branch, congressional, or independent commission investigations into the terrorist attacks of September 11, 2001, other terrorist attacks, and terrorism generally;

"(4) make a full and complete accounting of the circumstances surrounding the attacks, and the extent of the United States' preparedness for, and immediate response to, the attacks; and

"(5) investigate and report to the President and Congress on its findings, conclusions, and recommendations for corrective measures that can be taken to prevent acts of terrorism.

"SEC. 603. COMPOSITION OF COMMISSION.

"(a) MEMBERS.—The Commission shall be composed of 10 members, of whom—

"(1) 1 member shall be appointed by the President, who shall serve as chairman of the Commission;

"(2) 1 member shall be appointed by the leader of the Senate (majority or minority leader, as the case may be) of the Democratic Party, in consultation with the leader of the House of Representatives (majority or minority leader, as the case may be) of the Democratic Party, who shall serve as vice chairman of the Commission;

"(3) 2 members shall be appointed by the senior member of the Senate leadership of the Democratic Party;

"(4) 2 members shall be appointed by the senior member of the leadership of the House of Representatives of the Republican Party;

"(5) 2 members shall be appointed by the senior member of the Senate leadership of the Republican Party; and

"(6) 2 members shall be appointed by the senior member of the leadership of the House of Representatives of the Democratic Party.

"(b) QUALIFICATIONS; INITIAL MEETING.—

"(1) POLITICAL PARTY AFFILIATION.—Not more than 5 members of the Commission shall be from the same political party.

"(2) NONGOVERNMENTAL APPOINTEES.—An individual appointed to the Commission may not be an officer or employee of the Federal Government or any State or local government.

"(3) OTHER QUALIFICATIONS.—It is the sense of Congress that individuals appointed to the Commission should be prominent United States citizens, with national recognition and significant depth of experience in such professions as governmental service, law enforcement, the armed services, law, public administration, intelligence gathering, commerce (including aviation matters), and foreign affairs.

"(4) DEADLINE FOR APPOINTMENT.—All members of the Commission shall be appointed on or before December 15, 2002.

"(5) INITIAL MEETING.—The Commission shall meet and begin the operations of the Commission as soon as practicable.

"(c) QUORUM; VACANCIES.—After its initial meeting, the Commission shall meet upon the call of the chairman or a majority of its members. Six members of the Commission shall constitute a quorum. Any vacancy in the Commission shall not affect its powers, but shall be filled in the same manner in which the original appointment was made.

"SEC. 604. FUNCTIONS OF COMMISSION.

"(a) IN GENERAL.—The functions of the Commission are to—

"(1) conduct an investigation that—

"(A) investigates relevant facts and circumstances relating to the terrorist attacks of September 11, 2001, including any relevant legislation, Executive order, regulation, plan, policy, practice, or procedure; and

"(B) may include relevant facts and circumstances relating to—

"(i) intelligence agencies;

"(ii) law enforcement agencies;

"(iii) diplomacy;

"(iv) immigration, nonimmigrant visas, and border control;

"(v) the flow of assets to terrorist organizations;

"(vi) commercial aviation;

"(vii) the role of congressional oversight and resource allocation; and

"(viii) other areas of the public and private sectors determined relevant by the Commission for its inquiry;

"(2) identify, review, and evaluate the lessons learned from the terrorist attacks of September 11, 2001, regarding the structure, coordination, management policies, and procedures of the Federal Government, and, if appropriate, State and local governments and nongovernmental entities, relative to detecting, preventing, and responding to such terrorist attacks; and

"(3) submit to the President and Congress such reports as are required by this title containing such findings, conclusions, and recommendations as the Commission shall determine, including proposing organization, coordination, planning, management arrangements, procedures, rules, and regulations.

"(b) RELATIONSHIP TO INTELLIGENCE COMMITTEES' INQUIRY.—When investigating facts and circumstances relating to the intelligence community, the Commission shall—

"(1) first review the information compiled by, and the findings, conclusions, and recommendations of, the Joint Inquiry; and

"(2) after that review pursue any appropriate area of inquiry if the Commission determines that—

"(A) the Joint Inquiry had not investigated that area;

"(B) the Joint Inquiry's investigation of that area had not been complete; or

"(C) new information not reviewed by the Joint Inquiry had become available with respect to that area.

"SEC. 605. POWERS OF COMMISSION.

"(a) IN GENERAL.—

"(1) HEARINGS AND EVIDENCE.—The Commission or, on the authority of the Commission, any subcommittee or member thereof, may, for the purpose of carrying out this title—

"(A) hold such hearings and sit and act at such times and places, take such testimony, receive such evidence, administer such oaths; and

"(B) subject to paragraph (2)(A), require, by subpoena or otherwise, the attendance and testimony of such witnesses and the production of such books, records, correspondence, memoranda, papers, and documents, as the Commission or such designated subcommittee or designated member may determine advisable.

"(2) SUBPOENAS.—

"(A) ISSUANCE.—

"(i) IN GENERAL.—A subpoena may be issued under this subsection only—

"(I) by the agreement of the chairman and the vice chairman; or

"(II) by the affirmative vote of 6 members of the Commission.

"(ii) SIGNATURE.—Subject to clause (i), subpoenas issued under this subsection may be issued under the signature of the chairman or any member designated by a majority of the Commission, and may be served by any person designated by the chairman or by a member designated by a majority of the Commission.

"(B) ENFORCEMENT.—

"(i) IN GENERAL.—In the case of contumacy or failure to obey a subpoena issued under subsection (a), the United States district court for the judicial district in which the subpoenaed person resides, is served, or may be found, or where the subpoena is returnable, may issue an order requiring such person to appear at any designated place to testify or to produce documentary or other evidence. Any failure to obey the order of the court may be punished by the court as a contempt of that court.

"(ii) ADDITIONAL ENFORCEMENT.—In the case of any failure of any witness to comply with any subpoena or to testify when summoned under authority of this section, the Commission may, by majority vote, certify a statement of fact constituting such failure to the appropriate United States attorney, who may bring the matter before the grand jury for its action, under the same statutory authority and procedures as if the United States attorney had received a certification under sections 102 through 104 of the Revised Statutes of the United States (2 U.S.C. 192 through 194).

"(b) CONTRACTING.—The Commission may, to such extent and in such amounts as are provided in appropriation Acts, enter into contracts to enable the Commission to discharge its duties under this title.

"(c) INFORMATION FROM FEDERAL AGENCIES.—

"(1) IN GENERAL.—The Commission is authorized to secure directly from any executive department, bureau, agency, board, commission, office, independent establishment, or instrumentality of the Government, information, suggestions, estimates, and statistics for the purposes of this title. Each department, bureau, agency, board, commission, office, independent establishment, or instrumentality shall, to the extent authorized by law, furnish such information, suggestions, estimates, and statistics directly to the Commission, upon request made by the chairman, the chairman of any subcommittee created by a majority of the Commission, or any member designated by a majority of the Commission.

"(2) RECEIPT, HANDLING, STORAGE, AND DISSEMINATION.—Information shall only be received, handled, stored, and disseminated by members of the Commission and its staff consistent with all applicable statutes, regulations, and Executive orders.

"(d) ASSISTANCE FROM FEDERAL AGENCIES.—

"(1) GENERAL SERVICES ADMINISTRATION.—The Administrator of General Services shall provide to the Commission on a reimbursable basis administrative support and other services for the performance of the Commission's functions.

"(2) OTHER DEPARTMENTS AND AGENCIES.—In addition to the assistance prescribed in paragraph (1), departments and agencies of the United States may provide to the Commission such services, funds, facilities, staff, and other support services as they may determine advisable and as may be authorized by law.

"(e) GIFTS.—The Commission may accept, use, and dispose of gifts or donations of services or property.

"(f) POSTAL SERVICES.—The Commission may use the United States mails in the same manner and under the same conditions as departments and agencies of the United States.

"SEC. 606. NONAPPLICABILITY OF FEDERAL ADVISORY COMMITTEE ACT.

"(a) IN GENERAL.—The Federal Advisory Committee Act (5 U.S.C. App.) shall not apply to the Commission.

"(b) PUBLIC MEETINGS AND RELEASE OF PUBLIC VERSIONS OF REPORTS.—The Commission shall—

"(1) hold public hearings and meetings to the extent appropriate; and

"(2) release public versions of the reports required under section 610(a) and (b).

"(c) PUBLIC HEARINGS.—Any public hearings of the Commission shall be conducted in a manner consistent with the protection of information provided to or developed for or by the Commission as required by any applicable statute, regulation, or Executive order.

"SEC. 607. STAFF OF COMMISSION.

"(a) IN GENERAL.—

"(1) APPOINTMENT AND COMPENSATION.—The chairman, in consultation with vice chairman, in accordance with rules agreed upon by the Commission, may appoint and fix the compensation of a staff director and such other personnel as may be necessary to enable the Commission to carry out its functions, without regard to the provisions of title 5, United States Code, governing appointments in the competitive service, and without regard to the provisions of chapter 51 and subchapter III of chapter 53 of such title relating to classification and General Schedule pay rates, except that no rate of pay fixed under this subsection may exceed the equivalent of that payable for a position at level V of the Executive Schedule under section 5316 of title 5, United States Code.

"(2) PERSONNEL AS FEDERAL EMPLOYEES.—

"(A) IN GENERAL.—The executive director and any personnel of the Commission who are employees shall be employees under section 2105 of title 5, United States Code, for purposes of chapters 63, 81, 83, 84, 85, 87, 89, and 90 of that title.

"(B) MEMBERS OF COMMISSION.—Subparagraph (A) shall not be construed to apply to members of the Commission.

"(b) DETAILEES.—Any Federal Government employee may be detailed to the Commission without reimbursement from the Commission, and such detailee shall retain the rights, status, and privileges of his or her regular employment without interruption.

"(c) CONSULTANT SERVICES.—The Commission is authorized to procure the services of experts and consultants in accordance with section 3109 of title 5, United States Code, but at rates not to exceed the daily rate paid a person occupying a position at level IV of the Executive Schedule under section 5315 of title 5, United States Code.

"SEC. 608. COMPENSATION AND TRAVEL EXPENSES.

"(a) COMPENSATION.—Each member of the Commission may be compensated at not to exceed the daily equivalent of the annual rate of basic pay in effect for a position at level IV of the Executive Schedule under section 5315 of title 5, United States Code, for each day during which that member is engaged in the actual performance of the duties of the Commission.

"(b) TRAVEL EXPENSES.—While away from their homes or regular places of business in the performance of services for the Commission, members of the Commission shall be allowed travel expenses, including per diem in lieu of subsistence, in the same manner as persons employed intermittently in the Government service are allowed expenses under section 5703(b) [5703] of title 5, United States Code.

"SEC. 609. SECURITY CLEARANCES FOR COMMISSION MEMBERS AND STAFF.

"The appropriate Federal agencies or departments shall cooperate with the Commission in expeditiously providing to the Commission members and staff appropriate security clearances to the extent possible pursuant to existing procedures and requirements, except that no person shall be provided with access to classified information under this title without the appropriate security clearances.

"SEC. 610. REPORTS OF COMMISSION; TERMINATION.

"(a) INTERIM REPORTS.—The Commission may submit to the President and Congress interim reports containing such findings, conclusions, and recommendations for corrective measures as have been agreed to by a majority of Commission members.

"(b) FINAL REPORT.—Not later than 20 months after the date of the enactment of this Act [Nov. 27, 2002], the Commission shall submit to the President and Congress a final report containing such findings, conclusions, and recommendations for corrective measures as have been agreed to by a majority of Commission members.

"(c) TERMINATION.—

"(1) IN GENERAL.—The Commission, and all the authorities of this title, shall terminate 30 days after the date on which the final report is submitted under subsection (b).

"(2) ADMINISTRATIVE ACTIVITIES BEFORE TERMINATION.—The Commission may use the 30-day period referred to in paragraph (1) for the purpose of concluding its activities, including providing testimony to committees of Congress concerning its reports and disseminating the final report.

"SEC. 611. FUNDING.

"(a) TRANSFER FROM THE NATIONAL FOREIGN INTELLIGENCE PROGRAM.—Of the amounts authorized to be appropriated by this Act [see Tables for classification] and made available in public law 107–248 [see Tables for classification] (Department of Defense Appropriations Act, 2003) for the National Foreign Intelligence Program, not to exceed $3,000,000 shall be available for transfer to the Commission for purposes of the activities of the Commission under this title.

"(b) ADDITIONAL FUNDING.—In addition to the amounts made available to the Commission under subsection (a) and under chapter 2 of title II of the Emergency Wartime Supplemental Appropriations Act, 2003 (Public Law 108–11; 117 Stat. 591), of the amounts appropriated for the programs and activities of the Federal Government for fiscal year 2004 that remain available for obligation, not more than $1,000,000 shall be available for transfer to the Commission for purposes of the activities of the Commission under this title.

"(c) DURATION OF AVAILABILITY.—Amounts made available to the Commission under this section shall remain available until the termination of the Commission."

§ 102. Construction; severability

Any provision of this chapter held to be invalid or unenforceable by its terms, or as applied to any person or circumstance, shall be construed so as to give it the maximum effect permitted by law, unless such holding shall be one of utter invalidity or unenforceability, in which event such provision shall be deemed severable from this chapter and shall not affect the remainder thereof, or the application of such provision to other persons not similarly situated or to other, dissimilar circumstances.

(Pub. L. 107–296, §3, Nov. 25, 2002, 116 Stat. 2141.)

§ 103. Use of appropriated funds

Notwithstanding any other provision of this chapter, any report, notification, or consultation addressing directly or indirectly the use of appropriated funds and stipulated by this chapter to be submitted to, or held with, the Congress or any Congressional committee shall also be submitted to, or held with, the Committees on Appropriations of the Senate and the House of Representatives under the same conditions and with the same restrictions as stipulated by this chapter.

(Pub. L. 107–296, title XVII, §1714, as added Pub. L. 108–7, div. L, §103(5), Feb. 20, 2003, 117 Stat. 529.)

REFERENCES IN TEXT

This chapter, referred to in text, was in the original "this Act", meaning Pub. L. 107–296, Nov. 25, 2002, 116 Stat. 2135, known as the Homeland Security Act of 2002, which is classified principally to this chapter. For complete classification of this Act to the Code, see Short Title note set out under section 101 of this title and Tables.

PRIOR PROVISIONS

A prior section 1714 of Pub. L. 107–296 amended section 300aa–33 of Title 42, The Public Health and Welfare, prior to repeal by Pub. L. 108–7, div. L, §102(a), Feb. 20, 2003, 117 Stat. 528.

NOTIFICATIONS FOR REPROGRAMMING OR TRANSFER OF FUNDS

Pub. L. 109–90, title V, §503(e), Oct. 18, 2005, 119 Stat. 2082, provided that: "Hereafter, notwithstanding any other provision of law, notifications pursuant to this section or any other authority for reprogramming or transfer of funds shall be made solely to the Committees on Appropriations of the Senate and the House of Representatives."

SUBCHAPTER I—DEPARTMENT OF HOMELAND SECURITY

§111. Executive department; mission

(a) Establishment

There is established a Department of Homeland Security, as an executive department of the United States within the meaning of title 5.

(b) Mission

(1) In general

The primary mission of the Department is to—

(A) prevent terrorist attacks within the United States;

(B) reduce the vulnerability of the United States to terrorism;

(C) minimize the damage, and assist in the recovery, from terrorist attacks that do occur within the United States;

(D) carry out all functions of entities transferred to the Department, including by acting as a focal point regarding natural and manmade crises and emergency planning;

(E) ensure that the functions of the agencies and subdivisions within the Department that are not related directly to securing the homeland are not diminished or neglected except by a specific explicit Act of Congress;

(F) ensure that the overall economic security of the United States is not diminished by efforts, activities, and programs aimed at securing the homeland;

(G) ensure that the civil rights and civil liberties of persons are not diminished by efforts, activities, and programs aimed at securing the homeland; and

(H) monitor connections between illegal drug trafficking and terrorism, coordinate efforts to sever such connections, and otherwise contribute to efforts to interdict illegal drug trafficking.

(2) Responsibility for investigating and prosecuting terrorism

Except as specifically provided by law with respect to entities transferred to the Department under this chapter, primary responsibility for investigating and prosecuting acts of terrorism shall be vested not in the Department, but rather in Federal, State, and local law enforcement agencies with jurisdiction over the acts in question.

(Pub. L. 107–296, title I, §101, Nov. 25, 2002, 116 Stat. 2142; Pub. L. 108–458, title VIII, §8302, Dec. 17, 2004, 118 Stat. 3867.)

REFERENCES IN TEXT

This chapter, referred to in subsec. (b)(2), was in the original "this Act", meaning Pub. L. 107–296, Nov. 25, 2002, 116 Stat. 2135, known as the Homeland Security Act of 2002, which is classified principally to this chapter. For complete classification of this Act to the Code, see Short Title note set out under section 101 of this title and Tables.

AMENDMENTS

2004—Subsec. (b)(1)(G), (H). Pub. L. 108–458 added subpar. (G) and redesignated former subpar. (G) as (H).

TRANSFER OF CERTAIN OPM AUTHORITY TO DEPARTMENT OF HOMELAND SECURITY

Pub. L. 109–295, title V, §513, Oct. 4, 2006, 120 Stat. 1378, provided that: "Notwithstanding any other provision of law, the authority of the Office of Personnel Management to conduct personnel security and suitability background investigations, update investigations, and periodic reinvestigations of applicants for, or appointees in, positions in the Office of the Secretary and Executive Management, the Office of the Under Secretary for Management, Analysis and Operations, Immigration and Customs Enforcement, the Directorate for Preparedness, and the Directorate of Science and Technology of the Department of Homeland Security is transferred to the Department of Homeland Security: *Provided*, That on request of the Department of Homeland Security, the Office of Personnel Management shall cooperate with and assist the Department in any investigation or reinvestigation under this section: *Provided further*, That this section shall cease to be effective at such time as the President has selected a single agency to conduct security clearance investigations pursuant to section 3001(c) of the Intelligence Reform and Terrorism Prevention Act of 2004 (Public Law 108–458; 50 U.S.C. 435b) and the entity selected pursuant to section 3001(b) of such Act has reported to Congress that the agency selected pursuant to such section 3001(c) is capable of conducting all necessary investigations in a timely manner or has authorized the entities within the Department of Homeland Security covered by this section to conduct their own investigations pursuant to section 3001 of such Act."

[For transfer of all functions, personnel, assets, components, authorities, grant programs, and liabilities of the Directorate for Preparedness, as constituted on June 1, 2006, including the functions of the Under Secretary for Preparedness relating thereto, to the Federal Emergency Management Agency, with certain exceptions, see section 315(a)(2), (b) of this title.]

Similar provisions were contained in the following prior appropriation acts:

Pub. L. 109–90, title V, §516, Oct. 18, 2005, 119 Stat. 2084.

Pub. L. 108–334, title V, §518, Oct. 18, 2004, 118 Stat. 1318.

EX. ORD. NO. 13286. AMENDMENT OF EXECUTIVE ORDERS, AND OTHER ACTIONS, IN CONNECTION WITH THE TRANSFER OF CERTAIN FUNCTIONS TO THE SECRETARY OF HOMELAND SECURITY

Ex. Ord. No. 13286, Feb. 28, 2003, 68 F.R. 10619, as amended by Ex. Ord. No. 13442, §1, Aug. 13, 2007, 72 F.R. 45877, provided:

By the authority vested in me as President by the Constitution and the laws of the United States of America, including the Homeland Security Act of 2002 (Public Law 107–296) [see Tables for classification] and section 301 of title 3, United States Code, and in order to reflect the transfer of certain functions to, and other responsibilities vested in, the Secretary of Homeland Security, the transfer of certain agencies and agency components to the Department of Homeland Security, and the delegation of appropriate responsibilities to the Secretary of Homeland Security, it is hereby ordered as follows:

SECTION 1. [Amended Ex. Ord. No. 13276, set out as a note under section 1182 of Title 8, Aliens and Nationality.]

SEC. 2. [Amended Ex. Ord. No. 13274, set out as a note under section 301 of Title 49, Transportation.]

SEC. 3. [Amended Ex. Ord. No. 13271, formerly set out as a note under section 509 of Title 28, Judiciary and Judicial Procedure.]

SEC. 4. [Amended and revoked Ex. Ord. No. 13260, set out as a note under section 402 of Title 50, War and National Defense.]

SEC. 5. [Amended Ex. Ord. No. 13257, set out as a note under section 7103 of Title 22, Foreign Relations and Intercourse.]

SEC. 6. [Amended Ex. Ord. No. 13254, set out as a note under section 12501 of Title 42, The Public Health and Welfare.]

SEC. 7. [Amended Ex. Ord. No. 13231, set out as a note under section 121 of this title.]

SEC. 8. [Amended Ex. Ord. No. 13228, set out as a note under section 402 of Title 50, War and National Defense.]

SEC. 9. [Amended Ex. Ord. No. 13223, set out as a note under section 12302 of Title 10, Armed Forces.]

SEC. 10. [Amended Ex. Ord. No. 13212, set out as a note under section 13201 of Title 42, The Public Health and Welfare.]

SEC. 11. [Amended Ex. Ord. No. 13165, set out as a note under section 1701 of Title 21, Food and Drugs.]

SEC. 12. [Amended Ex. Ord. No. 13154.]

SEC. 13. [Amended Ex. Ord. No. 13133.]

SEC. 14. [Amended Ex. Ord. No. 13120, set out as a note under section 12304 of Title 10, Armed Forces.]

SEC. 15. [Amended Ex. Ord. No. 13112, set out as a note under section 4321 of Title 42, The Public Health and Welfare.]

SEC. 16. [Amended Ex. Ord. No. 13100, set out as a note under section 341 of Title 21, Food and Drugs.]

SEC. 17. [Amended Ex. Ord. No. 13076, set out as a note under section 12304 of Title 10, Armed Forces.]

SEC. 18. [Amended Ex. Ord. No. 13011, set out as a note under section 11101 of Title 40, Public Buildings, Property, and Works.]

SEC. 19. [Amended Ex. Ord. No. 12989, set out as a note under section 1324a of Title 8, Aliens and Nationality.]

SEC. 20. [Amended Ex. Ord. No. 12985, set out as a note preceding section 1121 of Title 10, Armed Forces.]

SEC. 21. [Amended Ex. Ord. No. 12982, set out as a note under section 12304 of Title 10, Armed Forces.]

SEC. 22. [Amended Ex. Ord. No. 12978, listed in a table under section 1701 of Title 50, War and National Defense.]

SEC. 23. [Amended Ex. Ord. No. 12977, set out as a note under section 121 of Title 40, Public Buildings, Property, and Works.]

SEC. 24. [Amended Ex. Ord. No. 12919, set out as a note under section 2153 of Title 50, Appendix, War and National Defense.]

SEC. 25. [Amended Ex. Ord. No. 12906, set out as a note under section 1457 of Title 43, Public Lands.]

SEC. 26. [Amended Ex. Ord. No. 12870, set out as a note under section 4727 of Title 15, Commerce and Trade.]

SEC. 27. [Amended Ex. Ord. No. 12835, set out as a note under section 1023 of Title 15, Commerce and Trade.]

SEC. 28. [Amended Ex. Ord. No. 12830, set out as a note preceding section 1121 of Title 10, Armed Forces.]

SEC. 29. [Amended Ex. Ord. No. 12824, set out as a note under section 492 of Title 14, Coast Guard.]

SEC. 30. [Amended Ex. Ord. No. 12807, set out as a note under section 1182 of Title 8, Aliens and Nationality.]

SEC. 31. [Amended Ex. Ord. No. 12793, set out as a note preceding section 1121 of Title 10, Armed Forces.]

SEC. 32. [Amended Ex. Ord. No. 12789, set out as a note under section 1364 of Title 8, Aliens and Nationality.]

SEC. 33. [Amended Ex. Ord. No. 12788, set out as a note under section 2391 of Title 10, Armed Forces.]

SEC. 34. [Amended Ex. Ord. No. 12777, set out as a note under section 1321 of Title 33, Navigation and Navigable Waters.]

SEC. 35. [Amended Ex. Ord. No. 12743, formerly set out as a note under section 12302 of Title 10, Armed Forces.]

SEC. 36. [Amended Ex. Ord. No. 12742, set out as a note under section 82 of Title 50, War and National Defense.]

SEC. 37. [Amended Ex. Ord. No. 12733, set out as a note under section 12304 of Title 10, Armed Forces.]

SEC. 38. [Amended Ex. Ord. No. 12728, set out as a note under section 12305 of Title 10, Armed Forces.]

SEC. 39. [Amended Ex. Ord. No. 12727, set out as a note under section 12304 of Title 10, Armed Forces.]

SEC. 40. [Amended Ex. Ord. No. 12699, set out as a note under section 7704 of Title 42, The Public Health and Welfare.]

SEC. 41. [Amended Ex. Ord. No. 12657, set out as a note under section 5195 of Title 42, The Public Health and Welfare.]

SEC. 42. [(a) to (i) amended Ex. Ord. No. 12656, set out as a note under section 5195 of Title 42, The Public Health and Welfare.]

Without prejudice to subsections (a) through (i) of this section, all responsibilities assigned to specific Federal officials pursuant to Executive Order 12656 that are substantially the same as any responsibility assigned to, or function transferred to, the Secretary of Homeland Security pursuant to the Homeland Security Act of 2002 (regardless of whether such responsibility or function is expressly required to be carried out through another official of the Department of Homeland Security or not pursuant to such Act), or intended or required to be carried out by an agency or an agency component transferred to the Department of Homeland Security pursuant to such Act, are hereby reassigned to the Secretary of Homeland Security.

SEC. 43. [Amended Ex. Ord. No. 12580, set out as a note under section 9615 of Title 42, The Public Health and Welfare.]

SEC. 44. [Amended Ex. Ord. No. 12555, set out as a note under section 2602 of Title 19, Customs Duties.]

SEC. 45. [Amended Ex. Ord. No. 12501, set out as a note under section 4101 of Title 15, Commerce and Trade.]

SEC. 46. [Amended Ex. Ord. No. 12472, set out as a note under section 5195 of Title 42, The Public Health and Welfare.]

SEC. 47. [Amended Ex. Ord. No. 12382, set out as a note under section 901 of Title 47, Telegraphs, Telephones, and Radiotelegraphs.]

SEC. 48. [Amended Ex. Ord. No. 12341, set out as a note under section 1522 of Title 8, Aliens and Nationality.]

SEC. 49. [Amended Ex. Ord. No. 12208, set out as a note under section 1157 of Title 8, Aliens and Nationality.]

SEC. 50. [Amended Ex. Ord. No. 12188, set out as a note under section 2171 of Title 19, Customs Duties.]

SEC. 51. [Amended Ex. Ord. No. 12160, set out as a note under section 3501 of Title 42, The Public Health and Welfare.]

SEC. 52. [Amended Ex. Ord. No. 12148, set out as a note under section 5195 of Title 42, The Public Health and Welfare.]

SEC. 53. [Amended Ex. Ord. No. 12146, set out as a note under section 509 of Title 28, Judiciary and Judicial Procedures.]

SEC. 54. [Amended Ex. Ord. No. 12002, set out as a note under section 2403 of Title 50, Appendix, War and National Defense.]

SEC. 55. [Amended Ex. Ord. No. 11965, set out as a note preceding section 1121 of Title 10, Armed Forces.]

SEC. 56. [Amended Ex. Ord. No. 11926, set out as a note preceding section 1121 of Title 10, Armed Forces.]

SEC. 57. [Amended Ex. Ord. No. 11858, set out as a note under section 2170 of Title 50, Appendix, War and National Defense.]

SEC. 58. [Amended Ex. Ord. No. 11800, formerly set out as a note under section 301a of Title 37, Pay and Allowances of the Uniformed Services.]

SEC. 59. [Amended Ex. Ord. No. 11645, set out as a note under section 475 of Title 14, Coast Guard.]

SEC. 60. [Amended Ex. Ord. No. 11623, set out as a note under section 460 of Title 50, Appendix, War and National Defense.]

SEC. 61. [Amended Ex. Ord. No. 11448, set out as a note preceding section 1121 of Title 10, Armed Forces.]

SEC. 62. [Amended Ex. Ord. No. 11446, set out as a note under section 7342 of Title 5, Government Organization and Employees.]

SEC. 63. [Amended Ex. Ord. No. 11438, set out as a note under section 1124 of Title 10, Armed Forces.]

SEC. 64. [Amended Ex. Ord. No. 11366, set out as a note under section 12303 of Title 10, Armed Forces.]

SEC. 65. [Amended Ex. Ord. No. 11239, set out as a note under former section 1051 of Title 33, Navigation and Navigable Waters.]

SEC. 66. [Amended Ex. Ord. No. 11231.]

SEC. 67. [Amended Ex. Ord. No. 11190, set out as a note under section 10149 of Title 10, Armed Forces.]

SEC. 68. [Amended Ex. Ord. No. 11139.]

SEC. 69. [Amended Ex. Ord. No. 11079, set out as a note under section 2603 of Title 10, Armed Forces.]

SEC. 70. [Amended Ex. Ord. No. 11046, set out as a note under section 3746 of Title 10, Armed Forces.]

SEC. 71. [Amended Ex. Ord. No. 11016.]

SEC. 72. [Amended Ex. Ord. No. 10977.]

SEC. 73. [Amended Ex. Ord. No. 10789, set out as a note under section 1431 of Title 50, War and National Defense.]

SEC. 74. [Amended Ex. Ord. No. 10694.]

SEC. 75. [Amended Ex. Ord. No. 10637, set out as a note under section 301 of Title 3, The President.]

SEC. 76. [Amended Ex. Ord. No. 10631, set out as a note under section 802 of Title 10, Armed Forces.]

SEC. 77. [Amended Ex. Ord. No. 10554, set out as a note under section 772 of Title 10, Armed Forces.]

SEC. 78. [Amended Ex. Ord. No. 10499.]

SEC. 79. [Amended Ex. Ord. No. 10448.]

SEC. 80. [Amended Ex. Ord. No. 10271, set out as a note under section 471 of Title 50, Appendix, War and National Defense.]

SEC. 81. [Amended Ex. Ord. No. 10179.]

SEC. 82. [Amended Ex. Ord. No. 10163.]

SEC. 83. [Amended Ex. Ord. No. 10113, set out as a note under section 418 of Title 37, Pay and Allowances of the Uniformed Services.]

SEC. 84. [Amended Ex. Ord. No. 4601.]

SEC. 85. *Designation as a Defense Agency of the United States.*

I hereby designate the Department of Homeland Security as a defense agency of the United States for the purposes of chapter 17 of title 35 of the United States Code.

SEC. 86. *Exception from the Provisions of the Government Employees Training Act.*

Those elements of the Department of Homeland Security that are supervised by the Under Secretary of Homeland Security for Information Analysis and Infrastructure Protection through the Department's Assistant Secretary for Information Analysis are, pursuant to section 4102(b)(1) of title 5, United States Code, and in the public interest, excepted from the following provisions of the Government Employees Training Act as codified in title 5: sections 4103(a)(1), 4108, 4115, 4117, and 4118, and that part of 4109(a) that provides "under the regulations prescribed under section 4118(a)(8) of this title and".

SEC. 87. *Functions of Certain Officials in the Coast Guard.*

The Commandant and the Assistant Commandant for Intelligence of the Coast Guard each shall be considered a "Senior Official of the Intelligence Community" for purposes of Executive Order 12333 of December 4, 1981 [50 U.S.C. 401 note], and all other relevant authorities.

SEC. 88. *Order of Succession.*

Subject to the provisions of subsection (b) of this section, the officers named in subsection (a) of this section, in the order listed, shall act as, and perform the functions and duties of the office of, the Secretary of Homeland Security (Secretary), if they are eligible to act as Secretary under the provisions of the Federal Vacancies Reform Act of 1998, 5 U.S.C. 3345 *et seq.* (Vacancies Act), during any period in which the Secretary has died, resigned, or otherwise become unable to perform the functions and duties of the office of Secretary.

(a) Order of Succession.

(i) Deputy Secretary of Homeland Security;

(ii) Under Secretary for National Protection and Programs;

(iii) Under Secretary for Management;

(iv) Assistant Secretary of Homeland Security (Policy);

(v) Under Secretary for Science and Technology;

(vi) General Counsel;

(vii) Assistant Secretary of Homeland Security (Transportation Security Administration);

(viii) Administrator of the Federal Emergency Management Agency;

(ix) Commissioner of U.S. Customs and Border Protection;

(x) Assistant Secretary of Homeland Security (U.S. Immigration and Customs Enforcement);

(xi) Director of U.S. Citizenship and Immigration Services;

(xii) Chief Financial Officer;

(xiii) Regional Administrator, Region V, Federal Emergency Management Agency;

(xiv) Regional Administrator, Region VI, Federal Emergency Management Agency;

(xv) Regional Administrator, Region VII, Federal Emergency Management Agency;

(xvi) Regional Administrator, Region IX, Federal Emergency Management Agency; and

(xvii) Regional Administrator, Region I, Federal Emergency Management Agency.

(b) Exceptions.

(i) No individual who is serving in an office listed in subsection (a) in an acting capacity, by virtue of so serving, shall act as Secretary pursuant to this section.

(ii) Notwithstanding the provisions of this section, the President retains discretion, to the extent permitted by the Vacancies Act, to depart from this order in designating an acting Secretary.

SEC. 89. *Savings Provision.*

Except as otherwise specifically provided above or in Executive Order 13284 of January 23, 2003 ("Amendment of Executive Orders, and Other Actions, in Connection With the Establishment of the Department of Homeland Security") [6 U.S.C. 121 note], references in any prior Executive Order relating to an agency or an agency component that is transferred to the Department of Homeland Security ("the Department"), or relating to a function that is transferred to the Secretary of Homeland Security, shall be deemed to refer, as appropriate, to the Department or its officers, employees, agents, organizational units, or functions.

SEC. 90. Nothing in this order shall be construed to impair or otherwise affect the authority of the Secretary of Defense with respect to the Department of Defense, including the chain of command for the armed forces of the United States under section 162(b) of title 10, United States Code, and the authority of the Secretary of Defense with respect to the Department of Defense under section 113(b) of that title.

SEC. 91. Nothing in this order shall be construed to limit or restrict the authorities of the Central Intelligence Agency and the Director of Central Intelligence pursuant to the National Security Act of 1947 [see Short Title note set out under 50 U.S.C. 401] and the CIA Act of 1949 [probably means the Central Intelligence Agency Act of 1949, see Short Title note set out under 50 U.S.C. 403a].

SEC. 92. This order shall become effective on March 1, 2003.

SEC. 93. This order does not create any right or benefit, substantive or procedural, enforceable at law or in equity, against the United States, its departments, agencies, or other entities, its officers or employees, or any other person.

GEORGE W. BUSH.

[Reference to the Director of Central Intelligence or the Director of the Central Intelligence Agency in the Director's capacity as the head of the intelligence community deemed to be a reference to the Director of National Intelligence. Reference to the Director of Central Intelligence or the Director of the Central Intelligence Agency in the Director's capacity as the head of the Central Intelligence Agency deemed to be a reference to the Director of the Central Intelligence Agency. See section 1081(a) and (b) of Pub. L. 108–458, set out as a note under section 401 of Title 50, War and National Defense.]

EXECUTIVE ORDER NO. 13362

Ex. Ord. No. 13362, Nov. 29, 2004, 69 F.R. 70173, which designated additional officers for the Department of Homeland Security order of succession, was revoked by Ex. Ord. No. 13442, §2, Aug. 13, 2007, 72 F.R. 45878.

§ 112. Secretary; functions

(a) Secretary

(1) In general

There is a Secretary of Homeland Security, appointed by the President, by and with the advice and consent of the Senate.

(2) Head of Department

The Secretary is the head of the Department and shall have direction, authority, and control over it.

(3) Functions vested in Secretary

All functions of all officers, employees, and organizational units of the Department are vested in the Secretary.

(b) Functions

The Secretary—

(1) except as otherwise provided by this chapter, may delegate any of the Secretary's functions to any officer, employee, or organizational unit of the Department;

(2) shall have the authority to make contracts, grants, and cooperative agreements, and to enter into agreements with other executive agencies, as may be necessary and proper to carry out the Secretary's responsibilities under this chapter or otherwise provided by law; and

(3) shall take reasonable steps to ensure that information systems and databases of the Department are compatible with each other and with appropriate databases of other Departments.

(c) Coordination with non-Federal entities

With respect to homeland security, the Secretary shall coordinate through the Office of State and Local Coordination[1] (established under section 361 of this title) (including the provision of training and equipment) with State and local government personnel, agencies, and authorities, with the private sector, and with other entities, including by—

(1) coordinating with State and local government personnel, agencies, and authorities, and with the private sector, to ensure adequate planning, equipment, training, and exercise activities;

(2) coordinating and, as appropriate, consolidating, the Federal Government's communications and systems of communications relating to homeland security with State and local government personnel, agencies, and authorities, the private sector, other entities, and the public; and

(3) distributing or, as appropriate, coordinating the distribution of, warnings and information to State and local government personnel, agencies, and authorities and to the public.

(d) Meetings of National Security Council

The Secretary may, subject to the direction of the President, attend and participate in meetings of the National Security Council.

(e) Issuance of regulations

The issuance of regulations by the Secretary shall be governed by the provisions of chapter 5 of title 5, except as specifically provided in this chapter, in laws granting regulatory authorities that are transferred by this chapter, and in laws enacted after November 25, 2002.

(f) Special Assistant to the Secretary

The Secretary shall appoint a Special Assistant to the Secretary who shall be responsible for—

(1) creating and fostering strategic communications with the private sector to enhance the primary mission of the Department to protect the American homeland;

(2) advising the Secretary on the impact of the Department's policies, regulations, processes, and actions on the private sector;

(3) interfacing with other relevant Federal agencies with homeland security missions to assess the impact of these agencies' actions on the private sector;

(4) creating and managing private sector advisory councils composed of representatives of industries and associations designated by the Secretary to—

(A) advise the Secretary on private sector products, applications, and solutions as they relate to homeland security challenges;

(B) advise the Secretary on homeland security policies, regulations, processes, and actions that affect the participating industries and associations; and

(C) advise the Secretary on private sector preparedness issues, including effective methods for—

(i) promoting voluntary preparedness standards to the private sector; and

(ii) assisting the private sector in adopting voluntary preparedness standards;

(5) working with Federal laboratories, federally funded research and development centers, other federally funded organizations, aca-

[1] So in original. Probably should be "Office of State and Local Government Coordination".

demia, and the private sector to develop innovative approaches to address homeland security challenges to produce and deploy the best available technologies for homeland security missions;

(6) promoting existing public-private partnerships and developing new public-private partnerships to provide for collaboration and mutual support to address homeland security challenges;

(7) assisting in the development and promotion of private sector best practices to secure critical infrastructure;

(8) providing information to the private sector regarding voluntary preparedness standards and the business justification for preparedness and promoting to the private sector the adoption of voluntary preparedness standards;

(9) coordinating industry efforts, with respect to functions of the Department of Homeland Security, to identify private sector resources and capabilities that could be effective in supplementing Federal, State, and local government agency efforts to prevent or respond to a terrorist attack;

(10) coordinating with the Directorate of Border and Transportation Security and the Assistant Secretary for Trade Development of the Department of Commerce on issues related to the travel and tourism industries; and

(11) consulting with the Office of State and Local Government Coordination and Preparedness on all matters of concern to the private sector, including the tourism industry.

(g) Standards policy

All standards activities of the Department shall be conducted in accordance with section 12(d) of the National Technology Transfer Advancement Act of 1995 (15 U.S.C. 272 note) and Office of Management and Budget Circular A–119.

(Pub. L. 107–296, title I, §102, Nov. 25, 2002, 116 Stat. 2142; Pub. L. 108–458, title VII, §7402, Dec. 17, 2004, 118 Stat. 3850; Pub. L. 110–53, title IX, §902, Aug. 3, 2007, 121 Stat. 371.)

REFERENCES IN TEXT

Section 12(d) of the National Technology Transfer Advancement Act of 1995, referred to in subsec. (g), probably means section 12(d) of the National Technology Transfer and Advancement Act of 1995, which is section 12(d) of Pub. L. 104–113, and which is set out as a note under section 272 of Title 15, Commerce and Trade.

AMENDMENTS

2007—Subsec. (f)(4)(C). Pub. L. 110–53, §902(b), added subpar. (C).

Subsec. (f)(8) to (11). Pub. L. 110–53, §902(a), added par. (8) and redesignated former pars. (8) to (10) as (9) to (11), respectively.

2004—Subsec. (f)(8) to (10). Pub. L. 108–458 added pars. (8) to (10).

REQUIRED COORDINATION

Pub. L. 108–458, title VII, §7405, Dec. 17, 2004, 118 Stat. 3851, provided that: "The Secretary of Homeland Security shall ensure that there is effective and ongoing coordination of Federal efforts to prevent, prepare for, and respond to acts of terrorism and other major disasters and emergencies among the divisions of the Department of Homeland Security, including the Directorate of Emergency Preparedness and Response and the Office for State and Local Government Coordination and Preparedness."

PROTECTIONS FOR HUMAN RESEARCH SUBJECTS OF THE DEPARTMENT OF HOMELAND SECURITY

Pub. L. 108–458, title VIII, §8306, Dec. 17, 2004, 118 Stat. 3869, provided that: "The Secretary of Homeland Security shall ensure that the Department of Homeland Security complies with the protections for human research subjects, as described in part 46 of title 45, Code of Federal Regulations, or in equivalent regulations as promulgated by such Secretary, with respect to research that is conducted or supported by the Department."

§113. Other officers

(a) Deputy Secretary; Under Secretaries

There are the following officers, appointed by the President, by and with the advice and consent of the Senate:

(1) A Deputy Secretary of Homeland Security, who shall be the Secretary's first assistant for purposes of subchapter III of chapter 33 of title 5.

(2) An Under Secretary for Science and Technology.

(3) An Under Secretary for Border and Transportation Security.

(4) An Administrator of the Federal Emergency Management Agency.

(5) A Director of the Bureau of Citizenship and Immigration Services.

(6) An Under Secretary for Management.

(7) A Director of the Office of Counternarcotics Enforcement.

(8) An Under Secretary responsible for overseeing critical infrastructure protection, cybersecurity, and other related programs of the Department.

(9) Not more than 12 Assistant Secretaries.

(10) A General Counsel, who shall be the chief legal officer of the Department.

(b) Inspector General

There shall be in the Department an Office of Inspector General and an Inspector General at the head of such office, as provided in the Inspector General Act of 1978 (5 U.S.C. App.).

(c) Commandant of the Coast Guard

To assist the Secretary in the performance of the Secretary's functions, there is a Commandant of the Coast Guard, who shall be appointed as provided in section 44 of title 14 and who shall report directly to the Secretary. In addition to such duties as may be provided in this chapter and as assigned to the Commandant by the Secretary, the duties of the Commandant shall include those required by section 2 of title 14.

(d) Other officers

To assist the Secretary in the performance of the Secretary's functions, there are the following officers, appointed by the President:

(1) A Director of the Secret Service.

(2) A Chief Information Officer.

(3) An Officer for Civil Rights and Civil Liberties.

(4) A Director for Domestic Nuclear Detection.

(e) Chief Financial Officer

There shall be in the Department a Chief Financial Officer, as provided in chapter 9 of title 31.

(f) Performance of specific functions

Subject to the provisions of this chapter, every officer of the Department shall perform the functions specified by law for the official's office or prescribed by the Secretary.

(Pub. L. 107–296, title I, § 103, Nov. 25, 2002, 116 Stat. 2144; Pub. L. 108–7, div. L, § 104(a), Feb. 20, 2003, 117 Stat. 529; Pub. L. 108–330, § 3(d)(1)(A), Oct. 16, 2004, 118 Stat. 1276; Pub. L. 108–458, title VII, § 7407(b), Dec. 17, 2004, 118 Stat. 3853; Pub. L. 109–295, title VI, § 612(b), Oct. 4, 2006, 120 Stat. 1410; Pub. L. 109–347, title V, § 501(b)(1), Oct. 13, 2006, 120 Stat. 1935; Pub. L. 110–53, title V, § 531(b)(2), Aug. 3, 2007, 121 Stat. 334; Pub. L. 110–388, § 1, Oct. 10, 2008, 122 Stat. 4144.)

REFERENCES IN TEXT

The Inspector General Act of 1978, referred to in subsec. (b), is Pub. L. 95–452, Oct. 12, 1978, 92 Stat. 1101, as amended, which is set out in the Appendix to Title 5, Government Organization and Employees.

AMENDMENTS

2008—Subsec. (d)(3) to (5). Pub. L. 110–388 redesignated pars. (4) and (5) as (3) and (4), respectively, and struck out former par. (3) which read as follows: "A Chief Human Capital Officer."

2007—Subsec. (a)(8) to (10). Pub. L. 110–53 added par. (8) and redesignated former pars. (8) and (9) as (9) and (10), respectively.

2006—Subsec. (a)(2) to (4). Pub. L. 109–295, § 612(b)(2), (3), redesignated pars. (3) to (5) as (2) to (4), respectively, and struck out former par. (2) which read as follows: "An Under Secretary for Information Analysis and Infrastructure Protection."

Subsec. (a)(5). Pub. L. 109–295, § 612(b)(3), redesignated par. (6) as (5). Former par. (5) redesignated (4).

Pub. L. 109–295, § 612(b)(1), added par. (5) and struck out former par. (5) which read as follows: "An Under Secretary for Emergency Preparedness and Response."

Subsec. (a)(6) to (10). Pub. L. 109–295, § 612(b)(3), redesignated pars. (7) to (10) as (6) to (9), respectively. Former par. (6) redesignated (5).

Subsec. (d)(5). Pub. L. 109–347 added par. (5).

2004—Subsec. (a)(8) to (10). Pub. L. 108–458 added par. (8) and redesignated former pars. (8) and (9) as (9) and (10), respectively.

Subsec. (d)(4), (5). Pub. L. 108–330, § 3(d)(1)(A)(i), redesignated par. (5) as (4) and struck out former par. (4) which read as follows: "A Chief Financial Officer."

Subsecs. (e), (f). Pub. L. 108–330, § 3(d)(1)(A)(ii), (iii), added subsec. (e) and redesignated former subsec. (e) as (f).

2003—Subsec. (b). Pub. L. 108–7 reenacted heading without change and amended text generally. Prior to amendment, text read as follows: "There is an Inspector General, who shall be appointed as provided in section 3(a) of the Inspector General Act of 1978."

CHANGE OF NAME

Any reference to the Administrator of the Federal Emergency Management Agency in title VI of Pub. L. 109–295 or an amendment by title VI to be considered to refer and apply to the Director of the Federal Emergency Management Agency until Mar. 31, 2007, see section 612(f)(2) of Pub. L. 109–295, set out as a note under section 313 of this title.

§ 114. Sensitive Security Information

Using funds made available in this Act, the Secretary of Homeland Security shall provide that each office within the Department that handles documents marked as Sensitive Security Information (SSI) shall have at least one employee in that office with authority to coordinate and make determinations on behalf of the agency that such documents meet the criteria for marking as SSI: *Provided*, That not later than December 31, 2005, the Secretary shall submit to the Committees on Appropriations of the Senate and the House of Representatives: (1) Department-wide policies for designating, coordinating and marking documents as SSI; (2) Department-wide auditing and accountability procedures for documents designated and marked as SSI; (3) the total number of SSI Coordinators within the Department; and (4) the total number of staff authorized to designate SSI documents within the Department: *Provided further*, That not later than January 31, 2006, the Secretary shall provide to the Committees on Appropriations of the Senate and the House of Representatives the title of all DHS documents that are designated as SSI in their entirety during the period October 1, 2005, through December 31, 2005: *Provided further*, That not later than January 31 of each succeeding year, starting on January 31, 2007, the Secretary shall provide annually a similar report to the Committees on Appropriations of the Senate and the House of Representatives on the titles of all DHS documents that are designated as SSI in their entirety during the period of January 1 through December 31 for the preceding year: *Provided further*, That the Secretary shall promulgate guidance that includes common but extensive examples of SSI that further define the individual categories of information cited under 49 CFR 1520(b)(1) through (16) and eliminates judgment by covered persons in the application of the SSI marking: *Provided further*, That such guidance shall serve as the primary basis and authority for the marking of DHS information as SSI by covered persons.

(Pub. L. 109–90, title V, § 537, Oct. 18, 2005, 119 Stat. 2088.)

REFERENCES IN TEXT

This Act, referred to in text, is Pub. L. 109–90, Oct. 18, 2005, 119 Stat. 2064, known as the Department of Homeland Security Appropriations Act, 2006. For complete classification of this Act to the Code, see Tables.

CODIFICATION

Section was enacted as part of the Department of Homeland Security Appropriations Act, 2006, and not as part of the Homeland Security Act of 2002 which comprises this chapter.

§ 115. Trade and customs revenue functions of the Department

(a) Trade and customs revenue functions

(1) Designation of appropriate official

The Secretary shall designate an appropriate senior official in the office of the Secretary who shall—

(A) ensure that the trade and customs revenue functions of the Department are coordinated within the Department and with other Federal departments and agencies, and that the impact on legitimate trade is taken

into account in any action impacting the functions; and

(B) monitor and report to Congress on the Department's mandate to ensure that the trade and customs revenue functions of the Department are not diminished, including how spending, operations, and personnel related to these functions have kept pace with the level of trade entering the United States.

(2) Director of Trade Policy

There shall be a Director of Trade Policy (in this subsection referred to as the "Director"), who shall be subject to the direction and control of the official designated pursuant to paragraph (1). The Director shall—

(A) advise the official designated pursuant to paragraph (1) regarding all aspects of Department policies relating to the trade and customs revenue functions of the Department;

(B) coordinate the development of Department-wide policies regarding trade and customs revenue functions and trade facilitation; and

(C) coordinate the trade and customs revenue-related policies of the Department with the policies of other Federal departments and agencies.

(b) Study; report

(1) In general

The Comptroller General of the United States shall conduct a study evaluating the extent to which the Department of Homeland Security is meeting its obligations under section 212(b) of this title with respect to the maintenance of customs revenue functions.

(2) Analysis

The study shall include an analysis of—

(A) the extent to which the customs revenue functions carried out by the former United States Customs Service have been consolidated with other functions of the Department (including the assignment of noncustoms revenue functions to personnel responsible for customs revenue collection), discontinued, or diminished following the transfer of the United States Customs Service to the Department;

(B) the extent to which staffing levels or resources attributable to customs revenue functions have decreased since the transfer of the United States Customs Service to the Department; and

(C) the extent to which the management structure created by the Department ensures effective trade facilitation and customs revenue collection.

(3) Report

Not later than 180 days after October 13, 2006, the Comptroller General shall submit to the appropriate congressional committees a report on the results of the study conducted under subsection (a).

(4) Maintenance of functions

Not later than September 30, 2007, the Secretary shall ensure that the requirements of section 212(b) of this title are fully satisfied and shall report to the Committee on Finance of the Senate and the Committee on Ways and Means of the House of Representatives regarding implementation of this paragraph.

(5) Definition

In this section, the term "customs revenue functions" means the functions described in section 212(b)(2) of this title.

(c) Consultation on trade and customs revenue functions

(1) Business community consultations

The Secretary shall consult with representatives of the business community involved in international trade, including seeking the advice and recommendations of the Commercial Operations Advisory Committee, on Department policies and actions that have a significant impact on international trade and customs revenue functions.

(2) Congressional consultation and notification

(A) In general

Subject to subparagraph (B), the Secretary shall notify the appropriate congressional committees not later than 30 days prior to the finalization of any Department policies, initiatives, or actions that will have a major impact on trade and customs revenue functions. Such notifications shall include a description of the proposed policies, initiatives, or actions and any comments or recommendations provided by the Commercial Operations Advisory Committee and other relevant groups regarding the proposed policies, initiatives, or actions.

(B) Exception

If the Secretary determines that it is important to the national security interest of the United States to finalize any Department policies, initiatives, or actions prior to the consultation described in subparagraph (A), the Secretary shall—

(i) notify and provide any recommendations of the Commercial Operations Advisory Committee received to the appropriate congressional committees not later than 45 days after the date on which the policies, initiatives, or actions are finalized; and

(ii) to the extent appropriate, modify the policies, initiatives, or actions based upon the consultations with the appropriate congressional committees.

(d) Notification of reorganization of customs revenue functions

(1) In general

Not less than 45 days prior to any change in the organization of any of the customs revenue functions of the Department, the Secretary shall notify the Committee on Appropriations, the Committee on Finance, and the Committee on Homeland Security and Governmental Affairs of the Senate, and the Committee on Appropriations, the Committee on Homeland Security, and the Committee on Ways and Means of the House of Representatives of the specific assets, functions, or personnel to be transferred as part of such reorganization, and the reason for such transfer. The notification shall also include—

(A) an explanation of how trade enforcement functions will be impacted by the reorganization;

(B) an explanation of how the reorganization meets the requirements of section 212(b) of this title that the Department not diminish the customs revenue and trade facilitation functions formerly performed by the United States Customs Service; and

(C) any comments or recommendations provided by the Commercial Operations Advisory Committee regarding such reorganization.

(2) Analysis

Any congressional committee referred to in paragraph (1) may request that the Commercial Operations Advisory Committee provide a report to the committee analyzing the impact of the reorganization and providing any recommendations for modifying the reorganization.

(3) Report

Not later than 1 year after any reorganization referred to in paragraph (1) takes place, the Secretary, in consultation with the Commercial Operations Advisory Committee, shall submit a report to the Committee on Finance of the Senate and the Committee on Ways and Means of the House of Representatives. Such report shall include an assessment of the impact of, and any suggested modifications to, such reorganization.

(Pub. L. 109–347, title IV, § 401, Oct. 13, 2006, 120 Stat. 1921.)

CODIFICATION

Section was enacted as part of the Security and Accountability For Every Port Act of 2006, also known as the SAFE Port Act, and not as part of the Homeland Security Act of 2002 which comprises this chapter.

DEFINITIONS

For definitions of terms used in this section, see section 901 of this title.

SUBCHAPTER II—INFORMATION ANALYSIS AND INFRASTRUCTURE PROTECTION

PART A—INFORMATION AND ANALYSIS AND INFRASTRUCTURE PROTECTION; ACCESS TO INFORMATION

AMENDMENTS

2007—Pub. L. 110–53, title V, § 531(b)(3), Aug. 3, 2007, 121 Stat. 334, substituted "Information and" for "Directorate for Information" in part heading.

§ 121. Information and Analysis and Infrastructure Protection

(a) Intelligence and analysis and infrastructure protection

There shall be in the Department an Office of Intelligence and Analysis and an Office of Infrastructure Protection.

(b) Under Secretary for Intelligence and Analysis and Assistant Secretary for Infrastructure Protection

(1) Office of Intelligence and Analysis

The Office of Intelligence and Analysis shall be headed by an Under Secretary for Intelligence and Analysis, who shall be appointed by the President, by and with the advice and consent of the Senate.

(2) Chief Intelligence Officer

The Under Secretary for Intelligence and Analysis shall serve as the Chief Intelligence Officer of the Department.

(3) Office of Infrastructure Protection

The Office of Infrastructure Protection shall be headed by an Assistant Secretary for Infrastructure Protection, who shall be appointed by the President.

(c) Discharge of responsibilities

The Secretary shall ensure that the responsibilities of the Department relating to information analysis and infrastructure protection, including those described in subsection (d), are carried out through the Under Secretary for Intelligence and Analysis or the Assistant Secretary for Infrastructure Protection, as appropriate.

(d) Responsibilities of Secretary relating to intelligence and analysis and infrastructure protection

The responsibilities of the Secretary relating to intelligence and analysis and infrastructure protection shall be as follows:

(1) To access, receive, and analyze law enforcement information, intelligence information, and other information from agencies of the Federal Government, State and local government agencies (including law enforcement agencies), and private sector entities, and to integrate such information, in support of the mission responsibilities of the Department and the functions of the National Counterterrorism Center established under section 119 of the National Security Act of 1947 (50 U.S.C. 404*o*), in order to—

(A) identify and assess the nature and scope of terrorist threats to the homeland;

(B) detect and identify threats of terrorism against the United States; and

(C) understand such threats in light of actual and potential vulnerabilities of the homeland.

(2) To carry out comprehensive assessments of the vulnerabilities of the key resources and critical infrastructure of the United States, including the performance of risk assessments to determine the risks posed by particular types of terrorist attacks within the United States (including an assessment of the probability of success of such attacks and the feasibility and potential efficacy of various countermeasures to such attacks).

(3) To integrate relevant information, analyses, and vulnerability assessments (whether such information, analyses, or assessments are provided or produced by the Department or others) in order to identify priorities for pro-

tective and support measures by the Department, other agencies of the Federal Government, State and local government agencies and authorities, the private sector, and other entities.

(4) To ensure, pursuant to section 122 of this title, the timely and efficient access by the Department to all information necessary to discharge the responsibilities under this section, including obtaining such information from other agencies of the Federal Government.

(5) To develop a comprehensive national plan for securing the key resources and critical infrastructure of the United States, including power production, generation, and distribution systems, information technology and telecommunications systems (including satellites), electronic financial and property record storage and transmission systems, emergency preparedness communications systems, and the physical and technological assets that support such systems.

(6) To recommend measures necessary to protect the key resources and critical infrastructure of the United States in coordination with other agencies of the Federal Government and in cooperation with State and local government agencies and authorities, the private sector, and other entities.

(7) To review, analyze, and make recommendations for improvements to the policies and procedures governing the sharing of information within the scope of the information sharing environment established under section 485 of this title, including homeland security information, terrorism information, and weapons of mass destruction information, and any policies, guidelines, procedures, instructions, or standards established under that section.

(8) To disseminate, as appropriate, information analyzed by the Department within the Department, to other agencies of the Federal Government with responsibilities relating to homeland security, and to agencies of State and local governments and private sector entities with such responsibilities in order to assist in the deterrence, prevention, preemption of, or response to, terrorist attacks against the United States.

(9) To consult with the Director of National Intelligence and other appropriate intelligence, law enforcement, or other elements of the Federal Government to establish collection priorities and strategies for information, including law enforcement-related information, relating to threats of terrorism against the United States through such means as the representation of the Department in discussions regarding requirements and priorities in the collection of such information.

(10) To consult with State and local governments and private sector entities to ensure appropriate exchanges of information, including law enforcement-related information, relating to threats of terrorism against the United States.

(11) To ensure that—

(A) any material received pursuant to this chapter is protected from unauthorized disclosure and handled and used only for the performance of official duties; and

(B) any intelligence information under this chapter is shared, retained, and disseminated consistent with the authority of the Director of National Intelligence to protect intelligence sources and methods under the National Security Act of 1947 (50 U.S.C. 401 et seq.) and related procedures and, as appropriate, similar authorities of the Attorney General concerning sensitive law enforcement information.

(12) To request additional information from other agencies of the Federal Government, State and local government agencies, and the private sector relating to threats of terrorism in the United States, or relating to other areas of responsibility assigned by the Secretary, including the entry into cooperative agreements through the Secretary to obtain such information.

(13) To establish and utilize, in conjunction with the chief information officer of the Department, a secure communications and information technology infrastructure, including data-mining and other advanced analytical tools, in order to access, receive, and analyze data and information in furtherance of the responsibilities under this section, and to disseminate information acquired and analyzed by the Department, as appropriate.

(14) To ensure, in conjunction with the chief information officer of the Department, that any information databases and analytical tools developed or utilized by the Department—

(A) are compatible with one another and with relevant information databases of other agencies of the Federal Government; and

(B) treat information in such databases in a manner that complies with applicable Federal law on privacy.

(15) To coordinate training and other support to the elements and personnel of the Department, other agencies of the Federal Government, and State and local governments that provide information to the Department, or are consumers of information provided by the Department, in order to facilitate the identification and sharing of information revealed in their ordinary duties and the optimal utilization of information received from the Department.

(16) To coordinate with elements of the intelligence community and with Federal, State, and local law enforcement agencies, and the private sector, as appropriate.

(17) To provide intelligence and information analysis and support to other elements of the Department.

(18) To coordinate and enhance integration among the intelligence components of the Department, including through strategic oversight of the intelligence activities of such components.

(19) To establish the intelligence collection, processing, analysis, and dissemination priorities, policies, processes, standards, guidelines, and procedures for the intelligence components of the Department, consistent with any directions from the President and, as applicable, the Director of National Intelligence.

(20) To establish a structure and process to support the missions and goals of the intelligence components of the Department.

(21) To ensure that, whenever possible, the Department—

(A) produces and disseminates unclassified reports and analytic products based on open-source information; and

(B) produces and disseminates such reports and analytic products contemporaneously with reports or similar information that the Department produced and disseminated in a classified format.

(22) To establish within the Office of Intelligence and Analysis an internal continuity of operations plan.

(23) Based on intelligence priorities set by the President, and guidance from the Secretary and, as appropriate, the Director of National Intelligence—

(A) to provide to the heads of each intelligence component of the Department guidance for developing the budget pertaining to the activities of such component; and

(B) to present to the Secretary a recommendation for a consolidated budget for the intelligence components of the Department, together with any comments from the heads of such components.

(24) To perform such other duties relating to such responsibilities as the Secretary may provide.

(25) To prepare and submit to the Committee on Homeland Security and Governmental Affairs of the Senate and the Committee on Homeland Security in the House of Representatives, and to other appropriate congressional committees having jurisdiction over the critical infrastructure or key resources, for each sector identified in the National Infrastructure Protection Plan, a report on the comprehensive assessments carried out by the Secretary of the critical infrastructure and key resources of the United States, evaluating threat, vulnerability, and consequence, as required under this subsection. Each such report—

(A) shall contain, if applicable, actions or countermeasures recommended or taken by the Secretary or the head of another Federal agency to address issues identified in the assessments;

(B) shall be required for fiscal year 2007 and each subsequent fiscal year and shall be submitted not later than 35 days after the last day of the fiscal year covered by the report; and

(C) may be classified.

(e) Staff

(1) In general

The Secretary shall provide the Office of Intelligence and Analysis and the Office of Infrastructure Protection with a staff of analysts having appropriate expertise and experience to assist such offices in discharging responsibilities under this section.

(2) Private sector analysts

Analysts under this subsection may include analysts from the private sector.

(3) Security clearances

Analysts under this subsection shall possess security clearances appropriate for their work under this section.

(f) Detail of personnel

(1) In general

In order to assist the Office of Intelligence and Analysis and the Office of Infrastructure Protection in discharging responsibilities under this section, personnel of the agencies referred to in paragraph (2) may be detailed to the Department for the performance of analytic functions and related duties.

(2) Covered agencies

The agencies referred to in this paragraph are as follows:

(A) The Department of State.

(B) The Central Intelligence Agency.

(C) The Federal Bureau of Investigation.

(D) The National Security Agency.

(E) The National Geospatial-Intelligence Agency.

(F) The Defense Intelligence Agency.

(G) Any other agency of the Federal Government that the President considers appropriate.

(3) Cooperative agreements

The Secretary and the head of the agency concerned may enter into cooperative agreements for the purpose of detailing personnel under this subsection.

(4) Basis

The detail of personnel under this subsection may be on a reimbursable or non-reimbursable basis.

(g) Functions transferred

In accordance with subchapter XII of this chapter, there shall be transferred to the Secretary, for assignment to the Office of Intelligence and Analysis and the Office of Infrastructure Protection under this section, the functions, personnel, assets, and liabilities of the following:

(1) The National Infrastructure Protection Center of the Federal Bureau of Investigation (other than the Computer Investigations and Operations Section), including the functions of the Attorney General relating thereto.

(2) The National Communications System of the Department of Defense, including the functions of the Secretary of Defense relating thereto.

(3) The Critical Infrastructure Assurance Office of the Department of Commerce, including the functions of the Secretary of Commerce relating thereto.

(4) The National Infrastructure Simulation and Analysis Center of the Department of Energy and the energy security and assurance program and activities of the Department, including the functions of the Secretary of Energy relating thereto.

(5) The Federal Computer Incident Response Center of the General Services Administration, including the functions of the Administrator of General Services relating thereto.

(Pub. L. 107–296, title II, §201, Nov. 25, 2002, 116 Stat. 2145; Pub. L. 110–53, title V, §§501(a)(2)(A), (b), 531(a), title X, § 1002(a), Aug. 3, 2007, 121 Stat. 309, 332, 374; Pub. L. 110–417, [div. A], title IX, § 931(b)(5), Oct. 14, 2008, 122 Stat. 4575; Pub. L. 111–84, div. A, title X, § 1073(c)(9), Oct. 28, 2009, 123 Stat. 2475.)

REFERENCES IN TEXT

This chapter, referred to in subsec. (d)(11), was in the original "this Act", meaning Pub. L. 107–296, Nov. 25, 2002, 116 Stat. 2135, known as the Homeland Security Act of 2002, which is classified principally to this chapter. For complete classification of this Act to the Code, see Short Title note set out under section 101 of this title and Tables.

The National Security Act of 1947, referred to in subsec. (d)(11)(B), is act July 26, 1947, ch. 343, 61 Stat. 495, as amended. For complete classification of this Act to the Code, see Short Title note set out under section 401 of Title 50, War and National Defense, and Tables.

CODIFICATION

Section is comprised of section 201 of Pub. L. 107–296. Subsec. (h) of section 201 of Pub. L. 107–296 amended section 401a of Title 50, War and National Defense.

AMENDMENTS

2009—Subsec. (f)(2)(E). Pub. L. 111–84 made technical amendment to directory language of Pub. L. 110–417. See 2008 amendment note below.

2008—Subsec. (f)(2)(E). Pub. L. 110–417, § 931(b)(5), as amended by Pub. L. 111–84, substituted "National Geospatial-Intelligence Agency" for "National Imagery and Mapping Agency".

2007—Pub. L. 110–53, § 531(a)(1), substituted "Information and" for "Directorate for Information" in section catchline.

Subsecs. (a) to (c). Pub. L. 110–53, § 531(a)(2), added subsecs. (a) to (c) and struck out former subsecs. (a) to (c) which related to, in subsec. (a), establishment and responsibilities of Directorate for Information Analysis and Infrastructure Protection, in subsec. (b), positions of Assistant Secretary for Information Analysis and Assistant Secretary for Infrastructure Protection, and, in subsec. (c), Secretary's duty to ensure that responsibilities regarding information analysis and infrastructure protection would be carried out through the Under Secretary for Information Analysis and Infrastructure Protection.

Subsec. (d). Pub. L. 110–53, § 531(a)(3), substituted "Secretary relating to intelligence and analysis and infrastructure protection" for "Under Secretary" in heading and "The responsibilities of the Secretary relating to intelligence and analysis and infrastructure protection" for "Subject to the direction and control of the Secretary, the responsibilities of the Under Secretary for Information Analysis and Infrastructure Protection" in introductory provisions.

Subsec. (d)(1). Pub. L. 110–53, § 501(b)(1), inserted ", in support of the mission responsibilities of the Department and the functions of the National Counterterrorism Center established under section 119 of the National Security Act of 1947 (50 U.S.C. 404*o*)," after "to integrate such information" in introductory provisions.

Subsec. (d)(7). Pub. L. 110–53, § 501(b)(2), added par. (7) and struck out former par. (7) which read as follows: "To review, analyze, and make recommendations for improvements in the policies and procedures governing the sharing of law enforcement information, intelligence information, intelligence-related information, and other information relating to homeland security within the Federal Government and between the Federal Government and State and local government agencies and authorities."

Pub. L. 110–53, § 501(a)(2)(A), redesignated par. (8) as (7) and struck out former par. (7) which read as follows: "To administer the Homeland Security Advisory System, including—

"(A) exercising primary responsibility for public advisories related to threats to homeland security; and

"(B) in coordination with other agencies of the Federal Government, providing specific warning information, and advice about appropriate protective measures and countermeasures, to State and local government agencies and authorities, the private sector, other entities, and the public."

Subsec. (d)(8). Pub. L. 110–53, § 501(a)(2)(A)(ii), redesignated par. (9) as (8). Former par. (8) redesignated (7).

Subsec. (d)(9). Pub. L. 110–53, § 531(a)(3)(C), substituted "Director of National Intelligence" for "Director of Central Intelligence".

Pub. L. 110–53, § 501(a)(2)(A)(ii), redesignated par. (10) as (9). Former par. (9) redesignated (8).

Subsec. (d)(10). Pub. L. 110–53, § 501(a)(2)(A)(ii), redesignated par. (11) as (10). Former par. (10) redesignated (9).

Subsec. (d)(11). Pub. L. 110–53, § 501(a)(2)(A)(ii), redesignated par. (12) as (11). Former par. (11) redesignated (10).

Subsec. (d)(11)(B). Pub. L. 110–53, § 531(a)(3)(D), substituted "Director of National Intelligence" for "Director of Central Intelligence".

Subsec. (d)(12) to (17). Pub. L. 110–53, § 501(a)(2)(A)(ii), redesignated pars. (13) to (18) as (12) to (17), respectively. Former par. (12) redesignated (11).

Subsec. (d)(18). Pub. L. 110–53, § 531(a)(3)(E), (F), added par. (18) and redesignated former par. (18) as (24).

Pub. L. 110–53, § 501(a)(2)(A)(ii), redesignated par. (19) as (18). Former par. (18) redesignated (17).

Subsec. (d)(19). Pub. L. 110–53, § 531(a)(3)(F), added par. (19).

Pub. L. 110–53, § 501(a)(2)(A)(ii), redesignated par. (19) as (18).

Subsec. (d)(20) to (23). Pub. L. 110–53, § 531(a)(3)(F), added pars. (20) to (23).

Subsec. (d)(24). Pub. L. 110–53, § 531(a)(3)(E), redesignated par. (18) as (24).

Subsec. (d)(25). Pub. L. 110–53, § 1002(a), added par. (25).

Subsec. (e)(1). Pub. L. 110–53, § 531(a)(4), substituted "provide the Office of Intelligence and Analysis and the Office of Infrastructure Protection" for "provide the Directorate" and "assist such offices in discharging" for "assist the Directorate in discharging".

Subsec. (f)(1). Pub. L. 110–53, § 531(a)(5), substituted "Office of Intelligence and Analysis and the Office of Infrastructure Protection" for "Directorate".

Subsec. (g). Pub. L. 110–53, § 531(a)(6), substituted "Office of Intelligence and Analysis and the Office of Infrastructure Protection" for "Under Secretary for Information Analysis and Infrastructure Protection" in introductory provisions.

EFFECTIVE DATE OF 2009 AMENDMENT

Pub. L. 111–84, div. A, title X, § 1073(c), Oct. 28, 2009, 123 Stat. 2474, provided that the amendment by section 1073(c)(9) is effective as of Oct. 14, 2008, and as if included in Pub. L. 110–417 as enacted.

REGULATIONS

Pub. L. 109–295, title V, § 550, Oct. 4, 2006, 120 Stat. 1388, as amended by Pub. L. 110–161, div. E, title V, § 534, Dec. 26, 2007, 121 Stat. 2075; Pub. L. 111–83, title V, § 550, Oct. 28, 2009, 123 Stat. 2177, provided that:

"(a) No later than six months after the date of enactment of this Act [Oct. 4, 2006], the Secretary of Homeland Security shall issue interim final regulations establishing risk-based performance standards for security of chemical facilities and requiring vulnerability assessments and the development and implementation of site security plans for chemical facilities: *Provided*, That such regulations shall apply to chemical facilities that, in the discretion of the Secretary, present high levels of security risk: *Provided further*, That such regulations shall permit each such facility, in developing and implementing site security plans, to select layered security measures that, in combination, appropriately address the vulnerability assessment and the risk-based performance standards for security for the facility: *Provided further*, That the Secretary may not disapprove a site security plan submitted under this section based on the presence or absence of a particular security measure, but the Secretary may disapprove a site security plan if the plan fails to satisfy the risk-based performance standards established by this section: *Provided further*, That the Secretary may approve alternative security programs established by private sector entities, Federal, State, or local authorities, or other applicable laws if the Secretary determines that the requirements of such programs meet the requirements of this section and the interim regulations: *Provided further*, That the Secretary shall review and approve each vulnerability assessment and site security plan required under this section: *Provided further*, That the Secretary shall not apply regulations issued pursuant to this section to facilities regulated pursuant to the Maritime Transportation Security Act of 2002, Public Law 107–295, as amended [see Tables for classification]; Public Water Systems, as defined by section 1401 of the Safe Drinking Water Act, Public Law 93–523, as amended [42 U.S.C. 300f]; Treatment Works as defined in section 212 of the Federal Water Pollution Control Act, Public Law 92–500, as amended [33 U.S.C. 1292]; any facility owned or operated by the Department of Defense or the Department of Energy, or any facility subject to regulation by the Nuclear Regulatory Commission.

"(b) Interim regulations issued under this section shall apply until the effective date of interim or final regulations promulgated under other laws that establish requirements and standards referred to in subsection (a) and expressly supersede this section: *Provided*, That the authority provided by this section shall terminate on October 4, 2010.

"(c) Notwithstanding any other provision of law and subsection (b), information developed under this section, including vulnerability assessments, site security plans, and other security related information, records, and documents shall be given protections from public disclosure consistent with similar information developed by chemical facilities subject to regulation under section 70103 of title 46, United States Code: *Provided*, That this subsection does not prohibit the sharing of such information, as the Secretary deems appropriate, with State and local government officials possessing the necessary security clearances, including law enforcement officials and first responders, for the purpose of carrying out this section, provided that such information may not be disclosed pursuant to any State or local law: *Provided further*, That in any proceeding to enforce this section, vulnerability assessments, site security plans, and other information submitted to or obtained by the Secretary under this section, and related vulnerability or security information, shall be treated as if the information were classified material.

"(d) Any person who violates an order issued under this section shall be liable for a civil penalty under section 70119(a) of title 46, United States Code: *Provided*, That nothing in this section confers upon any person except the Secretary a right of action against an owner or operator of a chemical facility to enforce any provision of this section.

"(e) The Secretary of Homeland Security shall audit and inspect chemical facilities for the purposes of determining compliance with the regulations issued pursuant to this section.

"(f) Nothing in this section shall be construed to supersede, amend, alter, or affect any Federal law that regulates the manufacture, distribution in commerce, use, sale, other treatment, or disposal of chemical substances or mixtures.

"(g) If the Secretary determines that a chemical facility is not in compliance with this section, the Secretary shall provide the owner or operator with written notification (including a clear explanation of deficiencies in the vulnerability assessment and site security plan) and opportunity for consultation, and issue an order to comply by such date as the Secretary determines to be appropriate under the circumstances: *Provided*, That if the owner or operator continues to be in noncompliance, the Secretary may issue an order for the facility to cease operation, until the owner or operator complies with the order.

"(h) This section shall not preclude or deny any right of any State or political subdivision thereof to adopt or enforce any regulation, requirement, or standard of performance with respect to chemical facility security that is more stringent than a regulation, requirement, or standard of performance issued under this section, or otherwise impair any right or jurisdiction of any State with respect to chemical facilities within that State, unless there is an actual conflict between this section and the law of that State."

TREATMENT OF INCUMBENT UNDER SECRETARY FOR INTELLIGENCE AND ANALYSIS

Pub. L. 110–53, title V, §531(c), Aug. 3, 2007, 121 Stat. 335, provided that: "The individual administratively performing the duties of the Under Secretary for Intelligence and Analysis as of the date of the enactment of this Act [Aug. 3, 2007] may continue to perform such duties after the date on which the President nominates an individual to serve as the Under Secretary pursuant to section 201 of the Homeland Security Act of 2002 [6 U.S.C. 121], as amended by this section, and until the individual so appointed assumes the duties of the position."

REPORTS TO BE SUBMITTED TO CERTAIN COMMITTEES

Pub. L. 110–53, title XXIV, §2403, Aug. 3, 2007, 121 Stat. 547, provided that: "The Committee on Commerce, Science, and Transportation of the Senate shall receive the reports required by the following provisions of law in the same manner and to the same extent that the reports are to be received by the Committee on Homeland Security and Governmental Affairs of the Senate:

"(1) Section 1016(j)(1) of the Intelligence Reform and Terrorist [Terrorism] Prevention Act of 2004 (6 U.S.C. 485(j)(1)).

"(2) Section 511(d) of this Act [121 Stat. 323].

"(3) Subsection (a)(3)(D) of section 2022 of the Homeland Security Act of 2002 [6 U.S.C. 612(a)(3)(D)], as added by section 101 of this Act.

"(4) Section 7215(d) of the Intelligence Reform and Terrorism Prevention Act of 2004 (6 U.S.C. 123(d)).

"(5) Section 7209(b)(1)(C) of the Intelligence Reform and Terrorism Prevention Act of 2004 [Pub. L. 108–458] (8 U.S.C. 1185 note).

"(6) Section 804(c) of this Act [42 U.S.C. 2000ee–3(c)].

"(7) Section 901(b) of this Act [121 Stat. 370].

"(8) Section 1002(a) of this Act [amending this section].

"(9) Title III of this Act [enacting sections 579 and 580 of this title and amending sections 194 and 572 of this title]."

SECURITY MANAGEMENT SYSTEMS DEMONSTRATION PROJECT

Pub. L. 110–53, title XXIV, §2404, Aug. 3, 2007, 121 Stat. 548, provided that:

"(a) DEMONSTRATION PROJECT REQUIRED.—Not later than 120 days after the date of enactment of this Act [Aug. 3, 2007], the Secretary of Homeland Security shall—

"(1) establish a demonstration project to conduct demonstrations of security management systems that—

"(A) shall use a management system standards approach; and

"(B) may be integrated into quality, safety, environmental and other internationally adopted management systems; and

"(2) enter into one or more agreements with a private sector entity to conduct such demonstrations of security management systems.

"(b) SECURITY MANAGEMENT SYSTEM DEFINED.—In this section, the term 'security management system' means a set of guidelines that address the security assessment needs of critical infrastructure and key resources that are consistent with a set of generally accepted management standards ratified and adopted by a standards making body."

EX. ORD. NO. 13231. CRITICAL INFRASTRUCTURE PROTECTION IN THE INFORMATION AGE

Ex. Ord. No. 13231, Oct. 16, 2001, 66 F.R. 53063, as amended by Ex. Ord. No. 13284, §2, Jan. 23, 2003, 68 F.R. 4075; Ex. Ord. No. 13286, §7, Feb. 28, 2003, 68 F.R. 10620; Ex. Ord. No. 13385, §5, Sept. 29, 2005, 70 F.R. 57990, provided:

By the authority vested in me as President by the Constitution and the laws of the United States of America, and in order to ensure protection of information systems for critical infrastructure, including emergency preparedness communications and the physical assets that support such systems, in the information age, it is hereby ordered as follows:

SECTION 1. *Policy*. The information technology revolution has changed the way business is transacted, government operates, and national defense is conducted. Those three functions now depend on an interdependent network of critical information infrastructures. It is the policy of the United States to protect against disruption of the operation of information systems for critical infrastructure and thereby help to protect the people, economy, essential human and government services, and national security of the United States, and to ensure that any disruptions that occur are infrequent, of minimal duration, and manageable, and cause the least damage possible. The implementation of this policy shall include a voluntary public-private partnership, involving corporate and nongovernmental organizations.

SEC. 2. *Continuing Authorities*. This order does not alter the existing authorities or roles of United States Government departments and agencies. Authorities set forth in 44 U.S.C. chapter 35, and other applicable law, provide senior officials with responsibility for the security of Federal Government information systems.

(a) Executive Branch Information Systems Security. The Director of the Office of Management and Budget (OMB) has the responsibility to develop and oversee the implementation of government-wide policies, principles, standards, and guidelines for the security of information systems that support the executive branch departments and agencies, except those noted in section 2(b) of this order. The Director of OMB shall advise the President and the appropriate department or agency head when there is a critical deficiency in the security practices within the purview of this section in an executive branch department or agency.

(b) National Security Information Systems. The Secretary of Defense and the Director of Central Intelligence (DCI) shall have responsibility to oversee, develop, and ensure implementation of policies, principles, standards, and guidelines for the security of information systems that support the operations under their respective control. In consultation with the Assistant to the President for National Security Affairs and the affected departments and agencies, the Secretary of Defense and the DCI shall develop policies, principles, standards, and guidelines for the security of national security information systems that support the operations of other executive branch departments and agencies with national security information.

(i) Policies, principles, standards, and guidelines developed under this subsection may require more stringent protection than those developed in accordance with section 2(a) of this order.

(ii) The Assistant to the President for National Security Affairs shall advise the President and the appropriate department or agency when there is a critical deficiency in the security practices of a department or agency within the purview of this section.

(iii) National Security Systems. The National Security Telecommunications and Information Systems Security Committee, as established by and consistent with NSD-42 and chaired by the Department of Defense, shall be designated as the "Committee on National Security Systems."

(c) Additional Responsibilities. The heads of executive branch departments and agencies are responsible and accountable for providing and maintaining adequate levels of security for information systems, including emergency preparedness communications systems, for programs under their control. Heads of such departments and agencies shall ensure the development and, within available appropriations, funding of programs that adequately address these mission systems, especially those critical systems that support the national security and other essential government programs. Additionally, security should enable, and not unnecessarily impede, department and agency business operations.

SEC. 3. *The National Infrastructure Advisory Council*. The National Infrastructure Advisory Council (NIAC), established on October 16, 2001, shall provide the President through the Secretary of Homeland Security with advice on the security of the critical infrastructure sectors and their information systems.

(a) Membership. The NIAC shall be composed of not more than 30 members appointed by the President, taking appropriate account of the benefits of having members (i) from the private sector, including but not limited to banking and finance, transportation, energy, communications, and emergency services organizations and institutions of higher learning, and State, local, and tribal governments, (ii) with senior leadership responsibilities for the reliability and availability, which include security, of the critical infrastructure and key resource sectors, (iii) with expertise relevant to the functions of the NIAC, and (iv) with experience equivalent to that of a chief executive of an organization. Unless otherwise determined by the President, no full-time officer or employee of the executive branch shall be appointed to serve as a member of the NIAC. The President shall designate from among the members of the NIAC a Chair and a Vice Chair, who shall perform the functions of the Chair if the Chair is absent, disabled, or in the instance of a vacancy in the Chair.

(b) Functions of the NIAC. The NIAC shall meet periodically to:

(i) enhance the partnership of the public and private sectors in protecting critical infrastructures and their information systems and provide reports on this issue to the President through the Secretary of Homeland Security, as appropriate;

(ii) propose and develop ways to encourage private industry to perform periodic risk assessments;

(iii) monitor the development and operations of private sector coordinating councils and their information sharing mechanisms and provide recommendations to the President through the Secretary of Homeland Security on how these organizations can best foster improved cooperation among the sectors, the Department of Homeland Security, and other Federal Government entities;

(iv) report to the President through the Secretary of Homeland Security, who shall ensure appropriate coordination with the Assistant to the President for Homeland Security and Counterterrorism, the Assistant to the President for Economic Policy, and the Assistant to the President for National Security Affairs under the terms of this order; and

(v) advise sector specific agencies with critical infrastructure responsibilities to include issues pertaining to sector and government coordinating councils and their information sharing mechanisms.

(c) Administration of the NIAC.

(i) The NIAC may hold hearings, conduct inquiries, and establish subcommittees, as appropriate.

(ii) Upon request of the Chair, and to the extent permitted by law, the heads of the executive departments and agencies shall provide the NIAC with information and advice relating to its functions.

(iii) Senior Federal Government officials may participate in the meetings of the NIAC, as appropriate.

(iv) Members shall serve without compensation for their work on the NIAC. However, members may be reimbursed for travel expenses, including per diem in lieu of subsistence, as authorized by law for persons serving intermittently in Federal Government service (5 U.S.C. 5701–5707).

(v) To the extent permitted by law and subject to the availability of appropriations, the Department of Homeland Security shall provide the NIAC with administrative services, staff, and other support services, and such funds as may be necessary for the performance of the NIAC's functions.

SEC. 4. *Judicial Review*. This order does not create any right or benefit, substantive or procedural, enforceable at law or in equity, against the United States, its departments, agencies, or other entities, its officers or employees, or any other person.

GEORGE W. BUSH.

EXTENSION OF TERM OF NATIONAL INFRASTRUCTURE ADVISORY COUNCIL

Term of the National Infrastructure Advisory Council extended until Sept. 30, 2005, by Ex. Ord. No. 13316, Sept. 17, 2003, 68 F.R. 55255, formerly set out as a note under section 14 of the Federal Advisory Committee Act in the Appendix to Title 5, Government Organizations and Employees.

Term of the National Infrastructure Advisory Council extended until Sept. 30, 2007, by Ex. Ord. No. 13385, Sept. 29, 2005, 70 F.R. 57989, formerly set out as a note under section 14 of the Federal Advisory Committee Act in the Appendix to Title 5.

Term of the National Infrastructure Advisory Council extended until Sept. 30, 2009, by Ex. Ord. No. 13446, Sept. 28, 2007, 72 F.R. 56175, formerly set out as a note under section 14 of the Federal Advisory Committee Act in the Appendix to Title 5.

Term of the National Infrastructure Advisory Council extended until Sept. 30, 2011, by Ex. Ord. No. 13511, Sept. 29, 2009, 74 F.R. 50909, set out as a note under section 14 of the Federal Advisory Committee Act in the Appendix to Title 5.

EX. ORD. NO. 13284. AMENDMENT OF EXECUTIVE ORDERS, AND OTHER ACTIONS, IN CONNECTION WITH THE ESTABLISHMENT OF THE DEPARTMENT OF HOMELAND SECURITY

Ex. Ord. No. 13284, Jan. 23, 2003, 68 F.R. 4075, provided:

By the authority vested in me as President by the Constitution and the laws of the United States of America, including the Homeland Security Act of 2002 (Public Law 107–296) [see Tables for classification], and the National Security Act of 1947, as amended (50 U.S.C. 401 *et seq.*), and in order to reflect responsibilities vested in the Secretary of Homeland Security and take other actions in connection with the establishment of the Department of Homeland Security, it is hereby ordered as follows:

SECTION 1. [Amended Ex. Ord. No. 13234.]

SEC. 2. [Amended Ex. Ord. No. 13231, set out above.]

SEC. 3. Executive Order 13228 of October 8, 2001 ("Establishing the Office of Homeland Security and the Homeland Security Council") [50 U.S.C. 402 note], is amended by inserting "the Secretary of Homeland Security," after "the Secretary of Transportation," in section 5(b). Further, during the period from January 24, 2003, until March 1, 2003, the Secretary of Homeland Security shall have the responsibility for coordinating the domestic response efforts otherwise assigned to the Assistant to the President for Homeland Security pursuant to section 3(g) of Executive Order 13228.

SEC. 4. [Amended Ex. Ord. No. 13224, listed in a table under section 1701 of Title 50, War and National Defense.]

SEC. 5. [Amended Ex. Ord. No. 13151, set out as a note under section 5195 of Title 42, The Public Health and Welfare.]

SEC. 6. [Amended Ex. Ord. No. 13122, set out as a note under section 3121 of Title 42, The Public Health and Welfare.]

SEC. 7. [Amended Ex. Ord. No. 13048, set out as a note under section 501 of Title 31, Money and Finance.]

SEC. 8. [Amended Ex. Ord. No. 12992, set out as a note under section 1708 of Title 21, Food and Drugs.]

SEC. 9. [Amended Ex. Ord. No. 12881, set out as a note under section 6601 of Title 42, The Public Health and Welfare.]

SEC. 10. [Amended Ex. Ord. No. 12859, set out as a note preceding section 101 of Title 3, The President.]

SEC. 11. [Amended Ex. Ord. No. 12590, set out as a note under former section 1201 of Title 21, Food and Drugs.]

SEC. 12. [Amended Ex. Ord. No. 12260, set out as a note under section 2511 of Title 19, Customs Duties.]

SEC. 13. [Amended Ex. Ord. No. 11958, set out as a note under section 2751 of Title 22, Foreign Relations and Intercourse.]

SEC. 14. [Amended Ex. Ord. No. 11423, set out as a note under section 301 of Title 3, The President.]

SEC. 15. [Amended Ex. Ord. No. 10865, set out as a note under section 435 of Title 50, War and National Defense.]

SEC. 16. [Amended Ex. Ord. No. 13011, set out as a note under section 11101 of Title 40, Public Buildings, Property, and Works.]

SEC. 17. Those elements of the Department of Homeland Security that are supervised by the Department's Under Secretary for Information Analysis and Infrastructure Protection through the Department's Assistant Secretary for Information Analysis, with the exception of those functions that involve no analysis of foreign intelligence information, are designated as elements of the Intelligence Community under section 201(h) of the Homeland Security Act of 2002 [Pub. L. 107–296, amending 50 U.S.C. 401a] and section 3(4) of the National Security Act of 1947, as amended (50 U.S.C. 401a[(4)]).

SEC. 18. [Amended Ex. Ord. No. 12333, set out as a note under section 401 of title 50, War and National Defense.]

SEC. 19. *Functions of Certain Officials in the Department of Homeland Security*.

The Secretary of Homeland Security, the Deputy Secretary of Homeland Security, the Under Secretary for Information Analysis and Infrastructure Protection, Department of Homeland Security, and the Assistant Secretary for Information Analysis, Department of Homeland Security, each shall be considered a "Senior Official of the Intelligence Community" for purposes of Executive Order 12333 [50 U.S.C. 401 note], and all other relevant authorities, and shall:

(a) recognize and give effect to all current clearances for access to classified information held by those who become employees of the Department of Homeland Security by operation of law pursuant to the Homeland Security Act of 2002 or by Presidential appointment;

(b) recognize and give effect to all current clearances for access to classified information held by those in the private sector with whom employees of the Department of Homeland Security may seek to interact in the discharge of their homeland security-related responsibilities;

(c) make all clearance and access determinations pursuant to Executive Order 12968 of August 2, 1995 [50 U.S.C. 435 note], or any successor Executive Order, as to employees of, and applicants for employment in, the Department of Homeland Security who do not then hold a current clearance for access to classified information; and

(d) ensure all clearance and access determinations for those in the private sector with whom employees of the Department of Homeland Security may seek to interact in the discharge of their homeland security-related responsibilities are made in accordance with Executive Order 12829 of January 6, 1993 [50 U.S.C. 435 note].

SEC. 20. Pursuant to the provisions of section 1.4 of Executive Order 12958 of April 17, 1995 ("Classified National Security Information") [50 U.S.C. 435 note], I hereby authorize the Secretary of Homeland Security to classify information originally as "Top Secret." Any delegation of this authority shall be in accordance with section 1.4 of that order or any successor Executive Orders.

SEC. 21. This order shall become effective on January 24, 2003.

SEC. 22. This order does not create any right or benefit, substantive or procedural, enforceable at law or equity, against the United States, its departments, agencies, or other entities, its officers or employees, or any other person.

GEORGE W. BUSH.

§ 122. Access to information

(a) In general

(1) Threat and vulnerability information

Except as otherwise directed by the President, the Secretary shall have such access as the Secretary considers necessary to all information, including reports, assessments, analyses, and unevaluated intelligence relating to threats of terrorism against the United States and to other areas of responsibility assigned by the Secretary, and to all information concerning infrastructure or other vulnerabilities of the United States to terrorism, whether or not such information has been analyzed, that may be collected, possessed, or prepared by any agency of the Federal Government.

(2) Other information

The Secretary shall also have access to other information relating to matters under the responsibility of the Secretary that may be collected, possessed, or prepared by an agency of the Federal Government as the President may further provide.

(b) Manner of access

Except as otherwise directed by the President, with respect to information to which the Secretary has access pursuant to this section—

(1) the Secretary may obtain such material upon request, and may enter into cooperative arrangements with other executive agencies to provide such material or provide Department officials with access to it on a regular or routine basis, including requests or arrangements involving broad categories of material, access to electronic databases, or both; and

(2) regardless of whether the Secretary has made any request or entered into any cooperative arrangement pursuant to paragraph (1), all agencies of the Federal Government shall promptly provide to the Secretary—

(A) all reports (including information reports containing intelligence which has not been fully evaluated), assessments, and analytical information relating to threats of terrorism against the United States and to other areas of responsibility assigned by the Secretary;

(B) all information concerning the vulnerability of the infrastructure of the United States, or other vulnerabilities of the United States, to terrorism, whether or not such information has been analyzed;

(C) all other information relating to significant and credible threats of terrorism against the United States, whether or not such information has been analyzed; and

(D) such other information or material as the President may direct.

(c) Treatment under certain laws

The Secretary shall be deemed to be a Federal law enforcement, intelligence, protective, national defense, immigration, or national security official, and shall be provided with all information from law enforcement agencies that is required to be given to the Director of Central Intelligence, under any provision of the following:

(1) The USA PATRIOT Act of 2001 (Public Law 107–56).

(2) Section 2517(6) of title 18.

(3) Rule 6(e)(3)(C) of the Federal Rules of Criminal Procedure.

(d) Access to intelligence and other information

(1) Access by elements of Federal Government

Nothing in this subchapter shall preclude any element of the intelligence community (as that term is defined in section 401a(4) of title 50,[1] or any other element of the Federal Government with responsibility for analyzing terrorist threat information, from receiving any intelligence or other information relating to terrorism.

(2) Sharing of information

The Secretary, in consultation with the Director of Central Intelligence, shall work to ensure that intelligence or other information relating to terrorism to which the Department has access is appropriately shared with the elements of the Federal Government referred to in paragraph (1), as well as with State and local governments, as appropriate.

(Pub. L. 107–296, title II, § 202, Nov. 25, 2002, 116 Stat. 2149.)

REFERENCES IN TEXT

The USA PATRIOT Act of 2001, referred to in subsec. (c)(1), is Pub. L. 107–56, Oct. 26, 2001, 115 Stat. 272, known as the Uniting and Strengthening America by Providing Appropriate Tools Required to Intercept and Obstruct Terrorism Act of 2001 or the USA PATRIOT Act. For complete classification of this Act to the Code, see Short Title of 2001 Amendment note set out under section 1 of Title 18, Crimes and Criminal Procedure, and Tables.

The Federal Rules of Criminal Procedure, referred to in subsec. (c)(3), are set out in the Appendix to Title 18, Crimes and Criminal Procedure.

This subchapter, referred to in subsec. (d)(1), was in the original "this title", meaning title II of Pub. L. 107–296, Nov. 25, 2002, 116 Stat. 2145, which enacted this subchapter, amended sections 1030, 2511, 2512, 2520, 2701 to 2703, and 3125 of Title 18, Crimes and Criminal Procedure, sections 3712 and 3722 of Title 42, The Public Health and Welfare, and section 401a of Title 50, War and National Defense, and enacted provisions set out as a note under section 101 of this title and listed in a Provisions for Review, Promulgation, or Amendment of Federal Sentencing Guidelines Relating to Specific Offenses table set out under section 994 of Title 28, Judiciary and Judicial Procedure. For complete classification of title II to the Code, see Tables.

CHANGE OF NAME

Reference to the Director of Central Intelligence or the Director of the Central Intelligence Agency in the Director's capacity as the head of the intelligence community deemed to be a reference to the Director of National Intelligence. Reference to the Director of Central Intelligence or the Director of the Central Intelligence Agency in the Director's capacity as the head of the Central Intelligence Agency deemed to be a ref-

[1] So in original. There probably should be a closing parenthesis after "50".

erence to the Director of the Central Intelligence Agency. See section 1081(a), (b) of Pub. L. 108–458, set out as a note under section 401 of Title 50, War and National Defense.

§ 123. Terrorist travel program

(a) Requirement to establish

Not later than 90 days after August 3, 2007, the Secretary of Homeland Security, in consultation with the Director of the National Counterterrorism Center and consistent with the strategy developed under section 7201,[1] shall establish a program to oversee the implementation of the Secretary's responsibilities with respect to terrorist travel.

(b) Head of the program

The Secretary of Homeland Security shall designate an official of the Department of Homeland Security to be responsible for carrying out the program. Such official shall be—

(1) the Assistant Secretary for Policy of the Department of Homeland Security; or

(2) an official appointed by the Secretary who reports directly to the Secretary.

(c) Duties

The official designated under subsection (b) shall assist the Secretary of Homeland Security in improving the Department's ability to prevent terrorists from entering the United States or remaining in the United States undetected by—

(1) developing relevant strategies and policies;

(2) reviewing the effectiveness of existing programs and recommending improvements, if necessary;

(3) making recommendations on budget requests and on the allocation of funding and personnel;

(4) ensuring effective coordination, with respect to policies, programs, planning, operations, and dissemination of intelligence and information related to terrorist travel—

(A) among appropriate subdivisions of the Department of Homeland Security, as determined by the Secretary and including—

(i) United States Customs and Border Protection;

(ii) United States Immigration and Customs Enforcement;

(iii) United States Citizenship and Immigration Services;

(iv) the Transportation Security Administration; and

(v) the United States Coast Guard; and

(B) between the Department of Homeland Security and other appropriate Federal agencies; and

(5) serving as the Secretary's primary point of contact with the National Counterterrorism Center for implementing initiatives related to terrorist travel and ensuring that the recommendations of the Center related to terrorist travel are carried out by the Department.

(d) Report

Not later than 180 days after August 3, 2007, the Secretary of Homeland Security shall submit to the Committee on Homeland Security and Governmental Affairs of the Senate and the Committee on Homeland Security of the House of Representatives a report on the implementation of this section.

(Pub. L. 108–458, title VII, § 7215, Dec. 17, 2004, 118 Stat. 3832; Pub. L. 110–53, title VII, § 722, Aug. 3, 2007, 121 Stat. 348.)

REFERENCES IN TEXT

Section 7201, referred to in subsec. (a), is section 7201 of Pub. L. 108–458, title VII, Dec. 17, 2004, 118 Stat. 3808, which enacted section 1776 of Title 8, Aliens and Nationality, and provisions set out as notes under section 1776 of Title 8 and sections 403–1 and 404o of Title 50, War and National Defense.

CODIFICATION

Section was enacted as part of the Intelligence Reform and Terrorism Prevention Act of 2004, and also as part of the 9/11 Commission Implementation Act of 2004, and not as part of the Homeland Security Act of 2002 which comprises this chapter.

AMENDMENTS

2007—Pub. L. 110–53 reenacted section catchline without change and amended text generally, substituting provisions relating to establishment of a program to oversee the implementation of the Secretary's responsibilities with respect to terrorist travel not later than 90 days after Aug. 3, 2007, and relating to the head of the program, such official's duties, and report on implementation for provisions relating to establishment of a program to oversee the implementation of the Department's responsibilities with respect to terrorist travel.

§ 124. Homeland Security Advisory System

(a) Requirement

The Secretary shall administer the Homeland Security Advisory System in accordance with this section to provide advisories or warnings regarding the threat or risk that acts of terrorism will be committed on the homeland to Federal, State, local, and tribal government authorities and to the people of the United States, as appropriate. The Secretary shall exercise primary responsibility for providing such advisories or warnings.

(b) Required elements

In administering the Homeland Security Advisory System, the Secretary shall—

(1) establish criteria for the issuance and revocation of such advisories or warnings;

(2) develop a methodology, relying on the criteria established under paragraph (1), for the issuance and revocation of such advisories or warnings;

(3) provide, in each such advisory or warning, specific information and advice regarding appropriate protective measures and countermeasures that may be taken in response to the threat or risk, at the maximum level of detail practicable to enable individuals, government entities, emergency response providers, and the private sector to act appropriately;

(4) whenever possible, limit the scope of each such advisory or warning to a specific region, locality, or economic sector believed to be under threat or at risk; and

(5) not, in issuing any advisory or warning, use color designations as the exclusive means of specifying homeland security threat condi-

[1] See References in Text note below.

tions that are the subject of the advisory or warning.

(Pub. L. 107–296, title II, §203, as added Pub. L. 110–53, title V, §501(a)(1), Aug. 3, 2007, 121 Stat. 306.)

§ 124a. Homeland security information sharing

(a) Information sharing

Consistent with section 485 of this title, the Secretary, acting through the Under Secretary for Intelligence and Analysis, shall integrate the information and standardize the format of the products of the intelligence components of the Department containing homeland security information, terrorism information, weapons of mass destruction information, or national intelligence (as defined in section 401a(5) of title 50) except for any internal security protocols or personnel information of such intelligence components, or other administrative processes that are administered by any chief security officer of the Department.

(b) Information sharing and knowledge management officers

For each intelligence component of the Department, the Secretary shall designate an information sharing and knowledge management officer who shall report to the Under Secretary for Intelligence and Analysis regarding coordinating the different systems used in the Department to gather and disseminate homeland security information or national intelligence (as defined in section 401a(5) of title 50).

(c) State, local, and private-sector sources of information

(1) Establishment of business processes

The Secretary, acting through the Under Secretary for Intelligence and Analysis or the Assistant Secretary for Infrastructure Protection, as appropriate, shall—

(A) establish Department-wide procedures for the review and analysis of information provided by State, local, and tribal governments and the private sector;

(B) as appropriate, integrate such information into the information gathered by the Department and other departments and agencies of the Federal Government; and

(C) make available such information, as appropriate, within the Department and to other departments and agencies of the Federal Government.

(2) Feedback

The Secretary shall develop mechanisms to provide feedback regarding the analysis and utility of information provided by any entity of State, local, or tribal government or the private sector that provides such information to the Department.

(d) Training and evaluation of employees

(1) Training

The Secretary, acting through the Under Secretary for Intelligence and Analysis or the Assistant Secretary for Infrastructure Protection, as appropriate, shall provide to employees of the Department opportunities for training and education to develop an understanding of—

(A) the definitions of homeland security information and national intelligence (as defined in section 401a(5) of title 50); and

(B) how information available to such employees as part of their duties—

(i) might qualify as homeland security information or national intelligence; and

(ii) might be relevant to the Office of Intelligence and Analysis and the intelligence components of the Department.

(2) Evaluations

The Under Secretary for Intelligence and Analysis shall—

(A) on an ongoing basis, evaluate how employees of the Office of Intelligence and Analysis and the intelligence components of the Department are utilizing homeland security information or national intelligence, sharing information within the Department, as described in this subchapter, and participating in the information sharing environment established under section 485 of this title; and

(B) provide to the appropriate component heads regular reports regarding the evaluations under subparagraph (A).

(Pub. L. 107–296, title II, §204, as added Pub. L. 110–53, title V, §501(a)(1), Aug. 3, 2007, 121 Stat. 307.)

REFERENCES IN TEXT

This subchapter, referred to in subsec. (d)(2)(A), was in the original "this title", meaning title II of Pub. L. 107–296, Nov. 25, 2002, 116 Stat. 2145, which enacted this subchapter, amended sections 1030, 2511, 2512, 2520, 2701 to 2703, and 3125 of Title 18, Crimes and Criminal Procedure, sections 3712 and 3722 of Title 42, The Public Health and Welfare, and section 401a of Title 50, War and National Defense, and enacted provisions set out as a note under section 101 of this title and listed in a Provisions for Review, Promulgation, or Amendment of Federal Sentencing Guidelines Relating to Specific Offenses table set out under section 994 of Title 28, Judiciary and Judicial Procedure. For complete classification of title II to the Code, see Tables.

RECEIPT OF INFORMATION FROM UNITED STATES SECRET SERVICE

Pub. L. 110–53, title V, §502(b), Aug. 3, 2007, 121 Stat. 311, provided that:

"(1) IN GENERAL.—The Under Secretary for Intelligence and Analysis shall receive from the United States Secret Service homeland security information, terrorism information, weapons of mass destruction information (as these terms are defined in Section [sic] 1016 of the Intelligence Reform and Terrorism Prevention Act of 2004 (6 U.S.C. 485)), or national intelligence, as defined in Section [sic] 3(5) of the National Security Act of 1947 (50 U.S.C. 401a(5)), as well as suspect information obtained in criminal investigations. The United States Secret Service shall cooperate with the Under Secretary for Intelligence and Analysis with respect to activities under sections 204 and 205 of the Homeland Security Act of 2002 [6 U.S.C. 124a, 124b].

"(2) SAVINGS CLAUSE.—Nothing in this Act [see Tables for classification] shall interfere with the operation of Section [sic] 3056(g) of Title 18, United States Code, or with the authority of the Secretary of Homeland Security or the Director of the United States Secret Service regarding the budget of the United States Secret Service."

§ 124b. Comprehensive information technology network architecture

(a) Establishment

The Secretary, acting through the Under Secretary for Intelligence and Analysis, shall establish, consistent with the policies and procedures developed under section 485 of this title, and consistent with the enterprise architecture of the Department, a comprehensive information technology network architecture for the Office of Intelligence and Analysis that connects the various databases and related information technology assets of the Office of Intelligence and Analysis and the intelligence components of the Department in order to promote internal information sharing among the intelligence and other personnel of the Department.

(b) Comprehensive information technology network architecture defined

The term "comprehensive information technology network architecture" means an integrated framework for evolving or maintaining existing information technology and acquiring new information technology to achieve the strategic management and information resources management goals of the Office of Intelligence and Analysis.

(Pub. L. 107–296, title II, §205, as added Pub. L. 110–53, title V, §501(a)(1), Aug. 3, 2007, 121 Stat. 308.)

§ 124c. Coordination with information sharing environment

(a) Guidance

All activities to comply with sections 124, 124a, and 124b of this title shall be—

(1) consistent with any policies, guidelines, procedures, instructions, or standards established under section 485 of this title;

(2) implemented in coordination with, as appropriate, the program manager for the information sharing environment established under that section;

(3) consistent with any applicable guidance issued by the Director of National Intelligence; and

(4) consistent with any applicable guidance issued by the Secretary relating to the protection of law enforcement information or proprietary information.

(b) Consultation

In carrying out the duties and responsibilities under this part, the Under Secretary for Intelligence and Analysis shall take into account the views of the heads of the intelligence components of the Department.

(Pub. L. 107–296, title II, §206, as added Pub. L. 110–53, title V, §501(a)(1), Aug. 3, 2007, 121 Stat. 309.)

§ 124d. Intelligence components

Subject to the direction and control of the Secretary, and consistent with any applicable guidance issued by the Director of National Intelligence, the responsibilities of the head of each intelligence component of the Department are as follows:

(1) To ensure that the collection, processing, analysis, and dissemination of information within the scope of the information sharing environment, including homeland security information, terrorism information, weapons of mass destruction information, and national intelligence (as defined in section 401a(5) of title 50), are carried out effectively and efficiently in support of the intelligence mission of the Department, as led by the Under Secretary for Intelligence and Analysis.

(2) To otherwise support and implement the intelligence mission of the Department, as led by the Under Secretary for Intelligence and Analysis.

(3) To incorporate the input of the Under Secretary for Intelligence and Analysis with respect to performance appraisals, bonus or award recommendations, pay adjustments, and other forms of commendation.

(4) To coordinate with the Under Secretary for Intelligence and Analysis in developing policies and requirements for the recruitment and selection of intelligence officials of the intelligence component.

(5) To advise and coordinate with the Under Secretary for Intelligence and Analysis on any plan to reorganize or restructure the intelligence component that would, if implemented, result in realignments of intelligence functions.

(6) To ensure that employees of the intelligence component have knowledge of, and comply with, the programs and policies established by the Under Secretary for Intelligence and Analysis and other appropriate officials of the Department and that such employees comply with all applicable laws and regulations.

(7) To perform such other activities relating to such responsibilities as the Secretary may provide.

(Pub. L. 107–296, title II, §207, as added Pub. L. 110–53, title V, §503(a), Aug. 3, 2007, 121 Stat. 311.)

§ 124e. Training for employees of intelligence components

The Secretary shall provide training and guidance for employees, officials, and senior executives of the intelligence components of the Department to develop knowledge of laws, regulations, operations, policies, procedures, and programs that are related to the functions of the Department relating to the collection, processing, analysis, and dissemination of information within the scope of the information sharing environment, including homeland security information, terrorism information, and weapons of mass destruction information, or national intelligence (as defined in section 401a(5) of title 50).

(Pub. L. 107–296, title II, §208, as added Pub. L. 110–53, title V, §503(a), Aug. 3, 2007, 121 Stat. 312.)

§ 124f. Intelligence training development for State and local government officials

(a) Curriculum

The Secretary, acting through the Under Secretary for Intelligence and Analysis, shall—

(1) develop a curriculum for training State, local, and tribal government officials, includ-

ing law enforcement officers, intelligence analysts, and other emergency response providers, in the intelligence cycle and Federal laws, practices, and regulations regarding the development, handling, and review of intelligence and other information; and

(2) ensure that the curriculum includes executive level training for senior level State, local, and tribal law enforcement officers, intelligence analysts, and other emergency response providers.

(b) Training

To the extent possible, the Federal Law Enforcement Training Center and other existing Federal entities with the capacity and expertise to train State, local, and tribal government officials based on the curriculum developed under subsection (a) shall be used to carry out the training programs created under this section. If such entities do not have the capacity, resources, or capabilities to conduct such training, the Secretary may approve another entity to conduct such training.

(c) Consultation

In carrying out the duties described in subsection (a), the Under Secretary for Intelligence and Analysis shall consult with the Director of the Federal Law Enforcement Training Center, the Attorney General, the Director of National Intelligence, the Administrator of the Federal Emergency Management Agency, and other appropriate parties, such as private industry, institutions of higher education, nonprofit institutions, and other intelligence agencies of the Federal Government.

(Pub. L. 107–296, title II, §209, as added Pub. L. 110–53, title V, §503(a), Aug. 3, 2007, 121 Stat. 312.)

§ 124g. Information sharing incentives

(a) Awards

In making cash awards under chapter 45 of title 5, the President or the head of an agency, in consultation with the program manager designated under section 485 of this title, may consider the success of an employee in appropriately sharing information within the scope of the information sharing environment established under that section, including homeland security information, terrorism information, and weapons of mass destruction information, or national intelligence (as defined in section 401a(5) of title 50[1], in a manner consistent with any policies, guidelines, procedures, instructions, or standards established by the President or, as appropriate, the program manager of that environment for the implementation and management of that environment.

(b) Other incentives

The head of each department or agency described in section 485(i) of this title, in consultation with the program manager designated under section 485 of this title, shall adopt best practices regarding effective ways to educate and motivate officers and employees of the Federal Government to participate fully in the information sharing environment, including—

(1) promotions and other nonmonetary awards; and

(2) publicizing information sharing accomplishments by individual employees and, where appropriate, the tangible end benefits that resulted.

(Pub. L. 107–296, title II, §210, as added Pub. L. 110–53, title V, §503(a), Aug. 3, 2007, 121 Stat. 313.)

§ 124h. Department of Homeland Security State, Local, and Regional Fusion Center Initiative

(a) Establishment

The Secretary, in consultation with the program manager of the information sharing environment established under section 485 of this title, the Attorney General, the Privacy Officer of the Department, the Officer for Civil Rights and Civil Liberties of the Department, and the Privacy and Civil Liberties Oversight Board established under section 2000ee of title 42, shall establish a Department of Homeland Security State, Local, and Regional Fusion Center Initiative to establish partnerships with State, local, and regional fusion centers.

(b) Department support and coordination

Through the Department of Homeland Security State, Local, and Regional Fusion Center Initiative, and in coordination with the principal officials of participating State, local, or regional fusion centers and the officers designated as the Homeland Security Advisors of the States, the Secretary shall—

(1) provide operational and intelligence advice and assistance to State, local, and regional fusion centers;

(2) support efforts to include State, local, and regional fusion centers into efforts to establish an information sharing environment;

(3) conduct tabletop and live training exercises to regularly assess the capability of individual and regional networks of State, local, and regional fusion centers to integrate the efforts of such networks with the efforts of the Department;

(4) coordinate with other relevant Federal entities engaged in homeland security-related activities;

(5) provide analytic and reporting advice and assistance to State, local, and regional fusion centers;

(6) review information within the scope of the information sharing environment, including homeland security information, terrorism information, and weapons of mass destruction information, that is gathered by State, local, and regional fusion centers, and to incorporate such information, as appropriate, into the Department's own such information;

(7) provide management assistance to State, local, and regional fusion centers;

(8) serve as a point of contact to ensure the dissemination of information within the scope of the information sharing environment, including homeland security information, terrorism information, and weapons of mass destruction information;

(9) facilitate close communication and coordination between State, local, and regional fusion centers and the Department;

[1] So in original. A closing parenthesis probably should precede the comma.

(10) provide State, local, and regional fusion centers with expertise on Department resources and operations;

(11) provide training to State, local, and regional fusion centers and encourage such fusion centers to participate in terrorism threat-related exercises conducted by the Department; and

(12) carry out such other duties as the Secretary determines are appropriate.

(c) Personnel assignment

(1) In general

The Under Secretary for Intelligence and Analysis shall, to the maximum extent practicable, assign officers and intelligence analysts from components of the Department to participating State, local, and regional fusion centers.

(2) Personnel sources

Officers and intelligence analysts assigned to participating fusion centers under this subsection may be assigned from the following Department components, in coordination with the respective component head and in consultation with the principal officials of participating fusion centers:

(A) Office of Intelligence and Analysis.

(B) Office of Infrastructure Protection.

(C) Transportation Security Administration.

(D) United States Customs and Border Protection.

(E) United States Immigration and Customs Enforcement.

(F) United States Coast Guard.

(G) Other components of the Department, as determined by the Secretary.

(3) Qualifying criteria

(A) In general

The Secretary shall develop qualifying criteria for a fusion center to participate in the assigning of Department officers or intelligence analysts under this section.

(B) Criteria

Any criteria developed under subparagraph (A) may include—

(i) whether the fusion center, through its mission and governance structure, focuses on a broad counterterrorism approach, and whether that broad approach is pervasive through all levels of the organization;

(ii) whether the fusion center has sufficient numbers of adequately trained personnel to support a broad counterterrorism mission;

(iii) whether the fusion center has—

(I) access to relevant law enforcement, emergency response, private sector, open source, and national security data; and

(II) the ability to share and analytically utilize that data for lawful purposes;

(iv) whether the fusion center is adequately funded by the State, local, or regional government to support its counterterrorism mission; and

(v) the relevancy of the mission of the fusion center to the particular source component of Department officers or intelligence analysts.

(4) Prerequisite

(A) Intelligence analysis, privacy, and civil liberties training

Before being assigned to a fusion center under this section, an officer or intelligence analyst shall undergo—

(i) appropriate intelligence analysis or information sharing training using an intelligence-led policing curriculum that is consistent with—

(I) standard training and education programs offered to Department law enforcement and intelligence personnel; and

(II) the Criminal Intelligence Systems Operating Policies under part 23 of title 28, Code of Federal Regulations (or any corresponding similar rule or regulation);

(ii) appropriate privacy and civil liberties training that is developed, supported, or sponsored by the Privacy Officer appointed under section 142 of this title and the Officer for Civil Rights and Civil Liberties of the Department, in consultation with the Privacy and Civil Liberties Oversight Board established under section 2000ee of title 42; and

(iii) such other training prescribed by the Under Secretary for Intelligence and Analysis.

(B) Prior work experience in area

In determining the eligibility of an officer or intelligence analyst to be assigned to a fusion center under this section, the Under Secretary for Intelligence and Analysis shall consider the familiarity of the officer or intelligence analyst with the State, locality, or region, as determined by such factors as whether the officer or intelligence analyst—

(i) has been previously assigned in the geographic area; or

(ii) has previously worked with intelligence officials or law enforcement or other emergency response providers from that State, locality, or region.

(5) Expedited security clearance processing

The Under Secretary for Intelligence and Analysis—

(A) shall ensure that each officer or intelligence analyst assigned to a fusion center under this section has the appropriate security clearance to contribute effectively to the mission of the fusion center; and

(B) may request that security clearance processing be expedited for each such officer or intelligence analyst and may use available funds for such purpose.

(6) Further qualifications

Each officer or intelligence analyst assigned to a fusion center under this section shall satisfy any other qualifications the Under Secretary for Intelligence and Analysis may prescribe.

(d) Responsibilities

An officer or intelligence analyst assigned to a fusion center under this section shall—

(1) assist law enforcement agencies and other emergency response providers of State, local, and tribal governments and fusion center personnel in using information within the scope of the information sharing environment, including homeland security information, terrorism information, and weapons of mass destruction information, to develop a comprehensive and accurate threat picture;

(2) review homeland security-relevant information from law enforcement agencies and other emergency response providers of State, local, and tribal government;

(3) create intelligence and other information products derived from such information and other homeland security-relevant information provided by the Department; and

(4) assist in the dissemination of such products, as coordinated by the Under Secretary for Intelligence and Analysis, to law enforcement agencies and other emergency response providers of State, local, and tribal government, other fusion centers, and appropriate Federal agencies.

(e) Border intelligence priority

(1) In general

The Secretary shall make it a priority to assign officers and intelligence analysts under this section from United States Customs and Border Protection, United States Immigration and Customs Enforcement, and the Coast Guard to participating State, local, and regional fusion centers located in jurisdictions along land or maritime borders of the United States in order to enhance the integrity of and security at such borders by helping Federal, State, local, and tribal law enforcement authorities to identify, investigate, and otherwise interdict persons, weapons, and related contraband that pose a threat to homeland security.

(2) Border intelligence products

When performing the responsibilities described in subsection (d), officers and intelligence analysts assigned to participating State, local, and regional fusion centers under this section shall have, as a primary responsibility, the creation of border intelligence products that—

(A) assist State, local, and tribal law enforcement agencies in deploying their resources most efficiently to help detect and interdict terrorists, weapons of mass destruction, and related contraband at land or maritime borders of the United States;

(B) promote more consistent and timely sharing of border security-relevant information among jurisdictions along land or maritime borders of the United States; and

(C) enhance the Department's situational awareness of the threat of acts of terrorism at or involving the land or maritime borders of the United States.

(f) Database access

In order to fulfill the objectives described under subsection (d), each officer or intelligence analyst assigned to a fusion center under this section shall have appropriate access to all relevant Federal databases and information systems, consistent with any policies, guidelines, procedures, instructions, or standards established by the President or, as appropriate, the program manager of the information sharing environment for the implementation and management of that environment.

(g) Consumer feedback

(1) In general

The Secretary shall create a voluntary mechanism for any State, local, or tribal law enforcement officer or other emergency response provider who is a consumer of the intelligence or other information products referred to in subsection (d) to provide feedback to the Department on the quality and utility of such intelligence products.

(2) Report

Not later than one year after August 3, 2007, and annually thereafter, the Secretary shall submit to the Committee on Homeland Security and Governmental Affairs of the Senate and the Committee on Homeland Security of the House of Representatives a report that includes a description of the consumer feedback obtained under paragraph (1) and, if applicable, how the Department has adjusted its production of intelligence products in response to that consumer feedback.

(h) Rule of construction

(1) In general

The authorities granted under this section shall supplement the authorities granted under section 121(d) of this title and nothing in this section shall be construed to abrogate the authorities granted under section 121(d) of this title.

(2) Participation

Nothing in this section shall be construed to require a State, local, or regional government or entity to accept the assignment of officers or intelligence analysts of the Department into the fusion center of that State, locality, or region.

(i) Guidelines

The Secretary, in consultation with the Attorney General, shall establish guidelines for fusion centers created and operated by State and local governments, to include standards that any such fusion center shall—

(1) collaboratively develop a mission statement, identify expectations and goals, measure performance, and determine effectiveness for that fusion center;

(2) create a representative governance structure that includes law enforcement officers and other emergency response providers and, as appropriate, the private sector;

(3) create a collaborative environment for the sharing of intelligence and information among Federal, State, local, and tribal government agencies (including law enforcement officers and other emergency response providers), the private sector, and the public, consistent with any policies, guidelines, procedures, instructions, or standards established by the President or, as appropriate, the program manager of the information sharing environment;

(4) leverage the databases, systems, and networks available from public and private sector entities, in accordance with all applicable laws, to maximize information sharing;

(5) develop, publish, and adhere to a privacy and civil liberties policy consistent with Federal, State, and local law;

(6) provide, in coordination with the Privacy Officer of the Department and the Officer for Civil Rights and Civil Liberties of the Department, appropriate privacy and civil liberties training for all State, local, tribal, and private sector representatives at the fusion center;

(7) ensure appropriate security measures are in place for the facility, data, and personnel;

(8) select and train personnel based on the needs, mission, goals, and functions of that fusion center;

(9) offer a variety of intelligence and information services and products to recipients of fusion center intelligence and information; and

(10) incorporate law enforcement officers, other emergency response providers, and, as appropriate, the private sector, into all relevant phases of the intelligence and fusion process, consistent with the mission statement developed under paragraph (1), either through full time representatives or liaison relationships with the fusion center to enable the receipt and sharing of information and intelligence.

(j) Definitions

In this section—

(1) the term "fusion center" means a collaborative effort of 2 or more Federal, State, local, or tribal government agencies that combines resources, expertise, or information with the goal of maximizing the ability of such agencies to detect, prevent, investigate, apprehend, and respond to criminal or terrorist activity;

(2) the term "information sharing environment" means the information sharing environment established under section 485 of this title;

(3) the term "intelligence analyst" means an individual who regularly advises, administers, supervises, or performs work in the collection, gathering, analysis, evaluation, reporting, production, or dissemination of information on political, economic, social, cultural, physical, geographical, scientific, or military conditions, trends, or forces in foreign or domestic areas that directly or indirectly affect national security;

(4) the term "intelligence-led policing" means the collection and analysis of information to produce an intelligence end product designed to inform law enforcement decision making at the tactical and strategic levels; and

(5) the term "terrorism information" has the meaning given that term in section 485 of this title.

(k) Authorization of appropriations

There is authorized to be appropriated $10,000,000 for each of fiscal years 2008 through 2012, to carry out this section, except for subsection (i), including for hiring officers and intelligence analysts to replace officers and intelligence analysts who are assigned to fusion centers under this section.

(Pub. L. 107–296, title II, § 210A, as added Pub. L. 110–53, title V, § 511(a), Aug. 3, 2007, 121 Stat. 317.)

TRAINING FOR PREDEPLOYED OFFICERS AND ANALYSTS

Pub. L. 110–53, title V, § 511(b), Aug. 3, 2007, 121 Stat. 323, provided that: "An officer or analyst assigned to a fusion center by the Secretary of Homeland Security before the date of the enactment of this Act [Aug. 3, 2007] shall undergo the training described in section 210A(c)(4)(A) of the Homeland Security Act of 2002 [6 U.S.C. 124h(c)(4)(A)], as added by subsection (a), by not later than 6 months after such date."

§ 124i. Homeland Security Information Sharing Fellows Program

(a) Establishment

(1) In general

The Secretary, acting through the Under Secretary for Intelligence and Analysis, and in consultation with the Chief Human Capital Officer, shall establish a fellowship program in accordance with this section for the purpose of—

(A) detailing State, local, and tribal law enforcement officers and intelligence analysts to the Department in accordance with subchapter VI of chapter 33 of title 5 to participate in the work of the Office of Intelligence and Analysis in order to become familiar with—

(i) the relevant missions and capabilities of the Department and other Federal agencies; and

(ii) the role, programs, products, and personnel of the Office of Intelligence and Analysis; and

(B) promoting information sharing between the Department and State, local, and tribal law enforcement officers and intelligence analysts by assigning such officers and analysts to—

(i) serve as a point of contact in the Department to assist in the representation of State, local, and tribal information requirements;

(ii) identify information within the scope of the information sharing environment, including homeland security information, terrorism information, and weapons of mass destruction information, that is of interest to State, local, and tribal law enforcement officers, intelligence analysts, and other emergency response providers;

(iii) assist Department analysts in preparing and disseminating products derived from information within the scope of the information sharing environment, including homeland security information, terrorism information, and weapons of mass destruction information, that are tailored to State, local, and tribal law enforcement officers and intelligence analysts and designed to prepare for and thwart acts of terrorism; and

(iv) assist Department analysts in preparing products derived from information within the scope of the information sharing environment, including homeland security information, terrorism information, and weapons of mass destruction information, that are tailored to State, local, and tribal emergency response providers and assist in the dissemination of such products through appropriate Department channels.

(2) Program name

The program under this section shall be known as the "Homeland Security Information Sharing Fellows Program".

(b) Eligibility

(1) In general

In order to be eligible for selection as an Information Sharing Fellow under the program under this section, an individual shall—

(A) have homeland security-related responsibilities;

(B) be eligible for an appropriate security clearance;

(C) possess a valid need for access to classified information, as determined by the Under Secretary for Intelligence and Analysis;

(D) be an employee of an eligible entity; and

(E) have undergone appropriate privacy and civil liberties training that is developed, supported, or sponsored by the Privacy Officer and the Officer for Civil Rights and Civil Liberties, in consultation with the Privacy and Civil Liberties Oversight Board established under section 2000ee of title 42.

(2) Eligible entities

In this subsection, the term "eligible entity" means—

(A) a State, local, or regional fusion center;

(B) a State or local law enforcement or other government entity that serves a major metropolitan area, suburban area, or rural area, as determined by the Secretary;

(C) a State or local law enforcement or other government entity with port, border, or agricultural responsibilities, as determined by the Secretary;

(D) a tribal law enforcement or other authority; or

(E) such other entity as the Secretary determines is appropriate.

(c) Optional participation

No State, local, or tribal law enforcement or other government entity shall be required to participate in the Homeland Security Information Sharing Fellows Program.

(d) Procedures for nomination and selection

(1) In general

The Under Secretary for Intelligence and Analysis shall establish procedures to provide for the nomination and selection of individuals to participate in the Homeland Security Information Sharing Fellows Program.

(2) Limitations

The Under Secretary for Intelligence and Analysis shall—

(A) select law enforcement officers and intelligence analysts representing a broad cross-section of State, local, and tribal agencies; and

(B) ensure that the number of Information Sharing Fellows selected does not impede the activities of the Office of Intelligence and Analysis.

(Pub. L. 107–296, title II, §210B, as added Pub. L. 110–53, title V, §512(a), Aug. 3, 2007, 121 Stat. 324.)

§ 124j. Rural Policing Institute

(a) In general

The Secretary shall establish a Rural Policing Institute, which shall be administered by the Federal Law Enforcement Training Center, to target training to law enforcement agencies and other emergency response providers located in rural areas. The Secretary, through the Rural Policing Institute, shall—

(1) evaluate the needs of law enforcement agencies and other emergency response providers in rural areas;

(2) develop expert training programs designed to address the needs of law enforcement agencies and other emergency response providers in rural areas as identified in the evaluation conducted under paragraph (1), including training programs about intelligence-led policing and protections for privacy, civil rights, and civil liberties;

(3) provide the training programs developed under paragraph (2) to law enforcement agencies and other emergency response providers in rural areas; and

(4) conduct outreach efforts to ensure that local and tribal governments in rural areas are aware of the training programs developed under paragraph (2) so they can avail themselves of such programs.

(b) Curricula

The training at the Rural Policing Institute established under subsection (a) shall—

(1) be configured in a manner so as not to duplicate or displace any law enforcement or emergency response program of the Federal Law Enforcement Training Center or a local or tribal government entity in existence on August 3, 2007; and

(2) to the maximum extent practicable, be delivered in a cost-effective manner at facilities of the Department, on closed military installations with adequate training facilities, or at facilities operated by the participants.

(c) Definition

In this section, the term "rural" means an area that is not located in a metropolitan statistical area, as defined by the Office of Management and Budget.

(d) Authorization of appropriations

There are authorized to be appropriated to carry out this section (including for contracts, staff, and equipment)—

(1) $10,000,000 for fiscal year 2008; and

(2) $5,000,000 for each of fiscal years 2009 through 2013.

(Pub. L. 107–296, title II, §210C, as added Pub. L. 110–53, title V, §513(a), Aug. 3, 2007, 121 Stat. 327.)

§ 124k. Interagency Threat Assessment and Coordination Group

(a) In general

To improve the sharing of information within the scope of the information sharing environment established under section 485 of this title with State, local, tribal, and private sector officials, the Director of National Intelligence, through the program manager for the information sharing environment, in coordination with the Secretary, shall coordinate and oversee the creation of an Interagency Threat Assessment and Coordination Group (referred to in this section as the "ITACG").

(b) Composition of ITACG

The ITACG shall consist of—

(1) an ITACG Advisory Council to set policy and develop processes for the integration, analysis, and dissemination of federally-coordinated information within the scope of the information sharing environment, including homeland security information, terrorism information, and weapons of mass destruction information; and

(2) an ITACG Detail comprised of State, local, and tribal homeland security and law enforcement officers and intelligence analysts detailed to work in the National Counterterrorism Center with Federal intelligence analysts for the purpose of integrating, analyzing, and assisting in the dissemination of federally-coordinated information within the scope of the information sharing environment, including homeland security information, terrorism information, and weapons of mass destruction information, through appropriate channels identified by the ITACG Advisory Council.

(c) Responsibilities of program manager

The program manager, in consultation with the Information Sharing Council, shall—

(1) monitor and assess the efficacy of the ITACG; and

(2) not later than 180 days after August 3, 2007, and at least annually thereafter, submit to the Secretary, the Attorney General, the Director of National Intelligence, the Committee on Homeland Security and Governmental Affairs of the Senate and the Committee on Homeland Security of the House of Representatives a report on the progress of the ITACG.

(d) Responsibilities of Secretary

The Secretary, or the Secretary's designee, in coordination with the Director of the National Counterterrorism Center and the ITACG Advisory Council, shall—

(1) create policies and standards for the creation of information products derived from information within the scope of the information sharing environment, including homeland security information, terrorism information, and weapons of mass destruction information, that are suitable for dissemination to State, local, and tribal governments and the private sector;

(2) evaluate and develop processes for the timely dissemination of federally-coordinated information within the scope of the information sharing environment, including homeland security information, terrorism information, and weapons of mass destruction information, to State, local, and tribal governments and the private sector;

(3) establish criteria and a methodology for indicating to State, local, and tribal governments and the private sector the reliability of information within the scope of the information sharing environment, including homeland security information, terrorism information, and weapons of mass destruction information, disseminated to them;

(4) educate the intelligence community about the requirements of the State, local, and tribal homeland security, law enforcement, and other emergency response providers regarding information within the scope of the information sharing environment, including homeland security information, terrorism information, and weapons of mass destruction information;

(5) establish and maintain the ITACG Detail, which shall assign an appropriate number of State, local, and tribal homeland security and law enforcement officers and intelligence analysts to work in the National Counterterrorism Center who shall—

(A) educate and advise National Counterterrorism Center intelligence analysts about the requirements of the State, local, and tribal homeland security and law enforcement officers, and other emergency response providers regarding information within the scope of the information sharing environment, including homeland security information, terrorism information, and weapons of mass destruction information;

(B) assist National Counterterrorism Center intelligence analysts in integrating, analyzing, and otherwise preparing versions of products derived from information within the scope of the information sharing environment, including homeland security information, terrorism information, and weapons of mass destruction information that are unclassified or classified at the lowest possible level and suitable for dissemination to State, local, and tribal homeland security and law enforcement agencies in order to help deter and prevent terrorist attacks;

(C) implement, in coordination with National Counterterrorism Center intelligence analysts, the policies, processes, procedures, standards, and guidelines developed by the ITACG Advisory Council;

(D) assist in the dissemination of products derived from information within the scope of the information sharing environment, including homeland security information, terrorism information, and weapons of mass destruction information, to State, local, and tribal jurisdictions only through appropriate channels identified by the ITACG Advisory Council; and

(E) report directly to the senior intelligence official from the Department under paragraph (6);

(6) detail a senior intelligence official from the Department of Homeland Security to the National Counterterrorism Center, who shall—

(A) manage the day-to-day operations of the ITACG Detail;

(B) report directly to the Director of the National Counterterrorism Center or the Director's designee; and

(C) in coordination with the Director of the Federal Bureau of Investigation, and subject to the approval of the Director of the National Counterterrorism Center, select a deputy from the pool of available detailees from the Federal Bureau of Investigation in the National Counterterrorism Center; and

(7) establish, within the ITACG Advisory Council, a mechanism to select law enforcement officers and intelligence analysts for placement in the National Counterterrorism Center consistent with paragraph (5), using criteria developed by the ITACG Advisory Council that shall encourage participation from a broadly representative group of State, local, and tribal homeland security and law enforcement agencies.

(e) Membership

The Secretary, or the Secretary's designee, shall serve as the chair of the ITACG Advisory Council, which shall include—

(1) representatives of—

(A) the Department;

(B) the Federal Bureau of Investigation;

(C) the National Counterterrorism Center;

(D) the Department of Defense;

(E) the Department of Energy;

(F) the Department of State; and

(G) other Federal entities as appropriate;

(2) the program manager of the information sharing environment, designated under section 485(f) of this title, or the program manager's designee; and

(3) executive level law enforcement and intelligence officials from State, local, and tribal governments.

(f) Criteria

The Secretary, in consultation with the Director of National Intelligence, the Attorney General, and the program manager of the information sharing environment established under section 485 of this title, shall—

(1) establish procedures for selecting members of the ITACG Advisory Council and for the proper handling and safeguarding of products derived from information within the scope of the information sharing environment, including homeland security information, terrorism information, and weapons of mass destruction information, by those members; and

(2) ensure that at least 50 percent of the members of the ITACG Advisory Council are from State, local, and tribal governments.

(g) Operations

(1) In general

Beginning not later than 90 days after August 3, 2007, the ITACG Advisory Council shall meet regularly, but not less than quarterly, at the facilities of the National Counterterrorism Center of the Office of the Director of National Intelligence.

(2) Management

Pursuant to section 404*o*(f)(E)[1] of title 50, the Director of the National Counterterrorism Center, acting through the senior intelligence official from the Department of Homeland Security detailed pursuant to subsection (d)(6), shall ensure that—

(A) the products derived from information within the scope of the information sharing environment, including homeland security information, terrorism information, and weapons of mass destruction information, prepared by the National Counterterrorism Center and the ITACG Detail for distribution to State, local, and tribal homeland security and law enforcement agencies reflect the requirements of such agencies and are produced consistently with the policies, processes, procedures, standards, and guidelines established by the ITACG Advisory Council;

(B) in consultation with the ITACG Advisory Council and consistent with sections 403-1(f)(1)(B)(iii) and 404*o*(f)(E)[1] of title 50, all products described in subparagraph (A) are disseminated through existing channels of the Department and the Department of Justice and other appropriate channels to State, local, and tribal government officials and other entities;

(C) all detailees under subsection (d)(5) have appropriate access to all relevant information within the scope of the information sharing environment, including homeland security information, terrorism information, and weapons of mass destruction information, available at the National Counterterrorism Center in order to accomplish the objectives under that paragraph;

(D) all detailees under subsection (d)(5) have the appropriate security clearances and are trained in the procedures for handling, processing, storing, and disseminating classified products derived from information within the scope of the information sharing environment, including homeland security information, terrorism information, and weapons of mass destruction information; and

(E) all detailees under subsection (d)(5) complete appropriate privacy and civil liberties training.

(h) Inapplicability of the Federal Advisory Committee Act

The Federal Advisory Committee Act (5 U.S.C. App.) shall not apply to the ITACG or any subsidiary groups thereof.

(i) Authorization of appropriations

There are authorized to be appropriated such sums as may be necessary for each of fiscal years 2008 through 2012 to carry out this section, including to obtain security clearances for the State, local, and tribal participants in the ITACG.

(Pub. L. 107–296, title II, §210D, as added Pub. L. 110–53, title V, §521(a), Aug. 3, 2007, 121 Stat. 328.)

[1] So in original. Probably should be section "404*o*(f)(1)(E)".

REFERENCES IN TEXT

The Federal Advisory Committee Act, referred to in subsec. (h), is Pub. L. 92–463, Oct. 6, 1972, 86 Stat. 770, which is set out in the Appendix to Title 5, Government Organization and Employees.

§ 124*l*. National asset database

(a) Establishment

(1) National asset database

The Secretary shall establish and maintain a national database of each system or asset that—

(A) the Secretary, in consultation with appropriate homeland security officials of the States, determines to be vital and the loss, interruption, incapacity, or destruction of which would have a negative or debilitating effect on the economic security, public health, or safety of the United States, any State, or any local government; or

(B) the Secretary determines is appropriate for inclusion in the database.

(2) Prioritized critical infrastructure list

In accordance with Homeland Security Presidential Directive–7, as in effect on January 1, 2007, the Secretary shall establish and maintain a single classified prioritized list of systems and assets included in the database under paragraph (1) that the Secretary determines would, if destroyed or disrupted, cause national or regional catastrophic effects.

(b) Use of database

The Secretary shall use the database established under subsection (a)(1) in the development and implementation of Department plans and programs as appropriate.

(c) Maintenance of database

(1) In general

The Secretary shall maintain and annually update the database established under subsection (a)(1) and the list established under subsection (a)(2), including—

(A) establishing data collection guidelines and providing such guidelines to the appropriate homeland security official of each State;

(B) regularly reviewing the guidelines established under subparagraph (A), including by consulting with the appropriate homeland security officials of States, to solicit feedback about the guidelines, as appropriate;

(C) after providing the homeland security official of a State with the guidelines under subparagraph (A), allowing the official a reasonable amount of time to submit to the Secretary any data submissions recommended by the official for inclusion in the database established under subsection (a)(1);

(D) examining the contents and identifying any submissions made by such an official that are described incorrectly or that do not meet the guidelines established under subparagraph (A); and

(E) providing to the appropriate homeland security official of each relevant State a list of submissions identified under subparagraph (D) for review and possible correction before the Secretary finalizes the decision of which submissions will be included in the database established under subsection (a)(1).

(2) Organization of information in database

The Secretary shall organize the contents of the database established under subsection (a)(1) and the list established under subsection (a)(2) as the Secretary determines is appropriate. Any organizational structure of such contents shall include the categorization of the contents—

(A) according to the sectors listed in National Infrastructure Protection Plan developed pursuant to Homeland Security Presidential Directive–7; and

(B) by the State and county of their location.

(3) Private sector integration

The Secretary shall identify and evaluate methods, including the Department's Protected Critical Infrastructure Information Program, to acquire relevant private sector information for the purpose of using that information to generate any database or list, including the database established under subsection (a)(1) and the list established under subsection (a)(2).

(4) Retention of classification

The classification of information required to be provided to Congress, the Department, or any other department or agency under this section by a sector-specific agency, including the assignment of a level of classification of such information, shall be binding on Congress, the Department, and that other Federal agency.

(d) Reports

(1) Report required

Not later than 180 days after August 3, 2007, and annually thereafter, the Secretary shall submit to the Committee on Homeland Security and Governmental Affairs of the Senate and the Committee on Homeland Security of the House of Representatives a report on the database established under subsection (a)(1) and the list established under subsection (a)(2).

(2) Contents of report

Each such report shall include the following:

(A) The name, location, and sector classification of each of the systems and assets on the list established under subsection (a)(2).

(B) The name, location, and sector classification of each of the systems and assets on such list that are determined by the Secretary to be most at risk to terrorism.

(C) Any significant challenges in compiling the list of the systems and assets included on such list or in the database established under subsection (a)(1).

(D) Any significant changes from the preceding report in the systems and assets included on such list or in such database.

(E) If appropriate, the extent to which such database and such list have been used, individually or jointly, for allocating funds by the Federal Government to prevent, reduce, mitigate, or respond to acts of terrorism.

(F) The amount of coordination between the Department and the private sector, through any entity of the Department that meets with representatives of private sector industries for purposes of such coordination, for the purpose of ensuring the accuracy of such database and such list.

(G) Any other information the Secretary deems relevant.

(3) Classified information

The report shall be submitted in unclassified form but may contain a classified annex.

(e) Inspector General study

By not later than two years after August 3, 2007, the Inspector General of the Department shall conduct a study of the implementation of this section.

(f) National Infrastructure Protection Consortium

The Secretary may establish a consortium to be known as the "National Infrastructure Protection Consortium". The Consortium may advise the Secretary on the best way to identify, generate, organize, and maintain any database or list of systems and assets established by the Secretary, including the database established under subsection (a)(1) and the list established under subsection (a)(2). If the Secretary establishes the National Infrastructure Protection Consortium, the Consortium may—

(1) be composed of national laboratories, Federal agencies, State and local homeland security organizations, academic institutions, or national Centers of Excellence that have demonstrated experience working with and identifying critical infrastructure and key resources; and

(2) provide input to the Secretary on any request pertaining to the contents of such database or such list.

(Pub. L. 107–296, title II, §210E, as added Pub. L. 110–53, title X, §1001(a), Aug. 3, 2007, 121 Stat. 372.)

DEADLINES FOR IMPLEMENTATION AND NOTIFICATION OF CONGRESS

Pub. L. 110–53, title X, §1001(b), Aug. 3, 2007, 121 Stat. 374, provided that: "Not later than 180 days after the date of the enactment of this Act [Aug. 3, 2007], the Secretary of Homeland Security shall submit the first report required under section 210E(d) of the Homeland Security Act of 2002 [6 U.S.C. 124*l*(d)], as added by subsection (a)."

PART B—CRITICAL INFRASTRUCTURE INFORMATION

§ 131. Definitions

In this part:

(1) Agency

The term "agency" has the meaning given it in section 551 of title 5.

(2) Covered Federal agency

The term "covered Federal agency" means the Department of Homeland Security.

(3) Critical infrastructure information

The term "critical infrastructure information" means information not customarily in the public domain and related to the security of critical infrastructure or protected systems—

(A) actual, potential, or threatened interference with, attack on, compromise of, or incapacitation of critical infrastructure or protected systems by either physical or computer-based attack or other similar conduct (including the misuse of or unauthorized access to all types of communications and data transmission systems) that violates Federal, State, or local law, harms interstate commerce of the United States, or threatens public health or safety;

(B) the ability of any critical infrastructure or protected system to resist such interference, compromise, or incapacitation, including any planned or past assessment, projection, or estimate of the vulnerability of critical infrastructure or a protected system, including security testing, risk evaluation thereto, risk management planning, or risk audit; or

(C) any planned or past operational problem or solution regarding critical infrastructure or protected systems, including repair, recovery, reconstruction, insurance, or continuity, to the extent it is related to such interference, compromise, or incapacitation.

(4) Critical infrastructure protection program

The term "critical infrastructure protection program" means any component or bureau of a covered Federal agency that has been designated by the President or any agency head to receive critical infrastructure information.

(5) Information Sharing and Analysis Organization

The term "Information Sharing and Analysis Organization" means any formal or informal entity or collaboration created or employed by public or private sector organizations, for purposes of—

(A) gathering and analyzing critical infrastructure information in order to better understand security problems and interdependencies related to critical infrastructure and protected systems, so as to ensure the availability, integrity, and reliability thereof;

(B) communicating or disclosing critical infrastructure information to help prevent, detect, mitigate, or recover from the effects of a[1] interference, compromise, or a[2] incapacitation problem related to critical infrastructure or protected systems; and

(C) voluntarily disseminating critical infrastructure information to its members, State, local, and Federal Governments, or any other entities that may be of assistance in carrying out the purposes specified in subparagraphs (A) and (B).

(6) Protected system

The term "protected system"—

(A) means any service, physical or computer-based system, process, or procedure

[1] So in original. Probably should be "an".

[2] So in original. The word "a" probably should not appear.

that directly or indirectly affects the viability of a facility of critical infrastructure; and

(B) includes any physical or computer-based system, including a computer, computer system, computer or communications network, or any component hardware or element thereof, software program, processing instructions, or information or data in transmission or storage therein, irrespective of the medium of transmission or storage.

(7) Voluntary

(A) In general

The term "voluntary", in the case of any submittal of critical infrastructure information to a covered Federal agency, means the submittal thereof in the absence of such agency's exercise of legal authority to compel access to or submission of such information and may be accomplished by a single entity or an Information Sharing and Analysis Organization on behalf of itself or its members.

(B) Exclusions

The term "voluntary"—

(i) in the case of any action brought under the securities laws as is defined in section 78c(a)(47) of title 15—

(I) does not include information or statements contained in any documents or materials filed with the Securities and Exchange Commission, or with Federal banking regulators, pursuant to section 78*l*(i) of title 15; and

(II) with respect to the submittal of critical infrastructure information, does not include any disclosure or writing that when made accompanied the solicitation of an offer or a sale of securities; and

(ii) does not include information or statements submitted or relied upon as a basis for making licensing or permitting determinations, or during regulatory proceedings.

(Pub. L. 107–296, title II, § 212, Nov. 25, 2002, 116 Stat. 2150.)

SHORT TITLE

For short title of this part as the "Critical Infrastructure Information Act of 2002", see section 211 of Pub. L. 107–296, set out as a note under section 101 of this title.

§ 132. Designation of critical infrastructure protection program

A critical infrastructure protection program may be designated as such by one of the following:

(1) The President.

(2) The Secretary of Homeland Security.

(Pub. L. 107–296, title II, § 213, Nov. 25, 2002, 116 Stat. 2152.)

§ 133. Protection of voluntarily shared critical infrastructure information

(a) Protection

(1) In general

Notwithstanding any other provision of law, critical infrastructure information (including the identity of the submitting person or entity) that is voluntarily submitted to a covered Federal agency for use by that agency regarding the security of critical infrastructure and protected systems, analysis, warning, interdependency study, recovery, reconstitution, or other informational purpose, when accompanied by an express statement specified in paragraph (2)—

(A) shall be exempt from disclosure under section 552 of title 5 (commonly referred to as the Freedom of Information Act);

(B) shall not be subject to any agency rules or judicial doctrine regarding ex parte communications with a decision making official;

(C) shall not, without the written consent of the person or entity submitting such information, be used directly by such agency, any other Federal, State, or local authority, or any third party, in any civil action arising under Federal or State law if such information is submitted in good faith;

(D) shall not, without the written consent of the person or entity submitting such information, be used or disclosed by any officer or employee of the United States for purposes other than the purposes of this part, except—

(i) in furtherance of an investigation or the prosecution of a criminal act; or

(ii) when disclosure of the information would be—

(I) to either House of Congress, or to the extent of matter within its jurisdiction, any committee or subcommittee thereof, any joint committee thereof or subcommittee of any such joint committee; or

(II) to the Comptroller General, or any authorized representative of the Comptroller General, in the course of the performance of the duties of the Government Accountability Office.[1]

(E) shall not, if provided to a State or local government or government agency—

(i) be made available pursuant to any State or local law requiring disclosure of information or records;

(ii) otherwise be disclosed or distributed to any party by said State or local government or government agency without the written consent of the person or entity submitting such information; or

(iii) be used other than for the purpose of protecting critical infrastructure or protected systems, or in furtherance of an investigation or the prosecution of a criminal act; and

(F) does not constitute a waiver of any applicable privilege or protection provided under law, such as trade secret protection.

(2) Express statement

For purposes of paragraph (1), the term "express statement", with respect to information or records, means—

(A) in the case of written information or records, a written marking on the informa-

[1] So in original. The period probably should be a semicolon.

tion or records substantially similar to the following: "This information is voluntarily submitted to the Federal Government in expectation of protection from disclosure as provided by the provisions of the Critical Infrastructure Information Act of 2002."; or

(B) in the case of oral information, a similar written statement submitted within a reasonable period following the oral communication.

(b) Limitation

No communication of critical infrastructure information to a covered Federal agency made pursuant to this part shall be considered to be an action subject to the requirements of the Federal Advisory Committee Act.

(c) Independently obtained information

Nothing in this section shall be construed to limit or otherwise affect the ability of a State, local, or Federal Government entity, agency, or authority, or any third party, under applicable law, to obtain critical infrastructure information in a manner not covered by subsection (a) of this section, including any information lawfully and properly disclosed generally or broadly to the public and to use such information in any manner permitted by law.

(d) Treatment of voluntary submittal of information

The voluntary submittal to the Government of information or records that are protected from disclosure by this part shall not be construed to constitute compliance with any requirement to submit such information to a Federal agency under any other provision of law.

(e) Procedures

(1) In general

The Secretary of the Department of Homeland Security shall, in consultation with appropriate representatives of the National Security Council and the Office of Science and Technology Policy, establish uniform procedures for the receipt, care, and storage by Federal agencies of critical infrastructure information that is voluntarily submitted to the Government. The procedures shall be established not later than 90 days after November 25, 2002.

(2) Elements

The procedures established under paragraph (1) shall include mechanisms regarding—

(A) the acknowledgement of receipt by Federal agencies of critical infrastructure information that is voluntarily submitted to the Government;

(B) the maintenance of the identification of such information as voluntarily submitted to the Government for purposes of and subject to the provisions of this part;

(C) the care and storage of such information; and

(D) the protection and maintenance of the confidentiality of such information so as to permit the sharing of such information within the Federal Government and with State and local governments, and the issuance of notices and warnings related to the protection of critical infrastructure and protected systems, in such manner as to protect from public disclosure the identity of the submitting person or entity, or information that is proprietary, business sensitive, relates specifically to the submitting person or entity, and is otherwise not appropriately in the public domain.

(f) Penalties

Whoever, being an officer or employee of the United States or of any department or agency thereof, knowingly publishes, divulges, discloses, or makes known in any manner or to any extent not authorized by law, any critical infrastructure information protected from disclosure by this part coming to him in the course of this employment or official duties or by reason of any examination or investigation made by, or return, report, or record made to or filed with, such department or agency or officer or employee thereof, shall be fined under title 18, imprisoned not more than 1 year, or both, and shall be removed from office or employment.

(g) Authority to issue warnings

The Federal Government may provide advisories, alerts, and warnings to relevant companies, targeted sectors, other governmental entities, or the general public regarding potential threats to critical infrastructure as appropriate. In issuing a warning, the Federal Government shall take appropriate actions to protect from disclosure—

(1) the source of any voluntarily submitted critical infrastructure information that forms the basis for the warning; or

(2) information that is proprietary, business sensitive, relates specifically to the submitting person or entity, or is otherwise not appropriately in the public domain.

(h) Authority to delegate

The President may delegate authority to a critical infrastructure protection program, designated under section 132 of this title, to enter into a voluntary agreement to promote critical infrastructure security, including with any Information Sharing and Analysis Organization, or a plan of action as otherwise defined in section 2158 of title 50, Appendix.

(Pub. L. 107–296, title II, §214, Nov. 25, 2002, 116 Stat. 2152; Pub. L. 108–271, §8(b), July 7, 2004, 118 Stat. 814.)

REFERENCES IN TEXT

The Critical Infrastructure Information Act of 2002, referred to in subsec. (a)(2)(A), is subtitle B (§211 et seq.) of title II of Pub. L. 107–296, Nov. 25, 2002, 116 Stat. 2150, which is classified generally to this part. For complete classification of this Act to the Code, see Short Title note set out under section 101 of this title and Tables.

The Federal Advisory Committee Act, referred to in subsec. (b), is Pub. L. 92–463, Oct. 6, 1972, 86 Stat. 770, as amended, which is set out in the Appendix to Title 5, Government Organization and Employees.

AMENDMENTS

2004—Subsec. (a)(1)(D)(ii)(II). Pub. L. 108–271 substituted "Government Accountability Office" for "General Accounting Office".

§134. No private right of action

Nothing in this part may be construed to create a private right of action for enforcement of any provision of this chapter.

(Pub. L. 107–296, title II, §215, Nov. 25, 2002, 116 Stat. 2155.)

PART C—INFORMATION SECURITY

§141. Procedures for sharing information

The Secretary shall establish procedures on the use of information shared under this subchapter that—

(1) limit the redissemination of such information to ensure that it is not used for an unauthorized purpose;

(2) ensure the security and confidentiality of such information;

(3) protect the constitutional and statutory rights of any individuals who are subjects of such information; and

(4) provide data integrity through the timely removal and destruction of obsolete or erroneous names and information.

(Pub. L. 107–296, title II, §221, Nov. 25, 2002, 116 Stat. 2155.)

REFERENCES IN TEXT

This subchapter, referred to in text, was in the original "this title", meaning title II of Pub. L. 107–296, Nov. 25, 2002, 116 Stat. 2145, which enacted this subchapter, amended sections 1030, 2511, 2512, 2520, 2701 to 2703, and 3125 of Title 18, Crimes and Criminal Procedure, sections 3712 and 3722 of Title 42, The Public Health and Welfare, and section 401a of Title 50, War and National Defense, and enacted provisions set out as a note under section 101 of this title and listed in a Provisions for Review, Promulgation, or Amendment of Federal Sentencing Guidelines Relating to Specific Offenses table set out under section 994 of Title 28, Judiciary and Judicial Procedure. For complete classification of title II to the Code, see Tables.

§142. Privacy officer

(a) Appointment and responsibilities

The Secretary shall appoint a senior official in the Department, who shall report directly to the Secretary, to assume primary responsibility for privacy policy, including—

(1) assuring that the use of technologies sustain, and do not erode, privacy protections relating to the use, collection, and disclosure of personal information;

(2) assuring that personal information contained in Privacy Act systems of records is handled in full compliance with fair information practices as set out in the Privacy Act of 1974 [5 U.S.C. 552a];

(3) evaluating legislative and regulatory proposals involving collection, use, and disclosure of personal information by the Federal Government;

(4) conducting a privacy impact assessment of proposed rules of the Department or that of the Department on the privacy of personal information, including the type of personal information collected and the number of people affected;

(5) coordinating with the Officer for Civil Rights and Civil Liberties to ensure that—

(A) programs, policies, and procedures involving civil rights, civil liberties, and privacy considerations are addressed in an integrated and comprehensive manner; and

(B) Congress receives appropriate reports on such programs, policies, and procedures; and

(6) preparing a report to Congress on an annual basis on activities of the Department that affect privacy, including complaints of privacy violations, implementation of the Privacy Act of 1974 [5 U.S.C. 552a], internal controls, and other matters.

(b) Authority to investigate

(1) In general

The senior official appointed under subsection (a) may—

(A) have access to all records, reports, audits, reviews, documents, papers, recommendations, and other materials available to the Department that relate to programs and operations with respect to the responsibilities of the senior official under this section;

(B) make such investigations and reports relating to the administration of the programs and operations of the Department as are, in the senior official's judgment, necessary or desirable;

(C) subject to the approval of the Secretary, require by subpoena the production, by any person other than a Federal agency, of all information, documents, reports, answers, records, accounts, papers, and other data and documentary evidence necessary to performance of the responsibilities of the senior official under this section; and

(D) administer to or take from any person an oath, affirmation, or affidavit, whenever necessary to performance of the responsibilities of the senior official under this section.

(2) Enforcement of subpoenas

Any subpoena issued under paragraph (1)(C) shall, in the case of contumacy or refusal to obey, be enforceable by order of any appropriate United States district court.

(3) Effect of oaths

Any oath, affirmation, or affidavit administered or taken under paragraph (1)(D) by or before an employee of the Privacy Office designated for that purpose by the senior official appointed under subsection (a) shall have the same force and effect as if administered or taken by or before an officer having a seal of office.

(c) Supervision and coordination

(1) In general

The senior official appointed under subsection (a) shall—

(A) report to, and be under the general supervision of, the Secretary; and

(B) coordinate activities with the Inspector General of the Department in order to avoid duplication of effort.

(2) Coordination with the Inspector General

(A) In general

Except as provided in subparagraph (B), the senior official appointed under subsection (a) may investigate any matter relating to possible violations or abuse concerning the administration of any program or operation of the Department relevant to the purposes under this section.

(B) Coordination

(i) Referral

Before initiating any investigation described under subparagraph (A), the senior official shall refer the matter and all related complaints, allegations, and information to the Inspector General of the Department.

(ii) Determinations and notifications by the Inspector General

(I) In general

Not later than 30 days after the receipt of a matter referred under clause (i), the Inspector General shall—

(aa) make a determination regarding whether the Inspector General intends to initiate an audit or investigation of the matter referred under clause (i); and

(bb) notify the senior official of that determination.

(II) Investigation not initiated

If the Inspector General notifies the senior official under subclause (I)(bb) that the Inspector General intended to initiate an audit or investigation, but does not initiate that audit or investigation within 90 days after providing that notification, the Inspector General shall further notify the senior official that an audit or investigation was not initiated. The further notification under this subclause shall be made not later than 3 days after the end of that 90-day period.

(iii) Investigation by senior official

The senior official may investigate a matter referred under clause (i) if—

(I) the Inspector General notifies the senior official under clause (ii)(I)(bb) that the Inspector General does not intend to initiate an audit or investigation relating to that matter; or

(II) the Inspector General provides a further notification under clause (ii)(II) relating to that matter.

(iv) Privacy training

Any employee of the Office of Inspector General who audits or investigates any matter referred under clause (i) shall be required to receive adequate training on privacy laws, rules, and regulations, to be provided by an entity approved by the Inspector General in consultation with the senior official appointed under subsection (a).

(d) Notification to Congress on removal

If the Secretary removes the senior official appointed under subsection (a) or transfers that senior official to another position or location within the Department, the Secretary shall—

(1) promptly submit a written notification of the removal or transfer to Houses of Congress; and

(2) include in any such notification the reasons for the removal or transfer.

(e) Reports by senior official to Congress

The senior official appointed under subsection (a) shall—

(1) submit reports directly to the Congress regarding performance of the responsibilities of the senior official under this section, without any prior comment or amendment by the Secretary, Deputy Secretary, or any other officer or employee of the Department or the Office of Management and Budget; and

(2) inform the Committee on Homeland Security and Governmental Affairs of the Senate and the Committee on Homeland Security of the House of Representatives not later than—

(A) 30 days after the Secretary disapproves the senior official's request for a subpoena under subsection (b)(1)(C) or the Secretary substantively modifies the requested subpoena; or

(B) 45 days after the senior official's request for a subpoena under subsection (b)(1)(C), if that subpoena has not either been approved or disapproved by the Secretary.

(Pub. L. 107–296, title II, § 222, Nov. 25, 2002, 116 Stat. 2155; Pub. L. 108–458, title VIII, § 8305, Dec. 17, 2004, 118 Stat. 3868; Pub. L. 110–53, title VIII, § 802, Aug. 3, 2007, 121 Stat. 358.)

REFERENCES IN TEXT

The Privacy Act of 1974, referred to in subsec. (a)(2), (6), is Pub. L. 93–579, Dec. 31, 1974, 88 Stat. 1896, as amended, which enacted section 552a of Title 5, Government Organization and Employees, and provisions set out as notes under section 552a of Title 5. For complete classification of this Act to the Code, see Short Title of 1974 Amendment note set out under section 552a of Title 5 and Tables.

AMENDMENTS

2007—Pub. L. 110–53 designated existing provisions as subsec. (a), inserted heading, and added subsecs. (b) to (e).

2004—Pub. L. 108–458, § 8305(1), inserted ", who shall report directly to the Secretary," after "in the Department" in introductory provisions.

Pars. (5), (6). Pub. L. 108–458, § 8305(2)–(4), added par. (5) and redesignated former par. (5) as (6).

§ 143. Enhancement of non-Federal cybersecurity

In carrying out the responsibilities under section 121 of this title, the Under Secretary for Intelligence and Analysis, in cooperation with the Assistant Secretary for Infrastructure Protection[1] shall—

(1) as appropriate, provide to State and local government entities, and upon request to private entities that own or operate critical information systems—

(A) analysis and warnings related to threats to, and vulnerabilities of, critical information systems; and

(B) in coordination with the Under Secretary for Emergency Preparedness and Response, crisis management support in response to threats to, or attacks on, critical information systems; and

[1] So in original. Probably should be followed by a comma.

(2) as appropriate, provide technical assistance, upon request, to the private sector and other government entities, in coordination with the Under Secretary for Emergency Preparedness and Response, with respect to emergency recovery plans to respond to major failures of critical information systems.

(Pub. L. 107–296, title II, § 223, Nov. 25, 2002, 116 Stat. 2156; Pub. L. 110–53, title V, § 531(b)(1)(A), Aug. 3, 2007, 121 Stat. 334.)

AMENDMENTS

2007—Pub. L. 110–53 substituted "Under Secretary for Intelligence and Analysis, in cooperation with the Assistant Secretary for Infrastructure Protection" for "Under Secretary for Information Analysis and Infrastructure Protection" in introductory provisions.

§ 144. NET Guard

The Assistant Secretary for Infrastructure Protection may establish a national technology guard, to be known as "NET Guard", comprised of local teams of volunteers with expertise in relevant areas of science and technology, to assist local communities to respond and recover from attacks on information systems and communications networks.

(Pub. L. 107–296, title II, § 224, Nov. 25, 2002, 116 Stat. 2156; Pub. L. 110–53, title V, § 531(b)(1)(B), Aug. 3, 2007, 121 Stat. 334.)

AMENDMENTS

2007—Pub. L. 110–53 substituted "Assistant Secretary for Infrastructure Protection" for "Under Secretary for Information Analysis and Infrastructure Protection".

§ 145. Cyber Security Enhancement Act of 2002

(a) Short title

This section may be cited as the "Cyber Security Enhancement Act of 2002".

(b) Amendment of sentencing guidelines relating to certain computer crimes

(1) Directive to the United States Sentencing Commission

Pursuant to its authority under section 994(p) of title 28 and in accordance with this subsection, the United States Sentencing Commission shall review and, if appropriate, amend its guidelines and its policy statements applicable to persons convicted of an offense under section 1030 of title 18.

(2) Requirements

In carrying out this subsection, the Sentencing Commission shall—

(A) ensure that the sentencing guidelines and policy statements reflect the serious nature of the offenses described in paragraph (1), the growing incidence of such offenses, and the need for an effective deterrent and appropriate punishment to prevent such offenses;

(B) consider the following factors and the extent to which the guidelines may or may not account for them—

(i) the potential and actual loss resulting from the offense;

(ii) the level of sophistication and planning involved in the offense;

(iii) whether the offense was committed for purposes of commercial advantage or private financial benefit;

(iv) whether the defendant acted with malicious intent to cause harm in committing the offense;

(v) the extent to which the offense violated the privacy rights of individuals harmed;

(vi) whether the offense involved a computer used by the government in furtherance of national defense, national security, or the administration of justice;

(vii) whether the violation was intended to or had the effect of significantly interfering with or disrupting a critical infrastructure; and

(viii) whether the violation was intended to or had the effect of creating a threat to public health or safety, or injury to any person;

(C) assure reasonable consistency with other relevant directives and with other sentencing guidelines;

(D) account for any additional aggravating or mitigating circumstances that might justify exceptions to the generally applicable sentencing ranges;

(E) make any necessary conforming changes to the sentencing guidelines; and

(F) assure that the guidelines adequately meet the purposes of sentencing as set forth in section 3553(a)(2) of title 18.

(c) Study and report on computer crimes

Not later than May 1, 2003, the United States Sentencing Commission shall submit a brief report to Congress that explains any actions taken by the Sentencing Commission in response to this section and includes any recommendations the Commission may have regarding statutory penalties for offenses under section 1030 of title 18.

(d) Emergency disclosure exception

(1) Omitted

(2) Reporting of disclosures

A government entity that receives a disclosure under section 2702(b) of title 18 shall file, not later than 90 days after such disclosure, a report to the Attorney General stating the paragraph of that section under which the disclosure was made, the date of the disclosure, the entity to which the disclosure was made, the number of customers or subscribers to whom the information disclosed pertained, and the number of communications, if any, that were disclosed. The Attorney General shall publish all such reports into a single report to be submitted to Congress 1 year after November 25, 2002.

(Pub. L. 107–296, title II, § 225, Nov. 25, 2002, 116 Stat. 2156.)

CODIFICATION

Section is comprised of section 225 of Pub. L. 107–296. Subsecs. (d)(1) and (e) to (j) of section 225 of Pub. L. 107–296 amended sections 1030, 2511, 2512, 2520, 2701 to 2703, and 3125 of Title 18, Crimes and Criminal Procedure.

PART D—OFFICE OF SCIENCE AND TECHNOLOGY

§ 161. Establishment of Office; Director

(a) Establishment

(1) In general

There is hereby established within the Department of Justice an Office of Science and Technology (hereinafter in this subchapter referred to as the "Office").

(2) Authority

The Office shall be under the general authority of the Assistant Attorney General, Office of Justice Programs, and shall be established within the National Institute of Justice.

(b) Director

The Office shall be headed by a Director, who shall be an individual appointed based on approval by the Office of Personnel Management of the executive qualifications of the individual.

(Pub. L. 107–296, title II, § 231, Nov. 25, 2002, 116 Stat. 2159.)

REFERENCES IN TEXT

This subchapter, referred to in subsec. (a)(1), was in the original "this title", meaning title II of Pub. L. 107–296, Nov. 25, 2002, 116 Stat. 2145, which enacted this subchapter, amended sections 1030, 2511, 2512, 2520, 2701 to 2703, and 3125 of Title 18, Crimes and Criminal Procedure, sections 3712 and 3722 of Title 42, The Public Health and Welfare, and section 401a of Title 50, War and National Defense, and enacted provisions set out as a note under section 101 of this title and listed in a Provisions for Review, Promulgation, or Amendment of Federal Sentencing Guidelines Relating to Specific Offenses table set out under section 994 of Title 28, Judiciary and Judicial Procedure. For complete classification of title II to the Code, see Tables.

§ 162. Mission of Office; duties

(a) Mission

The mission of the Office shall be—

(1) to serve as the national focal point for work on law enforcement technology; and

(2) to carry out programs that, through the provision of equipment, training, and technical assistance, improve the safety and effectiveness of law enforcement technology and improve access to such technology by Federal, State, and local law enforcement agencies.

(b) Duties

In carrying out its mission, the Office shall have the following duties:

(1) To provide recommendations and advice to the Attorney General.

(2) To establish and maintain advisory groups (which shall be exempt from the provisions of the Federal Advisory Committee Act (5 U.S.C. App.)) to assess the law enforcement technology needs of Federal, State, and local law enforcement agencies.

(3) To establish and maintain performance standards in accordance with the National Technology Transfer and Advancement Act of 1995 (Public Law 104–113) for, and test and evaluate law enforcement technologies that may be used by, Federal, State, and local law enforcement agencies.

(4) To establish and maintain a program to certify, validate, and mark or otherwise recognize law enforcement technology products that conform to standards established and maintained by the Office in accordance with the National Technology Transfer and Advancement Act of 1995 (Public Law 104–113). The program may, at the discretion of the Office, allow for supplier's declaration of conformity with such standards.

(5) To work with other entities within the Department of Justice, other Federal agencies, and the executive office of the President to establish a coordinated Federal approach on issues related to law enforcement technology.

(6) To carry out research, development, testing, evaluation, and cost-benefit analyses in fields that would improve the safety, effectiveness, and efficiency of law enforcement technologies used by Federal, State, and local law enforcement agencies, including, but not limited to—

(A) weapons capable of preventing use by unauthorized persons, including personalized guns;

(B) protective apparel;

(C) bullet-resistant and explosion-resistant glass;

(D) monitoring systems and alarm systems capable of providing precise location information;

(E) wire and wireless interoperable communication technologies;

(F) tools and techniques that facilitate investigative and forensic work, including computer forensics;

(G) equipment for particular use in counterterrorism, including devices and technologies to disable terrorist devices;

(H) guides to assist State and local law enforcement agencies;

(I) DNA identification technologies; and

(J) tools and techniques that facilitate investigations of computer crime.

(7) To administer a program of research, development, testing, and demonstration to improve the interoperability of voice and data public safety communications.

(8) To serve on the Technical Support Working Group of the Department of Defense, and on other relevant interagency panels, as requested.

(9) To develop, and disseminate to State and local law enforcement agencies, technical assistance and training materials for law enforcement personnel, including prosecutors.

(10) To operate the regional National Law Enforcement and Corrections Technology Centers and, to the extent necessary, establish additional centers through a competitive process.

(11) To administer a program of acquisition, research, development, and dissemination of advanced investigative analysis and forensic tools to assist State and local law enforcement agencies in combating cybercrime.

(12) To support research fellowships in support of its mission.

(13) To serve as a clearinghouse for information on law enforcement technologies.

(14) To represent the United States and State and local law enforcement agencies, as requested, in international activities concerning law enforcement technology.

(15) To enter into contracts and cooperative agreements and provide grants, which may require in-kind or cash matches from the recipient, as necessary to carry out its mission.

(16) To carry out other duties assigned by the Attorney General to accomplish the mission of the Office.

(c) Competition required

Except as otherwise expressly provided by law, all research and development carried out by or through the Office shall be carried out on a competitive basis.

(d) Information from Federal agencies

Federal agencies shall, upon request from the Office and in accordance with Federal law, provide the Office with any data, reports, or other information requested, unless compliance with such request is otherwise prohibited by law.

(e) Publications

Decisions concerning publications issued by the Office shall rest solely with the Director of the Office.

(f) Transfer of funds

The Office may transfer funds to other Federal agencies or provide funding to non-Federal entities through grants, cooperative agreements, or contracts to carry out its duties under this section: *Provided*, That any such transfer or provision of funding shall be carried out in accordance with section 605 of Public Law 107–77.

(g) Annual report

The Director of the Office shall include with the budget justification materials submitted to Congress in support of the Department of Justice budget for each fiscal year (as submitted with the budget of the President under section 1105(a) of title 31) a report on the activities of the Office. Each such report shall include the following:

(1) For the period of 5 fiscal years beginning with the fiscal year for which the budget is submitted—

(A) the Director's assessment of the needs of Federal, State, and local law enforcement agencies for assistance with respect to law enforcement technology and other matters consistent with the mission of the Office; and

(B) a strategic plan for meeting such needs of such law enforcement agencies.

(2) For the fiscal year preceding the fiscal year for which such budget is submitted, a description of the activities carried out by the Office and an evaluation of the extent to which those activities successfully meet the needs assessed under paragraph (1)(A) in previous reports.

(Pub. L. 107–296, title II, §232, Nov. 25, 2002, 116 Stat. 2159; Pub. L. 108–7, div. L, §103(1), Feb. 20, 2003, 117 Stat. 529.)

REFERENCES IN TEXT

The Federal Advisory Committee Act, referred to in subsec. (b)(2), is Pub. L. 92–463, Oct. 6, 1972, 86 Stat. 770, as amended, which is set out in the Appendix to Title 5, Government Organization and Employees.

The National Technology Transfer and Advancement Act of 1995, referred to in subsec. (b)(3), (4), is Pub. L. 104–113, Mar. 7, 1996, 110 Stat. 775, as amended. For complete classification of this Act to the Code, see Short Title of 1996 Amendment note set out under section 3701 of Title 15, Commerce and Trade, and Tables.

Section 605 of Public Law 107–77, referred to in subsec. (f), is section 605 of Pub. L. 107–77, title VI, Nov. 28, 2001, 115 Stat. 798, which is not classified to the Code.

AMENDMENTS

2003—Subsec. (f). Pub. L. 108–7 inserted before period at end ": *Provided*, That any such transfer or provision of funding shall be carried out in accordance with section 605 of Public Law 107–77".

§ 163. Definition of law enforcement technology

For the purposes of this subchapter, the term "law enforcement technology" includes investigative and forensic technologies, corrections technologies, and technologies that support the judicial process.

(Pub. L. 107–296, title II, §233, Nov. 25, 2002, 116 Stat. 2161.)

REFERENCES IN TEXT

This subchapter, referred to in text, was in the original "this title", meaning title II of Pub. L. 107–296, Nov. 25, 2002, 116 Stat. 2145, which enacted this subchapter, amended sections 1030, 2511, 2512, 2520, 2701 to 2703, and 3125 of Title 18, Crimes and Criminal Procedure, sections 3712 and 3722 of Title 42, The Public Health and Welfare, and section 401a of Title 50, War and National Defense, and enacted provisions set out as a note under section 101 of this title and listed in a Provisions for Review, Promulgation, or Amendment of Federal Sentencing Guidelines Relating to Specific Offenses table set out under section 994 of Title 28, Judiciary and Judicial Procedure. For complete classification of title II to the Code, see Tables.

§ 164. Abolishment of Office of Science and Technology of National Institute of Justice; transfer of functions

(a) Authority to transfer functions

The Attorney General may transfer to the Office any other program or activity of the Department of Justice that the Attorney General, in consultation with the Committee on the Judiciary of the Senate and the Committee on the Judiciary of the House of Representatives, determines to be consistent with the mission of the Office.

(b) Transfer of personnel and assets

With respect to any function, power, or duty, or any program or activity, that is established in the Office, those employees and assets of the element of the Department of Justice from which the transfer is made that the Attorney General determines are needed to perform that function, power, or duty, or for that program or activity, as the case may be, shall be transferred to the Office: *Provided*, That any such transfer shall be carried out in accordance with section 605 of Public Law 107–77.

(c) Report on implementation

Not later than 1 year after November 25, 2002, the Attorney General shall submit to the Committee on the Judiciary of the Senate and the Committee on the Judiciary of the House of Representatives a report on the implementation of this subchapter. The report shall—

(1) provide an accounting of the amounts and sources of funding available to the Office to

carry out its mission under existing authorizations and appropriations, and set forth the future funding needs of the Office; and

(2) include such other information and recommendations as the Attorney General considers appropriate.

(Pub. L. 107–296, title II, §234, Nov. 25, 2002, 116 Stat. 2161; Pub. L. 108–7, div. L, §103(2), Feb. 20, 2003, 117 Stat. 529.)

REFERENCES IN TEXT

Section 605 of Public Law 107–77, referred to in subsec. (b), is section 605 of Pub. L. 107–77, title VI, Nov. 28, 2001, 115 Stat. 798, which is not classified to the Code.

This subchapter, referred to in subsec. (c), was in the original "this title", meaning title II of Pub. L. 107–296, Nov. 25, 2002, 116 Stat. 2145, which enacted this subchapter, amended sections 1030, 2511, 2512, 2520, 2701 to 2703, and 3125 of Title 18, Crimes and Criminal Procedure, sections 3712 and 3722 of Title 42, The Public Health and Welfare, and section 401a of Title 50, War and National Defense, and enacted provisions set out as a note under section 101 of this title and listed in a Provisions for Review, Promulgation, or Amendment of Federal Sentencing Guidelines Relating to Specific Offenses table set out under section 994 of Title 28, Judiciary and Judicial Procedure. For complete classification of title II to the Code, see Tables.

AMENDMENTS

2003—Subsec. (b). Pub. L. 108–7 inserted before period at end ": *Provided*, That any such transfer shall be carried out in accordance with section 605 of Public Law 107–77".

§ 165. National Law Enforcement and Corrections Technology Centers

(a) In general

The Director of the Office shall operate and support National Law Enforcement and Corrections Technology Centers (hereinafter in this section referred to as "Centers") and, to the extent necessary, establish new centers through a merit-based, competitive process.

(b) Purpose of Centers

The purpose of the Centers shall be to—

(1) support research and development of law enforcement technology;

(2) support the transfer and implementation of technology;

(3) assist in the development and dissemination of guidelines and technological standards; and

(4) provide technology assistance, information, and support for law enforcement, corrections, and criminal justice purposes.

(c) Annual meeting

Each year, the Director shall convene a meeting of the Centers in order to foster collaboration and communication between Center participants.

(d) Report

Not later than 12 months after November 25, 2002, the Director shall transmit to the Congress a report assessing the effectiveness of the existing system of Centers and identify the number of Centers necessary to meet the technology needs of Federal, State, and local law enforcement in the United States.

(Pub. L. 107–296, title II, §235, Nov. 25, 2002, 116 Stat. 2162.)

SUBCHAPTER III—SCIENCE AND TECHNOLOGY IN SUPPORT OF HOMELAND SECURITY

§ 181. Under Secretary for Science and Technology

There shall be in the Department a Directorate of Science and Technology headed by an Under Secretary for Science and Technology.

(Pub. L. 107–296, title III, §301, Nov. 25, 2002, 116 Stat. 2163.)

§ 182. Responsibilities and authorities of the Under Secretary for Science and Technology

The Secretary, acting through the Under Secretary for Science and Technology, shall have the responsibility for—

(1) advising the Secretary regarding research and development efforts and priorities in support of the Department's missions;

(2) developing, in consultation with other appropriate executive agencies, a national policy and strategic plan for, identifying priorities, goals, objectives and policies for, and coordinating the Federal Government's civilian efforts to identify and develop countermeasures to chemical, biological,,[1] and other emerging terrorist threats, including the development of comprehensive, research-based definable goals for such efforts and development of annual measurable objectives and specific targets to accomplish and evaluate the goals for such efforts;

(3) supporting the Under Secretary for Intelligence and Analysis and the Assistant Secretary for Infrastructure Protection, by assessing and testing homeland security vulnerabilities and possible threats;

(4) conducting basic and applied research, development, demonstration, testing, and evaluation activities that are relevant to any or all elements of the Department, through both intramural and extramural programs, except that such responsibility does not extend to human health-related research and development activities;

(5) establishing priorities for, directing, funding, and conducting national research, development, test and evaluation, and procurement of technology and systems for—

(A) preventing the importation of chemical, biological,,[1] and related weapons and material; and

(B) detecting, preventing, protecting against, and responding to terrorist attacks;

(6) establishing a system for transferring homeland security developments or technologies to Federal, State, local government, and private sector entities;

(7) entering into work agreements, joint sponsorships, contracts, or any other agreements with the Department of Energy regarding the use of the national laboratories or sites and support of the science and technology base at those facilities;

(8) collaborating with the Secretary of Agriculture and the Attorney General as provided in section 8401 of title 7;

[1] So in original.

(9) collaborating with the Secretary of Health and Human Services and the Attorney General in determining any new biological agents and toxins that shall be listed as "select agents" in Appendix A of part 72 of title 42, Code of Federal Regulations, pursuant to section 262a of title 42;

(10) supporting United States leadership in science and technology;

(11) establishing and administering the primary research and development activities of the Department, including the long-term research and development needs and capabilities for all elements of the Department;

(12) coordinating and integrating all research, development, demonstration, testing, and evaluation activities of the Department;

(13) coordinating with other appropriate executive agencies in developing and carrying out the science and technology agenda of the Department to reduce duplication and identify unmet needs; and

(14) developing and overseeing the administration of guidelines for merit review of research and development projects throughout the Department, and for the dissemination of research conducted or sponsored by the Department.

(Pub. L. 107–296, title III, § 302, Nov. 25, 2002, 116 Stat. 2163; Pub. L. 109–347, title V, § 501(b)(2), Oct. 13, 2006, 120 Stat. 1935; Pub. L. 110–53, title V, § 531(b)(1)(C), Aug. 3, 2007, 121 Stat. 334.)

AMENDMENTS

2007—Par. (3). Pub. L. 110–53 substituted "Under Secretary for Intelligence and Analysis and the Assistant Secretary for Infrastructure Protection" for "Under Secretary for Information Analysis and Infrastructure Protection".

2006—Pars. (2), (5)(A). Pub. L. 109–347 struck out "radiological, nuclear" after "biological,".

§ 183. Functions transferred

In accordance with subchapter XII of this chapter, there shall be transferred to the Secretary the functions, personnel, assets, and liabilities of the following entities:

(1) The following programs and activities of the Department of Energy, including the functions of the Secretary of Energy relating thereto (but not including programs and activities relating to the strategic nuclear defense posture of the United States):

(A) The chemical and biological national security and supporting programs and activities of the nonproliferation and verification research and development program.

(B) The nuclear smuggling programs and activities within the proliferation detection program of the nonproliferation and verification research and development program. The programs and activities described in this subparagraph may be designated by the President either for transfer to the Department or for joint operation by the Secretary and the Secretary of Energy.

(C) The nuclear assessment program and activities of the assessment, detection, and cooperation program of the international materials protection and cooperation program.

(D) Such life sciences activities of the biological and environmental research program related to microbial pathogens as may be designated by the President for transfer to the Department.

(E) The Environmental Measurements Laboratory.

(F) The advanced scientific computing research program and activities at Lawrence Livermore National Laboratory.

(2) The National Bio-Weapons Defense Analysis Center of the Department of Defense, including the functions of the Secretary of Defense related thereto.

(Pub. L. 107–296, title III, § 303, Nov. 25, 2002, 116 Stat. 2164.)

§ 184. Conduct of certain public health-related activities

(a) In general

With respect to civilian human health-related research and development activities relating to countermeasures for chemical, biological, radiological, and nuclear and other emerging terrorist threats carried out by the Department of Health and Human Services (including the Public Health Service), the Secretary of Health and Human Services shall set priorities, goals, objectives, and policies and develop a coordinated strategy for such activities in collaboration with the Secretary of Homeland Security to ensure consistency with the national policy and strategic plan developed pursuant to section 182(2) of this title.

(b) Evaluation of progress

In carrying out subsection (a) of this section, the Secretary of Health and Human Services shall collaborate with the Secretary in developing specific benchmarks and outcome measurements for evaluating progress toward achieving the priorities and goals described in such subsection.

(Pub. L. 107–296, title III, § 304, Nov. 25, 2002, 116 Stat. 2165.)

CODIFICATION

Section is comprised of section 304 of Pub. L. 107–296. Subsec. (c) of section 304 of Pub. L. 107–296 amended section 233 of Title 42, The Public Health and Welfare.

§ 185. Federally funded research and development centers

The Secretary, acting through the Under Secretary for Science and Technology, shall have the authority to establish or contract with 1 or more federally funded research and development centers to provide independent analysis of homeland security issues, or to carry out other responsibilities under this chapter, including coordinating and integrating both the extramural and intramural programs described in section 188 of this title.

(Pub. L. 107–296, title III, § 305, Nov. 25, 2002, 116 Stat. 2168.)

REFERENCES IN TEXT

This chapter, referred to in text, was in the original "this Act", meaning Pub. L. 107–296, Nov. 25, 2002, 116

Stat. 2135, known as the Homeland Security Act of 2002, which is classified principally to this chapter. For complete classification of this Act to the Code, see Short Title note set out under section 101 of this title and Tables.

§186. Miscellaneous provisions

(a) Classification

To the greatest extent practicable, research conducted or supported by the Department shall be unclassified.

(b) Construction

Nothing in this subchapter shall be construed to preclude any Under Secretary of the Department from carrying out research, development, demonstration, or deployment activities, as long as such activities are coordinated through the Under Secretary for Science and Technology.

(c) Regulations

The Secretary, acting through the Under Secretary for Science and Technology, may issue necessary regulations with respect to research, development, demonstration, testing, and evaluation activities of the Department, including the conducting, funding, and reviewing of such activities.

(d) Notification of Presidential life sciences designations

Not later than 60 days before effecting any transfer of Department of Energy life sciences activities pursuant to section 183(1)(D) of this title, the President shall notify the appropriate congressional committees of the proposed transfer and shall include the reasons for the transfer and a description of the effect of the transfer on the activities of the Department of Energy.

(Pub. L. 107–296, title III, §306, Nov. 25, 2002, 116 Stat. 2168.)

§187. Homeland Security Advanced Research Projects Agency

(a) Definitions

In this section:

(1) Fund

The term "Fund" means the Acceleration Fund for Research and Development of Homeland Security Technologies established in subsection (c) of this section.

(2) Homeland security research

The term "homeland security research" means research relevant to the detection of, prevention of, protection against, response to, attribution of, and recovery from homeland security threats, particularly acts of terrorism.

(3) HSARPA

The term "HSARPA" means the Homeland Security Advanced Research Projects Agency established in subsection (b) of this section.

(4) Under Secretary

The term "Under Secretary" means the Under Secretary for Science and Technology.

(b) Homeland Security Advanced Research Projects Agency

(1) Establishment

There is established the Homeland Security Advanced Research Projects Agency.

(2) Director

HSARPA shall be headed by a Director, who shall be appointed by the Secretary. The Director shall report to the Under Secretary.

(3) Responsibilities

The Director shall administer the Fund to award competitive, merit-reviewed grants, cooperative agreements or contracts to public or private entities, including businesses, federally funded research and development centers, and universities. The Director shall administer the Fund to—

(A) support basic and applied homeland security research to promote revolutionary changes in technologies that would promote homeland security;

(B) advance the development, testing and evaluation, and deployment of critical homeland security technologies; and

(C) accelerate the prototyping and deployment of technologies that would address homeland security vulnerabilities.

(4) Targeted competitions

The Director may solicit proposals to address specific vulnerabilities identified by the Director.

(5) Coordination

The Director shall ensure that the activities of HSARPA are coordinated with those of other relevant research agencies, and may run projects jointly with other agencies.

(6) Personnel

In hiring personnel for HSARPA, the Secretary shall have the hiring and management authorities described in section 1101 of the Strom Thurmond National Defense Authorization Act for Fiscal Year 1999 (5 U.S.C. 3104 note; Public Law 105–261). The term of appointments for employees under subsection (c)(1) of that section may not exceed 5 years before the granting of any extension under subsection (c)(2) of that section.

(7) Demonstrations

The Director, periodically, shall hold homeland security technology demonstrations to improve contact among technology developers, vendors and acquisition personnel.

(c) Fund

(1) Establishment

There is established the Acceleration Fund for Research and Development of Homeland Security Technologies, which shall be administered by the Director of HSARPA.

(2) Authorization of appropriations

There are authorized to be appropriated $500,000,000 to the Fund for fiscal year 2003 and such sums as may be necessary thereafter.

(3) Coast Guard

Of the funds authorized to be appropriated under paragraph (2), not less than 10 percent of such funds for each fiscal year through fiscal year 2005 shall be authorized only for the Under Secretary, through joint agreement with the Commandant of the Coast Guard, to carry out research and development of improved ports, waterways and coastal security surveillance and perimeter protection capabilities for the purpose of minimizing the possibility that Coast Guard cutters, aircraft, helicopters, and personnel will be diverted from non-homeland security missions to the ports, waterways and coastal security mission.

(Pub. L. 107–296, title III, § 307, Nov. 25, 2002, 116 Stat. 2168.)

§ 188. Conduct of research, development, demonstration, testing and evaluation

(a) In general

The Secretary, acting through the Under Secretary for Science and Technology, shall carry out the responsibilities under section 182(4) of this title through both extramural and intramural programs.

(b) Extramural programs

(1) In general

The Secretary, acting through the Under Secretary for Science and Technology, shall operate extramural research, development, demonstration, testing, and evaluation programs so as to—

(A) ensure that colleges, universities, private research institutes, and companies (and consortia thereof) from as many areas of the United States as practicable participate;

(B) ensure that the research funded is of high quality, as determined through merit review processes developed under section 182(14) of this title; and

(C) distribute funds through grants, cooperative agreements, and contracts.

(2) University-based centers for homeland security

(A) Designation

The Secretary, acting through the Under Secretary for Science and Technology, shall designate a university-based center or several university-based centers for homeland security. The purpose of the center or these centers shall be to establish a coordinated, university-based system to enhance the Nation's homeland security.

(B) Criteria for designation

Criteria for the designation of colleges or universities as a center for homeland security, shall include, but are not limited to, demonstrated expertise in—

(i) The training of first responders.

(ii) Responding to incidents involving weapons of mass destruction and biological warfare.

(iii) Emergency and diagnostic medical services.

(iv) Chemical, biological, radiological, and nuclear countermeasures or detection.

(v) Animal and plant health and diagnostics.

(vi) Food safety.

(vii) Water and wastewater operations.

(viii) Port and waterway security.

(ix) Multi-modal transportation.

(x) Information security and information engineering.

(xi) Engineering.

(xii) Educational outreach and technical assistance.

(xiii) Border transportation and security.

(xiv) The public policy implications and public dissemination of homeland security related research and development.

(C) Discretion of Secretary

To the extent that exercising such discretion is in the interest of homeland security, and with respect to the designation of any given university-based center for homeland security, the Secretary may except certain criteria as specified in subparagraph (B) and consider additional criteria beyond those specified in subparagraph (B). Upon designation of a university-based center for homeland security, the Secretary shall that day publish in the Federal Register the criteria that were excepted or added in the selection process and the justification for the set of criteria that were used for that designation.

(D) Report to Congress

The Secretary shall report annually, from the date of enactment, to Congress concerning the implementation of this section. That report shall indicate which center or centers have been designated and how the designation or designations enhance homeland security, as well as report any decisions to revoke or modify such designations.

(E) Authorization of appropriations

There are authorized to be appropriated such sums as may be necessary to carry out this paragraph.

(c) Intramural programs

(1) Consultation

In carrying out the duties under section 182 of this title, the Secretary, acting through the Under Secretary for Science and Technology, may draw upon the expertise of any laboratory of the Federal Government, whether operated by a contractor or the Government.

(2) Laboratories

The Secretary, acting through the Under Secretary for Science and Technology, may establish a headquarters laboratory for the Department at any laboratory or site and may establish additional laboratory units at other laboratories or sites.

(3) Criteria for headquarters laboratory

If the Secretary chooses to establish a headquarters laboratory pursuant to paragraph (2), then the Secretary shall do the following:

(A) Establish criteria for the selection of the headquarters laboratory in consultation with the National Academy of Sciences, appropriate Federal agencies, and other experts.

(B) Publish the criteria in the Federal Register.

(C) Evaluate all appropriate laboratories or sites against the criteria.

(D) Select a laboratory or site on the basis of the criteria.

(E) Report to the appropriate congressional committees on which laboratory was selected, how the selected laboratory meets the published criteria, and what duties the headquarters laboratory shall perform.

(4) Limitation on operation of laboratories

No laboratory shall begin operating as the headquarters laboratory of the Department until at least 30 days after the transmittal of the report required by paragraph (3)(E).

(Pub. L. 107–296, title III, §308, Nov. 25, 2002, 116 Stat. 2170; Pub. L. 108–7, div. L, §101(1), Feb. 20, 2003, 117 Stat. 526.)

REFERENCES IN TEXT

The date of enactment, referred to in subsec. (b)(2)(D), probably means the date of enactment of this section by Pub. L. 107–296, which was approved Nov. 25, 2002.

AMENDMENTS

2003—Subsecs. (a) to (c)(1). Pub. L. 108–7 added subsecs. (a) to (c)(1) and struck out former subsecs. (a) to (c)(1) which related to the responsibilities of the Secretary, acting through the Under Secretary for Science and Technology, to carry out the responsibilities under section 182(4) of this title through both extramural and intramural programs, to operate extramural research, development, demonstration, testing, and evaluation programs, to establish a coordinated, university-based system to enhance the Nation's homeland security, and to draw upon the expertise of any laboratory of the Federal Government.

§ 189. Utilization of Department of Energy national laboratories and sites in support of homeland security activities

(a) Authority to utilize national laboratories and sites

(1) In general

In carrying out the missions of the Department, the Secretary may utilize the Department of Energy national laboratories and sites through any 1 or more of the following methods, as the Secretary considers appropriate:

(A) A joint sponsorship arrangement referred to in subsection (b) of this section.

(B) A direct contract between the Department and the applicable Department of Energy laboratory or site, subject to subsection (c) of this section.

(C) Any "work for others" basis made available by that laboratory or site.

(D) Any other method provided by law.

(2) Acceptance and performance by labs and sites

Notwithstanding any other law governing the administration, mission, use, or operations of any of the Department of Energy national laboratories and sites, such laboratories and sites are authorized to accept and perform work for the Secretary, consistent with resources provided, and perform such work on an equal basis to other missions at the laboratory and not on a noninterference basis with other missions of such laboratory or site.

(b) Joint sponsorship arrangements

(1) Laboratories

The Department may be a joint sponsor, under a multiple agency sponsorship arrangement with the Department of Energy, of 1 or more Department of Energy national laboratories in the performance of work.

(2) Sites

The Department may be a joint sponsor of a Department of Energy site in the performance of work as if such site were a federally funded research and development center and the work were performed under a multiple agency sponsorship arrangement with the Department.

(3) Primary sponsor

The Department of Energy shall be the primary sponsor under a multiple agency sponsorship arrangement referred to in paragraph (1) or (2).

(4) Lead agent

The Secretary of Energy shall act as the lead agent in coordinating the formation and performance of a joint sponsorship arrangement under this subsection between the Department and a Department of Energy national laboratory or site.

(5) Federal acquisition regulation

Any work performed by a Department of Energy national laboratory or site under a joint sponsorship arrangement under this subsection shall comply with the policy on the use of federally funded research and development centers under the Federal Acquisition Regulations.

(6) Funding

The Department shall provide funds for work at the Department of Energy national laboratories or sites, as the case may be, under a joint sponsorship arrangement under this subsection under the same terms and conditions as apply to the primary sponsor of such national laboratory under section 253(b)(1)(C) of title 41 or of such site to the extent such section applies to such site as a federally funded research and development center by reason of this subsection.

(c) Separate contracting

To the extent that programs or activities transferred by this chapter from the Department of Energy to the Department of Homeland Security are being carried out through direct contracts with the operator of a national laboratory or site of the Department of Energy, the Secretary of Homeland Security and the Secretary of Energy shall ensure that direct contracts for such programs and activities between the Department of Homeland Security and such operator are separate from the direct contracts of the Department of Energy with such operator.

(d) Authority with respect to cooperative research and development agreements and licensing agreements

In connection with any utilization of the Department of Energy national laboratories and sites under this section, the Secretary may permit the director of any such national laboratory or site to enter into cooperative research and development agreements or to negotiate licensing agreements with any person, any agency or instrumentality, of the United States, any unit of State or local government, and any other entity under the authority granted by section 3710a of title 15. Technology may be transferred to a non-Federal party to such an agreement consistent with the provisions of sections 3710 and 3710a of title 15.

(e) Reimbursement of costs

In the case of an activity carried out by the operator of a Department of Energy national laboratory or site in connection with any utilization of such laboratory or site under this section, the Department of Homeland Security shall reimburse the Department of Energy for costs of such activity through a method under which the Secretary of Energy waives any requirement for the Department of Homeland Security to pay administrative charges or personnel costs of the Department of Energy or its contractors in excess of the amount that the Secretary of Energy pays for an activity carried out by such contractor and paid for by the Department of Energy.

(f) Laboratory directed research and development by the Department of Energy

No funds authorized to be appropriated or otherwise made available to the Department in any fiscal year may be obligated or expended for laboratory directed research and development activities carried out by the Department of Energy unless such activities support the missions of the Department of Homeland Security.

(g) Office for National Laboratories

There is established within the Directorate of Science and Technology an Office for National Laboratories, which shall be responsible for the coordination and utilization of the Department of Energy national laboratories and sites under this section in a manner to create a networked laboratory system for the purpose of supporting the missions of the Department.

(h) Department of Energy coordination on homeland security related research

The Secretary of Energy shall ensure that any research, development, test, and evaluation activities conducted within the Department of Energy that are directly or indirectly related to homeland security are fully coordinated with the Secretary to minimize duplication of effort and maximize the effective application of Federal budget resources.

(Pub. L. 107–296, title III, §309, Nov. 25, 2002, 116 Stat. 2172.)

§ 190. Transfer of Plum Island Animal Disease Center, Department of Agriculture

(a) In general

In accordance with subchapter XII of this chapter, the Secretary of Agriculture shall transfer to the Secretary of Homeland Security the Plum Island Animal Disease Center of the Department of Agriculture, including the assets and liabilities of the Center.

(b) Continued Department of Agriculture access

On completion of the transfer of the Plum Island Animal Disease Center under subsection (a) of this section, the Secretary of Homeland Security and the Secretary of Agriculture shall enter into an agreement to ensure that the Department of Agriculture is able to carry out research, diagnostic, and other activities of the Department of Agriculture at the Center.

(c) Direction of activities

The Secretary of Agriculture shall continue to direct the research, diagnostic, and other activities of the Department of Agriculture at the Center described in subsection (b) of this section.

(d) Notification

(1) In general

At least 180 days before any change in the biosafety level at the Plum Island Animal Disease Center, the President shall notify Congress of the change and describe the reasons for the change.

(2) Limitation

No change described in paragraph (1) may be made earlier than 180 days after the completion of the transition period (as defined in section 541 of this title).

(Pub. L. 107–296, title III, §310, Nov. 25, 2002, 116 Stat. 2174.)

§ 191. Homeland Security Science and Technology Advisory Committee

(a) Establishment

There is established within the Department a Homeland Security Science and Technology Advisory Committee (in this section referred to as the "Advisory Committee"). The Advisory Committee shall make recommendations with respect to the activities of the Under Secretary for Science and Technology, including identifying research areas of potential importance to the security of the Nation.

(b) Membership

(1) Appointment

The Advisory Committee shall consist of 20 members appointed by the Under Secretary for Science and Technology, which shall include emergency first-responders or representatives of organizations or associations of emergency first-responders. The Advisory Committee shall also include representatives of citizen groups, including economically disadvantaged communities. The individuals appointed as members of the Advisory Committee—

(A) shall be eminent in fields such as emergency response, research, engineering, new product development, business, and management consulting;

(B) shall be selected solely on the basis of established records of distinguished service;

(C) shall not be employees of the Federal Government; and

(D) shall be so selected as to provide representation of a cross-section of the research, development, demonstration, and deployment activities supported by the Under Secretary for Science and Technology.

(2) National Research Council

The Under Secretary for Science and Technology may enter into an arrangement for the National Research Council to select members of the Advisory Committee, but only if the panel used by the National Research Council reflects the representation described in paragraph (1).

(c) Terms of office

(1) In general

Except as otherwise provided in this subsection, the term of office of each member of the Advisory Committee shall be 3 years.

(2) Original appointments

The original members of the Advisory Committee shall be appointed to three classes. One class of six shall have a term of 1 year, one class of seven a term of 2 years, and one class of seven a term of 3 years.

(3) Vacancies

A member appointed to fill a vacancy occurring before the expiration of the term for which the member's predecessor was appointed shall be appointed for the remainder of such term.

(d) Eligibility

A person who has completed two consecutive full terms of service on the Advisory Committee shall thereafter be ineligible for appointment during the 1-year period following the expiration of the second such term.

(e) Meetings

The Advisory Committee shall meet at least quarterly at the call of the Chair or whenever one-third of the members so request in writing. Each member shall be given appropriate notice of the call of each meeting, whenever possible not less than 15 days before the meeting.

(f) Quorum

A majority of the members of the Advisory Committee not having a conflict of interest in the matter being considered by the Advisory Committee shall constitute a quorum.

(g) Conflict of interest rules

The Advisory Committee shall establish rules for determining when 1 of its members has a conflict of interest in a matter being considered by the Advisory Committee.

(h) Reports

(1) Annual report

The Advisory Committee shall render an annual report to the Under Secretary for Science and Technology for transmittal to Congress on or before January 31 of each year. Such report shall describe the activities and recommendations of the Advisory Committee during the previous year.

(2) Additional reports

The Advisory Committee may render to the Under Secretary for transmittal to Congress such additional reports on specific policy matters as it considers appropriate.

(i) Federal Advisory Committee Act exemption

Section 14 of the Federal Advisory Committee Act shall not apply to the Advisory Committee.

(j) Termination

The Department of Homeland Security Science and Technology Advisory Committee shall terminate on December 31, 2008.

(Pub. L. 107–296, title III, § 311, Nov. 25, 2002, 116 Stat. 2174; Pub. L. 108–334, title V, § 520, Oct. 18, 2004, 118 Stat. 1318; Pub. L. 109–347, title III, § 302(a), Oct. 13, 2006, 120 Stat. 1920.)

REFERENCES IN TEXT

Section 14 of the Federal Advisory Committee Act, referred to in subsec. (i), is section 14 of Pub. L. 92–463, which is set out in the Appendix to Title 5, Government Organization and Employees.

AMENDMENTS

2006—Subsec. (j). Pub. L. 109–347 substituted "on December 31, 2008" for "3 years after the effective date of this chapter".

2004—Subsec. (c)(2). Pub. L. 108–334 amended heading and text of par. (2) generally. Prior to amendment, text read as follows: "The original members of the Advisory Committee shall be appointed to three classes of three members each. One class shall have a term of 1 year, 1 a term of 2 years, and the other a term of 3 years."

EFFECTIVE DATE OF 2006 AMENDMENT

Pub. L. 109–347, title III, § 302(b), Oct. 13, 2006, 120 Stat. 1921, provided that: "The amendment made by subsection (a) [amending this section] shall be effective as if enacted on the date of the enactment of the Homeland Security Act of 2002 (6 U.S.C. 101 et seq.) [Nov. 25, 2002]."

§ 192. Homeland Security Institute

(a) Establishment

The Secretary shall establish a federally funded research and development center to be known as the "Homeland Security Institute" (in this section referred to as the "Institute").

(b) Administration

The Institute shall be administered as a separate entity by the Secretary.

(c) Duties

The duties of the Institute shall be determined by the Secretary, and may include the following:

(1) Systems analysis, risk analysis, and simulation and modeling to determine the vulnerabilities of the Nation's critical infrastructures and the effectiveness of the systems deployed to reduce those vulnerabilities.

(2) Economic and policy analysis to assess the distributed costs and benefits of alternative approaches to enhancing security.

(3) Evaluation of the effectiveness of measures deployed to enhance the security of institutions, facilities, and infrastructure that may be terrorist targets.

(4) Identification of instances when common standards and protocols could improve the interoperability and effective utilization of tools developed for field operators and first responders.

(5) Assistance for Federal agencies and departments in establishing testbeds to evaluate the effectiveness of technologies under development and to assess the appropriateness of such technologies for deployment.

(6) Design of metrics and use of those metrics to evaluate the effectiveness of homeland security programs throughout the Federal Government, including all national laboratories.

(7) Design of and support for the conduct of homeland security-related exercises and simulations.

(8) Creation of strategic technology development plans to reduce vulnerabilities in the Nation's critical infrastructure and key resources.

(d) Consultation on Institute activities

In carrying out the duties described in subsection (c) of this section, the Institute shall consult widely with representatives from private industry, institutions of higher education, nonprofit institutions, other Government agencies, and federally funded research and development centers.

(e) Use of centers

The Institute shall utilize the capabilities of the National Infrastructure Simulation and Analysis Center.

(f) Annual reports

The Institute shall transmit to the Secretary and Congress an annual report on the activities of the Institute under this section.

(g) Termination

The Homeland Security Institute shall terminate 5 years after its establishment.

(Pub. L. 107–296, title III, § 312, Nov. 25, 2002, 116 Stat. 2176; Pub. L. 108–334, title V, § 519, Oct. 18, 2004, 118 Stat. 1318.)

AMENDMENTS

2004—Subsec. (g). Pub. L. 108–334 amended heading and text of subsec. (g) generally. Prior to amendment, text read as follows: "The Homeland Security Institute shall terminate 3 years after the effective date of this chapter."

§ 193. Technology clearinghouse to encourage and support innovative solutions to enhance homeland security

(a) Establishment of program

The Secretary, acting through the Under Secretary for Science and Technology, shall establish and promote a program to encourage technological innovation in facilitating the mission of the Department (as described in section 111 of this title).

(b) Elements of program

The program described in subsection (a) of this section shall include the following components:

(1) The establishment of a centralized Federal clearinghouse for information relating to technologies that would further the mission of the Department for dissemination, as appropriate, to Federal, State, and local government and private sector entities for additional review, purchase, or use.

(2) The issuance of announcements seeking unique and innovative technologies to advance the mission of the Department.

(3) The establishment of a technical assistance team to assist in screening, as appropriate, proposals submitted to the Secretary (except as provided in subsection (c)(2) of this section) to assess the feasibility, scientific and technical merits, and estimated cost of such proposals, as appropriate.

(4) The provision of guidance, recommendations, and technical assistance, as appropriate, to assist Federal, State, and local government and private sector efforts to evaluate and implement the use of technologies described in paragraph (1) or (2).

(5) The provision of information for persons seeking guidance on how to pursue proposals to develop or deploy technologies that would enhance homeland security, including information relating to Federal funding, regulation, or acquisition.

(c) Miscellaneous provisions

(1) In general

Nothing in this section shall be construed as authorizing the Secretary or the technical assistance team established under subsection (b)(3) of this section to set standards for technology to be used by the Department, any other executive agency, any State or local government entity, or any private sector entity.

(2) Certain proposals

The technical assistance team established under subsection (b)(3) of this section shall not consider or evaluate proposals submitted in response to a solicitation for offers for a pending procurement or for a specific agency requirement.

(3) Coordination

In carrying out this section, the Secretary shall coordinate with the Technical Support Working Group (organized under the April 1982 National Security Decision Directive Numbered 30).

(Pub. L. 107–296, title III, § 313, Nov. 25, 2002, 116 Stat. 2176.)

§ 194. Enhancement of public safety communications interoperability

(a) Coordination of public safety interoperable communications programs

(1) Program

The Secretary of Homeland Security, in consultation with the Secretary of Commerce and the Chairman of the Federal Communications Commission, shall establish a program to enhance public safety interoperable communications at all levels of government. Such program shall—

(A) establish a comprehensive national approach to achieving public safety interoperable communications;

(B) coordinate with other Federal agencies in carrying out subparagraph (A);

(C) develop, in consultation with other appropriate Federal agencies and State and local authorities, appropriate minimum capabilities for communications interoperability for Federal, State, and local public safety agencies;

(D) accelerate, in consultation with other Federal agencies, including the National Institute of Standards and Technology, the private sector, and nationally recognized standards organizations as appropriate, the development of national voluntary consensus standards for public safety interoperable communications, recognizing—

(i) the value, life cycle, and technical capabilities of existing communications infrastructure;

(ii) the need for cross-border interoperability between States and nations;

(iii) the unique needs of small, rural communities; and

(iv) the interoperability needs for daily operations and catastrophic events;

(E) encourage the development and implementation of flexible and open architectures incorporating, where possible, technologies that currently are commercially available, with appropriate levels of security, for short-term and long-term solutions to public safety communications interoperability;

(F) assist other Federal agencies in identifying priorities for research, development, and testing and evaluation with regard to public safety interoperable communications;

(G) identify priorities within the Department of Homeland Security for research, development, and testing and evaluation with regard to public safety interoperable communications;

(H) establish coordinated guidance for Federal grant programs for public safety interoperable communications;

(I) provide technical assistance to State and local public safety agencies regarding planning, acquisition strategies, interoperability architectures, training, and other functions necessary to achieve public safety communications interoperability;

(J) develop and disseminate best practices to improve public safety communications interoperability; and

(K) develop appropriate performance measures and milestones to systematically measure the Nation's progress toward achieving public safety communications interoperability, including the development of national voluntary consensus standards.

(2) Office for Interoperability and Compatibility

(A) Establishment of office

The Secretary may establish an Office for Interoperability and Compatibility within the Directorate of Science and Technology to carry out this subsection.

(B) Functions

If the Secretary establishes such office, the Secretary shall, through such office—

(i) carry out Department of Homeland Security responsibilities and authorities relating to the SAFECOM Program; and

(ii) carry out section 321[1] of this title.

(3) Authorization of appropriations

There are authorized to be appropriated to the Secretary to carry out this subsection—

(A) $22,105,000 for fiscal year 2005;

(B) $22,768,000 for fiscal year 2006;

(C) $23,451,000 for fiscal year 2007;

(D) $24,155,000 for fiscal year 2008; and

(E) $24,879,000 for fiscal year 2009.

(b) Report

Not later than 120 days after December 17, 2004, the Secretary shall report to the Congress on Department of Homeland Security plans for accelerating the development of national voluntary consensus standards for public safety interoperable communications, a schedule of milestones for such development, and achievements of such development.

(c) International interoperability

Not later than 18 months after December 17, 2004, the President shall establish a mechanism for coordinating cross-border interoperability issues between—

(1) the United States and Canada; and

(2) the United States and Mexico.

(d) Omitted

(e) Multiyear interoperability grants

(1) Multiyear commitments

In awarding grants to any State, region, local government, or Indian tribe for the purposes of enhancing interoperable communications capabilities for emergency response providers, the Secretary may commit to obligate Federal assistance beyond the current fiscal year, subject to the limitations and restrictions in this subsection.

(2) Restrictions

(A) Time limit

No multiyear interoperability commitment may exceed 3 years in duration.

(B) Amount of committed funds

The total amount of assistance the Secretary has committed to obligate for any future fiscal year under paragraph (1) may not exceed $150,000,000.

(3) Letters of intent

(A) Issuance

Pursuant to paragraph (1), the Secretary may issue a letter of intent to an applicant committing to obligate from future budget authority an amount, not more than the Federal Government's share of the project's cost, for an interoperability communications project (including interest costs and costs of formulating the project).

(B) Schedule

A letter of intent under this paragraph shall establish a schedule under which the Secretary will reimburse the applicant for the Federal Government's share of the project's costs, as amounts become available, if the applicant, after the Secretary issues the letter, carries out the project before receiving amounts under a grant issued by the Secretary.

(C) Notice to Secretary

An applicant that is issued a letter of intent under this subsection shall notify the Secretary of the applicant's intent to carry out a project pursuant to the letter before the project begins.

(D) Notice to Congress

The Secretary shall transmit a written notification to the Congress no later than 3 days before the issuance of a letter of intent under this section.

[1] See References in Text note below.

(E) **Limitations**

A letter of intent issued under this section is not an obligation of the Government under section 1501 of title 31 and is not deemed to be an administrative commitment for financing. An obligation or administrative commitment may be made only as amounts are provided in authorization and appropriations laws.

(F) **Statutory construction**

Nothing in this subsection shall be construed—

(i) to prohibit the obligation of amounts pursuant to a letter of intent under this subsection in the same fiscal year as the letter of intent is issued; or

(ii) to apply to, or replace, Federal assistance intended for interoperable communications that is not provided pursuant to a commitment under this subsection.

(f) Interoperable communications plans

Any applicant requesting funding assistance from the Secretary for interoperable communications for emergency response providers shall submit an Interoperable Communications Plan to the Secretary for approval. Such a plan shall—

(1) describe the current state of communications interoperability in the applicable jurisdictions among Federal, State, and local emergency response providers and other relevant private resources;

(2) describe the available and planned use of public safety frequency spectrum and resources for interoperable communications within such jurisdictions;

(3) describe how the planned use of spectrum and resources for interoperable communications is compatible with surrounding capabilities and interoperable communications plans of Federal, State, and local governmental entities, military installations, foreign governments, critical infrastructure, and other relevant entities;

(4) include a 5-year plan for the dedication of Federal, State, and local government and private resources to achieve a consistent, secure, and effective interoperable communications system, including planning, system design and engineering, testing and technology development, procurement and installation, training, and operations and maintenance;

(5) describe how such 5-year plan meets or exceeds any applicable standards and grant requirements established by the Secretary;

(6) include information on the governance structure used to develop the plan, including such information about all agencies and organizations that participated in developing the plan and the scope and timeframe of the plan; and

(7) describe the method by which multi-jurisdictional, multidisciplinary input is provided from all regions of the jurisdiction, including any high-threat urban areas located in the jurisdiction, and the process for continuing to incorporate such input.

(g) Definitions

In this section:

(1) **Interoperable communications**

The term "interoperable communications" means the ability of emergency response providers and relevant Federal, State, and local government agencies to communicate with each other as necessary, through a dedicated public safety network utilizing information technology systems and radio communications systems, and to exchange voice, data, and video with one another on demand, in real time, as necessary.

(2) **Emergency response providers**

The term "emergency response providers" has the meaning that term has under section 101 of this title.

(h) Omitted

(i) Sense of Congress regarding interoperable communications

(1) **Finding**

The Congress finds that—

(A) many first responders working in the same jurisdiction or in different jurisdictions cannot effectively and efficiently communicate with one another; and

(B) their inability to do so threatens the public's safety and may result in unnecessary loss of lives and property.

(2) **Sense of Congress**

It is the sense of Congress that interoperable emergency communications systems and radios should continue to be deployed as soon as practicable for use by the first responder community, and that upgraded and new digital communications systems and new digital radios must meet prevailing national, voluntary consensus standards for interoperability.

(Pub. L. 108–458, title VII, § 7303, Dec. 17, 2004, 118 Stat. 3843; Pub. L. 110–53, title III, § 301(c), Aug. 3, 2007, 121 Stat. 299.)

REFERENCES IN TEXT

Section 321 of this title, referred to in subsec. (a)(2)(B)(ii), was in the original a reference to section 510 of the Homeland Security Act of 2002, as added by section 7303(d) of Pub. L. 108–458, which was repealed by Pub. L. 109–295, title VI, § 611(5), Oct. 4, 2006, 120 Stat. 1395.

CODIFICATION

Section is comprised of section 7303 of Pub. L. 108–458. Subsec. (d) of section 7303 of Pub. L. 108–458 enacted section 321 of this title. Subsec. (h) of section 7303 of Pub. L. 108–458 amended sections 238 and 312 of this title.

Section was enacted as part of the Intelligence Reform and Terrorism Prevention Act of 2004, and also as part of the 9/11 Commission Implementation Act of 2004, and not as part of the Homeland Security Act of 2002 which comprises this chapter.

Section 301(c) of Pub. L. 110–53, which directed the amendment of section 7303 of the "Intelligence Reform and Terrorist Prevention Act of 2004", was executed to this section, which is section 7303 of the Intelligence Reform and Terrorism Prevention Act of 2004, to reflect the probable intent of Congress. See 2007 Amendment notes below.

AMENDMENTS

2007—Subsec. (f)(6), (7). Pub. L. 110–53, § 301(c)(1), added pars. (6) and (7). See Codification note above.

Subsec. (g)(1). Pub. L. 110–53, §301(c)(2), substituted "and video" for "or video". See Codification note above.

EFFECTIVE DATE

Pub. L. 108–458, title VII, §7308, Dec. 17, 2004, 118 Stat. 3849, provided that: "Notwithstanding any other provision of this Act [see Tables for classification], this subtitle [subtitle C (§§7301–7308) of title VII of Pub. L. 108–458, enacting this section and section 321 of this title, amending sections 238 and 312 of this title, and enacting provisions set out as notes under this section and section 5196 of Title 42, The Public Health and Welfare] shall take effect on the date of enactment of this Act [Dec. 17, 2004]."

TRANSFER OF FUNCTIONS

For transfer of the SAFECOM Program, excluding elements related to research, development, testing, and evaluation and standards, to the Director for Emergency Communications, see section 571(d)(1) of this title.

CROSS BORDER INTEROPERABILITY REPORTS

Pub. L. 110–53, title XXII, §2203, Aug. 3, 2007, 121 Stat. 541, provided that:

"(a) IN GENERAL.—Not later than 90 days after the date of enactment of this Act [Aug. 3, 2007], the Federal Communications Commission, in consultation with the Department of Homeland Security's Office of Emergency Communications, the Office of Management of [sic] Budget, and the Department of State shall report to the Senate Committee on Commerce, Science, and Transportation and the House of Representatives Committee on Energy and Commerce on—

"(1) the status of the mechanism established by the President under section 7303(c) of the Intelligence Reform and Terrorism Prevention Act of 2004 (6 U.S.C. 194(c)) for coordinating cross border interoperability issues between—

"(A) the United States and Canada; and

"(B) the United States and Mexico;

"(2) the status of treaty negotiations with Canada and Mexico regarding the coordination of the re-banding of 800 megahertz radios, as required under the final rule of the Federal Communication Commission in the 'Private Land Mobile Services; 800 MHz Public Safety Interface Proceeding' (WT Docket No. 02–55; ET Docket No. 00–258; ET Docket No. 95–18, RM–9498; RM–10024; FCC 04–100) including the status of any outstanding issues in the negotiations between—

"(A) the United States and Canada; and

"(B) the United States and Mexico;

"(3) communications between the Commission and the Department of State over possible amendments to the bilateral legal agreements and protocols that govern the coordination process for license applications seeking to use channels and frequencies above Line A;

"(4) the annual rejection rate for the last 5 years by the United States of applications for new channels and frequencies by Canadian private and public entities; and

"(5) any additional procedures and mechanisms that can be taken by the Commission to decrease the rejection rate for applications by United States private and public entities seeking licenses to use channels and frequencies above Line A.

"(b) UPDATED REPORTS TO BE FILED ON THE STATUS OF TREATY OF [SIC] NEGOTIATIONS.—The Federal Communications Commission, in conjunction with the Department of Homeland Security, the Office of Management of Budget, and the Department of State shall continually provide updated reports to the Committee on Commerce, Science, and Transportation of the Senate and the Committee on Energy and Commerce of the House of Representatives on the status of treaty negotiations under subsection (a)(2) until the appropriate United States treaty has been revised with each of—

"(1) Canada; and

"(2) Mexico.

"(c) INTERNATIONAL NEGOTIATIONS TO REMEDY SITUATION.—Not later than 90 days after the date of enactment of this Act [Aug. 3, 2007], the Secretary of the Department of State shall report to Congress on—

"(1) the current process for considering applications by Canada for frequencies and channels by United States communities above Line A;

"(2) the status of current negotiations to reform and revise such process;

"(3) the estimated date of conclusion for such negotiations;

"(4) whether the current process allows for automatic denials or dismissals of initial applications by the Government of Canada, and whether such denials or dismissals are currently occurring; and

"(5) communications between the Department of State and the Federal Communications Commission pursuant to subsection (a)(3)."

SUBMISSION OF REPORTS TO APPROPRIATE CONGRESSIONAL COMMITTEES

Pub. L. 110–53, title XXII, §2205, Aug. 3, 2007, 121 Stat. 543, provided that: "In addition to the committees specifically enumerated to receive reports under this title [enacting provisions set out as note under this section, section 701 of this title, and section 247d–3a of Title 42, The Public Health and Welfare, and amending provisions set out as a note under section 309 of Title 47, Telegraphs, Telephones, and Radiotelegraphs], any report transmitted under the provisions of this title shall also be transmitted to the appropriate congressional committees (as defined in section 2(2) of the Homeland Security Act of 2002 (6 U.S.C. 101(2)))."

REGIONAL MODEL STRATEGIC PLAN PILOT PROJECTS

Pub. L. 108–458, title VII, §7304, Dec. 17, 2004, 118 Stat. 3847, directed the Secretary of Homeland Security, not later than 90 days after Dec. 17, 2004, to establish not fewer than 2 pilot projects in high threat urban areas or regions likely to implement a national model strategic plan in order to develop a regional strategic plan to foster interagency communication and coordinate the gathering of all Federal, State, and local first responders in that area, consistent with the national strategic plan developed by the Department of Homeland Security, and to submit to Congress an interim report regarding the progress of the interagency communications pilot projects 6 months after Dec. 17, 2004, and a final report 18 months after Dec. 17, 2004.

§ 195. Office for Interoperability and Compatibility

(a) Clarification of responsibilities

The Director of the Office for Interoperability and Compatibility shall—

(1) assist the Secretary in developing and implementing the science and technology aspects of the program described in subparagraphs (D), (E), (F), and (G) of section 194(a)(1) of this title;

(2) in coordination with the Federal Communications Commission, the National Institute of Standards and Technology, and other Federal departments and agencies with responsibility for standards, support the creation of national voluntary consensus standards for interoperable emergency communications;

(3) establish a comprehensive research, development, testing, and evaluation program for improving interoperable emergency communications;

(4) establish, in coordination with the Director for Emergency Communications, requirements for interoperable emergency commu-

nications capabilities, which shall be nonproprietary where standards for such capabilities exist, for all public safety radio and data communications systems and equipment purchased using homeland security assistance administered by the Department, excluding any alert and warning device, technology, or system;

(5) carry out the Department's responsibilities and authorities relating to research, development, testing, evaluation, or standards-related elements of the SAFECOM Program;

(6) evaluate and assess new technology in real-world environments to achieve interoperable emergency communications capabilities;

(7) encourage more efficient use of existing resources, including equipment, to achieve interoperable emergency communications capabilities;

(8) test public safety communications systems that are less prone to failure, support new nonvoice services, use spectrum more efficiently, and cost less than existing systems;

(9) coordinate with the private sector to develop solutions to improve emergency communications capabilities and achieve interoperable emergency communications capabilities; and

(10) conduct pilot projects, in coordination with the Director for Emergency Communications, to test and demonstrate technologies, including data and video, that enhance—

(A) the ability of emergency response providers and relevant government officials to continue to communicate in the event of natural disasters, acts of terrorism, and other man-made disasters; and

(B) interoperable emergency communications capabilities.

(b) Coordination

The Director of the Office for Interoperability and Compatibility shall coordinate with the Director for Emergency Communications with respect to the SAFECOM program.

(c) Sufficiency of resources

The Secretary shall provide the Office for Interoperability and Compatibility the resources and staff necessary to carry out the responsibilities under this section.

(Pub. L. 107–296, title III, §314, as added Pub. L. 109–295, title VI, §672(a), Oct. 4, 2006, 120 Stat. 1441.)

§ 195a. Emergency communications interoperability research and development

(a) In general

The Under Secretary for Science and Technology, acting through the Director of the Office for Interoperability and Compatibility, shall establish a comprehensive research and development program to support and promote—

(1) the ability of emergency response providers and relevant government officials to continue to communicate in the event of natural disasters, acts of terrorism, and other man-made disasters; and

(2) interoperable emergency communications capabilities among emergency response providers and relevant government officials, including by—

(A) supporting research on a competitive basis, including through the Directorate of Science and Technology and Homeland Security Advanced Research Projects Agency; and

(B) considering the establishment of a Center of Excellence under the Department of Homeland Security Centers of Excellence Program focused on improving emergency response providers' communication capabilities.

(b) Purposes

The purposes of the program established under subsection (a) include—

(1) supporting research, development, testing, and evaluation on emergency communication capabilities;

(2) understanding the strengths and weaknesses of the public safety communications systems in use;

(3) examining how current and emerging technology can make emergency response providers more effective, and how Federal, State, local, and tribal government agencies can use this technology in a coherent and cost-effective manner;

(4) investigating technologies that could lead to long-term advancements in emergency communications capabilities and supporting research on advanced technologies and potential systemic changes to dramatically improve emergency communications; and

(5) evaluating and validating advanced technology concepts, and facilitating the development and deployment of interoperable emergency communication capabilities.

(c) Definitions

For purposes of this section, the term "interoperable", with respect to emergency communications, has the meaning given the term in section 578 of this title.

(Pub. L. 107–296, title III, §315, as added Pub. L. 109–295, title VI, §673(a), Oct. 4, 2006, 120 Stat. 1443.)

§ 195b. National Biosurveillance Integration Center

(a) Establishment

The Secretary shall establish, operate, and maintain a National Biosurveillance Integration Center (referred to in this section as the "NBIC"), which shall be headed by a Directing Officer, under an office or directorate of the Department that is in existence as of August 3, 2007.

(b) Primary mission

The primary mission of the NBIC is to—

(1) enhance the capability of the Federal Government to—

(A) rapidly identify, characterize, localize, and track a biological event of national concern by integrating and analyzing data relating to human health, animal, plant, food, and environmental monitoring systems (both national and international); and

(B) disseminate alerts and other information to Member Agencies and, in coordination with (and where possible through) Member Agencies, to agencies of State, local, and tribal governments, as appropriate, to enhance the ability of such agencies to respond to a biological event of national concern; and

(2) oversee development and operation of the National Biosurveillance Integration System.

(c) Requirements

The NBIC shall detect, as early as possible, a biological event of national concern that presents a risk to the United States or the infrastructure or key assets of the United States, including by—

(1) consolidating data from all relevant surveillance systems maintained by Member Agencies to detect biological events of national concern across human, animal, and plant species;

(2) seeking private sources of surveillance, both foreign and domestic, when such sources would enhance coverage of critical surveillance gaps;

(3) using an information technology system that uses the best available statistical and other analytical tools to identify and characterize biological events of national concern in as close to real-time as is practicable;

(4) providing the infrastructure for such integration, including information technology systems and space, and support for personnel from Member Agencies with sufficient expertise to enable analysis and interpretation of data;

(5) working with Member Agencies to create information technology systems that use the minimum amount of patient data necessary and consider patient confidentiality and privacy issues at all stages of development and apprise the Privacy Officer of such efforts; and

(6) alerting Member Agencies and, in coordination with (and where possible through) Member Agencies, public health agencies of State, local, and tribal governments regarding any incident that could develop into a biological event of national concern.

(d) Responsibilities of the Directing Officer of the NBIC

(1) In general

The Directing Officer of the NBIC shall—

(A) on an ongoing basis, monitor the availability and appropriateness of surveillance systems used by the NBIC and those systems that could enhance biological situational awareness or the overall performance of the NBIC;

(B) on an ongoing basis, review and seek to improve the statistical and other analytical methods used by the NBIC;

(C) receive and consider other relevant homeland security information, as appropriate; and

(D) provide technical assistance, as appropriate, to all Federal, regional, State, local, and tribal government entities and private sector entities that contribute data relevant to the operation of the NBIC.

(2) Assessments

The Directing Officer of the NBIC shall—

(A) on an ongoing basis, evaluate available data for evidence of a biological event of national concern; and

(B) integrate homeland security information with NBIC data to provide overall situational awareness and determine whether a biological event of national concern has occurred.

(3) Information sharing

(A) In general

The Directing Officer of the NBIC shall—

(i) establish a method of real-time communication with the National Operations Center;

(ii) in the event that a biological event of national concern is detected, notify the Secretary and disseminate results of NBIC assessments relating to that biological event of national concern to appropriate Federal response entities and, in coordination with relevant Member Agencies, regional, State, local, and tribal governmental response entities in a timely manner;

(iii) provide any report on NBIC assessments to Member Agencies and, in coordination with relevant Member Agencies, any affected regional, State, local, or tribal government, and any private sector entity considered appropriate that may enhance the mission of such Member Agencies, governments, or entities or the ability of the Nation to respond to biological events of national concern; and

(iv) share NBIC incident or situational awareness reports, and other relevant information, consistent with the information sharing environment established under section 485 of this title and any policies, guidelines, procedures, instructions, or standards established under that section.

(B) Consultation

The Directing Officer of the NBIC shall implement the activities described in subparagraph (A) consistent with the policies, guidelines, procedures, instructions, or standards established under section 485 of this title and in consultation with the Director of National Intelligence, the Under Secretary for Intelligence and Analysis, and other offices or agencies of the Federal Government, as appropriate.

(e) Responsibilities of the NBIC member agencies

(1)[1] In general

Each Member Agency shall—

(A) use its best efforts to integrate biosurveillance information into the NBIC, with the goal of promoting information sharing between Federal, State, local, and tribal governments to detect biological events of national concern;

(B) provide timely information to assist the NBIC in maintaining biological situational awareness for accurate detection and response purposes;

[1] So in original. No par. (2) has been enacted.

(C) enable the NBIC to receive and use biosurveillance information from member agencies to carry out its requirements under subsection (c);

(D) connect the biosurveillance data systems of that Member Agency to the NBIC data system under mutually agreed protocols that are consistent with subsection (c)(5);

(E) participate in the formation of strategy and policy for the operation of the NBIC and its information sharing;

(F) provide personnel to the NBIC under an interagency personnel agreement and consider the qualifications of such personnel necessary to provide human, animal, and environmental data analysis and interpretation support to the NBIC; and

(G) retain responsibility for the surveillance and intelligence systems of that department or agency, if applicable.

(f) Administrative authorities

(1) Hiring of experts

The Directing Officer of the NBIC shall hire individuals with the necessary expertise to develop and operate the NBIC.

(2) Detail of personnel

Upon the request of the Directing Officer of the NBIC, the head of any Federal department or agency may detail, on a reimbursable basis, any of the personnel of that department or agency to the Department to assist the NBIC in carrying out this section.

(g) NBIC interagency working group

The Directing Officer of the NBIC shall—

(1) establish an interagency working group to facilitate interagency cooperation and to advise the Directing Officer of the NBIC regarding recommendations to enhance the biosurveillance capabilities of the Department; and

(2) invite Member Agencies to serve on that working group.

(h) Relationship to other departments and agencies

The authority of the Directing Officer of the NBIC under this section shall not affect any authority or responsibility of any other department or agency of the Federal Government with respect to biosurveillance activities under any program administered by that department or agency.

(i) Authorization of appropriations

There are authorized to be appropriated such sums as are necessary to carry out this section.

(j) Definitions

In this section:

(1) The terms "biological agent" and "toxin" have the meanings given those terms in section 178 of title 18.

(2) The term "biological event of national concern" means—

(A) an act of terrorism involving a biological agent or toxin; or

(B) a naturally occurring outbreak of an infectious disease that may result in a national epidemic.

(3) The term "homeland security information" has the meaning given that term in section 482 of this title.

(4) The term "Member Agency" means any Federal department or agency that, at the discretion of the head of that department or agency, has entered a memorandum of understanding regarding participation in the NBIC.

(5) The term "Privacy Officer" means the Privacy Officer appointed under section 142 of this title.

(Pub. L. 107–296, title III, § 316, as added Pub. L. 110–53, title XI, § 1101(a), Aug. 3, 2007, 121 Stat. 375.)

DEADLINE FOR IMPLEMENTATION

Pub. L. 110–53, title XI, § 1101(c), Aug. 3, 2007, 121 Stat. 378, provided that: "The National Biosurveillance Integration Center under section 316 of the Homeland Security Act [of 2002, 6 U.S.C. 195b], as added by subsection (a), shall be fully operational by not later than September 30, 2008."

§ 195c. Promoting antiterrorism through international cooperation program

(a) Definitions

In this section:

(1) Director

The term "Director" means the Director selected under subsection (b)(2).

(2) International cooperative activity

The term "international cooperative activity" includes—

(A) coordinated research projects, joint research projects, or joint ventures;

(B) joint studies or technical demonstrations;

(C) coordinated field exercises, scientific seminars, conferences, symposia, and workshops;

(D) training of scientists and engineers;

(E) visits and exchanges of scientists, engineers, or other appropriate personnel;

(F) exchanges or sharing of scientific and technological information; and

(G) joint use of laboratory facilities and equipment.

(b) Science and Technology Homeland Security International Cooperative Programs Office

(1) Establishment

The Under Secretary shall establish the Science and Technology Homeland Security International Cooperative Programs Office.

(2) Director

The Office shall be headed by a Director, who—

(A) shall be selected, in consultation with the Assistant Secretary for International Affairs, by and shall report to the Under Secretary; and

(B) may be an officer of the Department serving in another position.

(3) Responsibilities

(A) Development of mechanisms

The Director shall be responsible for developing, in coordination with the Department of State and, as appropriate, the Department of Defense, the Department of Energy, and other Federal agencies, understandings and agreements to allow and to support international cooperative activity in support of homeland security.

(B) Priorities

The Director shall be responsible for developing, in coordination with the Office of International Affairs and other Federal agencies, strategic priorities for international cooperative activity for the Department in support of homeland security.

(C) Activities

The Director shall facilitate the planning, development, and implementation of international cooperative activity to address the strategic priorities developed under subparagraph (B) through mechanisms the Under Secretary considers appropriate, including grants, cooperative agreements, or contracts to or with foreign public or private entities, governmental organizations, businesses (including small businesses and socially and economically disadvantaged small businesses (as those terms are defined in sections 632 and 637 of title 15, respectively)), federally funded research and development centers, and universities.

(D) Identification of partners

The Director shall facilitate the matching of United States entities engaged in homeland security research with non-United States entities engaged in homeland security research so that they may partner in homeland security research activities.

(4) Coordination

The Director shall ensure that the activities under this subsection are coordinated with the Office of International Affairs and the Department of State and, as appropriate, the Department of Defense, the Department of Energy, and other relevant Federal agencies or interagency bodies. The Director may enter into joint activities with other Federal agencies.

(c) Matching funding

(1) In general

(A) Equitability

The Director shall ensure that funding and resources expended in international cooperative activity will be equitably matched by the foreign partner government or other entity through direct funding, funding of complementary activities, or the provision of staff, facilities, material, or equipment.

(B) Grant matching and repayment

(i) In general

The Secretary may require a recipient of a grant under this section—

(I) to make a matching contribution of not more than 50 percent of the total cost of the proposed project for which the grant is awarded; and

(II) to repay to the Secretary the amount of the grant (or a portion thereof), interest on such amount at an appropriate rate, and such charges for administration of the grant as the Secretary determines appropriate.

(ii) Maximum amount

The Secretary may not require that repayment under clause (i)(II) be more than 150 percent of the amount of the grant, adjusted for inflation on the basis of the Consumer Price Index.

(2) Foreign partners

Partners may include Israel, the United Kingdom, Canada, Australia, Singapore, and other allies in the global war on terrorism as determined to be appropriate by the Secretary of Homeland Security and the Secretary of State.

(3) Loans of equipment

The Director may make or accept loans of equipment for research and development and comparative testing purposes.

(d) Foreign reimbursements

If the Science and Technology Homeland Security International Cooperative Programs Office participates in an international cooperative activity with a foreign partner on a cost-sharing basis, any reimbursements or contributions received from that foreign partner to meet its share of the project may be credited to appropriate current appropriations accounts of the Directorate of Science and Technology.

(e) Report to Congress on international cooperative activities

Not later than one year after August 3, 2007, and every 5 years thereafter, the Under Secretary, acting through the Director, shall submit to Congress a report containing—

(1) a brief description of each grant, cooperative agreement, or contract made or entered into under subsection (b)(3)(C), including the participants, goals, and amount and sources of funding; and

(2) a list of international cooperative activities underway, including the participants, goals, expected duration, and amount and sources of funding, including resources provided to support the activities in lieu of direct funding.

(f) Animal and zoonotic diseases

As part of the international cooperative activities authorized in this section, the Under Secretary, in coordination with the Chief Medical Officer, the Department of State, and appropriate officials of the Department of Agriculture, the Department of Defense, and the Department of Health and Human Services, may enter into cooperative activities with foreign countries, including African nations, to strengthen American preparedness against foreign animal and zoonotic diseases overseas that could harm the Nation's agricultural and public health sectors if they were to reach the United States.

(g) Construction; authorities of the Secretary of State

Nothing in this section shall be construed to alter or affect the following provisions of law:

(1) Title V of the Foreign Relations Authorization Act, Fiscal Year 1979 (22 U.S.C. 2656a et seq.).

(2) Section 112b(c) of title 1.

(3) Section 2651a(e)(2) of title 22.

(4) Sections 2752 and 2767 of title 22.

(5) Section 2382(c) of title 22.

(h) Authorization of appropriations

There are authorized to be appropriated to carry out this section such sums as are necessary.

(Pub. L. 107–296, title III, §317, as added Pub. L. 110–53, title XIX, §1901(b)(1), Aug. 3, 2007, 121 Stat. 505.)

REFERENCES IN TEXT

The Foreign Relations Authorization Act, Fiscal Year 1979, referred to in subsec. (g)(1), is Pub. L. 95–426, Oct. 7, 1978, 92 Stat. 963. Title V of the Act is classified generally to sections 2656a to 2656d of Title 22, Foreign Relations and Intercourse. For complete classification of this Act to the Code, see Tables.

FINDINGS

Pub. L. 110–53, title XIX, §1901(a), Aug. 3, 2007, 121 Stat. 505, provided that: "Congress finds the following:

"(1) The development and implementation of technology is critical to combating terrorism and other high consequence events and implementing a comprehensive homeland security strategy.

"(2) The United States and its allies in the global war on terrorism share a common interest in facilitating research, development, testing, and evaluation of equipment, capabilities, technologies, and services that will aid in detecting, preventing, responding to, recovering from, and mitigating against acts of terrorism.

"(3) Certain United States allies in the global war on terrorism, including Israel, the United Kingdom, Canada, Australia, and Singapore have extensive experience with, and technological expertise in, homeland security.

"(4) The United States and certain of its allies in the global war on terrorism have a history of successful collaboration in developing mutually beneficial equipment, capabilities, technologies, and services in the areas of defense, agriculture, and telecommunications.

"(5) The United States and its allies in the global war on terrorism will mutually benefit from the sharing of technological expertise to combat domestic and international terrorism.

"(6) The establishment of an office to facilitate and support cooperative endeavors between and among government agencies, for-profit business entities, academic institutions, and nonprofit entities of the United States and its allies will safeguard lives and property worldwide against acts of terrorism and other high consequence events."

TRANSPARENCY OF FUNDS

Pub. L. 110–53, title XIX, §1902, Aug. 3, 2007, 121 Stat. 508, provided that: "For each Federal award (as that term is defined in section 2 of the Federal Funding Accountability and Transparency Act of 2006 [Pub. L. 109–282] (31 U.S.C. 6101 note)) under this title [enacting this section and provisions set out as notes under this section] or an amendment made by this title, the Director of the Office of Management and Budget shall ensure full and timely compliance with the requirements of the Federal Funding Accountability and Transparency Act of 2006 (31 U.S.C. 6101 note)."

SUBCHAPTER IV—DIRECTORATE OF BORDER AND TRANSPORTATION SECURITY

PART A—UNDER SECRETARY FOR BORDER AND TRANSPORTATION SECURITY

§201. Under Secretary for Border and Transportation Security

There shall be in the Department a Directorate of Border and Transportation Security headed by an Under Secretary for Border and Transportation Security.

(Pub. L. 107–296, title IV, §401, Nov. 25, 2002, 116 Stat. 2177.)

§202. Responsibilities

The Secretary, acting through the Under Secretary for Border and Transportation Security, shall be responsible for the following:

(1) Preventing the entry of terrorists and the instruments of terrorism into the United States.

(2) Securing the borders, territorial waters, ports, terminals, waterways, and air, land, and sea transportation systems of the United States, including managing and coordinating those functions transferred to the Department at ports of entry.

(3) Carrying out the immigration enforcement functions vested by statute in, or performed by, the Commissioner of Immigration and Naturalization (or any officer, employee, or component of the Immigration and Naturalization Service) immediately before the date on which the transfer of functions specified under section 251 of this title takes effect.

(4) Establishing and administering rules, in accordance with section 236 of this title, governing the granting of visas or other forms of permission, including parole, to enter the United States to individuals who are not a citizen or an alien lawfully admitted for permanent residence in the United States.

(5) Establishing national immigration enforcement policies and priorities.

(6) Except as provided in part C of this subchapter, administering the customs laws of the United States.

(7) Conducting the inspection and related administrative functions of the Department of Agriculture transferred to the Secretary of Homeland Security under section 231 of this title.

(8) In carrying out the foregoing responsibilities, ensuring the speedy, orderly, and efficient flow of lawful traffic and commerce.

(Pub. L. 107–296, title IV, §402, Nov. 25, 2002, 116 Stat. 2177.)

REFERENCES IN TEXT

Part C of this subchapter, referred to in par. (6), was in the original "subtitle C", meaning subtitle C (§421 et seq.) of title IV of Pub. L. 107–296, Nov. 25, 2002, 116 Stat. 2182, which enacted part C (§231 et seq.) of this subchapter and amended sections 2279e and 2279f of Title 7, Agriculture, and sections 115, 44901, and 47106 of Title 49, Transportation. For complete classification of subtitle C to the Code, see Tables.

The customs laws of the United States, referred to in par. (6), are classified generally to Title 19, Customs Duties.

§ 203. Functions transferred

In accordance with subchapter XII of this chapter (relating to transition provisions), there shall be transferred to the Secretary the functions, personnel, assets, and liabilities of—

(1) the United States Customs Service of the Department of the Treasury, including the functions of the Secretary of the Treasury relating thereto;

(2) the Transportation Security Administration of the Department of Transportation, including the functions of the Secretary of Transportation, and of the Under Secretary of Transportation for Security, relating thereto;

(3) the Federal Protective Service of the General Services Administration, including the functions of the Administrator of General Services relating thereto;

(4) the Federal Law Enforcement Training Center of the Department of the Treasury; and

(5) the Office for Domestic Preparedness of the Office of Justice Programs, including the functions of the Attorney General relating thereto.

(Pub. L. 107–296, title IV, § 403, Nov. 25, 2002, 116 Stat. 2178.)

PART B—UNITED STATES CUSTOMS SERVICE

§ 211. Establishment; Commissioner of Customs

(a) Establishment

There is established in the Department the United States Customs Service, under the authority of the Under Secretary for Border and Transportation Security, which shall be vested with those functions including, but not limited to those set forth in section 215(7) of this title, and the personnel, assets, and liabilities attributable to those functions.

(b) Commissioner of Customs

(1) In general

There shall be at the head of the Customs Service a Commissioner of Customs, who shall be appointed by the President, by and with the advice and consent of the Senate.

(2) Omitted

(3) Continuation in office

The individual serving as the Commissioner of Customs on the day before the effective date of this chapter may serve as the Commissioner of Customs on and after such effective date until a Commissioner of Customs is appointed under paragraph (1).

(Pub. L. 107–296, title IV, § 411, Nov. 25, 2002, 116 Stat. 2178.)

REFERENCES IN TEXT

The effective date of this chapter, referred to in subsec. (b)(3), is 60 days after Nov. 25, 2002, see section 4 of Pub. L. 107–296, set out as an Effective Date note under section 101 of this title.

CODIFICATION

Section is comprised of section 411 of Pub. L. 107–296. Subsec. (b)(2) of section 411 of Pub. L. 107–296 amended section 5314 of Title 5, Government Organization and Employees.

CHANGE OF NAME

Customs Service, referred to in subsecs. (a) and (b)(1), changed to Bureau of Customs and Border Protection by Reorganization Plan Modification for the Department of Homeland Security, eff. Mar. 1, 2003, H. Doc. No. 108–32, 108th Congress, 1st Session, set out as a note under section 542 of this title.

§ 212. Retention of Customs revenue functions by Secretary of the Treasury

(a) Retention of Customs revenue functions by Secretary of the Treasury

(1) Retention of authority

Notwithstanding section 203(a)(1)[1] of this title, authority related to Customs revenue functions that was vested in the Secretary of the Treasury by law before the effective date of this chapter under those provisions of law set forth in paragraph (2) shall not be transferred to the Secretary by reason of this chapter, and on and after the effective date of this chapter, the Secretary of the Treasury may delegate any such authority to the Secretary at the discretion of the Secretary of the Treasury. The Secretary of the Treasury shall consult with the Secretary regarding the exercise of any such authority not delegated to the Secretary.

(2) Statutes

The provisions of law referred to in paragraph (1) are the following: the Tariff Act of 1930 [19 U.S.C. 1202 et seq.]; section 249 of the Revised Statutes of the United States (19 U.S.C. 3); section 2 of the Act of March 4, 1923 (19 U.S.C. 6); section 13031 of the Consolidated Omnibus Budget Reconciliation Act of 1985 (19 U.S.C. 58c); section 251 of the Revised Statutes of the United States (19 U.S.C. 66); section 1 of the Act of June 26, 1930 (19 U.S.C. 68); the Foreign Trade Zones Act (19 U.S.C. 81a et seq.); section 1 of the Act of March 2, 1911 (19 U.S.C. 198); the Trade Act of 1974 [19 U.S.C. 2101 et seq.]; the Trade Agreements Act of 1979; the North American Free Trade Area Implementation Act; the Uruguay Round Agreements Act, the Caribbean Basin Economic Recovery Act [19 U.S.C. 2701 et seq.]; the Andean Trade Preference Act [19 U.S.C. 3201 et seq.]; the African Growth and Opportunity Act [19 U.S.C. 3701 et seq.]; and any other provision of law vesting customs revenue functions in the Secretary of the Treasury.

(b) Maintenance of Customs revenue functions

(1) Maintenance of functions

Notwithstanding any other provision of this chapter, the Secretary may not consolidate, discontinue, or diminish those functions described in paragraph (2) performed by the United States Customs Service (as established under section 211 of this title) on or after the effective date of this chapter, reduce the staffing level, or reduce the resources attributable to such functions, and the Secretary shall ensure that an appropriate management structure is implemented to carry out such functions.

(2) Functions

The functions referred to in paragraph (1) are those functions performed by the following

[1] So in original. Probably should be section "203(1)".

personnel, and associated support staff, of the United States Customs Service on the day before the effective date of this chapter: Import Specialists, Entry Specialists, Drawback Specialists, National Import Specialist, Fines and Penalties Specialists, attorneys of the Office of Regulations and Rulings, Customs Auditors, International Trade Specialists, Financial Systems Specialists.

(c) New personnel

The Secretary of the Treasury is authorized to appoint up to 20 new personnel to work with personnel of the Department in performing customs revenue functions.

(Pub. L. 107–296, title IV, §412, Nov. 25, 2002, 116 Stat. 2179.)

REFERENCES IN TEXT

The effective date of this chapter, referred to in subsecs. (a)(1) and (b), is 60 days after Nov. 25, 2002, see section 4 of Pub. L. 107–296, set out as an Effective Date note under section 101 of this title.

This chapter, referred to in subsecs. (a)(1) and (b)(1), was in the original "this Act", meaning Pub. L. 107–296, Nov. 25, 2002, 116 Stat. 2135, known as the Homeland Security Act of 2002, which is classified principally to this chapter. For complete classification of this Act to the Code, see Short Title note set out under section 101 of this title and Tables.

The Tariff Act of 1930, referred to in subsec. (a)(2), is act June 17, 1930, ch. 497, 46 Stat. 590, as amended, which is classified generally to chapter 4 (§1202 et seq.) of Title 19, Customs Duties. For complete classification of this Act to the Code, see section 1654 of Title 19 and Tables.

The Foreign Trade Zones Act, referred to in subsec. (a)(2), is act June 18, 1934, ch. 590, 48 Stat. 998, as amended, which is classified generally to chapter 1A (§81a et seq.) of Title 19, Customs Duties. For complete classification of this Act to the Code, see Tables.

The Trade Act of 1974, referred to in subsec. (a)(2), is Pub. L. 93–618, Jan. 3, 1975, 88 Stat. 1978, as amended, which is classified principally to chapter 12 (§2101 et seq.) of Title 19, Customs Duties. For complete classification of this Act to the Code, see References in Text note set out under section 2101 of Title 19 and Tables.

The Trade Agreements Act of 1979, referred to in subsec. (a)(2), is Pub. L. 96–39, July 26, 1979, 93 Stat. 144, as amended. For complete classification of this Act to the Code, see References in Text note set out under section 2501 of Title 19, Customs Duties, and Tables.

The North American Free Trade Area Implementation Act, referred to in subsec. (a)(2), probably means the North American Free Trade Agreement Implementation Act, Pub. L. 103–182, Dec. 8, 1993, 107 Stat. 2057, as amended. For complete classification of this Act to the Code, see Short Title note set out under section 3301 of Title 19, Customs Duties, and Tables.

The Uruguay Round Agreements Act, referred to in subsec. (a)(2), is Pub. L. 103–465, Dec. 8, 1994, 108 Stat. 4809, as amended. For complete classification of this Act to the Code, see Short Title note set out under section 3501 of Title 19, Customs Duties, and Tables.

The Caribbean Basin Economic Recovery Act, referred to in subsec. (a)(2), is title II of Pub. L. 98–67, Aug. 5, 1983, 97 Stat. 384, as amended, which is classified principally to chapter 15 (§2701 et seq.) of Title 19, Customs Duties. For complete classification of this Act to the Code, see Short Title note set out under section 2701 of Title 19 and Tables.

The Andean Trade Preference Act, referred to in subsec. (a)(2), is title II of Pub. L. 102–182, Dec. 4, 1991, 105 Stat. 1236, as amended, which is classified generally to chapter 20 (§3201 et seq.) of Title 19, Customs Duties. For complete classification of this Act to the Code, see Short Title note set out under section 3201 of Title 19 and Tables.

The African Growth and Opportunity Act, referred to in subsec. (a)(2), is title I of Pub. L. 106–200, May 18, 2000, 114 Stat. 252, as amended, which is classified principally to chapter 23 (§3701 et seq.) of Title 19, Customs Duties. For complete classification of this Act to the Code, see Short Title note set out under section 3701 of Title 19 and Tables.

CHANGE OF NAME

Customs Service, referred to in subsec. (b), changed to Bureau of Customs and Border Protection by Reorganization Plan Modification for the Department of Homeland Security, eff. Mar. 1, 2003, H. Doc. No. 108–32, 108th Congress, 1st Session, set out as a note under section 542 of this title.

§213. Preservation of Customs funds

Notwithstanding any other provision of this chapter, no funds available to the United States Customs Service or collected under paragraphs (1) through (8) of section 58c(a) of title 19 may be transferred for use by any other agency or office in the Department.

(Pub. L. 107–296, title IV, §413, Nov. 25, 2002, 116 Stat. 2180.)

CHANGE OF NAME

Customs Service, referred to in text, changed to Bureau of Customs and Border Protection by Reorganization Plan Modification for the Department of Homeland Security, eff. Mar. 1, 2003, H. Doc. No. 108–32, 108th Congress, 1st Session, set out as a note under section 542 of this title.

§214. Separate budget request for Customs

The President shall include in each budget transmitted to Congress under section 1105 of title 31 a separate budget request for the United States Customs Service.

(Pub. L. 107–296, title IV, §414, Nov. 25, 2002, 116 Stat. 2180.)

CHANGE OF NAME

Customs Service, referred to in text, changed to Bureau of Customs and Border Protection by Reorganization Plan Modification for the Department of Homeland Security, eff. Mar. 1, 2003, H. Doc. No. 108–32, 108th Congress, 1st Session, set out as a note under section 542 of this title.

LAND BORDER PROJECTS

Pub. L. 111–83, title II, Oct. 28, 2009, 123 Stat. 2148, provided in part: "That for fiscal year 2011 and thereafter, the annual budget submission of U.S. Customs and Border Protection for 'Construction and Facilities Management' shall, in consultation with the General Services Administration, include a detailed 5-year plan for all Federal land border port of entry projects with a yearly update of total projected future funding needs delineated by land port of entry."

Similar provisions were contained in the following prior appropriation act:

Pub. L. 110–329, div. D, title II, Sept. 30, 2008, 122 Stat. 3658.

§215. Definition

In this part, the term "customs revenue function" means the following:

(1) Assessing and collecting customs duties (including antidumping and countervailing duties and duties imposed under safeguard provisions), excise taxes, fees, and penalties due on imported merchandise, including classifying

and valuing merchandise for purposes of such assessment.

(2) Processing and denial of entry of persons, baggage, cargo, and mail, with respect to the assessment and collection of import duties.

(3) Detecting and apprehending persons engaged in fraudulent practices designed to circumvent the customs laws of the United States.

(4) Enforcing section 1337 of title 19 and provisions relating to import quotas and the marking of imported merchandise, and providing Customs Recordations for copyrights, patents, and trademarks.

(5) Collecting accurate import data for compilation of international trade statistics.

(6) Enforcing reciprocal trade agreements.

(7) Functions performed by the following personnel, and associated support staff, of the United States Customs Service on the day before the effective date of this chapter: Import Specialists, Entry Specialists, Drawback Specialists, National Import Specialist, Fines and Penalties Specialists, attorneys of the Office of Regulations and Rulings, Customs Auditors, International Trade Specialists, Financial Systems Specialists.

(8) Functions performed by the following offices, with respect to any function described in any of paragraphs (1) through (7), and associated support staff, of the United States Customs Service on the day before the effective date of this chapter: the Office of Information and Technology, the Office of Laboratory Services, the Office of the Chief Counsel, the Office of Congressional Affairs, the Office of International Affairs, and the Office of Training and Development.

(Pub. L. 107–296, title IV, §415, Nov. 25, 2002, 116 Stat. 2180.)

REFERENCES IN TEXT

This part, referred to in text, was in the original "this subtitle", meaning subtitle B (§§411–419) of title IV of Pub. L. 107–296, Nov. 25, 2002, 116 Stat. 2178, which enacted this part, amended section 5314 of Title 5, Government Organization and Employees, section 58c of Title 19, Customs Duties, and provisions set out as a note under section 2075 of Title 19. For complete classification of subtitle B to the Code, see Tables.

The effective date of this chapter, referred to in pars. (7) and (8), is 60 days after Nov. 25, 2002, see section 4 of Pub. L. 107–296, set out as an Effective Date note under section 101 of this title.

§216. GAO report to Congress

Not later than 3 months after the effective date of this chapter, the Comptroller General of the United States shall submit to Congress a report that sets forth all trade functions performed by the executive branch, specifying each agency that performs each such function.

(Pub. L. 107–296, title IV, §416, Nov. 25, 2002, 116 Stat. 2181.)

REFERENCES IN TEXT

The effective date of this chapter, referred to in text, is 60 days after Nov. 25, 2002, see section 4 of Pub. L. 107–296, set out as an Effective Date note under section 101 of this title.

§217. Allocation of resources by the Secretary

(a) In general

The Secretary shall ensure that adequate staffing is provided to assure that levels of customs revenue services provided on the day before the effective date of this chapter shall continue to be provided.

(b) Notification of Congress

The Secretary shall notify the Committee on Ways and Means of the House of Representatives and the Committee on Finance of the Senate at least 90 days prior to taking any action which would—

(1) result in any significant reduction in customs revenue services, including hours of operation, provided at any office within the Department or any port of entry;

(2) eliminate or relocate any office of the Department which provides customs revenue services; or

(3) eliminate any port of entry.

(c) Definition

In this section, the term "customs revenue services" means those customs revenue functions described in paragraphs (1) through (6) and paragraph (8) of section 215 of this title.

(Pub. L. 107–296, title IV, §417, Nov. 25, 2002, 116 Stat. 2181.)

REFERENCES IN TEXT

The effective date of this chapter, referred to in subsec. (a), is 60 days after Nov. 25, 2002, see section 4 of Pub. L. 107–296, set out as an Effective Date note under section 101 of this title.

§218. Reports to Congress

(a) Continuing reports

The United States Customs Service shall, on and after the effective date of this chapter, continue to submit to the Committee on Ways and Means of the House of Representatives and the Committee on Finance of the Senate any report required, on the day before such the[1] effective date of this chapter, to be so submitted under any provision of law.

(b) Report on conforming amendments

Not later than 60 days after November 25, 2002, the Secretary of the Treasury shall submit a report to the Committee on Finance of the Senate and the Committee on Ways and Means of the House of Representatives of proposed conforming amendments to the statutes set forth under section 212(a)(2) of this title in order to determine the appropriate allocation of legal authorities described under this subsection. The Secretary of the Treasury shall also identify those authorities vested in the Secretary of the Treasury that are exercised by the Commissioner of Customs on or before the effective date of this section.

(Pub. L. 107–296, title IV, §418, Nov. 25, 2002, 116 Stat. 2181.)

REFERENCES IN TEXT

The effective date of this chapter and the effective date of this section, referred to in text, is 60 days after

[1] So in original.

Nov. 25, 2002, see section 4 of Pub. L. 107–296, set out as an Effective Date note under section 101 of this title.

CHANGE OF NAME

Customs Service, referred to in subsec. (a), changed to Bureau of Customs and Border Protection by Reorganization Plan Modification for the Department of Homeland Security, eff. Mar. 1, 2003, H. Doc. No. 108–32, 108th Congress, 1st Session, set out as a note under section 542 of this title.

§ 220. Methamphetamine and methamphetamine precursor chemicals

(a) Compliance with performance plan requirements

As part of the annual performance plan required in the budget submission of the United States Customs and Border Protection under section 1115 of title 31, the Commissioner shall establish performance indicators relating to the seizure of methamphetamine and methamphetamine precursor chemicals in order to evaluate the performance goals of the United States Customs and Border Protection with respect to the interdiction of illegal drugs entering the United States.

(b) Study and report relating to methamphetamine and methamphetamine precursor chemicals

(1) Analysis

The Commissioner shall, on an ongoing basis, analyze the movement of methamphetamine and methamphetamine precursor chemicals into the United States. In conducting the analysis, the Commissioner shall—

(A) consider the entry of methamphetamine and methamphetamine precursor chemicals through ports of entry, between ports of entry, through international mails, and through international courier services;

(B) examine the export procedures of each foreign country where the shipments of methamphetamine and methamphetamine precursor chemicals originate and determine if changes in the country's customs over time provisions would alleviate the export of methamphetamine and methamphetamine precursor chemicals; and

(C) identify emerging trends in smuggling techniques and strategies.

(2) Report

Not later than September 30, 2007, and each 2-year period thereafter, the Commissioner, in the consultation with the Attorney General, United States Immigration and Customs Enforcement, the United States Drug Enforcement Administration, and the United States Department of State, shall submit a report to the Committee on Finance of the Senate, the Committee on Foreign Relations of the Senate, the Committee on the Judiciary of the Senate, the Committee on Ways and Means of the House of Representatives, the Committee on International Relations of the House of Representatives, and the Committee on the Judiciary of the House of Representatives, that includes—

(A) a comprehensive summary of the analysis described in paragraph (1); and

(B) a description of how the Untied[1] States Customs and Border Protection utilized the analysis described in paragraph (1) to target shipments presenting a high risk for smuggling or circumvention of the Combat Methamphetamine Epidemic Act of 2005 (Public Law 109–177).

(3) Availability of analysis

The Commissioner shall ensure that the analysis described in paragraph (1) is made available in a timely manner to the Secretary of State to facilitate the Secretary in fulfilling the Secretary's reporting requirements in section 722 of the Combat Methamphetamine Epidemic Act of 2005.

(c) Definition

In this section, the term "methamphetamine precursor chemicals" means the chemicals ephedrine, pseudoephedrine, or phenylpropanolamine, including each of the salts, optical isomers, and salts of optical isomers of such chemicals.

(Pub. L. 109–347, title VII, § 707, Oct. 13, 2006, 120 Stat. 1946.)

REFERENCES IN TEXT

The Combat Methamphetamine Epidemic Act of 2005, referred to in subsec. (b)(2)(B), is Pub. L. 109–177, title VII, Mar. 9, 2006, 120 Stat. 256. Section 722 of the Act amended sections 2291h, 2291j, and 2291j–1 of Title 22, Foreign Relations and Intercourse, and enacted provisions set out as a note under section 2291h of Title 22. For complete classification of this Act to the Code, see Short Title note set out under section 801 of Title 21, Food and Drugs, and Tables.

CODIFICATION

Section was enacted as part of the Security and Accountability For Every Port Act of 2006, also known as the SAFE Port Act, and not as part of the Homeland Security Act of 2002 which comprises this chapter.

CHANGE OF NAME

Committee on International Relations of House of Representatives changed to Committee on Foreign Affairs of House of Representatives by House Resolution No. 6, One Hundred Tenth Congress, Jan. 5, 2007.

DEFINITIONS

For definition of "Commissioner" as used in this section, see section 901 of this title.

PART C—MISCELLANEOUS PROVISIONS

§ 231. Transfer of certain agricultural inspection functions of the Department of Agriculture

(a) Transfer of agricultural import and entry inspection functions

There shall be transferred to the Secretary the functions of the Secretary of Agriculture relating to agricultural import and entry inspection activities under the laws specified in subsection (b) of this section.

(b) Covered animal and plant protection laws

The laws referred to in subsection (a) of this section are the following:

(1) The Act commonly known as the Virus-Serum-Toxin Act (the eighth paragraph under

[1] So in original.

the heading "Bureau of Animal Industry" in the Act of March 4, 1913; 21 U.S.C. 151 et seq.).

(2) Section 1 of the Act of August 31, 1922 (commonly known as the Honeybee Act; 7 U.S.C. 281).

(3) Title III of the Federal Seed Act (7 U.S.C. 1581 et seq.).

(4) The Plant Protection Act (7 U.S.C. 7701 et seq.).

(5) The Animal Health Protection Act (subtitle E of title X of Public Law 107–171; 7 U.S.C. 8301 et seq.).

(6) The Lacey Act Amendments of 1981 (16 U.S.C. 3371 et seq.).

(7) Section 11 of the Endangered Species Act of 1973 (16 U.S.C. 1540).

(c) Exclusion of quarantine activities

For purposes of this section, the term "functions" does not include any quarantine activities carried out under the laws specified in subsection (b) of this section.

(d) Effect of transfer

(1) Compliance with Department of Agriculture regulations

The authority transferred pursuant to subsection (a) of this section shall be exercised by the Secretary in accordance with the regulations, policies, and procedures issued by the Secretary of Agriculture regarding the administration of the laws specified in subsection (b) of this section.

(2) Rulemaking coordination

The Secretary of Agriculture shall coordinate with the Secretary whenever the Secretary of Agriculture prescribes regulations, policies, or procedures for administering the functions transferred under subsection (a) of this section under a law specified in subsection (b) of this section.

(3) Effective administration

The Secretary, in consultation with the Secretary of Agriculture, may issue such directives and guidelines as are necessary to ensure the effective use of personnel of the Department of Homeland Security to carry out the functions transferred pursuant to subsection (a) of this section.

(e) Transfer agreement

(1) Agreement required; revision

Before the end of the transition period, as defined in section 541 of this title, the Secretary of Agriculture and the Secretary shall enter into an agreement to effectuate the transfer of functions required by subsection (a) of this section. The Secretary of Agriculture and the Secretary may jointly revise the agreement as necessary thereafter.

(2) Required terms

The agreement required by this subsection shall specifically address the following:

(A) The supervision by the Secretary of Agriculture of the training of employees of the Secretary to carry out the functions transferred pursuant to subsection (a) of this section.

(B) The transfer of funds to the Secretary under subsection (f) of this section.

(3) Cooperation and reciprocity

The Secretary of Agriculture and the Secretary may include as part of the agreement the following:

(A) Authority for the Secretary to perform functions delegated to the Animal and Plant Health Inspection Service of the Department of Agriculture regarding the protection of domestic livestock and plants, but not transferred to the Secretary pursuant to subsection (a) of this section.

(B) Authority for the Secretary of Agriculture to use employees of the Department of Homeland Security to carry out authorities delegated to the Animal and Plant Health Inspection Service regarding the protection of domestic livestock and plants.

(f) Periodic transfer of funds to Department of Homeland Security

(1) Transfer of funds

Out of funds collected by fees authorized under sections 136 and 136a of title 21, the Secretary of Agriculture shall transfer, from time to time in accordance with the agreement under subsection (e) of this section, to the Secretary funds for activities carried out by the Secretary for which such fees were collected.

(2) Limitation

The proportion of fees collected pursuant to such sections that are transferred to the Secretary under this subsection may not exceed the proportion of the costs incurred by the Secretary to all costs incurred to carry out activities funded by such fees.

(g) Transfer of Department of Agriculture employees

Not later than the completion of the transition period defined under section 541 of this title, the Secretary of Agriculture shall transfer to the Secretary not more than 3,200 full-time equivalent positions of the Department of Agriculture.

(Pub. L. 107–296, title IV, §421, Nov. 25, 2002, 116 Stat. 2182.)

REFERENCES IN TEXT

The Virus-Serum-Toxin Act, referred to in subsec. (b)(1), is the eighth paragraph under the heading "Bureau of Animal Industry" in act Mar. 4, 1913, ch. 145, 37 Stat. 832, 833, as amended, which is classified generally to chapter 5 (§151 et seq.) of Title 21, Food and Drugs. For complete classification of this Act to the Code, see Short Title note set out under section 151 of Title 21 and Tables.

The Federal Seed Act, referred to in subsec. (b)(3), is act Aug. 9, 1939, ch. 615, 53 Stat. 1275, as amended. Title III of the Act is classified generally to subchapter III (§1581 et seq.) of chapter 37 of Title 7, Agriculture. For complete classification of this Act to the Code, see section 1551 of Title 7 and Tables.

The Plant Protection Act, referred to in subsec. (b)(4), is title IV of Pub. L. 106–224, June 20, 2000, 114 Stat. 438, as amended, which is classified principally to chapter 104 (§7701 et seq.) of Title 7, Agriculture. For complete classification of this Act to the Code, see Short Title note set out under section 7701 of Title 7 and Tables.

The Animal Health Protection Act, referred to in subsec. (b)(5), is subtitle E (§§10401–10418) of title X of

Pub. L. 107–171, May 13, 2002, 116 Stat. 494, which is classified principally to chapter 109 (§8301 et seq.) of Title 7, Agriculture. For complete classification of this Act to the Code, see Short Title note set out under section 8301 of Title 7 and Tables.

The Lacey Act Amendments of 1981, referred to in subsec. (b)(6), is Pub. L. 97–79, Nov. 16, 1981, 95 Stat. 1073, as amended, which enacted chapter 53 (§3371 et seq.) of Title 16, Conservation, amended section 1540 of Title 16 and section 42 of Title 18, Crimes and Criminal Procedure, repealed sections 667e and 851 to 856 of Title 16 and sections 43, 44, 3054, and 3112 of Title 18, and enacted provisions set out as notes under sections 1540 and 3371 of Title 16. For complete classification of this Act to the Code, see Short Title note set out under section 3371 of Title 16 and Tables.

CODIFICATION

Section is comprised of section 421 of Pub. L. 107–296. Subsec. (h) of section 421 of Pub. L. 107–296 amended sections 2279e and 2279f of Title 7, Agriculture.

§232. Functions of Administrator of General Services

(a) Operation, maintenance, and protection of Federal buildings and grounds

Nothing in this chapter may be construed to affect the functions or authorities of the Administrator of General Services with respect to the operation, maintenance, and protection of buildings and grounds owned or occupied by the Federal Government and under the jurisdiction, custody, or control of the Administrator. Except for the law enforcement and related security functions transferred under section 203(3) of this title, the Administrator shall retain all powers, functions, and authorities vested in the Administrator under chapter 1, except section 121(e)(2)(A), and chapters 5 to 11 of title 40 and other provisions of law that are necessary for the operation, maintenance, and protection of such buildings and grounds.

(b) Collection of rents and fees; Federal Buildings Fund

(1) Statutory construction

Nothing in this chapter may be construed—

(A) to direct the transfer of, or affect, the authority of the Administrator of General Services to collect rents and fees, including fees collected for protective services; or

(B) to authorize the Secretary or any other official in the Department to obligate amounts in the Federal Buildings Fund established by section 592 of title 40.

(2) Use of transferred amounts

Any amounts transferred by the Administrator of General Services to the Secretary out of rents and fees collected by the Administrator shall be used by the Secretary solely for the protection of buildings or grounds owned or occupied by the Federal Government.

(Pub. L. 107–296, title IV, §422, Nov. 25, 2002, 116 Stat. 2184.)

CODIFICATION

"Chapter 1, except section 121(e)(2)(A), and chapters 5 to 11 of title 40" substituted in subsec. (a) for "chapter 10 of title 40" and "section 592 of title 40" substituted in subsec. (b)(1)(B) for "section 490(f) of title 40" on authority of Pub. L. 107–217, §5(c), Aug. 21, 2002, 116 Stat. 1303, the first section of which enacted Title 40, Public Buildings, Property, and Works.

§233. Functions of Transportation Security Administration

(a) Consultation with Federal Aviation Administration

The Secretary and other officials in the Department shall consult with the Administrator of the Federal Aviation Administration before taking any action that might affect aviation safety, air carrier operations, aircraft airworthiness, or the use of airspace. The Secretary shall establish a liaison office within the Department for the purpose of consulting with the Administrator of the Federal Aviation Administration.

(b) Report to Congress

Not later than 60 days after November 25, 2002, the Secretary of Transportation shall transmit to Congress a report containing a plan for complying with the requirements of section 44901(d) of title 49.

(c) Limitations on statutory construction

(1) Grant of authority

Nothing in this chapter may be construed to vest in the Secretary or any other official in the Department any authority over transportation security that is not vested in the Under Secretary of Transportation for Security, or in the Secretary of Transportation under chapter 449 of title 49 on the day before November 25, 2002.

(2) Obligation of AIP funds

Nothing in this chapter may be construed to authorize the Secretary or any other official in the Department to obligate amounts made available under section 48103 of title 49.

(Pub. L. 107–296, title IV, §423, Nov. 25, 2002, 116 Stat. 2185.)

§234. Preservation of Transportation Security Administration as a distinct entity

(a) In general

Notwithstanding any other provision of this chapter, and subject to subsection (b) of this section, the Transportation Security Administration shall be maintained as a distinct entity within the Department under the Under Secretary for Border Transportation and Security.

(b) Sunset

Subsection (a) of this section shall cease to apply 2 years after November 25, 2002.

(Pub. L. 107–296, title IV, §424, Nov. 25, 2002, 116 Stat. 2185.)

§235. Coordination of information and information technology

(a) Definition of affected agency

In this section, the term "affected agency" means—

(1) the Department;

(2) the Department of Agriculture;

(3) the Department of Health and Human Services; and

(4) any other department or agency determined to be appropriate by the Secretary.

(b) Coordination

The Secretary, in coordination with the Secretary of Agriculture, the Secretary of Health and Human Services, and the head of each other department or agency determined to be appropriate by the Secretary, shall ensure that appropriate information (as determined by the Secretary) concerning inspections of articles that are imported or entered into the United States, and are inspected or regulated by 1 or more affected agencies, is timely and efficiently exchanged between the affected agencies.

(c) Report and plan

Not later than 18 months after November 25, 2002, the Secretary, in consultation with the Secretary of Agriculture, the Secretary of Health and Human Services, and the head of each other department or agency determined to be appropriate by the Secretary, shall submit to Congress—

(1) a report on the progress made in implementing this section; and

(2) a plan to complete implementation of this section.

(Pub. L. 107–296, title IV, §427, Nov. 25, 2002, 116 Stat. 2187.)

§236. Visa issuance

(a) Definition

In this subsection,[1] the term "consular office"[2] has the meaning given that term under section 101(a)(9) of the Immigration and Nationality Act (8 U.S.C. 1101(a)(9)).

(b) In general

Notwithstanding section 104(a) of the Immigration and Nationality Act (8 U.S.C. 1104(a)) or any other provision of law, and except as provided in subsection (c) of this section, the Secretary—

(1) shall be vested exclusively with all authorities to issue regulations with respect to, administer, and enforce the provisions of such Act [8 U.S.C. 1101 et seq.], and of all other immigration and nationality laws, relating to the functions of consular officers of the United States in connection with the granting or refusal of visas, and shall have the authority to refuse visas in accordance with law and to develop programs of homeland security training for consular officers (in addition to consular training provided by the Secretary of State), which authorities shall be exercised through the Secretary of State, except that the Secretary shall not have authority to alter or reverse the decision of a consular officer to refuse a visa to an alien; and

(2) shall have authority to confer or impose upon any officer or employee of the United States, with the consent of the head of the executive agency under whose jurisdiction such officer or employee is serving, any of the functions specified in paragraph (1).

(c) Authority of the Secretary of State

(1) In general

Notwithstanding subsection (b) of this section, the Secretary of State may direct a consular officer to refuse a visa to an alien if the Secretary of State deems such refusal necessary or advisable in the foreign policy or security interests of the United States.

(2) Construction regarding authority

Nothing in this section, consistent with the Secretary of Homeland Security's authority to refuse visas in accordance with law, shall be construed as affecting the authorities of the Secretary of State under the following provisions of law:

(A) Section 101(a)(15)(A) of the Immigration and Nationality Act (8 U.S.C. 1101(a)(15)(A)).

(B) Section 204(d)(2) of the Immigration and Nationality Act (8 U.S.C. 1154) (as it will take effect upon the entry into force of the Convention on Protection of Children and Cooperation in Respect to Inter-Country adoption).

(C) Section 212(a)(3)(B)(i)(IV)(bb) of the Immigration and Nationality Act (8 U.S.C. 1182(a)(3)(B)(i)(IV)(bb)).

(D) Section 212(a)(3)(B)(i)(VI) of the Immigration and Nationality Act (8 U.S.C. 1182(a)(3)(B)(i)(VI)).

(E) Section 212(a)(3)(B)(vi)(II) of the Immigration and Nationality Act (8 U.S.C. 1182(a)(3)(B)(vi)(II)).

(F) Section 212(a)(3)(C) of the Immigration and Nationality Act (8 U.S.C. 1182(a)(3)(C)).

(G) Section 212(a)(10)(C) of the Immigration and Nationality Act (8 U.S.C. 1182(a)(10)(C)).

(H) Section 212(f) of the Immigration and Nationality Act (8 U.S.C. 1182(f)).

(I) Section 219(a) of the Immigration and Nationality Act (8 U.S.C. 1189(a)).

(J) Section 237(a)(4)(C) of the Immigration and Nationality Act (8 U.S.C. 1227(a)(4)(C)).

(K) Section 401 of the Cuban Liberty and Democratic Solidarity (LIBERTAD) Act of 1996 [22 U.S.C. 6091].

(L) Section 613 of the Departments of Commerce, Justice, and State, the Judiciary and Related Agencies Appropriations Act, 1999[3] (as contained in section 101(b) of division A of Public Law 105–277) (Omnibus Consolidated and Emergency Supplemental Appropriations Act, 1999); 112 Stat. 2681; H.R. 4328 (originally H.R. 4276) as amended by section 617 of Public Law 106–553.

(M) Section 103(f) of the Chemical Weapon Convention Implementation Act of 1998 [22 U.S.C. 6713(f)] (112 Stat. 2681–865).

(N) Section 801 of H.R. 3427, the Admiral James W. Nance and Meg Donovan Foreign Relations Authorization Act, Fiscal Years 2000 and 2001 [8 U.S.C. 1182e], as enacted by reference in Public Law 106–113.

(O) Section 568 of the Foreign Operations, Export Financing, and Related Programs Appropriations Act, 2002 (Public Law 107–115).

(P) Section 51 of the State Department Basic Authorities Act of 1956 (22 U.S.C. 2723).

(d) Consular officers and chiefs of missions

(1) In general

Nothing in this section may be construed to alter or affect—

[1] So in original. Probably should be "section".

[2] So in original. Probably should be "'consular officer'".

[3] See References in Text note below.

(A) the employment status of consular officers as employees of the Department of State; or

(B) the authority of a chief of mission under section 207 of the Foreign Service Act of 1980 (22 U.S.C. 3927).

(2) Construction regarding delegation of authority

Nothing in this section shall be construed to affect any delegation of authority to the Secretary of State by the President pursuant to any proclamation issued under section 212(f) of the Immigration and Nationality Act (8 U.S.C. 1182(f)), consistent with the Secretary of Homeland Security's authority to refuse visas in accordance with law.

(e) Assignment of Homeland Security employees to diplomatic and consular posts

(1) In general

The Secretary is authorized to assign employees of the Department to each diplomatic and consular post at which visas are issued, unless the Secretary determines that such an assignment at a particular post would not promote homeland security.

(2) Functions

Employees assigned under paragraph (1) shall perform the following functions:

(A) Provide expert advice and training to consular officers regarding specific security threats relating to the adjudication of individual visa applications or classes of applications.

(B) Review any such applications, either on the initiative of the employee of the Department or upon request by a consular officer or other person charged with adjudicating such applications.

(C) Conduct investigations with respect to consular matters under the jurisdiction of the Secretary.

(3) Evaluation of consular officers

The Secretary of State shall evaluate, in consultation with the Secretary, as deemed appropriate by the Secretary, the performance of consular officers with respect to the processing and adjudication of applications for visas in accordance with performance standards developed by the Secretary for these procedures.

(4) Report

The Secretary shall, on an annual basis, submit a report to Congress that describes the basis for each determination under paragraph (1) that the assignment of an employee of the Department at a particular diplomatic post would not promote homeland security.

(5) Permanent assignment; participation in terrorist lookout committee

When appropriate, employees of the Department assigned to perform functions described in paragraph (2) may be assigned permanently to overseas diplomatic or consular posts with country-specific or regional responsibility. If the Secretary so directs, any such employee, when present at an overseas post, shall participate in the terrorist lookout committee established under section 304 of the Enhanced Border Security and Visa Entry Reform Act of 2002 (8 U.S.C. 1733).

(6) Training and hiring

(A) In general

The Secretary shall ensure, to the extent possible, that any employees of the Department assigned to perform functions under paragraph (2) and, as appropriate, consular officers, shall be provided the necessary training to enable them to carry out such functions, including training in foreign languages, interview techniques, and fraud detection techniques, in conditions in the particular country where each employee is assigned, and in other appropriate areas of study.

(B) Use of Center

The Secretary is authorized to use the National Foreign Affairs Training Center, on a reimbursable basis, to obtain the training described in subparagraph (A).

(7) Report

Not later than 1 year after November 25, 2002, the Secretary and the Secretary of State shall submit to Congress—

(A) a report on the implementation of this subsection; and

(B) any legislative proposals necessary to further the objectives of this subsection.

(8) Effective date

This subsection shall take effect on the earlier of—

(A) the date on which the President publishes notice in the Federal Register that the President has submitted a report to Congress setting forth a memorandum of understanding between the Secretary and the Secretary of State governing the implementation of this section; or

(B) the date occurring 1 year after November 25, 2002.

(f) No creation of private right of action

Nothing in this section shall be construed to create or authorize a private right of action to challenge a decision of a consular officer or other United States official or employee to grant or deny a visa.

(g) Study regarding use of foreign nationals

(1) In general

The Secretary of Homeland Security shall conduct a study of the role of foreign nationals in the granting or refusal of visas and other documents authorizing entry of aliens into the United States. The study shall address the following:

(A) The proper role, if any, of foreign nationals in the process of rendering decisions on such grants and refusals.

(B) Any security concerns involving the employment of foreign nationals.

(C) Whether there are cost-effective alternatives to the use of foreign nationals.

(2) Report

Not later than 1 year after November 25, 2002, the Secretary shall submit a report containing the findings of the study conducted under paragraph (1) to the Committee on the Judiciary, the Committee on International Relations, and the Committee on Government Reform of the House of Representatives, and the Committee on the Judiciary, the Committee on Foreign Relations, and the Committee on Government[4] Affairs of the Senate.

(h) Report

Not later than 120 days after November 25, 2002, the Director of the Office of Science and Technology Policy shall submit to Congress a report on how the provisions of this section will affect procedures for the issuance of student visas.

(i) Visa issuance program for Saudi Arabia

Notwithstanding any other provision of law, after November 25, 2002, all third party screening programs in Saudi Arabia shall be terminated. On-site personnel of the Department of Homeland Security shall review all visa applications prior to adjudication.

(Pub. L. 107–296, title IV, §428, Nov. 25, 2002, 116 Stat. 2187.)

REFERENCES IN TEXT

The Immigration and Nationality Act, referred to in subsec. (b)(1), is act June 27, 1952, ch. 477, 66 Stat. 163, as amended, which is classified principally to chapter 12 (§1101 et seq.) of Title 8, Aliens and Nationality. For complete classification of this Act to the Code, see Short Title note set out under section 1101 of Title 8 and Tables.

Section 613 of the Departments of Commerce, Justice, and State, the Judiciary and Related Agencies Appropriations Act, 1999, referred to in subsec. (c)(2)(L), probably means section 101(b) [title VI, §616] of Pub. L. 105–277, div. A, Oct. 21, 1998, 112 Stat. 2681–50, 2681–114, as amended, which prohibits use of funds for issuance of visas to persons alleged to have ordered, carried out, or materially assisted in extrajudicial and political killings in Haiti and to certain others and is not classified to the Code.

Section 103(f) of the Chemical Weapon Convention Implementation Act of 1998, referred to in subsec. (c)(2)(M), probably means section 103(f) of the Chemical Weapons Convention Implementation Act of 1998, which is classified to section 6713(f) of Title 22, Foreign Relations and Intercourse.

Section 568 of the Foreign Operations, Export Financing, and Related Programs Appropriations Act, 2002, referred to in subsec. (c)(2)(O), is section 568 of title V of Pub. L. 107–115, Jan. 10, 2002, 115 Stat. 2166, which is not classified to the Code.

CHANGE OF NAME

References to National Foreign Affairs Training Center considered to refer to George P. Shultz National Foreign Affairs Training Center, see section 1(b) of Pub. L. 107–132, set out as a note under section 4021 of this title.

Committee on International Relations of House of Representatives changed to Committee on Foreign Affairs of House of Representatives by House Resolution No. 6, One Hundred Tenth Congress, Jan. 5, 2007.

Committee on Government Reform of House of Representatives changed to Committee on Oversight and Government Reform of House of Representatives by House Resolution No. 6, One Hundred Tenth Congress, Jan. 5, 2007.

Committee on Governmental Affairs of Senate changed to Committee on Homeland Security and Governmental Affairs of Senate, effective Jan. 4, 2005, by Senate Resolution No. 445, One Hundred Eighth Congress, Oct. 9, 2004.

[4] So in original. Probably should be "Governmental".

§237. Information on visa denials required to be entered into electronic data system

(a) In general

Whenever a consular officer of the United States denies a visa to an applicant, the consular officer shall enter the fact and the basis of the denial and the name of the applicant into the interoperable electronic data system implemented under section 1722(a) of title 8.

(b) Prohibition

In the case of any alien with respect to whom a visa has been denied under subsection (a) of this section—

(1) no subsequent visa may be issued to the alien unless the consular officer considering the alien's visa application has reviewed the information concerning the alien placed in the interoperable electronic data system, has indicated on the alien's application that the information has been reviewed, and has stated for the record why the visa is being issued or a waiver of visa ineligibility recommended in spite of that information; and

(2) the alien may not be admitted to the United States without a visa issued in accordance with the procedures described in paragraph (1).

(Pub. L. 107–296, title IV, §429, Nov. 25, 2002, 116 Stat. 2191.)

§238. Office for Domestic Preparedness

(a) In general

The Office for Domestic Preparedness shall be within the Directorate of Border and Transportation Security.

(b) Director

There shall be a Director of the Office for Domestic Preparedness, who shall be appointed by the President, by and with the advice and consent of the Senate. The Director of the Office for Domestic Preparedness shall report directly to the Under Secretary for Border and Transportation Security.

(c) Responsibilities

The Office for Domestic Preparedness shall have the primary responsibility within the executive branch of Government for the preparedness of the United States for acts of terrorism, including—

(1) coordinating preparedness efforts at the Federal level, and working with all State, local, tribal, parish, and private sector emergency response providers on all matters pertaining to combating terrorism, including training, exercises, and equipment support;

(2) coordinating or, as appropriate, consolidating communications and systems of communications relating to homeland security at all levels of government;

(3) directing and supervising terrorism preparedness grant programs of the Federal Government (other than those programs administered by the Department of Health and Human Services) for all emergency response providers;

(4) incorporating the Strategy priorities into planning guidance on an agency level for the preparedness efforts of the Office for Domestic Preparedness;

(5) providing agency-specific training for agents and analysts within the Department, other agencies, and State and local agencies and international entities;

(6) as the lead executive branch agency for preparedness of the United States for acts of terrorism, cooperating closely with the Federal Emergency Management Agency, which shall have the primary responsibility within the executive branch to prepare for and mitigate the effects of nonterrorist-related disasters in the United States;

(7) assisting and supporting the Secretary, in coordination with other Directorates and entities outside the Department, in conducting appropriate risk analysis and risk management activities of State, local, and tribal governments consistent with the mission and functions of the Directorate;

(8) those elements of the Office of National Preparedness of the Federal Emergency Management Agency which relate to terrorism, which shall be consolidated within the Department in the Office for Domestic Preparedness established under this section; and

(9) helping to ensure the acquisition of interoperable communication technology by State and local governments and emergency response providers.

(d) Fiscal years 2003 and 2004

During fiscal year 2003 and fiscal year 2004, the Director of the Office for Domestic Preparedness established under this section shall manage and carry out those functions of the Office for Domestic Preparedness of the Department of Justice (transferred under this section) before September 11, 2001, under the same terms, conditions, policies, and authorities, and with the required level of personnel, assets, and budget before September 11, 2001.

(Pub. L. 107–296, title IV, §430, Nov. 25, 2002, 116 Stat. 2191; Pub. L. 108–458, title VII, §7303(h)(2), Dec. 17, 2004, 118 Stat. 3847.)

AMENDMENTS

2004—Subsec. (c)(9). Pub. L. 108–458 added par. (9).

§239. Office of Cargo Security Policy

(a) Establishment

There is established within the Department an Office of Cargo Security Policy (referred to in this section as the "Office").

(b) Purpose

The Office shall—

(1) coordinate all Department policies relating to cargo security; and

(2) consult with stakeholders and coordinate with other Federal agencies in the establishment of standards and regulations and to promote best practices.

(c) Director

(1) Appointment

The Office shall be headed by a Director, who shall—

(A) be appointed by the Secretary; and

(B) report to the Assistant Secretary for Policy.

(2) Responsibilities

The Director shall—

(A) advise the Assistant Secretary for Policy in the development of Department-wide policies regarding cargo security;

(B) coordinate all policies relating to cargo security among the agencies and offices within the Department relating to cargo security; and

(C) coordinate the cargo security policies of the Department with the policies of other executive agencies.

(Pub. L. 107–296, title IV, §431, as added Pub. L. 109–347, title III, §301(a), Oct. 13, 2006, 120 Stat. 1920.)

RULE OF CONSTRUCTION

Pub. L. 109–347, title III, §301(c), Oct. 13, 2006, 120 Stat. 1920, provided that: "Nothing in this section [enacting this section and section 1001 of this title] shall be construed to affect—

"(1) the authorities, functions, or capabilities of the Coast Guard to perform its missions; or

"(2) the requirement under section 888 of the Homeland Security Act (6 U.S.C. 468) that those authorities, functions, and capabilities be maintained intact."

PART D—IMMIGRATION ENFORCEMENT FUNCTIONS

§251. Transfer of functions to Under Secretary for Border and Transportation Security

In accordance with subchapter XII of this chapter (relating to transition provisions), there shall be transferred from the Commissioner of Immigration and Naturalization to the Under Secretary for Border and Transportation Security all functions performed under the following programs, and all personnel, assets, and liabilities pertaining to such programs, immediately before such transfer occurs:

(1) The Border Patrol program.

(2) The detention and removal program.

(3) The intelligence program.

(4) The investigations program.

(5) The inspections program.

(Pub. L. 107–296, title IV, §441, Nov. 25, 2002, 116 Stat. 2192.)

§252. Establishment of Bureau of Border Security

(a) Establishment of Bureau

(1) In general

There shall be in the Department of Homeland Security a bureau to be known as the "Bureau of Border Security".

(2) Assistant Secretary

The head of the Bureau of Border Security shall be the Assistant Secretary of the Bureau of Border Security, who—

(A) shall report directly to the Under Secretary for Border and Transportation Security; and

(B) shall have a minimum of 5 years professional experience in law enforcement, and a minimum of 5 years of management experience.

(3) Functions

The Assistant Secretary of the Bureau of Border Security—

(A) shall establish the policies for performing such functions as are—

(i) transferred to the Under Secretary for Border and Transportation Security by section 251 of this title and delegated to the Assistant Secretary by the Under Secretary for Border and Transportation Security; or

(ii) otherwise vested in the Assistant Secretary by law;

(B) shall oversee the administration of such policies; and

(C) shall advise the Under Secretary for Border and Transportation Security with respect to any policy or operation of the Bureau of Border Security that may affect the Bureau of Citizenship and Immigration Services established under part E of this subchapter, including potentially conflicting policies or operations.

(4) Program to collect information relating to foreign students

The Assistant Secretary of the Bureau of Border Security shall be responsible for administering the program to collect information relating to nonimmigrant foreign students and other exchange program participants described in section 1372 of title 8, including the Student and Exchange Visitor Information System established under that section, and shall use such information to carry out the enforcement functions of the Bureau.

(5) Managerial rotation program

(A) In general

Not later than 1 year after the date on which the transfer of functions specified under section 251 of this title takes effect, the Assistant Secretary of the Bureau of Border Security shall design and implement a managerial rotation program under which employees of such bureau holding positions involving supervisory or managerial responsibility and classified, in accordance with chapter 51 of title 5, as a GS–14 or above, shall—

(i) gain some experience in all the major functions performed by such bureau; and

(ii) work in at least one local office of such bureau.

(B) Report

Not later than 2 years after the date on which the transfer of functions specified under section 251 of this title takes effect, the Secretary shall submit a report to the Congress on the implementation of such program.

(b) Chief of Policy and Strategy

(1) In general

There shall be a position of Chief of Policy and Strategy for the Bureau of Border Security.

(2) Functions

In consultation with Bureau of Border Security personnel in local offices, the Chief of Policy and Strategy shall be responsible for—

(A) making policy recommendations and performing policy research and analysis on immigration enforcement issues; and

(B) coordinating immigration policy issues with the Chief of Policy and Strategy for the Bureau of Citizenship and Immigration Services (established under part E of this subchapter), as appropriate.

(c) Legal advisor

There shall be a principal legal advisor to the Assistant Secretary of the Bureau of Border Security. The legal advisor shall provide specialized legal advice to the Assistant Secretary of the Bureau of Border Security and shall represent the bureau in all exclusion, deportation, and removal proceedings before the Executive Office for Immigration Review.

(Pub. L. 107–296, title IV, § 442, Nov. 25, 2002, 116 Stat. 2193.)

REFERENCES IN TEXT

Part E of this subchapter, referred to in subsecs. (a)(3)(C) and (b)(2)(B), was in the original "subtitle E", meaning subtitle E (§§ 451–462) of title IV of Pub. L. 107–296, Nov. 25, 2002, 116 Stat. 2195, which enacted part E (§ 271 et seq.) of this subchapter, amended sections 1356 and 1573 of Title 8, Aliens and Nationality, and enacted provisions set out as a note under section 271 of this title. For complete classification of subtitle E to the Code, see Tables.

CHANGE OF NAME

Bureau of Border Security, referred to in section catchline and text, changed to Bureau of Immigration and Customs Enforcement by Reorganization Plan Modification for the Department of Homeland Security, eff. Mar. 1, 2003, H. Doc. No. 108–32, 108th Congress, 1st Session, set out as a note under section 542 of this title.

§ 253. Professional responsibility and quality review

The Under Secretary for Border and Transportation Security shall be responsible for—

(1) conducting investigations of noncriminal allegations of misconduct, corruption, and fraud involving any employee of the Bureau of Border Security that are not subject to investigation by the Inspector General for the Department;

(2) inspecting the operations of the Bureau of Border Security and providing assessments of the quality of the operations of such bureau as a whole and each of its components; and

(3) providing an analysis of the management of the Bureau of Border Security.

(Pub. L. 107–296, title IV, § 443, Nov. 25, 2002, 116 Stat. 2194.)

CHANGE OF NAME

Bureau of Border Security, referred to in text, changed to Bureau of Immigration and Customs Enforcement by Reorganization Plan Modification for the Department of Homeland Security, eff. Mar. 1, 2003, H. Doc. No. 108–32, 108th Congress, 1st Session, set out as a note under section 542 of this title.

§ 254. Employee discipline

The Under Secretary for Border and Transportation Security may, notwithstanding any other provision of law, impose disciplinary action, including termination of employment, pursuant to policies and procedures applicable to employees of the Federal Bureau of Investigation, on any employee of the Bureau of Border Security who willfully deceives the Congress or agency leadership on any matter.

(Pub. L. 107–296, title IV, § 444, Nov. 25, 2002, 116 Stat. 2194.)

CHANGE OF NAME

Bureau of Border Security, referred to in text, changed to Bureau of Immigration and Customs Enforcement by Reorganization Plan Modification for the Department of Homeland Security, eff. Mar. 1, 2003, H. Doc. No. 108–32, 108th Congress, 1st Session, set out as a note under section 542 of this title.

§ 255. Report on improving enforcement functions

(a) In general

The Secretary, not later than 1 year after being sworn into office, shall submit to the Committees on Appropriations and the Judiciary of the House of Representatives and of the Senate a report with a plan detailing how the Bureau of Border Security, after the transfer of functions specified under section 251 of this title takes effect, will enforce comprehensively, effectively, and fairly all the enforcement provisions of the Immigration and Nationality Act (8 U.S.C. 1101 et seq.) relating to such functions.

(b) Consultation

In carrying out subsection (a) of this section, the Secretary of Homeland Security shall consult with the Attorney General, the Secretary of State, the Director of the Federal Bureau of Investigation, the Secretary of the Treasury, the Secretary of Labor, the Commissioner of Social Security, the Director of the Executive Office for Immigration Review, and the heads of State and local law enforcement agencies to determine how to most effectively conduct enforcement operations.

(Pub. L. 107–296, title IV, § 445, Nov. 25, 2002, 116 Stat. 2194.)

REFERENCES IN TEXT

The Immigration and Nationality Act, referred to in subsec. (a), is act June 27, 1952, ch. 477, 66 Stat. 163, as amended, which is classified principally to chapter 12 (§ 1101 et seq.) of Title 8, Aliens and Nationality. For complete classification of this Act to the Code, see Short Title note set out under section 1101 of Title 8 and Tables.

CHANGE OF NAME

Bureau of Border Security, referred to in subsec. (a), changed to Bureau of Immigration and Customs Enforcement by Reorganization Plan Modification for the Department of Homeland Security, eff. Mar. 1, 2003, H. Doc. No. 108–32, 108th Congress, 1st Session, set out as a note under section 542 of this title.

§ 256. Sense of Congress regarding construction of fencing near San Diego, California

It is the sense of the Congress that completing the 14-mile border fence project required to be carried out under section 102(b) of the Illegal Immigration Reform and Immigrant Responsibility Act of 1996 (8 U.S.C. 1103 note) should be a priority for the Secretary.

(Pub. L. 107–296, title IV, § 446, Nov. 25, 2002, 116 Stat. 2195.)

REFERENCES IN TEXT

Section 102(b) of the Illegal Immigration Reform and Immigrant Responsibility Act of 1996, referred to in text, is section 102(b) of title I of div. C of Pub. L. 104–208, which is set out as a note under section 1103 of Title 8, Aliens and Nationality.

PART E—CITIZENSHIP AND IMMIGRATION SERVICES

§ 271. Establishment of Bureau of Citizenship and Immigration Services

(a) Establishment of Bureau

(1) In general

There shall be in the Department a bureau to be known as the "Bureau of Citizenship and Immigration Services".

(2) Director

The head of the Bureau of Citizenship and Immigration Services shall be the Director of the Bureau of Citizenship and Immigration Services, who—

(A) shall report directly to the Deputy Secretary;

(B) shall have a minimum of 5 years of management experience; and

(C) shall be paid at the same level as the Assistant Secretary of the Bureau of Border Security.

(3) Functions

The Director of the Bureau of Citizenship and Immigration Services—

(A) shall establish the policies for performing such functions as are transferred to the Director by this section or this chapter or otherwise vested in the Director by law;

(B) shall oversee the administration of such policies;

(C) shall advise the Deputy Secretary with respect to any policy or operation of the Bureau of Citizenship and Immigration Services that may affect the Bureau of Border Security of the Department, including potentially conflicting policies or operations;

(D) shall establish national immigration services policies and priorities;

(E) shall meet regularly with the Ombudsman described in section 272 of this title to correct serious service problems identified by the Ombudsman; and

(F) shall establish procedures requiring a formal response to any recommendations submitted in the Ombudsman's annual report to Congress within 3 months after its submission to Congress.

(4) Managerial rotation program

(A) In general

Not later than 1 year after the effective date specified in section 455,[1] the Director of the Bureau of Citizenship and Immigration Services shall design and implement a managerial rotation program under which employees of such bureau holding positions in-

[1] See References in Text note below.

volving supervisory or managerial responsibility and classified, in accordance with chapter 51 of title 5, as a GS–14 or above, shall—

(i) gain some experience in all the major functions performed by such bureau; and

(ii) work in at least one field office and one service center of such bureau.

(B) Report

Not later than 2 years after the effective date specified in section 455,[1] the Secretary shall submit a report to Congress on the implementation of such program.

(5) Pilot initiatives for backlog elimination

The Director of the Bureau of Citizenship and Immigration Services is authorized to implement innovative pilot initiatives to eliminate any remaining backlog in the processing of immigration benefit applications, and to prevent any backlog in the processing of such applications from recurring, in accordance with section 1573(a) of title 8. Such initiatives may include measures such as increasing personnel, transferring personnel to focus on areas with the largest potential for backlog, and streamlining paperwork.

(b) Transfer of functions from Commissioner

In accordance with subchapter XII of this chapter (relating to transition provisions), there are transferred from the Commissioner of Immigration and Naturalization to the Director of the Bureau of Citizenship and Immigration Services the following functions, and all personnel, infrastructure, and funding provided to the Commissioner in support of such functions immediately before the effective date specified in section 455:[1]

(1) Adjudications of immigrant visa petitions.

(2) Adjudications of naturalization petitions.

(3) Adjudications of asylum and refugee applications.

(4) Adjudications performed at service centers.

(5) All other adjudications performed by the Immigration and Naturalization Service immediately before the effective date specified in section 455.[1]

(c) Chief of Policy and Strategy

(1) In general

There shall be a position of Chief of Policy and Strategy for the Bureau of Citizenship and Immigration Services.

(2) Functions

In consultation with Bureau of Citizenship and Immigration Services personnel in field offices, the Chief of Policy and Strategy shall be responsible for—

(A) making policy recommendations and performing policy research and analysis on immigration services issues; and

(B) coordinating immigration policy issues with the Chief of Policy and Strategy for the Bureau of Border Security of the Department.

(d) Legal advisor

(1) In general

There shall be a principal legal advisor to the Director of the Bureau of Citizenship and Immigration Services.

(2) Functions

The legal advisor shall be responsible for—

(A) providing specialized legal advice, opinions, determinations, regulations, and any other assistance to the Director of the Bureau of Citizenship and Immigration Services with respect to legal matters affecting the Bureau of Citizenship and Immigration Services; and

(B) representing the Bureau of Citizenship and Immigration Services in visa petition appeal proceedings before the Executive Office for Immigration Review.

(e) Budget Officer

(1) In general

There shall be a Budget Officer for the Bureau of Citizenship and Immigration Services.

(2) Functions

(A) In general

The Budget Officer shall be responsible for—

(i) formulating and executing the budget of the Bureau of Citizenship and Immigration Services;

(ii) financial management of the Bureau of Citizenship and Immigration Services; and

(iii) collecting all payments, fines, and other debts for the Bureau of Citizenship and Immigration Services.

(f) Chief of Office of Citizenship

(1) In general

There shall be a position of Chief of the Office of Citizenship for the Bureau of Citizenship and Immigration Services.

(2) Functions

The Chief of the Office of Citizenship for the Bureau of Citizenship and Immigration Services shall be responsible for promoting instruction and training on citizenship responsibilities for aliens interested in becoming naturalized citizens of the United States, including the development of educational materials.

(g) Office of the FBI liaison

(1) In general

There shall be an Office of the FBI Liaison in the Department of Homeland Security.

(2) Functions

The Office of the FBI Liaison shall monitor the progress of the functions of the Federal Bureau of Investigation in the naturalization process to assist in the expeditious completion of all such functions pertaining to naturalization applications filed by, or on behalf of—

(A) current or former members of the Armed Forces under section 1439 or 1440 of title 8;

(B) current spouses of United States citizens who are currently serving on active duty in the Armed Forces, who qualify for naturalization under section 1430(b) of title 8, and surviving spouses and children who qualify for naturalization under section 1430(d) of title 8; or

(C) a deceased individual who is eligible for posthumous citizenship under section 1440–1 of title 8.

(3) Authorization of appropriations

There are authorized to be appropriated such sums as may be necessary to carry out this subsection.

(Pub. L. 107–296, title IV, §451, Nov. 25, 2002, 116 Stat. 2195; Pub. L. 110–382, §2(a), Oct. 9, 2008, 122 Stat. 4087.)

AMENDMENT OF SECTION

For termination of amendment by section 4 of Pub. L. 110–382, see Termination Date of 2008 Amendment note below.

REFERENCES IN TEXT

For the effective date specified in section 455, referred to in subsecs. (a)(4) and (b), see Effective Date note below.

AMENDMENTS

2008—Subsec. (g). Pub. L. 110–382, §§2(a), 4, temporarily added subsec. (g). See Termination Date of 2008 Amendment note below.

CHANGE OF NAME

Bureau of Border Security, referred to in subsecs. (a)(2)(C), (3)(C), and (c)(2)(B), changed to Bureau of Immigration and Customs Enforcement by Reorganization Plan Modification for the Department of Homeland Security, eff. Mar. 1, 2003, H. Doc. No. 108–32, 108th Congress, 1st Session, set out as a note under section 542 of this title.

TERMINATION DATE OF 2008 AMENDMENT

Pub. L. 110–382, §4, Oct. 9, 2008, 122 Stat. 4089, provided that: "This Act [amending this section and section 1439 of Title 8, Aliens and Nationality, and enacting provisions set out as notes under this section and section 1101 of Title 8] and the amendments made by this Act are repealed on the date that is 5 years after the date of the enactment of this Act [Oct. 9, 2008]."

EFFECTIVE DATE

Pub. L. 107–296, title IV, §455, Nov. 25, 2002, 116 Stat. 2200, provided that: "Notwithstanding section 4 [enacting provisions set out as a note under section 101 of this title], sections 451 through 456 [enacting this section and sections 272 to 275 of this title], and the amendments made by such sections, shall take effect on the date on which the transfer of functions specified under section 441 [enacting section 251 of this title] takes effect." [For date on which transfer of functions specified under section 441 takes effect, see section 251 of this title and Department of Homeland Security Reorganization Plan, Nov. 25, 2002, set out as a note under section 542 of this title.]

RULEMAKING

Pub. L. 110–382, §2(b), Oct. 9, 2008, 122 Stat. 4087, provided that: "Not later than 180 days after the date of the enactment of this Act [Oct. 9, 2008], the Secretary of Homeland Security, in consultation with the Attorney General, shall promulgate rules to carry out the amendment made by subsection (a) [amending this section]."

[Pub. L. 110–382, §4, Oct. 9, 2008, 122 Stat. 4089, provided that section 2(b) of Pub. L. 110–382, set out as a note above, is repealed 5 years after Oct. 9, 2008.]

§272. Citizenship and Immigration Services Ombudsman

(a) In general

Within the Department, there shall be a position of Citizenship and Immigration Services Ombudsman (in this section referred to as the "Ombudsman"). The Ombudsman shall report directly to the Deputy Secretary. The Ombudsman shall have a background in customer service as well as immigration law.

(b) Functions

It shall be the function of the Ombudsman—

(1) to assist individuals and employers in resolving problems with the Bureau of Citizenship and Immigration Services;

(2) to identify areas in which individuals and employers have problems in dealing with the Bureau of Citizenship and Immigration Services; and

(3) to the extent possible, to propose changes in the administrative practices of the Bureau of Citizenship and Immigration Services to mitigate problems identified under paragraph (2).

(c) Annual reports

(1) Objectives

Not later than June 30 of each calendar year, the Ombudsman shall report to the Committee on the Judiciary of the House of Representatives and the Senate on the objectives of the Office of the Ombudsman for the fiscal year beginning in such calendar year. Any such report shall contain full and substantive analysis, in addition to statistical information, and—

(A) shall identify the recommendations the Office of the Ombudsman has made on improving services and responsiveness of the Bureau of Citizenship and Immigration Services;

(B) shall contain a summary of the most pervasive and serious problems encountered by individuals and employers, including a description of the nature of such problems;

(C) shall contain an inventory of the items described in subparagraphs (A) and (B) for which action has been taken and the result of such action;

(D) shall contain an inventory of the items described in subparagraphs (A) and (B) for which action remains to be completed and the period during which each item has remained on such inventory;

(E) shall contain an inventory of the items described in subparagraphs (A) and (B) for which no action has been taken, the period during which each item has remained on such inventory, the reasons for the inaction, and shall identify any official of the Bureau of Citizenship and Immigration Services who is responsible for such inaction;

(F) shall contain recommendations for such administrative action as may be appropriate to resolve problems encountered by individuals and employers, including problems created by excessive backlogs in the adjudication and processing of immigration benefit petitions and applications; and

(G) shall include such other information as the Ombudsman may deem advisable.

(2) Report to be submitted directly

Each report required under this subsection shall be provided directly to the committees described in paragraph (1) without any prior comment or amendment from the Secretary, Deputy Secretary, Director of the Bureau of Citizenship and Immigration Services, or any other officer or employee of the Department or the Office of Management and Budget.

(d) Other responsibilities

The Ombudsman—

(1) shall monitor the coverage and geographic allocation of local offices of the Ombudsman;

(2) shall develop guidance to be distributed to all officers and employees of the Bureau of Citizenship and Immigration Services outlining the criteria for referral of inquiries to local offices of the Ombudsman;

(3) shall ensure that the local telephone number for each local office of the Ombudsman is published and available to individuals and employers served by the office; and

(4) shall meet regularly with the Director of the Bureau of Citizenship and Immigration Services to identify serious service problems and to present recommendations for such administrative action as may be appropriate to resolve problems encountered by individuals and employers.

(e) Personnel actions

(1) In general

The Ombudsman shall have the responsibility and authority—

(A) to appoint local ombudsmen and make available at least 1 such ombudsman for each State; and

(B) to evaluate and take personnel actions (including dismissal) with respect to any employee of any local office of the Ombudsman.

(2) Consultation

The Ombudsman may consult with the appropriate supervisory personnel of the Bureau of Citizenship and Immigration Services in carrying out the Ombudsman's responsibilities under this subsection.

(f) Responsibilities of Bureau of Citizenship and Immigration Services

The Director of the Bureau of Citizenship and Immigration Services shall establish procedures requiring a formal response to all recommendations submitted to such director by the Ombudsman within 3 months after submission to such director.

(g) Operation of local offices

(1) In general

Each local ombudsman—

(A) shall report to the Ombudsman or the delegate thereof;

(B) may consult with the appropriate supervisory personnel of the Bureau of Citizenship and Immigration Services regarding the daily operation of the local office of such ombudsman;

(C) shall, at the initial meeting with any individual or employer seeking the assistance of such local office, notify such individual or employer that the local offices of the Ombudsman operate independently of any other component of the Department and report directly to Congress through the Ombudsman; and

(D) at the local ombudsman's discretion, may determine not to disclose to the Bureau of Citizenship and Immigration Services contact with, or information provided by, such individual or employer.

(2) Maintenance of independent communications

Each local office of the Ombudsman shall maintain a phone, facsimile, and other means of electronic communication access, and a post office address, that is separate from those maintained by the Bureau of Citizenship and Immigration Services, or any component of the Bureau of Citizenship and Immigration Services.

(Pub. L. 107–296, title IV, §452, Nov. 25, 2002, 116 Stat. 2197.)

EFFECTIVE DATE

Section effective on the date on which the transfer of functions specified under section 251 of this title takes effect, see section 455 of Pub. L. 107–296, set out as a note under section 271 of this title.

§273. Professional responsibility and quality review

(a) In general

The Director of the Bureau of Citizenship and Immigration Services shall be responsible for—

(1) conducting investigations of noncriminal allegations of misconduct, corruption, and fraud involving any employee of the Bureau of Citizenship and Immigration Services that are not subject to investigation by the Inspector General for the Department;

(2) inspecting the operations of the Bureau of Citizenship and Immigration Services and providing assessments of the quality of the operations of such bureau as a whole and each of its components; and

(3) providing an analysis of the management of the Bureau of Citizenship and Immigration Services.

(b) Special considerations

In providing assessments in accordance with subsection (a)(2) of this section with respect to a decision of the Bureau of Citizenship and Immigration Services, or any of its components, consideration shall be given to—

(1) the accuracy of the findings of fact and conclusions of law used in rendering the decision;

(2) any fraud or misrepresentation associated with the decision; and

(3) the efficiency with which the decision was rendered.

(Pub. L. 107–296, title IV, §453, Nov. 25, 2002, 116 Stat. 2199.)

EFFECTIVE DATE

Section effective on the date on which the transfer of functions specified under section 251 of this title takes effect, see section 455 of Pub. L. 107–296, set out as a note under section 271 of this title.

§ 274. Employee discipline

The Director of the Bureau of Citizenship and Immigration Services may, notwithstanding any other provision of law, impose disciplinary action, including termination of employment, pursuant to policies and procedures applicable to employees of the Federal Bureau of Investigation, on any employee of the Bureau of Citizenship and Immigration Services who willfully deceives Congress or agency leadership on any matter.

(Pub. L. 107–296, title IV, § 454, Nov. 25, 2002, 116 Stat. 2200.)

EFFECTIVE DATE

Section effective on the date on which the transfer of functions specified under section 251 of this title takes effect, see section 455 of Pub. L. 107–296, set out as a note under section 271 of this title.

§ 275. Transition

(a) References

With respect to any function transferred by this part to, and exercised on or after the effective date specified in section 455[1] by, the Director of the Bureau of Citizenship and Immigration Services, any reference in any other Federal law, Executive order, rule, regulation, or delegation of authority, or any document of or pertaining to a component of government from which such function is transferred—

(1) to the head of such component is deemed to refer to the Director of the Bureau of Citizenship and Immigration Services; or

(2) to such component is deemed to refer to the Bureau of Citizenship and Immigration Services.

(b) Other transition issues

(1) Exercise of authorities

Except as otherwise provided by law, a Federal official to whom a function is transferred by this part may, for purposes of performing the function, exercise all authorities under any other provision of law that were available with respect to the performance of that function to the official responsible for the performance of the function immediately before the effective date specified in section 455.[1]

(2) Transfer and allocation of appropriations and personnel

The personnel of the Department of Justice employed in connection with the functions transferred by this part (and functions that the Secretary determines are properly related to the functions of the Bureau of Citizenship and Immigration Services), and the assets, liabilities, contracts, property, records, and unexpended balance of appropriations, authorizations, allocations, and other funds employed, held, used, arising from, available to, or to be made available to, the Immigration and Naturalization Service in connection with the functions transferred by this part, subject to section 1531 of title 31, shall be transferred to the Director of the Bureau of Citizenship and Immigration Services for allocation to the appropriate component of the Department. Unexpended funds transferred pursuant to this paragraph shall be used only for the purposes for which the funds were originally authorized and appropriated. The Secretary shall have the right to adjust or realign transfers of funds and personnel effected pursuant to this part for a period of 2 years after the effective date specified in section 455.[1]

(Pub. L. 107–296, title IV, § 456, Nov. 25, 2002, 116 Stat. 2200.)

REFERENCES IN TEXT

This part, referred to in text, was in the original "this subtitle", meaning subtitle E (§§ 451–462) of title IV of Pub. L. 107–296, Nov. 25, 2002, 116 Stat. 2195, which enacted this part, amended sections 1356 and 1573 of Title 8, Aliens and Nationality, and enacted provisions set out as a note under section 271 of this title. For complete classification of subtitle E to the Code, see Tables.

For the effective date specified in section 455, referred to in text, see section 455 of Pub. L. 107–296, set out as an Effective Date note under section 271 of this title.

CODIFICATION

In subsec. (b)(2), "section 1531 of title 31" substituted for "section 202 of the Budget and Accounting Procedures Act of 1950" on authority of Pub. L. 97–258, § 4(b), Sept. 13, 1982, 96 Stat. 1067, the first section of which enacted Title 31, Money and Finance.

EFFECTIVE DATE

Section effective on the date on which the transfer of functions specified under section 251 of this title takes effect, see section 455 of Pub. L. 107–296, set out as a note under section 271 of this title.

§ 276. Report on improving immigration services

(a) In general

The Secretary, not later than 1 year after the effective date of this chapter, shall submit to the Committees on the Judiciary and Appropriations of the House of Representatives and of the Senate a report with a plan detailing how the Bureau of Citizenship and Immigration Services, after the transfer of functions specified in this part takes effect, will complete efficiently, fairly, and within a reasonable time, the adjudications described in paragraphs (1) through (5) of section 271(b) of this title.

(b) Contents

For each type of adjudication to be undertaken by the Director of the Bureau of Citizenship and Immigration Services, the report shall include the following:

(1) Any potential savings of resources that may be implemented without affecting the quality of the adjudication.

(2) The goal for processing time with respect to the application.

(3) Any statutory modifications with respect to the adjudication that the Secretary considers advisable.

(c) Consultation

In carrying out subsection (a) of this section, the Secretary shall consult with the Secretary

[1] See References in Text note below.

of State, the Secretary of Labor, the Assistant Secretary of the Bureau of Border Security of the Department, and the Director of the Executive Office for Immigration Review to determine how to streamline and improve the process for applying for and making adjudications described in section 271(b) of this title and related processes.

(Pub. L. 107–296, title IV, § 459, Nov. 25, 2002, 116 Stat. 2201.)

REFERENCES IN TEXT

The effective date of this chapter, referred to in subsec. (a), is 60 days after Nov. 25, 2002, see section 4 of Pub. L. 107–296, set out as an Effective Date note under section 101 of this title.

CHANGE OF NAME

Bureau of Border Security, referred to in subsec. (c), changed to Bureau of Immigration and Customs Enforcement by Reorganization Plan Modification for the Department of Homeland Security, eff. Mar. 1, 2003, H. Doc. No. 108–32, 108th Congress, 1st Session, set out as a note under section 542 of this title.

§ 277. Report on responding to fluctuating needs

Not later than 30 days after November 25, 2002, the Attorney General shall submit to Congress a report on changes in law, including changes in authorizations of appropriations and in appropriations, that are needed to permit the Immigration and Naturalization Service, and, after the transfer of functions specified in this part takes effect, the Bureau of Citizenship and Immigration Services of the Department, to ensure a prompt and timely response to emergent, unforeseen, or impending changes in the number of applications for immigration benefits, and otherwise to ensure the accommodation of changing immigration service needs.

(Pub. L. 107–296, title IV, § 460, Nov. 25, 2002, 116 Stat. 2201.)

§ 278. Application of Internet-based technologies

(a) Establishment of tracking system

The Secretary, not later than 1 year after the effective date of this chapter, in consultation with the Technology Advisory Committee established under subsection (c) of this section, shall establish an Internet-based system, that will permit a person, employer, immigrant, or nonimmigrant who has filings with the Secretary for any benefit under the Immigration and Nationality Act (8 U.S.C. 1101 et seq.), access to online information about the processing status of the filing involved.

(b) Feasibility study for online filing and improved processing

(1) Online filing

The Secretary, in consultation with the Technology Advisory Committee established under subsection (c) of this section, shall conduct a feasibility study on the online filing of the filings described in subsection (a) of this section. The study shall include a review of computerization and technology of the Immigration and Naturalization Service relating to the immigration services and processing of filings related to immigrant services. The study shall also include an estimate of the timeframe and cost and shall consider other factors in implementing such a filing system, including the feasibility of fee payment online.

(2) Report

A report on the study under this subsection shall be submitted to the Committees on the Judiciary of the House of Representatives and the Senate not later than 1 year after the effective date of this chapter.

(c) Technology Advisory Committee

(1) Establishment

The Secretary shall establish, not later than 60 days after the effective date of this chapter, an advisory committee (in this section referred to as the "Technology Advisory Committee") to assist the Secretary in—

(A) establishing the tracking system under subsection (a) of this section; and

(B) conducting the study under subsection (b) of this section.

The Technology Advisory Committee shall be established after consultation with the Committees on the Judiciary of the House of Representatives and the Senate.

(2) Composition

The Technology Advisory Committee shall be composed of representatives from high technology companies capable of establishing and implementing the system in an expeditious manner, and representatives of persons who may use the tracking system described in subsection (a) of this section and the online filing system described in subsection (b)(1) of this section.

(Pub. L. 107–296, title IV, § 461, Nov. 25, 2002, 116 Stat. 2202.)

REFERENCES IN TEXT

The effective date of this chapter, referred to in subsecs. (a), (b)(2), and (c)(1), is 60 days after Nov. 25, 2002, see section 4 of Pub. L. 107–296, set out as an Effective Date note under section 101 of this title.

The Immigration and Nationality Act, referred to in subsec. (a), is act June 27, 1952, ch. 477, 66 Stat. 163, as amended, which is classified principally to chapter 12 (§ 1101 et seq.) of Title 8, Aliens and Nationality. For complete classification of this Act to the Code, see Short Title note set out under section 1101 of Title 8 and Tables.

TERMINATION OF ADVISORY COMMITTEES

Advisory committees established after Jan. 5, 1973, to terminate not later than the expiration of the 2-year period beginning on date of their establishment, unless, in the case of a committee established by the President or an officer of the Federal Government, such committee is renewed by appropriate action prior to expiration of such 2-year period, or in the case of a committee established by Congress, its duration is otherwise provided for by law. See section 14 of Pub. L. 92–463, Oct. 6, 1972, 86 Stat. 776, set out in the Appendix to Title 5, Government Organization and Employees.

§ 279. Children's affairs

(a) Transfer of functions

There are transferred to the Director of the Office of Refugee Resettlement of the Department of Health and Human Services functions under the immigration laws of the United States with respect to the care of unaccompanied alien children that were vested by statute in, or performed by, the Commissioner of Immigration and Naturalization (or any officer, employee, or component of the Immigration and Naturalization Service) immediately before the effective date specified in subsection (d) of this section.

(b) Functions

(1) In general

Pursuant to the transfer made by subsection (a) of this section, the Director of the Office of Refugee Resettlement shall be responsible for—

(A) coordinating and implementing the care and placement of unaccompanied alien children who are in Federal custody by reason of their immigration status, including developing a plan to be submitted to Congress on how to ensure that qualified and independent legal counsel is timely appointed to represent the interests of each such child, consistent with the law regarding appointment of counsel that is in effect on November 25, 2002;

(B) ensuring that the interests of the child are considered in decisions and actions relating to the care and custody of an unaccompanied alien child;

(C) making placement determinations for all unaccompanied alien children who are in Federal custody by reason of their immigration status;

(D) implementing the placement determinations;

(E) implementing policies with respect to the care and placement of unaccompanied alien children;

(F) identifying a sufficient number of qualified individuals, entities, and facilities to house unaccompanied alien children;

(G) overseeing the infrastructure and personnel of facilities in which unaccompanied alien children reside;

(H) reuniting unaccompanied alien children with a parent abroad in appropriate cases;

(I) compiling, updating, and publishing at least annually a state-by-state list of professionals or other entities qualified to provide guardian and attorney representation services for unaccompanied alien children;

(J) maintaining statistical information and other data on unaccompanied alien children for whose care and placement the Director is responsible, which shall include—

(i) biographical information, such as a child's name, gender, date of birth, country of birth, and country of habitual residence;

(ii) the date on which the child came into Federal custody by reason of his or her immigration status;

(iii) information relating to the child's placement, removal, or release from each facility in which the child has resided;

(iv) in any case in which the child is placed in detention or released, an explanation relating to the detention or release; and

(v) the disposition of any actions in which the child is the subject;

(K) collecting and compiling statistical information from the Department of Justice, the Department of Homeland Security, and the Department of State on each department's actions relating to unaccompanied alien children; and

(L) conducting investigations and inspections of facilities and other entities in which unaccompanied alien children reside, including regular follow-up visits to such facilities, placements, and other entities, to assess the continued suitability of such placements.

(2) Coordination with other entities; no release on own recognizance

In making determinations described in paragraph (1)(C), the Director of the Office of Refugee Resettlement—

(A) shall consult with appropriate juvenile justice professionals, the Director of the Bureau of Citizenship and Immigration Services, and the Assistant Secretary of the Bureau of Border Security to ensure that such determinations ensure that unaccompanied alien children described in such subparagraph—

(i) are likely to appear for all hearings or proceedings in which they are involved;

(ii) are protected from smugglers, traffickers, or others who might seek to victimize or otherwise engage them in criminal, harmful, or exploitive activity; and

(iii) are placed in a setting in which they are not likely to pose a danger to themselves or others; and

(B) shall not release such children upon their own recognizance.

(3) Duties with respect to foster care

In carrying out the duties described in paragraph (1), the Director of the Office of Refugee Resettlement is encouraged to use the refugee children foster care system established pursuant to section 412(d) of the Immigration and Nationality Act (8 U.S.C. 1522(d)) for the placement of unaccompanied alien children.

(4) Rule of construction

Nothing in paragraph (2)(B) may be construed to require that a bond be posted for an unaccompanied alien child who is released to a qualified sponsor.

(c) Rule of construction

Nothing in this section may be construed to transfer the responsibility for adjudicating benefit determinations under the Immigration and Nationality Act (8 U.S.C. 1101 et seq.) from the authority of any official of the Department of Justice, the Department of Homeland Security, or the Department of State.

(d) Effective date

Notwithstanding section 4,[1] this section shall take effect on the date on which the transfer of functions specified under section 251 of this title takes effect.

(e) References

With respect to any function transferred by this section, any reference in any other Federal

[1] See References in Text note below.

law, Executive order, rule, regulation, or delegation of authority, or any document of or pertaining to a component of government from which such function is transferred—

(1) to the head of such component is deemed to refer to the Director of the Office of Refugee Resettlement; or

(2) to such component is deemed to refer to the Office of Refugee Resettlement of the Department of Health and Human Services.

(f) Other transition issues

(1) Exercise of authorities

Except as otherwise provided by law, a Federal official to whom a function is transferred by this section may, for purposes of performing the function, exercise all authorities under any other provision of law that were available with respect to the performance of that function to the official responsible for the performance of the function immediately before the effective date specified in subsection (d) of this section.

(2) Savings provisions

Subsections (a), (b), and (c) of section 552 of this title shall apply to a transfer of functions under this section in the same manner as such provisions apply to a transfer of functions under this chapter to the Department of Homeland Security.

(3) Transfer and allocation of appropriations and personnel

The personnel of the Department of Justice employed in connection with the functions transferred by this section, and the assets, liabilities, contracts, property, records, and unexpended balance of appropriations, authorizations, allocations, and other funds employed, held, used, arising from, available to, or to be made available to, the Immigration and Naturalization Service in connection with the functions transferred by this section, subject to section 1531 of title 31, shall be transferred to the Director of the Office of Refugee Resettlement for allocation to the appropriate component of the Department of Health and Human Services. Unexpended funds transferred pursuant to this paragraph shall be used only for the purposes for which the funds were originally authorized and appropriated.

(g) Definitions

As used in this section—

(1) the term "placement" means the placement of an unaccompanied alien child in either a detention facility or an alternative to such a facility; and

(2) the term "unaccompanied alien child" means a child who—

(A) has no lawful immigration status in the United States;

(B) has not attained 18 years of age; and

(C) with respect to whom—

(i) there is no parent or legal guardian in the United States; or

(ii) no parent or legal guardian in the United States is available to provide care and physical custody.

(Pub. L. 107–296, title IV, §462, Nov. 25, 2002, 116 Stat. 2202; Pub. L. 110–457, title II, §235(f), Dec. 23, 2008, 122 Stat. 5081.)

REFERENCES IN TEXT

The Immigration and Nationality Act, referred to in subsec. (c), is act June 27, 1952, ch. 477, 66 Stat. 163, as amended, which is classified principally to chapter 12 (§1101 et seq.) of Title 8, Aliens and Nationality. For complete classification of this Act to the Code, see Short Title note set out under section 1101 of Title 8 and Tables.

Section 4, referred to in subsec. (d), is section 4 of Pub. L. 107–296, which is set out as an Effective Date note under section 101 of this title.

CODIFICATION

In subsec. (f)(3), "section 1531 of title 31" substituted for "section 202 of the Budget and Accounting Procedures Act of 1950" on authority of Pub. L. 97–258, §4(b), Sept. 13, 1982, 96 Stat. 1067, the first section of which enacted Title 31, Money and Finance.

AMENDMENTS

2008—Subsec. (b)(1)(L). Pub. L. 110–457, §235(f)(1), substituted ", including regular follow-up visits to such facilities, placements, and other entities, to assess the continued suitability of such placements." for period at end.

Subsec. (b)(3). Pub. L. 110–457, §235(f)(2)(A), substituted "paragraph (1)," for "paragraph (1)(G),".

Subsec. (b)(4). Pub. L. 110–457, §235(f)(2)(B), added par. (4).

CHANGE OF NAME

Bureau of Border Security, referred to in subsec. (b)(2)(A), changed to Bureau of Immigration and Customs Enforcement by Reorganization Plan Modification for the Department of Homeland Security, eff. Mar. 1, 2003, H. Doc. No. 108–32, 108th Congress, 1st Session, set out as a note under section 542 of this title.

PART F—GENERAL IMMIGRATION PROVISIONS

§291. Abolishment of INS

(a) In general

Upon completion of all transfers from the Immigration and Naturalization Service as provided for by this chapter, the Immigration and Naturalization Service of the Department of Justice is abolished.

(b) Prohibition

The authority provided by section 542 of this title may be used to reorganize functions or organizational units within the Bureau of Border Security or the Bureau of Citizenship and Immigration Services, but may not be used to recombine the two bureaus into a single agency or otherwise to combine, join, or consolidate functions or organizational units of the two bureaus with each other.

(Pub. L. 107–296, title IV, §471, Nov. 25, 2002, 116 Stat. 2205.)

CHANGE OF NAME

Bureau of Border Security, referred to in subsec. (b), changed to Bureau of Immigration and Customs Enforcement by Reorganization Plan Modification for the Department of Homeland Security, eff. Mar. 1, 2003, H. Doc. No. 108–32, 108th Congress, 1st Session, set out as a note under section 542 of this title.

§292. Voluntary separation incentive payments

(a) Definitions

For purposes of this section—

(1) the term "employee" means an employee (as defined by section 2105 of title 5) who—

(A) has completed at least 3 years of current continuous service with 1 or more covered entities; and

(B) is serving under an appointment without time limitation,

but does not include any person under subparagraphs (A)-(G) of section 663(a)(2) of Public Law 104-208 (5 U.S.C. 5597 note);

(2) the term "covered entity" means—

(A) the Immigration and Naturalization Service;

(B) the Bureau of Border Security of the Department of Homeland Security; and

(C) the Bureau of Citizenship and Immigration Services of the Department of Homeland Security; and

(3) the term "transfer date" means the date on which the transfer of functions specified under section 251 of this title takes effect.

(b) Strategic restructuring plan

Before the Attorney General or the Secretary obligates any resources for voluntary separation incentive payments under this section, such official shall submit to the appropriate committees of Congress a strategic restructuring plan, which shall include—

(1) an organizational chart depicting the covered entities after their restructuring pursuant to this chapter;

(2) a summary description of how the authority under this section will be used to help carry out that restructuring; and

(3) the information specified in section 663(b)(2) of Public Law 104-208 (5 U.S.C. 5597 note).

As used in the preceding sentence, the "appropriate committees of Congress" are the Committees on Appropriations, Government Reform, and the Judiciary of the House of Representatives, and the Committees on Appropriations, Governmental Affairs, and the Judiciary of the Senate.

(c) Authority

The Attorney General and the Secretary may, to the extent necessary to help carry out their respective strategic restructuring plan described in subsection (b) of this section, make voluntary separation incentive payments to employees. Any such payment—

(1) shall be paid to the employee, in a lump sum, after the employee has separated from service;

(2) shall be paid from appropriations or funds available for the payment of basic pay of the employee;

(3) shall be equal to the lesser of—

(A) the amount the employee would be entitled to receive under section 5595(c) of title 5; or

(B) an amount not to exceed $25,000, as determined by the Attorney General or the Secretary;

(4) may not be made except in the case of any qualifying employee who voluntarily separates (whether by retirement or resignation) before the end of—

(A) the 3-month period beginning on the date on which such payment is offered or made available to such employee; or

(B) the 3-year period beginning on November 25, 2002,

whichever occurs first;

(5) shall not be a basis for payment, and shall not be included in the computation, of any other type of Government benefit; and

(6) shall not be taken into account in determining the amount of any severance pay to which the employee may be entitled under section 5595 of title 5, based on any other separation.

(d) Additional agency contributions to the retirement fund

(1) In general

In addition to any payments which it is otherwise required to make, the Department of Justice and the Department of Homeland Security shall, for each fiscal year with respect to which it makes any voluntary separation incentive payments under this section, remit to the Office of Personnel Management for deposit in the Treasury of the United States to the credit of the Civil Service Retirement and Disability Fund the amount required under paragraph (2).

(2) Amount required

The amount required under this paragraph shall, for any fiscal year, be the amount under subparagraph (A) or (B), whichever is greater.

(A) First method

The amount under this subparagraph shall, for any fiscal year, be equal to the minimum amount necessary to offset the additional costs to the retirement systems under title 5 (payable out of the Civil Service Retirement and Disability Fund) resulting from the voluntary separation of the employees described in paragraph (3), as determined under regulations of the Office of Personnel Management.

(B) Second method

The amount under this subparagraph shall, for any fiscal year, be equal to 45 percent of the sum total of the final basic pay of the employees described in paragraph (3).

(3) Computations to be based on separations occurring in the fiscal year involved

The employees described in this paragraph are those employees who receive a voluntary separation incentive payment under this section based on their separating from service during the fiscal year with respect to which the payment under this subsection relates.

(4) Final basic pay defined

In this subsection, the term "final basic pay" means, with respect to an employee, the total amount of basic pay which would be payable for a year of service by such employee, computed using the employee's final rate of basic pay, and, if last serving on other than a full-time basis, with appropriate adjustment therefor.

(e) Effect of subsequent employment with the Government

An individual who receives a voluntary separation incentive payment under this section and who, within 5 years after the date of the separation on which the payment is based, accepts any compensated employment with the Government or works for any agency of the Government through a personal services contract, shall be required to pay, prior to the individual's first day of employment, the entire amount of the incentive payment. Such payment shall be made to the covered entity from which the individual separated or, if made on or after the transfer date, to the Deputy Secretary or the Under Secretary for Border and Transportation Security (for transfer to the appropriate component of the Department of Homeland Security, if necessary).

(f) Effect on employment levels

(1) Intended effect

Voluntary separations under this section are not intended to necessarily reduce the total number of full-time equivalent positions in any covered entity.

(2) Use of voluntary separations

A covered entity may redeploy or use the full-time equivalent positions vacated by voluntary separations under this section to make other positions available to more critical locations or more critical occupations.

(Pub. L. 107–296, title IV, §472, Nov. 25, 2002, 116 Stat. 2205.)

References in Text

Section 663 of Public Law 104–208, referred to in subsecs. (a)(1) and (b)(3), probably means Pub. L. 104–208, div. A, title I, §101(f) [title VI, §663], Sept. 30, 1996, 110 Stat. 3009–314, 3009–383, which is classified as a note under section 5597 of Title 5, Government Organization and Employees.

Change of Name

Bureau of Border Security, referred to in subsec. (a)(2)(B), changed to Bureau of Immigration and Customs Enforcement by Reorganization Plan Modification for the Department of Homeland Security, eff. Mar. 1, 2003, H. Doc. No. 108–32, 108th Congress, 1st Session, set out as a note under section 542 of this title.

Committee on Government Reform of House of Representatives changed to Committee on Oversight and Government Reform of House of Representatives by House Resolution No. 6, One Hundred Tenth Congress, Jan. 5, 2007.

Committee on Governmental Affairs of Senate changed to Committee on Homeland Security and Governmental Affairs of Senate, effective Jan. 4, 2005, by Senate Resolution No. 445, One Hundred Eighth Congress, Oct. 9, 2004.

§293. Authority to conduct a demonstration project relating to disciplinary action

(a) In general

The Attorney General and the Secretary may each, during a period ending not later than 5 years after November 25, 2002, conduct a demonstration project for the purpose of determining whether one or more changes in the policies or procedures relating to methods for disciplining employees would result in improved personnel management.

(b) Scope

A demonstration project under this section—

(1) may not cover any employees apart from those employed in or under a covered entity; and

(2) shall not be limited by any provision of chapter 43, 75, or 77 of title 5.

(c) Procedures

Under the demonstration project—

(1) the use of alternative means of dispute resolution (as defined in section 571 of title 5) shall be encouraged, whenever appropriate; and

(2) each covered entity under the jurisdiction of the official conducting the project shall be required to provide for the expeditious, fair, and independent review of any action to which section 4303 or subchapter II of chapter 75 of such title 5 would otherwise apply (except an action described in section 7512(5) of such title 5).

(d) Actions involving discrimination

Notwithstanding any other provision of this section, if, in the case of any matter described in section 7702(a)(1)(B) of title 5, there is no judicially reviewable action under the demonstration project within 120 days after the filing of an appeal or other formal request for review (referred to in subsection (c)(2) of this section), an employee shall be entitled to file a civil action to the same extent and in the same manner as provided in section 7702(e)(1) of such title 5 (in the matter following subparagraph (C) thereof).

(e) Certain employees

Employees shall not be included within any project under this section if such employees are—

(1) neither managers nor supervisors; and

(2) within a unit with respect to which a labor organization is accorded exclusive recognition under chapter 71 of title 5.

Notwithstanding the preceding sentence, an aggrieved employee within a unit (referred to in paragraph (2)) may elect to participate in a complaint procedure developed under the demonstration project in lieu of any negotiated grievance procedure and any statutory procedure (as such term is used in section 7121 of such title 5).

(f) Reports

The Government Accountability Office shall prepare and submit to the Committees on Government Reform and the Judiciary of the House of Representatives and the Committees on Governmental Affairs and the Judiciary of the Senate periodic reports on any demonstration project conducted under this section, such reports to be submitted after the second and fourth years of its operation. Upon request, the Attorney General or the Secretary shall furnish such information as the Government Accountability Office may require to carry out this subsection.

(g) Definition

In this section, the term "covered entity" has the meaning given such term in section 292(a)(2) of this title.

(Pub. L. 107–296, title IV, §473, Nov. 25, 2002, 116 Stat. 2208; Pub. L. 108–271, §8(b), July 7, 2004, 118 Stat. 814.)

AMENDMENTS

2004—Subsec. (f). Pub. L. 108–271 substituted "Government Accountability Office" for "General Accounting Office" in two places.

CHANGE OF NAME

Committee on Government Reform of House of Representatives changed to Committee on Oversight and Government Reform of House of Representatives by House Resolution No. 6, One Hundred Tenth Congress, Jan. 5, 2007.

Committee on Governmental Affairs of Senate changed to Committee on Homeland Security and Governmental Affairs of Senate, effective Jan. 4, 2005, by Senate Resolution No. 445, One Hundred Eighth Congress, Oct. 9, 2004.

§ 294. Sense of Congress

It is the sense of Congress that—

(1) the missions of the Bureau of Border Security and the Bureau of Citizenship and Immigration Services are equally important and, accordingly, they each should be adequately funded; and

(2) the functions transferred under this part should not, after such transfers take effect, operate at levels below those in effect prior to November 25, 2002.

(Pub. L. 107–296, title IV, § 474, Nov. 25, 2002, 116 Stat. 2209.)

CHANGE OF NAME

Bureau of Border Security, referred to in par. (1), changed to Bureau of Immigration and Customs Enforcement by Reorganization Plan Modification for the Department of Homeland Security, eff. Mar. 1, 2003, H. Doc. No. 108–32, 108th Congress, 1st Session, set out as a note under section 542 of this title.

§ 295. Director of Shared Services

(a) In general

Within the Office of Deputy Secretary, there shall be a Director of Shared Services.

(b) Functions

The Director of Shared Services shall be responsible for the coordination of resources for the Bureau of Border Security and the Bureau of Citizenship and Immigration Services, including—

(1) information resources management, including computer databases and information technology;

(2) records and file management; and

(3) forms management.

(Pub. L. 107–296, title IV, § 475, Nov. 25, 2002, 116 Stat. 2209.)

CHANGE OF NAME

Bureau of Border Security, referred to in subsec. (b), changed to Bureau of Immigration and Customs Enforcement by Reorganization Plan Modification for the Department of Homeland Security, eff. Mar. 1, 2003, H. Doc. No. 108–32, 108th Congress, 1st Session, set out as a note under section 542 of this title.

§ 296. Separation of funding

(a) In general

There shall be established separate accounts in the Treasury of the United States for appropriated funds and other deposits available for the Bureau of Citizenship and Immigration Services and the Bureau of Border Security.

(b) Separate budgets

To ensure that the Bureau of Citizenship and Immigration Services and the Bureau of Border Security are funded to the extent necessary to fully carry out their respective functions, the Director of the Office of Management and Budget shall separate the budget requests for each such entity.

(c) Fees

Fees imposed for a particular service, application, or benefit shall be deposited into the account established under subsection (a) of this section that is for the bureau with jurisdiction over the function to which the fee relates.

(d) Fees not transferable

No fee may be transferred between the Bureau of Citizenship and Immigration Services and the Bureau of Border Security for purposes not authorized by section 1356 of title 8.

(Pub. L. 107–296, title IV, § 476, Nov. 25, 2002, 116 Stat. 2209.)

CHANGE OF NAME

Bureau of Border Security, referred to in subsecs. (a), (b), and (d), changed to Bureau of Immigration and Customs Enforcement by Reorganization Plan Modification for the Department of Homeland Security, eff. Mar. 1, 2003, H. Doc. No. 108–32, 108th Congress, 1st Session, set out as a note under section 542 of this title.

§ 297. Reports and implementation plans

(a) Division of funds

The Secretary, not later than 120 days after the effective date of this chapter, shall submit to the Committees on Appropriations and the Judiciary of the House of Representatives and of the Senate a report on the proposed division and transfer of funds, including unexpended funds, appropriations, and fees, between the Bureau of Citizenship and Immigration Services and the Bureau of Border Security.

(b) Division of personnel

The Secretary, not later than 120 days after the effective date of this chapter, shall submit to the Committees on Appropriations and the Judiciary of the House of Representatives and of the Senate a report on the proposed division of personnel between the Bureau of Citizenship and Immigration Services and the Bureau of Border Security.

(c) Implementation plan

(1) In general

The Secretary, not later than 120 days after the effective date of this chapter, and every 6 months thereafter until the termination of fiscal year 2005, shall submit to the Committees on Appropriations and the Judiciary of the House of Representatives and of the Senate an implementation plan to carry out this chapter.

(2) Contents

The implementation plan should include details concerning the separation of the Bureau of Citizenship and Immigration Services and the Bureau of Border Security, including the following:

(A) Organizational structure, including the field structure.

(B) Chain of command.

(C) Procedures for interaction among such bureaus.

(D) Fraud detection and investigation.

(E) The processing and handling of removal proceedings, including expedited removal and applications for relief from removal.

(F) Recommendations for conforming amendments to the Immigration and Nationality Act (8 U.S.C. 1101 et seq.).

(G) Establishment of a transition team.

(H) Methods to phase in the costs of separating the administrative support systems of the Immigration and Naturalization Service in order to provide for separate administrative support systems for the Bureau of Citizenship and Immigration Services and the Bureau of Border Security.

(d) Comptroller General studies and reports

(1) Status reports on transition

Not later than 18 months after the date on which the transfer of functions specified under section 251 of this title takes effect, and every 6 months thereafter, until full implementation of this part has been completed, the Comptroller General of the United States shall submit to the Committees on Appropriations and on the Judiciary of the House of Representatives and the Senate a report containing the following:

(A) A determination of whether the transfers of functions made by parts D and E of this subchapter have been completed, and if a transfer of functions has not taken place, identifying the reasons why the transfer has not taken place.

(B) If the transfers of functions made by parts D and E of this subchapter have been completed, an identification of any issues that have arisen due to the completed transfers.

(C) An identification of any issues that may arise due to any future transfer of functions.

(2) Report on management

Not later than 4 years after the date on which the transfer of functions specified under section 251 of this title takes effect, the Comptroller General of the United States shall submit to the Committees on Appropriations and on the Judiciary of the House of Representatives and the Senate a report, following a study, containing the following:

(A) Determinations of whether the transfer of functions from the Immigration and Naturalization Service to the Bureau of Citizenship and Immigration Services and the Bureau of Border Security have improved, with respect to each function transferred, the following:

(i) Operations.

(ii) Management, including accountability and communication.

(iii) Financial administration.

(iv) Recordkeeping, including information management and technology.

(B) A statement of the reasons for the determinations under subparagraph (A).

(C) Any recommendations for further improvements to the Bureau of Citizenship and Immigration Services and the Bureau of Border Security.

(3) Report on fees

Not later than 1 year after November 25, 2002, the Comptroller General of the United States shall submit to the Committees on the Judiciary of the House of Representatives and of the Senate a report examining whether the Bureau of Citizenship and Immigration Services is likely to derive sufficient funds from fees to carry out its functions in the absence of appropriated funds.

(Pub. L. 107–296, title IV, § 477, Nov. 25, 2002, 116 Stat. 2209.)

REFERENCES IN TEXT

The effective date of this chapter, referred to in subsecs. (a), (b), and (c)(1), is 60 days after Nov. 25, 2002, see section 4 of Pub. L. 107–296, set out as an Effective Date note under section 101 of this title.

The Immigration and Nationality Act, referred to in subsec. (c)(2)(F), is act June 27, 1952, ch. 477, 66 Stat. 163, as amended, which is classified principally to chapter 12 (§ 1101 et seq.) of Title 8, Aliens and Nationality. For complete classification of this Act to the Code, see Short Title note set out under section 1101 of Title 8 and Tables.

Parts D and E of this subchapter, referred to in subsec. (d)(1)(A), (B), was in the original "subtitles D and E", meaning subtitles D (§§ 441–446) and E (§§ 451–462) of title IV of Pub. L. 107–296, Nov. 25, 2002, 116 Stat. 2192, 2195, which enacted parts D and E of this subchapter, amended sections 1356 and 1573 of Title 8, Aliens and Nationality, and enacted provisions set out as a note under section 271 of this title. For complete classification of subtitles D and E to the Code, see Tables.

CHANGE OF NAME

Bureau of Border Security, referred to in text, changed to Bureau of Immigration and Customs Enforcement by Reorganization Plan Modification for the Department of Homeland Security, eff. Mar. 1, 2003, H. Doc. No. 108–32, 108th Congress, 1st Session, set out as a note under section 542 of this title.

§ 298. Immigration functions

(a) Annual report

(1) In general

One year after November 25, 2002, and each year thereafter, the Secretary shall submit a report to the President, to the Committees on the Judiciary and Government Reform of the House of Representatives, and to the Committees on the Judiciary and Government Affairs of the Senate, on the impact the transfers made by this part has had on immigration functions.

(2) Matter included

The report shall address the following with respect to the period covered by the report:

(A) The aggregate number of all immigration applications and petitions received, and processed, by the Department.

(B) Region-by-region statistics on the aggregate number of immigration applications and petitions filed by an alien (or filed on behalf of an alien) and denied, disaggregated by category of denial and application or petition type.

(C) The quantity of backlogged immigration applications and petitions that have been processed, the aggregate number awaiting processing, and a detailed plan for eliminating the backlog.

(D) The average processing period for immigration applications and petitions, disaggregated by application or petition type.

(E) The number and types of immigration-related grievances filed with any official of the Department of Justice, and if those grievances were resolved.

(F) Plans to address grievances and improve immigration services.

(G) Whether immigration-related fees were used consistent with legal requirements regarding such use.

(H) Whether immigration-related questions conveyed by customers to the Department (whether conveyed in person, by telephone, or by means of the Internet) were answered effectively and efficiently.

(b) Sense of Congress regarding immigration services

It is the sense of Congress that—

(1) the quality and efficiency of immigration services rendered by the Federal Government should be improved after the transfers made by this part take effect; and

(2) the Secretary should undertake efforts to guarantee that concerns regarding the quality and efficiency of immigration services are addressed after such effective date.

(Pub. L. 107–296, title IV, §478, Nov. 25, 2002, 116 Stat. 2211.)

CHANGE OF NAME

Committee on Government Reform of House of Representatives changed to Committee on Oversight and Government Reform of House of Representatives by House Resolution No. 6, One Hundred Tenth Congress, Jan. 5, 2007.

Committee on Governmental Affairs of Senate changed to Committee on Homeland Security and Governmental Affairs of Senate, effective Jan. 4, 2005, by Senate Resolution No. 445, One Hundred Eighth Congress, Oct. 9, 2004.

SUBCHAPTER V—NATIONAL EMERGENCY MANAGEMENT

AMENDMENTS

2006—Pub. L. 109–295, title VI, §611(1), Oct. 4, 2006, 120 Stat. 1395, substituted "NATIONAL EMERGENCY MANAGEMENT" for "EMERGENCY PREPAREDNESS AND RESPONSE" in subchapter heading.

§311. Definitions

In this subchapter—

(1) the term "Administrator" means the Administrator of the Agency;

(2) the term "Agency" means the Federal Emergency Management Agency;

(3) the term "catastrophic incident" means any natural disaster, act of terrorism, or other man-made disaster that results in extraordinary levels of casualties or damage or disruption severely affecting the population (including mass evacuations), infrastructure, environment, economy, national morale, or government functions in an area;

(4) the terms "credentialed" and "credentialing" mean having provided, or providing, respectively, documentation that identifies personnel and authenticates and verifies the qualifications of such personnel by ensuring that such personnel possess a minimum common level of training, experience, physical and medical fitness, and capability appropriate for a particular position in accordance with standards created under section 320 of this title;

(5) the term "Federal coordinating officer" means a Federal coordinating officer as described in section 5143 of title 42;

(6) the term "interoperable" has the meaning given the term "interoperable communications" under section 194(g)(1) of this title;

(7) the term "National Incident Management System" means a system to enable effective, efficient, and collaborative incident management;

(8) the term "National Response Plan" means the National Response Plan or any successor plan prepared under section 314(a)(6)[1] of this title;

(9) the term "Regional Administrator" means a Regional Administrator appointed under section 317 of this title;

(10) the term "Regional Office" means a Regional Office established under section 317 of this title;

(11) the term "resources" means personnel and major items of equipment, supplies, and facilities available or potentially available for responding to a natural disaster, act of terrorism, or other man-made disaster;

(12) the term "surge capacity" means the ability to rapidly and substantially increase the provision of search and rescue capabilities, food, water, medicine, shelter and housing, medical care, evacuation capacity, staffing (including disaster assistance employees), and other resources necessary to save lives and protect property during a catastrophic incident;

(13) the term "tribal government" means the government of any entity described in section 101(11)(B) of this title; and

(14) the terms "typed" and "typing" mean having evaluated, or evaluating, respectively, a resource in accordance with standards created under section 320 of this title.

(Pub. L. 107–296, title V, §501, as added Pub. L. 109–295, title VI, §611(10), Oct. 4, 2006, 120 Stat. 1395; amended Pub. L. 110–53, title IV, §401(a), title V, §502(c)(1), Aug. 3, 2007, 121 Stat. 301, 311.)

REFERENCES IN TEXT

Section 314(a)(6) of this title, referred to in par. (8), was in the original "section 502(a)(6)" and was translated as meaning section 502 of Pub. L. 107–296 prior to its redesignation as section 504 by Pub. L. 109–295, §611(8), and not section 506 which was redesignated section 502 by Pub. L. 109–295, §611(9), and is classified to section 312 of this title, to reflect the probable intent of Congress.

[1] See References in Text note below.

PRIOR PROVISIONS

A prior section 311, Pub. L. 107–296, title V, §501, Nov. 25, 2002, 116 Stat. 2212, provided for an Under Secretary for Emergency Preparedness and Response, prior to repeal by Pub. L. 109–295, title VI, §611(2), Oct. 4, 2006, 120 Stat. 1395.

AMENDMENTS

2007—Pars. (4) to (12). Pub. L. 110–53, §401(a)(1)–(4), added pars. (4) and (11) and redesignated former pars. (4) to (10) as (5) to (10) and (12), respectively. Former par. (11) redesignated (13).

Par. (13). Pub. L. 110–53, §502(c)(1), substituted "101(11)(B)" for "101(10)(B)".

Pub. L. 110–53, §401(a)(1), redesignated par. (11) as (13).

Par. (14). Pub. L. 110–53, §401(a)(5)–(7), added par. (14).

CHANGE OF NAME

Any reference to the Administrator of the Federal Emergency Management Agency in title VI of Pub. L. 109–295 or an amendment by title VI to be considered to refer and apply to the Director of the Federal Emergency Management Agency until Mar. 31, 2007, see section 612(f)(2) of Pub. L. 109–295, set out as a note under section 313 of this title.

INTERIM ACTIONS

Pub. L. 109–295, title VI, §612(f)(1), Oct. 4, 2006, 120 Stat. 1411, provided that: "During the period beginning on the date of enactment of this Act [Oct. 4, 2006] and ending on March 31, 2007, the Secretary [of Homeland Security], the Under Secretary for Preparedness, and the Director of the Federal Emergency Management Agency shall take such actions as are necessary to provide for the orderly implementation of any amendment under this subtitle [subtitle A (§§611–614) of title VI of Pub. L. 109–295, see Tables for classification] that takes effect on March 31, 2007."

§312. Definition

In this subchapter, the term "Nuclear Incident Response Team" means a resource that includes—

(1) those entities of the Department of Energy that perform nuclear or radiological emergency support functions (including accident response, search response, advisory, and technical operations functions), radiation exposure functions at the medical assistance facility known as the Radiation Emergency Assistance Center/Training Site (REAC/TS), radiological assistance functions, and related functions; and

(2) those entities of the Environmental Protection Agency that perform such support functions (including radiological emergency response functions) and related functions.

(Pub. L. 107–296, title V, §502, formerly §506, Nov. 25, 2002, 116 Stat. 2214; renumbered §502, Pub. L. 109–295, title VI, §611(9), Oct. 4, 2006, 120 Stat. 1395.)

CODIFICATION

Section was formerly classified to section 316 of this title prior to renumbering by Pub. L. 109–295.

PRIOR PROVISIONS

A prior section 502 of Pub. L. 107–296 was renumbered section 504 and is classified to section 314 of this title.

§313. Federal Emergency Management Agency

(a) In general

There is in the Department the Federal Emergency Management Agency, headed by an Administrator.

(b) Mission

(1) Primary mission

The primary mission of the Agency is to reduce the loss of life and property and protect the Nation from all hazards, including natural disasters, acts of terrorism, and other man-made disasters, by leading and supporting the Nation in a risk-based, comprehensive emergency management system of preparedness, protection, response, recovery, and mitigation.

(2) Specific activities

In support of the primary mission of the Agency, the Administrator shall—

(A) lead the Nation's efforts to prepare for, protect against, respond to, recover from, and mitigate against the risk of natural disasters, acts of terrorism, and other man-made disasters, including catastrophic incidents;

(B) partner with State, local, and tribal governments and emergency response providers, with other Federal agencies, with the private sector, and with nongovernmental organizations to build a national system of emergency management that can effectively and efficiently utilize the full measure of the Nation's resources to respond to natural disasters, acts of terrorism, and other man-made disasters, including catastrophic incidents;

(C) develop a Federal response capability that, when necessary and appropriate, can act effectively and rapidly to deliver assistance essential to saving lives or protecting or preserving property or public health and safety in a natural disaster, act of terrorism, or other man-made disaster;

(D) integrate the Agency's emergency preparedness, protection, response, recovery, and mitigation responsibilities to confront effectively the challenges of a natural disaster, act of terrorism, or other man-made disaster;

(E) develop and maintain robust Regional Offices that will work with State, local, and tribal governments, emergency response providers, and other appropriate entities to identify and address regional priorities;

(F) under the leadership of the Secretary, coordinate with the Commandant of the Coast Guard, the Director of Customs and Border Protection, the Director of Immigration and Customs Enforcement, the National Operations Center, and other agencies and offices in the Department to take full advantage of the substantial range of resources in the Department;

(G) provide funding, training, exercises, technical assistance, planning, and other assistance to build tribal, local, State, regional, and national capabilities (including communications capabilities), necessary to respond to a natural disaster, act of terrorism, or other man-made disaster; and

(H) develop and coordinate the implementation of a risk-based, all-hazards strategy for preparedness that builds those common capabilities necessary to respond to natural disasters, acts of terrorism, and other man-made disasters while also building the unique capabilities necessary to respond to specific types of incidents that pose the greatest risk to our Nation.

(c) Administrator

(1) In general

The Administrator shall be appointed by the President, by and with the advice and consent of the Senate.

(2) Qualifications

The Administrator shall be appointed from among individuals who have—

(A) a demonstrated ability in and knowledge of emergency management and homeland security; and

(B) not less than 5 years of executive leadership and management experience in the public or private sector.

(3) Reporting

The Administrator shall report to the Secretary, without being required to report through any other official of the Department.

(4) Principal advisor on emergency management

(A) In general

The Administrator is the principal advisor to the President, the Homeland Security Council, and the Secretary for all matters relating to emergency management in the United States.

(B) Advice and recommendations

(i) In general

In presenting advice with respect to any matter to the President, the Homeland Security Council, or the Secretary, the Administrator shall, as the Administrator considers appropriate, inform the President, the Homeland Security Council, or the Secretary, as the case may be, of the range of emergency preparedness, protection, response, recovery, and mitigation options with respect to that matter.

(ii) Advice on request

The Administrator, as the principal advisor on emergency management, shall provide advice to the President, the Homeland Security Council, or the Secretary on a particular matter when the President, the Homeland Security Council, or the Secretary requests such advice.

(iii) Recommendations to Congress

After informing the Secretary, the Administrator may make such recommendations to Congress relating to emergency management as the Administrator considers appropriate.

(5) Cabinet status

(A) In general

The President may designate the Administrator to serve as a member of the Cabinet in the event of natural disasters, acts of terrorism, or other man-made disasters.

(B) Retention of authority

Nothing in this paragraph shall be construed as affecting the authority of the Secretary under this chapter.

(Pub. L. 107–296, title V, § 503, as added Pub. L. 109–295, title VI, § 611(11), Oct. 4, 2006, 120 Stat. 1396.)

REFERENCES IN TEXT

This chapter, referred to in subsec. (c)(5)(B), was in the original "this Act", meaning Pub. L. 107–296, Nov. 25, 2002, 116 Stat. 2135, known as the Homeland Security Act of 2002, which is classified principally to this chapter. For complete classification of this Act to the Code, see Short Title note set out under section 101 of this title and Tables.

PRIOR PROVISIONS

A prior section 313, Pub. L. 107–296, title V, § 503, Nov. 25, 2002, 116 Stat. 2213; Pub. L. 108–276, § 3(c)(3), July 21, 2004, 118 Stat. 853; Pub. L. 109–417, title III, § 301(c)(2), Dec. 19, 2006, 120 Stat. 2854, related to the transfer of certain functions to the Secretary of Homeland Security, prior to repeal by Pub. L. 109–295, title VI, § 611(3), Oct. 4, 2006, 120 Stat. 1395.

CHANGE OF NAME

Pub. L. 109–295, title VI, § 612(c), Oct. 4, 2006, 120 Stat. 1410, provided that: "Any reference to the Director of the Federal Emergency Management Agency, in any law, rule, regulation, certificate, directive, instruction, or other official paper shall be considered to refer and apply to the Administrator of the Federal Emergency Management Agency."

Pub. L. 109–295, title VI, § 612(f)(2), Oct. 4, 2006, 120 Stat. 1411, provided that: "Any reference to the Administrator of the Federal Emergency Management Agency in this title [see Tables for classification] or an amendment by this title shall be considered to refer and apply to the Director of the Federal Emergency Management Agency until March 31, 2007."

EFFECTIVE DATE

Section effective Mar. 31, 2007, see section 614(b)(1) of Pub. L. 109–295, set out as a note under section 701 of this title.

§ 314. Authority and responsibilities

(a) In general

The Administrator shall provide Federal leadership necessary to prepare for, protect against, respond to, recover from, or mitigate against a natural disaster, act of terrorism, or other man-made disaster, including—

(1) helping to ensure the effectiveness of emergency response providers to terrorist attacks, major disasters, and other emergencies;

(2) with respect to the Nuclear Incident Response Team (regardless of whether it is operating as an organizational unit of the Department pursuant to this subchapter)—

(A) establishing standards and certifying when those standards have been met;

(B) conducting joint and other exercises and training and evaluating performance; and

(C) providing funds to the Department of Energy and the Environmental Protection Agency, as appropriate, for homeland security planning, exercises and training, and equipment;

(3) providing the Federal Government's response to terrorist attacks and major disasters, including—

(A) managing such response;

(B) directing the Domestic Emergency Support Team and (when operating as an organizational unit of the Department pursuant to this subchapter) the Nuclear Incident Response Team;

(C) overseeing the Metropolitan Medical Response System; and

(D) coordinating other Federal response resources, including requiring deployment of the Strategic National Stockpile, in the event of a terrorist attack or major disaster;

(4) aiding the recovery from terrorist attacks and major disasters;

(5) building a comprehensive national incident management system with Federal, State, and local government personnel, agencies, and authorities, to respond to such attacks and disasters;

(6) consolidating existing Federal Government emergency response plans into a single, coordinated national response plan;

(7) helping ensure the acquisition of operable and interoperable communications capabilities by Federal, State, local, and tribal governments and emergency response providers;

(8) assisting the President in carrying out the functions under the Robert T. Stafford Disaster Relief and Emergency Assistance Act (42 U.S.C. 5121 et seq.) and carrying out all functions and authorities given to the Administrator under that Act;

(9) carrying out the mission of the Agency to reduce the loss of life and property and protect the Nation from all hazards by leading and supporting the Nation in a risk-based, comprehensive emergency management system of—

(A) mitigation, by taking sustained actions to reduce or eliminate long-term risks to people and property from hazards and their effects;

(B) preparedness, by planning, training, and building the emergency management profession to prepare effectively for, mitigate against, respond to, and recover from any hazard;

(C) response, by conducting emergency operations to save lives and property through positioning emergency equipment, personnel, and supplies, through evacuating potential victims, through providing food, water, shelter, and medical care to those in need, and through restoring critical public services; and

(D) recovery, by rebuilding communities so individuals, businesses, and governments can function on their own, return to normal life, and protect against future hazards;

(10) increasing efficiencies, by coordinating efforts relating to preparedness, protection, response, recovery, and mitigation;

(11) helping to ensure the effectiveness of emergency response providers in responding to a natural disaster, act of terrorism, or other man-made disaster;

(12) supervising grant programs administered by the Agency;

(13) administering and ensuring the implementation of the National Response Plan, including coordinating and ensuring the readiness of each emergency support function under the National Response Plan;

(14) coordinating with the National Advisory Council established under section 318 of this title;

(15) preparing and implementing the plans and programs of the Federal Government for—

(A) continuity of operations;

(B) continuity of government; and

(C) continuity of plans;

(16) minimizing, to the extent practicable, overlapping planning and reporting requirements applicable to State, local, and tribal governments and the private sector;

(17) maintaining and operating within the Agency the National Response Coordination Center or its successor;

(18) developing a national emergency management system that is capable of preparing for, protecting against, responding to, recovering from, and mitigating against catastrophic incidents;

(19) assisting the President in carrying out the functions under the national preparedness goal and the national preparedness system and carrying out all functions and authorities of the Administrator under the national preparedness System;

(20) carrying out all authorities of the Federal Emergency Management Agency and the Directorate of Preparedness of the Department as transferred under section 315 of this title; and

(21) otherwise carrying out the mission of the Agency as described in section 313(b) of this title.

(b) All-hazards approach

In carrying out the responsibilities under this section, the Administrator shall coordinate the implementation of a risk-based, all-hazards strategy that builds those common capabilities necessary to prepare for, protect against, respond to, recover from, or mitigate against natural disasters, acts of terrorism, and other man-made disasters, while also building the unique capabilities necessary to prepare for, protect against, respond to, recover from, or mitigate against the risks of specific types of incidents that pose the greatest risk to the Nation.

(Pub. L. 107–296, title V, §504, formerly §502, Nov. 25, 2002, 116 Stat. 2212; Pub. L. 108–276, §3(b)(1), July 21, 2004, 118 Stat. 852; Pub. L. 108–458, title VII, §7303(h)(1), Dec. 17, 2004, 118 Stat. 3846; renumbered §504 and amended Pub. L. 109–295, title VI, §611(8), (12), Oct. 4, 2006, 120 Stat. 1395, 1398; Pub. L. 109–417, title III, §301(c)(1), Dec. 19, 2006, 120 Stat. 2854.)

REFERENCES IN TEXT

The Robert T. Stafford Disaster Relief and Emergency Assistance Act, referred to in subsec. (a)(8), is Pub. L. 93–288, May 22, 1974, 88 Stat. 143, as amended, which is classified principally to chapter 68 (§5121 et seq.) of Title 42, The Public Health and Welfare. For complete classification of this Act to the Code, see Short Title note set out under section 5121 of Title 42 and Tables.

CODIFICATION

Section was formerly classified to section 312 of this title prior to renumbering by Pub. L. 109–295.

PRIOR PROVISIONS

A prior section 504 of Pub. L. 107–296 was renumbered section 517 and is classified to section 321f of this title.

AMENDMENTS

2006—Pub. L. 109–295, §611(12)(A), (B), inserted "Authority and" before "responsibilities" in section catchline, designated existing provisions as subsec. (a), inserted subsec. heading, and substituted "The Administrator shall provide Federal leadership necessary to prepare for, protect against, respond to, recover from, or mitigate against a natural disaster, act of terrorism, or other man-made disaster, including—" for "The Secretary, acting through the Under Secretary for Emergency Preparedness and Response, shall include—" in introductory provisions.

Subsec. (a)(3)(B). Pub. L. 109–417, which directed that section 502(3)(B) of Pub. L. 107–296 be amended by striking ", the National Disaster Medical System,", was executed by striking those words after "Domestic Emergency Support Team" in subsec. (a)(3)(B) of this section, to reflect the probable intent of Congress and the redesignation of section 502(3)(B) as 504(a)(3)(B) by Pub. L. 109–295, §611(8), (12)(B). See credits and Amendment note above.

Subsec. (a)(7) to (21). Pub. L. 109–295, §611(12)(C), (D), added pars. (7) to (21) and struck out former par. (7) which read as follows: "helping to ensure that emergency response providers acquire interoperable communications technology."

Subsec. (b). Pub. L. 109–295, §611(12)(D), added subsec. (b).

2004—Par. (3)(B). Pub. L. 108–276, §3(b)(1)(A), struck out "the Strategic National Stockpile," after "Domestic Emergency Support Team,".

Par. (3)(D). Pub. L. 108–276, §3(b)(1)(B), inserted ", including requiring deployment of the Strategic National Stockpile," after "resources".

Par. (7). Pub. L. 108–458 struck out "developing comprehensive programs for developing interoperative communications technology, and" before "helping" and substituted "acquire interoperable communications technology" for "acquire such technology".

EFFECTIVE DATE OF 2006 AMENDMENT

Pub. L. 109–417, title III, §301(f), Dec. 19, 2006, 120 Stat. 2855, provided that: "The amendments made by subsections (b) and (c) [amending this section and former section 313 of this title and enacting provisions set out as a note under section 300hh–11 of Title 42, The Public Health and Welfare] shall take effect on January 1, 2007."

Amendment by section 611(12) of Pub. L. 109–295 effective Mar. 31, 2007, see section 614(b)(2) of Pub. L. 109–295, set out as an Effective Date note under section 701 of this title.

EX. ORD. NO. 13347. INDIVIDUALS WITH DISABILITIES IN EMERGENCY PREPAREDNESS

Ex. Ord. No. 13347, July 22, 2004, 69 F.R. 44573, provided:

By the authority vested in me as President by the Constitution and the laws of the United States of America, and to strengthen emergency preparedness with respect to individuals with disabilities, it is hereby ordered as follows:

SECTION 1. *Policy.* To ensure that the Federal Government appropriately supports safety and security for individuals with disabilities in situations involving disasters, including earthquakes, tornadoes, fires, floods, hurricanes, and acts of terrorism, it shall be the policy of the United States that executive departments and agencies of the Federal Government (agencies):

(a) consider, in their emergency preparedness planning, the unique needs of agency employees with disabilities and individuals with disabilities whom the agency serves;

(b) encourage, including through the provision of technical assistance, as appropriate, consideration of the unique needs of employees and individuals with disabilities served by State, local, and tribal governments and private organizations and individuals in emergency preparedness planning; and

(c) facilitate cooperation among Federal, State, local, and tribal governments and private organizations and individuals in the implementation of emergency preparedness plans as they relate to individuals with disabilities.

SEC. 2. *Establishment of Council.* (a) There is hereby established, within the Department of Homeland Security for administrative purposes, the Interagency Coordinating Council on Emergency Preparedness and Individuals with Disabilities (the "Council"). The Council shall consist exclusively of the following members or their designees:

(i) the heads of executive departments, the Administrator of the Environmental Protection Agency, the Administrator of General Services, the Director of the Office of Personnel Management, and the Commissioner of Social Security; and

(ii) any other agency head as the Secretary of Homeland Security may, with the concurrence of the agency head, designate.

(b) The Secretary of Homeland Security shall chair the Council, convene and preside at its meetings, determine its agenda, direct its work, and, as appropriate to particular subject matters, establish and direct subgroups of the Council, which shall consist exclusively of Council members.

(c) A member of the Council may designate, to perform the Council functions of the member, an employee of the member's department or agency who is either an officer of the United States appointed by the President, or a full-time employee serving in a position with pay equal to or greater than the minimum rate payable for GS–15 of the General Schedule.

SEC. 3. *Functions of Council.* (a) The Council shall:

(i) coordinate implementation by agencies of the policy set forth in section 1 of this order;

(ii) whenever the Council obtains in the performance of its functions information or advice from any individual who is not a full-time or permanent part-time Federal employee, obtain such information and advice only in a manner that seeks individual advice and does not involve collective judgment or consensus advice or deliberation; and

(iii) at the request of any agency head (or the agency head's designee under section 2(c) of this order) who is a member of the Council, unless the Secretary of Homeland Security declines the request, promptly review and provide advice, for the purpose of furthering the policy set forth in section 1, on a proposed action by that agency.

(b) The Council shall submit to the President each year beginning 1 year after the date of this order, through the Assistant to the President for Homeland Security, a report that describes:

(i) the achievements of the Council in implementing the policy set forth in section 1;

(ii) the best practices among Federal, State, local, and tribal governments and private organizations and individuals for emergency preparedness planning with respect to individuals with disabilities; and

(iii) recommendations of the Council for advancing the policy set forth in section 1.

SEC. 4. *General.* (a) To the extent permitted by law:

(i) agencies shall assist and provide information to the Council for the performance of its functions under this order; and

(ii) the Department of Homeland Security shall provide funding and administrative support for the Council.

(b) Nothing in this order shall be construed to impair or otherwise affect the functions of the Director of the Office of Management and Budget relating to budget, administrative, or legislative proposals.

(c) This order is intended only to improve the internal management of the executive branch and is not intended to, and does not, create any right or benefit, substantive or procedural, enforceable at law or in equity by a party against the United States, its departments, agencies, instrumentalities, or entities, its officers or employees, or any other person.

GEORGE W. BUSH.

§314a. FEMA programs

Notwithstanding any other provision of Federal law, as of April 1, 2007, the Director of the Federal Emergency Management Agency shall be responsible for the radiological emergency preparedness program and the chemical stockpile emergency preparedness program.

(Pub. L. 109–347, title VI, §612, Oct. 13, 2006, 120 Stat. 1943.)

CODIFICATION

Section was enacted as part of the Security and Accountability For Every Port Act of 2006, also known as the SAFE Port Act, and not as part of the Homeland Security Act of 2002 which comprises this chapter.

CHANGE OF NAME

References to the Director of the Federal Emergency Management Agency considered to refer and apply to the Administrator of the Federal Emergency Management Agency, see section 612(c) of Pub. L. 109–295, set out as a note under section 313 of this title.

§315. Functions transferred

(a) In general

Except as provided in subsection (b), there are transferred to the Agency the following:

(1) All functions of the Federal Emergency Management Agency, including existing responsibilities for emergency alert systems and continuity of operations and continuity of government plans and programs as constituted on June 1, 2006, including all of its personnel, assets, components, authorities, grant programs, and liabilities, and including the functions of the Under Secretary for Federal Emergency Management relating thereto.

(2) The Directorate of Preparedness, as constituted on June 1, 2006, including all of its functions, personnel, assets, components, authorities, grant programs, and liabilities, and including the functions of the Under Secretary for Preparedness relating thereto.

(b) Exceptions

The following within the Preparedness Directorate shall not be transferred:

(1) The Office of Infrastructure Protection.

(2) The National Communications System.

(3) The National Cybersecurity Division.

(4) The Office of the Chief Medical Officer.

(5) The functions, personnel, assets, components, authorities, and liabilities of each component described under paragraphs (1) through (4).

(Pub. L. 107–296, title V, §505, as added Pub. L. 109–295, title VI, §611(13), Oct. 4, 2006, 120 Stat. 1400.)

PRIOR PROVISIONS

A prior section 505 of Pub. L. 107–296 was renumbered section 518 and is classified to section 321g of this title.

EFFECTIVE DATE

Section effective Mar. 31, 2007, see section 614(b)(3) of Pub. L. 109–295, set out as a note under section 701 of this title.

TRANSFER OF FUNCTIONS

For transfer of functions, personnel, assets, and liabilities of the Federal Emergency Management Agency, including the functions of the Director of the Federal Emergency Management Agency relating thereto, to the Secretary of Homeland Security, and for treatment of related references, see former section 313(1) and sections 551(d), 552(d), and 557 of this title and the Department of Homeland Security Reorganization Plan of November 25, 2002, as modified, set out as a note under section 542 of this title.

§316. Preserving the Federal Emergency Management Agency

(a) Distinct entity

The Agency shall be maintained as a distinct entity within the Department.

(b) Reorganization

Section 452 of this title shall not apply to the Agency, including any function or organizational unit of the Agency.

(c) Prohibition on changes to missions

(1) In general

The Secretary may not substantially or significantly reduce the authorities, responsibilities, or functions of the Agency or the capability of the Agency to perform those missions, authorities, responsibilities, except as otherwise specifically provided in an Act enacted after October 4, 2006.

(2) Certain transfers prohibited

No asset, function, or mission of the Agency may be diverted to the principal and continuing use of any other organization, unit, or entity of the Department, except for details or assignments that do not reduce the capability of the Agency to perform its missions.

(d) Reprogramming and transfer of funds

In reprogramming or transferring funds, the Secretary shall comply with any applicable provisions of any Act making appropriations for the Department for fiscal year 2007, or any succeeding fiscal year, relating to the reprogramming or transfer of funds.

(Pub. L. 107–296, title V, §506, as added Pub. L. 109–295, title VI, §611(13), Oct. 4, 2006, 120 Stat. 1400.)

PRIOR PROVISIONS

A prior section 506 of Pub. L. 107–296 was renumbered section 502 and is classified to section 312 of this title.

§317. Regional offices

(a) In general

There are in the Agency 10 regional offices, as identified by the Administrator.

(b) Management of regional offices

(1) Regional Administrator

Each Regional Office shall be headed by a Regional Administrator who shall be appointed by the Administrator, after consulting with State, local, and tribal government officials in the region. Each Regional Administrator shall report directly to the Administrator and be in the Senior Executive Service.

(2) Qualifications

(A) In general

Each Regional Administrator shall be appointed from among individuals who have a demonstrated ability in and knowledge of emergency management and homeland security.

(B) Considerations

In selecting a Regional Administrator for a Regional Office, the Administrator shall consider the familiarity of an individual with the geographical area and demographic characteristics of the population served by such Regional Office.

(c) Responsibilities

(1) In general

The Regional Administrator shall work in partnership with State, local, and tribal governments, emergency managers, emergency response providers, medical providers, the private sector, nongovernmental organizations, multijurisdictional councils of governments, and regional planning commissions and organizations in the geographical area served by the Regional Office to carry out the responsibilities of a Regional Administrator under this section.

(2) Responsibilities

The responsibilities of a Regional Administrator include—

(A) ensuring effective, coordinated, and integrated regional preparedness, protection, response, recovery, and mitigation activities and programs for natural disasters, acts of terrorism, and other man-made disasters (including planning, training, exercises, and professional development);

(B) assisting in the development of regional capabilities needed for a national catastrophic response system;

(C) coordinating the establishment of effective regional operable and interoperable emergency communications capabilities;

(D) staffing and overseeing 1 or more strike teams within the region under subsection (f), to serve as the focal point of the Federal Government's initial response efforts for natural disasters, acts of terrorism, and other man-made disasters within that region, and otherwise building Federal response capabilities to respond to natural disasters, acts of terrorism, and other man-made disasters within that region;

(E) designating an individual responsible for the development of strategic and operational regional plans in support of the National Response Plan;

(F) fostering the development of mutual aid and other cooperative agreements;

(G) identifying critical gaps in regional capabilities to respond to populations with special needs;

(H) maintaining and operating a Regional Response Coordination Center or its successor;

(I) coordinating with the private sector to help ensure private sector preparedness for natural disasters, acts of terrorism, and other man-made disasters;

(J) assisting State, local, and tribal governments, where appropriate, to preidentify and evaluate suitable sites where a multijurisdictional incident command system may quickly be established and operated from, if the need for such a system arises; and

(K) performing such other duties relating to such responsibilities as the Administrator may require.

(3) Training and exercise requirements

(A) Training

The Administrator shall require each Regional Administrator to undergo specific training periodically to complement the qualifications of the Regional Administrator. Such training, as appropriate, shall include training with respect to the National Incident Management System, the National Response Plan, and such other subjects as determined by the Administrator.

(B) Exercises

The Administrator shall require each Regional Administrator to participate as appropriate in regional and national exercises.

(d) Area offices

(1) In general

There is an Area Office for the Pacific and an Area Office for the Caribbean, as components in the appropriate Regional Offices.

(2) Alaska

The Administrator shall establish an Area Office in Alaska, as a component in the appropriate Regional Office.

(e) Regional Advisory Council

(1) Establishment

Each Regional Administrator shall establish a Regional Advisory Council.

(2) Nominations

A State, local, or tribal government located within the geographic area served by the Regional Office may nominate officials, including Adjutants General and emergency managers, to serve as members of the Regional Advisory Council for that region.

(3) Responsibilities

Each Regional Advisory Council shall—

(A) advise the Regional Administrator on emergency management issues specific to that region;

(B) identify any geographic, demographic, or other characteristics peculiar to any State, local, or tribal government within the region that might make preparedness, protection, response, recovery, or mitigation more complicated or difficult; and

(C) advise the Regional Administrator of any weaknesses or deficiencies in preparedness, protection, response, recovery, and mitigation for any State, local, and tribal government within the region of which the Regional Advisory Council is aware.

(f) Regional Office strike teams

(1) In general

In coordination with other relevant Federal agencies, each Regional Administrator shall oversee multi-agency strike teams authorized under section 5144 of title 42 that shall consist of—

(A) a designated Federal coordinating officer;

(B) personnel trained in incident management;

(C) public affairs, response and recovery, and communications support personnel;

(D) a defense coordinating officer;

(E) liaisons to other Federal agencies;

(F) such other personnel as the Administrator or Regional Administrator determines appropriate; and

(G) individuals from the agencies with primary responsibility for each of the emergency support functions in the National Response Plan.

(2) Other duties

The duties of an individual assigned to a Regional Office strike team from another relevant agency when such individual is not functioning as a member of the strike team shall be consistent with the emergency preparedness activities of the agency that employs such individual.

(3) Location of members

The members of each Regional Office strike team, including representatives from agencies other than the Department, shall be based primarily within the region that corresponds to that strike team.

(4) Coordination

Each Regional Office strike team shall coordinate the training and exercises of that strike team with the State, local, and tribal governments and private sector and nongovernmental entities which the strike team shall support when a natural disaster, act of terrorism, or other man-made disaster occurs.

(5) Preparedness

Each Regional Office strike team shall be trained as a unit on a regular basis and equipped and staffed to be well prepared to respond to natural disasters, acts of terrorism, and other man-made disasters, including catastrophic incidents.

(6) Authorities

If the Administrator determines that statutory authority is inadequate for the preparedness and deployment of individuals in strike teams under this subsection, the Administrator shall report to Congress regarding the additional statutory authorities that the Administrator determines are necessary.

(Pub. L. 107–296, title V, §507, as added Pub. L. 109–295, title VI, §611(13), Oct. 4, 2006, 120 Stat. 1401; amended Pub. L. 110–53, title IV, §404, Aug. 3, 2007, 121 Stat. 303.)

PRIOR PROVISIONS

A prior section 317, Pub. L. 107–296, title V, §507, Nov. 25, 2002, 116 Stat. 2214, related to the role of the Federal Emergency Management Agency, prior to repeal by Pub. L. 109–295, title VI, §611(4), Oct. 4, 2006, 120 Stat. 1395.

AMENDMENTS

2007—Subsec. (c)(2)(I) to (K). Pub. L. 110–53 added subpars. (I) and (J) and redesignated former subpar. (I) as (K).

EFFECTIVE DATE

Section effective Mar. 31, 2007, see section 614(b)(3) of Pub. L. 109–295, set out as a note under section 701 of this title.

§318. National Advisory Council

(a) Establishment

Not later than 60 days after October 4, 2006, the Secretary shall establish an advisory body under section 451(a) of this title to ensure effective and ongoing coordination of Federal preparedness, protection, response, recovery, and mitigation for natural disasters, acts of terrorism, and other man-made disasters, to be known as the National Advisory Council.

(b) Responsibilities

(1) In general

The National Advisory Council shall advise the Administrator on all aspects of emergency management. The National Advisory Council shall incorporate State, local, and tribal government and private sector input in the development and revision of the national preparedness goal, the national preparedness system, the National Incident Management System, the National Response Plan, and other related plans and strategies.

(2) Consultation on grants

To ensure input from and coordination with State, local, and tribal governments and emergency response providers, the Administrator shall regularly consult and work with the National Advisory Council on the administration and assessment of grant programs administered by the Department, including with respect to the development of program guidance and the development and evaluation of risk-assessment methodologies, as appropriate.

(c) Membership

(1) In general

The members of the National Advisory Council shall be appointed by the Administrator, and shall, to the extent practicable, represent a geographic (including urban and rural) and substantive cross section of officials, emergency managers, and emergency response providers from State, local, and tribal governments, the private sector, and nongovernmental organizations, including as appropriate—

(A) members selected from the emergency management field and emergency response providers, including fire service, law enforcement, hazardous materials response, emergency medical services, and emergency management personnel, or organizations representing such individuals;

(B) health scientists, emergency and inpatient medical providers, and public health professionals;

(C) experts from Federal, State, local, and tribal governments, and the private sector, representing standards-setting and accrediting organizations, including representatives from the voluntary consensus codes and standards development community, particularly those with expertise in the emergency preparedness and response field;

(D) State, local, and tribal government officials with expertise in preparedness, protection, response, recovery, and mitigation, including Adjutants General;

(E) elected State, local, and tribal government executives;

(F) experts in public and private sector infrastructure protection, cybersecurity, and communications;

(G) representatives of individuals with disabilities and other populations with special needs; and

(H) such other individuals as the Administrator determines to be appropriate.

(2) Coordination with the Departments of Health and Human Services and Transportation

In the selection of members of the National Advisory Council who are health or emergency medical services professionals, the Administrator shall work with the Secretary of Health and Human Services and the Secretary of Transportation.

(3) Ex officio members

The Administrator shall designate 1 or more officers of the Federal Government to serve as ex officio members of the National Advisory Council.

(4) Terms of office

(A) In general

Except as provided in subparagraph (B), the term of office of each member of the National Advisory Council shall be 3 years.

(B) Initial appointments

Of the members initially appointed to the National Advisory Council—

(i) one-third shall be appointed for a term of 1 year; and

(ii) one-third shall be appointed for a term of 2 years.

(d) Applicability of Federal Advisory Committee Act

(1) In general

Notwithstanding section 451(a) of this title and subject to paragraph (2), the Federal Advisory Committee Act (5 U.S.C. App.), including subsections (a), (b), and (d) of section 10 of such Act, and section 552b(c) of title 5 shall apply to the National Advisory Council.

(2) Termination

Section 14(a)(2) of the Federal Advisory Committee Act (5 U.S.C. App.) shall not apply to the National Advisory Council.

(Pub. L. 107–296, title V, §508, as added Pub. L. 109–295, title VI, §611(13), Oct. 4, 2006, 120 Stat. 1403; amended Pub. L. 110–53, title I, §102(a), Aug. 3, 2007, 121 Stat. 293.)

REFERENCES IN TEXT

The Federal Advisory Committee Act, referred to in subsec. (d), is Pub. L. 92–463, Oct. 6, 1972, 86 Stat. 770, as amended, which is set out in the Appendix to Title 5, Government Organization and Employees.

PRIOR PROVISIONS

A prior section 508 of Pub. L. 107–296 was renumbered section 519 and is classified to section 321h of this title.

AMENDMENTS

2007—Subsec. (b). Pub. L. 110–53 designated existing provisions as par. (1), inserted heading, and added par. (2).

EFFECTIVE DATE

Section effective Mar. 31, 2007, see section 614(b)(3) of Pub. L. 109–295, set out as a note under section 701 of this title.

§319. National Integration Center

(a) In general

There is established in the Agency a National Integration Center.

(b) Responsibilities

(1) In general

The Administrator, through the National Integration Center, and in consultation with other Federal departments and agencies and the National Advisory Council, shall ensure ongoing management and maintenance of the National Incident Management System, the National Response Plan, and any successor to such system or plan.

(2) Specific responsibilities

The National Integration Center shall periodically review, and revise as appropriate, the National Incident Management System and the National Response Plan, including—

(A) establishing, in consultation with the Director of the Corporation for National and Community Service, a process to better use volunteers and donations;

(B) improving the use of Federal, State, local, and tribal resources and ensuring the effective use of emergency response providers at emergency scenes; and

(C) revising the Catastrophic Incident Annex, finalizing and releasing the Catastrophic Incident Supplement to the National Response Plan, and ensuring that both effectively address response requirements in the event of a catastrophic incident.

(c) Incident management

(1) In general

(A) National Response Plan

The Secretary, acting through the Administrator, shall ensure that the National Response Plan provides for a clear chain of command to lead and coordinate the Federal response to any natural disaster, act of terrorism, or other man-made disaster.

(B) Administrator

The chain of the command specified in the National Response Plan shall—

(i) provide for a role for the Administrator consistent with the role of the Administrator as the principal emergency management advisor to the President, the Homeland Security Council, and the Secretary under section 313(c)(4) of this title and the responsibility of the Administrator under the Post-Katrina Emergency Management Reform Act of 2006, and the amendments made by that Act, relating to natural disasters, acts of terrorism, and other man-made disasters; and

(ii) provide for a role for the Federal Coordinating Officer consistent with the responsibilities under section 5143(b) of title 42.

(2) Principal Federal Official

The Principal Federal Official (or the successor thereto) shall not—

(A) direct or replace the incident command structure established at the incident; or

(B) have directive authority over the Senior Federal Law Enforcement Official, Federal Coordinating Officer, or other Federal and State officials.

(Pub. L. 107–296, title V, §509, as added Pub. L. 109–295, title VI, §611(13), Oct. 4, 2006, 120 Stat. 1405.)

REFERENCES IN TEXT

The Post-Katrina Emergency Management Reform Act of 2006, referred to in subsec. (c)(1)(B)(i), is title VI of Pub. L. 109–295, Oct. 4, 2006, 120 Stat. 1394. For complete classification of this Act to the Code, see Short Title note set out under section 701 of this title and Tables.

PRIOR PROVISIONS

A prior section 509 of Pub. L. 107–296 was renumbered section 520 and is classified to section 321i of this title.

CHANGE OF NAME

Any reference to the Administrator of the Federal Emergency Management Agency in title VI of Pub. L. 109–295 or an amendment by title VI to be considered to refer and apply to the Director of the Federal Emergency Management Agency until Mar. 31, 2007, see section 612(f)(2) of Pub. L. 109–295, set out as a note under section 313 of this title.

§320. Credentialing and typing

(a) In general

The Administrator shall enter into a memorandum of understanding with the administrators of the Emergency Management Assistance Compact, State, local, and tribal governments, and organizations that represent emergency response providers, to collaborate on developing standards for deployment capabilities, including for credentialing and typing of incident management personnel, emergency response providers, and other personnel (including temporary personnel) and resources likely needed to respond to natural disasters, acts of terrorism, and other man-made disasters.

(b) Distribution

(1) In general

Not later than 1 year after August 3, 2007, the Administrator shall provide the standards developed under subsection (a), including detailed written guidance, to—

(A) each Federal agency that has responsibilities under the National Response Plan to aid that agency with credentialing and typing incident management personnel, emergency response providers, and other personnel (including temporary personnel) and resources likely needed to respond to a natural disaster, act of terrorism, or other man-made disaster; and

(B) State, local, and tribal governments, to aid such governments with credentialing and typing of State, local, and tribal incident management personnel, emergency response providers, and other personnel (including temporary personnel) and resources likely needed to respond to a natural disaster, act of terrorism, or other man-made disaster.

(2) Assistance

The Administrator shall provide expertise and technical assistance to aid Federal, State, local, and tribal government agencies with credentialing and typing incident management personnel, emergency response providers, and other personnel (including temporary personnel) and resources likely needed to respond to a natural disaster, act of terrorism, or other man-made disaster.

(c) Credentialing and typing of personnel

Not later than 6 months after receiving the standards provided under subsection (b), each Federal agency with responsibilities under the National Response Plan shall ensure that incident management personnel, emergency response providers, and other personnel (including temporary personnel) and resources likely needed to respond to a natural disaster, act of terrorism, or other manmade disaster are credentialed and typed in accordance with this section.

(d) Consultation on health care standards

In developing standards for credentialing health care professionals under this section, the Administrator shall consult with the Secretary of Health and Human Services.

(Pub. L. 107–296, title V, §510, as added Pub. L. 109–295, title VI, §611(13), Oct. 4, 2006, 120 Stat. 1406; amended Pub. L. 110–53, title IV, §408, Aug. 3, 2007, 121 Stat. 304.)

PRIOR PROVISIONS

A prior section 510 of Pub. L. 107–296 was renumbered section 521 and is classified to section 321j of this title.

Another prior section 510 of Pub. L. 107–296 was classified to section 321 of this title, prior to repeal by Pub. L. 109–295.

AMENDMENTS

2007—Pub. L. 110–53 designated existing provisions as subsec. (a), inserted heading, substituted "for credentialing and typing of incident management personnel, emergency response providers, and other personnel (including temporary personnel) and" for "credentialing of personnel and typing of", and added subsecs. (b) to (d).

CHANGE OF NAME

Any reference to the Administrator of the Federal Emergency Management Agency in title VI of Pub. L. 109–295 or an amendment by title VI to be considered to refer and apply to the Director of the Federal Emergency Management Agency until Mar. 31, 2007, see section 612(f)(2) of Pub. L. 109–295, set out as a note under section 313 of this title.

§321. The National Infrastructure Simulation and Analysis Center

(a) Definition

In this section, the term "National Infrastructure Simulation and Analysis Center" means the National Infrastructure Simulation and Analysis Center established under section 5195c(d) of title 42.

(b) Authority

(1) In general

There is in the Department the National Infrastructure Simulation and Analysis Center which shall serve as a source of national expertise to address critical infrastructure protection and continuity through support for activities related to—

(A) counterterrorism, threat assessment, and risk mitigation; and

(B) a natural disaster, act of terrorism, or other man-made disaster.

(2) Infrastructure modeling

(A) Particular support

The support provided under paragraph (1) shall include modeling, simulation, and analysis of the systems and assets comprising critical infrastructure, in order to enhance preparedness, protection, response, recovery, and mitigation activities.

(B) Relationship with other agencies

Each Federal agency and department with critical infrastructure responsibilities under Homeland Security Presidential Directive 7, or any successor to such directive, shall establish a formal relationship, including an agreement regarding information sharing, between the elements of such agency or department and the National Infrastructure Simulation and Analysis Center, through the Department.

(C) Purpose

(i) In general

The purpose of the relationship under subparagraph (B) shall be to permit each Federal agency and department described in subparagraph (B) to take full advantage of the capabilities of the National Infrastructure Simulation and Analysis Center (particularly vulnerability and consequence analysis), consistent with its work load capacity and priorities, for real-time response to reported and projected natural disasters, acts of terrorism, and other man-made disasters.

(ii) Recipient of certain support

Modeling, simulation, and analysis provided under this subsection shall be provided to relevant Federal agencies and departments, including Federal agencies and departments with critical infrastructure responsibilities under Homeland Security Presidential Directive 7, or any successor to such directive.

(Pub. L. 107–296, title V, § 511, as added Pub. L. 109–295, title VI, § 611(13), Oct. 4, 2006, 120 Stat. 1406.)

PRIOR PROVISIONS

A prior section 321, Pub. L. 107–296, title V, § 510, as added Pub. L. 108–458, title VII, § 7303(d), Dec. 17, 2004, 118 Stat. 3844, related to urban and other high risk area communications capabilities, prior to repeal by Pub. L. 109–295, title VI, § 611(5), Oct. 4, 2006, 120 Stat. 1395.

§ 321a. Evacuation plans and exercises

(a) In general

Notwithstanding any other provision of law, and subject to subsection (d), grants made to States or local or tribal governments by the Department through the State Homeland Security Grant Program or the Urban Area Security Initiative may be used to—

(1) establish programs for the development and maintenance of mass evacuation plans under subsection (b) in the event of a natural disaster, act of terrorism, or other man-made disaster;

(2) prepare for the execution of such plans, including the development of evacuation routes and the purchase and stockpiling of necessary supplies and shelters; and

(3) conduct exercises of such plans.

(b) Plan development

In developing the mass evacuation plans authorized under subsection (a), each State, local, or tribal government shall, to the maximum extent practicable—

(1) establish incident command and decision making processes;

(2) ensure that State, local, and tribal government plans, including evacuation routes, are coordinated and integrated;

(3) identify primary and alternative evacuation routes and methods to increase evacuation capabilities along such routes such as conversion of two-way traffic to one-way evacuation routes;

(4) identify evacuation transportation modes and capabilities, including the use of mass and public transit capabilities, and coordinating and integrating evacuation plans for all populations including for those individuals located in hospitals, nursing homes, and other institutional living facilities;

(5) develop procedures for informing the public of evacuation plans before and during an evacuation, including individuals—

(A) with disabilities or other special needs, including the elderly;

(B) with limited English proficiency; or

(C) who might otherwise have difficulty in obtaining such information; and

(6) identify shelter locations and capabilities.

(c) Assistance

(1) In general

The Administrator may establish any guidelines, standards, or requirements determined appropriate to administer this section and to ensure effective mass evacuation planning for State, local, and tribal areas.

(2) Requested assistance

The Administrator shall make assistance available upon request of a State, local, or tribal government to assist hospitals, nursing homes, and other institutions that house individuals with special needs to establish, maintain, and exercise mass evacuation plans that are coordinated and integrated into the plans developed by that State, local, or tribal government under this section.

(d) Multipurpose funds

Nothing in this section may be construed to preclude a State, local, or tribal government from using grant funds in a manner that enhances preparedness for a natural or man-made disaster unrelated to an act of terrorism, if such use assists such government in building capabilities for terrorism preparedness.

(Pub. L. 107–296, title V, § 512, as added Pub. L. 109–295, title VI, § 611(13), Oct. 4, 2006, 120 Stat. 1407; amended Pub. L. 110–53, title I, § 102(b), Aug. 3, 2007, 121 Stat. 293.)

AMENDMENTS

2007—Subsec. (b)(5)(A). Pub. L. 110–53 inserted ", including the elderly" after "needs".

CHANGE OF NAME

Any reference to the Administrator of the Federal Emergency Management Agency in title VI of Pub. L. 109–295 or an amendment by title VI to be considered to refer and apply to the Director of the Federal Emergency Management Agency until Mar. 31, 2007, see section 612(f)(2) of Pub. L. 109–295, set out as a note under section 313 of this title.

§ 321b. Disability Coordinator

(a) In general

After consultation with organizations representing individuals with disabilities, the National Council on Disabilities, and the Interagency Coordinating Council on Preparedness and Individuals with Disabilities, established under Executive Order No. 13347, the Administrator shall appoint a Disability Coordinator. The Disability Coordinator shall report directly to the Administrator, in order to ensure that the needs of individuals with disabilities are being properly addressed in emergency preparedness and disaster relief.

(b) Responsibilities

The Disability Coordinator shall be responsible for—

(1) providing guidance and coordination on matters related to individuals with disabilities in emergency planning requirements and relief efforts in the event of a natural disaster, act of terrorism, or other man-made disaster;

(2) interacting with the staff of the Agency, the National Council on Disabilities, the Interagency Coordinating Council on Preparedness and Individuals with Disabilities established under Executive Order No. 13347, other agencies of the Federal Government, and State, local, and tribal government authorities regarding the needs of individuals with disabilities in emergency planning requirements and relief efforts in the event of a natural disaster, act of terrorism, or other man-made disaster;

(3) consulting with organizations that represent the interests and rights of individuals with disabilities about the needs of individuals with disabilities in emergency planning requirements and relief efforts in the event of a natural disaster, act of terrorism, or other man-made disaster;

(4) ensuring the coordination and dissemination of best practices and model evacuation plans for individuals with disabilities;

(5) ensuring the development of training materials and a curriculum for training of emergency response providers, State, local, and tribal government officials, and others on the needs of individuals with disabilities;

(6) promoting the accessibility of telephone hotlines and websites regarding emergency preparedness, evacuations, and disaster relief;

(7) working to ensure that video programming distributors, including broadcasters, cable operators, and satellite television services, make emergency information accessible to individuals with hearing and vision disabilities;

(8) ensuring the availability of accessible transportation options for individuals with disabilities in the event of an evacuation;

(9) providing guidance and implementing policies to ensure that the rights and wishes of individuals with disabilities regarding post-evacuation residency and relocation are respected;

(10) ensuring that meeting the needs of individuals with disabilities are included in the components of the national preparedness system established under section 744 of this title; and

(11) any other duties as assigned by the Administrator.

(Pub. L. 107–296, title V, § 513, as added Pub. L. 109–295, title VI, § 611(13), Oct. 4, 2006, 120 Stat. 1408.)

REFERENCES IN TEXT

Executive Order No. 13347, referred to in subsecs. (a) and (b)(2), is set out as a note under section 314 of this title.

CHANGE OF NAME

Any reference to the Administrator of the Federal Emergency Management Agency in title VI of Pub. L. 109–295 or an amendment by title VI to be considered to refer and apply to the Director of the Federal Emergency Management Agency until Mar. 31, 2007, see section 612(f)(2) of Pub. L. 109–295, set out as a note under section 313 of this title.

§ 321c. Department and Agency officials

(a) Deputy Administrators

The President may appoint, by and with the advice and consent of the Senate, not more than 4 Deputy Administrators to assist the Administrator in carrying out this subchapter.

(b) Cybersecurity and communications

There is in the Department an Assistant Secretary for Cybersecurity and Communications.

(c) United States Fire Administration

The Administrator of the United States Fire Administration shall have a rank equivalent to an assistant secretary of the Department.

(Pub. L. 107–296, title V, § 514, as added Pub. L. 109–295, title VI, § 611(13), Oct. 4, 2006, 120 Stat. 1409.)

EFFECTIVE DATE

Section effective Mar. 31, 2007, see section 614(b)(3) of Pub. L. 109–295, set out as a note under section 701 of this title.

§ 321d. National Operations Center

(a) Definition

In this section, the term "situational awareness" means information gathered from a variety of sources that, when communicated to emergency managers and decision makers, can form the basis for incident management decisionmaking.

(b) Establishment

The National Operations Center is the principal operations center for the Department and shall—

(1) provide situational awareness and a common operating picture for the entire Federal Government, and for State, local, and tribal governments as appropriate, in the event of a natural disaster, act of terrorism, or other man-made disaster; and

(2) ensure that critical terrorism and disaster-related information reaches government decision-makers.

(c) State and local fire service representation

(1) Establishment of position

The Secretary shall, in consultation with the Administrator of the United States Fire Administration, establish a fire service position at the National Operations Center established under subsection (b) to ensure the effective sharing of information between the Federal Government and State and local fire services.

(2) Designation of position

The Secretary shall designate, on a rotating basis, a State or local fire service official for the position described in paragraph (1).

(3) Management

The Secretary shall manage the position established pursuant to paragraph (1) in accordance with such rules, regulations, and practices as govern other similar rotating positions at the National Operations Center.

(Pub. L. 107–296, title V, § 515, as added Pub. L. 109–295, title VI, § 611(13), Oct. 4, 2006, 120 Stat. 1409; amended Pub. L. 110–376, § 8, Oct. 8, 2008, 122 Stat. 4060.)

AMENDMENTS

2008—Subsec. (c). Pub. L. 110–376 added subsec. (c).

§ 321e. Chief Medical Officer

(a) In general

There is in the Department a Chief Medical Officer, who shall be appointed by the President, by and with the advice and consent of the Senate.

(b) Qualifications

The individual appointed as Chief Medical Officer shall possess a demonstrated ability in and knowledge of medicine and public health.

(c) Responsibilities

The Chief Medical Officer shall have the primary responsibility within the Department for medical issues related to natural disasters, acts of terrorism, and other man-made disasters, including—

(1) serving as the principal advisor to the Secretary and the Administrator on medical and public health issues;

(2) coordinating the biodefense activities of the Department;

(3) ensuring internal and external coordination of all medical preparedness and response activities of the Department, including training, exercises, and equipment support;

(4) serving as the Department's primary point of contact with the Department of Agriculture, the Department of Defense, the Department of Health and Human Services, the Department of Transportation, the Department of Veterans Affairs, and other Federal departments or agencies, on medical and public health issues;

(5) serving as the Department's primary point of contact for State, local, and tribal governments, the medical community, and others within and outside the Department, with respect to medical and public health matters;

(6) discharging, in coordination with the Under Secretary for Science and Technology, the responsibilities of the Department related to Project Bioshield; and

(7) performing such other duties relating to such responsibilities as the Secretary may require.

(Pub. L. 107–296, title V, § 516, as added Pub. L. 109–295, title VI, § 611(13), Oct. 4, 2006, 120 Stat. 1409.)

CHANGE OF NAME

Any reference to the Administrator of the Federal Emergency Management Agency in title VI of Pub. L. 109–295 or an amendment by title VI to be considered to refer and apply to the Director of the Federal Emergency Management Agency until Mar. 31, 2007, see section 612(f)(2) of Pub. L. 109–295, set out as a note under section 313 of this title.

§ 321f. Nuclear incident response

(a) In general

At the direction of the Secretary (in connection with an actual or threatened terrorist attack, major disaster, or other emergency in the United States), the Nuclear Incident Response Team shall operate as an organizational unit of the Department. While so operating, the Nuclear Incident Response Team shall be subject to the direction, authority, and control of the Secretary.

(b) Rule of construction

Nothing in this subchapter shall be construed to limit the ordinary responsibility of the Secretary of Energy and the Administrator of the Environmental Protection Agency for organizing, training, equipping, and utilizing their respective entities in the Nuclear Incident Response Team, or (subject to the provisions of this subchapter) from exercising direction, authority, and control over them when they are not operating as a unit of the Department.

(Pub. L. 107–296, title V, § 517, formerly § 504, Nov. 25, 2002, 116 Stat. 2213; renumbered § 517, Pub. L. 109–295, title VI, § 611(6), Oct. 4, 2006, 120 Stat. 1395.)

CODIFICATION

Section was formerly classified to section 314 of this title prior to renumbering by Pub. L. 109–295.

§321g. Conduct of certain public health-related activities

(a) In general

With respect to all public health-related activities to improve State, local, and hospital preparedness and response to chemical, biological, radiological, and nuclear and other emerging terrorist threats carried out by the Department of Health and Human Services (including the Public Health Service), the Secretary of Health and Human Services shall set priorities and preparedness goals and further develop a coordinated strategy for such activities in collaboration with the Secretary.

(b) Evaluation of progress

In carrying out subsection (a), the Secretary of Health and Human Services shall collaborate with the Secretary in developing specific benchmarks and outcome measurements for evaluating progress toward achieving the priorities and goals described in such subsection.

(Pub. L. 107–296, title V, §518, formerly §505, Nov. 25, 2002, 116 Stat. 2213; renumbered §518, Pub. L. 109–295, title VI, §611(6), Oct. 4, 2006, 120 Stat. 1395.)

CODIFICATION

Section was formerly classified to section 315 of this title prior to renumbering by Pub. L. 109–295.

§321h. Use of national private sector networks in emergency response

To the maximum extent practicable, the Secretary shall use national private sector networks and infrastructure for emergency response to chemical, biological, radiological, nuclear, or explosive disasters, and other major disasters.

(Pub. L. 107–296, title V, §519, formerly §508, Nov. 25, 2002, 116 Stat. 2215; renumbered §519, Pub. L. 109–295, title VI, §611(6), Oct. 4, 2006, 120 Stat. 1395.)

CODIFICATION

Section was formerly classified to section 318 of this title prior to renumbering by Pub. L. 109–295.

§321i. Use of commercially available technology, goods, and services

It is the sense of Congress that—

(1) the Secretary should, to the maximum extent possible, use off-the-shelf commercially developed technologies to ensure that the Department's information technology systems allow the Department to collect, manage, share, analyze, and disseminate information securely over multiple channels of communication; and

(2) in order to further the policy of the United States to avoid competing commercially with the private sector, the Secretary should rely on commercial sources to supply the goods and services needed by the Department.

(Pub. L. 107–296, title V, §520, formerly §509, Nov. 25, 2002, 116 Stat. 2215; renumbered §520, Pub. L. 109–295, title VI, §611(6), Oct. 4, 2006, 120 Stat. 1395.)

CODIFICATION

Section was formerly classified to section 319 of this title prior to renumbering by Pub. L. 109–295.

§321j. Procurement of security countermeasures for Strategic National Stockpile

(a) Authorization of appropriations

For the procurement of security countermeasures under section 247d–6b(c) of title 42 (referred to in this section as the "security countermeasures program"), there is authorized to be appropriated up to $5,593,000,000 for the fiscal years 2004 through 2013. Of the amounts appropriated under the preceding sentence, not to exceed $3,418,000,000 may be obligated during the fiscal years 2004 through 2008, of which not to exceed $890,000,000 may be obligated during fiscal year 2004. None of the funds made available under this subsection shall be used to procure countermeasures to diagnose, mitigate, prevent, or treat harm resulting from any naturally occurring infectious disease or other public health threat that are not security countermeasures under section 247d–6b(c)(1)(B) of title 42.[1]

(b) Special reserve fund

For purposes of the security countermeasures program, the term "special reserve fund" means the "Biodefense Countermeasures" appropriations account or any other appropriation made under subsection (a).

(c) Availability

Amounts appropriated under subsection (a) become available for a procurement under the security countermeasures program only upon the approval by the President of such availability for the procurement in accordance with paragraph (6)(B) of such program.

(d) Related authorizations of appropriations

(1) Threat assessment capabilities

For the purpose of carrying out the responsibilities of the Secretary for terror threat assessment under the security countermeasures program, there are authorized to be appropriated such sums as may be necessary for each of the fiscal years 2004 through 2006, for the hiring of professional personnel within the Office of Intelligence and Analysis, who shall be analysts responsible for chemical, biological, radiological, and nuclear threat assessment (including but not limited to analysis of chemical, biological, radiological, and nuclear agents, the means by which such agents could be weaponized or used in a terrorist attack, and the capabilities, plans, and intentions of terrorists and other non-state actors who may have or acquire such agents). All such analysts shall meet the applicable standards and qualifications for the performance of intelligence activities promulgated by the Director of Central Intelligence pursuant to section 403–4[1] of title 50.

(2) Intelligence sharing infrastructure

For the purpose of carrying out the acquisition and deployment of secure facilities (including information technology and physical

[1] See References in Text note below.

infrastructure, whether mobile and temporary, or permanent) sufficient to permit the Secretary to receive, not later than 180 days after July 21, 2004, all classified information and products to which the Under Secretary for Intelligence and Analysis is entitled under part A of subchapter II of this chapter, there are authorized to be appropriated such sums as may be necessary for each of the fiscal years 2004 through 2006.

(Pub. L. 107–296, title V, § 521, formerly § 510, as added Pub. L. 108–276, § 3(b)(2), July 21, 2004, 118 Stat. 852; renumbered § 521, Pub. L. 109–295, title VI, § 611(7), Oct. 4, 2006, 120 Stat. 1395; amended Pub. L. 109–417, title IV, § 403(c), Dec. 19, 2006, 120 Stat. 2874; Pub. L. 110–53, title V, § 531(b)(1)(D), Aug. 3, 2007, 121 Stat. 334.)

REFERENCES IN TEXT

Section 247d–6b(c)(1)(B) of title 42, referred to in subsec. (a), was in the original "section 319F–2(c)(1)(B)", which was translated as meaning section 319F–2(c)(1)(B) of the Public Health Service Act, to reflect the probable intent of Congress.

Section 403–4 of title 50, referred to in subsec. (d)(1), was repealed and a new section 403–4 enacted by Pub. L. 108–458, title I, § 1011(a), Dec. 17, 2004, 118 Stat. 3660, and, as so enacted, section 403–4 no longer relates to promulgation of standards and qualifications for the performance of intelligence activities.

Part A of subchapter II of this chapter, referred to in subsec. (d)(2), was in the original "subtitle A of title II", meaning subtitle A of title II of Pub. L. 107–296, Nov. 25, 2002, 116 Stat. 2145, which is classified generally to part A (§ 121 et seq.) of subchapter II of this chapter. For complete classification of part A to the Code, see Tables.

CODIFICATION

Section was formerly classified to section 320 of this title prior to renumbering by Pub. L. 109–295.

AMENDMENTS

2007—Subsec. (d)(1). Pub. L. 110–53, § 531(b)(1)(D)(i), substituted "Office of Intelligence and Analysis" for "Directorate for Information Analysis and Infrastructure Protection".

Subsec. (d)(2). Pub. L. 110–53, § 531(b)(1)(D)(ii), substituted "Under Secretary for Intelligence and Analysis" for "Under Secretary for Information Analysis and Infrastructure Protection".

2006—Subsec. (a). Pub. L. 109–417, which directed amendment of section 510(a) of the Homeland Security Act of 2002, Pub. L. 107–296, by inserting a new last sentence, was executed to subsec. (a) of this section to reflect the probable intent of Congress and the redesignation of section 510(a) as 521(a) by Pub. L. 109–295, § 611(7).

CHANGE OF NAME

Reference to the Director of Central Intelligence or the Director of the Central Intelligence Agency in the Director's capacity as the head of the intelligence community deemed to be a reference to the Director of National Intelligence. Reference to the Director of Central Intelligence or the Director of the Central Intelligence Agency in the Director's capacity as the head of the Central Intelligence Agency deemed to be a reference to the Director of the Central Intelligence Agency. See section 1081(a), (b) of Pub. L. 108–458, set out as a note under section 401 of Title 50, War and National Defense.

§ 321k. Model standards and guidelines for critical infrastructure workers

(a) In general

Not later than 12 months after August 3, 2007, and in coordination with appropriate national professional organizations, Federal, State, local, and tribal government agencies, and private-sector and nongovernmental entities, the Administrator shall establish model standards and guidelines for credentialing critical infrastructure workers that may be used by a State to credential critical infrastructure workers that may respond to a natural disaster, act of terrorism, or other man-made disaster.

(b) Distribution and assistance

The Administrator shall provide the standards developed under subsection (a), including detailed written guidance, to State, local, and tribal governments, and provide expertise and technical assistance to aid such governments with credentialing critical infrastructure workers that may respond to a natural disaster, act of terrorism, or other manmade disaster.

(Pub. L. 107–296, title V, § 522, as added Pub. L. 110–53, title IV, § 409(a), Aug. 3, 2007, 121 Stat. 305.)

§ 321*l*. Guidance and recommendations

(a) In general

Consistent with their responsibilities and authorities under law, as of the day before August 3, 2007, the Administrator and the Assistant Secretary for Infrastructure Protection, in consultation with the private sector, may develop guidance or recommendations and identify best practices to assist or foster action by the private sector in—

(1) identifying potential hazards and assessing risks and impacts;

(2) mitigating the impact of a wide variety of hazards, including weapons of mass destruction;

(3) managing necessary emergency preparedness and response resources;

(4) developing mutual aid agreements;

(5) developing and maintaining emergency preparedness and response plans, and associated operational procedures;

(6) developing and conducting training and exercises to support and evaluate emergency preparedness and response plans and operational procedures;

(7) developing and conducting training programs for security guards to implement emergency preparedness and response plans and operations procedures; and

(8) developing procedures to respond to requests for information from the media or the public.

(b) Issuance and promotion

Any guidance or recommendations developed or best practices identified under subsection (a) shall be—

(1) issued through the Administrator; and

(2) promoted by the Secretary to the private sector.

(c) Small business concerns

In developing guidance or recommendations or identifying best practices under subsection (a), the Administrator and the Assistant Secretary for Infrastructure Protection shall take into consideration small business concerns (under the meaning given that term in section 632 of title 15), including any need for separate guidance or recommendations or best practices, as necessary and appropriate.

(d) Rule of construction

Nothing in this section may be construed to supersede any requirement established under any other provision of law.

(Pub. L. 107–296, title V, §523, as added Pub. L. 110–53, title IX, §901(a), Aug. 3, 2007, 121 Stat. 364.)

§321m. Voluntary private sector preparedness accreditation and certification program

(a) Establishment

(1) In general

The Secretary, acting through the officer designated under paragraph (2), shall establish and implement the voluntary private sector preparedness accreditation and certification program in accordance with this section.

(2) Designation of officer

The Secretary shall designate an officer responsible for the accreditation and certification program under this section. Such officer (hereinafter referred to in this section as the "designated officer") shall be one of the following:

(A) The Administrator, based on consideration of—

(i) the expertise of the Administrator in emergency management and preparedness in the United States; and

(ii) the responsibilities of the Administrator as the principal advisor to the President for all matters relating to emergency management in the United States.

(B) The Assistant Secretary for Infrastructure Protection, based on consideration of the expertise of the Assistant Secretary in, and responsibilities for—

(i) protection of critical infrastructure;

(ii) risk assessment methodologies; and

(iii) interacting with the private sector on the issues described in clauses (i) and (ii).

(C) The Under Secretary for Science and Technology, based on consideration of the expertise of the Under Secretary in, and responsibilities associated with, standards.

(3) Coordination

In carrying out the accreditation and certification program under this section, the designated officer shall coordinate with—

(A) the other officers of the Department referred to in paragraph (2), using the expertise and responsibilities of such officers; and

(B) the Special Assistant to the Secretary for the Private Sector, based on consideration of the expertise of the Special Assistant in, and responsibilities for, interacting with the private sector.

(b) Voluntary private sector preparedness standards; voluntary accreditation and certification program for the private sector

(1) Accreditation and certification program

Not later than 210 days after August 3, 2007, the designated officer shall—

(A) begin supporting the development and updating, as necessary, of voluntary preparedness standards through appropriate organizations that coordinate or facilitate the development and use of voluntary consensus standards and voluntary consensus standards development organizations; and

(B) in consultation with representatives of appropriate organizations that coordinate or facilitate the development and use of voluntary consensus standards, appropriate voluntary consensus standards development organizations, each private sector advisory council created under section 112(f)(4) of this title, appropriate representatives of State and local governments, including emergency management officials, and appropriate private sector advisory groups, such as sector coordinating councils and information sharing and analysis centers—

(i) develop and promote a program to certify the preparedness of private sector entities that voluntarily choose to seek certification under the program; and

(ii) implement the program under this subsection through any entity with which the designated officer enters into an agreement under paragraph (3)(A), which shall accredit third parties to carry out the certification process under this section.

(2) Program elements

(A) In general

(i) Program

The program developed and implemented under this subsection shall assess whether a private sector entity complies with voluntary preparedness standards.

(ii) Guidelines

In developing the program under this subsection, the designated officer shall develop guidelines for the accreditation and certification processes established under this subsection.

(B) Standards

The designated officer, in consultation with representatives of appropriate organizations that coordinate or facilitate the development and use of voluntary consensus standards, representatives of appropriate voluntary consensus standards development organizations, each private sector advisory council created under section 112(f)(4) of this title, appropriate representatives of State and local governments, including emergency management officials, and appropriate private sector advisory groups such as sector coordinating councils and information sharing and analysis centers—

(i) shall adopt one or more appropriate voluntary preparedness standards that promote preparedness, which may be tailored to address the unique nature of various sectors within the private sector, as necessary and appropriate, that shall be used in the accreditation and certification program under this subsection; and

(ii) after the adoption of one or more standards under clause (i), may adopt additional voluntary preparedness standards or modify or discontinue the use of voluntary preparedness standards for the accreditation and certification program, as necessary and appropriate to promote preparedness.

(C) Submission of recommendations

In adopting one or more standards under subparagraph (B), the designated officer may receive recommendations from any entity described in that subparagraph relating to appropriate voluntary preparedness standards, including appropriate sector specific standards, for adoption in the program.

(D) Small business concerns

The designated officer and any entity with which the designated officer enters into an agreement under paragraph (3)(A) shall establish separate classifications and methods of certification for small business concerns (under the meaning given that term in section 632 of title 15) for the program under this subsection.

(E) Considerations

In developing and implementing the program under this subsection, the designated officer shall—

(i) consider the unique nature of various sectors within the private sector, including preparedness standards, business continuity standards, or best practices, established—

(I) under any other provision of Federal law; or

(II) by any sector-specific agency, as defined under Homeland Security Presidential Directive–7; and

(ii) coordinate the program, as appropriate, with—

(I) other Department private sector related programs; and

(II) preparedness and business continuity programs in other Federal agencies.

(3) Accreditation and certification processes

(A) Agreement

(i) In general

Not later than 210 days after August 3, 2007, the designated officer shall enter into one or more agreements with a highly qualified nongovernmental entity with experience or expertise in coordinating and facilitating the development and use of voluntary consensus standards and in managing or implementing accreditation and certification programs for voluntary consensus standards, or a similarly qualified private sector entity, to carry out accreditations and oversee the certification process under this subsection. An entity entering into an agreement with the designated officer under this clause (hereinafter referred to in this section as a "selected entity") shall not perform certifications under this subsection.

(ii) Contents

A selected entity shall manage the accreditation process and oversee the certification process in accordance with the program established under this subsection and accredit qualified third parties to carry out the certification program established under this subsection.

(B) Procedures and requirements for accreditation and certification

(i) In general

Any selected entity shall collaborate to develop procedures and requirements for the accreditation and certification processes under this subsection, in accordance with the program established under this subsection and guidelines developed under paragraph (2)(A)(ii).

(ii) Contents and use

The procedures and requirements developed under clause (i) shall—

(I) ensure reasonable uniformity in any accreditation and certification processes if there is more than one selected entity; and

(II) be used by any selected entity in conducting accreditations and overseeing the certification process under this subsection.

(iii) Disagreement

Any disagreement among selected entities in developing procedures under clause (i) shall be resolved by the designated officer.

(C) Designation

A selected entity may accredit any qualified third party to carry out the certification process under this subsection.

(D) Disadvantaged business involvement

In accrediting qualified third parties to carry out the certification process under this subsection, a selected entity shall ensure, to the extent practicable, that the third parties include qualified small, minority, women-owned, or disadvantaged business concerns when appropriate. The term "disadvantaged business concern" means a small business that is owned and controlled by socially and economically disadvantaged individuals, as defined in section 124 of title 13, United States Code of Federal Regulations.

(E) Treatment of other certifications

At the request of any entity seeking certification, any selected entity may consider, as appropriate, other relevant certifications acquired by the entity seeking certification. If the selected entity determines that such other certifications are sufficient to meet the certification requirement or aspects of the certification requirement under this section, the selected entity may give credit to the entity seeking certification, as appropriate, to avoid unnecessarily duplicative certification requirements.

(F) Third parties

To be accredited under subparagraph (C), a third party shall—

(i) demonstrate that the third party has the ability to certify private sector entities in accordance with the procedures and requirements developed under subparagraph (B);

(ii) agree to perform certifications in accordance with such procedures and requirements;

(iii) agree not to have any beneficial interest in or any direct or indirect control over—

(I) a private sector entity for which that third party conducts a certification under this subsection; or

(II) any organization that provides preparedness consulting services to private sector entities;

(iv) agree not to have any other conflict of interest with respect to any private sector entity for which that third party conducts a certification under this subsection;

(v) maintain liability insurance coverage at policy limits in accordance with the requirements developed under subparagraph (B); and

(vi) enter into an agreement with the selected entity accrediting that third party to protect any proprietary information of a private sector entity obtained under this subsection.

(G) Monitoring

(i) In general

The designated officer and any selected entity shall regularly monitor and inspect the operations of any third party conducting certifications under this subsection to ensure that the third party is complying with the procedures and requirements established under subparagraph (B) and all other applicable requirements.

(ii) Revocation

If the designated officer or any selected entity determines that a third party is not meeting the procedures or requirements established under subparagraph (B), the selected entity shall—

(I) revoke the accreditation of that third party to conduct certifications under this subsection; and

(II) review any certification conducted by that third party, as necessary and appropriate.

(4) Annual review

(A) In general

The designated officer, in consultation with representatives of appropriate organizations that coordinate or facilitate the development and use of voluntary consensus standards, appropriate voluntary consensus standards development organizations, appropriate representatives of State and local governments, including emergency management officials, and each private sector advisory council created under section 112(f)(4) of this title, shall annually review the voluntary accreditation and certification program established under this subsection to ensure the effectiveness of such program (including the operations and management of such program by any selected entity and the selected entity's inclusion of qualified disadvantaged business concerns under paragraph (3)(D)) and make improvements and adjustments to the program as necessary and appropriate.

(B) Review of standards

Each review under subparagraph (A) shall include an assessment of the voluntary preparedness standard or standards used in the program under this subsection.

(5) Voluntary participation

Certification under this subsection shall be voluntary for any private sector entity.

(6) Public listing

The designated officer shall maintain and make public a listing of any private sector entity certified as being in compliance with the program established under this subsection, if that private sector entity consents to such listing.

(c) Rule of construction

Nothing in this section may be construed as—

(1) a requirement to replace any preparedness, emergency response, or business continuity standards, requirements, or best practices established—

(A) under any other provision of federal law; or

(B) by any sector-specific agency, as those agencies are defined under Homeland Security Presidential Directive-7; or

(2) exempting any private sector entity seeking certification or meeting certification requirements under subsection (b) from compliance with all applicable statutes, regulations, directives, policies, and industry codes of practice.

(Pub. L. 107–296, title V, §524, as added Pub. L. 110–53, title IX, §901(a), Aug. 3, 2007, 121 Stat. 365.)

DEADLINE FOR DESIGNATION OF OFFICER

Pub. L. 110–53, title IX, §901(c), Aug. 3, 2007, 121 Stat. 371, provided that: "The Secretary of Homeland Security shall designate the officer as described in section 524 of the Homeland Security Act of 2002 [6 U.S.C. 321m], as added by subsection (a), by not later than 30 days after the date of the enactment of this Act [Aug. 3, 2007]."

SUBCHAPTER VI—TREATMENT OF CHARITABLE TRUSTS FOR MEMBERS OF THE ARMED FORCES OF THE UNITED STATES AND OTHER GOVERNMENTAL ORGANIZATIONS

§331. Treatment of charitable trusts for members of the Armed Forces of the United States and other governmental organizations

(a) Findings

Congress finds the following:

(1) Members of the Armed Forces of the United States defend the freedom and security of our Nation.

(2) Members of the Armed Forces of the United States have lost their lives while battling the evils of terrorism around the world.

(3) Personnel of the Central Intelligence Agency (CIA) charged with the responsibility

of covert observation of terrorists around the world are often put in harm's way during their service to the United States.

(4) Personnel of the Central Intelligence Agency have also lost their lives while battling the evils of terrorism around the world.

(5) Employees of the Federal Bureau of Investigation (FBI) and other Federal agencies charged with domestic protection of the United States put their lives at risk on a daily basis for the freedom and security of our Nation.

(6) United States military personnel, CIA personnel, FBI personnel, and other Federal agents in the service of the United States are patriots of the highest order.

(7) CIA officer Johnny Micheal Spann became the first American to give his life for his country in the War on Terrorism declared by President George W. Bush following the terrorist attacks of September 11, 2001.

(8) Johnny Micheal Spann left behind a wife and children who are very proud of the heroic actions of their patriot father.

(9) Surviving dependents of members of the Armed Forces of the United States who lose their lives as a result of terrorist attacks or military operations abroad receive a $6,000 death benefit, plus a small monthly benefit.

(10) The current system of compensating spouses and children of American patriots is inequitable and needs improvement.

(b) Designation of Johnny Micheal Spann Patriot Trusts

Any charitable corporation, fund, foundation, or trust (or separate fund or account thereof) which otherwise meets all applicable requirements under law with respect to charitable entities and meets the requirements described in subsection (c) of this section shall be eligible to characterize itself as a "Johnny Micheal Spann Patriot Trust".

(c) Requirements for the designation of Johnny Micheal Spann Patriot Trusts

The requirements described in this subsection are as follows:

(1) Not taking into account funds or donations reasonably necessary to establish a trust, at least 85 percent of all funds or donations (including any earnings on the investment of such funds or donations) received or collected by any Johnny Micheal Spann Patriot Trust must be distributed to (or, if placed in a private foundation, held in trust for) surviving spouses, children, or dependent parents, grandparents, or siblings of 1 or more of the following:

(A) members of the Armed Forces of the United States;

(B) personnel, including contractors, of elements of the intelligence community, as defined in section 401a(4) of title 50;

(C) employees of the Federal Bureau of Investigation; and

(D) officers, employees, or contract employees of the United States Government,

whose deaths occur in the line of duty and arise out of terrorist attacks, military operations, intelligence operations, or law enforcement operations or accidents connected with activities occurring after September 11, 2001, and related to domestic or foreign efforts to curb international terrorism, including the Authorization for Use of Military Force (Public Law 107–40; 115 Stat. 224).

(2) Other than funds or donations reasonably necessary to establish a trust, not more than 15 percent of all funds or donations (or 15 percent of annual earnings on funds invested in a private foundation) may be used for administrative purposes.

(3) No part of the net earnings of any Johnny Micheal Spann Patriot Trust may inure to the benefit of any individual based solely on the position of such individual as a shareholder, an officer or employee of such Trust.

(4) None of the activities of any Johnny Micheal Spann Patriot Trust shall be conducted in a manner inconsistent with any law that prohibits attempting to influence legislation.

(5) No Johnny Micheal Spann Patriot Trust may participate in or intervene in any political campaign on behalf of (or in opposition to) any candidate for public office, including by publication or distribution of statements.

(6) Each Johnny Micheal Spann Patriot Trust shall comply with the instructions and directions of the Director of Central Intelligence, the Attorney General, or the Secretary of Defense relating to the protection of intelligence sources and methods, sensitive law enforcement information, or other sensitive national security information, including methods for confidentially disbursing funds.

(7) Each Johnny Micheal Spann Patriot Trust that receives annual contributions totaling more than $1,000,000 must be audited annually by an independent certified public accounting firm. Such audits shall be filed with the Internal Revenue Service, and shall be open to public inspection, except that the conduct, filing, and availability of the audit shall be consistent with the protection of intelligence sources and methods, of sensitive law enforcement information, and of other sensitive national security information.

(8) Each Johnny Micheal Spann Patriot Trust shall make distributions to beneficiaries described in paragraph (1) at least once every calendar year, beginning not later than 12 months after the formation of such Trust, and all funds and donations received and earnings not placed in a private foundation dedicated to such beneficiaries must be distributed within 36 months after the end of the fiscal year in which such funds, donations, and earnings are received.

(9)(A) When determining the amount of a distribution to any beneficiary described in paragraph (1), a Johnny Micheal Spann Patriot Trust should take into account the amount of any collateral source compensation that the beneficiary has received or is entitled to receive as a result of the death of an individual described in paragraph (1).

(B) Collateral source compensation includes all compensation from collateral sources, including life insurance, pension funds, death benefit programs, and payments by Federal,

State, or local governments related to the death of an individual described in paragraph (1).

(d) Treatment of Johnny Micheal Spann Patriot Trusts

Each Johnny Micheal Spann Patriot Trust shall refrain from conducting the activities described in clauses (i) and (ii) of section 431(20)(A) of title 2 so that a general solicitation of funds by an individual described in paragraph (1) of section 441i(e) of title 2 will be permissible if such solicitation meets the requirements of paragraph (4)(A) of such section.

(e) Notification of Trust beneficiaries

Notwithstanding any other provision of law, and in a manner consistent with the protection of intelligence sources and methods and sensitive law enforcement information, and other sensitive national security information, the Secretary of Defense, the Director of the Federal Bureau of Investigation, or the Director of Central Intelligence, or their designees, as applicable, may forward information received from an executor, administrator, or other legal representative of the estate of a decedent described in subparagraph (A), (B), (C), or (D) of subsection (c)(1) of this section, to a Johnny Micheal Spann Patriot Trust on how to contact individuals eligible for a distribution under subsection (c)(1) of this section for the purpose of providing assistance from such Trust: *Provided*, That, neither forwarding nor failing to forward any information under this subsection shall create any cause of action against any Federal department, agency, officer, agent, or employee.

(f) Regulations

Not later than 90 days after November 25, 2002, the Secretary of Defense, in coordination with the Attorney General, the Director of the Federal Bureau of Investigation, and the Director of Central Intelligence, shall prescribe regulations to carry out this section.

(Pub. L. 107–296, title VI, § 601, Nov. 25, 2002, 116 Stat. 2215.)

REFERENCES IN TEXT

The Authorization for Use of Military Force, referred to in subsec. (c)(1), is Pub. L. 107–40, Sept. 18, 2001, 115 Stat. 224, which is set out as a note under section 1541 of Title 50, War and National Defense.

CHANGE OF NAME

Reference to the Director of Central Intelligence or the Director of the Central Intelligence Agency in the Director's capacity as the head of the intelligence community deemed to be a reference to the Director of National Intelligence. Reference to the Director of Central Intelligence or the Director of the Central Intelligence Agency in the Director's capacity as the head of the Central Intelligence Agency deemed to be a reference to the Director of the Central Intelligence Agency. See section 1081(a), (b) of Pub. L. 108–458, set out as a note under section 401 of Title 50, War and National Defense.

SUBCHAPTER VII—MANAGEMENT

§ 341. Under Secretary for Management

(a) In general

The Under Secretary for Management shall serve as the Chief Management Officer and principal advisor to the Secretary on matters related to the management of the Department, including management integration and transformation in support of homeland security operations and programs. The Secretary, acting through the Under Secretary for Management, shall be responsible for the management and administration of the Department, including the following:

(1) The budget, appropriations, expenditures of funds, accounting, and finance.

(2) Procurement.

(3) Human resources and personnel.

(4) Information technology and communications systems.

(5) Facilities, property, equipment, and other material resources.

(6) Security for personnel, information technology and communications systems, facilities, property, equipment, and other material resources.

(7) Strategic management planning and annual performance planning and identification and tracking of performance measures relating to the responsibilities of the Department.

(8) Grants and other assistance management programs.

(9) The management integration and transformation process, as well as the transition process, to ensure an efficient and orderly consolidation of functions and personnel in the Department and transition, including—

(A) the development of a management integration strategy for the Department, and

(B) before December 1 of any year in which a Presidential election is held, the development of a transition and succession plan, to be made available to the incoming Secretary and Under Secretary for Management, to guide the transition of management functions to a new Administration.

(10) The conduct of internal audits and management analyses of the programs and activities of the Department.

(11) Any other management duties that the Secretary may designate.

(b) Immigration

(1) In general

In addition to the responsibilities described in subsection (a) of this section, the Under Secretary for Management shall be responsible for the following:

(A) Maintenance of all immigration statistical information of the Bureau of Border Security and the Bureau of Citizenship and Immigration Services. Such statistical information shall include information and statistics of the type contained in the publication entitled "Statistical Yearbook of the Immigration and Naturalization Service" prepared by the Immigration and Naturalization Service (as in effect immediately before the date on which the transfer of functions specified under section 251 of this title takes effect), including region-by-region statistics on the aggregate number of applications and petitions filed by an alien (or filed on behalf of an alien) and denied by such bureau, and the reasons for such denials, disaggregated by category of denial and application or petition type.

(B) Establishment of standards of reliability and validity for immigration statistics collected by such bureaus.

(2) Transfer of functions

In accordance with subchapter XII of this chapter, there shall be transferred to the Under Secretary for Management all functions performed immediately before such transfer occurs by the Statistics Branch of the Office of Policy and Planning of the Immigration and Naturalization Service with respect to the following programs:

(A) The Border Patrol program.

(B) The detention and removal program.

(C) The intelligence program.

(D) The investigations program.

(E) The inspections program.

(F) Adjudication of immigrant visa petitions.

(G) Adjudication of naturalization petitions.

(H) Adjudication of asylum and refugee applications.

(I) Adjudications performed at service centers.

(J) All other adjudications performed by the Immigration and Naturalization Service.

(c) Appointment and evaluation

The Under Secretary for Management shall—

(1) be appointed by the President, by and with the advice and consent of the Senate, from among persons who have—

(A) extensive executive level leadership and management experience in the public or private sector;

(B) strong leadership skills;

(C) a demonstrated ability to manage large and complex organizations; and

(D) a proven record in achieving positive operational results;

(2) enter into an annual performance agreement with the Secretary that shall set forth measurable individual and organizational goals; and

(3) be subject to an annual performance evaluation by the Secretary, who shall determine as part of each such evaluation whether the Under Secretary for Management has made satisfactory progress toward achieving the goals set out in the performance agreement required under paragraph (2).

(Pub. L. 107–296, title VII, §701, Nov. 25, 2002, 116 Stat. 2218; Pub. L. 110–53, title XXIV, §2405(a), (b), Aug. 3, 2007, 121 Stat. 548.)

AMENDMENTS

2007—Subsec. (a). Pub. L. 110–53, §2405(a)(1), inserted in introductory provisions "The Under Secretary for Management shall serve as the Chief Management Officer and principal advisor to the Secretary on matters related to the management of the Department, including management integration and transformation in support of homeland security operations and programs."

Subsec. (a)(7). Pub. L. 110–53, §2405(a)(2), added par. (7) and struck out former par. (7) which read as follows: "Identification and tracking of performance measures relating to the responsibilities of the Department."

Subsec. (a)(9). Pub. L. 110–53, §2405(a)(3), added par. (9) and struck out former par. (9) which read as follows: "The transition and reorganization process, to ensure an efficient and orderly transfer of functions and personnel to the Department, including the development of a transition plan."

Subsec. (c). Pub. L. 110–53, §2405(b), added subsec. (c).

CHANGE OF NAME

Bureau of Border Security, referred to in subsec. (b)(1)(A), changed to Bureau of Immigration and Customs Enforcement by Reorganization Plan Modification for the Department of Homeland Security, eff. Mar. 1, 2003, H. Doc. No. 108–32, 108th Congress, 1st Session, set out as a note under section 542 of this title.

DEADLINE FOR APPOINTMENT; INCUMBENT

Pub. L. 110–53, title XXIV, §2405(c), Aug. 3, 2007, 121 Stat. 549, provided that:

"(1) DEADLINE FOR APPOINTMENT.—Not later than 90 days after the date of the enactment of this Act [Aug. 3, 2007], the Secretary of Homeland Security shall name an individual who meets the qualifications of section 701 of the Homeland Security Act (6 U.S.C. 341), as amended by subsections (a) and (b), to serve as the Under Secretary of Homeland Security for Management. The Secretary may submit the name of the individual who serves in the position of Under Secretary of Homeland Security for Management on the date of enactment of this Act together with a statement that informs the Congress that the individual meets the qualifications of such section as so amended.

"(2) INCUMBENT.—The incumbent serving as Under Secretary of Homeland Security for Management on November 4, 2008, is authorized to continue serving in that position until a successor is confirmed, to ensure continuity in the management functions of the Department."

§342. Chief Financial Officer

(a) In general

The Chief Financial Officer shall perform functions as specified in chapter 9 of title 31 and, with respect to all such functions and other responsibilities that may be assigned to the Chief Financial Officer from time to time, shall also report to the Under Secretary for Management.

(b) Program analysis and evaluation function

(1) Establishment of Office of Program Analysis and Evaluation

Not later than 90 days after October 16, 2004, the Secretary shall establish an Office of Program Analysis and Evaluation within the Department (in this section referred to as the "Office").

(2) Responsibilities

The Office shall perform the following functions:

(A) Analyze and evaluate plans, programs, and budgets of the Department in relation to United States homeland security objectives, projected threats, vulnerability assessments, estimated costs, resource constraints, and the most recent homeland security strategy developed pursuant to section 454(b)(2) of this title.

(B) Develop and perform analyses and evaluations of alternative plans, programs, personnel levels, and budget submissions for the Department in relation to United States homeland security objectives, projected threats, vulnerability assessments, estimated costs, resource constraints, and the most recent homeland security strategy developed pursuant to section 454(b)(2) of this title.

(C) Establish policies for, and oversee the integration of, the planning, programming, and budgeting system of the Department.

(D) Review and ensure that the Department meets performance-based budget requirements established by the Office of Management and Budget.

(E) Provide guidance for, and oversee the development of, the Future Years Homeland Security Program of the Department, as specified under section 454 of this title.

(F) Ensure that the costs of Department programs, including classified programs, are presented accurately and completely.

(G) Oversee the preparation of the annual performance plan for the Department and the program and performance section of the annual report on program performance for the Department, consistent with sections 1115 and 1116, respectively, of title 31.

(H) Provide leadership in developing and promoting improved analytical tools and methods for analyzing homeland security planning and the allocation of resources.

(I) Any other responsibilities delegated by the Secretary consistent with an effective program analysis and evaluation function.

(3) Director of Program Analysis and Evaluation

There shall be a Director of Program Analysis and Evaluation, who—

(A) shall be a principal staff assistant to the Chief Financial Officer of the Department for program analysis and evaluation; and

(B) shall report to an official no lower than the Chief Financial Officer.

(4) Reorganization

(A) In general

The Secretary may allocate or reallocate the functions of the Office, or discontinue the Office, in accordance with section 452(a) of this title.

(B) Exemption from limitations

Section 452(b) of this title shall not apply to any action by the Secretary under this paragraph.

(c) Notification regarding transfer or reprogramming of funds

In any case in which appropriations available to the Department or any officer of the Department are transferred or reprogrammed and notice of such transfer or reprogramming is submitted to the Congress (including any officer, office, or Committee of the Congress), the Chief Financial Officer of the Department shall simultaneously submit such notice to the Select Committee on Homeland Security (or any successor to the jurisdiction of that committee) and the Committee on Government Reform of the House of Representatives, and to the Committee on Governmental Affairs of the Senate.

(Pub. L. 107–296, title VII, §702, Nov. 25, 2002, 116 Stat. 2219; Pub. L. 108–330, §§3(d)(1)(B), 6, 7, Oct. 16, 2004, 118 Stat. 1276, 1278, 1279.)

AMENDMENTS

2004—Pub. L. 108–330, §§6, 7, designated existing provisions as subsec. (a), inserted heading, and added subsecs. (b) and (c).

Pub. L. 108–330, §3(d)(1)(B), substituted "shall perform functions as specified in chapter 9 of title 31 and, with respect to all such functions and other responsibilities that may be assigned to the Chief Financial Officer from time to time, shall also report to the Under Secretary for Management" for "shall report to the Secretary, or to another official of the Department, as the Secretary may direct".

CHANGE OF NAME

Select Committee on Homeland Security, which was established by House Resolution 449, One Hundred Seventh Congress, June 19, 2002, and reestablished by section 4 of House Resolution 5, One Hundred Eighth Congress, Jan. 4, 2005, was not reestablished in the One Hundred Ninth Congress. Rule X(1)(i) of the Rules of the House of Representatives, One Hundred Ninth Congress, as amended by section 2 of House Resolution 5, One Hundred Ninth Congress, Jan. 4, 2005, established a Committee on Homeland Security. For jurisdiction of the Select Committee on Homeland Security and of the Committee on Homeland Security, see section 4 of House Resolution 5, One Hundred Eighth Congress, and Rule X(1)(i) of the Rules of the House, One Hundred Ninth Congress.

Committee on Government Reform of House of Representatives changed to Committee on Oversight and Government Reform of House of Representatives by House Resolution No. 6, One Hundred Tenth Congress, Jan. 5, 2007.

Committee on Governmental Affairs of Senate changed to Committee on Homeland Security and Governmental Affairs of Senate, effective Jan. 4, 2005, by Senate Resolution No. 445, One Hundred Eighth Congress, Oct. 9, 2004.

FINDINGS

Pub. L. 108–330, §2, Oct. 16, 2004, 118 Stat. 1275, provided that: "The Congress finds the following:

"(1) Influential financial management leadership is of vital importance to the mission success of the Department of Homeland Security. For this reason, the Chief Financial Officer of the Department must be a key figure in the Department's management.

"(2) To provide a sound financial leadership structure, the provisions of law enacted by the Chief Financial Officers Act of 1990 (Public Law 101–576) [see Short Title of 1990 Amendment note set out under section 501 of Title 31, Money and Finance] provide that the Chief Financial Officer of each of the Federal executive departments is to be a Presidential appointee who reports directly to the Secretary of that department on financial management matters. Because the Department of Homeland Security was only recently created, the provisions enacted by that Act must be amended to include the Department within these provisions.

"(3) The Department of Homeland Security was created by consolidation of 22 separate Federal agencies, each with its own accounting and financial management system. None of these systems was developed with a view to executing the mission of the Department of Homeland Security to prevent terrorist attacks within the United States, reduce the Nation's vulnerability to terrorism, and minimize the damage and assist in the recovery from terrorist attacks. For these reasons, a strong Chief Financial Officer is needed within the Department both to consolidate financial management operations, and to insure that management control systems are comprehensively designed to achieve the mission and execute the strategy of the Department.

"(4) The provisions of law enacted by the Chief Financial Officers Act of 1990 require agency Chief Financial Officers to improve the financial information available to agency managers and the Congress. Those provisions also specify that agency financial management systems must provide for the systematic measurement of performance. In the case of the Department of Homeland Security, therefore, it is vitally important that management control systems be designed with a clear view of a homeland security strategy, including the priorities of the Department in addressing those risks of terrorism deemed most significant based upon a comprehensive assessment of potential threats, vulnerabilities, criticality, and consequences. For this reason, Federal law should be amended to clearly state the responsibilities of the Chief Financial Officer of the Department of Homeland Security to provide management control information, for the benefit of managers within the Department and to help inform the Congress, that permits an assessment of the Department's performance in executing a homeland security strategy."

§ 343. Chief Information Officer

(a) In general

The Chief Information Officer shall report to the Secretary, or to another official of the Department, as the Secretary may direct.

(b) Geospatial information functions

(1) Definitions

As used in this subsection:

(A) Geospatial information

The term "geospatial information" means graphical or digital data depicting natural or manmade physical features, phenomena, or boundaries of the earth and any information related thereto, including surveys, maps, charts, remote sensing data, and images.

(B) Geospatial technology

The term "geospatial technology" means any technology utilized by analysts, specialists, surveyors, photogrammetrists, hydrographers, geodesists, cartographers, architects, or engineers for the collection, storage, retrieval, or dissemination of geospatial information, including—

(i) global satellite surveillance systems;
(ii) global position systems;
(iii) geographic information systems;
(iv) mapping equipment;
(v) geocoding technology; and
(vi) remote sensing devices.

(2) Office of Geospatial Management

(A) Establishment

The Office of Geospatial Management is established within the Office of the Chief Information Officer.

(B) Geospatial Information Officer

(i) Appointment

The Office of Geospatial Management shall be administered by the Geospatial Information Officer, who shall be appointed by the Secretary and serve under the direction of the Chief Information Officer.

(ii) Functions

The Geospatial Information Officer shall assist the Chief Information Officer in carrying out all functions under this section and in coordinating the geospatial information needs of the Department.

(C) Coordination of geospatial information

The Chief Information Officer shall establish and carry out a program to provide for the efficient use of geospatial information, which shall include—

(i) providing such geospatial information as may be necessary to implement the critical infrastructure protection programs;

(ii) providing leadership and coordination in meeting the geospatial information requirements of those responsible for planning, prevention, mitigation, assessment and response to emergencies, critical infrastructure protection, and other functions of the Department; and

(iii) coordinating with users of geospatial information within the Department to assure interoperability and prevent unnecessary duplication.

(D) Responsibilities

In carrying out this subsection, the responsibilities of the Chief Information Officer shall include—

(i) coordinating the geospatial information needs and activities of the Department;

(ii) implementing standards, as adopted by the Director of the Office of Management and Budget under the processes established under section 216 of the E-Government Act of 2002 (44 U.S.C. 3501 note), to facilitate the interoperability of geospatial information pertaining to homeland security among all users of such information within—

(I) the Department;
(II) State and local government; and
(III) the private sector;

(iii) coordinating with the Federal Geographic Data Committee and carrying out the responsibilities of the Department pursuant to Office of Management and Budget Circular A–16 and Executive Order 12906; and

(iv) making recommendations to the Secretary and the Executive Director of the Office for State and Local Government Coordination and Preparedness on awarding grants to—

(I) fund the creation of geospatial data; and

(II) execute information sharing agreements regarding geospatial data with State, local, and tribal governments.

(3) Authorization of appropriations

There are authorized to be appropriated such sums as may be necessary to carry out this subsection for each fiscal year.

(Pub. L. 107–296, title VII, § 703, Nov. 25, 2002, 116 Stat. 2219; Pub. L. 108–458, title VIII, § 8201(b), Dec. 17, 2004, 118 Stat. 3865.)

References in Text

Section 216 of the E-Government Act of 2002, referred to in subsec. (b)(2)(D)(ii), is section 216 of Pub. L. 107–347, which is set out in a note under section 3501 of Title 44, Public Printing and Documents.

Executive Order 12906, referred to in subsec. (b)(2)(D)(iii), is set out as a note under section 1457 of Title 43, Public Lands.

AMENDMENTS

2004—Pub. L. 108–458 designated existing provisions as subsec. (a), inserted heading, and added subsec. (b).

FINDINGS

Pub. L. 108–458, title VIII, §8201(a), Dec. 17, 2004, 118 Stat. 3865, provided that: "Congress makes the following findings:

"(1) Geospatial technologies and geospatial data improve government capabilities to detect, plan for, prepare for, and respond to disasters in order to save lives and protect property.

"(2) Geospatial data improves the ability of information technology applications and systems to enhance public security in a cost-effective manner.

"(3) Geospatial information preparedness in the United States, and specifically in the Department of Homeland Security, is insufficient because of—

"(A) inadequate geospatial data compatibility;

"(B) insufficient geospatial data sharing; and

"(C) technology interoperability barriers."

§344. Chief Human Capital Officer

The Chief Human Capital Officer shall report to the Secretary, or to another official of the Department, as the Secretary may direct and shall ensure that all employees of the Department are informed of their rights and remedies under chapters 12 and 23 of title 5 by—

(1) participating in the 2302(c) Certification Program of the Office of Special Counsel;

(2) achieving certification from the Office of Special Counsel of the Department's compliance with section 2302(c) of title 5; and

(3) informing Congress of such certification not later than 24 months after November 25, 2002.

(Pub. L. 107–296, title VII, §704, Nov. 25, 2002, 116 Stat. 2219.)

§345. Establishment of Officer for Civil Rights and Civil Liberties

(a) In general

The Officer for Civil Rights and Civil Liberties, who shall report directly to the Secretary, shall—

(1) review and assess information concerning abuses of civil rights, civil liberties, and profiling on the basis of race, ethnicity, or religion, by employees and officials of the Department;

(2) make public through the Internet, radio, television, or newspaper advertisements information on the responsibilities and functions of, and how to contact, the Officer;

(3) assist the Secretary, directorates, and offices of the Department to develop, implement, and periodically review Department policies and procedures to ensure that the protection of civil rights and civil liberties is appropriately incorporated into Department programs and activities;

(4) oversee compliance with constitutional, statutory, regulatory, policy, and other requirements relating to the civil rights and civil liberties of individuals affected by the programs and activities of the Department;

(5) coordinate with the Privacy Officer to ensure that—

(A) programs, policies, and procedures involving civil rights, civil liberties, and privacy considerations are addressed in an integrated and comprehensive manner; and

(B) Congress receives appropriate reports regarding such programs, policies, and procedures; and

(6) investigate complaints and information indicating possible abuses of civil rights or civil liberties, unless the Inspector General of the Department determines that any such complaint or information should be investigated by the Inspector General.

(b) Report

The Secretary shall submit to the President of the Senate, the Speaker of the House of Representatives, and the appropriate committees and subcommittees of Congress on an annual basis a report on the implementation of this section, including the use of funds appropriated to carry out this section, and detailing any allegations of abuses described under subsection (a)(1) of this section and any actions taken by the Department in response to such allegations.

(Pub. L. 107–296, title VII, §705, Nov. 25, 2002, 116 Stat. 2219; Pub. L. 108–458, title VIII, §8303, Dec. 17, 2004, 118 Stat. 3867.)

AMENDMENTS

2004—Subsec. (a). Pub. L. 108–458, §8303(1), reenacted heading without change and amended introductory provisions generally. Prior to amendment, introductory provisions read as follows: "The Secretary shall appoint in the Department an Officer for Civil Rights and Civil Liberties, who shall—".

Subsec. (a)(1). Pub. L. 108–458, §8303(2), amended par. (1) generally. Prior to amendment, par. (1) read as follows: "review and assess information alleging abuses of civil rights, civil liberties, and racial and ethnic profiling by employees and officials of the Department; and".

Subsec. (a)(3) to (6). Pub. L. 108–458, §8303(3), (4), added pars. (3) to (6).

§346. Consolidation and co-location of offices

Not later than 1 year after November 25, 2002, the Secretary shall develop and submit to Congress a plan for consolidating and co-locating—

(1) any regional offices or field offices of agencies that are transferred to the Department under this chapter, if such officers[1] are located in the same municipality; and

(2) portions of regional and field offices of other Federal agencies, to the extent such offices perform functions that are transferred to the Secretary under this chapter.

(Pub. L. 107–296, title VII, §706, Nov. 25, 2002, 116 Stat. 2220.)

REFERENCES IN TEXT

This chapter, referred to in pars. (1) and (2), was in the original "this Act", meaning Pub. L. 107–296, Nov. 25, 2002, 116 Stat. 2135, known as the Homeland Security Act of 2002, which is classified principally to this chapter. For complete classification of this Act to the Code, see Short Title note set out under section 101 of this title and Tables.

[1] So in original. Probably should be "offices".

§ 347. Quadrennial homeland security review

(a) Requirement

(1) Quadrennial reviews required

In fiscal year 2009, and every 4 years thereafter, the Secretary shall conduct a review of the homeland security of the Nation (in this section referred to as a "quadrennial homeland security review").

(2) Scope of reviews

Each quadrennial homeland security review shall be a comprehensive examination of the homeland security strategy of the Nation, including recommendations regarding the long-term strategy and priorities of the Nation for homeland security and guidance on the programs, assets, capabilities, budget, policies, and authorities of the Department.

(3) Consultation

The Secretary shall conduct each quadrennial homeland security review under this subsection in consultation with—

(A) the heads of other Federal agencies, including the Attorney General, the Secretary of State, the Secretary of Defense, the Secretary of Health and Human Services, the Secretary of the Treasury, the Secretary of Agriculture, and the Director of National Intelligence;

(B) key officials of the Department; and

(C) other relevant governmental and nongovernmental entities, including State, local, and tribal government officials, members of Congress, private sector representatives, academics, and other policy experts.

(4) Relationship with future years homeland security program

The Secretary shall ensure that each review conducted under this section is coordinated with the Future Years Homeland Security Program required under section 454 of this title.

(b) Contents of review

In each quadrennial homeland security review, the Secretary shall—

(1) delineate and update, as appropriate, the national homeland security strategy, consistent with appropriate national and Department strategies, strategic plans, and Homeland Security Presidential Directives, including the National Strategy for Homeland Security, the National Response Plan, and the Department Security Strategic Plan;

(2) outline and prioritize the full range of the critical homeland security mission areas of the Nation;

(3) describe the interagency cooperation, preparedness of Federal response assets, infrastructure, budget plan, and other elements of the homeland security program and policies of the Nation associated with the national homeland security strategy, required to execute successfully the full range of missions called for in the national homeland security strategy described in paragraph (1) and the homeland security mission areas outlined under paragraph (2);

(4) identify the budget plan required to provide sufficient resources to successfully execute the full range of missions called for in the national homeland security strategy described in paragraph (1) and the homeland security mission areas outlined under paragraph (2);

(5) include an assessment of the organizational alignment of the Department with the national homeland security strategy referred to in paragraph (1) and the homeland security mission areas outlined under paragraph (2); and

(6) review and assess the effectiveness of the mechanisms of the Department for executing the process of turning the requirements developed in the quadrennial homeland security review into an acquisition strategy and expenditure plan within the Department.

(c) Reporting

(1) In general

Not later than December 31 of the year in which a quadrennial homeland security review is conducted, the Secretary shall submit to Congress a report regarding that quadrennial homeland security review.

(2) Contents of report

Each report submitted under paragraph (1) shall include—

(A) the results of the quadrennial homeland security review;

(B) a description of the threats to the assumed or defined national homeland security interests of the Nation that were examined for the purposes of that review;

(C) the national homeland security strategy, including a prioritized list of the critical homeland security missions of the Nation;

(D) a description of the interagency cooperation, preparedness of Federal response assets, infrastructure, budget plan, and other elements of the homeland security program and policies of the Nation associated with the national homeland security strategy, required to execute successfully the full range of missions called for in the applicable national homeland security strategy referred to in subsection (b)(1) and the homeland security mission areas outlined under subsection (b)(2);

(E) an assessment of the organizational alignment of the Department with the applicable national homeland security strategy referred to in subsection (b)(1) and the homeland security mission areas outlined under subsection (b)(2), including the Department's organizational structure, management systems, budget and accounting systems, human resources systems, procurement systems, and physical and technical infrastructure;

(F) a discussion of the status of cooperation among Federal agencies in the effort to promote national homeland security;

(G) a discussion of the status of cooperation between the Federal Government and State, local, and tribal governments in preventing terrorist attacks and preparing for emergency response to threats to national homeland security;

(H) an explanation of any underlying assumptions used in conducting the review; and

(I) any other matter the Secretary considers appropriate.

(3) Public availability

The Secretary shall, consistent with the protection of national security and other sensitive matters, make each report submitted under paragraph (1) publicly available on the Internet website of the Department.

(d) Authorization of appropriations

There are authorized to be appropriated such sums as may be necessary to carry out this section.

(Pub. L. 107–296, title VII, §707, as added Pub. L. 110–53, title XXIV, §2401(a), Aug. 3, 2007, 121 Stat. 543.)

PREPARATION FOR FIRST QUADRENNIAL HOMELAND SECURITY REVIEW

Pub. L. 110–53, title XXIV, §2401(b), Aug. 3, 2007, 121 Stat. 546, provided that:

"(1) IN GENERAL.—During fiscal years 2007 and 2008, the Secretary of Homeland Security shall make preparations to conduct the first quadrennial homeland security review under section 707 of the Homeland Security Act of 2002 [6 U.S.C. 347], as added by subsection (a), in fiscal year 2009, including—

"(A) determining the tasks to be performed;

"(B) estimating the human, financial, and other resources required to perform each task;

"(C) establishing the schedule for the execution of all project tasks;

"(D) ensuring that these resources will be available as needed; and

"(E) all other preparations considered necessary by the Secretary.

"(2) REPORT.—Not later than 60 days after the date of enactment of this Act [Aug. 3, 2007], the Secretary shall submit to Congress and make publicly available on the Internet website of the Department of Homeland Security a detailed resource plan specifying the estimated budget and number of staff members that will be required for preparation of the first quadrennial homeland security review."

SUBCHAPTER VIII—COORDINATION WITH NON-FEDERAL ENTITIES; INSPECTOR GENERAL; UNITED STATES SECRET SERVICE; COAST GUARD; GENERAL PROVISIONS

PART A—COORDINATION WITH NON-FEDERAL ENTITIES

§361. Office for State and Local Government Coordination

(a) Establishment

There is established within the Office of the Secretary the Office for State and Local Government Coordination, to oversee and coordinate departmental programs for and relationships with State and local governments.

(b) Responsibilities

The Office established under subsection (a) of this section shall—

(1) coordinate the activities of the Department relating to State and local government;

(2) assess, and advocate for, the resources needed by State and local government to implement the national strategy for combating terrorism;

(3) provide State and local government with regular information, research, and technical support to assist local efforts at securing the homeland; and

(4) develop a process for receiving meaningful input from State and local government to assist the development of the national strategy for combating terrorism and other homeland security activities.

(Pub. L. 107–296, title VIII, §801, Nov. 25, 2002, 116 Stat. 2220.)

PART B—INSPECTOR GENERAL

§371. Repealed. Pub. L. 108–7, div. L, §104(c)(1), Feb. 20, 2003, 117 Stat. 531

Section, Pub. L. 107–296, title VIII, §811, Nov. 25, 2002, 116 Stat. 2221, related to authority of Secretary of Homeland Security with respect to Inspector General.

PART C—UNITED STATES SECRET SERVICE

§381. Functions transferred

In accordance with subchapter XII of this chapter, there shall be transferred to the Secretary the functions, personnel, assets, and obligations of the United States Secret Service, which shall be maintained as a distinct entity within the Department, including the functions of the Secretary of the Treasury relating thereto.

(Pub. L. 107–296, title VIII, §821, Nov. 25, 2002, 116 Stat. 2224.)

PART D—ACQUISITIONS

§391. Research and development projects

(a) Authority

Until September 30, 2010, and subject to subsection (d), the Secretary may carry out a pilot program under which the Secretary may exercise the following authorities:

(1) In general

When the Secretary carries out basic, applied, and advanced research and development projects, including the expenditure of funds for such projects, the Secretary may exercise the same authority (subject to the same limitations and conditions) with respect to such research and projects as the Secretary of Defense may exercise under section 2371 of title 10 (except for subsections (b) and (f)), after making a determination that the use of a contract, grant, or cooperative agreement for such project is not feasible or appropriate. The annual report required under subsection (b) of this section, as applied to the Secretary by this paragraph, shall be submitted to the President of the Senate and the Speaker of the House of Representatives.

(2) Prototype projects

The Secretary may, under the authority of paragraph (1), carry out prototype projects in accordance with the requirements and conditions provided for carrying out prototype projects under section 845 of the National Defense Authorization Act for Fiscal Year 1994 (Public Law 103–160). In applying the authorities of that section 845, subsection (c) of that section shall apply with respect to prototype projects under this paragraph, and the Secretary shall perform the functions of the Secretary of Defense under subsection (d) thereof.

(b) Report

Not later than 2 years after the effective date of this chapter, and annually thereafter, the Comptroller General shall report to the Committee on Government Reform of the House of Representatives and the Committee on Governmental Affairs of the Senate on—

(1) whether use of the authorities described in subsection (a) of this section attracts nontraditional Government contractors and results in the acquisition of needed technologies; and

(2) if such authorities were to be made permanent, whether additional safeguards are needed with respect to the use of such authorities.

(c) Procurement of temporary and intermittent services

The Secretary may—

(1) procure the temporary or intermittent services of experts or consultants (or organizations thereof) in accordance with section 3109(b) of title 5; and

(2) whenever necessary due to an urgent homeland security need, procure temporary (not to exceed 1 year) or intermittent personal services, including the services of experts or consultants (or organizations thereof), without regard to the pay limitations of such section 3109.

(d) Additional requirements

(1) In general

The authority of the Secretary under this section shall terminate September 30, 2010, unless before that date the Secretary—

(A) issues policy guidance detailing the appropriate use of that authority; and

(B) provides training to each employee that is authorized to exercise that authority.

(2) Report

The Secretary shall provide an annual report to the Committees on Appropriations of the Senate and the House of Representatives, the Committee on Homeland Security and Governmental Affairs of the Senate, and the Committee on Homeland Security of the House of Representatives detailing the projects for which the authority granted by subsection (a) was used, the rationale for its use, the funds spent using that authority, the outcome of each project for which that authority was used, and the results of any audits of such projects.

(e) Definition of nontraditional Government contractor

In this section, the term "nontraditional Government contractor" has the same meaning as the term "nontraditional defense contractor" as defined in section 845(e) of the National Defense Authorization Act for Fiscal Year 1994 (Public Law 103–160; 10 U.S.C. 2371 note).

(Pub. L. 107–296, title VIII, §831, Nov. 25, 2002, 116 Stat. 2224; Pub. L. 110–161, div. E, title V, §572, Dec. 26, 2007, 121 Stat. 2093; Pub. L. 110–329, div. D, title V, §537, Sept. 30, 2008, 122 Stat. 3687; Pub. L. 111–83, title V, §531, Oct. 28, 2009, 123 Stat. 2174.)

REFERENCES IN TEXT

Section 845 of the National Defense Authorization Act for Fiscal Year 1994, referred to in subsecs. (a)(2) and (e), is section 845 of Pub. L. 103–160, which is set out as a note under section 2371 of Title 10, Armed Forces.

The effective date of this chapter, referred to in subsec. (b), is 60 days after Nov. 25, 2002, see section 4 of Pub. L. 107–296, set out as an Effective Date note under section 101 of this title.

AMENDMENTS

2009—Subsec. (a). Pub. L. 111–83, §531(1), substituted "September 30, 2010," for "September 30, 2009" in introductory provisions.

Subsec. (d)(1). Pub. L. 111–83, §531(2), substituted "September 30, 2010," for "September 30, 2009," in introductory provisions.

2008—Subsec. (a). Pub. L. 110–329, §537(1), substituted "Until September 30, 2009 and subject to subsection (d)," for "Until September 30, 2008," in introductory provisions.

Subsecs. (d), (e). Pub. L. 110–329, §537(2), (3), added subsec. (d) and redesignated former subsec. (d) as (e).

2007—Subsec. (a). Pub. L. 110–161 substituted "Until September 30, 2008" for "During the 5-year period following the effective date of this chapter" in introductory provisions.

CHANGE OF NAME

Committee on Government Reform of House of Representatives changed to Committee on Oversight and Government Reform of House of Representatives by House Resolution No. 6, One Hundred Tenth Congress, Jan. 5, 2007.

Committee on Governmental Affairs of Senate changed to Committee on Homeland Security and Governmental Affairs of Senate, effective Jan. 4, 2005, by Senate Resolution No. 445, One Hundred Eighth Congress, Oct. 9, 2004.

§ 392. Personal services

The Secretary—

(1) may procure the temporary or intermittent services of experts or consultants (or organizations thereof) in accordance with section 3109 of title 5; and

(2) may, whenever necessary due to an urgent homeland security need, procure temporary (not to exceed 1 year) or intermittent personal services, including the services of experts or consultants (or organizations thereof), without regard to the pay limitations of such section 3109.

(Pub. L. 107–296, title VIII, §832, Nov. 25, 2002, 116 Stat. 2225.)

§ 393. Special streamlined acquisition authority

(a) Authority

(1) In general

The Secretary may use the authorities set forth in this section with respect to any procurement made during the period beginning on the effective date of this chapter and ending September 30, 2007, if the Secretary determines in writing that the mission of the Department (as described in section 111 of this title) would be seriously impaired without the use of such authorities.

(2) Delegation

The authority to make the determination described in paragraph (1) may not be delegated by the Secretary to an officer of the Department who is not appointed by the President with the advice and consent of the Senate.

(3) Notification

Not later than the date that is 7 days after the date of any determination under paragraph (1), the Secretary shall submit to the Committee on Government Reform of the House of Representatives and the Committee on Governmental Affairs of the Senate—

(A) notification of such determination; and

(B) the justification for such determination.

(b) Increased micro-purchase threshold for certain procurements

(1) In general

The Secretary may designate certain employees of the Department to make procurements described in subsection (a) of this section for which in the administration of section 428 of title 41 the amount specified in subsections (c), (d), and (f) of such section 428 shall be deemed to be $7,500.

(2) Number of employees

The number of employees designated under paragraph (1) shall be—

(A) fewer than the number of employees of the Department who are authorized to make purchases without obtaining competitive quotations, pursuant to section 428(c) of title 41;

(B) sufficient to ensure the geographic dispersal of the availability of the use of the procurement authority under such paragraph at locations reasonably considered to be potential terrorist targets; and

(C) sufficiently limited to allow for the careful monitoring of employees designated under such paragraph.

(3) Review

Procurements made under the authority of this subsection shall be subject to review by a designated supervisor on not less than a monthly basis. The supervisor responsible for the review shall be responsible for no more than 7 employees making procurements under this subsection.

(c) Simplified acquisition procedures

(1) In general

With respect to a procurement described in subsection (a) of this section, the Secretary may deem the simplified acquisition threshold referred to in section 403(11) of title 41 to be—

(A) in the case of a contract to be awarded and performed, or purchase to be made, within the United States, $200,000; and

(B) in the case of a contract to be awarded and performed, or purchase to be made, outside of the United States, $300,000.

(2) Omitted

(d) Application of certain commercial items authorities

(1) In general

With respect to a procurement described in subsection (a) of this section, the Secretary may deem any item or service to be a commercial item for the purpose of Federal procurement laws.

(2) Limitation

The $5,000,000 limitation provided in section 427(a)(2) of title 41 and section 253(g)(1)(B) of title 41 shall be deemed to be $7,500,000 for purposes of property or services under the authority of this subsection.

(3) Certain authority

Authority under a provision of law referred to in paragraph (2) that expires under section 4202(e) of the Clinger-Cohen Act of 1996 (divisions D and E of Public Law 104–106; 10 U.S.C. 2304 note) shall, notwithstanding such section, continue to apply for a procurement described in subsection (a) of this section.

(e) Report

Not later than 180 days after the end of fiscal year 2005, the Comptroller General shall submit to the Committee on Governmental Affairs of the Senate and the Committee on Government Reform of the House of Representatives a report on the use of the authorities provided in this section. The report shall contain the following:

(1) An assessment of the extent to which property and services acquired using authorities provided under this section contributed to the capacity of the Federal workforce to facilitate the mission of the Department as described in section 111 of this title.

(2) An assessment of the extent to which prices for property and services acquired using authorities provided under this section reflected the best value.

(3) The number of employees designated by each executive agency under subsection (b)(1) of this section.

(4) An assessment of the extent to which the Department has implemented subsections (b)(2) and (b)(3) of this section to monitor the use of procurement authority by employees designated under subsection (b)(1) of this section.

(5) Any recommendations of the Comptroller General for improving the effectiveness of the implementation of the provisions of this section.

(Pub. L. 107–296, title VIII, §833, Nov. 25, 2002, 116 Stat. 2225.)

REFERENCES IN TEXT

The effective date of this chapter, referred to in subsec. (a)(1), is 60 days after Nov. 25, 2002, see section 4 of Pub. L. 107–296, set out as an Effective Date note under section 101 of this title.

Section 4202(e) of the Clinger-Cohen Act of 1996, referred to in subsec. (d)(3), is section 4202(e) of Pub. L. 104–106, which is set out as a note under section 2304 of Title 10, Armed Forces.

CODIFICATION

Section is comprised of section 833 of Pub. L. 107–296. Subsec. (c)(2) of section 833 of Pub. L. 107–296 amended section 416 of Title 41, Public Contracts.

CHANGE OF NAME

Committee on Government Reform of House of Representatives changed to Committee on Oversight and Government Reform of House of Representatives by House Resolution No. 6, One Hundred Tenth Congress, Jan. 5, 2007.

Committee on Governmental Affairs of Senate changed to Committee on Homeland Security and Governmental Affairs of Senate, effective Jan. 4, 2005, by Senate Resolution No. 445, One Hundred Eighth Congress, Oct. 9, 2004.

§ 394. Unsolicited proposals

(a) Regulations required

Within 1 year of November 25, 2002, the Federal Acquisition Regulation shall be revised to include regulations with regard to unsolicited proposals.

(b) Content of regulations

The regulations prescribed under subsection (a) of this section shall require that before initiating a comprehensive evaluation, an agency contact point shall consider, among other factors, that the proposal—

(1) is not submitted in response to a previously published agency requirement; and

(2) contains technical and cost information for evaluation and overall scientific, technical or socioeconomic merit, or cost-related or price-related factors.

(Pub. L. 107–296, title VIII, § 834, Nov. 25, 2002, 116 Stat. 2227.)

§ 395. Prohibition on contracts with corporate expatriates

(a) In general

The Secretary may not enter into any contract with a foreign incorporated entity which is treated as an inverted domestic corporation under subsection (b) of this section, or any subsidiary of such an entity.

(b) Inverted domestic corporation

For purposes of this section, a foreign incorporated entity shall be treated as an inverted domestic corporation if, pursuant to a plan (or a series of related transactions)—

(1) the entity completes before, on, or after November 25, 2002, the direct or indirect acquisition of substantially all of the properties held directly or indirectly by a domestic corporation or substantially all of the properties constituting a trade or business of a domestic partnership;

(2) after the acquisition at least 80 percent of the stock (by vote or value) of the entity is held—

(A) in the case of an acquisition with respect to a domestic corporation, by former shareholders of the domestic corporation by reason of holding stock in the domestic corporation; or

(B) in the case of an acquisition with respect to a domestic partnership, by former partners of the domestic partnership by reason of holding a capital or profits interest in the domestic partnership; and

(3) the expanded affiliated group which after the acquisition includes the entity does not have substantial business activities in the foreign country in which or under the law of which the entity is created or organized when compared to the total business activities of such expanded affiliated group.

(c) Definitions and special rules

(1) Rules for application of subsection (b)

In applying subsection (b) of this section for purposes of subsection (a) of this section, the following rules shall apply:

(A) Certain stock disregarded

There shall not be taken into account in determining ownership for purposes of subsection (b)(2) of this section—

(i) stock held by members of the expanded affiliated group which includes the foreign incorporated entity; or

(ii) stock of such entity which is sold in a public offering related to the acquisition described in subsection (b)(1) of this section.

(B) Plan deemed in certain cases

If a foreign incorporated entity acquires directly or indirectly substantially all of the properties of a domestic corporation or partnership during the 4-year period beginning on the date which is 2 years before the ownership requirements of subsection (b)(2) of this section are met, such actions shall be treated as pursuant to a plan.

(C) Certain transfers disregarded

The transfer of properties or liabilities (including by contribution or distribution) shall be disregarded if such transfers are part of a plan a principal purpose of which is to avoid the purposes of this section.

(D) Special rule for related partnerships

For purposes of applying subsection (b) of this section to the acquisition of a domestic partnership, except as provided in regulations, all domestic partnerships which are under common control (within the meaning of section 482 of title 26) shall be treated as I[1] partnership.

(E) Treatment of certain rights

The Secretary shall prescribe such regulations as may be necessary to—

(i) treat warrants, options, contracts to acquire stock, convertible debt instruments, and other similar interests as stock; and

(ii) treat stock as not stock.

(2) Expanded affiliated group

The term "expanded affiliated group" means an affiliated group as defined in section 1504(a) of title 26 (without regard to section 1504(b) of such title), except that section 1504 of such title shall be applied by substituting "more than 50 percent" for "at least 80 percent" each place it appears.

(3) Foreign incorporated entity

The term "foreign incorporated entity" means any entity which is, or but for sub-

[1] So in original.

section (b) of this section would be, treated as a foreign corporation for purposes of title 26.

(4) Other definitions

The terms "person", "domestic", and "foreign" have the meanings given such terms by paragraphs (1), (4), and (5) of section 7701(a) of title 26, respectively.

(d) Waivers

The Secretary shall waive subsection (a) of this section with respect to any specific contract if the Secretary determines that the waiver is required in the interest of national security.

(Pub. L. 107–296, title VIII, §835, Nov. 25, 2002, 116 Stat. 2227; Pub. L. 108–7, div. L, §101(2), Feb. 20, 2003, 117 Stat. 528; Pub. L. 108–334, title V, §523, Oct. 18, 2004, 118 Stat. 1320.)

AMENDMENTS

2004—Subsec. (a). Pub. L. 108–334, §523(1), inserted before period at end ", or any subsidiary of such an entity".

Subsec. (b)(1). Pub. L. 108–334, §523(2), inserted "before, on, or" after "completes".

Subsec. (c)(1)(B). Pub. L. 108–334, §523(3), struck out "which is after November 25, 2002, and" after "beginning on the date".

Subsec. (d). Pub. L. 108–334, §523(4), substituted "national" for "homeland".

2003—Subsec. (d). Pub. L. 108–7 struck out ", or to prevent the loss of any jobs in the United States or prevent the Government from incurring any additional costs that otherwise would not occur" before period at end.

§396. Lead system integrator; financial interests

(a) In general

With respect to contracts entered into after July 1, 2007, and except as provided in subsection (b), no entity performing lead system integrator functions in the acquisition of a major system by the Department of Homeland Security may have any direct financial interest in the development or construction of any individual system or element of any system of systems.

(b) Exception

An entity described in subsection (a) may have a direct financial interest in the development or construction of an individual system or element of a system of systems if—

(1) the Secretary of Homeland Security certifies to the Committees on Appropriations of the Senate and the House of Representatives, the Committee on Homeland Security of the House of Representatives, the Committee on Transportation and Infrastructure of the House of Representatives, the Committee on Homeland Security and Governmental Affairs of the Senate, and the Committee on Commerce, Science and Transportation of the Senate that—

(A) the entity was selected by the Department of Homeland Security as a contractor to develop or construct the system or element concerned through the use of competitive procedures; and

(B) the Department took appropriate steps to prevent any organizational conflict of interest in the selection process; or

(2) the entity was selected by a subcontractor to serve as a lower-tier subcontractor, through a process over which the entity exercised no control.

(c) Construction

Nothing in this section shall be construed to preclude an entity described in subsection (a) from performing work necessary to integrate two or more individual systems or elements of a system of systems with each other.

(d) Regulations update

Not later than July 1, 2007, the Secretary of Homeland Security shall update the acquisition regulations of the Department of Homeland Security in order to specify fully in such regulations the matters with respect to lead system integrators set forth in this section. Included in such regulations shall be: (1) a precise and comprehensive definition of the term "lead system integrator", modeled after that used by the Department of Defense; and (2) a specification of various types of contracts and fee structures that are appropriate for use by lead system integrators in the production, fielding, and sustainment of complex systems.

(Pub. L. 110–28, title VI, §6405, May 25, 2007, 121 Stat. 176.)

CODIFICATION

Section was enacted as part of the U.S. Troop Readiness, Veterans' Care, Katrina Recovery, and Iraq Accountability Appropriations Act, 2007, and not as part of the Homeland Security Act of 2002 which comprises this chapter.

PART E—HUMAN RESOURCES MANAGEMENT

§411. Establishment of human resources management system

(a) Authority

(1) Sense of Congress

It is the sense of Congress that

(A) it is extremely important that employees of the Department be allowed to participate in a meaningful way in the creation of any human resources management system affecting them;

(B) such employees have the most direct knowledge of the demands of their jobs and have a direct interest in ensuring that their human resources management system is conducive to achieving optimal operational efficiencies;

(C) the 21st century human resources management system envisioned for the Department should be one that benefits from the input of its employees; and

(D) this collaborative effort will help secure our homeland.

(2), (3) Omitted

(b) Effect on personnel

(1) Nonseparation or nonreduction in grade or compensation of full-time personnel and part-time personnel holding permanent positions

Except as otherwise provided in this chapter, the transfer under this chapter of full-time personnel (except special Government employees) and part-time personnel holding permanent positions shall not cause any such employee to be separated or reduced in grade or compensation for 1 year after the date of transfer to the Department.

(2) Positions compensated in accordance with Executive Schedule

Any person who, on the day preceding such person's date of transfer pursuant to this chapter, held a position compensated in accordance with the Executive Schedule prescribed in chapter 53 of title 5 and who, without a break in service, is appointed in the Department to a position having duties comparable to the duties performed immediately preceding such appointment shall continue to be compensated in such new position at not less than the rate provided for such position, for the duration of the service of such person in such new position.

(3) Coordination rule

Any exercise of authority under chapter 97 of title 5, including under any system established under such chapter, shall be in conformance with the requirements of this subsection.

(Pub. L. 107–296, title VIII, §841, Nov. 25, 2002, 116 Stat. 2229.)

REFERENCES IN TEXT

This chapter, referred to in subsec. (b)(1), (2), was in the original "this Act", meaning Pub. L. 107–296, Nov. 25, 2002, 116 Stat. 2135, known as the Homeland Security Act of 2002, which is classified principally to this chapter. For complete classification of this Act to the Code, see Short Title note set out under section 101 of this title and Tables.

CODIFICATION

Section is comprised of section 841 of Pub. L. 107–296. Subsec. (a)(2), (3) of section 841 of Pub. L. 107–296 enacted chapter 97 (§9701) of Title 5, Government Organization and Employees.

§412. Labor-management relations

(a) Limitation on exclusionary authority

(1) In general

No agency or subdivision of an agency which is transferred to the Department pursuant to this chapter shall be excluded from the coverage of chapter 71 of title 5 as a result of any order issued under section 7103(b)(1) of such title 5 after June 18, 2002, unless—

(A) the mission and responsibilities of the agency (or subdivision) materially change; and

(B) a majority of the employees within such agency (or subdivision) have as their primary duty intelligence, counterintelligence, or investigative work directly related to terrorism investigation.

(2) Exclusions allowable

Nothing in paragraph (1) shall affect the effectiveness of any order to the extent that such order excludes any portion of an agency or subdivision of an agency as to which—

(A) recognition as an appropriate unit has never been conferred for purposes of chapter 71 of such title 5; or

(B) any such recognition has been revoked or otherwise terminated as a result of a determination under subsection (b)(1) of this section.

(b) Provisions relating to bargaining units

(1) Limitation relating to appropriate units

Each unit which is recognized as an appropriate unit for purposes of chapter 71 of title 5 as of the day before the effective date of this chapter (and any subdivision of any such unit) shall, if such unit (or subdivision) is transferred to the Department pursuant to this chapter, continue to be so recognized for such purposes, unless—

(A) the mission and responsibilities of such unit (or subdivision) materially change; and

(B) a majority of the employees within such unit (or subdivision) have as their primary duty intelligence, counterintelligence, or investigative work directly related to terrorism investigation.

(2) Limitation relating to positions or employees

No position or employee within a unit (or subdivision of a unit) as to which continued recognition is given in accordance with paragraph (1) shall be excluded from such unit (or subdivision), for purposes of chapter 71 of such title 5, unless the primary job duty of such position or employee—

(A) materially changes; and

(B) consists of intelligence, counterintelligence, or investigative work directly related to terrorism investigation.

In the case of any positions within a unit (or subdivision) which are first established on or after the effective date of this chapter and any employees first appointed on or after such date, the preceding sentence shall be applied disregarding subparagraph (A).

(c) Waiver

If the President determines that the application of subsections (a), (b), and (d) of this section would have a substantial adverse impact on the ability of the Department to protect homeland security, the President may waive the application of such subsections 10 days after the President has submitted to Congress a written explanation of the reasons for such determination.

(d) Coordination rule

No other provision of this chapter or of any amendment made by this chapter may be construed or applied in a manner so as to limit, supersede, or otherwise affect the provisions of this section, except to the extent that it does so by specific reference to this section.

(e) Rule of construction

Nothing in section 9701(e) of title 5 shall be considered to apply with respect to any agency or subdivision of any agency, which is excluded from the coverage of chapter 71 of title 5 by virtue of an order issued in accordance with section 7103(b) of such title 5 and the preceding provisions of this section (as applicable), or to any employees of any such agency or subdivision or to any individual or entity representing any such employees or any representatives thereof.

(Pub. L. 107–296, title VIII, §842, Nov. 25, 2002, 116 Stat. 2234.)

REFERENCES IN TEXT

The effective date of this chapter, referred to in subsec. (b), is 60 days after Nov. 25, 2002, see section 4 of Pub. L. 107–296, set out as an Effective Date note under section 101 of this title.

§413. Use of counternarcotics enforcement activities in certain employee performance appraisals

(a) In general

Each subdivision of the Department that is a National Drug Control Program Agency shall include as one of the criteria in its performance appraisal system, for each employee directly or indirectly involved in the enforcement of Federal, State, or local narcotics laws, the performance of that employee with respect to the enforcement of Federal, State, or local narcotics laws, relying to the greatest extent practicable on objective performance measures, including—

(1) the contribution of that employee to seizures of narcotics and arrests of violators of Federal, State, or local narcotics laws; and

(2) the degree to which that employee cooperated with or contributed to the efforts of other employees, either within the Department or other Federal, State, or local agencies, in counternarcotics enforcement.

(b) Definitions

For purposes of this section—

(1) the term "National Drug Control Program Agency" means—

(A) a National Drug Control Program Agency, as defined in section 1701(7) of title 21 (as last in effect); and

(B) any subdivision of the Department that has a significant counternarcotics responsibility, as determined by—

(i) the counternarcotics officer, appointed under section 458 of this title; or

(ii) if applicable, the counternarcotics officer's successor in function (as determined by the Secretary); and

(2) the term "performance appraisal system" means a system under which periodic appraisals of job performance of employees are made, whether under chapter 43 of title 5, or otherwise.

(Pub. L. 107–296, title VIII, §843, as added Pub. L. 108–458, title VII, §7408(a), Dec. 17, 2004, 118 Stat. 3854.)

REFERENCES IN TEXT

For repeal of section 1701 of title 21, referred to in subsec. (b)(1)(A), see section 1712 of Title 21, Food and Drugs.

§414. Homeland Security Rotation Program

(a)[1] Establishment

(1) In general

Not later than 180 days after October 4, 2006, the Secretary shall establish the Homeland Security Rotation Program (in this section referred to as the "Rotation Program") for employees of the Department. The Rotation Program shall use applicable best practices, including those from the Chief Human Capital Officers Council.

(2) Goals

The Rotation Program established by the Secretary shall—

(A) be established in accordance with the Human Capital Strategic Plan of the Department;

(B) provide middle and senior level employees in the Department the opportunity to broaden their knowledge through exposure to other components of the Department;

(C) expand the knowledge base of the Department by providing for rotational assignments of employees to other components;

(D) build professional relationships and contacts among the employees in the Department;

(E) invigorate the workforce with exciting and professionally rewarding opportunities;

(F) incorporate Department human capital strategic plans and activities, and address critical human capital deficiencies, recruitment and retention efforts, and succession planning within the Federal workforce of the Department; and

(G) complement and incorporate (but not replace) rotational programs within the Department in effect on October 4, 2006.

(3) Administration

(A) In general

The Chief Human Capital Officer shall administer the Rotation Program.

(B) Responsibilities

The Chief Human Capital Officer shall

(i) provide oversight of the establishment and implementation of the Rotation Program;

(ii) establish a framework that supports the goals of the Rotation Program and promotes cross-disciplinary rotational opportunities;

(iii) establish eligibility for employees to participate in the Rotation Program and select participants from employees who apply;

(iv) establish incentives for employees to participate in the Rotation Program, including promotions and employment preferences;

(v) ensure that the Rotation Program provides professional education and training;

(vi) ensure that the Rotation Program develops qualified employees and future leaders with broad-based experience throughout the Department;

(vii) provide for greater interaction among employees in components of the Department; and

(viii) coordinate with rotational programs within the Department in effect on October 4, 2006.

(4) Allowances, privileges, and benefits

All allowances, privileges, rights, seniority, and other benefits of employees participating in the Rotation Program shall be preserved.

[1] So in original. There is no subsec. (b).

(5) Reporting

Not later than 180 days after the date of the establishment of the Rotation Program, the Secretary shall submit a report on the status of the Rotation Program, including a description of the Rotation Program, the number of employees participating, and how the Rotation Program is used in succession planning and leadership development to the appropriate committees of Congress.

(Pub. L. 107–296, title VIII, §844, as added Pub. L. 109–295, title VI, §622(a), Oct. 4, 2006, 120 Stat. 1416.)

§415. Homeland Security Education Program

(a) Establishment

The Secretary, acting through the Administrator, shall establish a graduate-level Homeland Security Education Program in the National Capital Region to provide educational opportunities to senior Federal officials and selected State and local officials with homeland security and emergency management responsibilities. The Administrator shall appoint an individual to administer the activities under this section.

(b) Leveraging of existing resources

To maximize efficiency and effectiveness in carrying out the Program, the Administrator shall use existing Department-reviewed Master's Degree curricula in homeland security, including curricula pending accreditation, together with associated learning materials, quality assessment tools, digital libraries, exercise systems and other educational facilities, including the National Domestic Preparedness Consortium, the National Fire Academy, and the Emergency Management Institute. The Administrator may develop additional educational programs, as appropriate.

(c) Student enrollment

(1) Sources

The student body of the Program shall include officials from Federal, State, local, and tribal governments, and from other sources designated by the Administrator.

(2) Enrollment priorities and selection criteria

The Administrator shall establish policies governing student enrollment priorities and selection criteria that are consistent with the mission of the Program.

(3) Diversity

The Administrator shall take reasonable steps to ensure that the student body represents racial, gender, and ethnic diversity.

(d) Service commitment

(1) In general

Before any employee selected for the Program may be assigned to participate in the program, the employee shall agree in writing—

(A) to continue in the service of the agency sponsoring the employee during the 2-year period beginning on the date on which the employee completes the program, unless the employee is involuntarily separated from the service of that agency for reasons other than a reduction in force; and

(B) to pay to the Government the amount of the additional expenses incurred by the Government in connection with the employee's education if the employee is voluntarily separated from the service to the agency before the end of the period described in subparagraph (A).

(2) Payment of expenses

(A) Exemption

An employee who leaves the service of the sponsoring agency to enter into the service of another agency in any branch of the Government shall not be required to make a payment under paragraph (1)(B), unless the head of the agency that sponsored the education of the employee notifies that employee before the date on which the employee enters the service of the other agency that payment is required under that paragraph.

(B) Amount of payment

If an employee is required to make a payment under paragraph (1)(B), the agency that sponsored the education of the employee shall determine the amount of the payment, except that such amount may not exceed the pro rata share of the expenses incurred for the time remaining in the 2-year period.

(3) Recovery of payment

If an employee who is required to make a payment under this subsection does not make the payment, a sum equal to the amount of the expenses incurred by the Government for the education of that employee is recoverable by the Government from the employee or his estate by—

(A) setoff against accrued pay, compensation, amount of retirement credit, or other amount due the employee from the Government; or

(B) such other method as is provided by lay[1] for the recovery of amounts owing to the Government.

(Pub. L. 107–296, title VIII, §845, as added Pub. L. 109–295, title VI, §623(a), Oct. 4, 2006, 120 Stat. 1418.)

CHANGE OF NAME

The reference to the "Administrator" in text probably means the Administrator of the Federal Emergency Management Agency. Any reference to the Administrator of the Federal Emergency Management Agency in title VI of Pub. L. 109–295 or an amendment by title VI to be considered to refer and apply to the Director of the Federal Emergency Management Agency until Mar. 31, 2007, see section 612(f)(2) of Pub. L. 109–295, set out as a note under section 313 of this title.

PART F—FEDERAL EMERGENCY PROCUREMENT FLEXIBILITY

§421. Definition

In this part, the term "executive agency" has the meaning given that term under section 403(1) of title 41.

[1] So in original. Probably should be "law".

(Pub. L. 107–296, title VIII, §851, Nov. 25, 2002, 116 Stat. 2235.)

§422. Procurements for defense against or recovery from terrorism or nuclear, biological, chemical, or radiological attack

The authorities provided in this part apply to any procurement of property or services by or for an executive agency that, as determined by the head of the executive agency, are to be used to facilitate defense against or recovery from terrorism or nuclear, biological, chemical, or radiological attack, but only if a solicitation of offers for the procurement is issued during the 1-year period beginning on November 25, 2002.

(Pub. L. 107–296, title VIII, §852, Nov. 25, 2002, 116 Stat. 2235.)

§423. Increased simplified acquisition threshold for procurements in support of humanitarian or peacekeeping operations or contingency operations

(a) Temporary threshold amounts

For a procurement referred to in section 422 of this title that is carried out in support of a humanitarian or peacekeeping operation or a contingency operation, the simplified acquisition threshold definitions shall be applied as if the amount determined under the exception provided for such an operation in those definitions were—

(1) in the case of a contract to be awarded and performed, or purchase to be made, inside the United States, $200,000; or

(2) in the case of a contract to be awarded and performed, or purchase to be made, outside the United States, $300,000.

(b) Simplified acquisition threshold definitions

In this section, the term "simplified acquisition threshold definitions" means the following:

(1) Section 403(11) of title 41.

(2) Section 259(d) of title 41.

(3) Section 2302(7) of title 10.

(c) Small business reserve

For a procurement carried out pursuant to subsection (a) of this section, section 644(j) of title 15 shall be applied as if the maximum anticipated value identified therein is equal to the amounts referred to in subsection (a) of this section.

(Pub. L. 107–296, title VIII, §853, Nov. 25, 2002, 116 Stat. 2235.)

§424. Increased micro-purchase threshold for certain procurements

In the administration of section 428 of title 41 with respect to a procurement referred to in section 422 of this title, the amount specified in subsections (c), (d), and (f) of such section 428 shall be deemed to be $7,500.

(Pub. L. 107–296, title VIII, §854, Nov. 25, 2002, 116 Stat. 2236.)

§425. Application of certain commercial items authorities to certain procurements

(a) Authority

(1) In general

The head of an executive agency may apply the provisions of law listed in paragraph (2) to a procurement referred to in section 422 of this title without regard to whether the property or services are commercial items.

(2) Commercial item laws

The provisions of law referred to in paragraph (1) are as follows:

(A) Sections 427 and 430 of title 41.

(B) Section 2304(g) of title 10.

(C) Section 253(g) of title 41.

(b) Inapplicability of limitation on use of simplified acquisition procedures

(1) In general

The $5,000,000 limitation provided in section 427(a)(2) of title 41, section 2304(g)(1)(B) of title 10, and section 253(g)(1)(B) of title 41 shall not apply to purchases of property or services to which any of the provisions of law referred to in subsection (a) of this section are applied under the authority of this section.

(2) OMB guidance

The Director of the Office of Management and Budget shall issue guidance and procedures for the use of simplified acquisition procedures for a purchase of property or services in excess of $5,000,000 under the authority of this section.

(c) Continuation of authority for simplified purchase procedures

Authority under a provision of law referred to in subsection (a)(2) of this section that expires under section 4202(e) of the Clinger-Cohen Act of 1996 (divisions D and E of Public Law 104–106; 10 U.S.C. 2304 note) shall, notwithstanding such section, continue to apply for use by the head of an executive agency as provided in subsections (a) and (b) of this section.

(Pub. L. 107–296, title VIII, §855, Nov. 25, 2002, 116 Stat. 2236.)

REFERENCES IN TEXT

Section 4202(e) of the Clinger-Cohen Act of 1996, referred to in subsec. (c), is section 4202(e) of Pub. L. 104–106, which is set out as a note under section 2304 of Title 10, Armed Forces.

§426. Use of streamlined procedures

(a) Required use

The head of an executive agency shall, when appropriate, use streamlined acquisition authorities and procedures authorized by law for a procurement referred to in section 422 of this title, including authorities and procedures that are provided under the following provisions of law:

(1) Federal Property and Administrative Services Act of 1949

In title III of the Federal Property and Administrative Services Act of 1949 [41 U.S.C. 251 et seq.]:

(A) Paragraphs (1), (2), (6), and (7) of subsection (c) of section 303 (41 U.S.C. 253), relating to use of procedures other than competitive procedures under certain circumstances (subject to subsection (e) of such section).

(B) Section 303J (41 U.S.C. 253j), relating to orders under task and delivery order contracts.

(2) Title 10

In chapter 137 of title 10:

(A) Paragraphs (1), (2), (6), and (7) of subsection (c) of section 2304, relating to use of procedures other than competitive procedures under certain circumstances (subject to subsection (e) of such section).

(B) Section 2304c, relating to orders under task and delivery order contracts.

(3) Office of Federal Procurement Policy Act

Paragraphs (1)(B), (1)(D), and (2) of section 18(c) of the Office of Federal Procurement Policy Act (41 U.S.C. 416(c)), relating to inapplicability of a requirement for procurement notice.

(b) Waiver of certain small business threshold requirements

Subclause (II) of section 637(a)(1)(D)(i) of title 15 and clause (ii) of section 657a(b)(2)(A) of title 15 shall not apply in the use of streamlined acquisition authorities and procedures referred to in paragraphs (1)(A) and (2)(A) of subsection (a) of this section for a procurement referred to in section 422 of this title.

(Pub. L. 107–296, title VIII, §856, Nov. 25, 2002, 116 Stat. 2237.)

REFERENCES IN TEXT

The Federal Property and Administrative Services Act of 1949, referred to in subsec. (a)(1), is act June 30, 1949, ch. 288, 63 Stat. 377, as amended. Title III of the Act is classified generally to subchapter IV (§251 et seq.) of chapter 4 of Title 41, Public Contracts. For complete classification of this Act to the Code, see Tables.

§427. Review and report by Comptroller General

(a) Requirements

Not later than March 31, 2004, the Comptroller General shall—

(1) complete a review of the extent to which procurements of property and services have been made in accordance with this part; and

(2) submit a report on the results of the review to the Committee on Governmental Affairs of the Senate and the Committee on Government Reform of the House of Representatives.

(b) Content of report

The report under subsection (a)(2) of this section shall include the following matters:

(1) Assessment

The Comptroller General's assessment of—

(A) the extent to which property and services procured in accordance with this subchapter have contributed to the capacity of the workforce of Federal Government employees within each executive agency to carry out the mission of the executive agency; and

(B) the extent to which Federal Government employees have been trained on the use of technology.

(2) Recommendations

Any recommendations of the Comptroller General resulting from the assessment described in paragraph (1).

(c) Consultation

In preparing for the review under subsection (a)(1) of this section, the Comptroller shall consult with the Committee on Governmental Affairs of the Senate and the Committee on Government Reform of the House of Representatives on the specific issues and topics to be reviewed. The extent of coverage needed in areas such as technology integration, employee training, and human capital management, as well as the data requirements of the study, shall be included as part of the consultation.

(Pub. L. 107–296, title VIII, §857, Nov. 25, 2002, 116 Stat. 2237.)

REFERENCES IN TEXT

This subchapter, referred to in subsec. (b)(1)(A), was in the original "this title", meaning title VIII of Pub. L. 107–296, which enacted this subchapter, chapter 97 of Title 5, Government Organization and Employees, and section 8J of the Inspector General Act of 1978, Pub. L. 95–452, set out in the Appendix to Title 5, amended section 6 of the Inspector General Act of 1978, section 2517 of Title 18, Crimes and Criminal Procedure, Rule 6 of the Federal Rules of Criminal Procedure, set out in the Appendix to Title 18, section 1105 of Title 31, Money and Finance, section 416 of Title 41, Public Contracts, and sections 403–5d, 1806, and 1825 of Title 50, War and National Defense, enacted provisions set out as notes under section 101 of this title, section 6 of the Inspector General Act of 1978, and section 1105 of Title 31, amended provisions set out as notes under section 2517 of Title 18, section 40101 of Title 49, Transportation, and section 2301 of Title 50, and repealed provisions set out as a note under section 1113 of Title 31. For complete classification of title VIII to the Code, see Tables.

CHANGE OF NAME

Committee on Governmental Affairs of Senate changed to Committee on Homeland Security and Governmental Affairs of Senate, effective Jan. 4, 2005, by Senate Resolution No. 445, One Hundred Eighth Congress, Oct. 9, 2004.

Committee on Government Reform of House of Representatives changed to Committee on Oversight and Government Reform of House of Representatives by House Resolution No. 6, One Hundred Tenth Congress, Jan. 5, 2007.

§428. Identification of new entrants into the Federal marketplace

The head of each executive agency shall conduct market research on an ongoing basis to identify effectively the capabilities, including the capabilities of small businesses and new entrants into Federal contracting, that are available in the marketplace for meeting the requirements of the executive agency in furtherance of defense against or recovery from terrorism or nuclear, biological, chemical, or radiological attack. The head of the executive agency shall, to the maximum extent practicable, take advantage of commercially available market research methods, including use of commercial databases, to carry out the research.

(Pub. L. 107–296, title VIII, §858, Nov. 25, 2002, 116 Stat. 2238.)

PART G—SUPPORT ANTI-TERRORISM BY FOSTERING EFFECTIVE TECHNOLOGIES

§441. Administration

(a) In general

The Secretary shall be responsible for the administration of this part.

(b) Designation of qualified anti-terrorism technologies

The Secretary may designate anti-terrorism technologies that qualify for protection under the system of risk management set forth in this part in accordance with criteria that shall include, but not be limited to, the following:

(1) Prior United States Government use or demonstrated substantial utility and effectiveness.

(2) Availability of the technology for immediate deployment in public and private settings.

(3) Existence of extraordinarily large or extraordinarily unquantifiable potential third party liability risk exposure to the Seller or other provider of such anti-terrorism technology.

(4) Substantial likelihood that such anti-terrorism technology will not be deployed unless protections under the system of risk management provided under this part are extended.

(5) Magnitude of risk exposure to the public if such anti-terrorism technology is not deployed.

(6) Evaluation of all scientific studies that can be feasibly conducted in order to assess the capability of the technology to substantially reduce risks of harm.

(7) Anti-terrorism technology that would be effective in facilitating the defense against acts of terrorism, including technologies that prevent, defeat or respond to such acts.

(c) Regulations

The Secretary may issue such regulations, after notice and comment in accordance with section 553 of title 5, as may be necessary to carry out this part.

(Pub. L. 107–296, title VIII, §862, Nov. 25, 2002, 116 Stat. 2238.)

SHORT TITLE

For short title of this part as the "Support Anti-terrorism by Fostering Effective Technologies Act of 2002" or the "SAFETY Act", see section 861 of Pub. L. 107–296, set out as a Short Title note under section 101 of this title.

§442. Litigation management

(a) Federal cause of action

(1) In general

There shall exist a Federal cause of action for claims arising out of, relating to, or resulting from an act of terrorism when qualified anti-terrorism technologies have been deployed in defense against or response or recovery from such act and such claims result or may result in loss to the Seller. The substantive law for decision in any such action shall be derived from the law, including choice of law principles, of the State in which such acts of terrorism occurred, unless such law is inconsistent with or preempted by Federal law. Such Federal cause of action shall be brought only for claims for injuries that are proximately caused by sellers that provide qualified anti-terrorism technology to Federal and non-Federal government customers.

(2) Jurisdiction

Such appropriate district court of the United States shall have original and exclusive jurisdiction over all actions for any claim for loss of property, personal injury, or death arising out of, relating to, or resulting from an act of terrorism when qualified anti-terrorism technologies have been deployed in defense against or response or recovery from such act and such claims result or may result in loss to the Seller.

(b) Special rules

In an action brought under this section for damages the following provisions apply:

(1) Punitive damages

No punitive damages intended to punish or deter, exemplary damages, or other damages not intended to compensate a plaintiff for actual losses may be awarded, nor shall any party be liable for interest prior to the judgment.

(2) Noneconomic damages

(A) In general

Noneconomic damages may be awarded against a defendant only in an amount directly proportional to the percentage of responsibility of such defendant for the harm to the plaintiff, and no plaintiff may recover noneconomic damages unless the plaintiff suffered physical harm.

(B) Definition

For purposes of subparagraph (A), the term "noneconomic damages" means damages for losses for physical and emotional pain, suffering, inconvenience, physical impairment, mental anguish, disfigurement, loss of enjoyment of life, loss of society and companionship, loss of consortium, hedonic damages, injury to reputation, and any other nonpecuniary losses.

(c) Collateral sources

Any recovery by a plaintiff in an action under this section shall be reduced by the amount of collateral source compensation, if any, that the plaintiff has received or is entitled to receive as a result of such acts of terrorism that result or may result in loss to the Seller.

(d) Government contractor defense

(1) In general

Should a product liability or other lawsuit be filed for claims arising out of, relating to, or resulting from an act of terrorism when qualified anti-terrorism technologies approved by the Secretary, as provided in paragraphs (2) and (3) of this subsection, have been deployed in defense against or response or recovery from such act and such claims result or may result in loss to the Seller, there shall be a rebuttable presumption that the government contractor defense applies in such lawsuit. This presumption shall only be overcome by evidence showing that the Seller acted fraudulently or with willful misconduct in submitting information to the Secretary during the course of the Secretary's consideration of such technology under this subsection. This presumption of the government contractor defense shall apply regardless of whether the claim against the Seller arises from a sale of the product to Federal Government or non-Federal Government customers.

(2) Exclusive responsibility

The Secretary will be exclusively responsible for the review and approval of anti-terrorism technology for purposes of establishing a government contractor defense in any product liability lawsuit for claims arising out of, relating to, or resulting from an act of terrorism when qualified anti-terrorism technologies approved by the Secretary, as provided in this paragraph and paragraph (3), have been deployed in defense against or response or recovery from such act and such claims result or may result in loss to the Seller. Upon the Seller's submission to the Secretary for approval of anti-terrorism technology, the Secretary will conduct a comprehensive review of the design of such technology and determine whether it will perform as intended, conforms to the Seller's specifications, and is safe for use as intended. The Seller will conduct safety and hazard analyses on such technology and will supply the Secretary with all such information.

(3) Certificate

For anti-terrorism technology reviewed and approved by the Secretary, the Secretary will issue a certificate of conformance to the Seller and place the anti-terrorism technology on an Approved Product List for Homeland Security.

(e) Exclusion

Nothing in this section shall in any way limit the ability of any person to seek any form of recovery from any person, government, or other entity that—

(1) attempts to commit, knowingly participates in, aids and abets, or commits any act of terrorism, or any criminal act related to or resulting from such act of terrorism; or

(2) participates in a conspiracy to commit any such act of terrorism or any such criminal act.

(Pub. L. 107–296, title VIII, §863, Nov. 25, 2002, 116 Stat. 2239.)

§443. Risk management

(a) In general

(1) Liability insurance required

Any person or entity that sells or otherwise provides a qualified anti-terrorism technology to Federal and non-Federal Government customers ("Seller") shall obtain liability insurance of such types and in such amounts as shall be required in accordance with this section and certified by the Secretary to satisfy otherwise compensable third-party claims arising out of, relating to, or resulting from an act of terrorism when qualified anti-terrorism technologies have been deployed in defense against or response or recovery from such act.

(2) Maximum amount

For the total claims related to 1 such act of terrorism, the Seller is not required to obtain liability insurance of more than the maximum amount of liability insurance reasonably available from private sources on the world market at prices and terms that will not unreasonably distort the sales price of Seller's anti-terrorism technologies.

(3) Scope of coverage

Liability insurance obtained pursuant to this subsection shall, in addition to the Seller, protect the following, to the extent of their potential liability for involvement in the manufacture, qualification, sale, use, or operation of qualified anti-terrorism technologies deployed in defense against or response or recovery from an act of terrorism:

(A) Contractors, subcontractors, suppliers, vendors and customers of the Seller.

(B) Contractors, subcontractors, suppliers, and vendors of the customer.

(4) Third party claims

Such liability insurance under this section shall provide coverage against third party claims arising out of, relating to, or resulting from the sale or use of anti-terrorism technologies.

(b) Reciprocal waiver of claims

The Seller shall enter into a reciprocal waiver of claims with its contractors, subcontractors, suppliers, vendors and customers, and contractors and subcontractors of the customers, involved in the manufacture, sale, use or operation of qualified anti-terrorism technologies, under which each party to the waiver agrees to be responsible for losses, including business interruption losses, that it sustains, or for losses sustained by its own employees resulting from an activity resulting from an act of terrorism when qualified anti-terrorism technologies have been deployed in defense against or response or recovery from such act.

(c) Extent of liability

Notwithstanding any other provision of law, liability for all claims against a Seller arising out of, relating to, or resulting from an act of terrorism when qualified anti-terrorism technologies have been deployed in defense against or response or recovery from such act and such claims result or may result in loss to the Seller, whether for compensatory or punitive damages or for contribution or indemnity, shall not be in an amount greater than the limits of liability insurance coverage required to be maintained by the Seller under this section.

(Pub. L. 107–296, title VIII, §864, Nov. 25, 2002, 116 Stat. 2240.)

§444. Definitions

For purposes of this part, the following definitions apply:

(1) Qualified anti-terrorism technology

For purposes of this part, the term "qualified anti-terrorism technology" means any product, equipment, service (including support services), device, or technology (including information technology) designed, developed, modified, or procured for the specific purpose of preventing, detecting, identifying, or deterring acts of terrorism or limiting the harm such acts might otherwise cause, that is designated as such by the Secretary.

(2) Act of terrorism

(A) The term "act of terrorism" means any act that the Secretary determines meets the requirements under subparagraph (B), as such requirements are further defined and specified by the Secretary.

(B) REQUIREMENTS.—An act meets the requirements of this subparagraph if the act—

(i) is unlawful;

(ii) causes harm to a person, property, or entity, in the United States, or in the case of a domestic United States air carrier or a United States-flag vessel (or a vessel based principally in the United States on which United States income tax is paid and whose insurance coverage is subject to regulation in the United States), in or outside the United States; and

(iii) uses or attempts to use instrumentalities, weapons or other methods designed or intended to cause mass destruction, injury or other loss to citizens or institutions of the United States.

(3) Insurance carrier

The term "insurance carrier" means any corporation, association, society, order, firm, company, mutual, partnership, individual aggregation of individuals, or any other legal entity that provides commercial property and casualty insurance. Such term includes any affiliates of a commercial insurance carrier.

(4) Liability insurance

(A)[1] In general

The term "liability insurance" means insurance for legal liabilities incurred by the insured resulting from—

(i) loss of or damage to property of others;

(ii) ensuing loss of income or extra expense incurred because of loss of or damage to property of others;

(iii) bodily injury (including) to persons other than the insured or its employees; or

(iv) loss resulting from debt or default of another.

(5) Loss

The term "loss" means death, bodily injury, or loss of or damage to property, including business interruption loss.

(6) Non-Federal Government customers

The term "non-Federal Government customers" means any customer of a Seller that is not an agency or instrumentality of the United States Government with authority under Public Law 85–804 [50 U.S.C. 1431 et seq.] to provide for indemnification under certain circumstances for third-party claims against its contractors, including but not limited to State and local authorities and commercial entities.

(Pub. L. 107–296, title VIII, §865, Nov. 25, 2002, 116 Stat. 2241.)

REFERENCES IN TEXT

Public Law 85–804, referred to in par. (6), is Pub. L. 85–804, Aug. 28, 1958, 72 Stat. 972, as amended, which is classified generally to chapter 29 (§1431 et seq.) of Title 50, War and National Defense. For complete classification of this Act to the Code, see Tables.

PART H—MISCELLANEOUS PROVISIONS

§451. Advisory committees

(a) In general

The Secretary may establish, appoint members of, and use the services of, advisory committees, as the Secretary may deem necessary. An advisory committee established under this section may be exempted by the Secretary from Public Law 92–463, but the Secretary shall publish notice in the Federal Register announcing the establishment of such a committee and identifying its purpose and membership. Notwithstanding the preceding sentence, members of an advisory committee that is exempted by the Secretary under the preceding sentence who are special Government employees (as that term is defined in section 202 of title 18) shall be eligible for certifications under subsection (b)(3) of section 208 of title 18 for official actions taken as a member of such advisory committee.

(b) Termination

Any advisory committee established by the Secretary shall terminate 2 years after the date of its establishment, unless the Secretary makes a written determination to extend the advisory committee to a specified date, which shall not be more than 2 years after the date on which such determination is made. The Secretary may make any number of subsequent extensions consistent with this subsection.

(Pub. L. 107–296, title VIII, §871, Nov. 25, 2002, 116 Stat. 2243.)

REFERENCES IN TEXT

Public Law 92–463, referred to in subsec. (a), is Pub. L. 92–463, Oct. 6, 1972, 86 Stat. 770, as amended, known as the Federal Advisory Committee Act, which is set out in the Appendix to Title 5, Government Organization and Employees.

§452. Reorganization

(a) Reorganization

The Secretary may allocate or reallocate functions among the officers of the Department, and may establish, consolidate, alter, or discontinue organizational units within the Department, but only—

(1) pursuant to section 542(b) of this title; or

(2) after the expiration of 60 days after providing notice of such action to the appropriate congressional committees, which shall include an explanation of the rationale for the action.

(b) Limitations

(1) In general

Authority under subsection (a)(1) of this section does not extend to the abolition of any

[1] So in original. No subpar. (B) has been enacted.

agency, entity, organizational unit, program, or function established or required to be maintained by this chapter.

(2) Abolitions

Authority under subsection (a)(2) of this section does not extend to the abolition of any agency, entity, organizational unit, program, or function established or required to be maintained by statute.

(Pub. L. 107–296, title VIII, §872, Nov. 25, 2002, 116 Stat. 2243.)

§453. Use of appropriated funds

(a) Disposal of property

(1) Strict compliance

If specifically authorized to dispose of real property in this chapter or any other Act, the Secretary shall exercise this authority in strict compliance with subchapter IV of chapter 5 of title 40.

(2) Deposit of proceeds

The Secretary shall deposit the proceeds of any exercise of property disposal authority into the miscellaneous receipts of the Treasury in accordance with section 3302(b) of title 31.

(b) Gifts

Except as authorized by section 2601 of title 10 and by section 93 of title 14, gifts or donations of services or property of or for the Department may not be accepted, used, or disposed of unless specifically permitted in advance in an appropriations Act and only under the conditions and for the purposes specified in such appropriations Act.

(c) Budget request

Under section 1105 of title 31, the President shall submit to Congress a detailed budget request for the Department for fiscal year 2004, and for each subsequent fiscal year.

(Pub. L. 107–296, title VIII, §873, Nov. 25, 2002, 116 Stat. 2243; Pub. L. 108–7, div. L, §103(3), Feb. 20, 2003, 117 Stat. 529.)

CODIFICATION

In subsec. (a)(1), "subchapter IV of chapter 5 of title 40" substituted for "section 204 of the Federal Property and Administrative Services Act of 1949 (40 U.S.C. 485)" on authority of Pub. L. 107–217, §5(c), Aug. 21, 2002, 116 Stat. 1303, the first section of which enacted Title 40, Public Buildings, Property, and Works.

AMENDMENTS

2003—Subsec. (b). Pub. L. 108–7 substituted "Except as authorized by section 2601 of title 10 and by section 93 of title 14, gifts" for "Gifts".

§453a. Additional uses of appropriated funds

In fiscal year 2004 and thereafter, unless otherwise provided, funds may be used for purchase of uniforms without regard to the general purchase price limitation for the current fiscal year; purchase of insurance for official motor vehicles operated in foreign countries; entering into contracts with the Department of State to furnish health and medical services to employees and their dependents serving in foreign countries; services authorized by section 3109 of title 5; and the hire and purchase of motor vehicles, as authorized by section 1343 of title 31: *Provided*, That purchase for police-type use of passenger vehicles may be made without regard to the general purchase price limitation for the current fiscal year.

(Pub. L. 108–90, title V, §505, Oct. 1, 2003, 117 Stat. 1153.)

CODIFICATION

Section was enacted as part of the Department of Homeland Security Appropriations Act, 2004, and not as part of the Homeland Security Act of 2002 which comprises this chapter.

§453b. Requirement to buy certain items related to national security interests from American sources; exceptions

(a) Requirement

Except as provided in subsections (c) through (g), funds appropriated or otherwise available to the Department of Homeland Security may not be used for the procurement of an item described in subsection (b) if the item is not grown, reprocessed, reused, or produced in the United States.

(b) Covered items

An item referred to in subsection (a) is any of the following, if the item is directly related to the national security interests of the United States:

(1)[1] An article or item of—

(A) clothing and the materials and components thereof, other than sensors, electronics, or other items added to, and not normally associated with, clothing (and the materials and components thereof);

(B) tents, tarpaulins, covers, textile belts, bags, protective equipment (including but not limited to body armor), sleep systems, load carrying equipment (including but not limited to fieldpacks), textile marine equipment, parachutes, or bandages;

(C) cotton and other natural fiber products, woven silk or woven silk blends, spun silk yarn for cartridge cloth, synthetic fabric or coated synthetic fabric (including all textile fibers and yarns that are for use in such fabrics), canvas products, or wool (whether in the form of fiber or yarn or contained in fabrics, materials, or manufactured articles); or

(D) any item of individual equipment manufactured from or containing such fibers, yarns, fabrics, or materials.

(c) Availability exception

Subsection (a) does not apply to the extent that the Secretary of Homeland Security determines that satisfactory quality and sufficient quantity of any such article or item described in subsection (b)(1) grown, reprocessed, reused, or produced in the United States cannot be procured as and when needed at United States market prices. This section is not applicable to covered items that are, or include, materials determined to be non-available in accordance with

[1] So in original. No par. (2) has been enacted.

Federal Acquisition Regulation 25.104 Nonavailable Articles.

(d) De minimis exception

Notwithstanding subsection (a), the Secretary of Homeland Security may accept delivery of an item covered by subsection (b) that contains non-compliant fibers if the total value of non-compliant fibers contained in the end item does not exceed 10 percent of the total purchase price of the end item.

(e) Exception for certain procurements outside the United States

Subsection (a) does not apply to the following:

(1) Procurements by vessels in foreign waters.

(2) Emergency procurements.

(f) Exception for small purchases

Subsection (a) does not apply to purchases for amounts not greater than the simplified acquisition threshold referred to in section 2304(g) of title 10.

(g) Applicability to contracts and subcontracts for procurement of commercial items

This section is applicable to contracts and subcontracts for the procurement of commercial items not withstanding section 430 of title 41, with the exception of commercial items listed under subsections (b)(1)(C) and (b)(1)(D) above. For the purposes of this section, "commercial" shall be as defined in the Federal Acquisition Regulation—Part 2.

(h) Geographic coverage

In this section, the term "United States" includes the possessions of the United States.

(i) Notification required within 7 days after contract award if certain exceptions applied

In the case of any contract for the procurement of an item described in subsection (b)(1), if the Secretary of Homeland Security applies an exception set forth in subsection (c) with respect to that contract, the Secretary shall, not later than 7 days after the award of the contract, post a notification that the exception has been applied on the Internet site maintained by the General Services Administration known as FedBizOps.gov (or any successor site).

(j) Training during fiscal year 2009

(1) In general

The Secretary of Homeland Security shall ensure that each member of the acquisition workforce in the Department of Homeland Security who participates personally and substantially in the acquisition of textiles on a regular basis receives training during fiscal year 2009 on the requirements of this section and the regulations implementing this section.

(2) Inclusion of information in new training programs

The Secretary shall ensure that any training program for the acquisition workforce developed or implemented after February 17, 2009, includes comprehensive information on the requirements described in paragraph (1).

(k) Consistency with international agreements

This section shall be applied in a manner consistent with United States obligations under international agreements.

(*l*) Effective date

This section applies with respect to contracts entered into by the Department of Homeland Security 180 days after February 17, 2009.

(Pub. L. 111–5, div. A, title VI, §604, Feb. 17, 2009, 123 Stat. 165.)

CODIFICATION

Section was enacted as part of the American Recovery and Reinvestment Act of 2009, and not as part of the Homeland Security Act of 2002 which comprises this chapter.

§454. Future Years Homeland Security Program

(a) In general

Each budget request submitted to Congress for the Department under section 1105 of title 31 shall, at or about the same time, be accompanied by a Future Years Homeland Security Program.

(b) Contents

The Future Years Homeland Security Program under subsection (a) of this section shall—

(1) include the same type of information, organizational structure, and level of detail as the future years defense program submitted to Congress by the Secretary of Defense under section 221 of title 10;

(2) set forth the homeland security strategy of the Department, which shall be developed and updated as appropriate annually by the Secretary, that was used to develop program planning guidance for the Future Years Homeland Security Program; and

(3) include an explanation of how the resource allocations included in the Future Years Homeland Security Program correlate to the homeland security strategy set forth under paragraph (2).

(c) Effective date

This section shall take effect with respect to the preparation and submission of the fiscal year 2005 budget request for the Department and for any subsequent fiscal year, except that the first Future Years Homeland Security Program shall be submitted not later than 90 days after the Department's fiscal year 2005 budget request is submitted to Congress.

(Pub. L. 107–296, title VIII, §874, Nov. 25, 2002, 116 Stat. 2244; Pub. L. 108–330, §5, Oct. 16, 2004, 118 Stat. 1278.)

AMENDMENTS

2004—Subsec. (b). Pub. L. 108–330 added subsec. (b) and struck out heading and text of former subsec. (b). Text read as follows: "The Future Years Homeland Security Program under subsection (a) of this section shall be structured, and include the same type of information and level of detail, as the Future Years Defense Program submitted to Congress by the Department of Defense under section 221 of title 10."

§455. Miscellaneous authorities

(a) Seal

The Department shall have a seal, whose design is subject to the approval of the President.

(b) Participation of members of the Armed Forces

With respect to the Department, the Secretary shall have the same authorities that the Secretary of Transportation has with respect to the Department of Transportation under section 324 of title 49.

(c) Redelegation of functions

Unless otherwise provided in the delegation or by law, any function delegated under this chapter may be redelegated to any subordinate.

(Pub. L. 107–296, title VIII, § 875, Nov. 25, 2002, 116 Stat. 2244.)

§ 456. Military activities

Nothing in this chapter shall confer upon the Secretary any authority to engage in warfighting, the military defense of the United States, or other military activities, nor shall anything in this chapter limit the existing authority of the Department of Defense or the Armed Forces to engage in warfighting, the military defense of the United States, or other military activities.

(Pub. L. 107–296, title VIII, § 876, Nov. 25, 2002, 116 Stat. 2244.)

§ 457. Regulatory authority and preemption

(a) Regulatory authority

Except as otherwise provided in sections 186(c) and 441(c) of this title and section 1315 of title 40,[1] this chapter vests no new regulatory authority in the Secretary or any other Federal official, and transfers to the Secretary or another Federal official only such regulatory authority as exists on November 25, 2002, within any agency, program, or function transferred to the Department pursuant to this chapter, or that on November 25, 2002, is exercised by another official of the executive branch with respect to such agency, program, or function. Any such transferred authority may not be exercised by an official from whom it is transferred upon transfer of such agency, program, or function to the Secretary or another Federal official pursuant to this chapter. This chapter may not be construed as altering or diminishing the regulatory authority of any other executive agency, except to the extent that this chapter transfers such authority from the agency.

(b) Preemption of State or local law

Except as otherwise provided in this chapter, this chapter preempts no State or local law, except that any authority to preempt State or local law vested in any Federal agency or official transferred to the Department pursuant to this chapter shall be transferred to the Department effective on the date of the transfer to the Department of that Federal agency or official.

(Pub. L. 107–296, title VIII, § 877, Nov. 25, 2002, 116 Stat. 2244.)

REFERENCES IN TEXT

Section 1315 of title 40, referred to in subsec. (a), was in the original "1706(b)", meaning section 1706(b) of Pub. L. 107–296, which amended generally section 1315 of Title 40, Public Buildings, Property, and Works, and enacted provisions set out as a note under section 1315 of Title 40. For complete classification of section 1706(b) to the Code, see Tables.

This chapter, referred to in text, was in the original "this Act", meaning Pub. L. 107–296, Nov. 25, 2002, 116 Stat. 2135, known as the Homeland Security Act of 2002, which is classified principally to this chapter. For complete classification of this Act to the Code, see Short Title note set out under section 101 of this title and Tables.

[1] See References in Text note below.

§ 458. Office of Counternarcotics Enforcement

(a) Office

There is established in the Department an Office of Counternarcotics Enforcement, which shall be headed by a Director appointed by the President, by and with the advice and consent of the Senate.

(b) Assignment of personnel

(1) In general

The Secretary shall assign permanent staff to the Office, consistent with effective management of Department resources.

(2) Liaisons

The Secretary shall designate senior employees from each appropriate subdivision of the Department that has significant counternarcotics responsibilities to act as a liaison between that subdivision and the Office of Counternarcotics Enforcement.

(c) Limitation on concurrent employment

The Director of the Office of Counternarcotics Enforcement shall not be employed by, assigned to, or serve as the head of, any other branch of the Federal Government, any State or local government, or any subdivision of the Department other than the Office of Counternarcotics Enforcement.

(d) Responsibilities

The Secretary shall direct the Director of the Office of Counternarcotics Enforcement—

(1) to coordinate policy and operations within the Department, between the Department and other Federal departments and agencies, and between the Department and State and local agencies with respect to stopping the entry of illegal drugs into the United States;

(2) to ensure the adequacy of resources within the Department for stopping the entry of illegal drugs into the United States;

(3) to recommend the appropriate financial and personnel resources necessary to help the Department better fulfill its responsibility to stop the entry of illegal drugs into the United States;

(4) within the Joint Terrorism Task Force construct to track and sever connections between illegal drug trafficking and terrorism; and

(5) to be a representative of the Department on all task forces, committees, or other entities whose purpose is to coordinate the counternarcotics enforcement activities of the Department and other Federal, State or local agencies.

(e) Savings clause

Nothing in this section shall be construed to authorize direct control of the operations conducted by the Directorate of Border and Transportation Security, the Coast Guard, or joint terrorism task forces.

(f) Reports to Congress

(1) Annual budget review

The Director of the Office of Counternarcotics Enforcement shall, not later than 30 days after the submission by the President to Congress of any request for expenditures for the Department, submit to the Committees on Appropriations and the authorizing committees of jurisdiction of the House of Representatives and the Senate a review and evaluation of such request. The review and evaluation shall—

(A) identify any request or subpart of any request that affects or may affect the counternarcotics activities of the Department or any of its subdivisions, or that affects the ability of the Department or any subdivision of the Department to meet its responsibility to stop the entry of illegal drugs into the United States;

(B) describe with particularity how such requested funds would be or could be expended in furtherance of counternarcotics activities; and

(C) compare such requests with requests for expenditures and amounts appropriated by Congress in the previous fiscal year.

(2) Evaluation of counternarcotics activities

The Director of the Office of Counternarcotics Enforcement shall, not later than February 1 of each year, submit to the Committees on Appropriations and the authorizing committees of jurisdiction of the House of Representatives and the Senate a review and evaluation of the counternarcotics activities of the Department for the previous fiscal year. The review and evaluation shall—

(A) describe the counternarcotics activities of the Department and each subdivision of the Department (whether individually or in cooperation with other subdivisions of the Department, or in cooperation with other branches of the Federal Government or with State or local agencies), including the methods, procedures, and systems (including computer systems) for collecting, analyzing, sharing, and disseminating information concerning narcotics activity within the Department and between the Department and other Federal, State, and local agencies;

(B) describe the results of those activities, using quantifiable data whenever possible;

(C) state whether those activities were sufficient to meet the responsibility of the Department to stop the entry of illegal drugs into the United States, including a description of the performance measures of effectiveness that were used in making that determination; and

(D) recommend, where appropriate, changes to those activities to improve the performance of the Department in meeting its responsibility to stop the entry of illegal drugs into the United States.

(3) Classified or law enforcement sensitive information

Any content of a review and evaluation described in the reports required in this subsection that involves information classified under criteria established by an Executive order, or whose public disclosure, as determined by the Secretary, would be detrimental to the law enforcement or national security activities of the Department or any other Federal, State, or local agency, shall be presented to Congress separately from the rest of the review and evaluation.

(Pub. L. 107–296, title VIII, § 878, Nov. 25, 2002, 116 Stat. 2245; Pub. L. 108–458, title VII, § 7407(a), Dec. 17, 2004, 118 Stat. 3851; Pub. L. 109–469, title I, § 103(f)(2), Dec. 29, 2006, 120 Stat. 3510.)

AMENDMENTS

2006—Subsec. (c). Pub. L. 109–469, § 103(f)(2)(A), substituted "The" for "Except as provided in subsection (d) of this section, the".

Subsecs. (d) to (g). Pub. L. 109–469, § 103(f)(2)(B), redesignated subsecs. (e) to (g) as (d) to (f), respectively, and struck out heading and text of former subsec. (d). Text read as follows: "The Director of the Office of Counternarcotics Enforcement may be appointed as the United States Interdiction Coordinator by the Director of the Office of National Drug Control Policy, and shall be the only person at the Department eligible to be so appointed."

2004—Pub. L. 108–458 amended section catchline and text generally. Prior to amendment, text read as follows: "The Secretary shall appoint a senior official in the Department to assume primary responsibility for coordinating policy and operations within the Department and between the Department and other Federal departments and agencies with respect to interdicting the entry of illegal drugs into the United States, and tracking and severing connections between illegal drug trafficking and terrorism. Such official shall—

"(1) ensure the adequacy of resources within the Department for illicit drug interdiction; and

"(2) serve as the United States Interdiction Coordinator for the Director of National Drug Control Policy."

§ 459. Office of International Affairs

(a) Establishment

There is established within the Office of the Secretary an Office of International Affairs. The Office shall be headed by a Director, who shall be a senior official appointed by the Secretary.

(b) Duties of the Director

The Director shall have the following duties:

(1) To promote information and education exchange with nations friendly to the United States in order to promote sharing of best practices and technologies relating to homeland security. Such exchange shall include the following:

(A) Exchange of information on research and development on homeland security technologies.

(B) Joint training exercises of first responders.

(C) Exchange of expertise on terrorism prevention, response, and crisis management.

(2) To identify areas for homeland security information and training exchange where the United States has a demonstrated weakness and another friendly nation or nations have a demonstrated expertise.

(3) To plan and undertake international conferences, exchange programs, and training activities.

(4) To manage international activities within the Department in coordination with other

Federal officials with responsibility for counter-terrorism matters.

(Pub. L. 107–296, title VIII, §879, Nov. 25, 2002, 116 Stat. 2245.)

§460. Prohibition of the Terrorism Information and Prevention System

Any and all activities of the Federal Government to implement the proposed component program of the Citizen Corps known as Operation TIPS (Terrorism Information and Prevention System) are hereby prohibited.

(Pub. L. 107–296, title VIII, §880, Nov. 25, 2002, 116 Stat. 2245.)

§461. Review of pay and benefit plans

Notwithstanding any other provision of this chapter, the Secretary shall, in consultation with the Director of the Office of Personnel Management, review the pay and benefit plans of each agency whose functions are transferred under this chapter to the Department and, within 90 days after November 25, 2002, submit a plan to the President of the Senate and the Speaker of the House of Representatives and the appropriate committees and subcommittees of Congress, for ensuring, to the maximum extent practicable, the elimination of disparities in pay and benefits throughout the Department, especially among law enforcement personnel, that are inconsistent with merit system principles set forth in section 2301 of title 5.

(Pub. L. 107–296, title VIII, §881, Nov. 25, 2002, 116 Stat. 2246.)

§462. Office of National Capital Region Coordination

(a) Establishment

(1) In general

There is established within the Office of the Secretary the Office of National Capital Region Coordination, to oversee and coordinate Federal programs for and relationships with State, local, and regional authorities in the National Capital Region, as defined under section 2674(f)(2) of title 10.

(2) Director

The Office established under paragraph (1) shall be headed by a Director, who shall be appointed by the Secretary.

(3) Cooperation

The Secretary shall cooperate with the Mayor of the District of Columbia, the Governors of Maryland and Virginia, and other State, local, and regional officers in the National Capital Region to integrate the District of Columbia, Maryland, and Virginia into the planning, coordination, and execution of the activities of the Federal Government for the enhancement of domestic preparedness against the consequences of terrorist attacks.

(b) Responsibilities

The Office established under subsection (a)(1) of this section shall—

(1) coordinate the activities of the Department relating to the National Capital Region, including cooperation with the Office for State and Local Government Coordination;

(2) assess, and advocate for, the resources needed by State, local, and regional authorities in the National Capital Region to implement efforts to secure the homeland;

(3) provide State, local, and regional authorities in the National Capital Region with regular information, research, and technical support to assist the efforts of State, local, and regional authorities in the National Capital Region in securing the homeland;

(4) develop a process for receiving meaningful input from State, local, and regional authorities and the private sector in the National Capital Region to assist in the development of the homeland security plans and activities of the Federal Government;

(5) coordinate with Federal agencies in the National Capital Region on terrorism preparedness, to ensure adequate planning, information sharing, training, and execution of the Federal role in domestic preparedness activities;

(6) coordinate with Federal, State, local, and regional agencies, and the private sector in the National Capital Region on terrorism preparedness to ensure adequate planning, information sharing, training, and execution of domestic preparedness activities among these agencies and entities; and

(7) serve as a liaison between the Federal Government and State, local, and regional authorities, and private sector entities in the National Capital Region to facilitate access to Federal grants and other programs.

(c) Annual report

The Office established under subsection (a) of this section shall submit an annual report to Congress that includes—

(1) the identification of the resources required to fully implement homeland security efforts in the National Capital Region;

(2) an assessment of the progress made by the National Capital Region in implementing homeland security efforts; and

(3) recommendations to Congress regarding the additional resources needed to fully implement homeland security efforts in the National Capital Region.

(d) Limitation

Nothing contained in this section shall be construed as limiting the power of State and local governments.

(Pub. L. 107–296, title VIII, §882, Nov. 25, 2002, 116 Stat. 2246.)

§463. Requirement to comply with laws protecting equal employment opportunity and providing whistleblower protections

Nothing in this chapter shall be construed as exempting the Department from requirements applicable with respect to executive agencies—

(1) to provide equal employment protection for employees of the Department (including pursuant to the provisions in section 2302(b)(1) of title 5 and the Notification and Federal Employee Antidiscrimination and Retaliation Act of 2002 (Public Law 107–174)); or

(2) to provide whistleblower protections for employees of the Department (including pursuant to the provisions in section 2302(b)(8) and (9) of such title and the Notification and Federal Employee Antidiscrimination and Retaliation Act of 2002).

(Pub. L. 107–296, title VIII, § 883, Nov. 25, 2002, 116 Stat. 2247.)

REFERENCES IN TEXT

The Notification and Federal Employee Antidiscrimination and Retaliation Act of 2002, referred to in pars. (1) and (2), is Pub. L. 107–174, May 15, 2002, 116 Stat. 566, which is set out as a note under section 2301 of Title 5, Government Organization and Employees. For complete classification of this Act to the Code, see Tables.

§ 464. Federal Law Enforcement Training Center

(a) In general

The transfer of an authority or an agency under this chapter to the Department of Homeland Security does not affect training agreements already entered into with the Federal Law Enforcement Training Center with respect to the training of personnel to carry out that authority or the duties of that transferred agency.

(b) Continuity of operations

All activities of the Federal Law Enforcement Training Center transferred to the Department of Homeland Security under this chapter shall continue to be carried out at the locations such activities were carried out before such transfer.

(Pub. L. 107–296, title VIII, § 884, Nov. 25, 2002, 116 Stat. 2247.)

§ 464a. Acceptance and use of gifts

In fiscal year 2004 and thereafter, the Center is authorized to accept and use gifts of property, both real and personal, and to accept services, for authorized purposes.

(Pub. L. 108–90, title IV, Oct. 1, 2003, 117 Stat. 1150.)

REFERENCES IN TEXT

The Center, referred to in text, means the Federal Law Enforcement Training Center.

CODIFICATION

Section was enacted as part of the Department of Homeland Security Appropriations Act, 2004, and not as part of the Homeland Security Act of 2002 which comprises this chapter.

STANDARDS FOR MEASURING AND ASSESSING THE QUALITY AND EFFECTIVENESS OF FEDERAL LAW ENFORCEMENT TRAINING

Pub. L. 108–334, title V, § 506, Oct. 18, 2004, 118 Stat. 1316, provided that: "The Federal Law Enforcement Training Center shall establish an accrediting body, to include representatives from the Federal law enforcement community and non-Federal accreditation experts involved in law enforcement training, to establish standards for measuring and assessing the quality and effectiveness of Federal law enforcement training programs, facilities, and instructors."

Similar provisions were contained in the following prior appropriation acts:

Pub. L. 108–90, title V, § 509, Oct. 1, 2003, 117 Stat. 1154.

Pub. L. 108–7, div. J, title I, § 122, Feb. 20, 2003, 117 Stat. 439.

ANNUAL OUTSTANDING STUDENT AWARD

Pub. L. 108–7, div. J, title I, Feb. 20, 2003, 117 Stat. 431, provided in part: "That the [Federal Law Enforcement Training] Center is authorized to accept and use gifts of property, both real and personal, and to accept services, for authorized purposes, including funding of a gift of intrinsic value which shall be awarded annually by the Director of the Center to the outstanding student who graduated from a basic training program at the Center during the previous fiscal year, which shall be funded only by gifts received through the Center's gift authority".

Similar provisions were contained in the following prior appropriation acts:

Pub. L. 107–67, title I, Nov. 12, 2001, 115 Stat. 516.

Pub. L. 106–554, § 1(a)(3) [title I], Dec. 21, 2000, 114 Stat. 2763, 2763A–127.

Pub. L. 106–58, title I, Sept. 29, 1999, 113 Stat. 432.

Pub. L. 105–277, div. A, § 101(h) [title I], Oct. 21, 1998, 112 Stat. 2681–480, 2681–483.

Pub. L. 105–61, title I, Oct. 10, 1997, 111 Stat. 1275.

Pub. L. 104–208, div. A, title I, § 101(f) [title I], Sept. 30, 1996, 110 Stat. 3009–314, 3009–317.

Pub. L. 104–52, title I, Nov. 19, 1995, 109 Stat. 470.

Pub. L. 103–329, title I, Sept. 30, 1994, 108 Stat. 2383.

Pub. L. 103–123, title I, Oct. 28, 1993, 107 Stat. 1227.

Pub. L. 102–393, title I, Oct. 6, 1992, 106 Stat. 1730.

Pub. L. 102–141, title I, Oct. 28, 1991, 105 Stat. 835.

Pub. L. 101–509, title I, Nov. 5, 1990, 104 Stat. 1390.

Pub. L. 101–136, title I, Nov. 3, 1989, 103 Stat. 784.

§ 464b. Staffing accreditation function

In fiscal year 2004 and thereafter, the Center is authorized to accept detailees from other Federal agencies, on a non-reimbursable basis, to staff the accreditation function.

(Pub. L. 108–90, title IV, Oct. 1, 2003, 117 Stat. 1150.)

REFERENCES IN TEXT

The Center, referred to in text, means the Federal Law Enforcement Training Center.

CODIFICATION

Section was enacted as part of the Department of Homeland Security Appropriations Act, 2004, and not as part of the Homeland Security Act of 2002 which comprises this chapter.

PRIOR PROVISIONS

Similar provisions were contained in the following prior appropriation act:

Pub. L. 108–7, div. J, title I, Feb. 20, 2003, 117 Stat. 431.

§ 464c. Student housing

In fiscal year 2004 and thereafter, students attending training at any Center site shall reside in on-Center or Center-provided housing, insofar as available and in accordance with Center policy.

(Pub. L. 108–90, title IV, Oct. 1, 2003, 117 Stat. 1151.)

REFERENCES IN TEXT

The Center, referred to in text, means the Federal Law Enforcement Training Center.

CODIFICATION

Section was enacted as part of the Department of Homeland Security Appropriations Act, 2004, and not as part of the Homeland Security Act of 2002 which comprises this chapter.

PRIOR PROVISIONS

Similar provisions were contained in the following prior appropriation acts:

Pub. L. 108–7, div. J, title I, Feb. 20, 2003, 117 Stat. 431.
Pub. L. 107–67, title I, Nov. 12, 2001, 115 Stat. 517.
Pub. L. 106–554, §1(a)(3) [title I], Dec. 21, 2000, 114 Stat. 2763, 2763A–127.
Pub. L. 106–58, title I, Sept. 29, 1999, 113 Stat. 432.
Pub. L. 105–277, div. A, §101(h) [title I], Oct. 21, 1998, 112 Stat. 2681–480, 2681–483.
Pub. L. 105–61, title I, Oct. 10, 1997, 111 Stat. 1275.
Pub. L. 104–208, div. A, title I, §101(f) [title I], Sept. 30, 1996, 110 Stat. 3009–314, 3009–317.
Pub. L. 104–52, title I, Nov. 19, 1995, 109 Stat. 470.
Pub. L. 103–329, title I, Sept. 30, 1994, 108 Stat. 2383.
Pub. L. 103–123, title I, Oct. 28, 1993, 107 Stat. 1227.
Pub. L. 102–393, title I, Oct. 6, 1992, 106 Stat. 1730.
Pub. L. 102–141, title I, Oct. 28, 1991, 105 Stat. 835.
Pub. L. 101–509, title I, Nov. 5, 1990, 104 Stat. 1390.
Pub. L. 101–136, title I, Nov. 3, 1989, 103 Stat. 784.

§464d. Additional funds for training

In fiscal year 2004 and thereafter, funds appropriated in this account shall be available, at the discretion of the Director, for the following: training United States Postal Service law enforcement personnel and Postal police officers; State and local government law enforcement training on a space-available basis; training of foreign law enforcement officials on a space-available basis with reimbursement of actual costs to this appropriation, except that reimbursement may be waived by the Secretary for law enforcement training activities in foreign countries undertaken under section 801 of the Antiterrorism and Effective Death Penalty Act of 1996 (28 U.S.C. 509 note); training of private sector security officials on a space-available basis with reimbursement of actual costs to this appropriation; and travel expenses of non-Federal personnel to attend course development meetings and training sponsored by the Center.

(Pub. L. 108–90, title IV, Oct. 1, 2003, 117 Stat. 1151.)

References in Text

"Funds appropriated in this account", and "this appropriation", referred to in text, mean funds appropriated under the headings "Federal Law Enforcement Training Center" and "salaries and expenses" of title IV of the Department of Homeland Security Appropriations Act, 2004, Pub. L. 108–90.

Section 801 of the Antiterrorism and Effective Death Penalty Act of 1996, referred to in text, is section 801 of Pub. L. 104–132, which is set out as a note under section 509 of Title 28, Judiciary and Judicial Procedure.

The Center, referred to in text, means the Federal Law Enforcement Training Center.

Codification

Section was enacted as part of the Department of Homeland Security Appropriations Act, 2004, and not as part of the Homeland Security Act of 2002 which comprises this chapter.

Prior Provisions

Similar provisions were contained in the following prior appropriation acts:
Pub. L. 108–7, div. J, title I, Feb. 20, 2003, 117 Stat. 431.
Pub. L. 107–67, title I, Nov. 12, 2001, 115 Stat. 516.
Pub. L. 106–554, §1(a)(3) [title I], Dec. 21, 2000, 114 Stat. 2763, 2763A–127.
Pub. L. 106–58, title I, Sept. 29, 1999, 113 Stat. 432.
Pub. L. 105–277, div. A, §101(h) [title I], Oct. 21, 1998, 112 Stat. 2681–480, 2681–483.
Pub. L. 105–61, title I, Oct. 10, 1997, 111 Stat. 1276.
Pub. L. 104–208, div. A, title I, §101(f) [title I], Sept. 30, 1996, 110 Stat. 3009–314, 3009–317.
Pub. L. 104–52, title I, Nov. 19, 1995, 109 Stat. 470.
Pub. L. 103–329, title I, Sept. 30, 1994, 108 Stat. 2383.

§464e. Short-term medical services for students

In fiscal year 2004 and thereafter, the Center is authorized to provide short-term medical services for students undergoing training at the Center.

(Pub. L. 108–90, title IV, Oct. 1, 2003, 117 Stat. 1151.)

References in Text

The Center, referred to in text, means the Federal Law Enforcement Training Center.

Codification

Section was enacted as part of the Department of Homeland Security Appropriations Act, 2004, and not as part of the Homeland Security Act of 2002 which comprises this chapter.

Prior Provisions

Similar provisions were contained in the following prior appropriation acts:
Pub. L. 108–7, div. J, title I, Feb. 20, 2003, 117 Stat. 431.
Pub. L. 107–67, title I, Nov. 12, 2001, 115 Stat. 517.
Pub. L. 106–554, §1(a)(3) [title I], Dec. 21, 2000, 114 Stat. 2763, 2763A–127.
Pub. L. 106–58, title I, Sept. 29, 1999, 113 Stat. 433.
Pub. L. 105–277, div. A, §101(h) [title I], Oct. 21, 1998, 112 Stat. 2681–480, 2681–483.
Pub. L. 105–61, title I, Oct. 10, 1997, 111 Stat. 1276.
Pub. L. 104–208, div. A, title I, §101(f) [title I], Sept. 30, 1996, 110 Stat. 3009–314, 3009–318.
Pub. L. 104–52, title I, Nov. 19, 1995, 109 Stat. 470.
Pub. L. 103–329, title I, Sept. 30, 1994, 108 Stat. 2384.
Pub. L. 103–123, title I, Oct. 28, 1993, 107 Stat. 1228.
Pub. L. 102–393, title I, Oct. 6, 1992, 106 Stat. 1730.

§465. Joint Interagency Task Force

(a) Establishment

The Secretary may establish and operate a permanent Joint Interagency Homeland Security Task Force composed of representatives from military and civilian agencies of the United States Government for the purposes of anticipating terrorist threats against the United States and taking appropriate actions to prevent harm to the United States.

(b) Structure

It is the sense of Congress that the Secretary should model the Joint Interagency Homeland Security Task Force on the approach taken by the Joint Interagency Task Forces for drug interdiction at Key West, Florida and Alameda, California, to the maximum extent feasible and appropriate.

(Pub. L. 107–296, title VIII, §885, Nov. 25, 2002, 116 Stat. 2247.)

§466. Sense of Congress reaffirming the continued importance and applicability of the Posse Comitatus Act

(a) Findings

Congress finds the following:

(1) Section 1385 of title 18 (commonly known as the "Posse Comitatus Act") prohibits the use of the Armed Forces as a posse comitatus to execute the laws except in cases and under circumstances expressly authorized by the Constitution or Act of Congress.

(2) Enacted in 1878, the Posse Comitatus Act was expressly intended to prevent United States Marshals, on their own initiative, from calling on the Army for assistance in enforcing Federal law.

(3) The Posse Comitatus Act has served the Nation well in limiting the use of the Armed Forces to enforce the law.

(4) Nevertheless, by its express terms, the Posse Comitatus Act is not a complete barrier to the use of the Armed Forces for a range of domestic purposes, including law enforcement functions, when the use of the Armed Forces is authorized by Act of Congress or the President determines that the use of the Armed Forces is required to fulfill the President's obligations under the Constitution to respond promptly in time of war, insurrection, or other serious emergency.

(5) Existing laws, including chapter 15 of title 10 (commonly known as the "Insurrection Act"), and the Robert T. Stafford Disaster Relief and Emergency Assistance Act (42 U.S.C. 5121 et seq.), grant the President broad powers that may be invoked in the event of domestic emergencies, including an attack against the Nation using weapons of mass destruction, and these laws specifically authorize the President to use the Armed Forces to help restore public order.

(b) Sense of Congress

Congress reaffirms the continued importance of section 1385 of title 18, and it is the sense of Congress that nothing in this chapter should be construed to alter the applicability of such section to any use of the Armed Forces as a posse comitatus to execute the laws.

(Pub. L. 107–296, title VIII, §886, Nov. 25, 2002, 116 Stat. 2248.)

REFERENCES IN TEXT

The Robert T. Stafford Disaster Relief and Emergency Assistance Act, referred to in subsec. (a)(5), is Pub. L. 93–288, May 22, 1974, 88 Stat. 110, as amended, which is classified principally to chapter 68 (§5121 et seq.) of Title 42, The Public Health and Welfare. For complete classification of this Act to the Code, see Short Title note set out under section 5121 of Title 42 and Tables.

§467. Coordination with the Department of Health and Human Services under the Public Health Service Act

(a) In general

The annual Federal response plan developed by the Department shall be consistent with section 319 of the Public Health Service Act (42 U.S.C. 247d).

(b) Disclosures among relevant agencies

(1) In general

Full disclosure among relevant agencies shall be made in accordance with this subsection.

(2) Public health emergency

During the period in which the Secretary of Health and Human Services has declared the existence of a public health emergency under section 319(a) of the Public Health Service Act (42 U.S.C. 247d(a)), the Secretary of Health and Human Services shall keep relevant agencies, including the Department of Homeland Security, the Department of Justice, and the Federal Bureau of Investigation, fully and currently informed.

(3) Potential public health emergency

In cases involving, or potentially involving, a public health emergency, but in which no determination of an emergency by the Secretary of Health and Human Services under section 319(a) of the Public Health Service Act (42 U.S.C. 247d(a)), has been made, all relevant agencies, including the Department of Homeland Security, the Department of Justice, and the Federal Bureau of Investigation, shall keep the Secretary of Health and Human Services and the Director of the Centers for Disease Control and Prevention fully and currently informed.

(Pub. L. 107–296, title VIII, §887, Nov. 25, 2002, 116 Stat. 2248.)

§468. Preserving Coast Guard mission performance

(a) Definitions

In this section:

(1) Non-homeland security missions

The term "non-homeland security missions" means the following missions of the Coast Guard:

(A) Marine safety.

(B) Search and rescue.

(C) Aids to navigation.

(D) Living marine resources (fisheries law enforcement).

(E) Marine environmental protection.

(F) Ice operations.

(2) Homeland security missions

The term "homeland security missions" means the following missions of the Coast Guard:

(A) Ports, waterways and coastal security.

(B) Drug interdiction.

(C) Migrant interdiction.

(D) Defense readiness.

(E) Other law enforcement.

(b) Transfer

There are transferred to the Department the authorities, functions, personnel, and assets of the Coast Guard, which shall be maintained as a distinct entity within the Department, including the authorities and functions of the Secretary of Transportation relating thereto.

(c) Maintenance of status of functions and assets

Notwithstanding any other provision of this chapter, the authorities, functions, and capabilities of the Coast Guard to perform its missions shall be maintained intact and without significant reduction after the transfer of the Coast Guard to the Department, except as specified in subsequent Acts.

(d) Certain transfers prohibited

No mission, function, or asset (including for purposes of this subsection any ship, aircraft, or helicopter) of the Coast Guard may be diverted to the principal and continuing use of any other organization, unit, or entity of the Department, except for details or assignments that do not reduce the Coast Guard's capability to perform its missions.

(e) Changes to missions

(1) Prohibition

The Secretary may not substantially or significantly reduce the missions of the Coast Guard or the Coast Guard's capability to perform those missions, except as specified in subsequent Acts.

(2) Waiver

The Secretary may waive the restrictions under paragraph (1) for a period of not to exceed 90 days upon a declaration and certification by the Secretary to Congress that a clear, compelling, and immediate need exists for such a waiver. A certification under this paragraph shall include a detailed justification for the declaration and certification, including the reasons and specific information that demonstrate that the Nation and the Coast Guard cannot respond effectively if the restrictions under paragraph (1) are not waived.

(f) Annual review

(1) In general

The Inspector General of the Department shall conduct an annual review that shall assess thoroughly the performance by the Coast Guard of all missions of the Coast Guard (including non-homeland security missions and homeland security missions) with a particular emphasis on examining the non-homeland security missions.

(2) Report

The report under this paragraph shall be submitted to—

(A) the Committee on Governmental Affairs of the Senate;

(B) the Committee on Government Reform of the House of Representatives;

(C) the Committees on Appropriations of the Senate and the House of Representatives;

(D) the Committee on Commerce, Science, and Transportation of the Senate; and

(E) the Committee on Transportation and Infrastructure of the House of Representatives.

(g) Direct reporting to Secretary

Upon the transfer of the Coast Guard to the Department, the Commandant shall report directly to the Secretary without being required to report through any other official of the Department.

(h) Operation as a service in the Navy

None of the conditions and restrictions in this section shall apply when the Coast Guard operates as a service in the Navy under section 3 of title 14.

(i) Report on accelerating the Integrated Deepwater System

Not later than 90 days after November 25, 2002, the Secretary, in consultation with the Commandant of the Coast Guard, shall submit a report to the Committee on Commerce, Science, and Transportation of the Senate, the Committee on Transportation and Infrastructure of the House of Representatives, and the Committees on Appropriations of the Senate and the House of Representatives that—

(1) analyzes the feasibility of accelerating the rate of procurement in the Coast Guard's Integrated Deepwater System from 20 years to 10 years;

(2) includes an estimate of additional resources required;

(3) describes the resulting increased capabilities;

(4) outlines any increases in the Coast Guard's homeland security readiness;

(5) describes any increases in operational efficiencies; and

(6) provides a revised asset phase-in time line.

(Pub. L. 107–296, title VIII, § 888, Nov. 25, 2002, 116 Stat. 2249.)

CHANGE OF NAME

Committee on Governmental Affairs of Senate changed to Committee on Homeland Security and Governmental Affairs of Senate, effective Jan. 4, 2005, by Senate Resolution No. 445, One Hundred Eighth Congress, Oct. 9, 2004.

Committee on Government Reform of House of Representatives changed to Committee on Oversight and Government Reform of House of Representatives by House Resolution No. 6, One Hundred Tenth Congress, Jan. 5, 2007.

§ 469. Fees for credentialing and background investigations in transportation

(a) Fees

For fiscal year 2004 and thereafter, the Secretary of Homeland Security shall charge reasonable fees for providing credentialing and background investigations in the field of transportation: *Provided*, That the establishment and collection of fees shall be subject to the following requirements:

(1) such fees, in the aggregate, shall not exceed the costs incurred by the Department of Homeland Security associated with providing the credential or performing the background record checks;

(2) the Secretary shall charge fees in amounts that are reasonably related to the costs of providing services in connection with the activity or item for which the fee is charged;

(3) a fee may not be collected except to the extent such fee will be expended to pay for the costs of conducting or obtaining a criminal history record check and a review of available law enforcement databases and commercial databases and records of other governmental and international agencies; reviewing and adjudicating requests for waiver and appeals of agency decisions with respect to providing the credential, performing the background record check, and denying requests for waiver and appeals; and any other costs related to providing the credential or performing the background record check; and

(4) any fee collected shall be available for expenditure only to pay the costs incurred in

providing services in connection with the activity or item for which the fee is charged and shall remain available until expended.

(b) Recurrent training of aliens in operation of aircraft

(1) Process for reviewing threat assessments

Notwithstanding section 44939(e) of title 49, the Secretary shall establish a process to ensure that an alien (as defined in section 101(a)(3) of the Immigration and Nationality Act (8 U.S.C. 1101(a)(3)) applying for recurrent training in the operation of any aircraft is properly identified and has not, since the time of any prior threat assessment conducted pursuant to section 44939(a) of such title, become a risk to aviation or national security.

(2) Interruption of training

If the Secretary determines, in carrying out the process established under paragraph (1), that an alien is a present risk to aviation or national security, the Secretary shall immediately notify the person providing the training of the determination and that person shall not provide the training or if such training has commenced that person shall immediately terminate the training.

(3) Fees

The Secretary may charge reasonable fees under subsection (a) for providing credentialing and background investigations for aliens in connection with the process for recurrent training established under paragraph (1). Such fees shall be promulgated by notice in the Federal Register.

(Pub. L. 108–90, title V, §520, Oct. 1, 2003, 117 Stat. 1156; Pub. L. 110–329, div. D, title V, §543, Sept. 30, 2008, 122 Stat. 3609.)

CODIFICATION

Section was enacted as part of the Department of Homeland Security Appropriations Act, 2004, and not as part of the Homeland Security Act of 2002 which comprises this chapter.

AMENDMENTS

2008—Pub. L. 110–329 designated existing provisions as subsec. (a), inserted heading, and added subsec. (b).

§469a. Collection of fees from non-Federal participants in meetings

For fiscal year 2010 and thereafter, the Secretary of Homeland Security may collect fees from any non-Federal participant in a conference, seminar, exhibition, symposium, or similar meeting conducted by the Department of Homeland Security in advance of the conference, either directly or by contract, and those fees shall be credited to the appropriation or account from which the costs of the conference, seminar, exhibition, symposium, or similar meeting are paid and shall be available to pay the costs of the Department of Homeland Security with respect to the conference or to reimburse the Department for costs incurred with respect to the conference: *Provided*, That in the event the total amount of fees collected with respect to a conference exceeds the actual costs of the Department of Homeland Security with respect to the conference, the amount of such excess shall be deposited into the Treasury as miscellaneous receipts: *Provided further*, That the Secretary shall provide a report to the Committees on Appropriations of the Senate and the House of Representatives not later than January 5, 2011, providing the level of collections and a summary by agency of the purposes and levels of expenditures for the prior fiscal year, and shall report annually thereafter.

(Pub. L. 111–83, title V, §554, Oct. 28, 2009, 123 Stat. 2179.)

CODIFICATION

Section was enacted as part of the Department of Homeland Security Appropriations Act, 2010, and not as part of the Homeland Security Act of 2002 which comprises this chapter.

§470. Disclosures regarding homeland security grants

(a) Definitions

In this section:

(1) Homeland security grant

The term "homeland security grant" means any grant made or administered by the Department, including—

(A) the State Homeland Security Grant Program;

(B) the Urban Area Security Initiative Grant Program;

(C) the Law Enforcement Terrorism Prevention Program;

(D) the Citizen Corps; and

(E) the Metropolitan Medical Response System.

(2) Local government

The term "local government" has the meaning given the term in section 101 of this title.

(b) Required disclosures

Each State or local government that receives a homeland security grant shall, not later than 12 months after the later of October 13, 2006, and the date of receipt of such grant, and every 12 months thereafter until all funds provided under such grant are expended, submit a report to the Secretary that contains a list of all expenditures made by such State or local government using funds from such grant.

(Pub. L. 109–347, title VII, §702, Oct. 13, 2006, 120 Stat. 1943.)

CODIFICATION

Section was enacted as part of the Security and Accountability For Every Port Act of 2006, also known as the SAFE Port Act, and not as part of the Homeland Security Act of 2002 which comprises this chapter.

DEFINITIONS

For definitions of "Department" and "Secretary" as used in this section, see section 901 of this title.

PART I—INFORMATION SHARING

§481. Short title; findings; and sense of Congress

(a) Short title

This part may be cited as the "Homeland Security Information Sharing Act".

(b) Findings

Congress finds the following:

(1) The Federal Government is required by the Constitution to provide for the common defense, which includes terrorist attack.

(2) The Federal Government relies on State and local personnel to protect against terrorist attack.

(3) The Federal Government collects, creates, manages, and protects classified and sensitive but unclassified information to enhance homeland security.

(4) Some homeland security information is needed by the State and local personnel to prevent and prepare for terrorist attack.

(5) The needs of State and local personnel to have access to relevant homeland security information to combat terrorism must be reconciled with the need to preserve the protected status of such information and to protect the sources and methods used to acquire such information.

(6) Granting security clearances to certain State and local personnel is one way to facilitate the sharing of information regarding specific terrorist threats among Federal, State, and local levels of government.

(7) Methods exist to declassify, redact, or otherwise adapt classified information so it may be shared with State and local personnel without the need for granting additional security clearances.

(8) State and local personnel have capabilities and opportunities to gather information on suspicious activities and terrorist threats not possessed by Federal agencies.

(9) The Federal Government and State and local governments and agencies in other jurisdictions may benefit from such information.

(10) Federal, State, and local governments and intelligence, law enforcement, and other emergency preparation and response agencies must act in partnership to maximize the benefits of information gathering and analysis to prevent and respond to terrorist attacks.

(11) Information systems, including the National Law Enforcement Telecommunications System and the Terrorist Threat Warning System, have been established for rapid sharing of classified and sensitive but unclassified information among Federal, State, and local entities.

(12) Increased efforts to share homeland security information should avoid duplicating existing information systems.

(c) Sense of Congress

It is the sense of Congress that Federal, State, and local entities should share homeland security information to the maximum extent practicable, with special emphasis on hard-to-reach urban and rural communities.

(Pub. L. 107–296, title VIII, § 891, Nov. 25, 2002, 116 Stat. 2252.)

REFERENCES IN TEXT

This part, referred to in subsec. (a), was in the original "This subtitle", meaning subtitle I (§§ 891–899) of title VIII of Pub. L. 107–296, Nov. 25, 2002, 116 Stat. 2252, which enacted this part, amended section 2517 of Title 18, Crimes and Criminal Procedure, Rule 6 of the Federal Rules of Criminal Procedure, set out in the Appendix to Title 18, and sections 403–5d, 1806, and 1825 of Title 50, War and National Defense, and amended provisions set out as a note under section 2517 of Title 18. For complete classification of subtitle I to the Code, see Tables.

REPORTS TO CONGRESS

Pub. L. 110–28, title III, May 25, 2007, 121 Stat. 139, provided in part: "That starting July 1, 2007, the Secretary of Homeland Security shall submit quarterly reports to the Committees on Appropriations of the Senate and the House of Representatives detailing the information required in House Report 110–107."

§ 482. Facilitating homeland security information sharing procedures

(a) Procedures for determining extent of sharing of homeland security information

(1) The President shall prescribe and implement procedures under which relevant Federal agencies—

(A) share relevant and appropriate homeland security information with other Federal agencies, including the Department, and appropriate State and local personnel;

(B) identify and safeguard homeland security information that is sensitive but unclassified; and

(C) to the extent such information is in classified form, determine whether, how, and to what extent to remove classified information, as appropriate, and with which such personnel it may be shared after such information is removed.

(2) The President shall ensure that such procedures apply to all agencies of the Federal Government.

(3) Such procedures shall not change the substantive requirements for the classification and safeguarding of classified information.

(4) Such procedures shall not change the requirements and authorities to protect sources and methods.

(b) Procedures for sharing of homeland security information

(1) Under procedures prescribed by the President, all appropriate agencies, including the intelligence community, shall, through information sharing systems, share homeland security information with Federal agencies and appropriate State and local personnel to the extent such information may be shared, as determined in accordance with subsection (a) of this section, together with assessments of the credibility of such information.

(2) Each information sharing system through which information is shared under paragraph (1) shall—

(A) have the capability to transmit unclassified or classified information, though the procedures and recipients for each capability may differ;

(B) have the capability to restrict delivery of information to specified subgroups by geographic location, type of organization, position of a recipient within an organization, or a recipient's need to know such information;

(C) be configured to allow the efficient and effective sharing of information; and

(D) be accessible to appropriate State and local personnel.

(3) The procedures prescribed under paragraph (1) shall establish conditions on the use of information shared under paragraph (1)—

(A) to limit the redissemination of such information to ensure that such information is not used for an unauthorized purpose;

(B) to ensure the security and confidentiality of such information;

(C) to protect the constitutional and statutory rights of any individuals who are subjects of such information; and

(D) to provide data integrity through the timely removal and destruction of obsolete or erroneous names and information.

(4) The procedures prescribed under paragraph (1) shall ensure, to the greatest extent practicable, that the information sharing system through which information is shared under such paragraph include existing information sharing systems, including, but not limited to, the National Law Enforcement Telecommunications System, the Regional Information Sharing System, and the Terrorist Threat Warning System of the Federal Bureau of Investigation.

(5) Each appropriate Federal agency, as determined by the President, shall have access to each information sharing system through which information is shared under paragraph (1), and shall therefore have access to all information, as appropriate, shared under such paragraph.

(6) The procedures prescribed under paragraph (1) shall ensure that appropriate State and local personnel are authorized to use such information sharing systems—

(A) to access information shared with such personnel; and

(B) to share, with others who have access to such information sharing systems, the homeland security information of their own jurisdictions, which shall be marked appropriately as pertaining to potential terrorist activity.

(7) Under procedures prescribed jointly by the Director of Central Intelligence and the Attorney General, each appropriate Federal agency, as determined by the President, shall review and assess the information shared under paragraph (6) and integrate such information with existing intelligence.

(c) Sharing of classified information and sensitive but unclassified information with State and local personnel

(1) The President shall prescribe procedures under which Federal agencies may, to the extent the President considers necessary, share with appropriate State and local personnel homeland security information that remains classified or otherwise protected after the determinations prescribed under the procedures set forth in subsection (a) of this section.

(2) It is the sense of Congress that such procedures may include 1 or more of the following means:

(A) Carrying out security clearance investigations with respect to appropriate State and local personnel.

(B) With respect to information that is sensitive but unclassified, entering into nondisclosure agreements with appropriate State and local personnel.

(C) Increased use of information-sharing partnerships that include appropriate State and local personnel, such as the Joint Terrorism Task Forces of the Federal Bureau of Investigation, the Anti-Terrorism Task Forces of the Department of Justice, and regional Terrorism Early Warning Groups.

(3)(A) The Secretary shall establish a program to provide appropriate training to officials described in subparagraph (B) in order to assist such officials in—

(i) identifying sources of potential terrorist threats through such methods as the Secretary determines appropriate;

(ii) reporting information relating to such potential terrorist threats to the appropriate Federal agencies in the appropriate form and manner;

(iii) assuring that all reported information is systematically submitted to and passed on by the Department for use by appropriate Federal agencies; and

(iv) understanding the mission and roles of the intelligence community to promote more effective information sharing among Federal, State, and local officials and representatives of the private sector to prevent terrorist attacks against the United States.

(B) The officials referred to in subparagraph (A) are officials of State and local government agencies and representatives of private sector entities with responsibilities relating to the oversight and management of first responders, counterterrorism activities, or critical infrastructure.

(C) The Secretary shall consult with the Attorney General to ensure that the training program established in subparagraph (A) does not duplicate the training program established in section 908 of the USA PATRIOT Act (Public Law 107–56; 28 U.S.C. 509 note).

(D) The Secretary shall carry out this paragraph in consultation with the Director of Central Intelligence and the Attorney General.

(d) Responsible officials

For each affected Federal agency, the head of such agency shall designate an official to administer this chapter with respect to such agency.

(e) Federal control of information

Under procedures prescribed under this section, information obtained by a State or local government from a Federal agency under this section shall remain under the control of the Federal agency, and a State or local law authorizing or requiring such a government to disclose information shall not apply to such information.

(f) Definitions

As used in this section:

(1) The term "homeland security information" means any information possessed by a Federal, State, or local agency that—

(A) relates to the threat of terrorist activity;

(B) relates to the ability to prevent, interdict, or disrupt terrorist activity;

(C) would improve the identification or investigation of a suspected terrorist or terrorist organization; or

(D) would improve the response to a terrorist act.

(2) The term "intelligence community" has the meaning given such term in section 401a(4) of title 50.

(3) The term "State and local personnel" means any of the following persons involved in prevention, preparation, or response for terrorist attack:

(A) State Governors, mayors, and other locally elected officials.

(B) State and local law enforcement personnel and firefighters.

(C) Public health and medical professionals.

(D) Regional, State, and local emergency management agency personnel, including State adjutant generals.

(E) Other appropriate emergency response agency personnel.

(F) Employees of private-sector entities that affect critical infrastructure, cyber, economic, or public health security, as designated by the Federal Government in procedures developed pursuant to this section.

(4) The term "State" includes the District of Columbia and any commonwealth, territory, or possession of the United States.

(g) Construction

Nothing in this chapter shall be construed as authorizing any department, bureau, agency, officer, or employee of the Federal Government to request, receive, or transmit to any other Government entity or personnel, or transmit to any State or local entity or personnel otherwise authorized by this chapter to receive homeland security information, any information collected by the Federal Government solely for statistical purposes in violation of any other provision of law relating to the confidentiality of such information.

(Pub. L. 107–296, title VIII, § 892, Nov. 25, 2002, 116 Stat. 2253; Pub. L. 108–177, title III, § 316(a), Dec. 13, 2003, 117 Stat. 2610.)

AMENDMENTS

2003—Subsec. (c)(3). Pub. L. 108–177 added par. (3).

CHANGE OF NAME

Reference to the Director of Central Intelligence or the Director of the Central Intelligence Agency in the Director's capacity as the head of the intelligence community deemed to be a reference to the Director of National Intelligence. Reference to the Director of Central Intelligence or the Director of the Central Intelligence Agency in the Director's capacity as the head of the Central Intelligence Agency deemed to be a reference to the Director of the Central Intelligence Agency. See section 1081(a), (b) of Pub. L. 108–458, set out as a note under section 401 of Title 50, War and National Defense.

EX. ORD. NO. 13311. HOMELAND SECURITY INFORMATION SHARING

Ex. Ord. No. 13311, July 29, 2003, 68 F.R. 45149, as amended by Ex. Ord. No. 13388, § 8(a), Oct. 25, 2005, 70 F.R. 62025, provided:

By the authority vested in me by the Constitution and the laws of the United States, including sections 892 and 893 of the Homeland Security Act of 2002 (the "Act") (6 U.S.C. 482 and 483) and section 301 of title 3, United States Code, it is hereby ordered as follows:

SECTION 1. *Assignment of Functions*. (a) The functions of the President under section 892 of the Act are assigned to the Secretary of Homeland Security (the "Secretary"), except the functions of the President under subsections 892(a)(2) and 892(b)(7).

(b) Subject to section 2(b) of this order, the function of the President under section 893 of the Act is assigned to the Secretary.

(c) Procedures issued by the Secretary in the performance of the function of the President under section 892(a)(1) of the Act shall apply to all agencies of the Federal Government. Such procedures shall specify that the President may make, or may authorize another officer of the United States to make, exceptions to the procedures.

(d) The function of the President under section 892(b)(7) of the Act is delegated to the Attorney General and the Director of National Intelligence, to be exercised jointly.

(e) In performing the functions assigned to the Secretary by subsection (a) of this section, the Secretary shall coordinate with the Secretary of State, the Secretary of Defense, the Attorney General, the Secretary of Energy, the Director of the Office of Management and Budget, the Director of National Intelligence, the Archivist of the United States, and as the Secretary deems appropriate, other officers of the United States.

(f) A determination, under the procedures issued by the Secretary in the performance of the function of the President under section 892(a)(1) of the Act, as to whether, or to what extent, an individual who falls within the category of "State and local personnel" as defined in sections 892(f)(3) and (f)(4) of the Act shall have access to information classified pursuant to Executive Order 12958 of April 17, 1995 [50 U.S.C. 435 note], as amended, is a discretionary determination and shall be conclusive and not subject to review or appeal.

SEC. 2. *Rules of Construction*. Nothing in this order shall be construed to impair or otherwise affect:

(a) the authority of the Director of National Intelligence under section 102A(i)(1) of the National Security Act of 1947, as amended (50 U.S.C. 403–3(c)(7) [403–1(i)(1)]), to protect intelligence sources and methods from unauthorized disclosure;

(b) the functions of the Director of the Office of Management and Budget relating to budget, administrative, or legislative proposals; or

(c) the provisions of Executive Orders 12958 of April 17, 1995 [50 U.S.C. 435 note], as amended, and 12968 of August 2, 1995 [50 U.S.C. 435 note], as amended.

SEC. 3. *General Provision*. This order is intended only to improve the internal management of the Federal Government and is not intended to, and does not, create any right or benefit, substantive or procedural, enforceable at law or in equity, against the United States, its departments, agencies, or other entities, its officers or employees, or any other person.

GEORGE W. BUSH.

§ 483. Report

(a) Report required

Not later than 12 months after November 25, 2002, the President shall submit to the congressional committees specified in subsection (b) of this section a report on the implementation of section 482 of this title. The report shall include any recommendations for additional measures or appropriation requests, beyond the requirements of section 482 of this title, to increase the effectiveness of sharing of information between and among Federal, State, and local entities.

(b) Specified congressional committees

The congressional committees referred to in subsection (a) of this section are the following committees:

(1) The Permanent Select Committee on Intelligence and the Committee on the Judiciary of the House of Representatives.

(2) The Select Committee on Intelligence and the Committee on the Judiciary of the Senate.

(Pub. L. 107–296, title VIII, §893, Nov. 25, 2002, 116 Stat. 2255.)

DELEGATION OF FUNCTIONS

For assignment of function of President under this section, subject to certain limitations, to Secretary of Homeland Security, see Ex. Ord. No. 13311, §1(b), July 29, 2003, 68 F.R. 45149, set out as a note under section 482 of this title.

§484. Authorization of appropriations

There are authorized to be appropriated such sums as may be necessary to carry out section 482 of this title.

(Pub. L. 107–296, title VIII, §894, Nov. 25, 2002, 116 Stat. 2256.)

§485. Information sharing

(a) Definitions

In this section:

(1) Homeland security information

The term "homeland security information" has the meaning given that term in section 482(f) of this title.

(2) Information Sharing Council

The term "Information Sharing Council" means the Information Systems Council established by Executive Order 13356, or any successor body designated by the President, and referred to under subsection (g) of this section.

(3) Information sharing environment

The terms "information sharing environment" and "ISE" mean an approach that facilitates the sharing of terrorism and homeland security information, which may include any method determined necessary and appropriate for carrying out this section.

(4) Program manager

The term "program manager" means the program manager designated under subsection (f) of this section.

(5) Terrorism information

The term "terrorism information"—

(A) means all information, whether collected, produced, or distributed by intelligence, law enforcement, military, homeland security, or other activities relating to—

(i) the existence, organization, capabilities, plans, intentions, vulnerabilities, means of finance or material support, or activities of foreign or international terrorist groups or individuals, or of domestic groups or individuals involved in transnational terrorism;

(ii) threats posed by such groups or individuals to the United States, United States persons, or United States interests, or to those of other nations;

(iii) communications of or by such groups or individuals; or

(iv) groups or individuals reasonably believed to be assisting or associated with such groups or individuals; and

(B) includes weapons of mass destruction information.

(6) Weapons of mass destruction information

The term "weapons of mass destruction information" means information that could reasonably be expected to assist in the development, proliferation, or use of a weapon of mass destruction (including a chemical, biological, radiological, or nuclear weapon) that could be used by a terrorist or a terrorist organization against the United States, including information about the location of any stockpile of nuclear materials that could be exploited for use in such a weapon that could be used by a terrorist or a terrorist organization against the United States.

(b) Information sharing environment

(1) Establishment

The President shall—

(A) create an information sharing environment for the sharing of terrorism information in a manner consistent with national security and with applicable legal standards relating to privacy and civil liberties;

(B) designate the organizational and management structures that will be used to operate and manage the ISE; and

(C) determine and enforce the policies, directives, and rules that will govern the content and usage of the ISE.

(2) Attributes

The President shall, through the structures described in subparagraphs (B) and (C) of paragraph (1), ensure that the ISE provides and facilitates the means for sharing terrorism information among all appropriate Federal, State, local, and tribal entities, and the private sector through the use of policy guidelines and technologies. The President shall, to the greatest extent practicable, ensure that the ISE provides the functional equivalent of, or otherwise supports, a decentralized, distributed, and coordinated environment that—

(A) connects existing systems, where appropriate, provides no single points of failure, and allows users to share information among agencies, between levels of government, and, as appropriate, with the private sector;

(B) ensures direct and continuous online electronic access to information;

(C) facilitates the availability of information in a form and manner that facilitates its use in analysis, investigations and operations;

(D) builds upon existing systems capabilities currently in use across the Government;

(E) employs an information access management approach that controls access to data rather than just systems and networks, without sacrificing security;

(F) facilitates the sharing of information at and across all levels of security;

(G) provides directory services, or the functional equivalent, for locating people and information;

(H) incorporates protections for individuals' privacy and civil liberties;

(I) incorporates strong mechanisms to enhance accountability and facilitate oversight, including audits, authentication, and access controls;

(J) integrates the information within the scope of the information sharing environment, including any such information in legacy technologies;

(K) integrates technologies, including all legacy technologies, through Internet-based services, consistent with appropriate security protocols and safeguards, to enable connectivity among required users at the Federal, State, and local levels;

(L) allows the full range of analytic and operational activities without the need to centralize information within the scope of the information sharing environment;

(M) permits analysts to collaborate both independently and in a group (commonly known as "collective and noncollective collaboration"), and across multiple levels of national security information and controlled unclassified information;

(N) provides a resolution process that enables changes by authorized officials regarding rules and policies for the access, use, and retention of information within the scope of the information sharing environment; and

(O) incorporates continuous, real-time, and immutable audit capabilities, to the maximum extent practicable.

(c) Preliminary report

Not later than 180 days after December 17, 2004, the program manager shall, in consultation with the Information Sharing Council—

(1) submit to the President and Congress a description of the technological, legal, and policy issues presented by the creation of the ISE, and the way in which these issues will be addressed;

(2) establish an initial capability to provide electronic directory services, or the functional equivalent, to assist in locating in the Federal Government intelligence and terrorism information and people with relevant knowledge about intelligence and terrorism information; and

(3) conduct a review of relevant current Federal agency capabilities, databases, and systems for sharing information.

(d) Guidelines and requirements

As soon as possible, but in no event later than 270 days after December 17, 2004, the President shall—

(1) leverage all ongoing efforts consistent with establishing the ISE and issue guidelines for acquiring, accessing, sharing, and using information, including guidelines to ensure that information is provided in its most shareable form, such as by using tearlines to separate out data from the sources and methods by which the data are obtained;

(2) in consultation with the Privacy and Civil Liberties Oversight Board established under section 2000ee of title 42, issue guidelines that—

(A) protect privacy and civil liberties in the development and use of the ISE; and

(B) shall be made public, unless nondisclosure is clearly necessary to protect national security; and

(3) require the heads of Federal departments and agencies to promote a culture of information sharing by—

(A) reducing disincentives to information sharing, including over-classification of information and unnecessary requirements for originator approval, consistent with applicable laws and regulations; and

(B) providing affirmative incentives for information sharing.

(e) Implementation plan report

Not later than one year after December 17, 2004, the President shall, with the assistance of the program manager, submit to Congress a report containing an implementation plan for the ISE. The report shall include the following:

(1) A description of the functions, capabilities, resources, and conceptual design of the ISE, including standards.

(2) A description of the impact on enterprise architectures of participating agencies.

(3) A budget estimate that identifies the incremental costs associated with designing, testing, integrating, deploying, and operating the ISE.

(4) A project plan for designing, testing, integrating, deploying, and operating the ISE.

(5) The policies and directives referred to in subsection (b)(1)(C) of this section, as well as the metrics and enforcement mechanisms that will be utilized.

(6) Objective, systemwide performance measures to enable the assessment of progress toward achieving the full implementation of the ISE.

(7) A description of the training requirements needed to ensure that the ISE will be adequately implemented and properly utilized.

(8) A description of the means by which privacy and civil liberties will be protected in the design and operation of the ISE.

(9) The recommendations of the program manager, in consultation with the Information Sharing Council, regarding whether, and under what conditions, the ISE should be expanded to include other intelligence information.

(10) A delineation of the roles of the Federal departments and agencies that will participate in the ISE, including an identification of the agencies that will deliver the infrastructure needed to operate and manage the ISE (as distinct from individual department or agency components that are part of the ISE), with such delineation of roles to be consistent with—

(A) the authority of the Director of National Intelligence under this title,[1] and the amendments made by this title, to set standards for information sharing throughout the intelligence community; and

(B) the authority of the Secretary of Homeland Security and the Attorney General, and the role of the Department of Homeland Security and the Attorney General, in coordinating with State, local, and tribal officials and the private sector.

(11) The recommendations of the program manager, in consultation with the Information Sharing Council, for a future management structure for the ISE, including whether

[1] See References in Text note below.

the position of program manager should continue to remain in existence.

(f) Program manager

(1) Designation

Not later than 120 days after December 17, 2004, with notification to Congress, the President shall designate an individual as the program manager responsible for information sharing across the Federal Government. The individual designated as the program manager shall serve as program manager until removed from service or replaced by the President (at the President's sole discretion). The program manager, in consultation with the head of any affected department or agency, shall have and exercise governmentwide authority over the sharing of information within the scope of the information sharing environment, including homeland security information, terrorism information, and weapons of mass destruction information, by all Federal departments, agencies, and components, irrespective of the Federal department, agency, or component in which the program manager may be administratively located, except as otherwise expressly provided by law.

(2) Duties and responsibilities

(A) In general

The program manager shall, in consultation with the Information Sharing Council—

(i) plan for and oversee the implementation of, and manage, the ISE;

(ii) assist in the development of policies, as appropriate, to foster the development and proper operation of the ISE;

(iii) consistent with the direction and policies issued by the President, the Director of National Intelligence, and the Director of the Office of Management and Budget, issue governmentwide procedures, guidelines, instructions, and functional standards, as appropriate, for the management, development, and proper operation of the ISE;

(iv) identify and resolve information sharing disputes between Federal departments, agencies, and components; and

(v) assist, monitor, and assess the implementation of the ISE by Federal departments and agencies to ensure adequate progress, technological consistency and policy compliance; and regularly report the findings to Congress.

(B) Content of policies, procedures, guidelines, rules, and standards

The policies, procedures, guidelines, rules, and standards under subparagraph (A)(ii) shall—

(i) take into account the varying missions and security requirements of agencies participating in the ISE;

(ii) address development, implementation, and oversight of technical standards and requirements;

(iii) take into account ongoing and planned efforts that support development, implementation and management of the ISE;

(iv) address and facilitate information sharing between and among departments and agencies of the intelligence community, the Department of Defense, the homeland security community and the law enforcement community;

(v) address and facilitate information sharing between Federal departments and agencies and State, tribal, and local governments;

(vi) address and facilitate, as appropriate, information sharing between Federal departments and agencies and the private sector;

(vii) address and facilitate, as appropriate, information sharing between Federal departments and agencies with foreign partners and allies; and

(viii) ensure the protection of privacy and civil liberties.

(g) Information Sharing Council

(1) Establishment

There is established an Information Sharing Council that shall assist the President and the program manager in their duties under this section. The Information Sharing Council shall serve until removed from service or replaced by the President (at the sole discretion of the President) with a successor body.

(2) Specific duties

In assisting the President and the program manager in their duties under this section, the Information Sharing Council shall—

(A) advise the President and the program manager in developing policies, procedures, guidelines, roles, and standards necessary to establish, implement, and maintain the ISE;

(B) work to ensure coordination among the Federal departments and agencies participating in the ISE in the establishment, implementation, and maintenance of the ISE;

(C) identify and, as appropriate, recommend the consolidation and elimination of current programs, systems, and processes used by Federal departments and agencies to share information, and recommend, as appropriate, the redirection of existing resources to support the ISE;

(D) identify gaps, if any, between existing technologies, programs and systems used by Federal departments and agencies to share information and the parameters of the proposed information sharing environment;

(E) recommend solutions to address any gaps identified under subparagraph (D);

(F) recommend means by which the ISE can be extended to allow interchange of information between Federal departments and agencies and appropriate authorities of State and local governments;

(G) assist the program manager in identifying and resolving information sharing disputes between Federal departments, agencies, and components;

(H) identify appropriate personnel for assignment to the program manager to support staffing needs identified by the program manager; and

(I) recommend whether or not, and by which means, the ISE should be expanded so as to allow future expansion encompassing other relevant categories of information.

(3) Consultation

In performing its duties, the Information Sharing Council shall consider input from persons and entities outside the Federal Government having significant experience and expertise in policy, technical matters, and operational matters relating to the ISE.

(4) Inapplicability of Federal Advisory Committee Act

The Information Sharing Council (including any subsidiary group of the Information Sharing Council) shall not be subject to the requirements of the Federal Advisory Committee Act (5 U.S.C. App.).

(5) Detailees

Upon a request by the Director of National Intelligence, the departments and agencies represented on the Information Sharing Council shall detail to the program manager, on a reimbursable basis, appropriate personnel identified under paragraph (2)(H).

(h) Performance management reports

(1) In general

Not later than two years after December 17, 2004, and not later than June 30 of each year thereafter, the President shall submit to Congress a report on the state of the ISE and of information sharing across the Federal Government.

(2) Content

Each report under this subsection shall include—

(A) a progress report on the extent to which the ISE has been implemented, including how the ISE has fared on the performance measures and whether the performance goals set in the preceding year have been met;

(B) objective system-wide performance goals for the following year;

(C) an accounting of how much was spent on the ISE in the preceding year;

(D) actions taken to ensure that procurement of and investments in systems and technology are consistent with the implementation plan for the ISE;

(E) the extent to which all terrorism watch lists are available for combined searching in real time through the ISE and whether there are consistent standards for placing individuals on, and removing individuals from, the watch lists, including the availability of processes for correcting errors;

(F) the extent to which State, tribal, and local officials are participating in the ISE;

(G) the extent to which private sector data, including information from owners and operators of critical infrastructure, is incorporated in the ISE, and the extent to which individuals and entities outside the government are receiving information through the ISE;

(H) the measures taken by the Federal government to ensure the accuracy of information in the ISE, in particular the accuracy of information about individuals;

(I) an assessment of the privacy and civil liberties protections of the ISE, including actions taken in the preceding year to implement or enforce privacy and civil liberties protections; and

(J) an assessment of the security protections used in the ISE.

(i) Agency responsibilities

The head of each department or agency that possesses or uses intelligence or terrorism information, operates a system in the ISE, or otherwise participates (or expects to participate) in the ISE shall—

(1) ensure full department or agency compliance with information sharing policies, procedures, guidelines, rules, and standards established under subsections (b) and (f) of this section;

(2) ensure the provision of adequate resources for systems and activities supporting operation of and participation in the ISE;

(3) ensure full department or agency cooperation in the development of the ISE to implement governmentwide information sharing; and

(4) submit, at the request of the President or the program manager, any reports on the implementation of the requirements of the ISE within such department or agency.

(j) Report on the information sharing environment

(1) In general

Not later than 180 days after August 3, 2007, the President shall report to the Committee on Homeland Security and Governmental Affairs of the Senate, the Select Committee on Intelligence of the Senate, the Committee on Homeland Security of the House of Representatives, and the Permanent Select Committee on Intelligence of the House of Representatives on the feasibility of—

(A) eliminating the use of any marking or process (including "Originator Control") intended to, or having the effect of, restricting the sharing of information within the scope of the information sharing environment, including homeland security information, terrorism information, and weapons of mass destruction information, between and among participants in the information sharing environment, unless the President has—

(i) specifically exempted categories of information from such elimination; and

(ii) reported that exemption to the committees of Congress described in the matter preceding this subparagraph; and

(B) continuing to use Federal agency standards in effect on August 3, 2007, for the collection, sharing, and access to information within the scope of the information sharing environment, including homeland security information, terrorism information, and weapons of mass destruction information, relating to citizens and lawful permanent residents;

(C) replacing the standards described in subparagraph (B) with a standard that would allow mission-based or threat-based permission to access or share information within the scope of the information sharing environment, including homeland security information, terrorism information, and weapons of mass destruction information, for a particular purpose that the Federal Government, through an appropriate process established in consultation with the Privacy and Civil Liberties Oversight Board established under section 2000ee of title 42, has determined to be lawfully permissible for a particular agency, component, or employee (commonly known as an "authorized use" standard); and

(D) the use of anonymized data by Federal departments, agencies, or components collecting, possessing, disseminating, or handling information within the scope of the information sharing environment, including homeland security information, terrorism information, and weapons of mass destruction information, in any cases in which—

(i) the use of such information is reasonably expected to produce results materially equivalent to the use of information that is transferred or stored in a non-anonymized form; and

(ii) such use is consistent with any mission of that department, agency, or component (including any mission under a Federal statute or directive of the President) that involves the storage, retention, sharing, or exchange of personally identifiable information.

(2) Definition

In this subsection, the term "anonymized data" means data in which the individual to whom the data pertains is not identifiable with reasonable efforts, including information that has been encrypted or hidden through the use of other technology.

(k) Additional positions

The program manager is authorized to hire not more than 10 full-time employees to assist the program manager in—

(1) activities associated with the implementation of the information sharing environment, including—

(A) implementing the requirements under subsection (b)(2); and

(B) any additional implementation initiatives to enhance and expedite the creation of the information sharing environment; and

(2) identifying and resolving information sharing disputes between Federal departments, agencies, and components under subsection (f)(2)(A)(iv).

***(l)* Authorization of appropriations**

There is authorized to be appropriated to carry out this section $30,000,000 for each of fiscal years 2008 and 2009.

(Pub. L. 108–458, title I, § 1016, Dec. 17, 2004, 118 Stat. 3664; Pub. L. 110–53, title V, § 504, Aug. 3, 2007, 121 Stat. 313.)

REFERENCES IN TEXT

Executive Order 13356, referred to in subsec. (a)(2), which was formerly set out as a note below, was revoked by Ex. Ord. No. 13388, set out as a note below, which established an Information Sharing Council consistent with subsec. (g) of this section.

This title, referred to in subsec. (e)(10)(A), is title I of Pub. L. 108–458, Dec. 17, 2004, 118 Stat. 3643, known as the National Security Intelligence Reform Act of 2004. For complete classification of title I to the Code, see Short Title of 2004 Amendment note set out under section 401 of Title 50, War and National Defense, and Tables.

The Federal Advisory Committee Act, referred to in subsec. (g)(4), is Pub. L. 92–463, Oct. 6, 1972, 86 Stat. 770, as amended, which is set out in the Appendix to Title 5, Government Organization and Employees.

CODIFICATION

Section was enacted as part of the Intelligence Reform and Terrorism Prevention Act of 2004, and also as part of the National Security Intelligence Reform Act of 2004, and not as part of the Homeland Security Act of 2002 which comprises this chapter.

AMENDMENTS

2007—Subsec. (a)(1), (2). Pub. L. 110–53, § 504(1)(A), (B), added par. (1) and redesignated former par. (1) as (2). Former par. (2) redesignated (3).

Subsec. (a)(3). Pub. L. 110–53, § 504(1)(C), added par. (3) and struck out heading and text of former par. (3). Text read as follows: "The terms 'information sharing environment' and 'ISE' mean an approach that facilitates the sharing of terrorism information, which approach may include any methods determined necessary and appropriate for carrying out this section."

Pub. L. 110–53, § 504(1)(A), redesignated par. (2) as (3). Former par. (3) redesignated (4).

Subsec. (a)(4). Pub. L. 110–53, § 504(1)(A), redesignated par. (3) as (4). Former par. (4) redesignated (5).

Subsec. (a)(5). Pub. L. 110–53, § 504(1)(D), added par. (5) and struck out heading and text of former par (5). Text read as follows: "The term 'terrorism information' means all information, whether collected, produced, or distributed by intelligence, law enforcement, military, homeland security, or other activities relating to—

"(A) the existence, organization, capabilities, plans, intentions, vulnerabilities, means of finance or material support, or activities of foreign or international terrorist groups or individuals, or of domestic groups or individuals involved in transnational terrorism;

"(B) threats posed by such groups or individuals to the United States, United States persons, or United States interests, or to those of other nations;

"(C) communications of or by such groups or individuals; or

"(D) groups or individuals reasonably believed to be assisting or associated with such groups or individuals."

Pub. L. 110–53, § 504(1)(A), redesignated par. (4) as (5).

Subsec. (a)(6). Pub. L. 110–53, § 504(1)(E), added par. (6).

Subsec. (b)(2)(J) to (O). Pub. L. 110–53, § 504(2), added subpars. (J) to (O).

Subsec. (f)(1). Pub. L. 110–53, § 504(3)(A), substituted "until removed from service or replaced" for "during the two-year period beginning on the date of designation under this paragraph unless sooner removed from service and replaced" and "The program manager, in consultation with the head of any affected department or agency, shall have and exercise governmentwide authority over the sharing of information within the scope of the information sharing environment, including homeland security information, terrorism information, and weapons of mass destruction information, by all Federal departments, agencies, and components, irrespective of the Federal department, agency, or component in which the program manager may be administratively located, except as otherwise expressly provided by law" for "The program manager shall have and exercise governmentwide authority".

Subsec. (f)(2)(A)(ii) to (v). Pub. L. 110–53, § 504(3)(B), added cls. (ii) to (iv), redesignated former cl. (iii) as (v), and struck out former cl. (ii) which read as follows: "assist in the development of policies, procedures, guidelines, rules, and standards as appropriate to foster the development and proper operation of the ISE; and".

Subsec. (g)(1). Pub. L. 110–53, § 504(4)(A), substituted "until removed from service or replaced" for "during the two-year period beginning on the date of the initial designation of the program manager by the President under subsection (f)(1) of this section, unless sooner removed from service and replaced".

Subsec. (g)(2)(G) to (I). Pub. L. 110–53, § 504(4)(B), added subpars. (G) and (H) and redesignated former subpar. (G) as (I).

Subsec. (g)(4). Pub. L. 110–53, § 504(4)(C), inserted "(including any subsidiary group of the Information Sharing Council)" before "shall not be subject".

Subsec. (g)(5). Pub. L. 110–53, § 504(4)(D), added par. (5).

Subsec. (h)(1). Pub. L. 110–53, § 504(5), substituted "and not later than June 30 of each year thereafter" for "and annually thereafter".

Subsecs. (j) to (*l*). Pub. L. 110–53, § 504(6), added subsecs. (j) to (*l*) and struck out heading and text of former subsec. (j). Text read as follows: "There is authorized to be appropriated to carry out this section $20,000,000 for each of fiscal years 2005 and 2006."

EFFECTIVE DATE

For Determination by President that section takes effect on Apr. 21, 2005, see Memorandum of President of the United States, Apr. 21, 2005, 70 F.R. 23925, set out as a note under section 401 of Title 50, War and National Defense.

Section effective not later than six months after Dec. 17, 2004, except as otherwise expressly provided, see section 1097(a) of Pub. L. 108–458, set out as an Effective Date of 2004 Amendment; Transition Provisions note under section 401 of Title 50, War and National Defense.

PROCEDURES TO CLEAR INDIVIDUALS FROM TERRORIST DATABASE LISTS

Pub. L. 109–295, title V, § 556, Oct. 4, 2006, 120 Stat. 1391, provided that: "Not later than six months after the date of enactment of this Act [Oct. 4, 2006], the Secretary of Homeland Security shall establish revised procedures for expeditiously clearing individuals whose names have been mistakenly placed on a terrorist database list or who have names identical or similar to individuals on a terrorist database list. The Secretary shall advise Congress of the procedures established."

EXECUTIVE ORDER NO. 13356

Ex. Ord. No. 13356, Aug. 27, 2004, 69 F.R. 53599, which provided for strengthening the sharing of terrorism information to protect Americans, was revoked by Ex. Ord. No. 13388, § 8(b), Oct. 25, 2005, 70 F.R. 62025, set out below.

EX. ORD. NO. 13388. FURTHER STRENGTHENING THE SHARING OF TERRORISM INFORMATION TO PROTECT AMERICANS

Ex. Ord. No. 13388, Oct. 25, 2005, 70 F.R. 62023, provided:

By the authority vested in me as President by the Constitution and the laws of the United States of America, including section 1016 of the Intelligence Reform and Terrorism Prevention Act of 2004 (Public Law 108–458) [6 U.S.C. 485], and in order to further strengthen the effective conduct of United States counterterrorism activities and protect the territory, people, and interests of the United States of America, including against terrorist attacks, it is hereby ordered as follows:

SECTION 1. *Policy.* To the maximum extent consistent with applicable law, agencies shall, in the design and use of information systems and in the dissemination of information among agencies:

(a) give the highest priority to (i) the detection, prevention, disruption, preemption, and mitigation of the effects of terrorist activities against the territory, people, and interests of the United States of America; (ii) the interchange of terrorism information among agencies; (iii) the interchange of terrorism information between agencies and appropriate authorities of State, local, and tribal governments, and between agencies and appropriate private sector entities; and (iv) the protection of the ability of agencies to acquire additional such information; and

(b) protect the freedom, information privacy, and other legal rights of Americans in the conduct of activities implementing subsection (a).

SEC. 2. *Duties of Heads of Agencies Possessing or Acquiring Terrorism Information.* To implement the policy set forth in section 1 of this order, the head of each agency that possesses or acquires terrorism information:

(a) shall promptly give access to the terrorism information to the head of each other agency that has counterterrorism functions, and provide the terrorism information to each such agency, unless otherwise directed by the President, and consistent with (i) the statutory responsibilities of the agencies providing and receiving the information; (ii) any guidance issued by the Attorney General to fulfill the policy set forth in subsection 1(b) of this order; and (iii) other applicable law, including sections 102A(g) and (i) of the National Security Act of 1947 [50 U.S.C. 403–1(g), (i)], section 1016 of the Intelligence Reform and Terrorism Prevention Act of 2004 [6 U.S.C. 485] (including any policies, procedures, guidelines, rules, and standards issued pursuant thereto), sections 202 and 892 of the Homeland Security Act of 2002 [6 U.S.C. 122, 482], Executive Order 12958 of April 17, 1995, as amended [50 U.S.C. 435 note], and Executive Order 13311 of July 29, 2003 [6 U.S.C. 482 note]; and

(b) shall cooperate in and facilitate production of reports based on terrorism information with contents and formats that permit dissemination that maximizes the utility of the information in protecting the territory, people, and interests of the United States.

SEC. 3. *Preparing Terrorism Information for Maximum Distribution.* To assist in expeditious and effective implementation by agencies of the policy set forth in section 1 of this order, the common standards for the sharing of terrorism information established pursuant to section 3 of Executive Order 13356 of August 27, 2004 [formerly set out above], shall be used, as appropriate, in carrying out section 1016 of the Intelligence Reform and Terrorism Prevention Act of 2004.

SEC. 4. *Requirements for Collection of Terrorism Information Inside the United States.* To assist in expeditious and effective implementation by agencies of the policy set forth in section 1 of this order, the recommendations regarding the establishment of executive branch-wide collection and sharing requirements, procedures, and guidelines for terrorism information collected within the United States made pursuant to section 4 of Executive Order 13356 [formerly set out above] shall be used, as appropriate, in carrying out section 1016 of the Intelligence Reform and Terrorism Prevention Act of 2004.

SEC. 5. *Establishment and Functions of Information Sharing Council.* (a) Consistent with section 1016(g) of the Intelligence Reform and Terrorism Prevention Act of 2004, there is hereby established an Information Sharing Council (Council), chaired by the Program Manager to whom section 1016 of such Act refers, and composed exclusively of designees of: the Secretaries of State, the Treasury, Defense, Commerce, Energy, and Homeland Security; the Attorney General; the Director of National Intelligence; the Director of the Central Intelligence Agency; the Director of the Office of Management and Budget; the Director of the Federal Bureau of Investigation; the Director of the National Counterterrorism Center; and such other heads of departments or agencies as the Director of National Intelligence may designate.

(b) The mission of the Council is to (i) provide advice and information concerning the establishment of an interoperable terrorism information sharing environment to facilitate automated sharing of terrorism information among appropriate agencies to implement the policy set forth in section 1 of this order; and (ii) perform the duties set forth in section 1016(g) of the Intelligence Reform and Terrorism Prevention Act of 2004.

(c) To assist in expeditious and effective implementation by agencies of the policy set forth in section 1 of this order, the plan for establishment of a proposed interoperable terrorism information sharing environment reported under section 5(c) of Executive Order 13356 [formerly set out above] shall be used, as appropriate, in carrying out section 1016 of the Intelligence Reform and Terrorism Prevention Act of 2004.

SEC. 6. *Definitions*. As used in this order:

(a) the term "agency" has the meaning set forth for the term "executive agency" in section 105 of title 5, United States Code, together with the Department of Homeland Security, but includes the Postal Rate Commission and the United States Postal Service and excludes the Government Accountability Office; and

(b) the term "terrorism information" has the meaning set forth for such term in section 1016(a)(4) of the Intelligence Reform and Terrorism Prevention Act of 2004.

SEC. 7. *General Provisions*. (a) This order:

(i) shall be implemented in a manner consistent with applicable law, including Federal law protecting the information privacy and other legal rights of Americans, and subject to the availability of appropriations;

(ii) shall be implemented in a manner consistent with the authority of the principal officers of agencies as heads of their respective agencies, including under section 199 of the Revised Statutes (22 U.S.C. 2651), section 201 of the Department of Energy Organization Act (42 U.S.C. 7131), section 103 of the National Security Act of 1947 (50 U.S.C. 403–3), section 102(a) of the Homeland Security Act of 2002 (6 U.S.C. 112(a)), and sections 301 of title 5, 113(b) and 162(b) of title 10, 1501 of title 15, 503 of title 28, and 301(b) of title 31, United States Code;

(iii) shall be implemented consistent with the Presidential Memorandum of June 2, 2005, on "Strengthening Information Sharing, Access, and Integration—Organizational, Management, and Policy Development Structures for Creating the Terrorism Information Sharing Environment;" [not set out in the Code]

(iv) shall not be construed to impair or otherwise affect the functions of the Director of the Office of Management and Budget relating to budget, administrative, and legislative proposals; and

(v) shall be implemented in a manner consistent with section 102A of the National Security Act of 1947 [50 U.S.C. 403–1].

(b) This order is intended only to improve the internal management of the Federal Government and is not intended to, and does not, create any rights or benefits, substantive or procedural, enforceable at law or in equity by a party against the United States, its departments, agencies, instrumentalities, or entities, its officers, employees, or agents, or any other person.

SEC. 8. *Amendments and Revocation*. (a) [Amended Ex. Ord. No. 13311, set out as a note under section 482 of this title.]

(b) Executive Order 13356 of August 27, 2004 [formerly set out above], is hereby revoked.

GEORGE W. BUSH.

ASSIGNMENT OF CERTAIN FUNCTIONS UNDER THE INTELLIGENCE REFORM AND TERRORISM PREVENTION ACT OF 2004

Memorandum of President of the United States, Nov. 14, 2006, 71 F.R. 67029, provided:

Memorandum for the Director of National Intelligence

By the authority vested in me as President by the Constitution and laws of the United States, including section 301 of title 3, United States Code, the reporting function of the President under section 1016(e) of the Intelligence Reform and Terrorism Prevention Act of 2004 (Public Law 108–458, 118 Stat. 3638) is hereby assigned to the Director of National Intelligence (Director).

The Director shall perform such function in a manner consistent with the President's constitutional authority to withhold information the disclosure of which could impair foreign relations, national security, the deliberative processes of the Executive, or the performance of the Executive's constitutional duties.

Any reference in this memorandum to the provision of any Act shall be deemed to include references to any hereafter-enacted provision of law that is the same or substantially the same as such provision.

You are authorized and directed to publish this memorandum in the Federal Register.

GEORGE W. BUSH.

Memorandum of President of the United States, Apr. 10, 2007, 72 F.R. 18561, provided:

Memorandum for the Director of National Intelligence

By the authority vested in me as President by the Constitution and laws of the United States of America, including section 301 of title 3, United States Code, the functions of the President under section 1016(b) of the Intelligence Reform and Terrorism Prevention Act of 2004 (Public Law 108–458) (the "Act") are hereby assigned to the Director of National Intelligence (Director).

The Director shall perform such functions in a manner consistent with direction and guidance issued by the President, including (1) the Memorandum for the Heads of Executive Departments and Agencies of June 2, 2005, entitled "Strengthening Information Sharing, Access, and Integration—Organizational, Management, and Policy Development Structures for Creating the Terrorism Information Sharing Environment," and (2) the Memorandum for the Heads of Executive Departments and Agencies of December 16, 2005, entitled "Guidelines and Requirements in Support of the Information Sharing Environment;" provided that the Director shall ensure that the official within the Office of the Director of National Intelligence previously designated as the program manager responsible for information sharing across the Federal Government pursuant to the Act shall be the assistant to the Director in carrying out the functions delegated by this memorandum.

You are authorized and directed to publish this memorandum in the Federal Register.

GEORGE W. BUSH.

Memorandum of President of the United States, Sept. 8, 2007, 72 F.R. 52279, provided:

Memorandum for the Secretary of State[,] the Secretary of Defense[,] the Attorney General[,] the Secretary of Energy[,] the Secretary of Homeland Security[, and] the Director of National Intelligence

By the authority vested in me as President by the Constitution and laws of the United States, including section 301 of title 3, United States Code, the reporting functions of the President under subsections (h) and (j) of section 1016 of the Intelligence Reform and Terrorism Prevention Act of 2004 (Public Law 108–458), as amended by the Implementing Recommendations of the 9/11 Commission Act of 2007 (Public Law 110–53) (IRTPA), are hereby assigned to the Director of National Intelligence (Director). The Director shall consult the Secretaries of State, Defense, Energy, Homeland Security, and the Attorney General in performing such functions.

Heads of departments and agencies shall, to the extent permitted by law, furnish to the Director information that the Director requests to perform such functions, in the format and on the schedule specified by the Director.

The Director shall perform such functions in a manner consistent with the President's constitutional authority to withhold information the disclosure of which could impair foreign relations, national security, the deliberative processes of the Executive, and the performance of the Executive's constitutional duties.

Any reference in this memorandum to the provision of IRTPA shall be deemed to include references to any hereafter-enacted provision of law that is the same or substantially the same as such provision.

The Director is authorized and directed to publish this memorandum in the Federal Register.

GEORGE W. BUSH.

§ 486. Limitation of liability

A person who has completed a security awareness training course approved by or operated under a cooperative agreement with the Department of Homeland Security using funds made available in fiscal year 2006 and thereafter or in any prior appropriations Acts, who is enrolled in a program recognized or acknowledged by an Information Sharing and Analysis Center, and who reports a situation, activity or incident pursuant to that program to an appropriate authority, shall not be liable for damages in any action brought in a Federal or State court which result from any act or omission unless such person is guilty of gross negligence or willful misconduct.

(Pub. L. 109–90, title V, § 541, Oct. 18, 2005, 119 Stat. 2089.)

CODIFICATION

Section was enacted as part of the Department of Homeland Security Appropriations Act, 2006, and not as part of the Homeland Security Act of 2002 which comprises this chapter.

PART J—SECURE HANDLING OF AMMONIUM NITRATE

§ 488. Definitions

In this part:

(1) Ammonium nitrate

The term "ammonium nitrate" means—

(A) solid ammonium nitrate that is chiefly the ammonium salt of nitric acid and contains not less than 33 percent nitrogen by weight; and

(B) any mixture containing a percentage of ammonium nitrate that is equal to or greater than the percentage determined by the Secretary under section 488a(b) of this title.

(2) Ammonium nitrate facility

The term "ammonium nitrate facility" means any entity that produces, sells or otherwise transfers ownership of, or provides application services for ammonium nitrate.

(3) Ammonium nitrate purchaser

The term "ammonium nitrate purchaser" means any person who purchases ammonium nitrate from an ammonium nitrate facility.

(Pub. L. 107–296, title VIII, § 899A, as added Pub. L. 110–161, div. E, title V, § 563(a), Dec. 26, 2007, 121 Stat. 2083.)

§ 488a. Regulation of the sale and transfer of ammonium nitrate

(a) In general

The Secretary shall regulate the sale and transfer of ammonium nitrate by an ammonium nitrate facility in accordance with this part to prevent the misappropriation or use of ammonium nitrate in an act of terrorism.

(b) Ammonium nitrate mixtures

Not later than 90 days after December 26, 2007, the Secretary, in consultation with the heads of appropriate Federal departments and agencies (including the Secretary of Agriculture), shall, after notice and an opportunity for comment, establish a threshold percentage for ammonium nitrate in a substance.

(c) Registration of owners of ammonium nitrate facilities

(1) Registration

The Secretary shall establish a process by which any person that—

(A) owns an ammonium nitrate facility is required to register with the Department; and

(B) registers under subparagraph (A) is issued a registration number for purposes of this part.

(2) Registration information

Any person applying to register under paragraph (1) shall submit to the Secretary—

(A) the name, address, and telephone number of each ammonium nitrate facility owned by that person;

(B) the name of the person designated by that person as the point of contact for each such facility, for purposes of this part; and

(C) such other information as the Secretary may determine is appropriate.

(d) Registration of ammonium nitrate purchasers

(1) Registration

The Secretary shall establish a process by which any person that—

(A) intends to be an ammonium nitrate purchaser is required to register with the Department; and

(B) registers under subparagraph (A) is issued a registration number for purposes of this part.

(2) Registration information

Any person applying to register under paragraph (1) as an ammonium nitrate purchaser shall submit to the Secretary—

(A) the name, address, and telephone number of the applicant; and

(B) the intended use of ammonium nitrate to be purchased by the applicant.

(e) Records

(1) Maintenance of records

The owner of an ammonium nitrate facility shall—

(A) maintain a record of each sale or transfer of ammonium nitrate, during the two-year period beginning on the date of that sale or transfer; and

(B) include in such record the information described in paragraph (2).

(2) Specific information required

For each sale or transfer of ammonium nitrate, the owner of an ammonium nitrate facility shall—

(A) record the name, address, telephone number, and registration number issued under subsection (c) or (d) of each person that purchases ammonium nitrate, in a manner prescribed by the Secretary;

(B) if applicable, record the name, address, and telephone number of an agent acting on behalf of the person described in subparagraph (A), at the point of sale;

(C) record the date and quantity of ammonium nitrate sold or transferred; and

(D) verify the identity of the persons described in subparagraphs (A) and (B), as applicable, in accordance with a procedure established by the Secretary.

(3) Protection of information

In maintaining records in accordance with paragraph (1), the owner of an ammonium nitrate facility shall take reasonable actions to ensure the protection of the information included in such records.

(f) Exemption for explosive purposes

The Secretary may exempt from this part a person producing, selling, or purchasing ammonium nitrate exclusively for use in the production of an explosive under a license or permit issued under chapter 40 of title 18.

(g) Consultation

In carrying out this section, the Secretary shall consult with the Secretary of Agriculture, States, and appropriate private sector entities, to ensure that the access of agricultural producers to ammonium nitrate is not unduly burdened.

(h) Data confidentiality

(1) In general

Notwithstanding section 552 of title 5 or the USA PATRIOT ACT (Public Law 107–56; 115 Stat. 272), and except as provided in paragraph (2), the Secretary may not disclose to any person any information obtained under this part.

(2) Exception

The Secretary may disclose any information obtained by the Secretary under this part to—

(A) an officer or employee of the United States, or a person that has entered into a contract with the United States, who has a need to know the information to perform the duties of the officer, employee, or person; or

(B) to a State agency under section 488c of this title, under appropriate arrangements to ensure the protection of the information.

(i) Registration procedures and check of terrorist screening database

(1) Registration procedures

(A) Generally

The Secretary shall establish procedures to efficiently receive applications for registration numbers under this part, conduct the checks required under paragraph (2), and promptly issue or deny a registration number.

(B) Initial six-month registration period

The Secretary shall take steps to maximize the number of registration applications that are submitted and processed during the six-month period described in section 488e(e) of this title.

(2) Check of terrorist screening database

(A) Check required

The Secretary shall conduct a check of appropriate identifying information of any person seeking to register with the Department under subsection (c) or (d) against identifying information that appears in the terrorist screening database of the Department.

(B) Authority to deny registration number

If the identifying information of a person seeking to register with the Department under subsection (c) or (d) appears in the terrorist screening database of the Department, the Secretary may deny issuance of a registration number under this part.

(3) Expedited review of applications

(A) In general

Following the six-month period described in section 488e(e) of this title, the Secretary shall, to the extent practicable, issue or deny registration numbers under this part not later than 72 hours after the time the Secretary receives a complete registration application, unless the Secretary determines, in the interest of national security, that additional time is necessary to review an application.

(B) Notice of application status

In all cases, the Secretary shall notify a person seeking to register with the Department under subsection (c) or (d) of the status of the application of that person not later than 72 hours after the time the Secretary receives a complete registration application.

(4) Expedited appeals process

(A) Requirement

(i) Appeals process

The Secretary shall establish an expedited appeals process for persons denied a registration number under this part.

(ii) Time period for resolution

The Secretary shall, to the extent practicable, resolve appeals not later than 72 hours after receiving a complete request for appeal unless the Secretary determines, in the interest of national security, that additional time is necessary to resolve an appeal.

(B) Consultation

The Secretary, in developing the appeals process under subparagraph (A), shall consult with appropriate stakeholders.

(C) Guidance

The Secretary shall provide guidance regarding the procedures and information required for an appeal under subparagraph (A) to any person denied a registration number under this part.

(5) Restrictions on use and maintenance of information

(A) In general

Any information constituting grounds for denial of a registration number under this section shall be maintained confidentially by the Secretary and may be used only for making determinations under this section.

(B) Sharing of information

Notwithstanding any other provision of this part, the Secretary may share any such information with Federal, State, local, and tribal law enforcement agencies, as appropriate.

(6) Registration information

(A) Authority to require information

The Secretary may require a person applying for a registration number under this part to submit such information as may be necessary to carry out the requirements of this section.

(B) Requirement to update information

The Secretary may require persons issued a registration under this part to update registration information submitted to the Secretary under this part, as appropriate.

(7) Re-checks against terrorist screening database

(A) Re-checks

The Secretary shall, as appropriate, re-check persons provided a registration number pursuant to this part against the terrorist screening database of the Department, and may revoke such registration number if the Secretary determines such person may pose a threat to national security.

(B) Notice of revocation

The Secretary shall, as appropriate, provide prior notice to a person whose registration number is revoked under this section and such person shall have an opportunity to appeal, as provided in paragraph (4).

(Pub. L. 107–296, title VIII, § 899B, as added Pub. L. 110–161, div. E, title V, § 563(a), Dec. 26, 2007, 121 Stat. 2084.)

REFERENCES IN TEXT

The USA PATRIOT ACT, referred to in subsec. (h)(1), is Pub. L. 107–56, Oct. 26, 2001, 115 Stat. 272, also known as the Uniting and Strengthening America by Providing Appropriate Tools Required to Intercept and Obstruct Terrorism Act of 2001. For complete classification of this Act to the Code, see Short Title of 2001 Amendment note set out under section 1 of Title 18, Crimes and Criminal Procedure, and Tables.

§ 488b. Inspection and auditing of records

The Secretary shall establish a process for the periodic inspection and auditing of the records maintained by owners of ammonium nitrate facilities for the purpose of monitoring compliance with this part or for the purpose of deterring or preventing the misappropriation or use of ammonium nitrate in an act of terrorism.

(Pub. L. 107–296, title VIII, § 899C, as added Pub. L. 110–161, div. E, title V, § 563(a), Dec. 26, 2007, 121 Stat. 2087.)

§ 488c. Administrative provisions

(a) Cooperative agreements

The Secretary—

(1) may enter into a cooperative agreement with the Secretary of Agriculture, or the head of any State department of agriculture or its designee involved in agricultural regulation, in consultation with the State agency responsible for homeland security, to carry out the provisions of this part; and

(2) wherever possible, shall seek to cooperate with State agencies or their designees that oversee ammonium nitrate facility operations when seeking cooperative agreements to implement the registration and enforcement provisions of this part.

(b) Delegation

(1) Authority

The Secretary may delegate to a State the authority to assist the Secretary in the administration and enforcement of this part.

(2) Delegation required

At the request of a Governor of a State, the Secretary shall delegate to that State the authority to carry out functions under sections 488a and 488b of this title, if the Secretary determines that the State is capable of satisfactorily carrying out such functions.

(3) Funding

Subject to the availability of appropriations, if the Secretary delegates functions to a State under this subsection, the Secretary shall provide to that State sufficient funds to carry out the delegated functions.

(c) Provision of guidance and notification materials to ammonium nitrate facilities

(1) Guidance

The Secretary shall make available to each owner of an ammonium nitrate facility registered under section 488a(c)(1) of this title guidance on—

(A) the identification of suspicious ammonium nitrate purchases or transfers or attempted purchases or transfers;

(B) the appropriate course of action to be taken by the ammonium nitrate facility owner with respect to such a purchase or transfer or attempted purchase or transfer, including—

(i) exercising the right of the owner of the ammonium nitrate facility to decline sale of ammonium nitrate; and

(ii) notifying appropriate law enforcement entities; and

(C) additional subjects determined appropriate to prevent the misappropriation or use of ammonium nitrate in an act of terrorism.

(2) Use of materials and programs

In providing guidance under this subsection, the Secretary shall, to the extent practicable, leverage any relevant materials and programs.

(3) Notification materials

(A) In general

The Secretary shall make available materials suitable for posting at locations where ammonium nitrate is sold.

(B) Design of materials

Materials made available under subparagraph (A) shall be designed to notify prospective ammonium nitrate purchasers of—

(i) the record-keeping requirements under section 488a of this title; and

(ii) the penalties for violating such requirements.

(Pub. L. 107–296, title VIII, §899D, as added Pub. L. 110–161, div. E, title V, §563(a), Dec. 26, 2007, 121 Stat. 2087.)

§488d. Theft reporting requirement

Any person who is required to comply with section 488a(e) of this title who has knowledge of the theft or unexplained loss of ammonium nitrate shall report such theft or loss to the appropriate Federal law enforcement authorities not later than 1 calendar day of the date on which the person becomes aware of such theft or loss. Upon receipt of such report, the relevant Federal authorities shall inform State, local, and tribal law enforcement entities, as appropriate.

(Pub. L. 107–296, title VIII, §899E, as added Pub. L. 110–161, div. E, title V, §563(a), Dec. 26, 2007, 121 Stat. 2088.)

§488e. Prohibitions and penalty

(a) Prohibitions

(1) Taking possession

No person shall purchase ammonium nitrate from an ammonium nitrate facility unless such person is registered under subsection (c) or (d) of section 488a of this title, or is an agent of a person registered under subsection (c) or (d) of that section.

(2) Transferring possession

An owner of an ammonium nitrate facility shall not transfer possession of ammonium nitrate from the ammonium nitrate facility to any ammonium nitrate purchaser who is not registered under subsection (c) or (d) of section 488a of this title, or to any agent acting on behalf of an ammonium nitrate purchaser when such purchaser is not registered under subsection (c) or (d) of section 488a of this title.

(3) Other prohibitions

No person shall—

(A) purchase ammonium nitrate without a registration number required under subsection (c) or (d) of section 488a of this title;

(B) own or operate an ammonium nitrate facility without a registration number required under section 488a(c) of this title; or

(C) fail to comply with any requirement or violate any other prohibition under this part.

(b) Civil penalty

A person that violates this part may be assessed a civil penalty by the Secretary of not more than $50,000 per violation.

(c) Penalty considerations

In determining the amount of a civil penalty under this section, the Secretary shall consider—

(1) the nature and circumstances of the violation;

(2) with respect to the person who commits the violation, any history of prior violations, the ability to pay the penalty, and any effect the penalty is likely to have on the ability of such person to do business; and

(3) any other matter that the Secretary determines that justice requires.

(d) Notice and opportunity for a hearing

No civil penalty may be assessed under this part unless the person liable for the penalty has been given notice and an opportunity for a hearing on the violation for which the penalty is to be assessed in the county, parish, or incorporated city of residence of that person.

(e) Delay in application of prohibition

Paragraphs (1) and (2) of subsection (a) shall apply on and after the date that is 6 months after the date that the Secretary issues a final rule implementing this part.

(Pub. L. 107–296, title VIII, §899F, as added Pub. L. 110–161, div. E, title V, §563(a), Dec. 26, 2007, 121 Stat. 2088.)

§488f. Protection from civil liability

(a) In general

Notwithstanding any other provision of law, an owner of an ammonium nitrate facility that in good faith refuses to sell or transfer ammonium nitrate to any person, or that in good faith discloses to the Department or to appropriate law enforcement authorities an actual or attempted purchase or transfer of ammonium nitrate, based upon a reasonable belief that the person seeking purchase or transfer of ammonium nitrate may use the ammonium nitrate to create an explosive device to be employed in an act of terrorism (as defined in section 3077 of title 18), or to use ammonium nitrate for any other unlawful purpose, shall not be liable in any civil action relating to that refusal to sell ammonium nitrate or that disclosure.

(b) Reasonable belief

A reasonable belief that a person may use ammonium nitrate to create an explosive device to be employed in an act of terrorism under subsection (a) may not solely be based on the race, sex, national origin, creed, religion, status as a veteran, or status as a member of the Armed Forces of the United States of that person.

(Pub. L. 107–296, title VIII, §899G, as added Pub. L. 110–161, div. E, title V, §563(a), Dec. 26, 2007, 121 Stat. 2089.)

§488g. Preemption of other laws

(a) Other Federal regulations

Except as provided in section 488f of this title, nothing in this part affects any regulation issued by any agency other than an agency of the Department.

(b) State law

Subject to section 488f of this title, this part preempts the laws of any State to the extent that such laws are inconsistent with this part, except that this part shall not preempt any State law that provides additional protection against the acquisition of ammonium nitrate by terrorists or the use of ammonium nitrate in explosives in acts of terrorism or for other illicit purposes, as determined by the Secretary.

(Pub. L. 107–296, title VIII, §899H, as added Pub. L. 110–161, div. E, title V, §563(a), Dec. 26, 2007, 121 Stat. 2089.)

§488h. Deadlines for regulations

The Secretary—

(1) shall issue a proposed rule implementing this part not later than 6 months after December 26, 2007; and

(2) issue a final rule implementing this part not later than 1 year after December 26, 2007.

(Pub. L. 107–296, title VIII, § 899I, as added Pub. L. 110–161, div. E, title V, § 563(a), Dec. 26, 2007, 121 Stat. 2089.)

§ 488i. Authorization of appropriations

There are authorized to be appropriated to the Secretary—

(1) $2,000,000 for fiscal year 2008; and

(2) $10,750,000 for each of fiscal years 2009 through 2012.

(Pub. L. 107–296, title VIII, § 899J, as added Pub. L. 110–161, div. E, title V, § 563(a), Dec. 26, 2007, 121 Stat. 2090.)

SUBCHAPTER IX—NATIONAL HOMELAND SECURITY COUNCIL

§ 491. National Homeland Security Council

There is established within the Executive Office of the President a council to be known as the "Homeland Security Council" (in this subchapter referred to as the "Council").

(Pub. L. 107–296, title IX, § 901, Nov. 25, 2002, 116 Stat. 2258.)

§ 492. Function

The function of the Council shall be to advise the President on homeland security matters.

(Pub. L. 107–296, title IX, § 902, Nov. 25, 2002, 116 Stat. 2258.)

§ 493. Membership

(a) Members

The members of the Council shall be the following:

(1) The President.

(2) The Vice President.

(3) The Secretary of Homeland Security.

(4) The Attorney General.

(5) The Secretary of Defense.

(6) Such other individuals as may be designated by the President.

(b) Attendance of Chairman of Joint Chiefs of Staff at meetings

The Chairman of the Joint Chiefs of Staff (or, in the absence of the Chairman, the Vice Chairman of the Joint Chiefs of Staff) may, in the role of the Chairman of the Joint Chiefs of Staff as principal military adviser to the Council and subject to the direction of the President, attend and participate in meetings of the Council.

(Pub. L. 107–296, title IX, § 903, Nov. 25, 2002, 116 Stat. 2258; Pub. L. 109–163, div. A, title IX, § 908(b), Jan. 6, 2006, 119 Stat. 3404.)

AMENDMENTS

2006—Pub. L. 109–163 designated existing provisions as subsec. (a), inserted heading, and added subsec. (b).

§ 494. Other functions and activities

For the purpose of more effectively coordinating the policies and functions of the United States Government relating to homeland security, the Council shall—

(1) assess the objectives, commitments, and risks of the United States in the interest of homeland security and to[1] make resulting recommendations to the President;

(2) oversee and review homeland security policies of the Federal Government and to[1] make resulting recommendations to the President; and

(3) perform such other functions as the President may direct.

(Pub. L. 107–296, title IX, § 904, Nov. 25, 2002, 116 Stat. 2259.)

§ 495. Staff composition

The Council shall have a staff, the head of which shall be a civilian Executive Secretary, who shall be appointed by the President. The President is authorized to fix the pay of the Executive Secretary at a rate not to exceed the rate of pay payable to the Executive Secretary of the National Security Council.

(Pub. L. 107–296, title IX, § 905, Nov. 25, 2002, 116 Stat. 2259.)

§ 496. Relation to the National Security Council

The President may convene joint meetings of the Homeland Security Council and the National Security Council with participation by members of either Council or as the President may otherwise direct.

(Pub. L. 107–296, title IX, § 906, Nov. 25, 2002, 116 Stat. 2259.)

SUBCHAPTER X—CONSTRUCTION

§ 511. Information security responsibilities of certain agencies

(1) National security responsibilities

(A) Nothing in this chapter (including any amendment made by this chapter) shall supersede any authority of the Secretary of Defense, the Director of Central Intelligence, or other agency head, as authorized by law and as directed by the President, with regard to the operation, control, or management of national security systems, as defined by section 3532(3)[1] of title 44.

(B) Omitted

(2) Atomic Energy Act of 1954

Nothing in this chapter shall supersede any requirement made by or under the Atomic Energy Act of 1954 (42 U.S.C. 2011 et seq.). Restricted Data or Formerly Restricted Data shall be handled, protected, classified, downgraded, and declassified in conformity with the Atomic Energy Act of 1954 (42 U.S.C. 2011 et seq.).

(Pub. L. 107–296, title X, § 1001(c), Nov. 25, 2002, 116 Stat. 2267.)

REFERENCES IN TEXT

This chapter, referred to in text, was in the original "this Act", meaning Pub. L. 107–296, Nov. 25, 2002, 116 Stat. 2135, known as the Homeland Security Act of 2002,

[1] So in original. The word "to" probably should not appear.

[1] So in original. Probably should be section "3532(b)(2)".

which is classified principally to this chapter. For complete classification of this Act to the Code, see Tables.

The Atomic Energy Act of 1954, referred to in par. (2), is act Aug. 1, 1946, ch. 724, as added by act Aug. 30, 1954, ch. 1073, §1, 68 Stat. 921, and amended, which is classified generally to chapter 23 (§2011 et seq.) of Title 42, The Public Health and Welfare. For complete classification of this Act to the Code, see Short Title note set out under section 2011 of Title 42 and Tables.

CODIFICATION

Section is comprised of section 1001(c) of Pub. L. 107–296. Par. (1)(B) of section 1001(c) of Pub. L. 107–296 amended section 2224 of Title 10, Armed Forces.

CHANGE OF NAME

Reference to the Director of Central Intelligence or the Director of the Central Intelligence Agency in the Director's capacity as the head of the intelligence community deemed to be a reference to the Director of National Intelligence. Reference to the Director of Central Intelligence or the Director of the Central Intelligence Agency in the Director's capacity as the head of the Central Intelligence Agency deemed to be a reference to the Director of the Central Intelligence Agency. See section 1081(a), (b) of Pub. L. 108–458, set out as a note under section 401 of Title 50, War and National Defense.

SHORT TITLE

For short title of title X of Pub. L. 107–296, which enacted this subchapter, as the "Federal Information Security Management Act of 2002", see section 1001(a) of Pub. L. 107–296, set out as a note under section 101 of this title.

§512. Construction

Nothing in this chapter, or the amendments made by this chapter, affects the authority of the National Institute of Standards and Technology or the Department of Commerce relating to the development and promulgation of standards or guidelines under paragraphs (1) and (2) of section 278g–3(a) of title 15.

(Pub. L. 107–296, title X, §1006, Nov. 25, 2002, 116 Stat. 2273.)

REFERENCES IN TEXT

This chapter, referred to in text, was in the original "this Act", meaning Pub. L. 107–296, Nov. 25, 2002, 116 Stat. 2135, known as the Homeland Security Act of 2002, which is classified principally to this chapter. For complete classification of this Act to the Code, see Tables.

§513. Federal air marshal program

(1) Sense of Congress

It is the sense of Congress that the Federal air marshal program is critical to aviation security.

(2) Limitation on statutory construction

Nothing in this chapter, including any amendment made by this chapter, shall be construed as preventing the Under Secretary of Transportation for Security from implementing and training Federal air marshals.

(Pub. L. 107–296, title XIV, §1402(c), Nov. 25, 2002, 116 Stat. 2305.)

REFERENCES IN TEXT

This chapter, referred to in par. (2), was in the original "this Act", meaning Pub. L. 107–296, Nov. 25, 2002, 116 Stat. 2135, known as the Homeland Security Act of 2002, which is classified principally to this chapter. For complete classification of this Act to the Code, see Tables.

SUBCHAPTER XI—DEPARTMENT OF JUSTICE DIVISIONS

PART A—EXECUTIVE OFFICE FOR IMMIGRATION REVIEW

§521. Legal status of EOIR

(a)[1] Existence of EOIR

There is in the Department of Justice the Executive Office for Immigration Review, which shall be subject to the direction and regulation of the Attorney General under section 1103(g) of title 8.

(Pub. L. 107–296, title XI, §1101, Nov. 25, 2002, 116 Stat. 2273.)

EFFECTIVE DATE

Pub. L. 107–296, title XI, §1104, as added by Pub. L. 108–7, div. L, §105(a)(3), Feb. 20, 2003, 117 Stat. 531, provided that: "The provisions of this subtitle [subtitle A (§§1101–1104) of title XI of Pub. L. 107–296, enacting this part and amending section 1103 of Title 8, Immigration and Nationality] shall take effect on the date of the transfer of functions from the Commissioner of Immigration and Naturalization to officials of the Department of Homeland Security [functions transferred Mar. 1, 2003]".

§522. Statutory construction

Nothing in this chapter, any amendment made by this chapter, or in section 1103 of title 8, shall be construed to limit judicial deference to regulations, adjudications, interpretations, orders, decisions, judgments, or any other actions of the Secretary of Homeland Security or the Attorney General.

(Pub. L. 107–296, title XI, §1103, Nov. 25, 2002, 116 Stat. 2274.)

REFERENCES IN TEXT

This chapter, referred to in text, was in the original "this Act", meaning Pub. L. 107–296, Nov. 25, 2002, 116 Stat. 2135, known as the Homeland Security Act of 2002, which is classified principally to this chapter. For complete classification of this Act to the Code, see Tables.

PART B—TRANSFER OF THE BUREAU OF ALCOHOL, TOBACCO AND FIREARMS TO THE DEPARTMENT OF JUSTICE

§531. Bureau of Alcohol, Tobacco, Firearms, and Explosives

(a), (b) Transferred

(c) Transfer of authorities, functions, personnel, and assets to the Department of Justice

(1) Transferred

(2) Administration and revenue collection functions

There shall be retained within the Department of the Treasury the authorities, functions, personnel, and assets of the Bureau of Alcohol, Tobacco and Firearms relating to the administration and enforcement of chapters 51 and 52 of title 26, sections 4181 and 4182 of title 26, and title 27.

[1] So in original. No subsec. (b) has been enacted.

(3) Transferred

(d) Tax and Trade Bureau

(1) Establishment

There is established within the Department of the Treasury the Tax and Trade Bureau.

(2) Administrator

The Tax and Trade Bureau shall be headed by an Administrator, who shall perform such duties as assigned by the Under Secretary for Enforcement of the Department of the Treasury. The Administrator shall occupy a career-reserved position within the Senior Executive Service.

(3) Responsibilities

The authorities, functions, personnel, and assets of the Bureau of Alcohol, Tobacco and Firearms that are not transferred to the Department of Justice under this section shall be retained and administered by the Tax and Trade Bureau.

(Pub. L. 107–296, title XI, § 1111, Nov. 25, 2002, 116 Stat. 2274; Pub. L. 109–162, title XI, § 1187(b), Jan. 5, 2006, 119 Stat. 3127.)

AMENDMENTS

2006—Pub. L. 109–162 transferred section catchline and subsecs. (a)–(c)(1), (3), to section 599A of Title 28, Judiciary and Judicial Procedure.

§ 532. Explosives Training and Research Facility

(a) Establishment

There is established within the Bureau an Explosives Training and Research Facility at Fort AP Hill, Fredericksburg, Virginia.

(b) Purpose

The facility established under subsection (a) of this section shall be utilized to train Federal, State, and local law enforcement officers to—

(1) investigate bombings and explosions;

(2) properly handle, utilize, and dispose of explosive materials and devices;

(3) train canines on explosive detection; and

(4) conduct research on explosives.

(c) Authorization of appropriations

(1) In general

There are authorized to be appropriated such sums as may be necessary to establish and maintain the facility established under subsection (a) of this section.

(2) Availability of funds

Any amounts appropriated pursuant to paragraph (1) shall remain available until expended.

(Pub. L. 107–296, title XI, § 1114, Nov. 25, 2002, 116 Stat. 2280.)

§ 533. Transferred

CODIFICATION

Section, Pub. L. 107–296, title XI, § 1115, Nov. 25, 2002, 116 Stat. 2280, which related to a Personnel Management Demonstration Project, was transferred to section 599B of Title 28, Judiciary and Judicial Procedure, by Pub. L. 109–162, title XI, § 1187(b), (c)(2), Jan. 5, 2006, 119 Stat. 3127, 3128.

SUBCHAPTER XII—TRANSITION

PART A—REORGANIZATION PLAN

§ 541. Definitions

For purposes of this subchapter:

(1) The term "agency" includes any entity, organizational unit, program, or function.

(2) The term "transition period" means the 12-month period beginning on the effective date of this chapter.

(Pub. L. 107–296, title XV, § 1501, Nov. 25, 2002, 116 Stat. 2307.)

REFERENCES IN TEXT

The effective date of this chapter, referred to in par. (2), is 60 days after Nov. 25, 2002, see section 4 of Pub. L. 107–296, set out as an Effective Date note under section 101 of this title.

§ 542. Reorganization plan

(a) Submission of plan

Not later than 60 days after November 25, 2002, the President shall transmit to the appropriate congressional committees a reorganization plan regarding the following:

(1) The transfer of agencies, personnel, assets, and obligations to the Department pursuant to this chapter.

(2) Any consolidation, reorganization, or streamlining of agencies transferred to the Department pursuant to this chapter.

(b) Plan elements

The plan transmitted under subsection (a) of this section shall contain, consistent with this chapter, such elements as the President deems appropriate, including the following:

(1) Identification of any functions of agencies transferred to the Department pursuant to this chapter that will not be transferred to the Department under the plan.

(2) Specification of the steps to be taken by the Secretary to organize the Department, including the delegation or assignment of functions transferred to the Department among officers of the Department in order to permit the Department to carry out the functions transferred under the plan.

(3) Specification of the funds available to each agency that will be transferred to the Department as a result of transfers under the plan.

(4) Specification of the proposed allocations within the Department of unexpended funds transferred in connection with transfers under the plan.

(5) Specification of any proposed disposition of property, facilities, contracts, records, and other assets and obligations of agencies transferred under the plan.

(6) Specification of the proposed allocations within the Department of the functions of the agencies and subdivisions that are not related directly to securing the homeland.

(c) Modification of plan

The President may, on the basis of consultations with the appropriate congressional committees, modify or revise any part of the plan until that part of the plan becomes effective in accordance with subsection (d) of this section.

(d) Effective date

(1) In general

The reorganization plan described in this section, including any modifications or revisions of the plan under subsection (d) of this section, shall become effective for an agency on the earlier of—

(A) the date specified in the plan (or the plan as modified pursuant to subsection (d) of this section), except that such date may not be earlier than 90 days after the date the President has transmitted the reorganization plan to the appropriate congressional committees pursuant to subsection (a) of this section; or

(B) the end of the transition period.

(2) Statutory construction

Nothing in this subsection may be construed to require the transfer of functions, personnel, records, balances of appropriations, or other assets of an agency on a single date.

(3) Supersedes existing law

Paragraph (1) shall apply notwithstanding section 905(b) of title 5.

(Pub. L. 107–296, title XV, §1502, Nov. 25, 2002, 116 Stat. 2308.)

REFERENCES IN TEXT

This chapter, referred to in subsecs. (a) and (b), was in the original "this Act", meaning Pub. L. 107–296, Nov. 25, 2002, 116 Stat. 2135, known as the Homeland Security Act of 2002, which is classified principally to this chapter. For complete classification of this Act to the Code, see Short Title note set out under section 101 of this title and Tables.

DEPARTMENT OF HOMELAND SECURITY REORGANIZATION PLAN

November 25, 2002

H. Doc. No. 108–16, 108th Congress, 1st Session, provided:

INTRODUCTION

This Reorganization Plan is submitted pursuant to Section 1502 of the Department [sic] of Homeland Security Act of 2002 [6 U.S.C. 542] ("the Act"), which requires submission, not later than 60 days after enactment [Nov. 25, 2002], of a reorganization plan regarding two categories of information concerning plans for the Department of Homeland Security ("the Department" or "DHS"):

(1) The transfer of agencies, personnel, assets, and obligations to the Department pursuant to this Act [Pub. L. 107–296, Nov. 25, 2002, 116 Stat. 2135].

(2) Any consolidation, reorganization, or streamlining of agencies transferred to the Department pursuant to this Act. Section 1502(a).

Section 1502(b) of the Act identifies six elements, together with other elements "as the President deems appropriate," as among those for discussion in the plan. Each of the elements set out in the statute is identified *verbatim* below, followed by a discussion of current plans with respect to that element.

This plan is subject to modification pursuant to Section 1502(d) of the Act, which provides that on the basis of consultations with appropriate congressional committees the President may modify or revise any part of the plan until that part of the plan becomes effective. Additional details concerning the process for establishing the Department will become available in the coming weeks and months, and the President will work closely with Congress to modify this plan consistent with the Act.

PLAN ELEMENTS

(1) Identification of any functions of agencies transferred to the Department pursuant to this Act that will not be transferred to the Department under the plan.

Except as otherwise directed in the Act, all functions of agencies that are to be transferred to the Department pursuant to the Act will be transferred to the Department under the plan. The functions of agencies being transferred to the Department which the Act directs are not to be transferred are the following:

• Pursuant to Section 201(g)(1) of the Act [6 U.S.C. 121(g)(1)], the Computer Investigations and Operations Section ("CIOS") of the National Infrastructure Protection Center ("NIPC") of the Federal Bureau of Investigation ("FBI") will not transfer to the Department with the rest of NIPC. CIOS is the FBI headquarters entity responsible for managing all FBI computer intrusion field office cases (whether law enforcement or national security related).

• Pursuant to Sections 421(c) & (d) of the Act [6 U.S.C. 231(c), (d)], the regulatory responsibilities and quarantine activities relating to agricultural import and entry inspection activities of the United States Department of Agriculture ("the USDA") Animal and Plant Health Inspection Service ("APHIS") will remain with the USDA, as will the Secretary of Agriculture's authority to issue regulations, policies, and procedures regarding the functions transferred pursuant to Sections 421(a) & (b) of the Act.

• Pursuant to Subtitle B of Title IV of the Act [6 U.S.C. 211 et seq.], the authorities of the Secretary of the Treasury related to Customs revenue functions, as defined in the statute, will not transfer to the Department.

• Functions under the immigration laws of the United States with respect to the care of unaccompanied alien children will not transfer from the Department of Justice to DHS, but will instead transfer to the Department of Health and Human Services pursuant to Section 462 of the Act [6 U.S.C. 279].

(2) Specification of the steps to be taken by the Secretary to organize the Department, including the delegation or assignment of functions transferred to the Department among officers of the Department in order to permit the Department to carry out the functions transferred under the plan.

A. *Steps to be taken by the Secretary to organize the Department.* The President intends that the Secretary will carry out the following actions on the dates specified. All of the following transfers shall be deemed to be made to DHS, and all offices and positions to be established and all officers and officials to be appointed or named shall be deemed to be established, appointed, or named within DHS.

January 24, 2003 (effective date of the Act pursuant to Section 4 [6 U.S.C. 101 note]):

• Establish the Office of the Secretary.

• Begin to appoint, upon confirmation by the Senate, or transfer pursuant to the transfer provisions of the Act, as many of the following officers as may be possible:

(1) Deputy Secretary of Homeland Security

(2) Under Secretary for Information Analysis and Infrastructure Protection

(3) Under Secretary for Science and Technology

(4) Under Secretary for Border and Transportation Security

(5) Under Secretary for Emergency Preparedness and Response

(6) Director of the Bureau of Citizenship and Immigration Services

(7) Under Secretary for Management

(8) Not more than 12 Assistant Secretaries

(9) General Counsel

(10) Inspector General

(11) Commissioner of Customs

• Name, as soon as may be possible, officers to fill the following offices created by the Act:

(1) Assistant Secretary for Information Analysis

(2) Assistant Secretary for Infrastructure Protection

(3) Privacy Officer

(4) Director of the Secret Service

(5) Chief Information Officer

(6) Chief Human Capital Officer

(7) Chief Financial Officer

(8) Officer for Civil Rights and Civil Liberties

(9) Director of Shared Services

(10) Citizenship and Immigration Ombudsman

(11) Director of the Homeland Security Advanced Research Projects Agency

• Establish, within the Office of the Secretary, the Office for State and Local Government Coordination, the Office of International Affairs, and the Office of National Capital Region Coordination.

• Establish the Homeland Security Advanced Research Projects Agency and the Acceleration Fund for Research and Development of Homeland Security Technologies.

• Establish within the Directorate of Science and Technology the Office for National Laboratories.

• Establish the Bureau of Border Security [now Bureau of Immigration and Customs Enforcement], the Bureau of Citizenship and Immigration Services, and the Director of Shared Services.

• Establish the Transportation Security Oversight Board with the Secretary of Homeland Security as its Chair.

March 1, 2003:

• Transfer the Critical Infrastructure Assurance Office ("CIAO") of the Department of Commerce, the National Communications System ("the NCS"), the NIPC of the FBI (other than the CIOS), the National Infrastructure Simulation and Analysis Center ("NISAC"), the Energy Assurance Office ("EAO") of the Department of Energy, and the Federal Computer Incident Response Center of the General Services Administration ("FedCIRC").

• Transfer the Coast Guard.

• Transfer the Customs Service, the Transportation Security Administration ("the TSA"), functions of the Immigration and Naturalization Service ("the INS"), the Federal Protective Service ("the FPS"), the Office of Domestic Preparedness ("the ODP"), and the Federal Law Enforcement Training Center ("the FLETC").

• Transfer the functions of the Secretary of Agriculture relating to agricultural import and entry inspection activities under the laws specified in Section 421(b) of the Act [6 U.S.C. 231(b)] from the Animal and Plant Health Inspection Service.

• Transfer the United States Secret Service.

• Transfer the following programs and activities to the Directorate of Science and Technology:

° The chemical and biological national security and supporting programs and activities of the nonproliferation and verification research and development program of the Department of Energy.

° The life sciences activities related to microbial pathogens of the Biological and Environmental Research Program of the Department of Energy.

° The National Bio-Weapons Defense Analysis Center of the Department of Defense.

° The nuclear smuggling programs and activities within the proliferation detection program of the nonproliferation and verification research and development program of the Department of Energy.

° The nuclear assessment program and activities of the assessment, detection, and cooperation program of the international materials protection and cooperation program of the Department of Energy and the advanced scientific computing research program and activities at Lawrence Livermore National Laboratory of the Department of Energy.

° The Environmental Measurements Laboratory of the Department of Energy.

• Transfer the Federal Emergency Management Agency ("FEMA").

• Transfer the Integrated Hazard Information System of the National Oceanic and Atmospheric Administration, which shall be renamed "FIRESTAT."

• Transfer the National Domestic Preparedness Office of the FBI, including the functions of the Attorney General relating thereto.

• Transfer the Domestic Emergency Support Team of the Department of Justice, including the functions of the Attorney General relating thereto.

• Transfer the Metropolitan Medical Response System of the Department of Health and Human Services, including the functions of the Secretary of Health and Human Services and Assistant Secretary for Public Health Emergency Preparedness relating thereto.

• Transfer the National Disaster Medical System of the Department of Health and Human Services, including the functions of the Secretary of Health and Human Services and Assistant Secretary for Public Health Emergency Preparedness relating thereto.

• Transfer the Office of Emergency Preparedness and the Strategic National Stockpile of the Department of Health and Human Services, including the functions of the Secretary of Health and Human Services and Assistant Secretary for Public Health Emergency Preparedness relating thereto.

• Transfer to the Secretary the authority (in connection with an actual or threatened terrorist attack, major disaster, or other emergency in the United States) to direct the Nuclear Incident Response Team of the Department of Energy to operate as an organizational unit.

June 1, 2003:

• Transfer the Plum Island Animal Disease Center of USDA.

• Establish the Homeland Security Science and Technology Advisory Committee.

By September 30, 2003:

• Complete any incidental transfers, pursuant to Section 1516 of the Act [6 U.S.C. 556], of personnel, assets, and liabilities held, used, arising from, available, or to be made available, in connection with the functions transferred by the Act.

B. *Delegation or Assignment Among Officers of Functions Transferred to the Department.* The President intends that the Secretary will delegate or assign transferred functions within the Department as follows:

1. Information Analysis and Infrastructure Protection

a. *Under Secretary for Information Analysis and Infrastructure Protection ("IA and IP"):* Will be responsible for oversight of functions of NIPC, NCS, CIAO, NISAC, EAO, and FedCIRC transferred by the Act, the management of the Directorate's Information Analysis and Infrastructure Protection duties, and the administration of the Homeland Security Advisory System.

b. *Assistant Secretary for Information Analysis:* Will oversee the following Information Analysis functions:

• Identify and assess the nature and scope of terrorist threats to the homeland; detect and identify threats of terrorism against the United States; and, understand such threats in light of actual and potential vulnerabilities of the homeland.

• In coordination with the Assistant Secretary for Infrastructure Protection, integrate relevant information, analyses, and vulnerability assessments (whether such information, analyses, or assessments are provided or produced by the Department or others) in order to identify priorities for protective and support measures by the Department, other agencies of the Federal Government, State and local government agencies and authorities, the private sector, and other entities.

• Ensure the timely and efficient access by the Department to all information necessary to discharge the responsibilities under Section 201 of the Act [6 U.S.C. 121], including obtaining such information from other agencies of the Federal Government.

• Review, analyze, and make recommendations for improvements in the policies and procedures governing the sharing of law enforcement information, intelligence information, intelligence-related information, and other information relating to homeland security within the Federal Government and between the Federal Government and State and local government agencies and authorities.

• Disseminate, as appropriate, information analyzed by the Department within the Department, to other agencies of the Federal Government with responsibilities relating to homeland security, and to agencies of State and local governments and private sector entities with such responsibilities in order to assist in the deterrence, prevention, preemption of, or response to, terrorist attacks against the United States.

• Consult with the Director of Central Intelligence and other appropriate intelligence, law enforcement, or other elements of the Federal Government to establish collection priorities and strategies for information, including law enforcement-related information, relating to threats of terrorism against the United States through such means as the representation of the Department in discussions regarding requirements and priorities in the collection of such information.

• Consult with State and local governments and private sector entities to ensure appropriate exchanges of information, including law enforcement-related information, relating to threats of terrorism against the United States.

• Ensure that—

1. Any material received pursuant to the Act is protected from unauthorized disclosure and handled and used only for the performance of official duties; and

2. Any intelligence information under the Act is shared, retained, and disseminated consistent with the authority of the Director of Central Intelligence to protect intelligence sources and methods under the National Security Act of 1947 (50 U.S.C. Section 401, et seq.) and related procedures and, as appropriate, similar authorities of the Attorney General concerning sensitive law enforcement information.

• Request additional information from other agencies of the Federal Government, State and local government agencies, and the private sector relating to threats of terrorism in the United States, or relating to other areas of responsibility assigned by the Secretary, including the entry into cooperative agreements through the Secretary to obtain such information.

• Establish and utilize, in conjunction with the Chief Information Officer of the Department, a secure communications and information technology infrastructure, including data-mining and other advanced analytical tools, in order to access, receive, and analyze data and information in furtherance of statutory responsibilities, and to disseminate information acquired and analyzed by the Department, as appropriate.

• Ensure, in conjunction with the Chief Information Officer of the Department, that any information databases and analytical tools developed or utilized by the Department—

1. Are compatible with one another and with relevant information databases of other agencies of the Federal Government; and

2. Treat information in such databases in a manner that complies with applicable Federal law on privacy.

• Coordinate training and other support to the elements and personnel of the Department, other agencies of the Federal Government, and State and local governments that provide information to the Department, or are consumers of information provided by the Department, in order to facilitate the identification and sharing of information revealed in their ordinary duties and the optimal utilization of information received from the Department.

• Coordinate with elements of the intelligence community and with Federal, State, and local law enforcement agencies, and the private sector, as appropriate.

• Provide intelligence and information analysis and support to other elements of the Department.

c. *Assistant Secretary for Infrastructure Protection:* Will oversee the following Infrastructure Protection functions:

• Carry out comprehensive assessments of the vulnerabilities of the key resources and critical infrastructure of the United States, including the performance of risk assessments to determine the risks posed by particular types of terrorist attacks within the United States (including an assessment of the probability of success of such attacks and the feasibility and potential efficacy of various countermeasures to such attacks).

• In coordination with the Assistant Secretary for Information Analysis, integrate relevant information, analyses, and vulnerability assessments (whether such information, analyses, or assessments are provided or produced by the Department or others) in order to identify priorities for protective and support measures by the Department, other agencies of the Federal Government, State and local government agencies and authorities, the private sector, and other entities.

• Develop a comprehensive national plan for securing the key resources and critical infrastructure of the United States, including power production, generation, and distribution systems, information technology and telecommunications systems (including satellites), electronic financial and property record storage and transmission systems, emergency preparedness communications systems, and the physical and technological assets that support such systems.

• Recommend measures necessary to protect the key resources and critical infrastructure of the United States in coordination with other agencies of the Federal Government and in cooperation with State and local government agencies and authorities, the private sector, and other entities.

• In coordination with the Under Secretary for Emergency Preparedness and Response, provide to State and local government entities, and upon request to private entities that own or operate critical information systems, crisis management support in response to threats to, or attacks on, critical information systems.

• Provide technical assistance, upon request, to the private sector and other government entities, in coordination with the Under Secretary for Emergency Preparedness and Response, with respect to emergency recovery plans to respond to major failures of critical information systems.

• Coordinate with other agencies of the Federal Government to provide specific warning information, and advice about appropriate protective measures and countermeasures, to State and local government agencies and authorities, the private sector, other entities, and the public.

2. Science and Technology

Under Secretary for Science and Technology: Will be responsible for performing the functions set forth in Section 302 of the Act [6 U.S.C. 182], including the following:

• Advise the Secretary regarding research and development efforts and priorities in support of the Department's missions.

• Develop, in consultation with other appropriate executive agencies, a national policy and strategic plan for identifying priorities, goals, objectives, and policies for, and coordinating the Federal Government's civilian efforts with respect to, identifying and developing countermeasures to chemical, biological, radiological, nuclear, and other emerging terrorist threats, including the development of comprehensive, research-based definable goals for such efforts and of annual measurable objectives and specific targets to accomplish and evaluate the goals for such efforts.

• Support the Under Secretary for Information Analysis and Infrastructure Protection by assessing and testing homeland security vulnerabilities and possible threats.

• Conduct basic and applied research, development, demonstration, testing, and evaluation activities that are relevant to any or all elements of the Department, through both intramural and extramural programs, except that such responsibility does not extend to human health-related research and development activities.

• Establish priorities for directing, funding, and conducting national research, development, test and evaluation, and procurement of technology and systems for—

1. preventing the importation of chemical, biological, radiological, nuclear, and related weapons and material; and

2. detecting, preventing, protecting against, and responding to terrorist attacks.

• Establish a system for transferring homeland security developments or technologies to Federal, State, and local governments, and to private sector entities.

• Enter into work agreements, joint sponsorships, contracts, or any other agreements with the Department of Energy regarding the use of the national laboratories or sites and support of the science and technology base at those facilities.

• Collaborate with the Secretary of Agriculture and the Attorney General as provided in Section 212 of the Agricultural Bioterrorism Protection Act of 2002 (7 U.S.C. §8401), as amended by Section 1709(b) of the Act.

• Collaborate with the Secretary of Health and Human Services and the Attorney General in determining any new biological agents and toxins that shall be listed as "select agents" in Appendix A of part 72 of title 42, Code of Federal Regulations, pursuant to Section 351A of the Public Health Service Act (42 U.S.C. §262a).

• Support United States leadership in science and technology.

• Establish and administer the primary research and development activities of the Department, including the long-term research and development needs and capabilities for all elements of the Department.

• Coordinate and integrate all research, development, demonstration, testing, and evaluation activities of the Department.

• Coordinate with other appropriate executive agencies in developing and carrying out the science and technology agenda of the Department to reduce duplication and identify unmet needs.

• Develop and oversee the administration of guidelines for merit review of research and development projects throughout the Department, and for the dissemination of research conducted or sponsored by the Department.

3. Border and Transportation Security

The Directorate of Border and Transportation Security ("BTS") will include the following: the Bureau of Border Security [now Bureau of Immigration and Customs Enforcement]; the Office for Domestic Preparedness; the Customs Service [now Bureau of Customs and Border Protection]; the Transportation Security Administration; FLETC; and FPS.

The BTS Directorate will also have in place the key leaders of the new Directorate to include:

a. *Under Secretary for BTS:* Will be responsible for oversight of all responsibilities set forth in Section 402 of the Act [6 U.S.C. 202], including the following:

• Prevent the entry of terrorists and the instruments of terrorism into the United States.

• Secure the borders, territorial waters, ports, terminals, waterways, and air, land, and sea transportation systems of the United States, including managing and coordinating those functions transferred to the Department at ports of entry.

• Establish and administer rules, in accordance with Section 428 of the Act [6 U.S.C. 236], governing the granting of visas or other forms of permission, including parole, to enter the United States to individuals who are not a citizen or an alien lawfully admitted for permanent residence in the United States.

• Establish national immigration enforcement policies and priorities.

• Administer the customs laws of the United States, except as otherwise provided in the Act.

• Conduct the inspection and related administrative functions of the USDA transferred to the Secretary of Homeland Security under Section 421 of the Act [6 U.S.C. 231].

• In carrying out the foregoing responsibilities, ensure the speedy, orderly, and efficient flow of lawful traffic and commerce.

• Carry out the immigration enforcement functions specified under Section 441 of the Act [6 U.S.C. 251] that were vested by statute in, or performed by, the Commissioner of the INS (or any officer, employee, or component of the INS) immediately before the date on which the transfer of functions takes place.

b. *Assistant Secretary for Border Security:* Will report directly to the Under Secretary for Border and Transportation Security, and whose responsibilities will include the following:

• Establish and oversee the administration of the policies for performing such functions as are—

1. transferred to the Under Secretary for Border and Transportation Security by Section 441 of the Act and delegated to the Assistant Secretary by the Under Secretary for Border and Transportation Security; or

2. otherwise vested in the Assistant Secretary by law.

• Advise the Under Secretary for Border and Transportation Security with respect to any policy or operation of the Bureau of Border Security [now Bureau of Immigration and Customs Enforcement] that may affect the Bureau of Citizenship and Immigration.

c. *Director of the Office for Domestic Preparedness*—Will report directly to the Under Secretary for Border and Transportation Security and will have the primary responsibility within the Executive Branch of the Federal Government for the preparedness of the United States for acts of terrorism, including the following responsibilities:

• Coordinate preparedness efforts at the Federal level, and work with all State, local, tribal, parish, and private sector emergency response providers on all matters pertaining to combating terrorism, including training, exercises, and equipment support.

• Coordinate or, as appropriate, consolidate communications and systems of communications relating to homeland security at all levels of government.

• Direct and supervise terrorism preparedness grant programs of the Federal Government (other than those programs administered by the Department of Health and Human Services) for all emergency response providers.

• Incorporate homeland security priorities into planning guidance on an agency level for the preparedness efforts of the Office for Domestic Preparedness.

• Provide agency-specific training for agents and analysts within the Department, other agencies, and State and local agencies, and international entities.

• As the lead executive branch agency for preparedness of the United States for acts of terrorism, cooperate closely with the FEMA, which shall have the primary responsibility within the executive branch to prepare for and mitigate the effects of nonterrorist-related disasters in the United States.

• Assist and support the Secretary, in coordination with other Directorates and entities outside the Department, in conducting appropriate risk analysis and risk management activities of State, local, and tribal governments consistent with the mission and functions of the Directorate.

• Supervise those elements of the Office of National Preparedness of FEMA that relate to terrorism, which shall be consolidated within the Department in the ODP established pursuant to Section 430 of the Act [6 U.S.C. 238].

4. Emergency Preparedness and Response

The Emergency Preparedness and Response Directorate will be headed by the Under Secretary for Emergency Preparedness and Response.

Under Secretary for EP&R: Will be responsible for all of those functions included within Section 502 [now 504] of the Act [6 U.S.C. 314], including:

• Helping to ensure the effectiveness of emergency response providers to terrorist attacks, major disasters, and other emergencies.

• With respect to the Nuclear Incident Response Team (regardless of whether it is operating as an organizational unit of the Department pursuant to the Act):

1. Establishing standards and certifying when those standards have been met;

2. Conducting joint and other exercises and training and evaluating performance; and,

3. Providing funds to the Department of Energy and the Environmental Protection Agency, as appropriate, for homeland security planning, exercises and training, and equipment.

• Providing the Federal Government's response to terrorist attacks and major disasters, including:

1. Managing such response;

2. Directing the Domestic Emergency Support Team, the Strategic National Stockpile, the National Disaster Medical System, and (when operating as an organizational unit of the Department pursuant to the Act) the Nuclear Incident Response Team;

3. Overseeing the Metropolitan Medical Response System; and

4. Coordinating other Federal response resources in the event of a terrorist attack or major disaster.

• Aiding the recovery from terrorist attacks and major disasters;

• Building a comprehensive national incident management system with Federal, State, and local government personnel, agencies, and authorities, to respond to such attacks and disasters.

• Consolidating existing Federal Government emergency response plans into a single, coordinated national response plan; and

• Developing comprehensive programs for developing interoperative communications technology, and helping to ensure that emergency response providers acquire such technology.

5. Other Officers and Functions

a. *Director of the Bureau of Citizenship and Immigration Services:* Will report directly to the Deputy Secretary; and will be responsible for the following:

• Establishing the policies for performing such functions as are transferred to the Director by Section 451 of the Act [6 U.S.C. 271] or otherwise vested in the Director by law.

• Oversight of the administration of such policies.

• Advising the Deputy Secretary with respect to any policy or operation of the Bureau of Citizenship and Immigration Services that may affect the Bureau of Border Security [now Bureau of Immigration and Customs Enforcement] of the Department, including potentially conflicting policies or operations.

• Establishing national immigration services policies and priorities.

• Meeting regularly with the Ombudsman described in Section 452 of the Act [6 U.S.C. 272] to correct serious service problems identified by the Ombudsman.

• Establishing procedures requiring a formal response to any recommendations submitted in the Ombudsman's annual report to Congress within three months after its submission to Congress.

b. *Citizenship and Immigration Services Ombudsman:* Will report directly to the Deputy Secretary; and will be responsible for the following:

• Assisting individuals and employers in resolving problems with the Bureau of Citizenship and Immigration Services;

• Identifying areas in which individuals and employers have problems in dealing with the Bureau of Citizenship and Immigration Services; and

• Proposing changes in the administrative practices of the Bureau of Citizenship and Immigration Services to mitigate identified problems.

(3) Specification of the funds available to each agency that will be transferred to the Department as a result of transfers under the plan.

• The attached tables [not set out in the Code] provide estimates of the funds available to the agencies and entities that will be transferred to the Department by operation of the Act. The two tables include total funding (mandatory and discretionary including fees) and discretionary funding net of fees. The tables provide the enacted levels for 2002 and 2002 supplementals, and the President's requested levels for 2003.

Because of the current state of the 2003 budget process, information concerning the funds that will be available to each transferring agency on the date of the proposed transfers is not currently available and will not likely be available during the time period in which the President is to submit this Reorganization Plan. As additional information becomes available, it will be provided as may be required in accordance with the procedures under the Act for modification of this Plan or other applicable law.

(4) Specification of the proposed allocations within the Department of unexpended funds transferred in connection with transfers under the plan.

• The attached tables [not set out in the Code] provide estimates of the unobligated balances as of September 30, 2002, for the agencies and programs that will be transferred to the Department. The first table provides estimates of unobligated balances for the accounts that are moving to the Department in whole. The second table provides estimates of the unobligated balances in the accounts of which only a portion will be transferring to the new Department. These latter estimates, however, are of the unobligated balances for the full account, only a portion of which are associated with the activities that will be transferred to the Department. In addition, these unobligated balances are based on the Department of Treasury's estimates as of September 30, 2002, which are the latest available figures. Since October 1, 2002, Departments and agencies (except the Department of Defense) have been operating under continuing resolutions, and, as such, have been spending these balances to maintain current operations.

Authority to reallocate unexpended funds of agencies transferred under this Plan is found in H.J. Res. 124 [Pub. L. 107–294, Nov. 23, 2002, 116 Stat. 2062], the continuing resolution in effect currently and until January 11, 2003. The resolution provides authority for the Office of Management and Budget to transfer an amount not to exceed $140,000,000 from unobligated balances of appropriations enacted before October 1, 2002 "for organizations and entities that will be transferred to the new Department and for salaries and expenses associated with the initiation of the Department." Such authority may be exercised upon providing 15 days' notice to the Appropriations Committees. We anticipate that it may be necessary to provide funding through such transfers both for transferring entities and for salaries and expenses associated with the initiation of the Department, including, for example, those associated with establishing the Office of the Secretary and other new offices provided for in the Act. Any plan to use such funding will follow the procedures required under the continuing resolution, including the provision of at least 15 days' notice to the Appropriations Committees.

(5) Specification of any proposed disposition of property, facilities, contracts, records, and other assets and obligations of agencies transferred under the plan.

- There is no intention to dispose of property, facility, contracts, records, and other assets and obligations of agencies transferred under the plan. All of such assets and obligations will transfer with each agency pursuant to Section 1511(d)(1) of the Act [6 U.S.C. 551(d)(1)].
- Prior to and during the transition period (as defined by Section 1501(a)(2) of the Act [6 U.S.C. 541(a)(2)]), the Department may identify property, facilities, contracts, records, and other assets and obligations of agencies transferred that would be candidates for disposition due to duplication, non-use, obsolescence, and the like. If and when any such proposed dispositions are identified, we will follow provisions of the Act relating to modification of this plan or further notification of Congress.

(6) Specification of the proposed allocations within the Department of the functions of the agencies and subdivisions that are not related directly to securing the homeland.

- As agencies and subdivisions are transferred into the Department, any functions of those entities that are not directly related to securing the homeland will continue to be allocated to the agencies and subdivisions in which they are currently incorporated.

[Bureau of Border Security renamed Bureau of Immigration and Customs Enforcement, and Customs Service renamed Bureau of Customs and Border Protection, by Reorganization Plan Modification for the Department of Homeland Security, H. Doc. No. 108–32, 108th Congress, 1st Session, set out below.]

[For transfer of functions of Strategic National Stockpile to Secretary of Health and Human Services, with certain exceptions, see section 3(c)(1), (2) of Pub. L. 108–276, set out as a note under section 247d–6b of Title 42, The Public Health and Welfare.]

MESSAGE OF THE PRESIDENT

38 Weekly Compilation of Presidential Documents 2095, Dec. 2, 2002; H. Doc. No. 108–16, provided:

THE WHITE HOUSE, *Washington, November 25, 2002.*

Dear Mr. Speaker: (Dear Mr. President:)[1]

Pursuant to section 1502 of the Homeland Security Act of 2002 [6 U.S.C. 542], I submit herewith the enclosed Reorganization Plan for the Department of Homeland Security. The Reorganization Plan provides information concerning the elements identified in section 1502(b), and is subject to modification pursuant to section 1502(d) of the Act. In accordance with section 1502(a) of the Act, please transmit this Reorganization Plan to the appropriate congressional committees.

The details of this Plan are set forth in the enclosed letter from the Director of the Office of Management and Budget. I concur with his comments and observations.

Sincerely,

GEORGE W. BUSH.

[1] **Editorial note.** This is the text of identical letters addressed to the Speaker of the House of Representatives and the President of the Senate.

Enclosure.

REORGANIZATION PLAN MODIFICATION FOR THE DEPARTMENT OF HOMELAND SECURITY

January 30, 2003

H. Doc. No. 108–32, 108th Congress, 1st Session, provided:

INTRODUCTION

This Reorganization Plan Modification is submitted pursuant to the Homeland Security Act ("the Act") of 2002 [Pub. L. 107–296, Nov. 25, 2002, 116 Stat. 2135]. All elements of the Department of Homeland Security Reorganization Plan of November 25, 2002 ("the Plan") [set out above] remain as submitted except for those modifications addressed herein.

PURPOSE OF MODIFICATION

This modification of the Plan is to establish and specify organizational units within the Border and Transportation Security Directorate. This modification presents a structural change, but does not consolidate, discontinue, or diminish transferred agencies' current operations in the field.

PLAN MODIFICATIONS

(a) *Rename the "Bureau of Border Security" the "Bureau of Immigration and Customs Enforcement."* As required by the Act, this Bureau will be headed by an Assistant Secretary who will report directly to the Undersecretary for Border and Transportation Security.

This Bureau will comprise Immigration Naturalization Service (INS) interior enforcement functions, including the detention and removal program, the intelligence program, and the investigations program. At the same time, pursuant to this modification, the interior enforcement resources and missions of the Customs Service and the Federal Protective Service will be added to this Bureau. The mission of the Bureau is:

1. To enforce the full range of immigration and customs laws within the interior of the United States; and,

2. To protect specified federal buildings.

The Assistant Secretary will:

1. Establish and oversee the administration of the policies for performing the detention and removal program, the intelligence program, and the investigation program functions as are—

(a) transferred to the Under Secretary for Border and Transportation Security by Section 441 of the Act [6 U.S.C. 251] and delegated to the Assistant Secretary by the Under Secretary for Border and Transportation Security; or

(b) otherwise vested in the Assistant Secretary by law.

2. Advise the Under Secretary for Border and Transportation Security with respect to any policy or operation of the Bureau that may affect the Bureau of Citizenship and Immigration Services established under subtitle E of the Act [probably means subtitle E of title IV of the Act, 6 U.S.C. 271 et seq.], including potentially conflicting policies and operations.

(b) *Rename the "Customs Service" the "Bureau of Customs and Border Protection."* This Bureau will be headed by the Commissioner of Customs and will report to the Under Secretary for Border and Transportation Security.

The Bureau will contain the resources and missions relating to borders and ports of entry of the Customs Service, the INS, including the Border Patrol and the inspections program, and the agricultural inspections function of the Agricultural Quarantine Inspection program.

The Commissioner will:

1. Establish and oversee the administration of the policies for performing the Border Patrol and inspections program functions as are—

(a) transferred to the Under Secretary for Border and Transportation Security by Section 441 of the Act [6 U.S.C. 251] and delegated to the Commissioner by the Under Secretary for Border and Transportation Security; or

(b) otherwise vested in the Assistant Secretary [probably should be "Commissioner"] by law.

2. Advise the Under Secretary for Border and Transportation Security with respect to any policy or operation of the Bureau that may affect the Bureau of Citizenship and Immigration Services established under subtitle E of the Act [probably means subtitle E of title IV of the Act, 6 U.S.C. 271 et seq.], including potentially conflicting policies and operations.

IMPLEMENTATION DATE

March 1, 2003

ELEMENTS REQUIRED BY THE ACT TO BE SUBMITTED WITH MODIFIED PLAN

(1) *Identification of any functions of agencies transferred to the Department pursuant to this Act that will not be transferred to the Department under the plan.*

None.

(2) *Specification of the steps to be taken by the Secretary to organize the Department, including the delegation or assignment of functions transferred to the Department among officers of the Department in order to permit the Department to carry out the functions transferred under the plan.*

See plan modifications above.

(3) *Specification of the funds available to each agency that will be transferred to the Department as a result of transfers under the plan.*

The table attached at Tab A [not set out in the Code] provides estimates of the funds available to the agencies affected by this modification that will be transferred to the Department by operation of the Act. The table includes total funding (mandatory and discretionary including fees) and discretionary funding net of fees. The table provides the President's requested levels for 2003.

Because of the current state of the 2003 budget process, information concerning the funds that will be available to each transferring agency on the date of the proposed transfers is not currently available. As additional information becomes available, it will be provided as may be required in accordance with the procedures under the Act for modification of this Plan or other applicable law.

(4) *Specification of the proposed allocations within the Department of unexpended funds transferred in connection with transfers under the plan.*

The table attached at Tab B [not set out in the Code] provides updated estimates of the unobligated balances as of September 30, 2002, for the agencies affected by this modification that will be transferred to the Department. Since October 1, 2002, these agencies have been operating under continuing resolutions, and, as such, have been spending these balances to maintain current operations. As additional information becomes available, it will be provided as may be required in accordance with the procedures under the Act for modification of this Plan or other applicable law.

(5) *Specification of any proposed disposition of property, facilities, contracts, records, and other assets and obligations of agencies transferred under the plan.*

There is no intention to dispose of property, facilities, contracts, records, and other assets and obligations of agencies transferred under this modification. All such assets and obligations will transfer with each agency pursuant to Section 1511(d)(1) of the Act [6 U.S.C. 551(d)(1)].

(6) *Specification of the proposed allocations within the Department of the functions of the agencies and subdivisions that are not related directly to securing the homeland.*

The functions of the agencies affected by this modification that are not directly related to securing the homeland will continue to be performed by the bureaus formed by this planned reorganization.

MESSAGE OF THE PRESIDENT

39 Weekly Compilation of Presidential Documents 136, Feb. 3, 2003; H. Doc. No. 108–32, provided:

THE WHITE HOUSE, *Washington, January 30, 2003.*

Dear Mr. Speaker: (Dear Mr. President:)[1]

Pursuant to section 1502 of the Homeland Security Act of 2002 [6 U.S.C. 542] (Public Law 107–296) (the "Act"), I submit herewith the enclosed Reorganization Plan Modification for the Department of Homeland Security (DHS), which represents a modification of certain aspects of the DHS Reorganization Plan [set out above] I submitted to you on November 25, 2002. The modification involves organizational units within the DHS Border and Transportation Security Directorate. The enclosed Reorganization Plan Modification provides information concerning the elements identified in section 1502(b), and is itself subject to modification pursuant to section 1502(d) of the Act. In accordance with section 1502(a) of the Act, please transmit this Reorganization Plan Modification to the appropriate congressional committees.

Sincerely,

GEORGE W. BUSH.

[1] **Editorial note.** This is the text of identical letters addressed to the Speaker of the House of Representatives and the President of the Senate.

§ 543. Review of congressional committee structures

It is the sense of Congress that each House of Congress should review its committee structure in light of the reorganization of responsibilities within the executive branch by the establishment of the Department.

(Pub. L. 107–296, title XV, § 1503, Nov. 25, 2002, 116 Stat. 2309.)

PART B—TRANSITIONAL PROVISIONS

§ 551. Transitional authorities

(a) Provision of assistance by officials

Until the transfer of an agency to the Department, any official having authority over or functions relating to the agency immediately before the effective date of this chapter shall provide to the Secretary such assistance, including the use of personnel and assets, as the Secretary may request in preparing for the transfer and integration of the agency into the Department.

(b) Services and personnel

During the transition period, upon the request of the Secretary, the head of any executive agency may, on a reimbursable basis, provide services or detail personnel to assist with the transition.

(c) Acting officials

(1) During the transition period, pending the advice and consent of the Senate to the appoint-

ment of an officer required by this chapter to be appointed by and with such advice and consent, the President may designate any officer whose appointment was required to be made by and with such advice and consent and who was such an officer immediately before the effective date of this chapter (and who continues in office) or immediately before such designation, to act in such office until the same is filled as provided in this chapter. While so acting, such officers shall receive compensation at the higher of—

(A) the rates provided by this chapter for the respective offices in which they act; or

(B) the rates provided for the offices held at the time of designation.

(2) Nothing in this chapter shall be understood to require the advice and consent of the Senate to the appointment by the President to a position in the Department of any officer whose agency is transferred to the Department pursuant to this chapter and whose duties following such transfer are germane to those performed before such transfer.

(d) Transfer of personnel, assets, obligations, and functions

Upon the transfer of an agency to the Department—

(1) the personnel, assets, and obligations held by or available in connection with the agency shall be transferred to the Secretary for appropriate allocation, subject to the approval of the Director of the Office of Management and Budget and in accordance with the provisions of section 1531(a)(2) of title 31; and

(2) the Secretary shall have all functions relating to the agency that any other official could by law exercise in relation to the agency immediately before such transfer, and shall have in addition all functions vested in the Secretary by this chapter or other law.

(e) Prohibition on use of transportation trust funds

(1) In general

Notwithstanding any other provision of this chapter, no funds derived from the Highway Trust Fund, Airport and Airway Trust Fund, Inland Waterway Trust Fund, or Harbor Maintenance Trust Fund, may be transferred to, made available to, or obligated by the Secretary or any other official in the Department.

(2) Limitation

This subsection shall not apply to security-related funds provided to the Federal Aviation Administration for fiscal years preceding fiscal year 2003 for (A) operations, (B) facilities and equipment, or (C) research, engineering, and development, and to any funds provided to the Coast Guard from the Sport Fish Restoration and Boating Trust Fund for boating safety programs.

(Pub. L. 107–296, title XV, § 1511, Nov. 25, 2002, 116 Stat. 2309; Pub. L. 108–7, div. L, § 103(4), Feb. 20, 2003, 117 Stat. 529; Pub. L. 109–59, title XI, § 11115(b)(2)(F), Aug. 10, 2005, 119 Stat. 1950.)

REFERENCES IN TEXT

The effective date of this chapter, referred to in subsecs. (a) and (c)(1), is 60 days after Nov. 25, 2002, see section 4 of Pub. L. 107–296, set out as an Effective Date note under section 101 of this title.

AMENDMENTS

2005—Subsec. (e)(2). Pub. L. 109–59 substituted "Sport Fish Restoration and Boating Trust Fund" for "Aquatic Resources Trust Fund of the Highway Trust Fund".

2003—Subsec. (e)(2). Pub. L. 108–7 inserted before period at end ", and to any funds provided to the Coast Guard from the Aquatic Resources Trust Fund of the Highway Trust Fund for boating safety programs".

EFFECTIVE DATE OF 2005 AMENDMENT

Pub. L. 109–59, title XI, § 11115(d), Aug. 10, 2005, 119 Stat. 1950, provided that: "The amendments made by this section [amending this section and sections 9503 and 9504 of Title 26, Internal Revenue Code] shall take effect on October 1, 2005."

§ 552. Savings provisions

(a) Completed administrative actions

(1) Completed administrative actions of an agency shall not be affected by the enactment of this chapter or the transfer of such agency to the Department, but shall continue in effect according to their terms until amended, modified, superseded, terminated, set aside, or revoked in accordance with law by an officer of the United States or a court of competent jurisdiction, or by operation of law.

(2) For purposes of paragraph (1), the term "completed administrative action" includes orders, determinations, rules, regulations, personnel actions, permits, agreements, grants, contracts, certificates, licenses, registrations, and privileges.

(b) Pending proceedings

Subject to the authority of the Secretary under this chapter—

(1) pending proceedings in an agency, including notices of proposed rulemaking, and applications for licenses, permits, certificates, grants, and financial assistance, shall continue notwithstanding the enactment of this chapter or the transfer of the agency to the Department, unless discontinued or modified under the same terms and conditions and to the same extent that such discontinuance could have occurred if such enactment or transfer had not occurred; and

(2) orders issued in such proceedings, and appeals therefrom, and payments made pursuant to such orders, shall issue in the same manner and on the same terms as if this chapter had not been enacted or the agency had not been transferred, and any such orders shall continue in effect until amended, modified, superseded, terminated, set aside, or revoked by an officer of the United States or a court of competent jurisdiction, or by operation of law.

(c) Pending civil actions

Subject to the authority of the Secretary under this chapter, pending civil actions shall continue notwithstanding the enactment of this chapter or the transfer of an agency to the Department, and in such civil actions, proceedings shall be had, appeals taken, and judgments rendered and enforced in the same manner and with the same effect as if such enactment or transfer had not occurred.

(d) References

References relating to an agency that is transferred to the Department in statutes, Executive orders, rules, regulations, directives, or delegations of authority that precede such transfer or the effective date of this chapter shall be deemed to refer, as appropriate, to the Department, to its officers, employees, or agents, or to its corresponding organizational units or functions. Statutory reporting requirements that applied in relation to such an agency immediately before the effective date of this chapter shall continue to apply following such transfer if they refer to the agency by name.

(e) Employment provisions

(1) Notwithstanding the generality of the foregoing (including subsections (a) and (d) of this section), in and for the Department the Secretary may, in regulations prescribed jointly with the Director of the Office of Personnel Management, adopt the rules, procedures, terms, and conditions, established by statute, rule, or regulation before the effective date of this chapter, relating to employment in any agency transferred to the Department pursuant to this chapter; and

(2) except as otherwise provided in this chapter, or under authority granted by this chapter, the transfer pursuant to this chapter of personnel shall not alter the terms and conditions of employment, including compensation, of any employee so transferred.

(f) Statutory reporting requirements

Any statutory reporting requirement that applied to an agency, transferred to the Department under this chapter, immediately before the effective date of this chapter shall continue to apply following that transfer if the statutory requirement refers to the agency by name.

(Pub. L. 107–296, title XV, §1512, Nov. 25, 2002, 116 Stat. 2310.)

REFERENCES IN TEXT

The effective date of this chapter, referred to in subsecs. (d), (e)(1), and (f), is 60 days after Nov. 25, 2002, see section 4 of Pub. L. 107–296, set out as an Effective Date note under section 101 of this title.

§552a. Savings provision of certain transfers made under the Homeland Security Act of 2002

The transfer of functions under subtitle B of title XI of the Homeland Security Act of 2002 (Public Law 107–296) [6 U.S.C. 531 et seq.] shall not affect any pending or completed administrative actions, including orders, determinations, rules, regulations, personnel actions, permits, agreements, grants, contracts, certificates, licenses, or registrations, in effect on the date immediately prior to the date of such transfer, or any proceeding, unless and until amended, modified, superseded, terminated, set aside, or revoked. Pending civil actions shall not be affected by such transfer of functions.

(Pub. L. 108–7, div. L, §106, Feb. 20, 2003, 117 Stat. 531.)

REFERENCES IN TEXT

The Homeland Security Act of 2002, referred to in text, is Pub. L. 107–296, Nov. 25, 2002, 116 Stat. 2135, as amended, which is classified principally to this chapter. Subtitle B of title XI of the Act is classified principally to part B (§531 et seq.) of subchapter XI of this chapter. For complete classification of this Act to the Code, see Short Title note set out under section 101 of this title and Tables.

CODIFICATION

Section was enacted as part of the Homeland Security Act Amendments of 2003 and also as part of the Consolidated Appropriations Resolution, 2003, and not as part of the Homeland Security Act of 2002 which comprises this chapter.

§553. Terminations

Except as otherwise provided in this chapter, whenever all the functions vested by law in any agency have been transferred pursuant to this chapter, each position and office the incumbent of which was authorized to receive compensation at the rates prescribed for an office or position at level II, III, IV, or V, of the Executive Schedule, shall terminate.

(Pub. L. 107–296, title XV, §1513, Nov. 25, 2002, 116 Stat. 2311.)

REFERENCES IN TEXT

Levels II, III, IV, and V, of the Executive Schedule, referred to in text, are set out in sections 5313, 5314, 5315, and 5316, respectively, of Title 5, Government Organization and Employees.

§554. National identification system not authorized

Nothing in this chapter shall be construed to authorize the development of a national identification system or card.

(Pub. L. 107–296, title XV, §1514, Nov. 25, 2002, 116 Stat. 2311.)

§555. Continuity of Inspector General oversight

Notwithstanding the transfer of an agency to the Department pursuant to this chapter, the Inspector General that exercised oversight of such agency prior to such transfer shall continue to exercise oversight of such agency during the period of time, if any, between the transfer of such agency to the Department pursuant to this chapter and the appointment of the Inspector General of the Department of Homeland Security in accordance with section 113(b) of this title.

(Pub. L. 107–296, title XV, §1515, Nov. 25, 2002, 116 Stat. 2311.)

§556. Incidental transfers

The Director of the Office of Management and Budget, in consultation with the Secretary, is authorized and directed to make such additional incidental dispositions of personnel, assets, and liabilities held, used, arising from, available, or to be made available, in connection with the functions transferred by this chapter, as the Director may determine necessary to accomplish the purposes of this chapter.

(Pub. L. 107–296, title XV, §1516, Nov. 25, 2002, 116 Stat. 2311.)

§557. Reference

With respect to any function transferred by or under this chapter (including under a reorganization plan that becomes effective under section 542 of this title) and exercised on or after the effective date of this chapter, reference in any other Federal law to any department, commission, or agency or any officer or office the functions of which are so transferred shall be deemed to refer to the Secretary, other official, or component of the Department to which such function is so transferred.

(Pub. L. 107–296, title XV, § 1517, Nov. 25, 2002, 116 Stat. 2311.)

REFERENCES IN TEXT

The effective date of this chapter, referred to in text, is 60 days after Nov. 25, 2002, see section 4 of Pub. L. 107–296, set out as an Effective Date note under section 101 of this title.

SUBCHAPTER XIII—EMERGENCY COMMUNICATIONS

CODIFICATION

This subchapter is comprised of title XVIII of Pub. L. 107–296, as added by Pub. L. 109–295, title VI, § 671(b), Oct. 4, 2006, 120 Stat. 1433. Another title XVIII of Pub. L. 107–296 was renumbered title XIX and is classified to subchapter XIV (§ 591 et seq.) of this chapter.

§ 571. Office of Emergency Communications

(a) In general

There is established in the Department an Office of Emergency Communications.

(b) Director

The head of the office shall be the Director for Emergency Communications. The Director shall report to the Assistant Secretary for Cybersecurity and Communications.

(c) Responsibilities

The Director for Emergency Communications shall—

(1) assist the Secretary in developing and implementing the program described in section 194(a)(1) of this title, except as provided in section 195 of this title;

(2) administer the Department's responsibilities and authorities relating to the SAFECOM Program, excluding elements related to research, development, testing, and evaluation and standards;

(3) administer the Department's responsibilities and authorities relating to the Integrated Wireless Network program;

(4) conduct extensive, nationwide outreach to support and promote the ability of emergency response providers and relevant government officials to continue to communicate in the event of natural disasters, acts of terrorism, and other man-made disasters;

(5) conduct extensive, nationwide outreach and foster the development of interoperable emergency communications capabilities by State, regional, local, and tribal governments and public safety agencies, and by regional consortia thereof;

(6) provide technical assistance to State, regional, local, and tribal government officials with respect to use of interoperable emergency communications capabilities;

(7) coordinate with the Regional Administrators regarding the activities of Regional Emergency Communications Coordination Working Groups under section 575 of this title;

(8) promote the development of standard operating procedures and best practices with respect to use of interoperable emergency communications capabilities for incident response, and facilitate the sharing of information on such best practices for achieving, maintaining, and enhancing interoperable emergency communications capabilities for such response;

(9) coordinate, in cooperation with the National Communications System, the establishment of a national response capability with initial and ongoing planning, implementation, and training for the deployment of communications equipment for relevant State, local, and tribal governments and emergency response providers in the event of a catastrophic loss of local and regional emergency communications services;

(10) assist the President, the National Security Council, the Homeland Security Council, and the Director of the Office of Management and Budget in ensuring the continued operation of the telecommunications functions and responsibilities of the Federal Government, excluding spectrum management;

(11) establish, in coordination with the Director of the Office for Interoperability and Compatibility, requirements for interoperable emergency communications capabilities, which shall be nonproprietary where standards for such capabilities exist, for all public safety radio and data communications systems and equipment purchased using homeland security assistance administered by the Department, excluding any alert and warning device, technology, or system;

(12) review, in consultation with the Assistant Secretary for Grants and Training, all interoperable emergency communications plans of Federal, State, local, and tribal governments, including Statewide and tactical interoperability plans, developed pursuant to homeland security assistance administered by the Department, but excluding spectrum allocation and management related to such plans;

(13) develop and update periodically, as appropriate, a National Emergency Communications Plan under section 572 of this title;

(14) perform such other duties of the Department necessary to support and promote the ability of emergency response providers and relevant government officials to continue to communicate in the event of natural disasters, acts of terrorism, and other man-made disasters; and

(15) perform other duties of the Department necessary to achieve the goal of and maintain and enhance interoperable emergency communications capabilities.

(d) Performance of previously transferred functions

The Secretary shall transfer to, and administer through, the Director for Emergency Communications the following programs and responsibilities:

(1) The SAFECOM Program, excluding elements related to research, development, testing, and evaluation and standards.

(2) The responsibilities of the Chief Information Officer related to the implementation of the Integrated Wireless Network.

(3) The Interoperable Communications Technical Assistance Program.

(e) Coordination

The Director for Emergency Communications shall coordinate—

(1) as appropriate, with the Director of the Office for Interoperability and Compatibility with respect to the responsibilities described in section 195 of this title; and

(2) with the Administrator of the Federal Emergency Management Agency with respect to the responsibilities described in this subchapter.

(f) Sufficiency of resources plan

(1) Report

Not later than 120 days after October 4, 2006, the Secretary shall submit to Congress a report on the resources and staff necessary to carry out fully the responsibilities under this subchapter.

(2) Comptroller General review

The Comptroller General shall review the validity of the report submitted by the Secretary under paragraph (1). Not later than 60 days after the date on which such report is submitted, the Comptroller General shall submit to Congress a report containing the findings of such review.

(Pub. L. 107–296, title XVIII, § 1801, as added Pub. L. 109–295, title VI, § 671(b), Oct. 4, 2006, 120 Stat. 1433.)

CODIFICATION

Another section 1801 of Pub. L. 107–296 was renumbered section 1901 and is classified to section 591 of this title.

CHANGE OF NAME

Any reference to the Administrator of the Federal Emergency Management Agency in title VI of Pub. L. 109–295 or an amendment by title VI to be considered to refer and apply to the Director of the Federal Emergency Management Agency until Mar. 31, 2007, see section 612(f)(2) of Pub. L. 109–295, set out as a note under section 313 of this title.

SAVINGS CLAUSE

Pub. L. 109–295, title VI, § 675, Oct. 4, 2006, 120 Stat. 1444, provided that: "Nothing in this subtitle [subtitle D (§§ 671–675) of title VI of Pub. L. 109–295, enacting this subchapter and sections 195 and 195a of this title and provisions set out as a note under section 101 of this title] shall be construed to transfer to the Office of Emergency Communications any function, personnel, asset, component, authority, grant program, or liability of the Federal Emergency Management Agency as constituted on June 1, 2006."

§ 572. National Emergency Communications Plan

(a) In general

The Secretary, acting through the Director for Emergency Communications, and in cooperation with the Department of National Communications System (as appropriate), shall, in cooperation with State, local, and tribal governments, Federal departments and agencies, emergency response providers, and the private sector, develop not later than 180 days after the completion of the baseline assessment under section 573 of this title, and periodically update, a National Emergency Communications Plan to provide recommendations regarding how the United States should—

(1) support and promote the ability of emergency response providers and relevant government officials to continue to communicate in the event of natural disasters, acts of terrorism, and other man-made disasters; and

(2) ensure, accelerate, and attain interoperable emergency communications nationwide.

(b) Coordination

The Emergency Communications Preparedness Center under section 576 of this title shall coordinate the development of the Federal aspects of the National Emergency Communications Plan.

(c) Contents

The National Emergency Communications Plan shall—

(1) include recommendations developed in consultation with the Federal Communications Commission and the National Institute of Standards and Technology for a process for expediting national voluntary consensus standards for emergency communications equipment for the purchase and use by public safety agencies of interoperable emergency communications equipment and technologies;

(2) identify the appropriate capabilities necessary for emergency response providers and relevant government officials to continue to communicate in the event of natural disasters, acts of terrorism, and other man-made disasters;

(3) identify the appropriate interoperable emergency communications capabilities necessary for Federal, State, local, and tribal governments in the event of natural disasters, acts of terrorism, and other man-made disasters;

(4) recommend both short-term and long-term solutions for ensuring that emergency response providers and relevant government officials can continue to communicate in the event of natural disasters, acts of terrorism, and other man-made disasters;

(5) recommend both short-term and long-term solutions for deploying interoperable emergency communications systems for Federal, State, local, and tribal governments throughout the Nation, including through the provision of existing and emerging technologies;

(6) identify how Federal departments and agencies that respond to natural disasters, acts of terrorism, and other man-made disasters can work effectively with State, local, and tribal governments, in all States, and with other entities;

(7) identify obstacles to deploying interoperable emergency communications capabilities nationwide and recommend short-term and long-term measures to overcome those obstacles, including recommendations for multijurisdictional coordination among Federal, State, local, and tribal governments;

(8) recommend goals and timeframes for the deployment of emergency, command-level

communications systems based on new and existing equipment across the United States and develop a timetable for the deployment of interoperable emergency communications systems nationwide;

(9) recommend appropriate measures that emergency response providers should employ to ensure the continued operation of relevant governmental communications infrastructure in the event of natural disasters, acts of terrorism, or other man-made disasters; and

(10) set a date, including interim benchmarks, as appropriate, by which State, local, and tribal governments, Federal departments and agencies, and emergency response providers expect to achieve a baseline level of national interoperable communications, as that term is defined under section 194(g)(1) of this title.

(Pub. L. 107–296, title XVIII, § 1802, as added Pub. L. 109–295, title VI, § 671(b), Oct. 4, 2006, 120 Stat. 1435; amended Pub. L. 110–53, title III, § 301(d), Aug. 3, 2007, 121 Stat. 300.)

CODIFICATION

Another section 1802 of Pub. L. 107–296 was renumbered section 1902 and is classified to section 592 of this title.

AMENDMENTS

2007—Subsec. (c)(10). Pub. L. 110–53 added par. (10).

§ 573. Assessments and reports

(a) Baseline assessment

Not later than 1 year after October 4, 2006, and not less than every 5 years thereafter, the Secretary, acting through the Director for Emergency Communications, shall conduct an assessment of Federal, State, local, and tribal governments that—

(1) defines the range of capabilities needed by emergency response providers and relevant government officials to continue to communicate in the event of natural disasters, acts of terrorism, and other man-made disasters;

(2) defines the range of interoperable emergency communications capabilities needed for specific events;

(3) assesses the current available capabilities to meet such communications needs;

(4) identifies the gap between such current capabilities and defined requirements; and

(5) includes a national interoperable emergency communications inventory to be completed by the Secretary of Homeland Security, the Secretary of Commerce, and the Chairman of the Federal Communications Commission that—

(A) identifies for each Federal department and agency—

(i) the channels and frequencies used;

(ii) the nomenclature used to refer to each channel or frequency used; and

(iii) the types of communications systems and equipment used; and

(B) identifies the interoperable emergency communications systems in use by public safety agencies in the United States.

(b) Classified annex

The baseline assessment under this section may include a classified annex including information provided under subsection (a)(5)(A).

(c) Savings clause

In conducting the baseline assessment under this section, the Secretary may incorporate findings from assessments conducted before, or ongoing on, October 4, 2006.

(d) Progress reports

Not later than one year after October 4, 2006, and biennially thereafter, the Secretary, acting through the Director for Emergency Communications, shall submit to Congress a report on the progress of the Department in achieving the goals of, and carrying out its responsibilities under, this subchapter, including—

(1) a description of the findings of the most recent baseline assessment conducted under subsection (a);

(2) a determination of the degree to which interoperable emergency communications capabilities have been attained to date and the gaps that remain for interoperability to be achieved;

(3) an evaluation of the ability to continue to communicate and to provide and maintain interoperable emergency communications by emergency managers, emergency response providers, and relevant government officials in the event of—

(A) natural disasters, acts of terrorism, or other man-made disasters, including Incidents of National Significance declared by the Secretary under the National Response Plan; and

(B) a catastrophic loss of local and regional communications services;

(4) a list of best practices relating to the ability to continue to communicate and to provide and maintain interoperable emergency communications in the event of natural disasters, acts of terrorism, or other man-made disasters; and

(A)[1] an evaluation of the feasibility and desirability of the Department developing, on its own or in conjunction with the Department of Defense, a mobile communications capability, modeled on the Army Signal Corps, that could be deployed to support emergency communications at the site of natural disasters, acts of terrorism, or other man-made disasters.

(Pub. L. 107–296, title XVIII, § 1803, as added Pub. L. 109–295, title VI, § 671(b), Oct. 4, 2006, 120 Stat. 1437.)

CODIFICATION

Another section 1803 of Pub. L. 107–296 was renumbered section 1903 and is classified to section 593 of this title.

§ 574. Coordination of Department emergency communications grant programs

(a) Coordination of grants and standards programs

The Secretary, acting through the Director for Emergency Communications, shall ensure that grant guidelines for the use of homeland security assistance administered by the Department relating to interoperable emergency commu-

[1] So in original. Probably should be "(5)".

nications are coordinated and consistent with the goals and recommendations in the National Emergency Communications Plan under section 572 of this title.

(b) Denial of eligibility for grants

(1) In general

The Secretary, acting through the Assistant Secretary for Grants and Planning, and in consultation with the Director for Emergency Communications, may prohibit any State, local, or tribal government from using homeland security assistance administered by the Department to achieve, maintain, or enhance emergency communications capabilities, if—

(A) such government has not complied with the requirement to submit a Statewide Interoperable Communications Plan as required by section 194(f) of this title;

(B) such government has proposed to upgrade or purchase new equipment or systems that do not meet or exceed any applicable national voluntary consensus standards and has not provided a reasonable explanation of why such equipment or systems will serve the needs of the applicant better than equipment or systems that meet or exceed such standards; and

(C) as of the date that is 3 years after the date of the completion of the initial National Emergency Communications Plan under section 572 of this title, national voluntary consensus standards for interoperable emergency communications capabilities have not been developed and promulgated.

(2) Standards

The Secretary, in coordination with the Federal Communications Commission, the National Institute of Standards and Technology, and other Federal departments and agencies with responsibility for standards, shall support the development, promulgation, and updating as necessary of national voluntary consensus standards for interoperable emergency communications.

(Pub. L. 107–296, title XVIII, §1804, as added Pub. L. 109–295, title VI, §671(b), Oct. 4, 2006, 120 Stat. 1438.)

CODIFICATION

Another section 1804 of Pub. L. 107–296 was renumbered section 1904 and is classified to section 594 of this title.

§575. Regional emergency communications coordination

(a) In general

There is established in each Regional Office a Regional Emergency Communications Coordination Working Group (in this section referred to as an "RECC Working Group"). Each RECC Working Group shall report to the relevant Regional Administrator and coordinate its activities with the relevant Regional Advisory Council.

(b) Membership

Each RECC Working Group shall consist of the following:

(1) Non-Federal

Organizations representing the interests of the following:

(A) State officials.

(B) Local government officials, including sheriffs.

(C) State police departments.

(D) Local police departments.

(E) Local fire departments.

(F) Public safety answering points (9–1–1 services).

(G) State emergency managers, homeland security directors, or representatives of State Administrative Agencies.

(H) Local emergency managers or homeland security directors.

(I) Other emergency response providers as appropriate.

(2) Federal

Representatives from the Department, the Federal Communications Commission, and other Federal departments and agencies with responsibility for coordinating interoperable emergency communications with or providing emergency support services to State, local, and tribal governments.

(c) Coordination

Each RECC Working Group shall coordinate its activities with the following:

(1) Communications equipment manufacturers and vendors (including broadband data service providers).

(2) Local exchange carriers.

(3) Local broadcast media.

(4) Wireless carriers.

(5) Satellite communications services.

(6) Cable operators.

(7) Hospitals.

(8) Public utility services.

(9) Emergency evacuation transit services.

(10) Ambulance services.

(11) HAM and amateur radio operators.

(12) Representatives from other private sector entities and nongovernmental organizations as the Regional Administrator determines appropriate.

(d) Duties

The duties of each RECC Working Group shall include—

(1) assessing the survivability, sustainability, and interoperability of local emergency communications systems to meet the goals of the National Emergency Communications Plan;

(2) reporting annually to the relevant Regional Administrator, the Director for Emergency Communications, the Chairman of the Federal Communications Commission, and the Assistant Secretary for Communications and Information of the Department of Commerce on the status of its region in building robust and sustainable interoperable voice and data emergency communications networks and, not later than 60 days after the completion of the initial National Emergency Communications Plan under section 572 of this title, on the progress of the region in meeting the goals of such plan;

(3) ensuring a process for the coordination of effective multijurisdictional, multi-agency emergency communications networks for use during natural disasters, acts of terrorism,

and other man-made disasters through the expanded use of emergency management and public safety communications mutual aid agreements; and

(4) coordinating the establishment of Federal, State, local, and tribal support services and networks designed to address the immediate and critical human needs in responding to natural disasters, acts of terrorism, and other man-made disasters.

(Pub. L. 107–296, title XVIII, §1805, as added Pub. L. 109–295, title VI, §671(b), Oct. 4, 2006, 120 Stat. 1439.)

CODIFICATION

Another section 1805 of Pub. L. 107–296 was renumbered section 1905 and is classified to section 595 of this title.

§576. Emergency Communications Preparedness Center

(a) Establishment

There is established the Emergency Communications Preparedness Center (in this section referred to as the "Center").

(b) Operation

The Secretary, the Chairman of the Federal Communications Commission, the Secretary of Defense, the Secretary of Commerce, the Attorney General of the United States, and the heads of other Federal departments and agencies or their designees shall jointly operate the Center in accordance with the Memorandum of Understanding entitled, "Emergency Communications Preparedness Center (ECPC) Charter".

(c) Functions

The Center shall—

(1) serve as the focal point for interagency efforts and as a clearinghouse with respect to all relevant intergovernmental information to support and promote (including specifically by working to avoid duplication, hindrances, and counteractive efforts among the participating Federal departments and agencies)—

(A) the ability of emergency response providers and relevant government officials to continue to communicate in the event of natural disasters, acts of terrorism, and other man-made disasters; and

(B) interoperable emergency communications;

(2) prepare and submit to Congress, on an annual basis, a strategic assessment regarding the coordination efforts of Federal departments and agencies to advance—

(A) the ability of emergency response providers and relevant government officials to continue to communicate in the event of natural disasters, acts of terrorism, and other man-made disasters; and

(B) interoperable emergency communications;

(3) consider, in preparing the strategic assessment under paragraph (2), the goals stated in the National Emergency Communications Plan under section 572 of this title; and

(4) perform such other functions as are provided in the Emergency Communications Preparedness Center (ECPC) Charter described in subsection (b)(1).[1]

(Pub. L. 107–296, title XVIII, §1806, as added Pub. L. 109–295, title VI, §671(b), Oct. 4, 2006, 120 Stat. 1440.)

CODIFICATION

Another section 1806 of Pub. L. 107–296 was renumbered section 1906 and is classified to section 596 of this title.

§577. Urban and other high risk area communications capabilities

(a) In general

The Secretary, in consultation with the Chairman of the Federal Communications Commission and the Secretary of Defense, and with appropriate State, local, and tribal government officials, shall provide technical guidance, training, and other assistance, as appropriate, to support the rapid establishment of consistent, secure, and effective interoperable emergency communications capabilities in the event of an emergency in urban and other areas determined by the Secretary to be at consistently high levels of risk from natural disasters, acts of terrorism, and other man-made disasters.

(b) Minimum capabilities

The interoperable emergency communications capabilities established under subsection (a) shall ensure the ability of all levels of government, emergency response providers, the private sector, and other organizations with emergency response capabilities—

(1) to communicate with each other in the event of an emergency;

(2) to have appropriate and timely access to the Information Sharing Environment described in section 485 of this title; and

(3) to be consistent with any applicable State or Urban Area homeland strategy or plan.

(Pub. L. 107–296, title XVIII, §1807, as added Pub. L. 109–295, title VI, §671(b), Oct. 4, 2006, 120 Stat. 1441.)

§578. Definition

In this subchapter, the term "interoperable" has the meaning given the term "interoperable communications" under section 194(g)(1) of this title.

(Pub. L. 107–296, title XVIII, §1808, as added Pub. L. 109–295, title VI, §671(b), Oct. 4, 2006, 120 Stat. 1441.)

§579. Interoperable Emergency Communications Grant Program

(a) Establishment

The Secretary shall establish the Interoperable Emergency Communications Grant Program to make grants to States to carry out initiatives to improve local, tribal, statewide, regional, national and, where appropriate, international interoperable emergency communications, including communications in collective

---

[1] So in original. Subsection (b) of this section does not contain a paragraph (1).

response to natural disasters, acts of terrorism, and other man-made disasters.

(b) Policy

The Director for Emergency Communications shall ensure that a grant awarded to a State under this section is consistent with the policies established pursuant to the responsibilities and authorities of the Office of Emergency Communications under this subchapter, including ensuring that activities funded by the grant—

(1) comply with the statewide plan for that State required by section 194(f) of this title; and

(2) comply with the National Emergency Communications Plan under section 572 of this title, when completed.

(c) Administration

(1) In general

The Administrator of the Federal Emergency Management Agency shall administer the Interoperable Emergency Communications Grant Program pursuant to the responsibilities and authorities of the Administrator under subchapter V.

(2) Guidance

In administering the grant program, the Administrator shall ensure that the use of grants is consistent with guidance established by the Director of Emergency Communications pursuant to section 194(a)(1)(H) of this title.

(d) Use of funds

A State that receives a grant under this section shall use the grant to implement that State's Statewide Interoperability Plan required under section 194(f) of this title and approved under subsection (e), and to assist with activities determined by the Secretary to be integral to interoperable emergency communications.

(e) Approval of plans

(1) Approval as condition of grant

Before a State may receive a grant under this section, the Director of Emergency Communications shall approve the State's Statewide Interoperable Communications Plan required under section 194(f) of this title.

(2) Plan requirements

In approving a plan under this subsection, the Director of Emergency Communications shall ensure that the plan—

(A) is designed to improve interoperability at the city, county, regional, State and interstate level;

(B) considers any applicable local or regional plan; and

(C) complies, to the maximum extent practicable, with the National Emergency Communications Plan under section 572 of this title.

(3) Approval of revisions

The Director of Emergency Communications may approve revisions to a State's plan if the Director determines that doing so is likely to further interoperability.

(f) Limitations on uses of funds

(1) In general

The recipient of a grant under this section may not use the grant—

(A) to supplant State or local funds;

(B) for any State or local government cost-sharing contribution; or

(C) for recreational or social purposes.

(2) Penalties

In addition to other remedies currently available, the Secretary may take such actions as necessary to ensure that recipients of grant funds are using the funds for the purpose for which they were intended.

(g) Limitations on award of grants

(1) National emergency communications plan required

The Secretary may not award a grant under this section before the date on which the Secretary completes and submits to Congress the National Emergency Communications Plan required under section 572 of this title.

(2) Voluntary consensus standards

The Secretary may not award a grant to a State under this section for the purchase of equipment that does not meet applicable voluntary consensus standards, unless the State demonstrates that there are compelling reasons for such purchase.

(h) Award of grants

In approving applications and awarding grants under this section, the Secretary shall consider—

(1) the risk posed to each State by natural disasters, acts of terrorism, or other manmade disasters, including—

(A) the likely need of a jurisdiction within the State to respond to such risk in nearby jurisdictions;

(B) the degree of threat, vulnerability, and consequences related to critical infrastructure (from all critical infrastructure sectors) or key resources identified by the Administrator or the State homeland security and emergency management plans, including threats to, vulnerabilities of, and consequences from damage to critical infrastructure and key resources in nearby jurisdictions;

(C) the size of the population and density of the population of the State, including appropriate consideration of military, tourist, and commuter populations;

(D) whether the State is on or near an international border;

(E) whether the State encompasses an economically significant border crossing; and

(F) whether the State has a coastline bordering an ocean, a major waterway used for interstate commerce, or international waters; and

(2) the anticipated effectiveness of the State's proposed use of grant funds to improve interoperability.

(i) Opportunity to amend applications

In considering applications for grants under this section, the Administrator shall provide applicants with a reasonable opportunity to correct defects in the application, if any, before making final awards.

(j) Minimum grant amounts

(1) States

In awarding grants under this section, the Secretary shall ensure that for each fiscal year, except as provided in paragraph (2), no State receives a grant in an amount that is less than the following percentage of the total amount appropriated for grants under this section for that fiscal year:

(A) For fiscal year 2008, 0.50 percent.

(B) For fiscal year 2009, 0.50 percent.

(C) For fiscal year 2010, 0.45 percent.

(D) For fiscal year 2011, 0.40 percent.

(E) For fiscal year 2012 and each subsequent fiscal year, 0.35 percent.

(2) Territories and possessions

In awarding grants under this section, the Secretary shall ensure that for each fiscal year, American Samoa, the Commonwealth of the Northern Mariana Islands, Guam, and the Virgin Islands each receive grants in amounts that are not less than 0.08 percent of the total amount appropriated for grants under this section for that fiscal year.

(k) Certification

Each State that receives a grant under this section shall certify that the grant is used for the purpose for which the funds were intended and in compliance with the State's approved Statewide Interoperable Communications Plan.

(*l*) State responsibilities

(1) Availability of funds to local and tribal governments

Not later than 45 days after receiving grant funds, any State that receives a grant under this section shall obligate or otherwise make available to local and tribal governments—

(A) not less than 80 percent of the grant funds;

(B) with the consent of local and tribal governments, eligible expenditures having a value of not less than 80 percent of the amount of the grant; or

(C) grant funds combined with other eligible expenditures having a total value of not less than 80 percent of the amount of the grant.

(2) Allocation of funds

A State that receives a grant under this section shall allocate grant funds to tribal governments in the State to assist tribal communities in improving interoperable communications, in a manner consistent with the Statewide Interoperable Communications Plan. A State may not impose unreasonable or unduly burdensome requirements on a tribal government as a condition of providing grant funds or resources to the tribal government.

(3) Penalties

If a State violates the requirements of this subsection, in addition to other remedies available to the Secretary, the Secretary may terminate or reduce the amount of the grant awarded to that State or transfer grant funds previously awarded to the State directly to the appropriate local or tribal government.

(m) Reports

(1) Annual reports by State grant recipients

A State that receives a grant under this section shall annually submit to the Director of Emergency Communications a report on the progress of the State in implementing that State's Statewide Interoperable Communications Plans required under section 194(f) of this title and achieving interoperability at the city, county, regional, State, and interstate levels. The Director shall make the reports publicly available, including by making them available on the Internet website of the Office of Emergency Communications, subject to any redactions that the Director determines are necessary to protect classified or other sensitive information.

(2) Annual reports to Congress

At least once each year, the Director of Emergency Communications shall submit to Congress a report on the use of grants awarded under this section and any progress in implementing Statewide Interoperable Communications Plans and improving interoperability at the city, county, regional, State, and interstate level, as a result of the award of such grants.

(n) Rule of construction

Nothing in this section shall be construed or interpreted to preclude a State from using a grant awarded under this section for interim or long-term Internet Protocol-based interoperable solutions.

(*o*) Authorization of appropriations

There are authorized to be appropriated for grants under this section—

(1) for fiscal year 2008, such sums as may be necessary;

(2) for each of fiscal years 2009 through 2012, $400,000,000; and

(3) for each subsequent fiscal year, such sums as may be necessary.

(Pub. L. 107–296, title XVIII, §1809, as added Pub. L. 110–53, title III, §301(a), Aug. 3, 2007, 121 Stat. 296.)

§580. Border interoperability demonstration project

(a) In general

(1) Establishment

The Secretary, acting through the Director of the Office of Emergency Communications (referred to in this section as the "Director"), and in coordination with the Federal Communications Commission and the Secretary of Commerce, shall establish an International Border Community Interoperable Communications Demonstration Project (referred to in this section as the "demonstration project").

(2) Minimum number of communities

The Director shall select no fewer than 6 communities to participate in a demonstration project.

(3) Location of communities

No fewer than 3 of the communities selected under paragraph (2) shall be located on the northern border of the United States and no fewer than 3 of the communities selected under paragraph (2) shall be located on the southern border of the United States.

(b) Conditions

The Director, in coordination with the Federal Communications Commission and the Secretary of Commerce, shall ensure that the project is carried out as soon as adequate spectrum is available as a result of the 800 megahertz rebanding process in border areas, and shall ensure that the border projects do not impair or impede the rebanding process, but under no circumstances shall funds be distributed under this section unless the Federal Communications Commission and the Secretary of Commerce agree that these conditions have been met.

(c) Program requirements

Consistent with the responsibilities of the Office of Emergency Communications under section 571 of this title, the Director shall foster local, tribal, State, and Federal interoperable emergency communications, as well as interoperable emergency communications with appropriate Canadian and Mexican authorities in the communities selected for the demonstration project. The Director shall—

(1) identify solutions to facilitate interoperable communications across national borders expeditiously;

(2) help ensure that emergency response providers can communicate with each other in the event of natural disasters, acts of terrorism, and other man-made disasters;

(3) provide technical assistance to enable emergency response providers to deal with threats and contingencies in a variety of environments;

(4) identify appropriate joint-use equipment to ensure communications access;

(5) identify solutions to facilitate communications between emergency response providers in communities of differing population densities; and

(6) take other actions or provide equipment as the Director deems appropriate to foster interoperable emergency communications.

(d) Distribution of funds

(1) In general

The Secretary shall distribute funds under this section to each community participating in the demonstration project through the State, or States, in which each community is located.

(2) Other participants

A State shall make the funds available promptly to the local and tribal governments and emergency response providers selected by the Secretary to participate in the demonstration project.

(3) Report

Not later than 90 days after a State receives funds under this subsection the State shall report to the Director on the status of the distribution of such funds to local and tribal governments.

(e) Maximum period of grants

The Director may not fund any participant under the demonstration project for more than 3 years.

(f) Transfer of information and knowledge

The Director shall establish mechanisms to ensure that the information and knowledge gained by participants in the demonstration project are transferred among the participants and to other interested parties, including other communities that submitted applications to the participant in the project.

(g) Authorization of appropriations

There is authorized to be appropriated for grants under this section such sums as may be necessary.

(Pub. L. 107–296, title XVIII, §1810, as added Pub. L. 110–53, title III, §302(a), Aug. 3, 2007, 121 Stat. 300.)

SUBCHAPTER XIV—DOMESTIC NUCLEAR DETECTION OFFICE

CODIFICATION

This subchapter is comprised of title XIX, formerly title XVIII, of Pub. L. 107–296, as added by Pub. L. 109–347, title V, §501(a), Oct. 13, 2006, 120 Stat. 1932, and renumbered title XIX by Pub. L. 110–53, title I, §104(a)(1), Aug. 3, 2007, 121 Stat. 294.

§591. Domestic Nuclear Detection Office

(a) Establishment

There shall be established in the Department a Domestic Nuclear Detection Office (referred to in this subchapter as the "Office"). The Secretary may request that the Secretary of Defense, the Secretary of Energy, the Secretary of State, the Attorney General, the Nuclear Regulatory Commission, and the directors of other Federal agencies, including elements of the Intelligence Community, provide for the reimbursable detail of personnel with relevant expertise to the Office.

(b) Director

The Office shall be headed by a Director for Domestic Nuclear Detection, who shall be appointed by the President.

(Pub. L. 107–296, title XIX, §1901, formerly title XVIII, §1801, as added Pub. L. 109–347, title V, §501(a), Oct. 13, 2006, 120 Stat. 1932; renumbered title XIX, §1901, Pub. L. 110–53, title I, §104(a)(1), (2), Aug. 3, 2007, 121 Stat. 294.)

§592. Mission of Office

(a)[1] Mission

The Office shall be responsible for coordinating Federal efforts to detect and protect against the unauthorized importation, possession, storage, transportation, development, or use of a nuclear explosive device, fissile material, or radiological material in the United States, and to protect against attack using such devices or materials against the people, territory, or interests of the United States and, to this end, shall—

[1] So in original. No subsec. (b) has been enacted.

(1) serve as the primary entity of the United States Government to further develop, acquire, and support the deployment of an enhanced domestic system to detect and report on attempts to import, possess, store, transport, develop, or use an unauthorized nuclear explosive device, fissile material, or radiological material in the United States, and improve that system over time;

(2) enhance and coordinate the nuclear detection efforts of Federal, State, local, and tribal governments and the private sector to ensure a managed, coordinated response;

(3) establish, with the approval of the Secretary and in coordination with the Attorney General, the Secretary of Defense, and the Secretary of Energy, additional protocols and procedures for use within the United States to ensure that the detection of unauthorized nuclear explosive devices, fissile material, or radiological material is promptly reported to the Attorney General, the Secretary, the Secretary of Defense, the Secretary of Energy, and other appropriate officials or their respective designees for appropriate action by law enforcement, military, emergency response, or other authorities;

(4) develop, with the approval of the Secretary and in coordination with the Attorney General, the Secretary of State, the Secretary of Defense, and the Secretary of Energy, an enhanced global nuclear detection architecture with implementation under which—

(A) the Office will be responsible for the implementation of the domestic portion of the global architecture;

(B) the Secretary of Defense will retain responsibility for implementation of Department of Defense requirements within and outside the United States; and

(C) the Secretary of State, the Secretary of Defense, and the Secretary of Energy will maintain their respective responsibilities for policy guidance and implementation of the portion of the global architecture outside the United States, which will be implemented consistent with applicable law and relevant international arrangements;

(5) ensure that the expertise necessary to accurately interpret detection data is made available in a timely manner for all technology deployed by the Office to implement the global nuclear detection architecture;

(6) conduct, support, coordinate, and encourage an aggressive, expedited, evolutionary, and transformational program of research and development to generate and improve technologies to detect and prevent the illicit entry, transport, assembly, or potential use within the United States of a nuclear explosive device or fissile or radiological material, and coordinate with the Under Secretary for Science and Technology on basic and advanced or transformational research and development efforts relevant to the mission of both organizations;

(7) carry out a program to test and evaluate technology for detecting a nuclear explosive device and fissile or radiological material, in coordination with the Secretary of Defense and the Secretary of Energy, as appropriate, and establish performance metrics for evaluating the effectiveness of individual detectors and detection systems in detecting such devices or material—

(A) under realistic operational and environmental conditions; and

(B) against realistic adversary tactics and countermeasures;

(8) support and enhance the effective sharing and use of appropriate information generated by the intelligence community, law enforcement agencies, counterterrorism community, other government agencies, and foreign governments, as well as provide appropriate information to such entities;

(9) further enhance and maintain continuous awareness by analyzing information from all Office mission-related detection systems; and

(10) perform other duties as assigned by the Secretary.

(Pub. L. 107–296, title XIX, § 1902, formerly title XVIII, § 1802, as added Pub. L. 109–347, title V, § 501(a), Oct. 13, 2006, 120 Stat. 1932; renumbered title XIX, § 1902, Pub. L. 110–53, title I, § 104(a)(1), (2), Aug. 3, 2007, 121 Stat. 294.)

§ 592a. Technology research and development investment strategy for nuclear and radiological detection

(a) In general

Not later than 1 year after October 13, 2006, the Secretary, the Secretary of Energy, the Secretary of Defense, and the Director of National Intelligence shall submit to Congress a research and development investment strategy for nuclear and radiological detection.

(b) Contents

The strategy under subsection (a) shall include—

(1) a long term technology roadmap for nuclear and radiological detection applicable to the mission needs of the Department, the Department of Energy, the Department of Defense, and the Office of the Director of National Intelligence;

(2) budget requirements necessary to meet the roadmap; and

(3) documentation of how the Department, the Department of Energy, the Department of Defense, and the Office of the Director of National Intelligence will execute this strategy.

(c) Initial report

Not later than 1 year after October 13, 2006, the Secretary shall submit a report to the appropriate congressional committees on—

(1) the impact of this title,[1] and the amendments made by this title, on the responsibilities under section 182 of this title; and

(2) the efforts of the Department to coordinate, integrate, and establish priorities for conducting all basic and applied research, development, testing, and evaluation of technology and systems to detect, prevent, protect, and respond to chemical, biological, radiological, and nuclear terrorist attacks.

(d) Annual report

The Director for Domestic Nuclear Detection and the Under Secretary for Science and Tech-

[1] See References in Text note below.

nology shall jointly and annually notify Congress that the strategy and technology road map for nuclear and radiological detection developed under subsections (a) and (b) is consistent with the national policy and strategic plan for identifying priorities, goals, objectives, and policies for coordinating the Federal Government's civilian efforts to identify and develop countermeasures to terrorist threats from weapons of mass destruction that are required under section 182(2) of this title.

(Pub. L. 109–347, title V, § 502, Oct. 13, 2006, 120 Stat. 1935.)

REFERENCES IN TEXT

This title, referred to in subsec. (c)(1), is title V of Pub. L. 109–347, Oct. 13, 2006, 120 Stat. 1932, which enacted this subchapter and this section and amended sections 113 and 182 of this title. For complete classification of title V to the Code, see Tables.

CODIFICATION

Section was enacted as part of the Security and Accountability For Every Port Act of 2006, also known as the SAFE Port Act, and not as part of the Homeland Security Act of 2002 which comprises this chapter.

DEFINITIONS

For definitions of terms used in this section, see section 901 of this title.

§ 593. Hiring authority

In hiring personnel for the Office, the Secretary shall have the hiring and management authorities provided in section 1101 of the Strom Thurmond National Defense Authorization Act for Fiscal Year 1999 (5 U.S.C. 3104 note). The term of appointments for employees under subsection (c)(1) of such section may not exceed 5 years before granting any extension under subsection (c)(2) of such section.

(Pub. L. 107–296, title XIX, § 1903, formerly title XVIII, § 1803, as added Pub. L. 109–347, title V, § 501(a), Oct. 13, 2006, 120 Stat. 1934; renumbered title XIX, § 1903, Pub. L. 110–53, title I, § 104(a)(1), (2), Aug. 3, 2007, 121 Stat. 294.)

REFERENCES IN TEXT

Section 1101 of the Strom Thurmond National Defense Authorization Act for Fiscal Year 1999, referred to in text, is section 1101 of Pub. L. 105–261, which is set out as a note under section 3104 of Title 5, Government Organization and Employees.

§ 594. Testing authority

(a) In general

The Director shall coordinate with the responsible Federal agency or other entity to facilitate the use by the Office, by its contractors, or by other persons or entities, of existing Government laboratories, centers, ranges, or other testing facilities for the testing of materials, equipment, models, computer software, and other items as may be related to the missions identified in section 592 of this title. Any such use of Government facilities shall be carried out in accordance with all applicable laws, regulations, and contractual provisions, including those governing security, safety, and environmental protection, including, when applicable, the provisions of section 189 of this title. The Office may direct that private sector entities utilizing Government facilities in accordance with this section pay an appropriate fee to the agency that owns or operates those facilities to defray additional costs to the Government resulting from such use.

(b) Confidentiality of test results

The results of tests performed with services made available shall be confidential and shall not be disclosed outside the Federal Government without the consent of the persons for whom the tests are performed.

(c) Fees

Fees for services made available under this section shall not exceed the amount necessary to recoup the direct and indirect costs involved, such as direct costs of utilities, contractor support, and salaries of personnel that are incurred by the United States to provide for the testing.

(d) Use of fees

Fees received for services made available under this section may be credited to the appropriation from which funds were expended to provide such services.

(Pub. L. 107–296, title XIX, § 1904, formerly title XVIII, § 1804, as added Pub. L. 109–347, title V, § 501(a), Oct. 13, 2006, 120 Stat. 1934; renumbered title XIX, § 1904, and amended Pub. L. 110–53, title I, § 104(a)(1)–(3), Aug. 3, 2007, 121 Stat. 294.)

AMENDMENTS

2007—Subsec. (a). Pub. L. 110–53, § 104(a)(3), made technical amendment to reference in original act which appears in text as reference to section 592 of this title.

§ 595. Relationship to other Department entities and Federal agencies

The authority of the Director under this subchapter shall not affect the authorities or responsibilities of any officer of the Department or of any officer of any other department or agency of the United States with respect to the command, control, or direction of the functions, personnel, funds, assets, and liabilities of any entity within the Department or any Federal department or agency.

(Pub. L. 107–296, title XIX, § 1905, formerly title XVIII, § 1805, as added Pub. L. 109–347, title V, § 501(a), Oct. 13, 2006, 120 Stat. 1934; renumbered title XIX, § 1905, Pub. L. 110–53, title I, § 104(a)(1), (2), Aug. 3, 2007, 121 Stat. 294.)

§ 596. Contracting and grant making authorities

The Secretary, acting through the Director for Domestic Nuclear Detection, in carrying out the responsibilities under paragraphs (6) and (7) of section 592(a) of this title, shall—

(1) operate extramural and intramural programs and distribute funds through grants, cooperative agreements, and other transactions and contracts;

(2) ensure that activities under paragraphs (6) and (7) of section 592(a) of this title include investigations of radiation detection equipment in configurations suitable for deployment at seaports, which may include underwater or water surface detection equipment and detection equipment that can be mounted

on cranes and straddle cars used to move shipping containers; and

(3) have the authority to establish or contract with 1 or more federally funded research and development centers to provide independent analysis of homeland security issues and carry out other responsibilities under this subchapter.

(Pub. L. 107–296, title XIX, § 1906, formerly title XVIII, § 1806, as added Pub. L. 109–347, title V, § 501(a), Oct. 13, 2006, 120 Stat. 1935; renumbered title XIX, § 1906, and amended Pub. L. 110–53, title I, § 104(a)(1), (2), (4), Aug. 3, 2007, 121 Stat. 294.)

AMENDMENTS

2007—Pub. L. 110–53, § 104(a)(4), made technical amendment to reference in original act which appears in two places in text as reference to section 592(a) of this title.

§ 596a. Joint annual interagency review of global nuclear detection architecture

(a) Annual review

(1) In general

The Secretary, the Attorney General, the Secretary of State, the Secretary of Defense, the Secretary of Energy, and the Director of National Intelligence shall jointly ensure interagency coordination on the development and implementation of the global nuclear detection architecture by ensuring that, not less frequently than once each year—

(A) each relevant agency, office, or entity—

(i) assesses its involvement, support, and participation in the development, revision, and implementation of the global nuclear detection architecture; and

(ii) examines and evaluates components of the global nuclear detection architecture (including associated strategies and acquisition plans) relating to the operations of that agency, office, or entity, to determine whether such components incorporate and address current threat assessments, scenarios, or intelligence analyses developed by the Director of National Intelligence or other agencies regarding threats relating to nuclear or radiological weapons of mass destruction; and

(B) each agency, office, or entity deploying or operating any nuclear or radiological detection technology under the global nuclear detection architecture—

(i) evaluates the deployment and operation of nuclear or radiological detection technologies under the global nuclear detection architecture by that agency, office, or entity;

(ii) identifies performance deficiencies and operational or technical deficiencies in nuclear or radiological detection technologies deployed under the global nuclear detection architecture; and

(iii) assesses the capacity of that agency, office, or entity to implement the responsibilities of that agency, office, or entity under the global nuclear detection architecture.

(2) Technology

Not less frequently than once each year, the Secretary shall examine and evaluate the development, assessment, and acquisition of radiation detection technologies deployed or implemented in support of the domestic portion of the global nuclear detection architecture.

(b) Annual report on joint interagency review

(1) In general

Not later than March 31 of each year, the Secretary, the Attorney General, the Secretary of State, the Secretary of Defense, the Secretary of Energy, and the Director of National Intelligence, shall jointly submit a report regarding the implementation of this section and the results of the reviews required under subsection (a) to—

(A) the President;

(B) the Committee on Appropriations, the Committee on Armed Services, the Select Committee on Intelligence, and the Committee on Homeland Security and Governmental Affairs of the Senate; and

(C) the Committee on Appropriations, the Committee on Armed Services, the Permanent Select Committee on Intelligence, the Committee on Homeland Security, and the Committee on Science and Technology of the House of Representatives.

(2) Form

The annual report submitted under paragraph (1) shall be submitted in unclassified form to the maximum extent practicable, but may include a classified annex.

(c) Definition

In this section, the term "global nuclear detection architecture" means the global nuclear detection architecture developed under section 592 of this title.

(Pub. L. 107–296, title XIX, § 1907, as added Pub. L. 110–53, title XI, § 1103(a), Aug. 3, 2007, 121 Stat. 379.)

SUBCHAPTER XV—HOMELAND SECURITY GRANTS

§ 601. Definitions

In this subchapter, the following definitions shall apply:

(1) Administrator

The term "Administrator" means the Administrator of the Federal Emergency Management Agency.

(2) Appropriate committees of Congress

The term "appropriate committees of Congress" means—

(A) the Committee on Homeland Security and Governmental Affairs of the Senate; and

(B) those committees of the House of Representatives that the Speaker of the House of Representatives determines appropriate.

(3) Critical infrastructure sectors

The term "critical infrastructure sectors" means the following sectors, in both urban and rural areas:

(A) Agriculture and food.

(B) Banking and finance.
(C) Chemical industries.
(D) Commercial facilities.
(E) Commercial nuclear reactors, materials, and waste.
(F) Dams.
(G) The defense industrial base.
(H) Emergency services.
(I) Energy.
(J) Government facilities.
(K) Information technology.
(L) National monuments and icons.
(M) Postal and shipping.
(N) Public health and health care.
(O) Telecommunications.
(P) Transportation systems.
(Q) Water.

(4) Directly eligible tribe

The term "directly eligible tribe" means—

(A) any Indian tribe—

(i) that is located in the continental United States;

(ii) that operates a law enforcement or emergency response agency with the capacity to respond to calls for law enforcement or emergency services;

(iii)(I) that is located on or near an international border or a coastline bordering an ocean (including the Gulf of Mexico) or international waters;

(II) that is located within 10 miles of a system or asset included on the prioritized critical infrastructure list established under section 124*l*(a)(2) of this title or has such a system or asset within its territory;

(III) that is located within or contiguous to 1 of the 50 most populous metropolitan statistical areas in the United States; or

(IV) the jurisdiction of which includes not less than 1,000 square miles of Indian country, as that term is defined in section 1151 of title 18; and

(iv) that certifies to the Secretary that a State has not provided funds under section 604 or 605 of this title to the Indian tribe or consortium of Indian tribes for the purpose for which direct funding is sought; and

(B) a consortium of Indian tribes, if each tribe satisfies the requirements of subparagraph (A).

(5) Eligible metropolitan area

The term "eligible metropolitan area" means any of the 100 most populous metropolitan statistical areas in the United States.

(6) High-risk urban area

The term "high-risk urban area" means a high-risk urban area designated under section 604(b)(3)(A) of this title.

(7) Indian tribe

The term "Indian tribe" has the meaning given that term in section 450b(e) of title 25.

(8) Metropolitan statistical area

The term "metropolitan statistical area" means a metropolitan statistical area, as defined by the Office of Management and Budget.

(9) National Special Security Event

The term "National Special Security Event" means a designated event that, by virtue of its political, economic, social, or religious significance, may be the target of terrorism or other criminal activity.

(10) Population

The term "population" means population according to the most recent United States census population estimates available at the start of the relevant fiscal year.

(11) Population density

The term "population density" means population divided by land area in square miles.

(12) Qualified intelligence analyst

The term "qualified intelligence analyst" means an intelligence analyst (as that term is defined in section 124h(j) of this title), including law enforcement personnel—

(A) who has successfully completed training to ensure baseline proficiency in intelligence analysis and production, as determined by the Secretary, which may include training using a curriculum developed under section 124f of this title; or

(B) whose experience ensures baseline proficiency in intelligence analysis and production equivalent to the training required under subparagraph (A), as determined by the Secretary.

(13) Target capabilities

The term "target capabilities" means the target capabilities for Federal, State, local, and tribal government preparedness for which guidelines are required to be established under section 746(a) of this title.

(14) Tribal government

The term "tribal government" means the government of an Indian tribe.

(Pub. L. 107–296, title XX, § 2001, as added Pub. L. 110–53, title I, § 101, Aug. 3, 2007, 121 Stat. 271.)

PART A—GRANTS TO STATES AND HIGH-RISK URBAN AREAS

§ 603. Homeland security grant programs

(a) Grants authorized

The Secretary, through the Administrator, may award grants under sections 604 and 605 of this title to State, local, and tribal governments.

(b) Programs not affected

This part shall not be construed to affect any of the following Federal programs:

(1) Firefighter and other assistance programs authorized under the Federal Fire Prevention and Control Act of 1974 (15 U.S.C. 2201 et seq.).

(2) Grants authorized under the Robert T. Stafford Disaster Relief and Emergency Assistance Act (42 U.S.C. 5121 et seq.).

(3) Emergency Management Performance Grants under the amendments made by title II of the Implementing Recommendations of the 9/11 Commission Act of 2007.

(4) Grants to protect critical infrastructure, including port security grants authorized under section 70107 of title 46 and the grants authorized under title[1] XIV and XV of the Im-

[1] So in original. Probably should be "titles".

plementing Recommendations of the 9/11 Commission Act of 2007 [6 U.S.C. 1131 et seq., 1151 et seq.] and the amendments made by such titles.

(5) The Metropolitan Medical Response System authorized under section 723 of this title.

(6) The Interoperable Emergency Communications Grant Program authorized under subchapter XIII.

(7) Grant programs other than those administered by the Department.

(c) Relationship to other laws

(1) In general

The grant programs authorized under sections 604 and 605 of this title shall supercede all grant programs authorized under section 3714 of title 42.

(2) Allocation

The allocation of grants authorized under section 604 or 605 of this title shall be governed by the terms of this part and not by any other provision of law.

(Pub. L. 107–296, title XX, § 2002, as added Pub. L. 110–53, title I, § 101, Aug. 3, 2007, 121 Stat. 273.)

REFERENCES IN TEXT

The Federal Fire Prevention and Control Act of 1974, referred to in subsec. (b)(1), is Pub. L. 93–498, Oct. 29, 1974, 88 Stat. 1535, which is classified principally to chapter 49 (§ 2201 et seq.) of Title 15, Commerce and Trade. For complete classification of this Act to the Code, see Short Title note set out under section 2201 of Title 15 and Tables.

The Robert T. Stafford Disaster Relief and Emergency Assistance Act, referred to in subsec. (b)(2), is Pub. L. 93–288, May 22, 1974, 88 Stat. 143, which is classified principally to chapter 68 (§ 5121 et seq.) of Title 42, The Public Health and Welfare. For complete classification of this Act to the Code, see Short Title note set out under section 5121 of Title 42 and Tables.

The Implementing Recommendations of the 9/11 Commission Act of 2007, referred to in subsec. (b)(3), (4), is Pub. L. 110–53, Aug. 3, 2007, 121 Stat. 266. Title II of the Act amended section 762 of this title and section 5196c of Title 42, The Public Health and Welfare. Title XIV of the Act is classified generally to subchapter III (§ 1131 et seq.) of chapter 4 of this title. Title XV of the Act is classified principally to subchapter IV (§ 1151 et seq.) of chapter 4 of this title. For complete classification of this Act to the Code, see Short Title of 2007 Amendment note set out under section 101 of this title and Tables.

§ 604. Urban Area Security Initiative

(a) Establishment

There is established an Urban Area Security Initiative to provide grants to assist high-risk urban areas in preventing, preparing for, protecting against, and responding to acts of terrorism.

(b) Assessment and designation of high-risk urban areas

(1) In general

The Administrator shall designate high-risk urban areas to receive grants under this section based on procedures under this subsection.

(2) Initial assessment

(A) In general

For each fiscal year, the Administrator shall conduct an initial assessment of the relative threat, vulnerability, and consequences from acts of terrorism faced by each eligible metropolitan area, including consideration of—

(i) the factors set forth in subparagraphs (A) through (H) and (K) of section 608(a)(1) of this title; and

(ii) information and materials submitted under subparagraph (B).

(B) Submission of information by eligible metropolitan areas

Prior to conducting each initial assessment under subparagraph (A), the Administrator shall provide each eligible metropolitan area with, and shall notify each eligible metropolitan area of, the opportunity to—

(i) submit information that the eligible metropolitan area believes to be relevant to the determination of the threat, vulnerability, and consequences it faces from acts of terrorism; and

(ii) review the risk assessment conducted by the Department of that eligible metropolitan area, including the bases for the assessment by the Department of the threat, vulnerability, and consequences from acts of terrorism faced by that eligible metropolitan area, and remedy erroneous or incomplete information.

(3) Designation of high-risk urban areas

(A) Designation

(i) In general

For each fiscal year, after conducting the initial assessment under paragraph (2), and based on that assessment, the Administrator shall designate high-risk urban areas that may submit applications for grants under this section.

(ii) Additional areas

Notwithstanding paragraph (2), the Administrator may—

(I) in any case where an eligible metropolitan area consists of more than 1 metropolitan division (as that term is defined by the Office of Management and Budget) designate more than 1 high-risk urban area within a single eligible metropolitan area; and

(II) designate an area that is not an eligible metropolitan area as a high-risk urban area based on the assessment by the Administrator of the relative threat, vulnerability, and consequences from acts of terrorism faced by the area.

(iii) Rule of construction

Nothing in this subsection may be construed to require the Administrator to—

(I) designate all eligible metropolitan areas that submit information to the Administrator under paragraph (2)(B)(i) as high-risk urban areas; or

(II) designate all areas within an eligible metropolitan area as part of the high-risk urban area.

(B) Jurisdictions included in high-risk urban areas

(i) In general

In designating high-risk urban areas under subparagraph (A), the Administrator shall determine which jurisdictions, at a minimum, shall be included in each high-risk urban area.

(ii) Additional jurisdictions

A high-risk urban area designated by the Administrator may, in consultation with the State or States in which such high-risk urban area is located, add additional jurisdictions to the high-risk urban area.

(c) Application

(1) In general

An area designated as a high-risk urban area under subsection (b) may apply for a grant under this section.

(2) Minimum contents of application

In an application for a grant under this section, a high-risk urban area shall submit—

(A) a plan describing the proposed division of responsibilities and distribution of funding among the local and tribal governments in the high-risk urban area;

(B) the name of an individual to serve as a high-risk urban area liaison with the Department and among the various jurisdictions in the high-risk urban area; and

(C) such information in support of the application as the Administrator may reasonably require.

(3) Annual applications

Applicants for grants under this section shall apply or reapply on an annual basis.

(4) State review and transmission

(A) In general

To ensure consistency with State homeland security plans, a high-risk urban area applying for a grant under this section shall submit its application to each State within which any part of that high-risk urban area is located for review before submission of such application to the Department.

(B) Deadline

Not later than 30 days after receiving an application from a high-risk urban area under subparagraph (A), a State shall transmit the application to the Department.

(C) Opportunity for State comment

If the Governor of a State determines that an application of a high-risk urban area is inconsistent with the State homeland security plan of that State, or otherwise does not support the application, the Governor shall—

(i) notify the Administrator, in writing, of that fact; and

(ii) provide an explanation of the reason for not supporting the application at the time of transmission of the application.

(5) Opportunity to amend

In considering applications for grants under this section, the Administrator shall provide applicants with a reasonable opportunity to correct defects in the application, if any, before making final awards.

(d) Distribution of awards

(1) In general

If the Administrator approves the application of a high-risk urban area for a grant under this section, the Administrator shall distribute the grant funds to the State or States in which that high-risk urban area is located.

(2) State distribution of funds

(A) In general

Not later than 45 days after the date that a State receives grant funds under paragraph (1), that State shall provide the high-risk urban area awarded that grant not less than 80 percent of the grant funds. Any funds retained by a State shall be expended on items, services, or activities that benefit the high-risk urban area.

(B) Funds retained

A State shall provide each relevant high-risk urban area with an accounting of the items, services, or activities on which any funds retained by the State under subparagraph (A) were expended.

(3) Interstate urban areas

If parts of a high-risk urban area awarded a grant under this section are located in 2 or more States, the Administrator shall distribute to each such State—

(A) a portion of the grant funds in accordance with the proposed distribution set forth in the application; or

(B) if no agreement on distribution has been reached, a portion of the grant funds determined by the Administrator to be appropriate.

(4) Certifications regarding distribution of grant funds to high-risk urban areas

A State that receives grant funds under paragraph (1) shall certify to the Administrator that the State has made available to the applicable high-risk urban area the required funds under paragraph (2).

(e) Authorization of appropriations

There are authorized to be appropriated for grants under this section—

(1) $850,000,000 for fiscal year 2008;

(2) $950,000,000 for fiscal year 2009;

(3) $1,050,000,000 for fiscal year 2010;

(4) $1,150,000,000 for fiscal year 2011;

(5) $1,300,000,000 for fiscal year 2012; and

(6) such sums as are necessary for fiscal year 2013, and each fiscal year thereafter.

(Pub. L. 107–296, title XX, §2003, as added Pub. L. 110–53, title I, §101, Aug. 3, 2007, 121 Stat. 274.)

§605. State Homeland Security Grant Program

(a) Establishment

There is established a State Homeland Security Grant Program to assist State, local, and tribal governments in preventing, preparing for, protecting against, and responding to acts of terrorism.

(b) Application

(1) In general

Each State may apply for a grant under this section, and shall submit such information in support of the application as the Administrator may reasonably require.

(2) Minimum contents of application

The Administrator shall require that each State include in its application, at a minimum—

(A) the purpose for which the State seeks grant funds and the reasons why the State needs the grant to meet the target capabilities of that State;

(B) a description of how the State plans to allocate the grant funds to local governments and Indian tribes; and

(C) a budget showing how the State intends to expend the grant funds.

(3) Annual applications

Applicants for grants under this section shall apply or reapply on an annual basis.

(c) Distribution to local and tribal governments

(1) In general

Not later than 45 days after receiving grant funds, any State receiving a grant under this section shall make available to local and tribal governments, consistent with the applicable State homeland security plan—

(A) not less than 80 percent of the grant funds;

(B) with the consent of local and tribal governments, items, services, or activities having a value of not less than 80 percent of the amount of the grant; or

(C) with the consent of local and tribal governments, grant funds combined with other items, services, or activities having a total value of not less than 80 percent of the amount of the grant.

(2) Certifications regarding distribution of grant funds to local governments

A State shall certify to the Administrator that the State has made the distribution to local and tribal governments required under paragraph (1).

(3) Extension of period

The Governor of a State may request in writing that the Administrator extend the period under paragraph (1) for an additional period of time. The Administrator may approve such a request if the Administrator determines that the resulting delay in providing grant funding to the local and tribal governments is necessary to promote effective investments to prevent, prepare for, protect against, or respond to acts of terrorism.

(4) Exception

Paragraph (1) shall not apply to the District of Columbia, the Commonwealth of Puerto Rico, American Samoa, the Commonwealth of the Northern Mariana Islands, Guam, or the Virgin Islands.

(5) Direct funding

If a State fails to make the distribution to local or tribal governments required under paragraph (1) in a timely fashion, a local or tribal government entitled to receive such distribution may petition the Administrator to request that grant funds be provided directly to the local or tribal government.

(d) Multistate applications

(1) In general

Instead of, or in addition to, any application for a grant under subsection (b), 2 or more States may submit an application for a grant under this section in support of multistate efforts to prevent, prepare for, protect against, and respond to acts of terrorism.

(2) Administration of grant

If a group of States applies for a grant under this section, such States shall submit to the Administrator at the time of application a plan describing—

(A) the division of responsibilities for administering the grant; and

(B) the distribution of funding among the States that are parties to the application.

(e) Minimum allocation

(1) In general

In allocating funds under this section, the Administrator shall ensure that—

(A) except as provided in subparagraph (B), each State receives, from the funds appropriated for the State Homeland Security Grant Program established under this section, not less than an amount equal to—

(i) 0.375 percent of the total funds appropriated for grants under this section and section 604 of this title in fiscal year 2008;

(ii) 0.365 percent of the total funds appropriated for grants under this section and section 604 of this title in fiscal year 2009;

(iii) 0.36 percent of the total funds appropriated for grants under this section and section 604 of this title in fiscal year 2010;

(iv) 0.355 percent of the total funds appropriated for grants under this section and section 604 of this title in fiscal year 2011; and

(v) 0.35 percent of the total funds appropriated for grants under this section and section 604 of this title in fiscal year 2012 and in each fiscal year thereafter; and

(B) for each fiscal year, American Samoa, the Commonwealth of the Northern Mariana Islands, Guam, and the Virgin Islands each receive, from the funds appropriated for the State Homeland Security Grant Program established under this section, not less than an amount equal to 0.08 percent of the total funds appropriated for grants under this section and section 604 of this title.

(2) Effect of multistate award on State minimum

Any portion of a multistate award provided to a State under subsection (d) shall be considered in calculating the minimum State allocation under this subsection.

(f) Authorization of appropriations

There are authorized to be appropriated for grants under this section—

(1) $950,000,000 for each of fiscal years 2008 through 2012; and

(2) such sums as are necessary for fiscal year 2013, and each fiscal year thereafter.

(Pub. L. 107–296, title XX, § 2004, as added Pub. L. 110–53, title I, § 101, Aug. 3, 2007, 121 Stat. 277.)

§ 606. Grants to directly eligible tribes

(a) In general

Notwithstanding section 605(b) of this title, the Administrator may award grants to directly eligible tribes under section 605 of this title.

(b) Tribal applications

A directly eligible tribe may apply for a grant under section 605 of this title by submitting an application to the Administrator that includes, as appropriate, the information required for an application by a State under section 605(b) of this title.

(c) Consistency with State plans

(1) In general

To ensure consistency with any applicable State homeland security plan, a directly eligible tribe applying for a grant under section 605 of this title shall provide a copy of its application to each State within which any part of the tribe is located for review before the tribe submits such application to the Department.

(2) Opportunity for comment

If the Governor of a State determines that the application of a directly eligible tribe is inconsistent with the State homeland security plan of that State, or otherwise does not support the application, not later than 30 days after the date of receipt of that application the Governor shall—

(A) notify the Administrator, in writing, of that fact; and

(B) provide an explanation of the reason for not supporting the application.

(d) Final authority

The Administrator shall have final authority to approve any application of a directly eligible tribe. The Administrator shall notify each State within the boundaries of which any part of a directly eligible tribe is located of the approval of an application by the tribe.

(e) Prioritization

The Administrator shall allocate funds to directly eligible tribes in accordance with the factors applicable to allocating funds among States under section 608 of this title.

(f) Distribution of awards to directly eligible tribes

If the Administrator awards funds to a directly eligible tribe under this section, the Administrator shall distribute the grant funds directly to the tribe and not through any State.

(g) Minimum allocation

(1) In general

In allocating funds under this section, the Administrator shall ensure that, for each fiscal year, directly eligible tribes collectively receive, from the funds appropriated for the State Homeland Security Grant Program established under section 605 of this title, not less than an amount equal to 0.1 percent of the total funds appropriated for grants under sections 604 and 605 of this title.

(2) Exception

This subsection shall not apply in any fiscal year in which the Administrator—

(A) receives fewer than 5 applications under this section; or

(B) does not approve at least 2 applications under this section.

(h) Tribal liaison

A directly eligible tribe applying for a grant under section 605 of this title shall designate an individual to serve as a tribal liaison with the Department and other Federal, State, local, and regional government officials concerning preventing, preparing for, protecting against, and responding to acts of terrorism.

(i) Eligibility for other funds

A directly eligible tribe that receives a grant under section 605 of this title may receive funds for other purposes under a grant from the State or States within the boundaries of which any part of such tribe is located and from any high-risk urban area of which it is a part, consistent with the homeland security plan of the State or high-risk urban area.

(j) State obligations

(1) In general

States shall be responsible for allocating grant funds received under section 605 of this title to tribal governments in order to help those tribal communities achieve target capabilities not achieved through grants to directly eligible tribes.

(2) Distribution of grant funds

With respect to a grant to a State under section 605 of this title, an Indian tribe shall be eligible for funding directly from that State, and shall not be required to seek funding from any local government.

(3) Imposition of requirements

A State may not impose unreasonable or unduly burdensome requirements on an Indian tribe as a condition of providing the Indian tribe with grant funds or resources under section 605 of this title.

(k) Rule of construction

Nothing in this section shall be construed to affect the authority of an Indian tribe that receives funds under this part.

(Pub. L. 107–296, title XX, § 2005, as added Pub. L. 110–53, title I, § 101, Aug. 3, 2007, 121 Stat. 279.)

§ 607. Terrorism prevention

(a) Law enforcement terrorism prevention program

(1) In general

The Administrator shall ensure that not less than 25 percent of the total combined funds appropriated for grants under sections 604 and 605 of this title is used for law enforcement terrorism prevention activities.

(2) Law enforcement terrorism prevention activities

Law enforcement terrorism prevention activities include—

(A) information sharing and analysis;

(B) target hardening;

(C) threat recognition;

(D) terrorist interdiction;

(E) overtime expenses consistent with a State homeland security plan, including for the provision of enhanced law enforcement operations in support of Federal agencies, including for increased border security and border crossing enforcement;

(F) establishing, enhancing, and staffing with appropriately qualified personnel State, local, and regional fusion centers that comply with the guidelines established under section 124h(i) of this title;

(G) paying salaries and benefits for personnel, including individuals employed by the grant recipient on the date of the relevant grant application, to serve as qualified intelligence analysts;

(H) any other activity permitted under the Fiscal Year 2007 Program Guidance of the Department for the Law Enforcement Terrorism Prevention Program; and

(I) any other terrorism prevention activity authorized by the Administrator.

(3) Participation of underrepresented communities in fusion centers

The Administrator shall ensure that grant funds described in paragraph (1) are used to support the participation, as appropriate, of law enforcement and other emergency response providers from rural and other underrepresented communities at risk from acts of terrorism in fusion centers.

(b) Office for State and Local Law Enforcement

(1) Establishment

There is established in the Policy Directorate of the Department an Office for State and Local Law Enforcement, which shall be headed by an Assistant Secretary for State and Local Law Enforcement.

(2) Qualifications

The Assistant Secretary for State and Local Law Enforcement shall have an appropriate background with experience in law enforcement, intelligence, and other counterterrorism functions.

(3) Assignment of personnel

The Secretary shall assign to the Office for State and Local Law Enforcement permanent staff and, as appropriate and consistent with sections 316(c)(2), 381, and 468(d) of this title, other appropriate personnel detailed from other components of the Department to carry out the responsibilities under this subsection.

(4) Responsibilities

The Assistant Secretary for State and Local Law Enforcement shall—

(A) lead the coordination of Department-wide policies relating to the role of State and local law enforcement in preventing, preparing for, protecting against, and responding to natural disasters, acts of terrorism, and other man-made disasters within the United States;

(B) serve as a liaison between State, local, and tribal law enforcement agencies and the Department;

(C) coordinate with the Office of Intelligence and Analysis to ensure the intelligence and information sharing requirements of State, local, and tribal law enforcement agencies are being addressed;

(D) work with the Administrator to ensure that law enforcement and terrorism-focused grants to State, local, and tribal government agencies, including grants under sections 604 and 605 of this title, the Commercial Equipment Direct Assistance Program, and other grants administered by the Department to support fusion centers and law enforcement-oriented programs, are appropriately focused on terrorism prevention activities;

(E) coordinate with the Science and Technology Directorate, the Federal Emergency Management Agency, the Department of Justice, the National Institute of Justice, law enforcement organizations, and other appropriate entities to support the development, promulgation, and updating, as necessary, of national voluntary consensus standards for training and personal protective equipment to be used in a tactical environment by law enforcement officers; and

(F) conduct, jointly with the Administrator, a study to determine the efficacy and feasibility of establishing specialized law enforcement deployment teams to assist State, local, and tribal governments in responding to natural disasters, acts of terrorism, or other man-made disasters and report on the results of that study to the appropriate committees of Congress.

(5) Rule of construction

Nothing in this subsection shall be construed to diminish, supercede, or replace the responsibilities, authorities, or role of the Administrator.

(Pub. L. 107–296, title XX, § 2006, as added Pub. L. 110–53, title I, § 101, Aug. 3, 2007, 121 Stat. 280.)

§ 608. Prioritization

(a) In general

In allocating funds among States and high-risk urban areas applying for grants under section 604 or 605 of this title, the Administrator shall consider, for each State or high-risk urban area—

(1) its relative threat, vulnerability, and consequences from acts of terrorism, including consideration of—

(A) its population, including appropriate consideration of military, tourist, and commuter populations;

(B) its population density;

(C) its history of threats, including whether it has been the target of a prior act of terrorism;

(D) its degree of threat, vulnerability, and consequences related to critical infrastructure (for all critical infrastructure sectors) or key resources identified by the Administrator or the State homeland security plan, including threats, vulnerabilities, and consequences related to critical infrastructure or key resources in nearby jurisdictions;

(E) the most current threat assessments available to the Department;

(F) whether the State has, or the high-risk urban area is located at or near, an international border;

(G) whether it has a coastline bordering an ocean (including the Gulf of Mexico) or international waters;

(H) its likely need to respond to acts of terrorism occurring in nearby jurisdictions;

(I) the extent to which it has unmet target capabilities;

(J) in the case of a high-risk urban area, the extent to which that high-risk urban area includes—

(i) those incorporated municipalities, counties, parishes, and Indian tribes within the relevant eligible metropolitan area, the inclusion of which will enhance regional efforts to prevent, prepare for, protect against, and respond to acts of terrorism; and

(ii) other local and tribal governments in the surrounding area that are likely to be called upon to respond to acts of terrorism within the high-risk urban area; and

(K) such other factors as are specified in writing by the Administrator; and

(2) the anticipated effectiveness of the proposed use of the grant by the State or high-risk urban area in increasing the ability of that State or high-risk urban area to prevent, prepare for, protect against, and respond to acts of terrorism, to meet its target capabilities, and to otherwise reduce the overall risk to the high-risk urban area, the State, or the Nation.

(b) Types of threat

In assessing threat under this section, the Administrator shall consider the following types of threat to critical infrastructure sectors and to populations in all areas of the United States, urban and rural:

(1) Biological.

(2) Chemical.

(3) Cyber.

(4) Explosives.

(5) Incendiary.

(6) Nuclear.

(7) Radiological.

(8) Suicide bombers.

(9) Such other types of threat determined relevant by the Administrator.

(Pub. L. 107–296, title XX, § 2007, as added Pub. L. 110–53, title I, § 101, Aug. 3, 2007, 121 Stat. 282.)

§ 609. Use of funds

(a) Permitted uses

The Administrator shall permit the recipient of a grant under section 604 or 605 of this title to use grant funds to achieve target capabilities related to preventing, preparing for, protecting against, and responding to acts of terrorism, consistent with a State homeland security plan and relevant local, tribal, and regional homeland security plans, through—

(1) developing and enhancing homeland security, emergency management, or other relevant plans, assessments, or mutual aid agreements;

(2) designing, conducting, and evaluating training and exercises, including training and exercises conducted under section 321a of this title and section 748 of this title;

(3) protecting a system or asset included on the prioritized critical infrastructure list established under section 124*l*(a)(2) of this title;

(4) purchasing, upgrading, storing, or maintaining equipment, including computer hardware and software;

(5) ensuring operability and achieving interoperability of emergency communications;

(6) responding to an increase in the threat level under the Homeland Security Advisory System, or to the needs resulting from a National Special Security Event;

(7) establishing, enhancing, and staffing with appropriately qualified personnel State, local, and regional fusion centers that comply with the guidelines established under section 124h(i) of this title;

(8) enhancing school preparedness;

(9) supporting public safety answering points;

(10) paying salaries and benefits for personnel, including individuals employed by the grant recipient on the date of the relevant grant application, to serve as qualified intelligence analysts, regardless of whether such analysts are current or new full-time employees or contract employees;

(11) paying expenses directly related to administration of the grant, except that such expenses may not exceed 3 percent of the amount of the grant;

(12) any activity permitted under the Fiscal Year 2007 Program Guidance of the Department for the State Homeland Security Grant Program, the Urban Area Security Initiative (including activities permitted under the full-time counterterrorism staffing pilot), or the Law Enforcement Terrorism Prevention Program; and

(13) any other appropriate activity, as determined by the Administrator.

(b) Limitations on use of funds

(1) In general

Funds provided under section 604 or 605 of this title may not be used—

(A) to supplant State or local funds, except that nothing in this paragraph shall prohibit the use of grant funds provided to a State or high-risk urban area for otherwise permissible uses under subsection (a) on the basis that a State or high-risk urban area has previously used State or local funds to support the same or similar uses; or

(B) for any State or local government cost-sharing contribution.

(2) Personnel

(A) In general

Not more than 50 percent of the amount awarded to a grant recipient under section 604 or 605 of this title in any fiscal year may be used to pay for personnel, including overtime and backfill costs, in support of the permitted uses under subsection (a).

(B) Waiver

At the request of the recipient of a grant under section 604 or 605 of this title, the Administrator may grant a waiver of the limitation under subparagraph (A).

(3) Limitations on discretion

(A) In general

With respect to the use of amounts awarded to a grant recipient under section 604 or 605 of this title for personnel costs in accordance with paragraph (2) of this subsection, the Administrator may not—

(i) impose a limit on the amount of the award that may be used to pay for personnel, or personnel-related, costs that is higher or lower than the percent limit imposed in paragraph (2)(A); or

(ii) impose any additional limitation on the portion of the funds of a recipient that may be used for a specific type, purpose, or category of personnel, or personnel-related, costs.

(B) Analysts

If amounts awarded to a grant recipient under section 604 or 605 of this title are used for paying salary or benefits of a qualified intelligence analyst under subsection (a)(10), the Administrator shall make such amounts available without time limitations placed on the period of time that the analyst can serve under the grant.

(4) Construction

(A) In general

A grant awarded under section 604 or 605 of this title may not be used to acquire land or to construct buildings or other physical facilities.

(B) Exceptions

(i) In general

Notwithstanding subparagraph (A), nothing in this paragraph shall prohibit the use of a grant awarded under section 604 or 605 of this title to achieve target capabilities related to preventing, preparing for, protecting against, or responding to acts of terrorism, including through the alteration or remodeling of existing buildings for the purpose of making such buildings secure against acts of terrorism.

(ii) Requirements for exception

No grant awarded under section 604 or 605 of this title may be used for a purpose described in clause (i) unless—

(I) specifically approved by the Administrator;

(II) any construction work occurs under terms and conditions consistent with the requirements under section 5196(j)(9) of title 42; and

(III) the amount allocated for purposes under clause (i) does not exceed the greater of $1,000,000 or 15 percent of the grant award.

(5) Recreation

Grants awarded under this part may not be used for recreational or social purposes.

(c) Multiple-purpose funds

Nothing in this part shall be construed to prohibit State, local, or tribal governments from using grant funds under sections 604 and 605 of this title in a manner that enhances preparedness for disasters unrelated to acts of terrorism, if such use assists such governments in achieving target capabilities related to preventing, preparing for, protecting against, or responding to acts of terrorism.

(d) Reimbursement of costs

(1) Paid-on-call or volunteer reimbursement

In addition to the activities described in subsection (a), a grant under section 604 or 605 of this title may be used to provide a reasonable stipend to paid-on-call or volunteer emergency response providers who are not otherwise compensated for travel to or participation in training or exercises related to the purposes of this part. Any such reimbursement shall not be considered compensation for purposes of rendering an emergency response provider an employee under the Fair Labor Standards Act of 1938 (29 U.S.C. 201 et seq.).

(2) Performance of Federal duty

An applicant for a grant under section 604 or 605 of this title may petition the Administrator to use the funds from its grants under those sections for the reimbursement of the cost of any activity relating to preventing, preparing for, protecting against, or responding to acts of terrorism that is a Federal duty and usually performed by a Federal agency, and that is being performed by a State or local government under agreement with a Federal agency.

(e) Flexibility in unspent homeland security grant funds

Upon request by the recipient of a grant under section 604 or 605 of this title, the Administrator may authorize the grant recipient to transfer all or part of the grant funds from uses specified in the grant agreement to other uses authorized under this section, if the Administrator determines that such transfer is in the interests of homeland security.

(f) Equipment standards

If an applicant for a grant under section 604 or 605 of this title proposes to upgrade or purchase, with assistance provided under that grant, new equipment or systems that do not meet or exceed any applicable national voluntary consensus standards developed under section 747 of this title, the applicant shall include in its application an explanation of why such equipment or systems will serve the needs of the applicant better than equipment or systems that meet or exceed such standards.

(Pub. L. 107–296, title XX, §2008, as added Pub. L. 110–53, title I, §101, Aug. 3, 2007, 121 Stat. 283; amended Pub. L. 110–412, §2, Oct. 14, 2008, 122 Stat. 4336.)

REFERENCES IN TEXT

The Fair Labor Standards Act of 1938, referred to in subsec. (d)(1), is act June 25, 1938, ch. 676, 52 Stat. 1060, which is classified generally to chapter 8 (§201 et seq.) of Title 29, Labor. For complete classification of this Act to the Code, see section 201 of Title 29 and Tables.

AMENDMENTS

2008—Subsec. (a). Pub. L. 110–412, §2(1)(A), substituted "The Administrator shall permit the recipient of a grant under section 604 or 605 of this title to use grant funds" for "Grants awarded under section 604 or 605 of this title may be used" in introductory provisions.

Subsec. (a)(10). Pub. L. 110–412, § 2(1)(B), inserted ", regardless of whether such analysts are current or new full-time employees or contract employees" after "analysts".

Subsec. (b)(3) to (5). Pub. L. 110–412, § 2(2), added par. (3) and redesignated former pars. (3) and (4) as (4) and (5), respectively.

PART B—GRANTS ADMINISTRATION

§ 611. Administration and coordination

(a) Regional coordination

The Administrator shall ensure that—

(1) all recipients of grants administered by the Department to prevent, prepare for, protect against, or respond to natural disasters, acts of terrorism, or other man-made disasters (excluding assistance provided under section 203, title IV, or title V of the Robert T. Stafford Disaster Relief and Emergency Assistance Act (42 U.S.C. 5133, 5170 et seq., and 5191 et seq.)) coordinate, as appropriate, their prevention, preparedness, and protection efforts with neighboring State, local, and tribal governments; and

(2) all high-risk urban areas and other recipients of grants administered by the Department to prevent, prepare for, protect against, or respond to natural disasters, acts of terrorism, or other man-made disasters (excluding assistance provided under section 203, title IV, or title V of the Robert T. Stafford Disaster Relief and Emergency Assistance Act (42 U.S.C. 5133, 5170 et seq., and 5191 et seq.)) that include or substantially affect parts or all of more than 1 State coordinate, as appropriate, across State boundaries, including, where appropriate, through the use of regional working groups and requirements for regional plans.

(b) Planning committees

(1) In general

Any State or high-risk urban area receiving a grant under section 604 or 605 of this title shall establish a planning committee to assist in preparation and revision of the State, regional, or local homeland security plan and to assist in determining effective funding priorities for grants under sections 604 and 605 of this title.

(2) Composition

(A) In general

The planning committee shall include representatives of significant stakeholders, including—

(i) local and tribal government officials; and

(ii) emergency response providers, which shall include representatives of the fire service, law enforcement, emergency medical response, and emergency managers.

(B) Geographic representation

The members of the planning committee shall be a representative group of individuals from the counties, cities, towns, and Indian tribes within the State or high-risk urban area, including, as appropriate, representatives of rural, high-population, and high-threat jurisdictions.

(3) Existing planning committees

Nothing in this subsection may be construed to require that any State or high-risk urban area create a planning committee if that State or high-risk urban area has established and uses a multijurisdictional planning committee or commission that meets the requirements of this subsection.

(c) Interagency coordination

(1) In general

Not later than 12 months after August 3, 2007, the Secretary (acting through the Administrator), the Attorney General, the Secretary of Health and Human Services, and the heads of other agencies providing assistance to State, local, and tribal governments for preventing, preparing for, protecting against, and responding to natural disasters, acts of terrorism, and other man-made disasters, shall jointly—

(A) compile a comprehensive list of Federal grant programs for State, local, and tribal governments for preventing, preparing for, protecting against, and responding to natural disasters, acts of terrorism, and other man-made disasters;

(B) compile the planning, reporting, application, and other requirements and guidance for the grant programs described in subparagraph (A);

(C) develop recommendations, as appropriate, to—

(i) eliminate redundant and duplicative requirements for State, local, and tribal governments, including onerous application and ongoing reporting requirements;

(ii) ensure accountability of the programs to the intended purposes of such programs;

(iii) coordinate allocation of grant funds to avoid duplicative or inconsistent purchases by the recipients;

(iv) make the programs more accessible and user friendly to applicants; and

(v) ensure the programs are coordinated to enhance the overall preparedness of the Nation;

(D) submit the information and recommendations under subparagraphs (A), (B), and (C) to the appropriate committees of Congress; and

(E) provide the appropriate committees of Congress, the Comptroller General, and any officer or employee of the Government Accountability Office with full access to any information collected or reviewed in preparing the submission under subparagraph (D).

(2) Scope of task

Nothing in this subsection shall authorize the elimination, or the alteration of the purposes, as delineated by statute, regulation, or guidance, of any grant program that exists on August 3, 2007, nor authorize the review or preparation of proposals on the elimination, or the alteration of such purposes, of any such grant program.

(d) Sense of Congress

It is the sense of Congress that, in order to ensure that the Nation is most effectively able to prevent, prepare for, protect against, and respond to all hazards, including natural disasters, acts of terrorism, and other man-made disasters—

(1) the Department should administer a coherent and coordinated system of both terrorism-focused and all-hazards grants;

(2) there should be a continuing and appropriate balance between funding for terrorism-focused and all-hazards preparedness, as reflected in the authorizations of appropriations for grants under the amendments made by titles I and II, as applicable, of the Implementing Recommendations of the 9/11 Commission Act of 2007; and

(3) with respect to terrorism-focused grants, it is necessary to ensure both that the target capabilities of the highest risk areas are achieved quickly and that basic levels of preparedness, as measured by the attainment of target capabilities, are achieved nationwide.

(Pub. L. 107–296, title XX, § 2021, as added Pub. L. 110–53, title I, § 101, Aug. 3, 2007, 121 Stat. 285.)

REFERENCES IN TEXT

The Robert T. Stafford Disaster Relief and Emergency Assistance Act, referred to in subsec. (a), is Pub. L. 93–288, May 22, 1974, 88 Stat. 143. Section 203 of the Act is classified to section 5133 of Title 42, The Public Health and Welfare. Titles IV and V of the Act are classified generally to subchapters IV (§ 5170 et seq.) and IV–A (§ 5191 et seq.), respectively, of chapter 68 of Title 42. For complete classification of this Act to the Code, see Short Title note set out under section 5121 of Title 42 and Tables.

The Implementing Recommendations of the 9/11 Commission Act of 2007, referred to in subsec. (d)(2), is Pub. L. 110–53, Aug. 3, 2007, 121 Stat. 266. Title I of the Act enacted this subchapter and amended sections 318, 321a, 594, 596, and 752 of this title. Title II of the Act amended section 762 of this title and section 5196c of Title 42, The Public Health and Welfare. For complete classification of titles I and II to the Code, see Tables.

§ 612. Accountability

(a) Audits of grant programs

(1) Compliance requirements

(A) Audit requirement

Each recipient of a grant administered by the Department that expends not less than $500,000 in Federal funds during its fiscal year shall submit to the Administrator a copy of the organization-wide financial and compliance audit report required under chapter 75 of title 31.

(B) Access to information

The Department and each recipient of a grant administered by the Department shall provide the Comptroller General and any officer or employee of the Government Accountability Office with full access to information regarding the activities carried out related to any grant administered by the Department.

(C) Improper payments

Consistent with the Improper Payments Information Act of 2002 (31 U.S.C. 3321 note), for each of the grant programs under sections 604 and 605 of this title and section 762 of this title, the Administrator shall specify policies and procedures for—

(i) identifying activities funded under any such grant program that are susceptible to significant improper payments; and

(ii) reporting any improper payments to the Department.

(2) Agency program review

(A) In general

Not less than once every 2 years, the Administrator shall conduct, for each State and high-risk urban area receiving a grant administered by the Department, a programmatic and financial review of all grants awarded by the Department to prevent, prepare for, protect against, or respond to natural disasters, acts of terrorism, or other man-made disasters, excluding assistance provided under section 203, title IV, or title V of the Robert T. Stafford Disaster Relief and Emergency Assistance Act (42 U.S.C. 5133, 5170 et seq., and 5191 et seq.).

(B) Contents

Each review under subparagraph (A) shall, at a minimum, examine—

(i) whether the funds awarded were used in accordance with the law, program guidance, and State homeland security plans or other applicable plans; and

(ii) the extent to which funds awarded enhanced the ability of a grantee to prevent, prepare for, protect against, and respond to natural disasters, acts of terrorism, and other man-made disasters.

(C) Authorization of appropriations

In addition to any other amounts authorized to be appropriated to the Administrator, there are authorized to be appropriated to the Administrator for reviews under this paragraph—

(i) $8,000,000 for each of fiscal years 2008, 2009, and 2010; and

(ii) such sums as are necessary for fiscal year 2011, and each fiscal year thereafter.

(3) Office of Inspector General performance audits

(A) In general

In order to ensure the effective and appropriate use of grants administered by the Department, the Inspector General of the Department each year shall conduct audits of a sample of States and high-risk urban areas that receive grants administered by the Department to prevent, prepare for, protect against, or respond to natural disasters, acts of terrorism, or other man-made disasters, excluding assistance provided under section 203, title IV, or title V of the Robert T. Stafford Disaster Relief and Emergency Assistance Act (42 U.S.C. 5133, 5170 et seq., and 5191 et seq.).

(B) Determining samples

The sample selected for audits under subparagraph (A) shall be—

(i) of an appropriate size to—

(I) assess the overall integrity of the grant programs described in subparagraph (A); and

(II) act as a deterrent to financial mismanagement; and

(ii) selected based on—

(I) the size of the grants awarded to the recipient;

(II) the past grant management performance of the recipient;

(III) concerns identified by the Administrator, including referrals from the Administrator; and

(IV) such other factors as determined by the Inspector General of the Department.

(C) Comprehensive auditing

During the 7-year period beginning on August 3, 2007, the Inspector General of the Department shall conduct not fewer than 1 audit of each State that receives funds under a grant under section 604 or 605 of this title.

(D) Report by the Inspector General

(i) In general

The Inspector General of the Department shall submit to the appropriate committees of Congress an annual consolidated report regarding the audits completed during the fiscal year before the date of that report.

(ii) Contents

Each report submitted under clause (i) shall describe, for the fiscal year before the date of that report—

(I) the audits conducted under subparagraph (A);

(II) the findings of the Inspector General with respect to the audits conducted under subparagraph (A);

(III) whether the funds awarded were used in accordance with the law, program guidance, and State homeland security plans and other applicable plans; and

(IV) the extent to which funds awarded enhanced the ability of a grantee to prevent, prepare for, protect against, and respond to natural disasters, acts of terrorism and other man-made disasters.

(iii) Deadline

For each year, the report required under clause (i) shall be submitted not later than December 31.

(E) Public availability on website

The Inspector General of the Department shall make each audit conducted under subparagraph (A) available on the website of the Inspector General, subject to redaction as the Inspector General determines necessary to protect classified and other sensitive information.

(F) Provision of information to Administrator

The Inspector General of the Department shall provide to the Administrator any findings and recommendations from audits conducted under subparagraph (A).

(G) Evaluation of grants management and oversight

Not later than 1 year after August 3, 2007, the Inspector General of the Department shall review and evaluate the grants management and oversight practices of the Federal Emergency Management Agency, including assessment of and recommendations relating to—

(i) the skills, resources, and capabilities of the workforce; and

(ii) any additional resources and staff necessary to carry out such management and oversight.

(H) Authorization of appropriations

In addition to any other amounts authorized to be appropriated to the Inspector General of the Department, there are authorized to be appropriated to the Inspector General of the Department for audits under subparagraph (A)—

(i) $8,500,000 for each of fiscal years 2008, 2009, and 2010; and

(ii) such sums as are necessary for fiscal year 2011, and each fiscal year thereafter.

(4) Performance assessment

In order to ensure that States and high-risk urban areas are using grants administered by the Department appropriately to meet target capabilities and preparedness priorities, the Administrator shall—

(A) ensure that any such State or high-risk urban area conducts or participates in exercises under section 748(b) of this title;

(B) use performance metrics in accordance with the comprehensive assessment system under section 749 of this title and ensure that any such State or high-risk urban area regularly tests its progress against such metrics through the exercises required under subparagraph (A);

(C) use the remedial action management program under section 750 of this title; and

(D) ensure that each State receiving a grant administered by the Department submits a report to the Administrator on its level of preparedness, as required by section 752(c) of this title.

(5) Consideration of assessments

In conducting program reviews and performance audits under paragraphs (2) and (3), the Administrator and the Inspector General of the Department shall take into account the performance assessment elements required under paragraph (4).

(6) Recovery audits

The Administrator shall conduct a recovery audit (as that term is defined by the Director of the Office of Management and Budget under section 3561 of title 31) for any grant administered by the Department with a total value of not less than $1,000,000, if the Administrator finds that—

(A) a financial audit has identified improper payments that can be recouped; and

(B) it is cost effective to conduct a recovery audit to recapture the targeted funds.

(7) Remedies for noncompliance

(A) In general

If, as a result of a review or audit under this subsection or otherwise, the Administrator finds that a recipient of a grant under this subchapter has failed to substantially comply with any provision of law or with any regulations or guidelines of the Department regarding eligible expenditures, the Administrator shall—

(i) reduce the amount of payment of grant funds to the recipient by an amount equal to the amount of grants funds that were not properly expended by the recipient;

(ii) limit the use of grant funds to programs, projects, or activities not affected by the failure to comply;

(iii) refer the matter to the Inspector General of the Department for further investigation;

(iv) terminate any payment of grant funds to be made to the recipient; or

(v) take such other action as the Administrator determines appropriate.

(B) Duration of penalty

The Administrator shall apply an appropriate penalty under subparagraph (A) until such time as the Administrator determines that the grant recipient is in full compliance with the law and with applicable guidelines or regulations of the Department.

(b) Reports by grant recipients

(1) Quarterly reports on homeland security spending

(A) In general

As a condition of receiving a grant under section 604 or 605 of this title, a State, high-risk urban area, or directly eligible tribe shall, not later than 30 days after the end of each Federal fiscal quarter, submit to the Administrator a report on activities performed using grant funds during that fiscal quarter.

(B) Contents

Each report submitted under subparagraph (A) shall at a minimum include, for the applicable State, high-risk urban area, or directly eligible tribe, and each subgrantee thereof—

(i) the amount obligated to that recipient under section 604 or 605 of this title in that quarter;

(ii) the amount of funds received and expended under section 604 or 605 of this title by that recipient in that quarter; and

(iii) a summary description of expenditures made by that recipient using such funds, and the purposes for which such expenditures were made.

(C) End-of-year report

The report submitted under subparagraph (A) by a State, high-risk urban area, or directly eligible tribe relating to the last quarter of any fiscal year shall include—

(i) the amount and date of receipt of all funds received under the grant during that fiscal year;

(ii) the identity of, and amount provided to, any subgrantee for that grant during that fiscal year;

(iii) the amount and the dates of disbursements of all such funds expended in compliance with section 611(a)(1) of this title or under mutual aid agreements or other sharing arrangements that apply within the State, high-risk urban area, or directly eligible tribe, as applicable, during that fiscal year; and

(iv) how the funds were used by each recipient or subgrantee during that fiscal year.

(2) Annual report

Any State applying for a grant under section 605 of this title shall submit to the Administrator annually a State preparedness report, as required by section 752(c) of this title.

(c) Reports by the Administrator

(1) Federal Preparedness Report

The Administrator shall submit to the appropriate committees of Congress annually the Federal Preparedness Report required under section 752(a) of this title.

(2) Risk assessment

(A) In general

For each fiscal year, the Administrator shall provide to the appropriate committees of Congress a detailed and comprehensive explanation of the methodologies used to calculate risk and compute the allocation of funds for grants administered by the Department, including—

(i) all variables included in the risk assessment and the weights assigned to each such variable;

(ii) an explanation of how each such variable, as weighted, correlates to risk, and the basis for concluding there is such a correlation; and

(iii) any change in the methodologies from the previous fiscal year, including changes in variables considered, weighting of those variables, and computational methods.

(B) Classified annex

The information required under subparagraph (A) shall be provided in unclassified form to the greatest extent possible, and may include a classified annex if necessary.

(C) Deadline

For each fiscal year, the information required under subparagraph (A) shall be provided on the earlier of—

(i) October 31; or

(ii) 30 days before the issuance of any program guidance for grants administered by the Department.

(3) Tribal funding report

At the end of each fiscal year, the Administrator shall submit to the appropriate committees of Congress a report setting forth the amount of funding provided during that fiscal year to Indian tribes under any grant program administered by the Department, whether provided directly or through a subgrant from a State or high-risk urban area.

(Pub. L. 107–296, title XX, § 2022, as added Pub. L. 110–53, title I, § 101, Aug. 3, 2007, 121 Stat. 287.)

REFERENCES IN TEXT

The Improper Payments Information Act of 2002, referred to in subsec. (a)(1)(C), is Pub. L. 107–300, Nov. 26, 2002, 116 Stat. 2350, which is set out as a note under section 3321 of Title 31, Money and Finance.

The Robert T. Stafford Disaster Relief and Emergency Assistance Act, referred to in subsec. (a)(2)(A), (3)(A), is Pub. L. 93–288, May 22, 1974, 88 Stat. 143. Section 203 of the Act is classified to section 5133 of Title 42, The Public Health and Welfare. Titles IV and V of the Act are classified generally to subchapters IV (§ 5170 et seq.) and IV–A (§ 5191 et seq.), respectively, of chapter 68 of Title 42. For complete classification of this Act to the Code, see Short Title note set out under section 5121 of Title 42 and Tables.

CHAPTER 2—NATIONAL EMERGENCY MANAGEMENT

§ 701. Definitions

In this title—[1]

(1) the term "Administrator" means the Administrator of the Agency;

(2) the term "Agency" means the Federal Emergency Management Agency;

(3) the term "appropriate committees of Congress" means—

(A) the Committee on Homeland Security and Governmental Affairs of the Senate; and

(B) those committees of the House of Representatives that the Speaker of the House of Representatives determines appropriate;

(4) the term "catastrophic incident" means any natural disaster, act of terrorism, or other man-made disaster that results in extraordinary levels of casualties or damage or disruption severely affecting the population (including mass evacuations), infrastructure, environment, economy, national morale, or government functions in an area;

(5) the term "Department" means the Department of Homeland Security;

(6) the terms "emergency" and "major disaster" have the meanings given the terms in section 5122 of title 42;

(7) the term "emergency management" means the governmental function that coordinates and integrates all activities necessary to build, sustain, and improve the capability to prepare for, protect against, respond to, recover from, or mitigate against threatened or actual natural disasters, acts of terrorism, or other man-made disasters;

(8) the term "emergency response provider" has the meaning given the term in section 101 of this title;

(9) the term "Federal coordinating officer" means a Federal coordinating officer as described in section 5143 of title 42;

(10) the term "individual with a disability" has the meaning given the term in section 12102 of title 42;

(11) the terms "local government" and "State" have the meaning given the terms in section 101 of this title;

(12) the term "National Incident Management System" means a system to enable effec-

[1] See References in Text note below.

tive, efficient, and collaborative incident management;

(13) the term "National Response Plan" means the National Response Plan or any successor plan prepared under section 314(a)(6) of this title;

(14) the term "Secretary" means the Secretary of Homeland Security;

(15) the term "surge capacity" means the ability to rapidly and substantially increase the provision of search and rescue capabilities, food, water, medicine, shelter and housing, medical care, evacuation capacity, staffing (including disaster assistance employees), and other resources necessary to save lives and protect property during a catastrophic incident; and

(16) the term "tribal government" means the government of an Indian tribe or authorized tribal organization, or in Alaska a Native village or Alaska Regional Native Corporation.

(Pub. L. 109–295, title VI, § 602, Oct. 4, 2006, 120 Stat. 1394.)

REFERENCES IN TEXT

This title, referred to in text, is title VI of Pub. L. 109–295, Oct. 4, 2006, 120 Stat. 1355, known as the Post-Katrina Emergency Management Reform Act of 2006. For complete classification of title VI to the Code, see Short Title note set out below and Tables.

Section 314(a)(6) of this title, referred to in par. (13), was in the original "section 502(a)(6) of the Homeland Security Act 2002" and was translated as meaning section 502 of Pub. L. 107-296 prior to its redesignation as section 504 by Pub. L. 109–295, § 611(8), and not section 506 of Pub. L. 107–296 which was redesignated section 502 by Pub. L. 109–295, § 611(9), and is classified to section 312 of this title, to reflect the probable intent of Congress.

CHANGE OF NAME

Any reference to the Administrator of the Federal Emergency Management Agency in title VI of Pub. L. 109–295 or an amendment by title VI to be considered to refer and apply to the Director of the Federal Emergency Management Agency until Mar. 31, 2007, see section 612(f)(2) of Pub. L. 109–295, set out as a note under section 313 of this title.

EFFECTIVE DATE

Pub. L. 109–295, title VI, § 614, Oct. 4, 2006, 120 Stat. 1411, provided that:

"(a) IN GENERAL.—Except as provided in subsection (b), this title [see Tables for classification] and the amendments made by this title shall take effect on the date of enactment of this Act [Oct. 4, 2006].

"(b) EXCEPTIONS.—The following shall take effect on March 31, 2007:

"(1) The amendments made by section 611(11) [enacting section 313 of this title].

"(2) The amendments made by section 611(12) [amending section 314 of this title].

"(3) Sections 505, 507, 508, and 514 of the Homeland Security Act of 2002 [sections 315, 317, 318, and 321c of this title], as amended by section 611(13) of this Act.

"(4) The amendments made by subsection (a) [sic].

"(5) The amendments made by subsection (b)(1) [sic]."

SHORT TITLE

Pub. L. 109–295, title VI, § 601, Oct. 4, 2006, 120 Stat. 1394, provided that: "This title [see Tables for classification] may be cited as the 'Post-Katrina Emergency Management Reform Act of 2006'."

CLARIFICATION OF CONGRESSIONAL INTENT

Pub. L. 110–53, title XXII, § 2202, Aug. 3, 2007, 121 Stat. 541, provided that: "The Federal departments and agencies (including independent agencies) identified under the provisions of this title [enacting provisions set out as notes under section 194 of this title and section 247d–3a of Title 42, The Public Health and Welfare, and amending provisions set out as a note under section 309 of Title 47, Telegraphs, Telephones, and Radiotelegraphs] and title III of this Act [enacting sections 579 and 580 of this title and amending sections 194 and 572 of this title] and title VI of Public Law 109–295 [see Short Title note set out above] shall carry out their respective duties and responsibilities in a manner that does not impede the implementation of requirements specified under this title and title III of this Act and title VI of Public Law 109–295. Notwithstanding the obligations under section 1806 of Public Law 109–295 [probably means Pub. L. 107–296; 6 U.S.C. 576], the provisions of this title and title III of this Act and title VI of Public Law 109–295 shall not preclude or obstruct any such department or agency from exercising its other authorities related to emergency communications matters."

NATIONAL WEATHER SERVICE

Pub. L. 109–295, title VI, § 613, Oct. 4, 2006, 120 Stat. 1411, provided that: "Nothing in this title [see Tables for classification] shall alter or otherwise affect the authorities and activities of the National Weather Service to protect life and property, including under the Act of October 1, 1890 (26 Stat. 653-55) [15 U.S.C. 312 et seq.]."

REFERENCES IN PUB. L. 109–295

Pub. L. 109–295, title VI, § 699A, Oct. 4, 2006, 120 Stat. 1463, provided that: "Except as expressly provided otherwise, any reference to 'this Act' contained in this title [see Tables for classification] shall be treated as referring only to the provisions of this title."

SUBCHAPTER I—PERSONNEL PROVISIONS

PART A—FEDERAL EMERGENCY MANAGEMENT AGENCY PERSONNEL

§ 711. Surge Capacity Force

(a) Establishment

(1) In general

Not later than 6 months after October 4, 2006, the Administrator shall prepare and submit to the appropriate committees of Congress a plan to establish and implement a Surge Capacity Force for deployment of individuals to respond to natural disasters, acts of terrorism, and other man-made disasters, including catastrophic incidents.

(2) Authority

(A) In general

Except as provided in subparagraph (B), the plan shall provide for individuals in the Surge Capacity Force to be trained and deployed under the authorities set forth in the Robert T. Stafford Disaster Relief and Emergency Assistance Act [42 U.S.C. 5121 et seq.].

(B) Exception

If the Administrator determines that the existing authorities are inadequate for the training and deployment of individuals in the Surge Capacity Force, the Administrator shall report to Congress as to the additional statutory authorities that the Administrator determines necessary.

(b) Employees designated to serve

The plan shall include procedures under which the Secretary shall designate employees of the

Department who are not employees of the Agency and shall, in conjunction with the heads of other Executive agencies, designate employees of those other Executive agencies, as appropriate, to serve on the Surge Capacity Force.

(c) Capabilities

The plan shall ensure that the Surge Capacity Force—

(1) includes a sufficient number of individuals credentialed in accordance with section 320 of this title that are capable of deploying rapidly and efficiently after activation to prepare for, respond to, and recover from natural disasters, acts of terrorism, and other man-made disasters, including catastrophic incidents; and

(2) includes a sufficient number of full-time, highly trained individuals credentialed in accordance with section 320 of this title to lead and manage the Surge Capacity Force.

(d) Training

The plan shall ensure that the Administrator provides appropriate and continuous training to members of the Surge Capacity Force to ensure such personnel are adequately trained on the Agency's programs and policies for natural disasters, acts of terrorism, and other man-made disasters.

(e) No impact on agency personnel ceiling

Surge Capacity Force members shall not be counted against any personnel ceiling applicable to the Federal Emergency Management Agency.

(f) Expenses

The Administrator may provide members of the Surge Capacity Force with travel expenses, including per diem in lieu of subsistence, at rates authorized for employees of agencies under subchapter I of chapter 57 of title 5 for the purpose of participating in any training that relates to service as a member of the Surge Capacity Force.

(g) Immediate implementation of Surge Capacity Force involving Federal employees

As soon as practicable after October 4, 2006, the Administrator shall develop and implement—

(1) the procedures under subsection (b); and

(2) other elements of the plan needed to establish the portion of the Surge Capacity Force consisting of individuals designated under those procedures.

(Pub. L. 109–295, title VI, §624, Oct. 4, 2006, 120 Stat. 1419.)

References in Text

The Robert T. Stafford Disaster Relief and Emergency Assistance Act, referred to in subsec. (a)(2)(A), is Pub. L. 93–288, May 22, 1974, 88 Stat. 143, as amended, which is classified principally to chapter 68 (§5121 et seq.) of Title 42, The Public Health and Welfare. For complete classification of this Act to the Code, see Short Title note set out under section 5121 of Title 42 and Tables.

Part B—Emergency Management Capabilities

§ 721. Evacuation preparedness technical assistance

The Administrator, in coordination with the heads of other appropriate Federal agencies, shall provide evacuation preparedness technical assistance to State, local, and tribal governments, including the preparation of hurricane evacuation studies and technical assistance in developing evacuation plans, assessing storm surge estimates, evacuation zones, evacuation clearance times, transportation capacity, and shelter capacity.

(Pub. L. 109–295, title VI, §632, Oct. 4, 2006, 120 Stat. 1421.)

§ 722. Urban Search and Rescue Response System

(a) In general

There is in the Agency a system known as the Urban Search and Rescue Response System.

(b) Authorization of appropriations

There is authorized to be appropriated to carry out the system for fiscal year 2008, an amount equal to the amount appropriated for the system for fiscal year 2007 and an additional $20,000,000.

(Pub. L. 109–295, title VI, §634, Oct. 4, 2006, 120 Stat. 1421.)

§ 723. Metropolitan Medical Response Grant Program

(a) In general

There is a Metropolitan Medical Response Program.

(b) Purposes

The program shall include each purpose of the program as it existed on June 1, 2006.

(c) Authorization of appropriations

There is authorized to be appropriated to carry out the program for fiscal year 2008, an amount equal to the amount appropriated for the program for fiscal year 2007 and an additional $30,000,000.

(Pub. L. 109–295, title VI, §635, Oct. 4, 2006, 120 Stat. 1421.)

§ 724. Logistics

The Administrator shall develop an efficient, transparent, and flexible logistics system for procurement and delivery of goods and services necessary for an effective and timely response to natural disasters, acts of terrorism, and other man-made disasters and for real-time visibility of items at each point throughout the logistics system.

(Pub. L. 109–295, title VI, §636, Oct. 4, 2006, 120 Stat. 1422.)

§ 725. Prepositioned equipment program

(a) In general

The Administrator shall establish a prepositioned equipment program to preposition standardized emergency equipment in at least 11 locations to sustain and replenish critical assets used by State, local, and tribal governments in response to (or rendered inoperable by the effects of) natural disasters, acts of terrorism, and other man-made disasters.

(b) Notice

The Administrator shall notify State, local, and tribal officials in an area in which a location for the prepositioned equipment program will be closed not later than 60 days before the date of such closure.

(Pub. L. 109–295, title VI, § 637, Oct. 4, 2006, 120 Stat. 1422.)

§ 726. Basic life supporting first aid and education

The Administrator shall enter into agreements with organizations to provide funds to emergency response providers to provide education and training in life supporting first aid to children.

(Pub. L. 109–295, title VI, § 639, Oct. 4, 2006, 120 Stat. 1423.)

§ 727. Improvements to information technology systems

(a) Measures to improve information technology systems

The Administrator, in coordination with the Chief Information Officer of the Department, shall take appropriate measures to update and improve the information technology systems of the Agency, including measures to—

(1) ensure that the multiple information technology systems of the Agency (including the National Emergency Management Information System, the Logistics Information Management System III, and the Automated Deployment Database) are, to the extent practicable, fully compatible and can share and access information, as appropriate, from each other;

(2) ensure technology enhancements reach the headquarters and regional offices of the Agency in a timely fashion, to allow seamless integration;

(3) develop and maintain a testing environment that ensures that all system components are properly and thoroughly tested before their release;

(4) ensure that the information technology systems of the Agency have the capacity to track disaster response personnel, mission assignments task orders, commodities, and supplies used in response to a natural disaster, act of terrorism, or other man-made disaster;

(5) make appropriate improvements to the National Emergency Management Information System to address shortcomings in such system on October 4, 2006; and

(6) provide training, manuals, and guidance on information technology systems to personnel, including disaster response personnel, to help ensure employees can properly use information technology systems.

(b) Report

Not later than 270 days after October 4, 2006, the Administrator shall submit to the appropriate committees of Congress a report describing the implementation of this section, including a description of any actions taken, improvements made, and remaining problems and a description of any additional funding needed to make necessary and appropriate improvements to the information technology systems of the Agency.

(Pub. L. 109–295, title VI, § 640, Oct. 4, 2006, 120 Stat. 1423.)

§ 728. Disclosure of certain information to law enforcement agencies

In the event of circumstances requiring an evacuation, sheltering, or mass relocation, the Administrator may disclose information in any individual assistance database of the Agency in accordance with section 552a(b) of title 5 (commonly referred to as the "Privacy Act") to any law enforcement agency of the Federal Government or a State, local, or tribal government in order to identify illegal conduct or address public safety or security issues, including compliance with sex offender notification laws.

(Pub. L. 109–295, title VI, § 640a, Oct. 4, 2006, 120 Stat. 1424.)

SUBCHAPTER II—COMPREHENSIVE PREPAREDNESS SYSTEM

PART A—NATIONAL PREPAREDNESS SYSTEM

§ 741. Definitions

In this part:

(1) Capability

The term "capability" means the ability to provide the means to accomplish one or more tasks under specific conditions and to specific performance standards. A capability may be achieved with any combination of properly planned, organized, equipped, trained, and exercised personnel that achieves the intended outcome.

(2) Credentialed; credentialing

The terms "credentialed" and "credentialing" have the meanings given those terms in section 311 of this title.

(3) Hazard

The term "hazard" has the meaning given that term under section 5195a(a)(1) of title 42.

(4) Mission assignment

The term "mission assignment" means a work order issued to a Federal agency by the Agency, directing completion by that agency of a specified task and setting forth funding, other managerial controls, and guidance.

(5) National preparedness goal

The term "national preparedness goal" means the national preparedness goal established under section 743 of this title.

(6) National preparedness system

The term "national preparedness system" means the national preparedness system established under section 744 of this title.

(7) National training program

The term "national training program" means the national training program established under section 748(a) of this title.

(8) Operational readiness

The term "operational readiness" means the capability of an organization, an asset, a system, or equipment to perform the missions or functions for which it is organized or designed.

(9) Performance measure

The term "performance measure" means a quantitative or qualitative characteristic used to gauge the results of an outcome compared to its intended purpose.

(10) Performance metric

The term "performance metric" means a particular value or characteristic used to measure the outcome that is generally expressed in terms of a baseline and a target.

(11) Prevention

The term "prevention" means any activity undertaken to avoid, prevent, or stop a threatened or actual act of terrorism.

(12) Resources

The term "resources" has the meaning given that term in section 311 of this title.

(13) Type

The term "type" means a classification of resources that refers to the capability of a resource.

(14) Typed; typing

The terms "typed" and "typing" have the meanings given those terms in section 311 of this title.

(Pub. L. 109–295, title VI, § 641, Oct. 4, 2006, 120 Stat. 1424; Pub. L. 110–53, title IV, § 401(b), Aug. 3, 2007, 121 Stat. 302.)

AMENDMENTS

2007—Pars. (2) to (14). Pub. L. 110–53 added pars. (2) and (12) to (14) and redesignated former pars. (2) to (10) as (3) to (11), respectively.

§ 742. National preparedness

In order to prepare the Nation for all hazards, including natural disasters, acts of terrorism, and other man-made disasters, the President, consistent with the declaration of policy under section 5195 of title 42 and title V of the Homeland Security Act of 2002 (6 U.S.C. 311 et seq.), as amended by this Act, shall develop a national preparedness goal and a national preparedness system.

(Pub. L. 109–295, title VI, § 642, Oct. 4, 2006, 120 Stat. 1425.)

REFERENCES IN TEXT

The Homeland Security Act of 2002, referred to in text, is Pub. L. 107–296, Nov. 25, 2002, 116 Stat. 2135, as amended. Title V of the Act is classified generally to subchapter V (§ 311 et seq.) of chapter 1 of this title. For complete classification of this Act to the Code, see Short Title note set out under section 101 of this title and Tables.

This Act, referred to in text, means title VI of Pub. L. 109–295, Oct. 4, 2006, 120 Stat. 1394, known as the Post-Katrina Emergency Management Reform Act of 2006. For complete classification of this Act to the Code, see Short Title and References in Pub. L. 109–295 notes set out under section 701 of this title and Tables.

§ 743. National preparedness goal

(a) Establishment

The President, acting through the Administrator, shall complete, revise, and update, as necessary, a national preparedness goal that defines the target level of preparedness to ensure the Nation's ability to prevent, respond to, recover from, and mitigate against natural disasters, acts of terrorism, and other man-made disasters.

(b) National Incident Management System and National Response Plan

The national preparedness goal, to the greatest extent practicable, shall be consistent with the National Incident Management System and the National Response Plan.

(Pub. L. 109–295, title VI, § 643, Oct. 4, 2006, 120 Stat. 1425.)

§ 744. Establishment of national preparedness system

(a) Establishment

The President, acting through the Administrator, shall develop a national preparedness system to enable the Nation to meet the national preparedness goal.

(b) Components

The national preparedness system shall include the following components:

(1) Target capabilities and preparedness priorities.

(2) Equipment and training standards.

(3) Training and exercises.

(4) Comprehensive assessment system.

(5) Remedial action management program.

(6) Federal response capability inventory.

(7) Reporting requirements.

(8) Federal preparedness.

(c) National planning scenarios

The national preparedness system may include national planning scenarios.

(Pub. L. 109–295, title VI, § 644, Oct. 4, 2006, 120 Stat. 1425.)

§ 745. National planning scenarios

(a) In general

The Administrator, in coordination with the heads of appropriate Federal agencies and the National Advisory Council, may develop planning scenarios to reflect the relative risk requirements presented by all hazards, including natural disasters, acts of terrorism, and other man-made disasters, in order to provide the foundation for the flexible and adaptive development of target capabilities and the identification of target capability levels to meet the national preparedness goal.

(b) Development

In developing, revising, and replacing national planning scenarios, the Administrator shall ensure that the scenarios—

(1) reflect the relative risk of all hazards and illustrate the potential scope, magnitude, and complexity of a broad range of representative hazards; and

(2) provide the minimum number of representative scenarios necessary to identify and define the tasks and target capabilities required to respond to all hazards.

(Pub. L. 109–295, title VI, § 645, Oct. 4, 2006, 120 Stat. 1425.)

§ 746. Target capabilities and preparedness priorities

(a) Establishment of guidelines on target capabilities

Not later than 180 days after October 4, 2006, the Administrator, in coordination with the heads of appropriate Federal agencies, the National Council on Disability, and the National Advisory Council, shall complete, revise, and update, as necessary, guidelines to define risk-based target capabilities for Federal, State, local, and tribal government preparedness that will enable the Nation to prevent, respond to, recover from, and mitigate against all hazards, including natural disasters, acts of terrorism, and other man-made disasters.

(b) Distribution of guidelines

The Administrator shall ensure that the guidelines are provided promptly to the appropriate committees of Congress and the States.

(c) Objectives

The Administrator shall ensure that the guidelines are specific, flexible, and measurable.

(d) Terrorism risk assessment

With respect to analyzing and assessing the risk of acts of terrorism, the Administrator shall consider—

(1) the variables of threat, vulnerability, and consequences related to population (including transient commuting and tourist populations), areas of high population density, critical infrastructure, coastline, and international borders; and

(2) the most current risk assessment available from the Chief Intelligence Officer of the Department of the threats of terrorism against the United States.

(e) Preparedness priorities

In establishing the guidelines under subsection (a), the Administrator shall establish preparedness priorities that appropriately balance the risk of all hazards, including natural disasters, acts of terrorism, and other man-made disasters, with the resources required to prevent, respond to, recover from, and mitigate against the hazards.

(f) Mutual aid agreements

The Administrator may provide support for the development of mutual aid agreements within States.

(Pub. L. 109–295, title VI, §646, Oct. 4, 2006, 120 Stat. 1426.)

§ 747. Equipment and training standards

(a) Equipment standards

(1) In general

The Administrator, in coordination with the heads of appropriate Federal agencies and the National Advisory Council, shall support the development, promulgation, and updating, as necessary, of national voluntary consensus standards for the performance, use, and validation of equipment used by Federal, State, local, and tribal governments and nongovernmental emergency response providers.

(2) Requirements

The national voluntary consensus standards shall—

(A) be designed to achieve equipment and other capabilities consistent with the national preparedness goal, including the safety and health of emergency response providers;

(B) to the maximum extent practicable, be consistent with existing national voluntary consensus standards;

(C) take into account, as appropriate, threats that may not have been contemplated when the existing standards were developed; and

(D) focus on maximizing operability, interoperability, interchangeability, durability, flexibility, efficiency, efficacy, portability, sustainability, and safety.

(b) Training standards

The Administrator shall—

(1) support the development, promulgation, and regular updating, as necessary, of national voluntary consensus standards for training; and

(2) ensure that the training provided under the national training program is consistent with the standards.

(c) Consultation with standards organizations

In carrying out this section, the Administrator shall consult with representatives of relevant public and private sector national voluntary consensus standards development organizations.

(Pub. L. 109–295, title VI, §647, Oct. 4, 2006, 120 Stat. 1426.)

§ 748. Training and exercises

(a) National training program

(1) In general

Beginning not later than 180 days after October 4, 2006, the Administrator, in coordination with the heads of appropriate Federal agencies, the National Council on Disability, and the National Advisory Council, shall carry out a national training program to implement the national preparedness goal, National Incident Management System, National Response Plan, and other related plans and strategies.

(2) Training partners

In developing and implementing the national training program, the Administrator shall—

(A) work with government training facilities, academic institutions, private organizations, and other entities that provide specialized, state-of-the-art training for emergency managers or emergency response providers; and

(B) utilize, as appropriate, training courses provided by community colleges, State and local public safety academies, State and private universities, and other facilities.

(b) National exercise program

(1) In general

Beginning not later than 180 days after October 4, 2006, the Administrator, in coordination with the heads of appropriate Federal agencies, the National Council on Disability, and the National Advisory Council, shall carry out a national exercise program to test and evaluate the national preparedness goal, National Incident Management System, National Response Plan, and other related plans and strategies.

(2) Requirements

The national exercise program—

(A) shall be—

(i) as realistic as practicable, based on current risk assessments, including credible threats, vulnerabilities, and consequences, and designed to stress the national preparedness system;

(ii) designed, as practicable, to simulate the partial or complete incapacitation of a State, local, or tribal government;

(iii) carried out, as appropriate, with a minimum degree of notice to involved parties regarding the timing and details of such exercises, consistent with safety considerations;

(iv) designed to provide for the systematic evaluation of readiness and enhance operational understanding of the incident command system and relevant mutual aid agreements;

(v) designed to address the unique requirements of populations with special needs, including the elderly; and

(vi) designed to promptly develop after-action reports and plans for quickly incorporating lessons learned into future operations; and

(B) shall include a selection of model exercises that State, local, and tribal governments can readily adapt for use and provide assistance to State, local, and tribal governments with the design, implementation, and evaluation of exercises (whether a model exercise program or an exercise designed locally) that—

(i) conform to the requirements under subparagraph (A);

(ii) are consistent with any applicable State, local, or tribal strategy or plan; and

(iii) provide for systematic evaluation of readiness.

(3) National level exercises

The Administrator shall periodically, but not less than biennially, perform national exercises for the following purposes:

(A) To test and evaluate the capability of Federal, State, local, and tribal governments to detect, disrupt, and prevent threatened or actual catastrophic acts of terrorism, especially those involving weapons of mass destruction.

(B) To test and evaluate the readiness of Federal, State, local, and tribal governments to respond and recover in a coordinated and unified manner to catastrophic incidents.

(Pub. L. 109–295, title VI, §648, Oct. 4, 2006, 120 Stat. 1427; Pub. L. 110–53, title IV, §§402, 403, Aug. 3, 2007, 121 Stat. 302, 303.)

AMENDMENTS

2007—Subsec. (b)(2)(A)(iv) to (vi). Pub. L. 110–53, §402, added cls. (iv) to (vi) and struck out former cls. (iv) and (v) which read as follows:

"(iv) designed to provide for systematic evaluation of readiness; and

"(v) designed to address the unique requirements of populations with special needs; and".

Subsec. (b)(2)(B). Pub. L. 110–53, §403, in introductory provisions, substituted "shall include a selection of model exercises that State, local, and tribal governments can readily adapt for use and provide assistance to State, local, and tribal governments with the design, implementation, and evaluation of exercises (whether a model exercise program or an exercise designed locally)" for "shall provide assistance to State, local, and tribal governments with the design, implementation, and evaluation of exercises".

§749. Comprehensive assessment system

(a) Establishment

The Administrator, in coordination with the National Council on Disability and the National Advisory Council, shall establish a comprehensive system to assess, on an ongoing basis, the Nation's prevention capabilities and overall preparedness, including operational readiness.

(b) Performance metrics and measures

The Administrator shall ensure that each component of the national preparedness system, National Incident Management System, National Response Plan, and other related plans and strategies, and the reports required under section 752 of this title is developed, revised, and updated with clear and quantifiable performance metrics, measures, and outcomes.

(c) Contents

The assessment system established under subsection (a) shall assess—

(1) compliance with the national preparedness system, National Incident Management System, National Response Plan, and other related plans and strategies;

(2) capability levels at the time of assessment against target capability levels defined pursuant to the guidelines established under section 746(a) of this title;

(3) resource needs to meet the desired target capability levels defined pursuant to the guidelines established under section 746(a) of this title; and

(4) performance of training, exercises, and operations.

(Pub. L. 109–295, title VI, §649, Oct. 4, 2006, 120 Stat. 1428.)

§750. Remedial action management program

The Administrator, in coordination with the National Council on Disability and the National Advisory Council, shall establish a remedial action management program to—

(1) analyze training, exercises, and real-world events to identify and disseminate lessons learned and best practices;

(2) generate and disseminate, as appropriate, after action reports to participants in exercises and real-world events; and

(3) conduct remedial action tracking and long-term trend analysis.

(Pub. L. 109–295, title VI, §650, Oct. 4, 2006, 120 Stat. 1428.)

§ 751. Federal response capability inventory

(a) In general

In accordance with section 5196(h)(1)(C) of title 42, the Administrator shall accelerate the completion of the inventory of Federal response capabilities.

(b) Contents

For each Federal agency with responsibilities under the National Response Plan, the inventory shall include—

(1) for each capability—

(A) the performance parameters of the capability;

(B) the timeframe within which the capability can be brought to bear on an incident; and

(C) the readiness of the capability to respond to all hazards, including natural disasters, acts of terrorism, and other man-made disasters;

(2) a list of personnel credentialed in accordance with section 320 of this title;

(3) a list of resources typed in accordance with section 320 of this title; and

(4) emergency communications assets maintained by the Federal Government and, if appropriate, State, local, and tribal governments and the private sector.

(c) Department of Defense

The Administrator, in coordination with the Secretary of Defense, shall develop a list of organizations and functions within the Department of Defense that may be used, pursuant to the authority provided under the National Response Plan and sections 5170a, 5170b, and 5192 of title 42, to provide support to civil authorities during natural disasters, acts of terrorism, and other man-made disasters.

(d) Database

The Administrator shall establish an inventory database to allow—

(1) real-time exchange of information regarding—

(A) capabilities;

(B) readiness;

(C) the compatibility of equipment;

(D) credentialed personnel; and

(E) typed resources;

(2) easy identification and rapid deployment of capabilities, credentialed personnel, and typed resources during an incident; and

(3) the sharing of the inventory described in subsection (a) with other Federal agencies, as appropriate.

(Pub. L. 109–295, title VI, § 651, Oct. 4, 2006, 120 Stat. 1429; Pub. L. 110–53, title IV, § 405, Aug. 3, 2007, 121 Stat. 303.)

AMENDMENTS

2007—Subsec. (b). Pub. L. 110–53, § 405(1)(A), substituted "For each Federal agency with responsibilities under the National Response Plan, the inventory" for "The inventory" in introductory provisions.

Subsec. (b)(2) to (4). Pub. L. 110–53, § 405(1)(B)–(D), added pars. (2) and (3) and redesignated former par. (2) as (4).

Subsec. (d)(1). Pub. L. 110–53, § 405(2)(A), substituted "regarding—" for "regarding capabilities, readiness, or the compatibility of equipment;" in introductory provisions and added subpars. (A) to (E).

Subsec. (d)(2). Pub. L. 110–53, § 405(2)(B), inserted "of capabilities, credentialed personnel, and typed resources" after "rapid deployment".

Subsec. (d)(3). Pub. L. 110–53, § 405(2)(C), substituted "the inventory described in subsection (a)" for "inventories".

§ 752. Reporting requirements

(a) Federal preparedness report

(1) In general

Not later than 12 months after October 4, 2006, and annually thereafter, the Administrator, in coordination with the heads of appropriate Federal agencies, shall submit to the appropriate committees of Congress a report on the Nation's level of preparedness for all hazards, including natural disasters, acts of terrorism, and other man-made disasters.

(2) Contents

Each report shall include—

(A) an assessment of how Federal assistance supports the national preparedness system;

(B) the results of the comprehensive assessment carried out under section 749 of this title;

(C) a review of the inventory described in section 751 of this title, including the number and type of credentialed personnel in each category of personnel trained and ready to respond to a natural disaster, act of terrorism, or other man-made disaster;

(D) an assessment of resource needs to meet preparedness priorities established under section 746(e) of this title, including—

(i) an estimate of the amount of Federal, State, local, and tribal expenditures required to attain the preparedness priorities; and

(ii) the extent to which the use of Federal assistance during the preceding fiscal year achieved the preparedness priorities;

(E) an evaluation of the extent to which grants administered by the Department, including grants under title XX of the Homeland Security Act of 2002 [6 U.S.C. 601 et seq.]—

(i) have contributed to the progress of State, local, and tribal governments in achieving target capabilities; and

(ii) have led to the reduction of risk from natural disasters, acts of terrorism, or other man-made disasters nationally and in State, local, and tribal jurisdictions; and

(F) a discussion of whether the list of credentialed personnel of the Agency described in section 751(b)(2) of this title—

(i) complies with the strategic human capital plan developed under section 10102 of title 5; and

(ii) is sufficient to respond to a natural disaster, act of terrorism, or other man-made disaster, including a catastrophic incident.

(b) Catastrophic resource report

(1) In general

The Administrator shall develop and submit to the appropriate committees of Congress annually an estimate of the resources of the Agency and other Federal agencies needed for and devoted specifically to developing the capabilities of Federal, State, local, and tribal governments necessary to respond to a catastrophic incident.

(2) Contents

Each estimate under paragraph (1) shall include the resources both necessary for and devoted to—

(A) planning;

(B) training and exercises;

(C) Regional Office enhancements;

(D) staffing, including for surge capacity during a catastrophic incident;

(E) additional logistics capabilities;

(F) other responsibilities under the catastrophic incident annex and the catastrophic incident supplement of the National Response Plan;

(G) State, local, and tribal government catastrophic incident preparedness; and

(H) covering increases in the fixed costs or expenses of the Agency, including rent or property acquisition costs or expenses, taxes, contributions to the working capital fund of the Department, and security costs for the year after the year in which such estimate is submitted.

(c) State preparedness report

(1) In general

Not later than 15 months after October 4, 2006, and annually thereafter, a State receiving Federal preparedness assistance administered by the Department shall submit a report to the Administrator on the State's level of preparedness.

(2) Contents

Each report shall include—

(A) an assessment of State compliance with the national preparedness system, National Incident Management System, National Response Plan, and other related plans and strategies;

(B) an assessment of current capability levels and a description of target capability levels; and

(C) a discussion of the extent to which target capabilities identified in the applicable State homeland security plan and other applicable plans remain unmet and an assessment of resources needed to meet the preparedness priorities established under section 746(e) of this title, including—

(i) an estimate of the amount of expenditures required to attain the preparedness priorities; and

(ii) the extent to which the use of Federal assistance during the preceding fiscal year achieved the preparedness priorities.

(Pub. L. 109–295, title VI, § 652, Oct. 4, 2006, 120 Stat. 1429; Pub. L. 110–53, title I, § 103, title IV, § 406, Aug. 3, 2007, 121 Stat. 293, 304.)

REFERENCES IN TEXT

The Homeland Security Act of 2002, referred to in subsec. (a)(2)(E), is Pub. L. 107–296, Nov. 25, 2002, 116 Stat. 2135. Title XX of the Act is classified generally to subchapter XV (§ 601 et seq.) of chapter 1 of this title. For complete classification of this Act to the Code, see Short Title note set out under section 101 of this title and Tables.

AMENDMENTS

2007—Subsec. (a)(2)(C). Pub. L. 110–53, § 406(1), substituted "section 751 of this title, including the number and type of credentialed personnel in each category of personnel trained and ready to respond to a natural disaster, act of terrorism, or other man-made disaster" for "section 751(a) of this title".

Subsec. (a)(2)(E). Pub. L. 110–53, § 103(a), added subpar. (E).

Subsec. (a)(2)(F). Pub. L. 110–53, § 406(2)–(4), added subpar. (F).

Subsec. (c)(2)(C). Pub. L. 110–53, § 103(b), which directed amendment of subpar. (D) by substituting "a discussion of the extent to which target capabilities identified in the applicable State homeland security plan and other applicable plans remain unmet and an assessment of resources needed" for "an assessment of resource needs", was executed by making the substitution in subpar. (C) to reflect the probable intent of Congress.

§ 753. Federal preparedness

(a) Agency responsibility

In support of the national preparedness system, the President shall ensure that each Federal agency with responsibilities under the National Response Plan—

(1) has the operational capability to meet the national preparedness goal, including—

(A) the personnel to make and communicate decisions;

(B) organizational structures that are assigned, trained, and exercised for the missions of the agency;

(C) sufficient physical resources; and

(D) the command, control, and communication channels to make, monitor, and communicate decisions;

(2) complies with the National Incident Management System, including credentialing of personnel and typing of resources likely needed to respond to a natural disaster, act of terrorism, or other man-made disaster in accordance with section 320 of this title;

(3) develops, trains, and exercises rosters of response personnel to be deployed when the agency is called upon to support a Federal response;

(4) develops deliberate operational plans and the corresponding capabilities, including crisis planning, to respond effectively to natural disasters, acts of terrorism, and other man-made disasters in support of the National Response Plan to ensure a coordinated Federal response; and

(5) regularly updates, verifies the accuracy of, and provides to the Administrator the information in the inventory required under section 751 of this title.

(b) Operational plans

An operations plan developed under subsection (a)(4) shall meet the following requirements:

(1) The operations plan shall be coordinated under a unified system with a common terminology, approach, and framework.

(2) The operations plan shall be developed, in coordination with State, local, and tribal government officials, to address both regional and national risks.

(3) The operations plan shall contain, as appropriate, the following elements:

(A) Concepts of operations.

(B) Critical tasks and responsibilities.

(C) Detailed resource and personnel requirements, together with sourcing requirements.

(D) Specific provisions for the rapid integration of the resources and personnel of the agency into the overall response.

(4) The operations plan shall address, as appropriate, the following matters:

(A) Support of State, local, and tribal governments in conducting mass evacuations, including—

(i) transportation and relocation;

(ii) short- and long-term sheltering and accommodation;

(iii) provisions for populations with special needs, keeping families together, and expeditious location of missing children; and

(iv) policies and provisions for pets.

(B) The preparedness and deployment of public health and medical resources, including resources to address the needs of evacuees and populations with special needs.

(C) The coordination of interagency search and rescue operations, including land, water, and airborne search and rescue operations.

(D) The roles and responsibilities of the Senior Federal Law Enforcement Official with respect to other law enforcement entities.

(E) The protection of critical infrastructure.

(F) The coordination of maritime salvage efforts among relevant agencies.

(G) The coordination of Department of Defense and National Guard support of civilian authorities.

(H) To the extent practicable, the utilization of Department of Defense, National Air and Space Administration, National Oceanic and Atmospheric Administration, and commercial aircraft and satellite remotely sensed imagery.

(I) The coordination and integration of support from the private sector and nongovernmental organizations.

(J) The safe disposal of debris, including hazardous materials, and, when practicable, the recycling of debris.

(K) The identification of the required surge capacity.

(L) Specific provisions for the recovery of affected geographic areas.

(c) Mission assignments

To expedite the provision of assistance under the National Response Plan, the President shall ensure that the Administrator, in coordination with Federal agencies with responsibilities under the National Response Plan, develops prescripted mission assignments, including logistics, communications, mass care, health services, and public safety.

(d) Certification

The President shall certify to the Committee on Homeland Security and Governmental Affairs of the Senate and the Committee on Homeland Security and the Committee on Transportation and Infrastructure of the House of Representatives on an annual basis that each Federal agency with responsibilities under the National Response Plan complies with subsections (a) and (b).

(e) Construction

Nothing in this section shall be construed to limit the authority of the Secretary of Defense with regard to—

(1) the command, control, training, planning, equipment, exercises, or employment of Department of Defense forces; or

(2) the allocation of Department of Defense resources.

(Pub. L. 109–295, title VI, §653, Oct. 4, 2006, 120 Stat. 1430; Pub. L. 110–53, title IV, §407, Aug. 3, 2007, 121 Stat. 304.)

AMENDMENTS

2007—Subsec. (a). Pub. L. 110–53, §407(1)(A), struck out "coordinating, primary, or supporting" before "responsibilities" in introductory provisions.

Subsec. (a)(2). Pub. L. 110–53, §407(1)(B), inserted ", including credentialing of personnel and typing of resources likely needed to respond to a natural disaster, act of terrorism, or other man-made disaster in accordance with section 320 of this title" before semicolon at end.

Subsec. (a)(5). Pub. L. 110–53, §407(1)(C)–(E), added par. (5).

Subsec. (d). Pub. L. 110–53, §407(2), inserted "to the Committee on Homeland Security and Governmental Affairs of the Senate and the Committee on Homeland Security and the Committee on Transportation and Infrastructure of the House of Representatives" after "certify" and struck out "coordinating, primary, or supporting" before "responsibilities".

§ 754. Use of existing resources

In establishing the national preparedness goal and national preparedness system, the Administrator shall use existing preparedness documents, planning tools, and guidelines to the extent practicable and consistent with this Act.

(Pub. L. 109–295, title VI, §654, Oct. 4, 2006, 120 Stat. 1432.)

REFERENCES IN TEXT

This Act, referred to in text, means title VI of Pub. L. 109–295, Oct. 4, 2006, 120 Stat. 1394, known as the Post-Katrina Emergency Management Reform Act of 2006. For complete classification of title VI to the Code, see Short Title note set out under section 701 of this title and Tables.

PART B—ADDITIONAL PREPAREDNESS

§ 761. Emergency Management Assistance Compact grants

(a) In general

The Administrator may make grants to administer the Emergency Management Assistance Compact consented to by the Joint Resolution entitled "Joint Resolution granting the consent of Congress to the Emergency Management Assistance Compact" (Public Law 104–321; 110 Stat. 3877).

(b) Uses

A grant under this section shall be used—

(1) to carry out recommendations identified in the Emergency Management Assistance Compact after-action reports for the 2004 and 2005 hurricane season;

(2) to administer compact operations on behalf of all member States and territories;

(3) to continue coordination with the Agency and appropriate Federal agencies;

(4) to continue coordination with State, local, and tribal government entities and their respective national organizations; and

(5) to assist State and local governments, emergency response providers, and organizations representing such providers with credentialing emergency response providers and the typing of emergency response resources.

(c) Coordination

The Administrator shall consult with the Administrator of the Emergency Management Assistance Compact to ensure effective coordination of efforts in responding to requests for assistance.

(d) Authorization

There is authorized to be appropriated to carry out this section $4,000,000 for fiscal year 2008. Such sums shall remain available until expended.

(Pub. L. 109–295, title VI, § 661, Oct. 4, 2006, 120 Stat. 1432.)

REFERENCES IN TEXT

The Joint Resolution entitled "Joint Resolution granting the consent of Congress to the Emergency Management Assistance Compact", referred to in subsec. (a), is Pub. L. 104–321, Oct. 19, 1996, 110 Stat. 3877, which is not classified to the Code.

§ 762. Emergency management performance grants program

(a) Definitions

In this section—

(1) the term "program" means the emergency management performance grants program described in subsection (b); and

(2) the term "State" has the meaning given that term in section 102 of the Robert T. Stafford Disaster Relief and Emergency Assistance Act (42 U.S.C. 5122).

(b) In general

The Administrator of the Federal Emergency Management Agency shall continue implementation of an emergency management performance grants program, to make grants to States to assist State, local, and tribal governments in preparing for all hazards, as authorized by the Robert T. Stafford Disaster Relief and Emergency Assistance Act (42 U.S.C. 5121 et seq.).

(c) Federal share

Except as otherwise specifically provided by title VI of the Robert T. Stafford Disaster Relief and Emergency Assistance Act [42 U.S.C. 5195 et seq.], the Federal share of the cost of an activity carried out using funds made available under the program shall not exceed 50 percent.

(d) Apportionment

For fiscal year 2008, and each fiscal year thereafter, the Administrator shall apportion the amounts appropriated to carry out the program among the States as follows:

(1) Baseline amount

The Administrator shall first apportion 0.25 percent of such amounts to each of American Samoa, the Commonwealth of the Northern Mariana Islands, Guam, and the Virgin Islands and 0.75 percent of such amounts to each of the remaining States.

(2) Remainder

The Administrator shall apportion the remainder of such amounts in the ratio that—

(A) the population of each State; bears to

(B) the population of all States.

(e) Consistency in allocation

Notwithstanding subsection (d), in any fiscal year before fiscal year 2013 in which the appropriation for grants under this section is equal to or greater than the appropriation for emergency management performance grants in fiscal year 2007, no State shall receive an amount under this section for that fiscal year less than the amount that State received in fiscal year 2007.

(f) Authorization of appropriations

There is authorized to be appropriated to carry out the program—

(1) for fiscal year 2008, $400,000,000;

(2) for fiscal year 2009, $535,000,000;

(3) for fiscal year 2010, $680,000,000;

(4) for fiscal year 2011, $815,000,000; and

(5) for fiscal year 2012, $950,000,000.

(Pub. L. 109–295, title VI, § 662, Oct. 4, 2006, 120 Stat. 1433; Pub. L. 110–53, title II, § 201, Aug. 3, 2007, 121 Stat. 294.)

REFERENCES IN TEXT

The Robert T. Stafford Disaster Relief and Emergency Assistance Act, referred to in subsecs. (b) and (c), is Pub. L. 93–288, May 22, 1974, 88 Stat. 143, which is classified principally to chapter 68 (§ 5121 et seq.) of Title 42, The Public Health and Welfare. Title VI of the Act is classified generally to subchapter IV–B (§ 5195 et seq.) of chapter 68 of Title 42. For complete classification of this Act to the Code, see Short Title note set out under section 5121 of Title 42 and Tables.

AMENDMENTS

2007—Pub. L. 110–53 amended section catchline and text generally. Prior to amendment, text read as follows: "There is authorized to be appropriated for the Emergency Management Performance Grants Program for fiscal year 2008, an amount equal to the amount appropriated for the program for fiscal year 2007 and an additional $175,000,000."

§ 763. Transfer of Noble Training Center

The Noble Training Center is transferred to the Center for Domestic Preparedness. The Center for Domestic Preparedness shall integrate the Noble Training Center into the program structure of the Center for Domestic Preparedness.

(Pub. L. 109–295, title VI, § 663, Oct. 4, 2006, 120 Stat. 1433.)

§ 764. National exercise simulation center

The President shall establish a national exercise simulation center that—

(1) uses a mix of live, virtual, and constructive simulations to—

(A) prepare elected officials, emergency managers, emergency response providers, and emergency support providers at all levels of government to operate cohesively;

(B) provide a learning environment for the homeland security personnel of all Federal agencies;

(C) assist in the development of operational procedures and exercises, particularly those based on catastrophic incidents; and

(D) allow incident commanders to exercise decisionmaking in a simulated environment; and

(2) uses modeling and simulation for training, exercises, and command and control functions at the operational level.

(Pub. L. 109–295, title VI, § 664, Oct. 4, 2006, 120 Stat. 1433.)

PART C—MISCELLANEOUS AUTHORITIES

§ 771. National Disaster Recovery Strategy

(a) In general

The Administrator, in coordination with the Secretary of Housing and Urban Development, the Administrator of the Environmental Protection Agency, the Secretary of Agriculture, the Secretary of Commerce, the Secretary of the Treasury, the Secretary of Transportation, the Administrator of the Small Business Administration, the Assistant Secretary for Indian Affairs of the Department of the Interior, and the heads of other appropriate Federal agencies, State, local, and tribal government officials (including through the National Advisory Council), and representatives of appropriate nongovernmental organizations shall develop, coordinate, and maintain a National Disaster Recovery Strategy to serve as a guide to recovery efforts after major disasters and emergencies.

(b) Contents

The National Disaster Recovery Strategy shall—

(1) outline the most efficient and cost-effective Federal programs that will meet the recovery needs of States, local and tribal governments, and individuals and households affected by a major disaster;

(2) clearly define the role, programs, authorities, and responsibilities of each Federal agency that may be of assistance in providing assistance in the recovery from a major disaster;

(3) promote the use of the most appropriate and cost-effective building materials (based on the hazards present in an area) in any area affected by a major disaster, with the goal of encouraging the construction of disaster-resistant buildings; and

(4) describe in detail the programs that may be offered by the agencies described in paragraph (2), including—

(A) discussing funding issues;

(B) detailing how responsibilities under the National Disaster Recovery Strategy will be shared; and

(C) addressing other matters concerning the cooperative effort to provide recovery assistance.

(c) Report

(1) In general

Not later than 270 days after October 4, 2006, the Administrator shall submit to the appropriate committees of Congress a report describing in detail the National Disaster Recovery Strategy and any additional authorities necessary to implement any portion of the National Disaster Recovery Strategy.

(2) Update

The Administrator shall submit to the appropriate committees of Congress a report updating the report submitted under paragraph (1)—

(A) on the same date that any change is made to the National Disaster Recovery Strategy; and

(B) on a periodic basis after the submission of the report under paragraph (1), but not less than once every 5 years after the date of the submission of the report under paragraph (1).

(Pub. L. 109–295, title VI, § 682, Oct. 4, 2006, 120 Stat. 1445.)

§ 772. National Disaster Housing Strategy

(a) In general

The Administrator, in coordination with representatives of the Federal agencies, governments, and organizations listed in subsection (b)(2) of this section, the National Advisory Council, the National Council on Disability, and other entities at the Administrator's discretion, shall develop, coordinate, and maintain a National Disaster Housing Strategy.

(b) Contents

The National Disaster Housing Strategy shall—

(1) outline the most efficient and cost effective Federal programs that will best meet the short-term and long-term housing needs of individuals and households affected by a major disaster;

(2) clearly define the role, programs, authorities, and responsibilities of each entity in providing housing assistance in the event of a major disaster, including—

(A) the Agency;

(B) the Department of Housing and Urban Development;

(C) the Department of Agriculture;

(D) the Department of Veterans Affairs;

(E) the Department of Health and Human Services;

(F) the Bureau of Indian Affairs;

(G) any other Federal agency that may provide housing assistance in the event of a major disaster;

(H) the American Red Cross; and

(I) State, local, and tribal governments;

(3) describe in detail the programs that may be offered by the entities described in paragraph (2), including—

(A) outlining any funding issues;

(B) detailing how responsibilities under the National Disaster Housing Strategy will be shared; and

(C) addressing other matters concerning the cooperative effort to provide housing assistance during a major disaster;

(4) consider methods through which housing assistance can be provided to individuals and households where employment and other resources for living are available;

(5) describe programs directed to meet the needs of special needs and low-income populations and ensure that a sufficient number of housing units are provided for individuals with disabilities;

(6) describe plans for the operation of clusters of housing provided to individuals and households, including access to public services, site management, security, and site density;

(7) describe plans for promoting the repair or rehabilitation of existing rental housing, including through lease agreements or other means, in order to improve the provision of housing to individuals and households under section 408 of the Robert T. Stafford Disaster Relief and Emergency Assistance Act (42 U.S.C. 5174); and

(8) describe any additional authorities necessary to carry out any portion of the strategy.

(c) Guidance

The Administrator should develop and make publicly available guidance on—

(1) types of housing assistance available under the Robert T. Stafford Disaster Relief and Emergency Assistance Act (42 U.S.C. 5121 et seq.) to individuals and households affected by an emergency or major disaster;

(2) eligibility for such assistance (including, where appropriate, the continuation of such assistance); and

(3) application procedures for such assistance.

(d) Report

(1) In general

Not later than 270 days after October 4, 2006, the Administrator shall submit to the appropriate committees of Congress a report describing in detail the National Disaster Housing Strategy, including programs directed to meeting the needs of special needs populations.

(2) Updated report

The Administrator shall submit to the appropriate committees of Congress a report updating the report submitted under paragraph (1)—

(A) on the same date that any change is made to the National Disaster Housing Strategy; and

(B) on a periodic basis after the submission of the report under paragraph (1), but not less than once every 5 years after the date of the submission of the report under paragraph (1).

(Pub. L. 109–295, title VI, §683, Oct. 4, 2006, 120 Stat. 1446.)

REFERENCES IN TEXT

The Robert T. Stafford Disaster Relief and Emergency Assistance Act, referred to in subsec. (c)(1), is Pub. L. 93–288, May 22, 1974, 88 Stat. 143, as amended, which is classified principally to chapter 68 (§5121 et seq.) of Title 42, The Public Health and Welfare. For complete classification of this Act to the Code, see Short Title note set out under section 5121 of Title 42 and Tables.

§ 773. Individuals with disabilities guidelines

Not later than 90 days after October 4, 2006, and in coordination with the National Advisory Council, the National Council on Disability, the Interagency Coordinating Council on Preparedness and Individuals With Disabilities established under Executive Order No. 13347, and the Disability Coordinator (established under section 321b of this title), the Administrator shall develop guidelines to accommodate individuals with disabilities, which shall include guidelines for—

(1) the accessibility of, and communications and programs in, shelters, recovery centers, and other facilities; and

(2) devices used in connection with disaster operations, including first aid stations, mass feeding areas, portable payphone stations, portable toilets, and temporary housing.

(Pub. L. 109–295, title VI, §689(a), Oct. 4, 2006, 120 Stat. 1448.)

REFERENCES IN TEXT

Executive Order No. 13347, referred to in text, is set out as a note under section 314 of this title.

§ 774. Reunification

(a) Definitions

In this section:

(1) Child Locator Center

The term "Child Locator Center" means the National Emergency Child Locator Center established under subsection (b).

(2) Declared event

The term "declared event" means a major disaster or emergency.

(3) Displaced adult

The term "displaced adult" means an individual 21 years of age or older who is displaced from the habitual residence of that individual as a result of a declared event.

(4) Displaced child

The term "displaced child" means an individual under 21 years of age who is displaced from the habitual residence of that individual as a result of a declared event.

(b) National Emergency Child Locator Center

(1) In general

Not later than 180 days after October 4, 2006, the Administrator, in coordination with the Attorney General of the United States, shall establish within the National Center for Missing and Exploited Children the National Emergency Child Locator Center. In establishing the National Emergency Child Locator Center, the Administrator shall establish procedures to make all relevant information available to the National Emergency Child Locator Center in a timely manner to facilitate the expeditious identification and reunification of children with their families.

(2) Purposes

The purposes of the Child Locator Center are to—

(A) enable individuals to provide to the Child Locator Center the name of and other identifying information about a displaced child or a displaced adult who may have information about the location of a displaced child;

(B) enable individuals to receive information about other sources of information about displaced children and displaced adults; and

(C) assist law enforcement in locating displaced children.

(3) Responsibilities and duties

The responsibilities and duties of the Child Locator Center are to—

(A) establish a toll-free telephone number to receive reports of displaced children and information about displaced adults that may assist in locating displaced children;

(B) create a website to provide information about displaced children;

(C) deploy its staff to the location of a declared event to gather information about displaced children;

(D) assist in the reunification of displaced children with their families;

(E) provide information to the public about additional resources for disaster assistance;

(F) work in partnership with Federal, State, and local law enforcement agencies;

(G) provide technical assistance in locating displaced children;

(H) share information on displaced children and displaced adults with governmental agencies and nongovernmental organizations providing disaster assistance;

(I) use its resources to gather information about displaced children;

(J) refer reports of displaced adults to—

(i) an entity designated by the Attorney General to provide technical assistance in locating displaced adults; and

(ii) the National Emergency Family Registry and Locator System as defined under section 775(a) of this title;

(K) enter into cooperative agreements with Federal and State agencies and other organizations such as the American Red Cross as necessary to implement the mission of the Child Locator Center; and

(L) develop an emergency response plan to prepare for the activation of the Child Locator Center.

(c) Omitted

(d) Report

Not later than 270 days after October 4, 2006, the Administrator shall submit to the Committee on Homeland Security and Governmental Affairs and the Committee on the Judiciary of the Senate and the Committee on Transportation and Infrastructure and the Committee on the Judiciary of the House of Representatives a report describing in detail the status of the Child Locator Center, including funding issues and any difficulties or issues in establishing the Center or completing the cooperative agreements described in subsection (b)(3)(K).

(Pub. L. 109–295, title VI, §689b, Oct. 4, 2006, 120 Stat. 1449.)

CODIFICATION

Section is comprised of section 689b of Pub. L. 109–295. Subsec. (c) of section 689b of Pub. L. 109–295 amended section 5772 of Title 42, The Public Health and Welfare.

§775. National Emergency Family Registry and Locator System

(a) Definitions

In this section—

(1) the term "displaced individual" means an individual displaced by an emergency or major disaster; and

(2) the term "National Emergency Family Registry and Locator System" means the National Emergency Family Registry and Locator System established under subsection (b).

(b) Establishment

Not later than 180 days after October 4, 2006, the Administrator shall establish a National Emergency Family Registry and Locator System to help reunify families separated after an emergency or major disaster.

(c) Operation of System

The National Emergency Family Registry and Locator System shall—

(1) allow a displaced adult (including medical patients) to voluntarily register (and allow an adult that is the parent or guardian of a displaced child to register such child), by submitting personal information to be entered into a database (such as the name, current location of residence, and any other relevant information that could be used by others seeking to locate that individual);

(2) ensure that information submitted under paragraph (1) is accessible to those individuals named by a displaced individual and to those law enforcement officials;

(3) be accessible through the Internet and through a toll-free number, to receive reports of displaced individuals; and

(4) include a means of referring displaced children to the National Emergency Child Locator Center established under section 774 of this title.

(d) Publication of information

Not later than 210 days after October 4, 2006, the Administrator shall establish a mechanism to inform the public about the National Emergency Family Registry and Locator System and its potential usefulness for assisting to reunite displaced individuals with their families.

(e) Coordination

Not later than 90 days after October 4, 2006, the Administrator shall enter a memorandum of understanding with the Department of Justice, the National Center for Missing and Exploited Children, the Department of Health and Human Services, and the American Red Cross and other relevant private organizations that will enhance the sharing of information to facilitate reuniting displaced individuals (including medical patients) with their families.

(f) Report

Not later than 270 days after October 4, 2006, the Administrator shall submit to the appropriate committees of Congress a report describing in detail the status of the National Emergency Family Registry and Locator System, including any difficulties or issues in establishing the System, including funding issues.

(Pub. L. 109–295, title VI, §689c, Oct. 4, 2006, 120 Stat. 1451.)

§ 776. Individuals and households pilot program

(a) Pilot program

(1) In general

The President, acting through the Administrator, in coordination with State, local, and tribal governments, shall establish and conduct a pilot program. The pilot program shall be designed to make better use of existing rental housing, located in areas covered by a major disaster declaration, in order to provide timely and cost-effective temporary housing assistance to individuals and households eligible for assistance under section 5174 of title 42 where alternative housing options are less available or less cost-effective.

(2) Administration

(A) In general

For the purposes of the pilot program under this section, the Administrator may—

(i) enter into lease agreements with owners of multi-family rental property located in areas covered by a major disaster declaration to house individuals and households eligible for assistance under section 5174 of title 42;

(ii) make improvements to properties under such lease agreements;

(iii) use the pilot program where the program is cost effective in that the cost to the Government for the lease agreements is in proportion to the savings to the Government by not providing alternative housing; and

(iv) limit repairs to those required to ensure that the housing units shall meet Federal housing quality standards.

(B) Improvements to leased properties

Under the terms of any lease agreement for a property described under subparagraph (A)(ii), the value of the contribution of the Agency to such improvements—

(i) shall be deducted from the value of the lease agreement; and

(ii) may not exceed the value of the lease agreement.

(3) Consultation

In administering the pilot program under this section, the Administrator may consult with State, local, and tribal governments.

(4) Report

(A) In general

Not later than March 31, 2009, the Administrator shall submit to the appropriate committees of Congress a report regarding the effectiveness of the pilot program.

(B) Contents

The Administrator shall include in the report—

(i) an assessment of the effectiveness of the pilot program under this section, including an assessment of cost-savings to the Federal Government and any benefits to individuals and households eligible for assistance under section 5174 of title 42 under the pilot program;

(ii) findings and conclusions of the Administrator with respect to the pilot program;

(iii) an assessment of additional authorities needed to aid the Agency in its mission of providing disaster housing assistance to individuals and households eligible for assistance under section 5174 of title 42, either under the pilot program under this section or other potential housing programs; and

(iv) any recommendations of the Administrator for additional authority to continue or make permanent the pilot program.

(b) Pilot program project approval

The Administrator shall not approve a project under the pilot program after December 31, 2008.

(Pub. L. 109–295, title VI, §689i, Oct. 4, 2006, 120 Stat. 1454.)

§ 777. Public assistance pilot program

(a) Pilot program

(1) In general

The President, acting through the Administrator, and in coordination with State and local governments, shall establish and conduct a pilot program to—

(A) reduce the costs to the Federal Government of providing assistance to States and local governments under sections 5170b(a)(3)(A), 5172, and 5173 of title 42;

(B) increase flexibility in the administration of sections 5170b(a)(3)(A), 5172, and 5173 of title 42; and

(C) expedite the provision of assistance to States and local governments provided under sections 5170b(a)(3)(A), 5172, and 5173 of title 42.

(2) Participation

Only States and local governments that elect to participate in the pilot program may participate in the pilot program for a particular project.

(3) Innovative administration

(A) In general

For purposes of the pilot program, the Administrator shall establish new procedures to administer assistance provided under the sections referred to in paragraph (1).

(B) New procedures

The new procedures established under subparagraph (A) may include 1 or more of the following:

(i) Notwithstanding section 5172(c)(1)(A) of title 42, providing an option for a State or local government to elect to receive an in-lieu contribution in an amount equal to 90 percent of the Federal share of the Federal estimate of the cost of repair, restoration, reconstruction, or replacement of a public facility owned or controlled by the State or local government and of management expenses.

(ii) Making grants on the basis of estimates agreed to by the local government (or where no local government is involved, by the State government) and the Administrator to provide financial incentives and disincentives for the local government (or where no local government is involved, for the State government) for the timely or cost effective completion of projects under sections 5170b(a)(3)(A), 5172, and 5173 of title 42.

(iii) Increasing the Federal share for removal of debris and wreckage for States and local governments that have a debris management plan approved by the Administrator and have pre-qualified 1 or more debris and wreckage removal contractors before the date of declaration of the major disaster.

(iv) Using a sliding scale for the Federal share for removal of debris and wreckage based on the time it takes to complete debris and wreckage removal.

(v) Using a financial incentive to recycle debris.

(vi) Reimbursing base wages for employees and extra hires of a State or local government involved in or administering debris and wreckage removal.

(4) Waiver

The Administrator may waive such regulations or rules applicable to the provisions of assistance under the sections referred to in paragraph (1) as the Administrator determines are necessary to carry out the pilot program under this section.

(b) Report

(1) In general

Not later than March 31, 2009, the Administrator shall submit to the appropriate committees of Congress a report regarding the effectiveness of the pilot program under this section.

(2) Contents

The report submitted under paragraph (1) shall include—

(A) an assessment by the Administrator of any administrative or financial benefits of the pilot program;

(B) an assessment by the Administrator of the effect, including any savings in time and cost, of the pilot program;

(C) any identified legal or other obstacles to increasing the amount of debris recycled after a major disaster;

(D) any other findings and conclusions of the Administrator with respect to the pilot program; and

(E) any recommendations of the Administrator for additional authority to continue or make permanent the pilot program.

(c) Deadline for initiation of implementation

The Administrator shall initiate implementation of the pilot program under this section not later than 90 days after October 4, 2006.

(d) Pilot program project duration

The Administrator may not approve a project under the pilot program under this section after December 31, 2008.

(Pub. L. 109–295, title VI, § 689j, Oct. 4, 2006, 120 Stat. 1455.)

PART D—PREVENTION OF FRAUD, WASTE, AND ABUSE

§ 791. Advance contracting

(a) Initial report

(1) In general

Not later than 180 days after October 4, 2006, the Administrator shall submit a report under paragraph (2) identifying—

(A) recurring disaster response requirements, including specific goods and services, for which the Agency is capable of contracting for in advance of a natural disaster or act of terrorism or other man-made disaster in a cost effective manner;

(B) recurring disaster response requirements, including specific goods and services, for which the Agency can not contract in advance of a natural disaster or act of terrorism or other man-made disaster in a cost effective manner; and

(C) a contracting strategy that maximizes the use of advance contracts to the extent practical and cost-effective.

(2) Submission

The report under paragraph (1) shall be submitted to the appropriate committees of Congress.

(b) Entering into contracts

(1) In general

Not later than 1 year after October 4, 2006, the Administrator shall enter into 1 or more contracts for each type of goods or services identified under subsection (a)(1)(A), and in accordance with the contracting strategy identified in subsection (a)(1)(C). Any contract for goods or services identified in subsection (a)(1)(A) previously awarded may be maintained in fulfilling this requirement.

(2) Considered factors

Before entering into any contract under this subsection, the Administrator shall consider section 5150 of title 42.

(3) Prenegotiated Federal contracts for goods and services

The Administrator, in coordination with State and local governments and other Federal agencies, shall establish a process to ensure that Federal prenegotiated contracts for goods and services are coordinated with State and local governments, as appropriate.

(4) Prenegotiated State and local contracts for goods and services

The Administrator shall encourage State and local governments to establish prenegotiated contracts with vendors for goods and services in advance of natural disasters and acts of terrorism or other man-made disasters.

(c) Maintenance of contracts

After the date described under subsection (b), the Administrator shall have the responsibility to maintain contracts for appropriate levels of goods and services in accordance with subsection (a)(1)(C).

(d) Report on contracts not using competitive procedures

At the end of each fiscal quarter, beginning with the first fiscal quarter occurring at least 90 days after October 4, 2006, the Administrator shall submit a report on each disaster assistance contract entered into by the Agency by other than competitive procedures to the appropriate committees of Congress.

(Pub. L. 109–295, title VI, §691, Oct. 4, 2006, 120 Stat. 1457.)

§ 792. Limitations on tiering of subcontractors

(a) Regulations

The Secretary shall promulgate regulations applicable to contracts described in subsection (c) to minimize the excessive use by contractors of subcontractors or tiers of subcontractors to perform the principal work of the contract.

(b) Specific requirement

At a minimum, the regulations promulgated under subsection (a) shall preclude a contractor from using subcontracts for more than 65 percent of the cost of the contract or the cost of any individual task or delivery order (not including overhead and profit), unless the Secretary determines that such requirement is not feasible or practicable.

(c) Covered contracts

This section applies to any cost-reimbursement type contract or task or delivery order in an amount greater than the simplified acquisition threshold (as defined by section 403 of title 41) entered into by the Department to facilitate response to or recovery from a natural disaster or act of terrorism or other man-made disaster.

(Pub. L. 109–295, title VI, §692, Oct. 4, 2006, 120 Stat. 1458.)

§ 793. Oversight and accountability of Federal disaster expenditures

(a) Authority of Administrator to designate funds for oversight activities

The Administrator may designate up to 1 percent of the total amount provided to a Federal agency for a mission assignment as oversight funds to be used by the recipient agency for performing oversight of activities carried out under the Agency reimbursable mission assignment process. Such funds shall remain available until expended.

(b) Use of funds

(1) Types of oversight activities

Oversight funds may be used for the following types of oversight activities related to Agency mission assignments:

(A) Monitoring, tracking, and auditing expenditures of funds.

(B) Ensuring that sufficient management and internal control mechanisms are available so that Agency funds are spent appropriately and in accordance with all applicable laws and regulations.

(C) Reviewing selected contracts and other activities.

(D) Investigating allegations of fraud involving Agency funds.

(E) Conducting and participating in fraud prevention activities with other Federal, State, and local government personnel and contractors.

(2) Plans and reports

Oversight funds may be used to issue the plans required under subsection (e) and the reports required under subsection (f).

(c) Restriction on use of funds

Oversight funds may not be used to finance existing agency oversight responsibilities related to direct agency appropriations used for disaster response, relief, and recovery activities.

(d) Methods of oversight activities

(1) In general

Oversight activities may be carried out by an agency under this section either directly or by contract. Such activities may include evaluations and financial and performance audits.

(2) Coordination of oversight activities

To the extent practicable, evaluations and audits under this section shall be performed by the inspector general of the agency.

(e) Development of oversight plans

(1) In general

If an agency receives oversight funds for a fiscal year, the head of the agency shall prepare a plan describing the oversight activities for disaster response, relief, and recovery anticipated to be undertaken during the subsequent fiscal year.

(2) Selection of oversight activities

In preparing the plan, the head of the agency shall select oversight activities based upon a risk assessment of those areas that present the greatest risk of fraud, waste, and abuse.

(3) Schedule

The plan shall include a schedule for conducting oversight activities, including anticipated dates of completion.

(f) Federal disaster assistance accountability reports

A Federal agency receiving oversight funds under this section shall submit annually to the Administrator and the appropriate committees of Congress a consolidated report regarding the use of such funds, including information summarizing oversight activities and the results achieved.

(g) Definition

In this section, the term "oversight funds" means funds referred to in subsection (a) that are designated for use in performing oversight activities.

(Pub. L. 109–295, title VI, § 693, Oct. 4, 2006, 120 Stat. 1458.)

§ 794. Limitation on length of certain noncompetitive contracts

(a) Regulations

The Secretary shall promulgate regulations applicable to contracts described in subsection (c) to restrict the contract period of any such contract entered into using procedures other than competitive procedures pursuant to the exception provided in paragraph (2) of section 253(c) of title 41 to the minimum contract period necessary—

(1) to meet the urgent and compelling requirements of the work to be performed under the contract; and

(2) to enter into another contract for the required goods or services through the use of competitive procedures.

(b) Specific contract period

The regulations promulgated under subsection (a) shall require the contract period to not to exceed[1] 150 days, unless the Secretary determines that exceptional circumstances apply.

(c) Covered contracts

This section applies to any contract in an amount greater than the simplified acquisition threshold (as defined by section 403 of title 41) entered into by the Department to facilitate response to or recovery from a natural disaster, act of terrorism, or other man-made disaster.

(Pub. L. 109–295, title VI, § 695, Oct. 4, 2006, 120 Stat. 1460.)

§ 795. Fraud, waste, and abuse controls

(a) In general

The Administrator shall ensure that—

(1) all programs within the Agency administering Federal disaster relief assistance develop and maintain proper internal management controls to prevent and detect fraud, waste, and abuse;

(2) application databases used by the Agency to collect information on eligible recipients must record disbursements;

(3) such tracking is designed to highlight and identify ineligible applications; and

(4) the databases used to collect information from applications for such assistance must be integrated with disbursements and payment records.

(b) Audits and reviews required

The Administrator shall ensure that any database or similar application processing system for Federal disaster relief assistance programs administered by the Agency undergoes a review by the Inspector General of the Agency to determine the existence and implementation of such internal controls required under this section and the amendments made by this section.

(Pub. L. 109–295, title VI, § 696, Oct. 4, 2006, 120 Stat. 1460.)

REFERENCES IN TEXT

For the amendments made by this section, referred to in subsec. (b), see Codification note below.

[1] So in original. Probably should be "period not to exceed".

CODIFICATION

Section is comprised of section 696 of Pub. L. 109–295. Subsec. (c) of section 696 of Pub. L. 109–295 amended section 5174 of Title 42, The Public Health and Welfare.

§ 796. Registry of disaster response contractors

(a) Definitions

In this section—

(1) the term "registry" means the registry created under subsection (b); and

(2) the terms "small business concern", "small business concern owned and controlled by socially and economically disadvantaged individuals", "small business concern owned and controlled by women", and "small business concern owned and controlled by service-disabled veterans" have the meanings given those terms under the Small Business Act (15 U.S.C. 631 et seq.).

(b) Registry

(1) In general

The Administrator shall establish and maintain a registry of contractors who are willing to perform debris removal, distribution of supplies, reconstruction, and other disaster or emergency relief activities.

(2) Contents

The registry shall include, for each business concern—

(A) the name of the business concern;

(B) the location of the business concern;

(C) the area served by the business concern;

(D) the type of good or service provided by the business concern;

(E) the bonding level of the business concern; and

(F) whether the business concern is—

(i) a small business concern;

(ii) a small business concern owned and controlled by socially and economically disadvantaged individuals;

(iii) a small business concern owned and controlled by women; or

(iv) a small business concern owned and controlled by service-disabled veterans.

(3) Source of information

(A) Submission

Information maintained in the registry shall be submitted on a voluntary basis and be kept current by the submitting business concerns.

(B) Attestation

Each business concern submitting information to the registry shall submit—

(i) an attestation that the information is true; and

(ii) documentation supporting such attestation.

(C) Verification

The Administrator shall verify that the documentation submitted by each business concern supports the information submitted by that business concern.

(4) Availability of registry

The registry shall be made generally available on the Internet site of the Agency.

(5) Consultation of registry

As part of the acquisition planning for contracting for debris removal, distribution of supplies in a disaster, reconstruction, and other disaster or emergency relief activities, a Federal agency shall consult the registry.

(Pub. L. 109–295, title VI, §697, Oct. 4, 2006, 120 Stat. 1461.)

REFERENCES IN TEXT

The Small Business Act, referred to in subsec. (a)(2), is Pub. L. 85–536, §2(1 et seq.), July 18, 1958, 72 Stat. 384, which is classified generally to chapter 14A (§631 et seq.) of Title 15, Commerce and Trade. For complete classification of this Act to the Code, see Short Title note set out under section 631 of Title 15 and Tables.

§797. Fraud prevention training program

The Administrator shall develop and implement a program to provide training on the prevention of waste, fraud, and abuse of Federal disaster relief assistance relating to the response to or recovery from natural disasters and acts of terrorism or other man-made disasters and ways to identify such potential waste, fraud, and abuse.

(Pub. L. 109–295, title VI, §698, Oct. 4, 2006, 120 Stat. 1462.)

PART E—AUTHORIZATION OF APPROPRIATIONS

§811. Authorization of appropriations

There are authorized to be appropriated to carry out this title[1] and the amendments made by this title for the administration and operations of the Agency—

(1) for fiscal year 2008, an amount equal to the amount appropriated for fiscal year 2007 for administration and operations of the Agency, multiplied by 1.1;

(2) for fiscal year 2009, an amount equal to the amount described in paragraph (1), multiplied by 1.1, and

(3) for fiscal year 2010, an amount equal to the amount described in paragraph (2), multiplied by 1.1.

(Pub. L. 109–295, title VI, §699, Oct. 4, 2006, 120 Stat. 1462.)

REFERENCES IN TEXT

This title, referred to in text, is title VI of Pub. L. 109–295, Oct. 4, 2006, 120 Stat. 1355, known as the Post-Katrina Emergency Management Reform Act of 2006. For complete classification of title VI to the Code, see Short Title note set out under section 701 of this title and Tables.

[1] See References in Text note below.

CHAPTER 3—SECURITY AND ACCOUNTABILITY FOR EVERY PORT

§901. Definitions

In this Act:

(1) Appropriate congressional committees

Except as otherwise provided, the term "appropriate congressional committees" means—

(A) the Committee on Appropriations of the Senate;

(B) the Committee on Commerce, Science, and Transportation of the Senate;

(C) the Committee on Finance of the Senate;

(D) the Committee on Homeland Security and Governmental Affairs of the Senate;

(E) the Committee on Appropriations of the House of Representatives;

(F) the Committee on Homeland Security of the House of Representatives;

(G) the Committee on Transportation and Infrastructure of the House of Representatives;

(H) the Committee on Ways and Means of the House of Representatives; and

(I) other congressional committees, as appropriate.

(2) Commercial Operations Advisory Committee

The term "Commercial Operations Advisory Committee" means the Advisory Committee established pursuant to section 9503(c) of the Omnibus Budget Reconciliation Act of 1987 (19 U.S.C. 2071 note) or any successor committee.

(3) Commercial seaport personnel

The term "commercial seaport personnel" includes any person engaged in an activity relating to the loading or unloading of cargo or passengers, the movement or tracking of cargo, the maintenance and repair of intermodal equipment, the operation of cargo-related equipment (whether or not integral to the vessel), and the handling of mooring lines on the dock when a vessel is made fast or let go in the United States.

(4) Commissioner

The term "Commissioner" means the Commissioner responsible for the United States Customs and Border Protection of the Department of Homeland Security.

(5) Container

The term "container" has the meaning given the term in the International Convention for Safe Containers, with annexes, done at Geneva, December 2, 1972 (29 UST 3707).

(6) Container security device

The term "container security device" means a device, or system, designed, at a minimum, to identify positively a container, to detect and record the unauthorized intrusion of a container, and to secure a container against tampering throughout the supply chain. Such a device, or system, shall have a low false alarm rate as determined by the Secretary.

(7) Department

The term "Department" means the Department of Homeland Security.

(8) Examination

The term "examination" means an inspection of cargo to detect the presence of misdeclared, restricted, or prohibited items that utilizes nonintrusive imaging and detection technology.

(9) Inspection

The term "inspection" means the comprehensive process used by the United States Customs and Border Protection to assess goods entering the United States to appraise them for duty purposes, to detect the presence of restricted or prohibited items, and to ensure compliance with all applicable laws. The process may include screening, conducting an examination, or conducting a search.

(10) International supply chain

The term "international supply chain" means the end-to-end process for shipping goods to or from the United States beginning at the point of origin (including manufacturer, supplier, or vendor) through a point of distribution to the destination.

(11) Radiation detection equipment

The term "radiation detection equipment" means any technology that is capable of detecting or identifying nuclear and radiological material or nuclear and radiological explosive devices.

(12) Scan

The term "scan" means utilizing nonintrusive imaging equipment, radiation detection equipment, or both, to capture data, including images of a container.

(13) Screening

The term "screening" means a visual or automated review of information about goods, including manifest or entry documentation accompanying a shipment being imported into the United States, to determine the presence of misdeclared, restricted, or prohibited items and assess the level of threat posed by such cargo.

(14) Search

The term "search" means an intrusive examination in which a container is opened and its contents are devanned and visually inspected for the presence of misdeclared, restricted, or prohibited items.

(15) Secretary

The term "Secretary" means the Secretary of Homeland Security.

(16) Transportation disruption

The term "transportation disruption" means any significant delay, interruption, or stoppage in the flow of trade caused by a natural disaster, heightened threat level, an act of terrorism, or any transportation security incident (as defined in section 70101(6) of title 46).

(17) Transportation security incident

The term "transportation security incident" has the meaning given the term in section 70101(6) of title 46.

(Pub. L. 109–347, §2, Oct. 13, 2006, 120 Stat. 1886.)

REFERENCES IN TEXT

This Act, referred to in text, is Pub. L. 109–347, Oct. 13, 2006, 120 Stat. 1884, known as the Security and Accountability For Every Port Act of 2006 or the SAFE Port Act. For complete classification of this Act to the Code, see Tables.

Section 9503(c) of the Omnibus Budget Reconciliation Act of 1987, referred to in par. (2), is section 9503(c) of title IX of Pub. L. 100–203, which is set out as a note under section 2071 of Title 19, Customs Duties.

SHORT TITLE

Pub. L. 109–347, §1(a), Oct. 13, 2006, 120 Stat. 1884, provided that: "This Act [see Tables for classification] may be cited as the 'Security and Accountability For Every Port Act of 2006' or the 'SAFE Port Act'."

SUBCHAPTER I—SECURITY OF UNITED STATES SEAPORTS

PART A—PORT SECURITY GRANTS; TRAINING AND EXERCISE PROGRAMS

§911. Port Security Training Program

(a) In general

The Secretary, acting through the Under Secretary for Preparedness and in coordination with the Commandant of the Coast Guard, shall establish a Port Security Training Program (referred to in this section as the "Training Program") for the purpose of enhancing the capabilities of each facility required to submit a plan under section 70103(c) of title 46 to prevent, prepare for, respond to, mitigate against, and recover from threatened or actual acts of terrorism, natural disasters, and other emergencies.

(b) Requirements

The Training Program shall provide validated training that—

(1) reaches multiple disciplines, including Federal, State, and local government officials, commercial seaport personnel and management, and governmental and nongovernmental emergency response providers;

(2) provides training at the awareness, performance, and management and planning levels;

(3) utilizes multiple training mediums and methods;

(4) addresses port security topics, including—

(A) facility security plans and procedures, including how security plans and procedures are adjusted when threat levels increase;

(B) facility security force operations and management;

(C) physical security and access control at facilities;

(D) methods of security for preventing and countering cargo theft;

(E) container security;

(F) recognition and detection of weapons, dangerous substances, and devices;

(G) operation and maintenance of security equipment and systems;

(H) security threats and patterns;

(I) security incident procedures, including procedures for communicating with governmental and nongovernmental emergency response providers; and

(J) evacuation procedures;

(5) is consistent with, and supports implementation of, the National Incident Management System, the National Response Plan, the National Infrastructure Protection Plan, the National Preparedness Guidance, the National Preparedness Goal, the National Maritime Transportation Security Plan, and other such national initiatives;

(6) is evaluated against clear and consistent performance measures;

(7) addresses security requirements under facility security plans; and

(8) educates, trains, and involves individuals in neighborhoods around facilities required to submit a plan under section 70103(c) of title 46 on how to observe and report security risks.

(c) Omitted

(d) Consultation

The Secretary shall ensure that, in carrying out the Program, the Office of Grants and Training shall consult with commercial seaport personnel and management.

(e) Training partners

In developing and delivering training under the Training Program, the Secretary, in coordination with the Maritime Administration of the Department of Transportation, and consistent with section 109 of the Maritime Transportation Security Act of 2002 (46 U.S.C. 70101 note), shall—

(1) work with government training facilities, academic institutions, private organizations, employee organizations, and other entities that provide specialized, state-of-the-art training for governmental and nongovernmental emergency responder providers or commercial seaport personnel and management; and

(2) utilize, as appropriate, government training facilities, courses provided by community colleges, public safety academies, State and private universities, and other facilities.

(Pub. L. 109–347, title I, §113, Oct. 13, 2006, 120 Stat. 1895.)

REFERENCES IN TEXT

Section 109 of the Maritime Transportation Security Act of 2002, referred to in subsec. (e), is section 109 of title I of Pub. L. 107–295, which is set out as a note under section 70101 of Title 46, Shipping.

CODIFICATION

Section is comprised of section 113 of Pub. L. 109–347. Subsec. (c) of section 113 of Pub. L. 109–347 amended section 70103 of Title 46, Shipping.

§912. Port Security Exercise Program

(a) In general

The Secretary, acting through the Under Secretary for Preparedness and in coordination with the Commandant of the Coast Guard, shall establish a Port Security Exercise Program (referred to in this section as the "Exercise Program") for the purpose of testing and evaluating the capabilities of Federal, State, local, and foreign governments, commercial seaport personnel and management, governmental and nongovernmental emergency response providers, the private sector, or any other organization or entity, as the Secretary determines to be appropriate, to prevent, prepare for, mitigate against, respond to, and recover from acts of terrorism, natural disasters, and other emergencies at facilities required to submit a plan under section 70103(c) of title 46.

(b) Requirements

The Secretary shall ensure that the Exercise Program—

(1) conducts, on a periodic basis, port security exercises at such facilities that are—

(A) scaled and tailored to the needs of each facility;

(B) live, in the case of the most at-risk facilities;

(C) as realistic as practicable and based on current risk assessments, including credible threats, vulnerabilities, and consequences;

(D) consistent with the National Incident Management System, the National Response Plan, the National Infrastructure Protection Plan, the National Preparedness Guidance, the National Preparedness Goal, the National Maritime Transportation Security Plan, and other such national initiatives;

(E) evaluated against clear and consistent performance measures;

(F) assessed to learn best practices, which shall be shared with appropriate Federal, State, and local officials, commercial seaport personnel and management, governmental and nongovernmental emergency response providers, and the private sector; and

(G) followed by remedial action in response to lessons learned; and

(2) assists State and local governments and facilities in designing, implementing, and evaluating exercises that—

(A) conform to the requirements of paragraph (1); and

(B) are consistent with any applicable Area Maritime Transportation Security Plan and State or Urban Area Homeland Security Plan.

(c) Improvement plan

The Secretary shall establish a port security exercise improvement plan process to—

(1) identify and analyze each port security exercise for lessons learned and best practices;

(2) disseminate lessons learned and best practices to participants in the Exercise Program;

(3) monitor the implementation of lessons learned and best practices by participants in the Exercise Program; and

(4) conduct remedial action tracking and long-term trend analysis.

(Pub. L. 109–347, title I, §114, Oct. 13, 2006, 120 Stat. 1896.)

§913. Facility exercise requirements

The Secretary of the Department in which the Coast Guard is operating shall require each high risk facility to conduct live or full-scale exercises described in section 105.220(c) of title 33, Code of Federal Regulations, not less frequently than once every 2 years, in accordance with the facility security plan required under section 70103(c) of title 46.

(Pub. L. 109–347, title I, §115, Oct. 13, 2006, 120 Stat. 1897.)

PART B—PORT OPERATIONS

§921. Domestic radiation detection and imaging

(a) Scanning containers

Subject to section 1318 of title 19, not later than December 31, 2007, all containers entering the United States through the 22 ports through which the greatest volume of containers enter the United States by vessel shall be scanned for radiation. To the extent practicable, the Secretary shall deploy next generation radiation detection technology.

(b) Strategy

The Secretary shall develop a strategy for the deployment of radiation detection capabilities that includes—

(1) a risk-based prioritization of ports of entry at which radiation detection equipment will be deployed;

(2) a proposed timeline of when radiation detection equipment will be deployed at each port of entry identified under paragraph (1);

(3) the type of equipment to be used at each port of entry identified under paragraph (1), including the joint deployment and utilization of radiation detection equipment and nonintrusive imaging equipment;

(4) standard operating procedures for examining containers with such equipment, including sensor alarming, networking, and communications and response protocols;

(5) operator training plans;

(6) an evaluation of the environmental health and safety impacts of nonintrusive imaging technology and a radiation risk reduction plan, in consultation with the Nuclear Regulatory Commission, the Occupational Safety and Health Administration, and the National Institute for Occupational Safety and Health, that seeks to minimize radiation exposure of workers and the public to levels as low as reasonably achievable;

(7) the policy of the Department for using nonintrusive imaging equipment in tandem with radiation detection equipment; and

(8) a classified annex that—

(A) details plans for covert testing; and

(B) outlines the risk-based prioritization of ports of entry identified under paragraph (1).

(c) Report

Not later than 90 days after October 13, 2006, the Secretary shall submit the strategy developed under subsection (b) to the appropriate congressional committees.

(d) Update

Not later than 180 days after the date of the submission of the report under subsection (c), the Secretary shall provide a more complete evaluation under subsection (b)(6).

(e) Other weapons of mass destruction threats

Not later than 180 days after October 13, 2006, the Secretary shall submit to the appropriate congressional committees a report on the feasibility of, and a strategy for, the development of equipment to detect and prevent shielded nuclear and radiological threat material and chemical, biological, and other weapons of mass destruction from entering the United States.

(f) Standards

The Secretary, acting through the Director for Domestic Nuclear Detection and in collaboration with the National Institute of Standards and Technology, shall publish technical capability standards and recommended standard operating procedures for the use of nonintrusive imaging and radiation detection equipment in the United States. Such standards and procedures—

(1) should take into account relevant standards and procedures utilized by other Federal departments or agencies as well as those developed by international bodies; and

(2) shall not be designed so as to endorse specific companies or create sovereignty conflicts with participating countries.

(g) Implementation

Not later than 3 years after October 13, 2006, the Secretary shall fully implement the strategy developed under subsection (b).

(h) Expansion to other United States ports of entry

(1) In general

As soon as practicable after—

(A) implementation of the program for the examination of containers for radiation at ports of entry described in subsection (a); and

(B) submission of the strategy developed under subsection (b) (and updating, if any, of that strategy under subsection (c)),

but not later than December 31, 2008, the Secretary shall expand the strategy developed under subsection (b), in a manner consistent with the requirements of subsection (b), to provide for the deployment of radiation detection capabilities at all other United States ports of entry not covered by the strategy developed under subsection (b).

(2) Risk assessment

In expanding the strategy under paragraph (1), the Secretary shall identify and assess the risks to those other ports of entry in order to determine what equipment and practices will best mitigate the risks.

(i) Intermodal Rail Radiation Detection Test Center

(1) Establishment

In accordance with subsection (b), and in order to comply with this section, the Secretary shall establish an Intermodal Rail Radiation Detection Test Center (referred to in this subsection as the "Test Center").

(2) Projects

The Secretary shall conduct multiple, concurrent projects at the Test Center to rapidly identify and test concepts specific to the challenges posed by on-dock rail.

(3) Location

The Test Center shall be located within a public port facility at which a majority of the containerized cargo is directly laden from (or unladen to) on-dock, intermodal rail.

(Pub. L. 109–347, title I, §121, Oct. 13, 2006, 120 Stat. 1898.)

§921a. Integration of detection equipment and technologies

(a) Responsibility of Secretary

The Secretary of Homeland Security shall have responsibility for ensuring that domestic chemical, biological, radiological, and nuclear detection equipment and technologies are integrated, as appropriate, with other border security systems and detection technologies.

(b) Report

Not later than 6 months after August 3, 2007, the Secretary shall submit a report to Congress that contains a plan to develop a departmental technology assessment process to determine and certify the technology readiness levels of chemical, biological, radiological, and nuclear detection technologies before the full deployment of such technologies within the United States.

(Pub. L. 110–53, title XI, §1104, Aug. 3, 2007, 121 Stat. 380.)

CODIFICATION

Section was enacted as part of the Implementing Recommendations of the 9/11 Commission Act of 2007, and not as part of the Security and Accountability For Every Port Act of 2006, also known as the SAFE Port Act, which comprises this chapter.

§922. Inspection of car ferries entering from abroad

Not later than 120 days after October 13, 2006, the Secretary, acting through the Commissioner, and in coordination with the Secretary of State and in cooperation with ferry operators and appropriate foreign government officials, shall seek to develop a plan for the inspection of passengers and vehicles before such passengers board, or such vehicles are loaded onto, a ferry bound for a United States facility required to submit a plan under section 70103(c) of title 46.

(Pub. L. 109–347, title I, §122, Oct. 13, 2006, 120 Stat. 1899.)

§923. Random searches of containers

Not later than 1 year after October 13, 2006, the Secretary, acting through the Commissioner, shall develop and implement a plan, utilizing best practices for empirical scientific research design and random sampling, to conduct random searches of containers in addition to any targeted or preshipment inspection of such containers required by law or regulation or conducted under any other program conducted by the Secretary. Nothing in this section shall be construed to mean that implementation of the random sampling plan precludes additional searches of containers not inspected pursuant to the plan.

(Pub. L. 109–347, title I, §123, Oct. 13, 2006, 120 Stat. 1899.)

§924. Threat assessment screening of port truck drivers

Not later than 90 days after October 13, 2006, the Secretary shall implement a threat assessment screening, including name-based checks against terrorist watch lists and immigration status check, for all port truck drivers with access to secure areas of a port who have a commercial driver's license but do not have a current and valid hazardous materials endorsement issued in accordance with section 1572 of title 49, Code of Federal Regulations, that is the same as the threat assessment screening required for facility employees and longshoremen by the Commandant of the Coast Guard under Coast Guard Notice USCG–2006–24189 (Federal Register, Vol. 71, No. 82, Friday, April 28, 2006).

(Pub. L. 109–347, title I, §125, Oct. 13, 2006, 120 Stat. 1900.)

§ 925. Border Patrol unit for United States Virgin Islands

(a) In general

The Secretary may establish at least 1 Border Patrol unit for the United States Virgin Islands.

(b) Report

Not later than 180 days after October 13, 2006, the Secretary shall submit a report to the appropriate congressional committees that includes the schedule, if any, for carrying out subsection (a).

(Pub. L. 109–347, title I, § 126, Oct. 13, 2006, 120 Stat. 1900.)

§ 926. Center of Excellence for Maritime Domain Awareness

(a) Establishment

The Secretary shall establish a university-based Center for Excellence for Maritime Domain Awareness following the merit-review processes and procedures that have been established by the Secretary for selecting university program centers of excellence.

(b) Duties

The Center established under subsection (a) shall—

(1) prioritize its activities based on the "National Plan To Improve Maritime Domain Awareness" published by the Department in October 2005;

(2) recognize the extensive previous and ongoing work and existing competence in the field of maritime domain awareness at numerous academic and research institutions, such as the Naval Postgraduate School;

(3) leverage existing knowledge and continue development of a broad base of expertise within academia and industry in maritime domain awareness; and

(4) provide educational, technical, and analytical assistance to Federal agencies with responsibilities for maritime domain awareness, including the Coast Guard, to focus on the need for interoperability, information sharing, and common information technology standards and architecture.

(Pub. L. 109–347, title I, § 128, Oct. 13, 2006, 120 Stat. 1900.)

SUBCHAPTER II—SECURITY OF THE INTERNATIONAL SUPPLY CHAIN

PART A—GENERAL PROVISIONS

§ 941. Strategic plan to enhance the security of the international supply chain

(a) Strategic plan

The Secretary, in consultation with appropriate Federal, State, local, and tribal government agencies and private sector stakeholders responsible for security matters that affect or relate to the movement of containers through the international supply chain, shall develop, implement, and update, as appropriate, a strategic plan to enhance the security of the international supply chain.

(b) Requirements

The strategic plan required under subsection (a) shall—

(1) describe the roles, responsibilities, and authorities of Federal, State, local, and tribal government agencies and private-sector stakeholders that relate to the security of the movement of containers through the international supply chain;

(2) identify and address gaps and unnecessary overlaps in the roles, responsibilities, or authorities described in paragraph (1);

(3) identify and make recommendations regarding legislative, regulatory, and organizational changes necessary to improve coordination among the entities or to enhance the security of the international supply chain;

(4) provide measurable goals, including objectives, mechanisms, and a schedule, for furthering the security of commercial operations from point of origin to point of destination;

(5) build on available resources and consider costs and benefits;

(6) provide incentives for additional voluntary measures to enhance cargo security, as recommended by the Commissioner;

(7) consider the impact of supply chain security requirements on small- and medium-sized companies;

(8) include a process for sharing intelligence and information with private-sector stakeholders to assist in their security efforts;

(9) identify a framework for prudent and measured response in the event of a transportation security incident involving the international supply chain;

(10) provide protocols for the expeditious resumption of the flow of trade in accordance with section 942 of this title;

(11) consider the linkages between supply chain security and security programs within other systems of movement, including travel security and terrorism finance programs; and

(12) expand upon and relate to existing strategies and plans, including the National Response Plan, the National Maritime Transportation Security Plan, the National Strategy for Maritime Security, and the 8 supporting plans of the Strategy, as required by Homeland Security Presidential Directive 13.

(c) Consultation

In developing protocols under subsection (b)(10), the Secretary shall consult with Federal, State, local, and private sector stakeholders, including the National Maritime Security Advisory Committee and the Commercial Operations Advisory Committee.

(d) Communication

To the extent practicable, the strategic plan developed under subsection (a) shall provide for coordination with, and lines of communication among, appropriate Federal, State, local, and private-sector stakeholders on law enforcement actions, intermodal rerouting plans, and other strategic infrastructure issues resulting from a transportation security incident or transportation disruption.

(e) Utilization of Advisory Committees

As part of the consultations described in subsection (a), the Secretary shall, to the extent practicable, utilize the Homeland Security Advisory Committee, the National Maritime Security Advisory Committee, and the Commercial Operations Advisory Committee to review, as necessary, the draft strategic plan and any subsequent updates to the strategic plan.

(f) International standards and practices

In furtherance of the strategic plan required under subsection (a), the Secretary is encouraged to consider proposed or established standards and practices of foreign governments and international organizations, including the International Maritime Organization, the World Customs Organization, the International Labor Organization, and the International Organization for Standardization, as appropriate, to establish standards and best practices for the security of containers moving through the international supply chain.

(g) Report

(1) Initial report

Not later than 270 days after October 13, 2006, the Secretary shall submit to the appropriate congressional committees a report that contains the strategic plan required by subsection (a).

(2) Final report

Not later than 3 years after the date on which the strategic plan is submitted under paragraph (1), the Secretary shall submit a report to the appropriate congressional committees that contains an update of the strategic plan.

(Pub. L. 109–347, title II, §201, Oct. 13, 2006, 120 Stat. 1901.)

§942. Post-incident resumption of trade

(a) In general

The Secretary shall develop and update, as necessary, protocols for the resumption of trade in accordance with section 941(b)(10) of this title in the event of a transportation disruption or a transportation security incident. The protocols shall include—

(1) the identification of the appropriate initial incident commander, if the Commandant of the Coast Guard is not the appropriate person, and lead departments, agencies, or offices to execute such protocols;

(2) a plan to redeploy resources and personnel, as necessary, to reestablish the flow of trade;

(3) a plan to provide training for the periodic instruction of personnel of the United States Customs and Border Protection, the Coast Guard, and the Transportation Security Administration in trade resumption functions and responsibilities; and

(4) appropriate factors for establishing prioritization of vessels and cargo determined by the President to be critical for response and recovery, including factors relating to public health, national security, and economic need.

(b) Vessels

In determining the prioritization of vessels accessing facilities (as defined under section 70101 of title 46), the Commandant of the Coast Guard may, to the extent practicable and consistent with the protocols and plans required under this section to ensure the safe and secure transit of vessels to ports in the United States after a transportation security incident, give priority to a vessel—

(1) that has an approved security plan under section 70103(c) of title 46 or a valid international ship security certificate, as provided under part 104 of title 33, Code of Federal Regulations;

(2) that is manned by individuals who are described in section 70105(b)(2)(B) of title 46; and

(3) that is operated by validated participants in the Customs-Trade Partnership Against Terrorism program.

(c) Cargo

In determining the prioritization of the resumption of the flow of cargo and consistent with the protocols established under this section, the Commissioner may give preference to cargo—

(1) entering a port of entry directly from a foreign seaport designated under the Container Security Initiative;

(2) from the supply chain of a validated C–TPAT participant and other private sector entities, as appropriate; or

(3) that has undergone—

(A) a nuclear or radiological detection scan;

(B) an x-ray, density, or other imaging scan; and

(C) a system to positively identify the container at the last port of departure prior to arrival in the United States, which data has been evaluated and analyzed by personnel of the United States Customs and Border Protection.

(d) Coordination

The Secretary shall ensure that there is appropriate coordination among the Commandant of the Coast Guard, the Commissioner, and other Federal officials following a maritime disruption or maritime transportation security incident in order to provide for the resumption of trade.

(e) Communication

Consistent with section 941 of this title, the Commandant of the Coast Guard, Commissioner, and other appropriate Federal officials, shall promptly communicate any revised procedures or instructions intended for the private sector following a maritime disruption or maritime transportation security incident.

(Pub. L. 109–347, title II, §202, Oct. 13, 2006, 120 Stat. 1903.)

§943. Automated Targeting System

(a) In general

The Secretary, acting through the Commissioner, shall—

(1) identify and seek the submission of data related to the movement of a shipment of cargo through the international supply chain; and

(2) analyze the data described in paragraph (1) to identify high-risk cargo for inspection.

(b) Requirement

The Secretary, acting through the Commissioner, shall require the electronic transmission to the Department of additional data elements for improved high-risk targeting, including appropriate security elements of entry data, as determined by the Secretary, to be provided as advanced information with respect to cargo destined for importation into the United States prior to loading of such cargo on vessels at foreign seaports.

(c) Consideration

The Secretary, acting through the Commissioner, shall—

(1) consider the cost, benefit, and feasibility of—

(A) requiring additional nonmanifest documentation;

(B) reducing the time period allowed by law for revisions to a container cargo manifest;

(C) reducing the time period allowed by law for submission of certain elements of entry data, for vessel or cargo; and

(D) such other actions the Secretary considers beneficial for improving the information relied upon for the Automated Targeting System and any successor targeting system in furthering the security and integrity of the international supply chain; and

(2) consult with stakeholders, including the Commercial Operations Advisory Committee, and identify to them the need for such information, and the appropriate timing of its submission.

(d) Regulations

The Secretary shall promulgate regulations to carry out this section. In promulgating such regulations, the Secretary shall adhere to the parameters applicable to the development of regulations under section 343(a) of the Trade Act of 2002 (19 U.S.C. 2071 note), including provisions relating to consultation, technology, analysis, use of information, confidentiality, and timing requirements.

(e) System improvements

The Secretary, acting through the Commissioner, shall—

(1) conduct, through an independent panel, a review of the effectiveness and capabilities of the Automated Targeting System;

(2) consider future iterations of the Automated Targeting System, which would incorporate smart features, such as more complex algorithms and real-time intelligence, instead of relying solely on rule sets that are periodically updated;

(3) ensure that the Automated Targeting System has the capability to electronically compare manifest and other available data for cargo entered into or bound for the United States to detect any significant anomalies between such data and facilitate the resolution of such anomalies;

(4) ensure that the Automated Targeting System has the capability to electronically identify, compile, and compare select data elements for cargo entered into or bound for the United States following a maritime transportation security incident, in order to efficiently identify cargo for increased inspection or expeditious release; and

(5) develop a schedule to address the recommendations of the Comptroller General of the United States, the Inspector General of the Department of the Treasury, and the Inspector General of the Department with respect to the operation of the Automated Targeting System.

(f) Secure transmission of certain information

All information required by the Department from supply chain partners shall be transmitted in a secure fashion, as determined by the Secretary, so as to protect the information from unauthorized access.

(g) Authorization of appropriations

There are authorized to be appropriated to the United States Customs and Border Protection to carry out the Automated Targeting System for identifying high-risk oceanborne container cargo for inspection—

(1) $33,200,000 for fiscal year 2008;

(2) $35,700,000 for fiscal year 2009; and

(3) $37,485,000 for fiscal year 2010.

(Pub. L. 109–347, title II, § 203, Oct. 13, 2006, 120 Stat. 1904.)

REFERENCES IN TEXT

Section 343(a) of the Trade Act of 2002, referred to in subsec. (d), is section 343(a) of title III of div. A of Pub. L. 107–210, which is set out as a note under section 2071 of Title 19, Customs Duties.

§ 944. Container security standards and procedures

(a) Establishment

(1) In general

Not later than 90 days after October 13, 2006, the Secretary shall initiate a rulemaking proceeding to establish minimum standards and procedures for securing containers in transit to the United States.

(2) Interim rule

Not later than 180 days after October 13, 2006, the Secretary shall issue an interim final rule pursuant to the proceeding described in paragraph (1).

(3) Missed deadline

If the Secretary is unable to meet the deadline established pursuant to paragraph (2), the Secretary shall submit a letter to the appropriate congressional committees explaining why the Secretary is unable to meet that deadline and describing what must be done before such minimum standards and procedures can be established.

(4) Deadline for enforcement

(A) Enforcement of rule

Not later than 2 years after the date on which the standards and procedures are established pursuant to paragraph (1), all containers bound for ports of entry in the United States shall meet such standards and procedures.

(B) Interim requirement

If the interim final rule described in paragraph (2) is not issued by April 1, 2008, then—

(i) effective not later than October 15, 2008, all containers in transit to the United

States shall be required to meet the requirements of International Organization for Standardization Publicly Available Specification 17712 standard for sealing containers; and

(ii) the requirements of this subparagraph shall cease to be effective upon the effective date of the interim final rule issued pursuant to this subsection.

(b) Review and enhancement

The Secretary shall regularly review and enhance the standards and procedures established pursuant to subsection (a), as appropriate, based on tests of technologies as they become commercially available to detect container intrusion and the highest consequence threats, particularly weapons of mass destruction.

(c) International cargo security standards

The Secretary, in consultation with the Secretary of State, the Secretary of Energy, and other Federal Government officials, as appropriate, and with the Commercial Operations Advisory Committee, the Homeland Security Advisory Committee, and the National Maritime Security Advisory Committee, is encouraged to promote and establish international standards for the security of containers moving through the international supply chain with foreign governments and international organizations, including the International Maritime Organization, the International Organization for Standardization, the International Labor Organization, and the World Customs Organization.

(d) International trade and other obligations

In carrying out this section, the Secretary shall consult with appropriate Federal departments and agencies and private sector stakeholders and ensure that actions under this section do not violate international trade obligations or other international obligations of the United States.

(Pub. L. 109–347, title II, §204, Oct. 13, 2006, 120 Stat. 1905; Pub. L. 110–53, title XVII, §1701(b), Aug. 3, 2007, 121 Stat. 491.)

AMENDMENTS

2007—Subsec. (a)(4). Pub. L. 110–53, which directed amendment of par. (4) by substituting "(1) Deadline for enforcement" and subpar. (A) designation and heading for "(1) Deadline for enforcement", was executed by inserting the subpar. (A) designation and heading before "Not later than" and making no change in the par. designation or heading, to reflect the probable intent of Congress.

Subsec. (a)(4)(B). Pub. L. 110–53, §1701(b)(2), added subpar. (B).

§945. Container Security Initiative

(a) Establishment

The Secretary, acting through the Commissioner, shall establish and implement a program (referred to in this section as the "Container Security Initiative" or "CSI") to identify and examine or search maritime containers that pose a security risk before loading such containers in a foreign port for shipment to the United States, either directly or through a foreign port.

(b) Assessment

The Secretary, acting through the Commissioner, may designate foreign seaports to participate in the Container Security Initiative after the Secretary has assessed the costs, benefits, and other factors associated with such designation, including—

(1) the level of risk for the potential compromise of containers by terrorists, or other threats as determined by the Secretary;

(2) the volume of cargo being imported to the United States directly from, or being transshipped through, the foreign seaport;

(3) the results of the Coast Guard assessments conducted pursuant to section 70108 of title 46;

(4) the commitment of the government of the country in which the foreign seaport is located to cooperating with the Department in sharing critical data and risk management information and to maintain programs to ensure employee integrity; and

(5) the potential for validation of security practices at the foreign seaport by the Department.

(c) Notification

The Secretary shall notify the appropriate congressional committees of the designation of a foreign port under the Container Security Initiative or the revocation of such a designation before notifying the public of such designation or revocation.

(d) Negotiations

The Secretary, in cooperation with the Secretary of State and in consultation with the United States Trade Representative, may enter into negotiations with the government of each foreign nation in which a seaport is designated under the Container Security Initiative to ensure full compliance with the requirements under the Container Security Initiative.

(e) Overseas inspections

(1) Requirements and procedures

The Secretary shall—

(A) establish minimum technical capability criteria and standard operating procedures for the use of nonintrusive inspection and nuclear and radiological detection systems in conjunction with CSI;

(B) require each port designated under CSI to operate nonintrusive inspection and nuclear and radiological detection systems in accordance with the technical capability criteria and standard operating procedures established under subparagraph (A);

(C) continually monitor the technologies, processes, and techniques used to inspect cargo at ports designated under CSI to ensure adherence to such criteria and the use of such procedures; and

(D) consult with the Secretary of Energy in establishing the minimum technical capability criteria and standard operating procedures established under subparagraph (A) pertaining to radiation detection technologies to promote consistency in detection systems at foreign ports designated under CSI.

(2) Constraints

The criteria and procedures established under paragraph (1)(A)—

(A) shall be consistent, as practicable, with relevant standards and procedures utilized by other Federal departments or agencies, or developed by international bodies if the United States consents to such standards and procedures;

(B) shall not apply to activities conducted under the Megaports Initiative of the Department of Energy; and

(C) shall not be designed to endorse the product or technology of any specific company or to conflict with the sovereignty of a country in which a foreign seaport designated under the Container Security Initiative is located.

(f) Savings provision

The authority of the Secretary under this section shall not affect any authority or duplicate any efforts or responsibilities of the Federal Government with respect to the deployment of radiation detection equipment outside of the United States.

(g) Coordination

The Secretary shall—

(1) coordinate with the Secretary of Energy, as necessary, to provide radiation detection equipment required to support the Container Security Initiative through the Department of Energy's Second Line of Defense Program and Megaports Initiative; or

(2) work with the private sector or host governments, when possible, to obtain radiation detection equipment that meets the Department's and the Department of Energy's technical specifications for such equipment.

(h) Staffing

The Secretary shall develop a human capital management plan to determine adequate staffing levels in the United States and in foreign seaports including, as appropriate, the remote location of personnel in countries in which foreign seaports are designated under the Container Security Initiative.

(i) Annual discussions

The Secretary, in coordination with the appropriate Federal officials, shall hold annual discussions with foreign governments of countries in which foreign seaports designated under the Container Security Initiative are located regarding best practices, technical assistance, training needs, and technological developments that will assist in ensuring the efficient and secure movement of international cargo.

(j) Lesser risk port

The Secretary, acting through the Commissioner, may treat cargo loaded in a foreign seaport designated under the Container Security Initiative as presenting a lesser risk than similar cargo loaded in a foreign seaport that is not designated under the Container Security Initiative, for the purpose of clearing such cargo into the United States.

(k) Prohibition

(1) In general

The Secretary shall issue a "do not load" order, using existing authorities, to prevent the onload of any cargo loaded at a port designated under CSI that has been identified as high risk, including by the Automated Targeting System, unless the cargo is determined to no longer be high risk through—

(A) a scan of the cargo with nonintrusive imaging equipment and radiation detection equipment;

(B) a search of the cargo; or

(C) additional information received by the Department.

(2) Rule of construction

Nothing in this subsection shall be construed to interfere with the ability of the Secretary to deny entry of any cargo into the United States.

(*l*) Report

(1) In general

Not later than September 30, 2007, the Secretary, acting through the Commissioner, shall, in consultation with other appropriate government officials and the Commercial Operations Advisory Committee, submit a report to the appropriate congressional committees on the effectiveness of, and the need for any improvements to, the Container Security Initiative. The report shall include—

(A) a description of the technical assistance delivered to, as well as needed at, each designated seaport;

(B) a description of the human capital management plan at each designated seaport;

(C) a summary of the requests made by the United States to foreign governments to conduct physical or nonintrusive inspections of cargo at designated seaports, and whether each such request was granted or denied by the foreign government;

(D) an assessment of the effectiveness of screening, scanning, and inspection protocols and technologies utilized at designated seaports and the effect on the flow of commerce at such seaports, as well as any recommendations for improving the effectiveness of screening, scanning, and inspection protocols and technologies utilized at designated seaports;

(E) a description and assessment of the outcome of any security incident involving a foreign seaport designated under the Container Security Initiative;

(F) the rationale for the continuance of each port designated under CSI;

(G) a description of the potential for remote targeting to decrease the number of personnel who are deployed at foreign ports under CSI; and

(H) a summary and assessment of the aggregate number and extent of trade compliance lapses at each seaport designated under the Container Security Initiative.

(2) Updated report

Not later than September 30, 2010, the Secretary, acting through the Commissioner, shall, in consultation with other appropriate government officials and the Commercial Operations Advisory Committee, submit an updated report to the appropriate congressional committees on the effectiveness of, and the need for any improvements to, the Container Security Initiative. The updated report shall address each of the elements required to be included in the report provided for under paragraph (1).

(m) Authorization of appropriations

There are authorized to be appropriated to the United States Customs and Border Protection to carry out the provisions of this section—

(1) $144,000,000 for fiscal year 2008;

(2) $146,000,000 for fiscal year 2009; and

(3) $153,300,000 for fiscal year 2010.

(Pub. L. 109–347, title II, §205, Oct. 13, 2006, 120 Stat. 1906.)

PART B—CUSTOMS-TRADE PARTNERSHIP AGAINST TERRORISM

§961. Establishment

(a) Establishment

The Secretary, acting through the Commissioner, is authorized to establish a voluntary government-private sector program (to be known as the "Customs–Trade Partnership Against Terrorism" or "C–TPAT") to strengthen and improve the overall security of the international supply chain and United States border security, and to facilitate the movement of secure cargo through the international supply chain, by providing benefits to participants meeting or exceeding the program requirements. Participants in C–TPAT shall include Tier 1 participants, Tier 2 participants, and Tier 3 participants.

(b) Minimum security requirements

The Secretary, acting through the Commissioner, shall review the minimum security requirements of C–TPAT at least once every year and update such requirements as necessary.

(Pub. L. 109–347, title II, §211, Oct. 13, 2006, 120 Stat. 1909.)

§962. Eligible entities

Importers, customs brokers, forwarders, air, sea, land carriers, contract logistics providers, and other entities in the international supply chain and intermodal transportation system are eligible to apply to voluntarily enter into partnerships with the Department under C–TPAT.

(Pub. L. 109–347, title II, §212, Oct. 13, 2006, 120 Stat. 1909.)

§963. Minimum requirements

An applicant seeking to participate in C–TPAT shall—

(1) demonstrate a history of moving cargo in the international supply chain;

(2) conduct an assessment of its supply chain based upon security criteria established by the Secretary, acting through the Commissioner, including—

(A) business partner requirements;

(B) container security;

(C) physical security and access controls;

(D) personnel security;

(E) procedural security;

(F) security training and threat awareness; and

(G) information technology security;

(3) implement and maintain security measures and supply chain security practices meeting security criteria established by the Commissioner; and

(4) meet all other requirements established by the Commissioner, in consultation with the Commercial Operations Advisory Committee.

(Pub. L. 109–347, title II, §213, Oct. 13, 2006, 120 Stat. 1909.)

§964. Tier 1 participants in C–TPAT

(a) Benefits

The Secretary, acting through the Commissioner, shall offer limited benefits to a Tier 1 participant who has been certified in accordance with the guidelines referred to in subsection (b). Such benefits may include a reduction in the score assigned pursuant to the Automated Targeting System of not greater than 20 percent of the high-risk threshold established by the Secretary.

(b) Guidelines

Not later than 180 days after October 13, 2006, the Secretary, acting through the Commissioner, shall update the guidelines for certifying a C–TPAT participant's security measures and supply chain security practices under this section. Such guidelines shall include a background investigation and extensive documentation review.

(c) Timeframe

To the extent practicable, the Secretary, acting through the Commissioner, shall complete the Tier 1 certification process within 90 days of receipt of an application for participation in C–TPAT.

(Pub. L. 109–347, title II, §214, Oct. 13, 2006, 120 Stat. 1910.)

§965. Tier 2 participants in C–TPAT

(a) Validation

The Secretary, acting through the Commissioner, shall validate the security measures and supply chain security practices of a Tier 1 participant in accordance with the guidelines referred to in subsection (c). Such validation shall include on-site assessments at appropriate foreign locations utilized by the Tier 1 participant in its supply chain and shall, to the extent practicable, be completed not later than 1 year after certification as a Tier 1 participant.

(b) Benefits

The Secretary, acting through the Commissioner, shall extend benefits to each C–TPAT participant that has been validated as a Tier 2 participant under this section, which may include—

(1) reduced scores in the Automated Targeting System;

(2) reduced examinations of cargo; and

(3) priority searches of cargo.

(c) Guidelines

Not later than 180 days after October 13, 2006, the Secretary, acting through the Commissioner, shall develop a schedule and update the guidelines for validating a participant's security measures and supply chain security practices under this section.

(Pub. L. 109–347, title II, § 215, Oct. 13, 2006, 120 Stat. 1910.)

§ 966. Tier 3 participants in C–TPAT

(a) In general

The Secretary, acting through the Commissioner, shall establish a third tier of C–TPAT participation that offers additional benefits to participants who demonstrate a sustained commitment to maintaining security measures and supply chain security practices that exceed the guidelines established for validation as a Tier 2 participant in C–TPAT under section 965 of this title.

(b) Criteria

The Secretary, acting through the Commissioner, shall designate criteria for validating a C–TPAT participant as a Tier 3 participant under this section. Such criteria may include—

(1) compliance with any additional guidelines established by the Secretary that exceed the guidelines established pursuant to section 965 of this title for validating a C–TPAT participant as a Tier 2 participant, particularly with respect to controls over access to cargo throughout the supply chain;

(2) submission of additional information regarding cargo prior to loading, as determined by the Secretary;

(3) utilization of container security devices, technologies, policies, or practices that meet standards and criteria established by the Secretary; and

(4) compliance with any other cargo requirements established by the Secretary.

(c) Benefits

The Secretary, acting through the Commissioner, in consultation with the Commercial Operations Advisory Committee and the National Maritime Security Advisory Committee, shall extend benefits to each C–TPAT participant that has been validated as a Tier 3 participant under this section, which may include—

(1) the expedited release of a Tier 3 participant's cargo in destination ports within the United States during all threat levels designated by the Secretary;

(2) further reduction in examinations of cargo;

(3) priority for examinations of cargo; and

(4) further reduction in the risk score assigned pursuant to the Automated Targeting System; and

(5) inclusion in joint incident management exercises, as appropriate.

(d) Deadline

Not later than 2 years after October 13, 2006, the Secretary, acting through the Commissioner, shall designate appropriate criteria pursuant to subsection (b) and provide benefits to validated Tier 3 participants pursuant to subsection (c).

(Pub. L. 109–347, title II, § 216, Oct. 13, 2006, 120 Stat. 1910.)

§ 967. Consequences for lack of compliance

(a) In general

If at any time a C–TPAT participant's security measures and supply chain security practices fail to meet any of the requirements under this part, the Commissioner may deny the participant benefits otherwise available under this part, in whole or in part. The Commissioner shall develop procedures that provide appropriate protections to C–TPAT participants before benefits are revoked. Such procedures may not limit the ability of the Commissioner to take actions to protect the national security of the United States.

(b) False or misleading information

If a C–TPAT participant knowingly provides false or misleading information to the Commissioner during the validation process provided for under this part, the Commissioner shall suspend or expel the participant from C–TPAT for an appropriate period of time. The Commissioner, after the completion of the process under subsection (c), may publish in the Federal Register a list of participants who have been suspended or expelled from C–TPAT pursuant to this subsection, and may make such list available to C–TPAT participants.

(c) Right of appeal

(1) In general

A C–TPAT participant may appeal a decision of the Commissioner pursuant to subsection (a). Such appeal shall be filed with the Secretary not later than 90 days after the date of the decision, and the Secretary shall issue a determination not later than 180 days after the appeal is filed.

(2) Appeals of other decisions

A C–TPAT participant may appeal a decision of the Commissioner pursuant to subsection (b). Such appeal shall be filed with the Secretary not later than 30 days after the date of the decision, and the Secretary shall issue a determination not later than 180 days after the appeal is filed.

(Pub. L. 109–347, title II, § 217, Oct. 13, 2006, 120 Stat. 1911.)

§ 968. Third party validations

(a) Plan

The Secretary, acting through the Commissioner, shall develop a plan to implement a 1-year voluntary pilot program to test and assess the feasibility, costs, and benefits of using third party entities to conduct validations of C–TPAT participants.

(b) Consultations

Not later than 120 days after October 13, 2006, after consulting with private sector stakeholders, including the Commercial Operations Advisory Committee, the Secretary shall submit a report to the appropriate congressional committees on the plan described in subsection (a).

(c) Pilot program

(1) In general

Not later than 1 year after the consultations described in subsection (b), the Secretary shall carry out the 1-year pilot program to conduct validations of C–TPAT participants using third party entities described in subsection (a).

(2) Authority of the Secretary

The decision to validate a C–TPAT participant is solely within the discretion of the Secretary, or the Secretary's designee.

(d) Certification of third party entities

The Secretary shall certify a third party entity to conduct validations under subsection (c) if the entity—

(1) demonstrates to the satisfaction of the Secretary that the entity has the ability to perform validations in accordance with standard operating procedures and requirements designated by the Secretary; and

(2) agrees—

(A) to perform validations in accordance with such standard operating procedures and requirements (and updates to such procedures and requirements); and

(B) to maintain liability insurance coverage at policy limits and in accordance with conditions to be established by the Secretary; and

(3) signs an agreement to protect all proprietary information of C–TPAT participants with respect to which the entity will conduct validations.

(e) Information for establishing limits of liability insurance

A third party entity seeking a certificate under subsection (d) shall submit to the Secretary necessary information for establishing the limits of liability insurance required to be maintained by the entity under this Act.

(f) Additional requirements

The Secretary shall ensure that—

(1) any third party entity certified under this section does not have—

(A) any beneficial interest in or any direct or indirect control over the C–TPAT participant for which the validation services are performed; or

(B) any other conflict of interest with respect to the C–TPAT participant; and

(2) the C–TPAT participant has entered into a contract with the third party entity under which the C–TPAT participant agrees to pay all costs associated with the validation.

(g) Monitoring

(1) In general

The Secretary shall regularly monitor and inspect the operations of a third party entity conducting validations under subsection (c) to ensure that the entity is meeting the minimum standard operating procedures and requirements for the validation of C–TPAT participants established by the Secretary and all other applicable requirements for validation services.

(2) Revocation

If the Secretary determines that a third party entity is not meeting the minimum standard operating procedures and requirements designated by the Secretary under subsection (d)(1), the Secretary shall—

(A) revoke the entity's certificate of conformance issued under subsection (d)(1); and

(B) review any validations conducted by the entity.

(h) Limitation on authority

The Secretary may only grant a C–TPAT validation by a third party entity pursuant to subsection (c) if the C–TPAT participant voluntarily submits to validation by such third party entity.

(i) Report

Not later than 30 days after the completion of the pilot program conducted pursuant to subsection (c), the Secretary shall submit a report to the appropriate congressional committees that contains—

(1) the results of the pilot program, including the extent to which the pilot program ensured sufficient protection for proprietary commercial information;

(2) the cost and efficiency associated with validations under the pilot program;

(3) the impact of the pilot program on the rate of validations conducted under C–TPAT;

(4) any impact on national security of the pilot program; and

(5) any recommendations by the Secretary based upon the results of the pilot program.

(Pub. L. 109–347, title II, §218, Oct. 13, 2006, 120 Stat. 1912.)

REFERENCES IN TEXT

This Act, referred to in subsec. (e), is Pub. L. 109–347, Oct. 13, 2006, 120 Stat. 1884, known as the Security and Accountability For Every Port Act of 2006 or the SAFE Port Act. For complete classification of this Act to the Code, see Tables.

§969. Revalidation

The Secretary, acting through the Commissioner, shall develop and implement—

(1) a revalidation process for Tier 2 and Tier 3 participants;

(2) a framework based upon objective criteria for identifying participants for periodic revalidation not less frequently than once during each 4-year period following the initial validation; and

(3) an annual plan for revalidation that includes—

(A) performance measures;

(B) an assessment of the personnel needed to perform the revalidations; and

(C) the number of participants that will be revalidated during the following year.

(Pub. L. 109–347, title II, §219, Oct. 13, 2006, 120 Stat. 1913.)

§970. Noncontainerized cargo

The Secretary, acting through the Commissioner, shall consider the potential for participation in C–TPAT by importers of noncontainerized cargoes that otherwise meet the requirements under this part.

(Pub. L. 109–347, title II, §220, Oct. 13, 2006, 120 Stat. 1914.)

§971. C–TPAT program management

(a) In general

The Secretary, acting through the Commissioner, shall establish sufficient internal quality controls and record management to support the management systems of C–TPAT. In managing the program, the Secretary shall ensure that the program includes:

(1) Strategic plan

A 5-year plan to identify outcome-based goals and performance measures of the program.

(2) Annual plan

An annual plan for each fiscal year designed to match available resources to the projected workload.

(3) Standardized work program

A standardized work program to be used by agency personnel to carry out the certifications, validations, and revalidations of participants. The Secretary shall keep records and monitor staff hours associated with the completion of each such review.

(b) Documentation of reviews

The Secretary, acting through the Commissioner, shall maintain a record management system to document determinations on the reviews of each C–TPAT participant, including certifications, validations, and revalidations.

(c) Confidential information safeguards

In consultation with the Commercial Operations Advisory Committee, the Secretary, acting through the Commissioner, shall develop and implement procedures to ensure the protection of confidential data collected, stored, or shared with government agencies or as part of the application, certification, validation, and revalidation processes.

(d) Resource management staffing plan

The Secretary, acting through the Commissioner, shall—

(1) develop a staffing plan to recruit and train staff (including a formalized training program) to meet the objectives identified in the strategic plan of the C–TPAT program; and

(2) provide cross-training in postincident trade resumption for personnel who administer the C–TPAT program.

(e) Report to Congress

In connection with the President's annual budget submission for the Department, the Secretary shall report to the appropriate congressional committees on the progress made by the Commissioner to certify, validate, and revalidate C–TPAT participants. Such report shall be due on the same date that the President's budget is submitted to the Congress.

(Pub. L. 109–347, title II, §221, Oct. 13, 2006, 120 Stat. 1914.)

§972. Additional personnel

For fiscal years 2008 and 2009, the Commissioner shall increase by not less than 50 the number of full-time personnel engaged in the validation and revalidation of C–TPAT participants (over the number of such personnel on the last day of the previous fiscal year), and shall provide appropriate training and support to such additional personnel.

(Pub. L. 109–347, title II, §222, Oct. 13, 2006, 120 Stat. 1914.)

§973. Authorization of appropriations

(a) C–TPAT

There are authorized to be appropriated to the United States Customs and Border Protection to carry out the provisions of sections 961 through 971 of this title to remain available until expended—

(1) $65,000,000 for fiscal year 2008;

(2) $72,000,000 for fiscal year 2009; and

(3) $75,600,000 for fiscal year 2010.

(b) Additional personnel

In addition to any amounts otherwise appropriated to the United States Customs and Border Protection, there are authorized to be appropriated for the purpose of meeting the staffing requirement provided for in section 972 of this title, to remain available until expended—

(1) $8,500,000 for fiscal year 2008;

(2) $17,600,000 for fiscal year 2009;

(3) $19,000,000 for fiscal year 2010;

(4) $20,000,000 for fiscal year 2011; and

(5) $21,000,000 for fiscal year 2012.

(Pub. L. 109–347, title II, §223, Oct. 13, 2006, 120 Stat. 1915.)

PART C—MISCELLANEOUS PROVISIONS

§981. Pilot integrated scanning system

(a) Designations

Not later than 90 days after October 13, 2006, the Secretary shall designate 3 foreign seaports through which containers pass or are transshipped to the United States for the establishment of pilot integrated scanning systems that couple nonintrusive imaging equipment and radiation detection equipment. In making the designations under this subsection, the Secretary shall consider 3 distinct ports with unique features and differing levels of trade volume.

(b) Coordination

The Secretary shall—

(1) coordinate with the Secretary of Energy, as necessary, to provide radiation detection equipment through the Department of Energy's Second Line of Defense and Megaports programs; or

(2) work with the private sector or, when possible, host governments to obtain radiation detection equipment that meets both the Department's and the Department of Energy's technical specifications for such equipment.

(c) Pilot system implementation

Not later than 1 year after October 13, 2006, the Secretary shall achieve a full-scale implementation of the pilot integrated scanning system at the ports designated under subsection (a), which—

(1) shall scan all containers destined for the United States that are loaded in such ports;

(2) shall electronically transmit the images and information to appropriate United States Government personnel in the country in which the port is located or in the United States for evaluation and analysis;

(3) shall resolve every radiation alarm according to established Department procedures;

(4) shall utilize the information collected to enhance the Automated Targeting System or other relevant programs;

(5) shall store the information for later retrieval and analysis; and

(6) may provide an automated notification of questionable or high-risk cargo as a trigger for further inspection by appropriately trained personnel.

(d) Report

Not later than 180 days after achieving full-scale implementation under subsection (c), the Secretary, in consultation with the Secretary of State and, as appropriate, the Secretary of Energy, shall submit a report to the appropriate congressional committees, that includes—

(1) an evaluation of the lessons derived from the pilot system implemented under this subsection;

(2) an analysis of the efficacy of the Automated Targeting System or other relevant programs in utilizing the images captured to examine high-risk containers;

(3) an evaluation of the effectiveness of the integrated scanning system in detecting shielded and unshielded nuclear and radiological material;

(4) an evaluation of software and other technologies that are capable of automatically identifying potential anomalies in scanned containers; and

(5) an analysis of the need and feasibility of expanding the integrated scanning system to other container security initiative ports, including—

(A) an analysis of the infrastructure requirements;

(B) a projection of the effect on current average processing speed of containerized cargo;

(C) an evaluation of the scalability of the system to meet both current and future forecasted trade flows;

(D) the ability of the system to automatically maintain and catalog appropriate data for reference and analysis in the event of a transportation disruption;

(E) an analysis of requirements, including costs, to install and maintain an integrated scanning system;

(F) the ability of administering personnel to efficiently manage and utilize the data produced by a nonintrusive scanning system;

(G) the ability to safeguard commercial data generated by, or submitted to, a non-intrusive scanning system; and

(H) an assessment of the reliability of currently available technology to implement an integrated scanning system.

(Pub. L. 109–347, title II, §231, Oct. 13, 2006, 120 Stat. 1915.)

§981a. Pilot integrated scanning system

(a) Designations

(1) In general

Not later than 90 days after October 4, 2006, the Secretary of Homeland Security (referred to in this section as the "Secretary") shall designate three foreign seaports through which containers pass or are transshipped to the United States to pilot an integrated scanning system that couples nonintrusive imaging equipment and radiation detection equipment, which may be provided by the Megaports Initiative of the Department of Energy. In making designations under this subsection, the Secretary shall consider three distinct ports with unique features and differing levels of trade volume.

(2) Collaboration and cooperation

The Secretary shall collaborate with the Secretary of Energy and cooperate with the private sector and host foreign government to implement the pilot program under this subsection.

(b) Implementation

Not later than one year after October 4, 2006, the Secretary shall achieve a full-scale implementation of the pilot integrated screening system, which shall—

(1) scan all containers destined for the United States that transit through the terminal;

(2) electronically transmit the images and information to the container security initiative personnel in the host country and/or Customs and Border Protection personnel in the United States for evaluation and analysis;

(3) resolve every radiation alarm according to established Department procedures;

(4) utilize the information collected to enhance the Automated Targeting System or other relevant programs; and

(5) store the information for later retrieval and analysis.

(c) Evaluation

The Secretary shall evaluate the pilot program in subsection (b) to determine whether such a system—

(1) has a sufficiently low false alarm rate for use in the supply chain;

(2) is capable of being deployed and operated at ports overseas, including consideration of cost, personnel, and infrastructure required to operate the system;

(3) is capable of integrating, where necessary, with existing systems;

(4) does not significantly impact trade capacity and flow of cargo at foreign or United States ports; and

(5) provides an automated notification of questionable or high-risk cargo as a trigger for further inspection by appropriately trained personnel.

(d) Report

Not later than 120 days after achieving full-scale implementation under subsection (b), the Secretary, in consultation with the Secretary of Energy and the Secretary of State, shall submit a report, to the appropriate congressional committees, that includes—

(1) an evaluation of the lessons derived from the pilot program implemented under this section;

(2) an analysis of the efficacy of the Automated Targeted System or other relevant programs in utilizing the images captured to examine high-risk containers;

(3) an evaluation of software that is capable of automatically identifying potential anomalies in scanned containers; and

(4) a plan and schedule to expand the integrated scanning system developed under this section to other container security initiative ports.

(e) Implementation

If the Secretary determines the available technology meets the criteria outlined in subsection (c), the Secretary, in cooperation with the Secretary of State, shall seek to secure the cooperation of foreign governments to initiate and maximize the use of such technology at foreign ports to scan all cargo bound for the United States as quickly as possible.

(Pub. L. 109–295, title V, §558, Oct. 4, 2006, 120 Stat. 1392.)

CODIFICATION

Section was enacted as part of the Department of Homeland Security Appropriations Act, 2007, and not as part of the Security and Accountability For Every Port Act of 2006, also known as the SAFE Port Act, which comprises this chapter.

§ 982. Screening and scanning of cargo containers

(a) One hundred percent screening of cargo containers and 100 percent scanning of high-risk containers

(1) Screening of cargo containers

The Secretary shall ensure that 100 percent of the cargo containers originating outside the United States and unloaded at a United States seaport undergo a screening to identify high-risk containers.

(2) Scanning of high-risk containers

The Secretary shall ensure that 100 percent of the containers that have been identified as high-risk under paragraph (1), or through other means, are scanned or searched before such containers leave a United States seaport facility.

(b) Full-scale implementation

(1) In general

A container that was loaded on a vessel in a foreign port shall not enter the United States (either directly or via a foreign port) unless the container was scanned by nonintrusive imaging equipment and radiation detection equipment at a foreign port before it was loaded on a vessel.

(2) Application

Paragraph (1) shall apply with respect to containers loaded on a vessel in a foreign country on or after the earlier of—

(A) July 1, 2012; or

(B) such other date as may be established by the Secretary under paragraph (3).

(3) Establishment of earlier deadline

The Secretary shall establish a date under (2)(B)[1] pursuant to the lessons learned through the pilot integrated scanning systems established under section 981 of this title.

(4) Extensions

The Secretary may extend the date specified in paragraph (2)(A) or (2)(B) for 2 years, and may renew the extension in additional 2-year increments, for containers loaded in a port or ports, if the Secretary certifies to Congress that at least two of the following conditions exist:

(A) Systems to scan containers in accordance with paragraph (1) are not available for purchase and installation.

(B) Systems to scan containers in accordance with paragraph (1) do not have a sufficiently low false alarm rate for use in the supply chain.

(C) Systems to scan containers in accordance with paragraph (1) cannot be purchased, deployed, or operated at ports overseas, including, if applicable, because a port does not have the physical characteristics to install such a system.

(D) Systems to scan containers in accordance with paragraph (1) cannot be integrated, as necessary, with existing systems.

(E) Use of systems that are available to scan containers in accordance with paragraph (1) will significantly impact trade capacity and the flow of cargo.

(F) Systems to scan containers in accordance with paragraph (1) do not adequately provide an automated notification of questionable or high-risk cargo as a trigger for further inspection by appropriately trained personnel.

(5) Exemption for military cargo

Notwithstanding any other provision in the section, supplies bought by the Secretary of Defense and transported in compliance section 2631 of title 10 and military cargo of foreign countries are exempt from the requirements of this section.

(6) Report on extensions

An extension under paragraph (4) for a port or ports shall take effect upon the expiration of the 60-day period beginning on the date the Secretary provides a report to Congress that—

(A) states what container traffic will be affected by the extension;

(B) provides supporting evidence to support the Secretary's certification of the basis for the extension; and

(C) explains what measures the Secretary is taking to ensure that scanning can be implemented as early as possible at the port or ports that are the subject of the report.

(7) Report on renewal of extension

If an extension under paragraph (4) takes effect, the Secretary shall, after one year, submit a report to Congress on whether the Secretary expects to seek to renew the extension.

---

[1] So in original. Probably should be "paragraph (2)(B)".

(8) Scanning technology standards

In implementing paragraph (1), the Secretary shall—

(A) establish technological and operational standards for systems to scan containers;

(B) ensure that the standards are consistent with the global nuclear detection architecture developed under the Homeland Security Act of 2002 [6 U.S.C. 101 et seq.]; and

(C) coordinate with other Federal agencies that administer scanning or detection programs at foreign ports.

(9) International trade and other obligations

In carrying out this subsection, the Secretary shall consult with appropriate Federal departments and agencies and private sector stakeholders, and ensure that actions under this section do not violate international trade obligations, and are consistent with the World Customs Organization framework, or other international obligations of the United States.

(c) Report

Not later than 6 months after the submission of a report under section 981(d) of this title, and every 6 months thereafter, the Secretary shall submit a report to the appropriate congressional committees describing the status of full-scale deployment under subsection (b) and the cost of deploying the system at each foreign port at which the integrated scanning systems are deployed.

(Pub. L. 109–347, title II, §232, Oct. 13, 2006, 120 Stat. 1916; Pub. L. 110–53, title XVII, §1701(a), Aug. 3, 2007, 121 Stat. 489.)

REFERENCES IN TEXT

The Homeland Security Act of 2002, referred to in subsec. (b)(8)(B), is Pub. L. 107–296, Nov. 25, 2002, 116 Stat. 2135, which is classified principally to chapter 1 (§101 et seq.) of this title. For complete classification of this Act to the Code, see Short Title note set out under section 101 of this title and Tables.

AMENDMENTS

2007—Subsec. (b). Pub. L. 110–53 reenacted heading without change and amended text of subsec. (b) generally. Prior to amendment, text related to full deployment of an integrated scanning system after the Secretary had determined that such system had met section 981(c) requirements, had a sufficiently low false alarm rate, was capable of being deployed overseas, was capable of integrating with existing systems, would not significantly impact trade flow, and had provided for automated notification of high-risk cargo.

§983. Inspection technology and training

(1) In general

The Secretary, in coordination with the Secretary of State, the Secretary of Energy, and appropriate representatives of other Federal agencies, may provide technical assistance, equipment, and training to facilitate the implementation of supply chain security measures at ports designated under the Container Security Initiative.

(2) Acquisition and training

Unless otherwise prohibited by law, the Secretary may—

(A) lease, loan, provide, or otherwise assist in the deployment of nonintrusive inspection and radiation detection equipment at foreign land and sea ports under such terms and conditions as the Secretary prescribes, including nonreimbursable loans or the transfer of ownership of equipment; and

(B) provide training and technical assistance for domestic or foreign personnel responsible for operating or maintaining such equipment.

(Pub. L. 109–347, title II, §233(a), Oct. 13, 2006, 120 Stat. 1917.)

§984. Pilot program to improve the security of empty containers

(a) In general

The Secretary shall conduct a 1-year pilot program to assess the risk posed by and improve the security of empty containers at United States seaports to ensure the safe and secure delivery of cargo and to prevent potential acts of terrorism involving such containers. The pilot program shall include the use of visual searches of empty containers at United States seaports.

(b) Report

Not later than 90 days after the completion of the pilot program under paragraph (1), the Secretary shall prepare and submit to the appropriate congressional committees a report that contains—

(1) the results of the pilot program; and

(2) the determination of the Secretary on whether to expand the pilot program.

(Pub. L. 109–347, title II, §235, Oct. 13, 2006, 120 Stat. 1919.)

§985. Information sharing relating to supply chain security cooperation

(a) Purposes

The purposes of this section are—

(1) to establish continuing liaison and to provide for supply chain security cooperation between Department and the private sector; and

(2) to provide for regular and timely interchange of information between the private sector and the Department concerning developments and security risks in the supply chain environment.

(b) System

The Secretary shall develop a system to collect from and share appropriate risk information related to the supply chain with the private sector entities determined appropriate by the Secretary.

(c) Consultation

In developing the system under subsection (b), the Secretary shall consult with the Commercial Operations Advisory Committee and a broad range of public and private sector entities likely to utilize the system, including importers, exporters, carriers, customs brokers, and freight forwarders, among other parties.

(d) Independently obtained information

Nothing in this section shall be construed to limit or otherwise affect the ability of a Federal, State, or local government entity, under applicable law, to obtain supply chain security information, including any information lawfully and properly disclosed generally or broadly to the public and to use such information in any manner permitted by law.

(e) Authority to issue warnings

The Secretary may provide advisories, alerts, and warnings to relevant companies, targeted sectors, other governmental entities, or the general public regarding potential risks to the supply chain as appropriate. In issuing a warning, the Secretary shall take appropriate actions to protect from disclosure—

(1) the source of any voluntarily submitted supply chain security information that forms the basis for the warning; and

(2) information that is proprietary, business sensitive, relates specifically to the submitting person or entity, or is otherwise not appropriately in the public domain.

(Pub. L. 109–347, title II, § 236, Oct. 13, 2006, 120 Stat. 1919.)

SUBCHAPTER III—ADMINISTRATION

§ 1001. Designation of liaison office of Department of State

The Secretary of State shall designate a liaison office within the Department of State to assist the Secretary, as appropriate, in negotiating cargo security-related international agreements.

(Pub. L. 109–347, title III, § 301(b), Oct. 13, 2006, 120 Stat. 1920.)

RULE OF CONSTRUCTION

Nothing in this section to be construed to affect the authorities, functions, or capabilities of the Coast Guard to perform its missions or the requirement under section 468 of this title that those authorities, functions, and capabilities be maintained intact, see section 301(c) of Pub. L. 109–347, set out as a note under section 239 of this title.

§ 1002. Homeland Security Science and Technology Advisory Committee

The Under Secretary for Science and Technology shall utilize the Homeland Security Science and Technology Advisory Committee, as appropriate, to provide outside expertise in advancing cargo security technology.

(Pub. L. 109–347, title III, § 302(c), Oct. 13, 2006, 120 Stat. 1921.)

§ 1003. Research, development, test, and evaluation efforts in furtherance of maritime and cargo security

(a) In general

The Secretary shall—

(1) direct research, development, testing, and evaluation efforts in furtherance of maritime and cargo security;

(2) coordinate with public and private sector entities to develop and test technologies, and process innovations in furtherance of these objectives; and

(3) evaluate such technologies.

(b) Coordination

The Secretary, in coordination with the Under Secretary for Science and Technology, the Assistant Secretary for Policy, the Commandant of the Coast Guard, the Director for Domestic Nuclear Detection, the Chief Financial Officer, and the heads of other appropriate offices or entities of the Department, shall ensure that—

(1) research, development, testing, and evaluation efforts funded by the Department in furtherance of maritime and cargo security are coordinated within the Department and with other appropriate Federal agencies to avoid duplication of efforts; and

(2) the results of such efforts are shared throughout the Department and with other Federal, State, and local agencies, as appropriate.

(Pub. L. 109–347, title III, § 303, Oct. 13, 2006, 120 Stat. 1921.)

CHAPTER 4—TRANSPORTATION SECURITY

SUBCHAPTER I—TRANSPORTATION SECURITY PLANNING AND INFORMATION SHARING

SUBCHAPTER II—TRANSPORTATION SECURITY ENHANCEMENTS

SUBCHAPTER III—PUBLIC TRANSPORTATION SECURITY

SUBCHAPTER IV—SURFACE TRANSPORTATION SECURITY

PART A—GENERAL PROVISIONS

PART B—RAILROAD SECURITY

SUBCHAPTER I—TRANSPORTATION SECURITY PLANNING AND INFORMATION SHARING

§ 1101. Definitions

For purposes of this subchapter, the following terms apply:

(1) Department

The term "Department" means the Department of Homeland Security.

(2) Secretary

The term "Secretary" means the Secretary of Homeland Security.

(Pub. L. 110–53, title XII, §1201, Aug. 3, 2007, 121 Stat. 381.)

REFERENCES IN TEXT

This subchapter, referred to in text, was in the original "this title", meaning title XII of Pub. L. 110–53, Aug. 3, 2007, 121 Stat. 381, which enacted this subchapter, amended section 114 of Title 49, Transportation, and enacted provisions set out as a note under section 114 of Title 49. For complete classification of title XII to the Code, see Tables.

SHORT TITLE

Pub. L. 110–53, title XIV, §1401, Aug. 3, 2007, 121 Stat. 400, provided that: "This title [enacting subchapter III of this chapter] may be cited as the 'National Transit Systems Security Act of 2007'."

EX. ORD. NO. 13416. STRENGTHENING SURFACE TRANSPORTATION SECURITY

Ex. Ord. No. 13416, Dec. 5, 2006, 71 F.R. 71033, provided:

By the authority vested in me as President by the Constitution and the laws of the United States of America, and to strengthen the security of the Nation's surface transportation systems and thereby enhance the protection of the people, property, and territory of the United States of America against terrorist attacks, it is hereby ordered as follows:

SECTION 1. *Policy*. The security of our Nation's surface transportation systems is a national priority, vital to our economy, and essential to the security of our Nation. Federal, State, local, and tribal governments, the private sector, and the public share responsibility for the security of surface transportation. It is the policy of the United States to protect the people, property, and territory of the United States by facilitating the implementation of a comprehensive, coordinated, and efficient security program to protect surface transportation systems within and adjacent to the United States against terrorist attacks.

SEC. 2. *Definitions*. For purposes of this order:

(a) "agencies" means those executive departments enumerated in 5 U.S.C. 101, independent establishments as defined by 5 U.S.C. 104(1), government corporations as defined by 5 U.S.C. 103(1), and the United States Postal Service;

(b) "Secretary" means the Secretary of Homeland Security;

(c) "security guideline" means any security-related guidance that the Secretary recommends, for implementation on a voluntary basis, to enhance the security of surface transportation;

(d) "security requirement" means any "regulatory action" as defined in section 3 of Executive Order 12866 of September 30, 1993, as amended (Regulatory Planning and Review), including security directives when appropriate, to implement measures to enhance the security of surface transportation;

(e) "surface transportation modes" means mass transit, commuter and long-distance passenger rail, freight rail, commercial vehicles (including intercity buses), and pipelines, and related infrastructure (including roads and highways), that are within the territory of the United States, but does not include electric grids; and

(f) "surface transportation" means any conveyance of people, goods, or commodities using one or more surface transportation modes.

SEC. 3. *Functions of the Secretary of Homeland Security*. The Secretary is the principal Federal official responsible for infrastructure protection activities for surface transportation. To implement the policy set forth in section 1 of this order, the Secretary shall, consistent with the National Infrastructure Protection Plan (NIPP), in coordination with the Secretary of Transportation, and in consultation with the heads of other relevant agencies:

(a) assess the security of each surface transportation mode and evaluate the effectiveness and efficiency of current Federal Government surface transportation security initiatives;

(b) building upon current security initiatives, not later than December 31, 2006, develop a comprehensive transportation systems sector specific plan, as defined in the NIPP;

(c) not later than 90 days after the comprehensive transportation systems sector specific plan is completed, develop an annex to such plan that addresses each surface transportation mode, which shall also include, at a minimum—

(i) an identification of existing security guidelines and security requirements and any security gaps, a description of how the transportation systems sector specific plan will be implemented for such mode, and the respective roles, responsibilities, and authorities of Federal, State, local, and tribal governments and the private sector;

(ii) schedules and protocols for annual reviews of the effectiveness of surface transportation security-related information sharing mechanisms in bringing about the timely exchange of surface transportation security information among Federal, State, local, and tribal governments and the private sector, as appropriate; and

(iii) a process for assessing (A) compliance with any security guidelines and security requirements issued by the Secretary for surface transportation, and (B) the need for revision of such guidelines and requirements to ensure their continuing effectiveness;

(d) in consultation with State, local, and tribal government officials and the private sector, not later than 180 days after the date of this order, identify surface transportation modes, or components thereof, that are subject to high risk of terrorist attack, draft appropriate security guidelines or security requirements to mitigate such risks, and ensure that, prior to their issuance, draft security requirements are transmitted to the Office of Management and Budget for review in accordance with Executive Order 12866 and draft security guidelines receive appropriate interagency review;

(e) develop, implement, and lead a process, in collaboration with other agencies, State, local, and tribal governments, and the private sector, as appropriate, to coordinate research, development, testing, and evaluation of technologies (including alternative uses for commercial off-the-shelf technologies and products) relating to the protection of surface transportation, including—

(i) determining product and technology needs to inform the requirements for and prioritization of research, development, testing, and evaluation, based on the security guidelines and security requirements developed pursuant to subsection (c) of this section and evolving terrorist threats to the security of surface transportation;

(ii) collecting information on existing and planned research, development, testing, and evaluation efforts; and

(iii) not later than 180 days after the date of this order, consistent with section 313 of the Homeland Security Act of 2002, as amended (6 U.S.C. 193), establishing and making available to Federal, State, local, and tribal government entities, and private sector owners and operators of surface transportation systems, lists of available technologies and products relating to the protection of surface transportation; and

(f) use security grants authorized by law to assist in implementing security requirements and security guidelines issued pursuant to law and consistent with subsection (c) of this section.

SEC. 4. *Duties of Heads of Other Agencies.* Heads of agencies, as appropriate, shall provide such assistance and information as the Secretary may request to implement this order.

SEC. 5. *General Provisions.* This order:

(a) shall be implemented consistent with applicable law and the authorities of agencies, or heads of agencies, vested by law, and subject to the availability of appropriations;

(b) shall not be construed to impair or otherwise affect the functions of the Director of the Office of Management and Budget relating to budget, administrative, and legislative proposals; and

(c) is not intended to, and does not, create any rights or benefits, substantive or procedural, enforceable at law or in equity by a party against the United States, its agencies, instrumentalities, or entities, its officers, employees, or agents, or any other person.

GEORGE W. BUSH.

§ 1102. National Domestic Preparedness Consortium

(a) In general

The Secretary is authorized to establish, operate, and maintain a National Domestic Preparedness Consortium within the Department.

(b) Members

Members of the National Domestic Preparedness Consortium shall consist of—

(1) the Center for Domestic Preparedness;

(2) the National Energetic Materials Research and Testing Center, New Mexico Institute of Mining and Technology;

(3) the National Center for Biomedical Research and Training, Louisiana State University;

(4) the National Emergency Response and Rescue Training Center, Texas A&M University;

(5) the National Exercise, Test, and Training Center, Nevada Test Site;

(6) the Transportation Technology Center, Incorporated, in Pueblo, Colorado; and

(7) the National Disaster Preparedness Training Center, University of Hawaii.

(c) Duties

The National Domestic Preparedness Consortium shall identify, develop, test, and deliver training to State, local, and tribal emergency response providers, provide on-site and mobile training at the performance and management and planning levels, and facilitate the delivery of training by the training partners of the Department.

(d) Authorization of appropriations

There are authorized to be appropriated to the Secretary—

(1) for the Center for Domestic Preparedness—

(A) $57,000,000 for fiscal year 2008;

(B) $60,000,000 for fiscal year 2009;

(C) $63,000,000 for fiscal year 2010; and

(D) $66,000,000 for fiscal year 2011; and

(2) for the National Energetic Materials Research and Testing Center, the National Center for Biomedical Research and Training, the National Emergency Response and Rescue Training Center, the National Exercise, Test, and Training Center, the Transportation Technology Center, Incorporated, and the National Disaster Preparedness Training Center each—

(A) $22,000,000 for fiscal year 2008;

(B) $23,000,000 for fiscal year 2009;

(C) $24,000,000 for fiscal year 2010; and

(D) $25,500,000 for fiscal year 2011.

(e) Savings provision

From the amounts appropriated pursuant to this section, the Secretary shall ensure that future amounts provided to each of the following entities are not less than the amounts provided to each such entity for participation in the Consortium in fiscal year 2007—

(1) the Center for Domestic Preparedness;

(2) the National Energetic Materials Research and Testing Center, New Mexico Institute of Mining and Technology;

(3) the National Center for Biomedical Research and Training, Louisiana State University;

(4) the National Emergency Response and Rescue Training Center, Texas A&M University; and

(5) the National Exercise, Test, and Training Center, Nevada Test Site.

(Pub. L. 110–53, title XII, § 1204, Aug. 3, 2007, 121 Stat. 386.)

§ 1103. National Transportation Security Center of Excellence

(a) Establishment

The Secretary shall establish a National Transportation Security Center of Excellence to conduct research and education activities, and to develop or provide professional security training, including the training of transportation employees and transportation professionals.

(b) Designation

The Secretary shall select one of the institutions identified in subsection (c) as the lead institution responsible for coordinating the National Transportation Security Center of Excellence.

(c) Member institutions

(1) Consortium

The institution of higher education selected under subsection (b) shall execute agreements with the other institutions of higher education identified in this subsection and other institutions designated by the Secretary to develop a consortium to assist in accomplishing the goals of the Center.

(2) Members

The National Transportation Security Center of Excellence shall consist of—

(A) Texas Southern University in Houston, Texas;

(B) the National Transit Institute at Rutgers, The State University of New Jersey;

(C) Tougaloo College;

(D) the Connecticut Transportation Institute at the University of Connecticut;

(E) the Homeland Security Management Institute, Long Island University;

(F) the Mack-Blackwell National Rural Transportation Study Center at the University of Arkansas; and

(G) any additional institutions or facilities designated by the Secretary.

(3) Certain inclusions

To the extent practicable, the Secretary shall ensure that an appropriate number of any additional consortium colleges or universities designated by the Secretary under this subsection are Historically Black Colleges and Universities, Hispanic Serving Institutions, and Indian Tribally Controlled Colleges and Universities.

(d) Authorization of appropriations

There are authorized to be appropriated to carry out this section—

(1) $18,000,000 for fiscal year 2008;

(2) $18,000,000 for fiscal year 2009;

(3) $18,000,000 for fiscal year 2010; and

(4) $18,000,000 for fiscal year 2011.

(Pub. L. 110–53, title XII, § 1205, Aug. 3, 2007, 121 Stat. 387.)

§ 1104. Immunity for reports of suspected terrorist activity or suspicious behavior and response

(a) Immunity for reports of suspected terrorist activity or suspicious behavior

(1) In general

Any person who, in good faith and based on objectively reasonable suspicion, makes, or causes to be made, a voluntary report of covered activity to an authorized official shall be immune from civil liability under Federal, State, and local law for such report.

(2) False reports

Paragraph (1) shall not apply to any report that the person knew to be false or was made with reckless disregard for the truth at the time that person made that report.

(b) Immunity for response

(1) In general

Any authorized official who observes, or receives a report of, covered activity and takes reasonable action in good faith to respond to such activity shall have qualified immunity from civil liability for such action, consistent with applicable law in the relevant jurisdiction. An authorized official as defined by subsection (d)(1)(A) not entitled to assert the defense of qualified immunity shall nevertheless be immune from civil liability under Federal, State, and local law if such authorized official takes reasonable action, in good faith, to respond to the reported activity.

(2) Savings clause

Nothing in this subsection shall affect the ability of any authorized official to assert any defense, privilege, or immunity that would otherwise be available, and this subsection shall not be construed as affecting any such defense, privilege, or immunity.

(c) Attorney fees and costs

Any person or authorized official found to be immune from civil liability under this section shall be entitled to recover from the plaintiff all reasonable costs and attorney fees.

(d) Definitions

In this section:

(1) Authorized official

The term "authorized official" means—

(A) any employee or agent of a passenger transportation system or other person with responsibilities relating to the security of such systems;

(B) any officer, employee, or agent of the Department of Homeland Security, the Department of Transportation, or the Department of Justice with responsibilities relating to the security of passenger transportation systems; or

(C) any Federal, State, or local law enforcement officer.

(2) Covered activity

The term "covered activity" means any suspicious transaction, activity, or occurrence that involves, or is directed against, a passenger transportation system or vehicle or its passengers indicating that an individual may be engaging, or preparing to engage, in a violation of law relating to—

(A) a threat to a passenger transportation system or passenger safety or security; or

(B) an act of terrorism (as that term is defined in section 3077 of title 18).

(3) Passenger transportation

The term "passenger transportation" means—

(A) public transportation, as defined in section 5302 of title 49;

(B) over-the-road bus transportation, as defined in subchapter IV, and school bus transportation;

(C) intercity passenger rail[1] transportation[2] as defined in section 24102 of title 49;

(D) the transportation of passengers onboard a passenger vessel[2] as defined in section 2101 of title 46;

(E) other regularly scheduled waterborne transportation service of passengers by vessel of at least 20 gross tons; and

(F) air transportation, as defined in section 40102 of title 49, of passengers.

(4) Passenger transportation system

The term "passenger transportation system" means an entity or entities organized to provide passenger transportation using vehicles, including the infrastructure used to provide such transportation.

(5) Vehicle

The term "vehicle" has the meaning given to that term in section 1992(16)[3] of title 18.

(e) Effective date

This section shall take effect on October 1, 2006, and shall apply to all activities and claims occurring on or after such date.

(Pub. L. 110–53, title XII, §1206, Aug. 3, 2007, 121 Stat. 388.)

REFERENCES IN TEXT

Subchapter IV, referred to in subsec. (d)(3)(B), was in the original "title XV of this Act", meaning title XV of Pub. L. 110–53, Aug. 3, 2007, 121 Stat. 422, which is classified principally to subchapter IV (§1151 et seq.) of this chapter. For complete classification of title XV to the Code, see References in Text note set out under section 1151 of this title and Tables.

SUBCHAPTER II—TRANSPORTATION SECURITY ENHANCEMENTS

§1111. Definitions

For purposes of this subchapter, the following terms apply:

(1) Appropriate congressional committees

The term "appropriate congressional committees" means the Committee on Commerce, Science, and Transportation, the Committee on Banking, Housing, and Urban Affairs, and the Committee on Homeland Security and Governmental Affairs of the Senate and the Committee on Homeland Security and the Committee on Transportation and Infrastructure of the House of Representatives.

(2) Department

The term "Department" means the Department of Homeland Security.

(3) Secretary

The term "Secretary" means the Secretary of Homeland Security.

(4) State

The term "State" means any one of the 50 States, the District of Columbia, Puerto Rico, the Northern Mariana Islands, the Virgin Islands, Guam, American Samoa, and any other territory or possession of the United States.

(5) Terrorism

The term "terrorism" has the meaning that term has in section 101 of this title.

(6) United States

The term "United States" means the 50 States, the District of Columbia, Puerto Rico, the Northern Mariana Islands, the Virgin Islands, Guam, American Samoa, and any other territory or possession of the United States.

(Pub. L. 110–53, title XIII, §1301, Aug. 3, 2007, 121 Stat. 389.)

REFERENCES IN TEXT

This subchapter, referred to in text, was in the original "this title", meaning title XIII of Pub. L. 110–53, Aug. 3, 2007, 121 Stat. 389, which enacted this subchapter and amended section 70105 of Title 46, Shipping, and sections 114 and 46301 of Title 49, Transportation. For complete classification of title XIII to the Code, see Tables.

§1112. Authorization of Visible Intermodal Prevention and Response teams

(a) In general

The Secretary, acting through the Administrator of the Transportation Security Administration, may develop Visible Intermodal Prevention and Response (referred to in this section as "VIPR") teams to augment the security of any mode of transportation at any location within the United States. In forming a VIPR team, the Secretary—

(1) may use any asset of the Department, including Federal air marshals, surface transportation security inspectors, canine detection teams, and advanced screening technology;

(2) may determine when a VIPR team shall be deployed, as well as the duration of the deployment;

(3) shall, prior to and during the deployment, consult with local security and law enforcement officials in the jurisdiction where the VIPR team is or will be deployed, to develop and agree upon the appropriate operational protocols and provide relevant information about the mission of the VIPR team, as appropriate; and

(4) shall, prior to and during the deployment, consult with all transportation entities directly affected by the deployment of a VIPR team, as appropriate, including railroad carriers, air carriers, airport owners, over-the-

[1] So in original. Probably should be "intercity rail passenger".

[2] So in original. Probably should be followed by a comma.

[3] So in original. Probably should be section "1992(d)(16)".

road bus operators and terminal owners and operators, motor carriers, public transportation agencies, owners or operators of highways, port operators and facility owners, vessel owners and operators and pipeline operators.

(b) Authorization of appropriations

There are authorized to be appropriated to the Secretary to carry out this section such sums as necessary for fiscal years 2007 through 2011.

(Pub. L. 110–53, title XIII, §1303, Aug. 3, 2007, 121 Stat. 392.)

§1113. Surface transportation security inspectors

(a) In general

The Secretary, acting through the Administrator of the Transportation Security Administration, is authorized to train, employ, and utilize surface transportation security inspectors.

(b) Mission

The Secretary shall use surface transportation security inspectors to assist surface transportation carriers, operators, owners, entities, and facilities to enhance their security against terrorist attack and other security threats and to assist the Secretary in enforcing applicable surface transportation security regulations and directives.

(c) Authorities

Surface transportation security inspectors employed pursuant to this section shall be authorized such powers and delegated such responsibilities as the Secretary determines appropriate, subject to subsection (e).

(d) Requirements

The Secretary shall require that surface transportation security inspectors have relevant transportation experience and other security and inspection qualifications, as determined appropriate.

(e) Limitations

(1) Inspectors

Surface transportation inspectors shall be prohibited from issuing fines to public transportation agencies, as defined in subchapter III, for violations of the Department's regulations or orders except through the process described in paragraph (2).

(2) Civil penalties

The Secretary shall be prohibited from assessing civil penalties against public transportation agencies, as defined in subchapter III, for violations of the Department's regulations or orders, except in accordance with the following:

(A) In the case of a public transportation agency that is found to be in violation of a regulation or order issued by the Secretary, the Secretary shall seek correction of the violation through a written notice to the public transportation agency and shall give the public transportation agency reasonable opportunity to correct the violation or propose an alternative means of compliance acceptable to the Secretary.

(B) If the public transportation agency does not correct the violation or propose an alternative means of compliance acceptable to the Secretary within a reasonable time period that is specified in the written notice, the Secretary may take any action authorized in section 114 of title 49.

(3) Limitation on Secretary

The Secretary shall not initiate civil enforcement actions for violations of administrative and procedural requirements pertaining to the application for, and expenditure of, funds awarded under transportation security grant programs under this Act.

(f) Number of inspectors

The Secretary shall employ up to a total of—

(1) 100 surface transportation security inspectors in fiscal year 2007;

(2) 150 surface transportation security inspectors in fiscal year 2008;

(3) 175 surface transportation security inspectors in fiscal year 2009; and

(4) 200 surface transportation security inspectors in fiscal years 2010 and 2011.

(g) Coordination

The Secretary shall ensure that the mission of the surface transportation security inspectors is consistent with any relevant risk assessments required by this Act or completed by the Department, the modal plans required under section 114(t)[1] of title 49, the Memorandum of Understanding between the Department and the Department of Transportation on Roles and Responsibilities, dated September 28, 2004, and any and all subsequent annexes to this Memorandum of Understanding, and other relevant documents setting forth the Department's transportation security strategy, as appropriate.

(h) Consultation

The Secretary shall periodically consult with the surface transportation entities which are or may be inspected by the surface transportation security inspectors, including, as appropriate, railroad carriers, over-the-road bus operators and terminal owners and operators, motor carriers, public transportation agencies, owners or operators of highways, and pipeline operators on—

(1) the inspectors' duties, responsibilities, authorities, and mission; and

(2) strategies to improve transportation security and to ensure compliance with transportation security requirements.

(i) Report

Not later than September 30, 2008, the Department of Homeland Security Inspector General shall transmit a report to the appropriate congressional committees on the performance and effectiveness of surface transportation security inspectors, whether there is a need for additional inspectors, and other recommendations.

(j) Authorization of appropriations

There are authorized to be appropriated to the Secretary to carry out this section—

(1) $11,400,000 for fiscal year 2007;

(2) $17,100,000 for fiscal year 2008;

(3) $19,950,000 for fiscal year 2009;

[1] See References in Text note below.

(4) $22,800,000 for fiscal year 2010; and

(5) $22,800,000 for fiscal year 2011.

(Pub. L. 110–53, title XIII, § 1304, Aug. 3, 2007, 121 Stat. 393.)

REFERENCES IN TEXT

This Act, referred to in subsecs. (e)(3) and (g), is Pub. L. 110–53, Aug. 3, 2007, 121 Stat. 266, known as the Implementing Recommendations of the 9/11 Commission Act of 2007, which enacted this chapter and enacted and amended numerous other sections and notes in the Code. For complete classification of this Act to the Code, see Short Title of 2007 Amendment note set out under section 101 of this title and Tables.

Section 114(t) of title 49, referred to in subsec. (g), was redesignated section 114(s) of title 49 by Pub. L. 110–161, div. E, title V, § 568(a), Dec. 26, 2007, 121 Stat. 2092.

§ 1114. Surface transportation security technology information sharing

(a) In general

(1) Information sharing

The Secretary, in consultation with the Secretary of Transportation, shall establish a program to provide appropriate information that the Department has gathered or developed on the performance, use, and testing of technologies that may be used to enhance railroad, public transportation, and surface transportation security to surface transportation entities, including railroad carriers, over-the-road bus operators and terminal owners and operators, motor carriers, public transportation agencies, owners or operators of highways, pipeline operators, and State, local, and tribal governments that provide security assistance to such entities.

(2) Designation of qualified antiterrorism technologies

The Secretary shall include in such information provided in paragraph (1) whether the technology is designated as a qualified antiterrorism technology under the Support Antiterrorism by Fostering Effective Technologies Act of 2002 (Public Law 107–296) [6 U.S.C. 441 et seq.], as appropriate.

(b) Purpose

The purpose of the program is to assist eligible grant recipients under this Act and others, as appropriate, to purchase and use the best technology and equipment available to meet the security needs of the Nation's surface transportation system.

(c) Coordination

The Secretary shall ensure that the program established under this section makes use of and is consistent with other Department technology testing, information sharing, evaluation, and standards-setting programs, as appropriate.

(Pub. L. 110–53, title XIII, § 1305, Aug. 3, 2007, 121 Stat. 394.)

REFERENCES IN TEXT

The Support Anti-Terrorism by Fostering Effective Technologies Act of 2002, referred to in subsec. (a)(2), is subtitle G (§§ 861–865) of title VIII of Pub. L. 107–296, Nov. 25, 2002, 116 Stat. 2238, also known as the SAFETY Act, which is classified generally to part G (§ 441 et seq.) of subchapter VIII of chapter 1 of this title. For complete classification of this Act to the Code, see Short Title note set out under section 101 of this title and Tables.

This Act, referred to in subsecs. (b), is Pub. L. 110–53, Aug. 3, 2007, 121 Stat. 266, known as the Implementing Recommendations of the 9/11 Commission Act of 2007, which enacted this chapter and enacted and amended numerous other sections and notes in the Code. For complete classification of this Act to the Code, see Short Title of 2007 Amendment note set out under section 101 of this title and Tables.

§ 1115. TSA personnel limitations

Any statutory limitation on the number of employees in the Transportation Security Administration does not apply to employees carrying out this chapter.

(Pub. L. 110–53, title XIII, § 1306, Aug. 3, 2007, 121 Stat. 395.)

REFERENCES IN TEXT

This chapter, referred to in text, was in the original a reference to titles XII, XIII, XIV, and XV of Pub. L. 110–53, which enacted this chapter, amended section 1992 of Title 18, Crimes and Criminal Procedure, section 70105 of Title 46, Shipping, and sections 114, 5103a, 14504, 20106, 20109, 24301, 28101, 31105, and 46301 of Title 49, Transportation, enacted provisions set out as notes under section 1101 of this title and sections 114, 13908, and 14504 of Title 49, and amended provisions set out as a note under section 14504 of Title 49. For complete classification of titles XII to XV to the Code, see Tables.

§ 1116. National explosives detection canine team training program

(a) Definitions

For purposes of this section, the term "explosives detection canine team" means a canine and a canine handler that are trained to detect explosives, radiological materials, chemical, nuclear or biological weapons, or other threats as defined by the Secretary.

(b) In general

(1) Increased capacity

Not later than 180 days after August 3, 2007, the Secretary of Homeland Security shall—

(A) begin to increase the number of explosives detection canine teams certified by the Transportation Security Administration for the purposes of transportation-related security by up to 200 canine teams annually by the end of 2010; and

(B) encourage State, local, and tribal governments and private owners of high-risk transportation facilities to strengthen security through the use of highly trained explosives detection canine teams.

(2) Explosives detection canine teams

The Secretary of Homeland Security shall increase the number of explosives detection canine teams by—

(A) using the Transportation Security Administration's National Explosives Detection Canine Team Training Center, including expanding and upgrading existing facilities, procuring and breeding additional canines, and increasing staffing and oversight commensurate with the increased training and deployment capabilities;

(B) partnering with other Federal, State, or local agencies, nonprofit organizations, universities, or the private sector to increase the training capacity for canine detection teams;

(C) procuring explosives detection canines trained by nonprofit organizations, universities, or the private sector provided they are trained in a manner consistent with the standards and requirements developed pursuant to subsection (c) or other criteria developed by the Secretary; or

(D) a combination of subparagraphs (A), (B), and (C), as appropriate.

(c) Standards for explosives detection canine teams

(1) In general

Based on the feasibility in meeting the ongoing demand for quality explosives detection canine teams, the Secretary shall establish criteria, including canine training curricula, performance standards, and other requirements approved by the Transportation Security Administration necessary to ensure that explosives detection canine teams trained by nonprofit organizations, universities, and private sector entities are adequately trained and maintained.

(2) Expansion

In developing and implementing such curriculum, performance standards, and other requirements, the Secretary shall—

(A) coordinate with key stakeholders, including international, Federal, State, and local officials, and private sector and academic entities to develop best practice guidelines for such a standardized program, as appropriate;

(B) require that explosives detection canine teams trained by nonprofit organizations, universities, or private sector entities that are used or made available by the Secretary be trained consistent with specific training criteria developed by the Secretary; and

(C) review the status of the private sector programs on at least an annual basis to ensure compliance with training curricula, performance standards, and other requirements.

(d) Deployment

The Secretary shall—

(1) use the additional explosives detection canine teams as part of the Department's efforts to strengthen security across the Nation's transportation network, and may use the canine teams on a more limited basis to support other homeland security missions, as determined appropriate by the Secretary;

(2) make available explosives detection canine teams to all modes of transportation, for high-risk areas or to address specific threats, on an as-needed basis and as otherwise determined appropriate by the Secretary;

(3) encourage, but not require, any transportation facility or system to deploy TSA-certified explosives detection canine teams developed under this section; and

(4) consider specific needs and training requirements for explosives detection canine teams to be deployed across the Nation's transportation network, including in venues of multiple modes of transportation, as appropriate.

(e) Canine procurement

The Secretary, acting through the Administrator of the Transportation Security Administration, shall work to ensure that explosives detection canine teams are procured as efficiently as possible and at the best price, while maintaining the needed level of quality, including, if appropriate, through increased domestic breeding.

(f) Study

Not later than 1 year after August 3, 2007, the Comptroller General shall report to the appropriate congressional committees on the utilization of explosives detection canine teams to strengthen security and the capacity of the national explosive detection canine team program.

(g) Authorization

There are authorized to be appropriated to the Secretary such sums as may be necessary to carry out this section for fiscal years 2007 through 2011.

(Pub. L. 110–53, title XIII, § 1307, Aug. 3, 2007, 121 Stat. 395.)

§ 1117. Roles of the Department of Homeland Security and the Department of Transportation

The Secretary of Homeland Security is the principal Federal official responsible for transportation security. The roles and responsibilities of the Department of Homeland Security and the Department of Transportation in carrying out this chapter are the roles and responsibilities of such Departments pursuant to the Aviation and Transportation Security Act (Public Law 107–71); the Intelligence Reform and Terrorism Prevention Act of 2004 (Public Law 108–458); the National Infrastructure Protection Plan required by Homeland Security Presidential Directive–7; The[1] Homeland Security Act of 2002 [6 U.S.C. 101 et seq.]; The[1] National Response Plan; Executive Order No. 13416: Strengthening Surface Transportation Security, dated December 5, 2006; the Memorandum of Understanding between the Department and the Department of Transportation on Roles and Responsibilities, dated September 28, 2004, and any and all subsequent annexes to this Memorandum of Understanding; and any other relevant agreements between the two Departments.

(Pub. L. 110–53, title XIII, § 1310, Aug. 3, 2007, 121 Stat. 400.)

REFERENCES IN TEXT

This chapter, referred to in text, was in the original a reference to titles XII, XIII, XIV, and XV of Pub. L. 110–53, which enacted this chapter, amended section 1992 of Title 18, Crimes and Criminal Procedure, section 70105 of Title 46, Shipping, and sections 114, 5103a, 14504, 20106, 20109, 24301, 28101, 31105, and 46301 of Title 49, Transportation, enacted provisions set out as notes under section 1101 of this title and sections 114, 13908, and 14504 of Title 49, and amended provisions set out as a note under section 14504 of Title 49. For complete

[1] So in original. Probably should not be capitalized.

classification of titles XII to XV to the Code, see Tables.

The Aviation and Transportation Security Act, referred to in text, is Pub. L. 107–71, Nov. 19, 2001, 115 Stat. 597. For complete classification of this Act to the Code, see Short Title of 2001 Amendment note set out under section 40101 of Title 49, Transportation, and Tables.

The Intelligence Reform and Terrorism Prevention Act of 2004, referred to in text, is Pub. L. 108–458, Dec. 17, 2004, 118 Stat. 3638. For complete classification of this Act to the Code, see Short Title of 2004 Amendment note set out under section 401 of Title 50, War and National Defense, and Tables.

The Homeland Security Act of 2002, referred to in text, is Pub. L. 107–296, Nov. 25, 2002, 116 Stat. 2135, which is classified principally to chapter 1 (§ 101 et seq.) of this title. For complete classification of this Act to the Code, see Short Title note set out under section 101 of this title and Tables.

Executive Order No. 13416, referred to in text, is set out as a note under section 1101 of this title.

SUBCHAPTER III—PUBLIC TRANSPORTATION SECURITY

§ 1131. Definitions

For purposes of this subchapter, the following terms apply:

(1) Appropriate congressional committees

The term "appropriate congressional committees" means the Committee on Banking, Housing, and Urban Affairs, and the Committee on Homeland Security and Governmental Affairs of the Senate and the Committee on Homeland Security and the Committee on Transportation and Infrastructure of the House of Representatives.

(2) Department

The term "Department" means the Department of Homeland Security.

(3) Disadvantaged businesses concerns

The term "disadvantaged business concerns" means small businesses that are owned and controlled by socially and economically disadvantaged individuals as defined in section[1] 124, title 13, Code of Federal Regulations.

(4) Frontline employee

The term "frontline employee" means an employee of a public transportation agency who is a transit vehicle driver or operator, dispatcher, maintenance and maintenance support employee, station attendant, customer service employee, security employee, or transit police, or any other employee who has direct contact with riders on a regular basis, and any other employee of a public transportation agency that the Secretary determines should receive security training under section 1137 of this title.

(5) Public transportation agency

The term "public transportation agency" means a publicly owned operator of public transportation eligible to receive Federal assistance under chapter 53 of title 49.

(6) Secretary

The term "Secretary" means the Secretary of Homeland Security.

[1] So in original. Probably should be "part".

(Pub. L. 110–53, title XIV, § 1402, Aug. 3, 2007, 121 Stat. 400.)

SHORT TITLE

For short title of this subchapter as the "National Transit Systems Security Act of 2007", see section 1401 of Pub. L. 110–53, set out as a note under section 1101 of this title.

§ 1132. Findings

Congress finds that—

(1) 182 public transportation systems throughout the world have been primary targets of terrorist attacks;

(2) more than 6,000 public transportation agencies operate in the United States;

(3) people use public transportation vehicles 33,000,000 times each day;

(4) the Federal Transit Administration has invested $93,800,000,000 since 1992 for construction and improvements;

(5) the Federal investment in transit security has been insufficient; and

(6) greater Federal investment in transit security improvements per passenger boarding is necessary to better protect the American people, given transit's vital importance in creating mobility and promoting our Nation's economy.

(Pub. L. 110–53, title XIV, § 1403, Aug. 3, 2007, 121 Stat. 401.)

§ 1133. National Strategy for Public Transportation Security

(a) National Strategy

Not later than 9 months after August 3, 2007, and based upon the previous and ongoing security assessments conducted by the Department and the Department of Transportation, the Secretary, consistent with and as required by section 114(t)[1] of title 49, shall develop and implement the modal plan for public transportation, entitled the "National Strategy for Public Transportation Security".

(b) Purpose

(1) Guidelines

In developing the National Strategy for Public Transportation Security, the Secretary shall establish guidelines for public transportation security that—

(A) minimize security threats to public transportation systems; and

(B) maximize the abilities of public transportation systems to mitigate damage resulting from terrorist attack or other major incident.

(2) Assessments and consultations

In developing the National Strategy for Public Transportation Security, the Secretary shall—

(A) use established and ongoing public transportation security assessments as the basis of the National Strategy for Public Transportation Security; and

(B) consult with all relevant stakeholders, including public transportation agencies,

[1] See References in Text note below.

nonprofit labor organizations representing public transportation employees, emergency responders, public safety officials, and other relevant parties.

(c) Contents

In the National Strategy for Public Transportation Security, the Secretary shall describe prioritized goals, objectives, policies, actions, and schedules to improve the security of public transportation.

(d) Responsibilities

The Secretary shall include in the National Strategy for Public Transportation Security a description of the roles, responsibilities, and authorities of Federal, State, and local agencies, tribal governments, and appropriate stakeholders. The plan shall also include—

(1) the identification of, and a plan to address, gaps and unnecessary overlaps in the roles, responsibilities, and authorities of Federal agencies; and

(2) a process for coordinating existing or future security strategies and plans for public transportation, including the National Infrastructure Protection Plan required by Homeland Security Presidential Directive–7; Executive Order No. 13416: Strengthening Surface Transportation Security dated December 5, 2006; the Memorandum of Understanding between the Department and the Department of Transportation on Roles and Responsibilities dated September 28, 2004; and subsequent annexes and agreements.

(e) Adequacy of existing plans and strategies

In developing the National Strategy for Public Transportation Security, the Secretary shall use relevant existing risk assessments and strategies developed by the Department or other Federal agencies, including those developed or implemented pursuant to section 114(t)[1] of title 49 or Homeland Security Presidential Directive–7.

(f) Funding

There is authorized to be appropriated to the Secretary to carry out this section $2,000,000 for fiscal year 2008.

(Pub. L. 110–53, title XIV, § 1404, Aug. 3, 2007, 121 Stat. 401.)

REFERENCES IN TEXT

Section 114(t) of title 49, referred to in subsecs. (a) and (e), was redesignated section 114(s) of title 49 by Pub. L. 110–161, div. E, title V, § 568(a), Dec. 26, 2007, 121 Stat. 2092.

Executive Order No. 13416, referred to in subsec. (d)(2), is set out as a note under section 1101 of this title.

§ 1134. Security assessments and plans

(a) Public transportation security assessments

(1) Submission

Not later than 30 days after August 3, 2007, the Administrator of the Federal Transit Administration of the Department of Transportation shall submit all public transportation security assessments and all other relevant information to the Secretary.

(2) Secretarial review

Not later than 60 days after receiving the submission under paragraph (1), the Secretary shall review and augment the security assessments received, and conduct additional security assessments as necessary to ensure that at a minimum, all high risk public transportation agencies, as determined by the Secretary, will have a completed security assessment.

(3) Content

The Secretary shall ensure that each completed security assessment includes—

(A) identification of critical assets, infrastructure, and systems and their vulnerabilities; and

(B) identification of any other security weaknesses, including weaknesses in emergency response planning and employee training.

(b) Bus and rural public transportation systems

Not later than 180 days after August 3, 2007, the Secretary shall—

(1) conduct security assessments, based on a representative sample, to determine the specific needs of—

(A) local bus-only public transportation systems; and

(B) public transportation systems that receive funds under section 5311 of title 49; and

(2) make the representative assessments available for use by similarly situated systems.

(c) Security plans

(1) Requirement for plan

(A) High risk agencies

The Secretary shall require public transportation agencies determined by the Secretary to be at high risk for terrorism to develop a comprehensive security plan. The Secretary shall provide technical assistance and guidance to public transportation agencies in preparing and implementing security plans under this section.

(B) Other agencies

Provided that no public transportation agency that has not been designated high risk shall be required to develop a security plan, the Secretary may also establish a security program for public transportation agencies not designated high risk by the Secretary, to assist those public transportation agencies which request assistance, including—

(i) guidance to assist such agencies in conducting security assessments and preparing and implementing security plans; and

(ii) a process for the Secretary to review and approve such assessments and plans, as appropriate.

(2) Contents of plan

The Secretary shall ensure that security plans include, as appropriate—

(A) a prioritized list of all items included in the public transportation agency's security assessment that have not yet been addressed;

(B) a detailed list of any additional capital and operational improvements identified by the Department or the public transportation agency and a certification of the public transportation agency's technical capacity for operating and maintaining any security equipment that may be identified in such list;

(C) specific procedures to be implemented or used by the public transportation agency in response to a terrorist attack, including evacuation and passenger communication plans and appropriate evacuation and communication measures for the elderly and individuals with disabilities;

(D) a coordinated response plan that establishes procedures for appropriate interaction with State and local law enforcement agencies, emergency responders, and Federal officials in order to coordinate security measures and plans for response in the event of a terrorist attack or other major incident;

(E) a strategy and timeline for conducting training under section 1137 of this title;

(F) plans for providing redundant and other appropriate backup systems necessary to ensure the continued operation of critical elements of the public transportation system in the event of a terrorist attack or other major incident;

(G) plans for providing service capabilities throughout the system in the event of a terrorist attack or other major incident in the city or region which the public transportation system serves;

(H) methods to mitigate damage within a public transportation system in case of an attack on the system, including a plan for communication and coordination with emergency responders; and

(I) other actions or procedures as the Secretary determines are appropriate to address the security of the public transportation system.

(3) Review

Not later than 6 months after receiving the plans required under this section, the Secretary shall—

(A) review each security plan submitted;

(B) require the public transportation agency to make any amendments needed to ensure that the plan meets the requirements of this section; and

(C) approve any security plan that meets the requirements of this section.

(4) Exemption

The Secretary shall not require a public transportation agency to develop a security plan under paragraph (1) if the agency does not receive a grant under section 1135 of this title.

(5) Waiver

The Secretary may waive the exemption provided in paragraph (4) to require a public transportation agency to develop a security plan under paragraph (1) in the absence of grant funds under section 1135 of this title if not less than 3 days after making the determination the Secretary provides the appropriate congressional committees and the public transportation agency written notification detailing the need for the security plan, the reasons grant funding has not been made available, and the reason the agency has been designated high risk.

(d) Consistency with other plans

The Secretary shall ensure that the security plans developed by public transportation agencies under this section are consistent with the security assessments developed by the Department and the National Strategy for Public Transportation Security developed under section 1133 of this title.

(e) Updates

Not later than September 30, 2008, and annually thereafter, the Secretary shall—

(1) update the security assessments referred to in subsection (a);

(2) update the security improvement priorities required under subsection (f); and

(3) require public transportation agencies to update the security plans required under subsection (c) as appropriate.

(f) Security improvement priorities

(1) In general

Beginning in fiscal year 2008 and each fiscal year thereafter, the Secretary, after consultation with management and nonprofit employee labor organizations representing public transportation employees as appropriate, and with appropriate State and local officials, shall utilize the information developed or received in this section to establish security improvement priorities unique to each individual public transportation agency that has been assessed.

(2) Allocations

The Secretary shall use the security improvement priorities established in paragraph (1) as the basis for allocating risk-based grant funds under section 1135 of this title, unless the Secretary notifies the appropriate congressional committees that the Secretary has determined an adjustment is necessary to respond to an urgent threat or other significant national security factors.

(g) Shared facilities

The Secretary shall encourage the development and implementation of coordinated assessments and security plans to the extent a public transportation agency shares facilities (such as tunnels, bridges, stations, or platforms) with another public transportation agency, a freight or passenger railroad carrier, or over-the-road bus operator that are geographically close or otherwise co-located.

(h) Nondisclosure of information

(1) Submission of information to Congress

Nothing in this section shall be construed as authorizing the withholding of any information from Congress.

(2) Disclosure of independently furnished information

Nothing in this section shall be construed as affecting any authority or obligation of a Federal agency to disclose any record or information that the Federal agency obtains from a public transportation agency under any other Federal law.

(i) Determination

In response to a petition by a public transportation agency or at the discretion of the Secretary, the Secretary may recognize existing procedures, protocols, and standards of a public transportation agency that the Secretary determines meet all or part of the requirements of this section regarding security assessments or security plans.

(Pub. L. 110–53, title XIV, § 1405, Aug. 3, 2007, 121 Stat. 402.)

§ 1135. Public transportation security assistance

(a) Security assistance program

(1) In general

The Secretary shall establish a program for making grants to eligible public transportation agencies for security improvements described in subsection (b).

(2) Eligibility

A public transportation agency is eligible for a grant under this section if the Secretary has performed a security assessment or the agency has developed a security plan under section 1134 of this title. Grant funds shall only be awarded for permissible uses under subsection (b) to—

(A) address items included in a security assessment; or

(B) further a security plan.

(b) Uses of funds

A recipient of a grant under subsection (a) shall use the grant funds for one or more of the following:

(1) Capital uses of funds, including—

(A) tunnel protection systems;

(B) perimeter protection systems, including access control, installation of improved lighting, fencing, and barricades;

(C) redundant critical operations control systems;

(D) chemical, biological, radiological, or explosive detection systems, including the acquisition of canines used for such detection;

(E) surveillance equipment;

(F) communications equipment, including mobile service equipment to provide access to wireless Enhanced 911 (E911) emergency services in an underground fixed guideway system;

(G) emergency response equipment, including personal protective equipment;

(H) fire suppression and decontamination equipment;

(I) global positioning or tracking and recovery equipment, and other automated-vehicle-locator-type system equipment;

(J) evacuation improvements;

(K) purchase and placement of bomb-resistant trash cans throughout public transportation facilities, including subway exits, entrances, and tunnels;

(L) capital costs associated with security awareness, security preparedness, and security response training, including training under section 1137 of this title and exercises under section 1136 of this title;

(M) security improvements for public transportation systems, including extensions thereto, in final design or under construction;

(N) security improvements for stations and other public transportation infrastructure, including stations and other public transportation infrastructure owned by State or local governments; and

(O) other capital security improvements determined appropriate by the Secretary.

(2) Operating uses of funds, including—

(A) security training, including training under section 1137 of this title and training developed by institutions of higher education and by nonprofit employee labor organizations, for public transportation employees, including frontline employees;

(B) live or simulated exercises under section 1136 of this title;

(C) public awareness campaigns for enhanced public transportation security;

(D) canine patrols for chemical, radiological, biological, or explosives detection;

(E) development of security plans under section 1134 of this title;

(F) overtime reimbursement including reimbursement of State, local, and tribal governments, for costs for enhanced security personnel during significant national and international public events;

(G) operational costs, including reimbursement of State, local, and tribal governments for costs for personnel assigned to full-time or part-time security or counterterrorism duties related to public transportation, provided that this expense totals no more than 10 percent of the total grant funds received by a public transportation agency in any 1 year; and

(H) other operational security costs determined appropriate by the Secretary, excluding routine, ongoing personnel costs, other than those set forth in this section.

(c) Department of Homeland Security responsibilities

In carrying out the responsibilities under subsection (a), the Secretary shall—

(1) determine the requirements for recipients of grants under this section, including application requirements;

(2) pursuant to subsection (a)(2), select the recipients of grants based solely on risk; and

(3) pursuant to subsection (b), establish the priorities for which grant funds may be used under this section.

(d) Distribution of grants

Not later than 90 days after August 3, 2007, the Secretary and the Secretary of Transportation shall determine the most effective and efficient way to distribute grant funds to the recipients of grants determined by the Secretary under subsection (a). Subject to the determination made by the Secretaries, the Secretary may transfer funds to the Secretary of Transportation for the purposes of disbursing funds to the grant recipient.

(e) Subject to certain terms and conditions

Except as otherwise specifically provided in this section, a grant provided under this section shall be subject to the terms and conditions applicable to a grant made under section 5307 of title 49, as in effect on January 1, 2007, and such other terms and conditions as are determined necessary by the Secretary.

(f) Limitation on uses of funds

Grants made under this section may not be used to make any State or local government cost-sharing contribution under any other Federal law.

(g) Annual reports

Each recipient of a grant under this section shall report annually to the Secretary on the use of the grant funds.

(h) Guidelines

Before distribution of funds to recipients of grants, the Secretary shall issue guidelines to ensure that, to the extent that recipients of grants under this section use contractors or subcontractors, such recipients shall use small, minority, women-owned, or disadvantaged business concerns as contractors or subcontractors to the extent practicable.

(i) Coordination with State homeland security plans

In establishing security improvement priorities under section 1134 of this title and in awarding grants for capital security improvements and operational security improvements under subsection (b), the Secretary shall act consistently with relevant State homeland security plans.

(j) Multistate transportation systems

In cases in which a public transportation system operates in more than one State, the Secretary shall give appropriate consideration to the risks of the entire system, including those portions of the States into which the system crosses, in establishing security improvement priorities under section 1134 of this title and in awarding grants for capital security improvements and operational security improvements under subsection (b).

(k) Congressional notification

Not later than 3 days before the award of any grant under this section, the Secretary shall notify simultaneously, the appropriate congressional committees of the intent to award such grant.

***(l)* Return of misspent grant funds**

The Secretary shall establish a process to require the return of any misspent grant funds received under this section determined to have been spent for a purpose other than those specified in the grant award.

(m) Authorization of appropriations

(1) There are authorized to be appropriated to the Secretary to make grants under this section—

(A) such sums as are necessary for fiscal year 2007;

(B) $650,000,000 for fiscal year 2008, except that not more than 50 percent of such funds may be used for operational costs under subsection (b)(2);

(C) $750,000,000 for fiscal year 2009, except that not more than 30 percent of such funds may be used for operational costs under subsection (b)(2);

(D) $900,000,000 for fiscal year 2010, except that not more than 20 percent of such funds may be used for operational costs under subsection (b)(2); and

(E) $1,100,000,000 for fiscal year 2011, except that not more than 10 percent of such funds may be used for operational costs under subsection (b)(2).

(2) PERIOD OF AVAILABILITY.—Sums appropriated to carry out this section shall remain available until expended.

(3) WAIVER.—The Secretary may waive the limitation on operational costs specified in subparagraphs (B) through (E) of paragraph (1) if the Secretary determines that such a waiver is required in the interest of national security, and if the Secretary provides a written justification to the appropriate congressional committees prior to any such action.

(4) EFFECTIVE DATE.—Funds provided for fiscal year 2007 transit security grants under Public Law 110–28 shall be allocated based on security assessments that are in existence as of August 3, 2007.

(Pub. L. 110–53, title XIV, § 1406, Aug. 3, 2007, 121 Stat. 405.)

REFERENCES IN TEXT

Public Law 110–28, referred to in subsec. (m)(4), is Pub. L. 110–28, May 25, 2007, 121 Stat. 112, known as the U.S. Troop Readinesss, Veterans' Care, Katrina Recovery, and Iraq Accountability Appropriations Act, 2007. For complete classification of this Act to the Code, see Tables.

§ 1136. Security exercises

(a) In general

The Secretary shall establish a program for conducting security exercises for public transportation agencies for the purpose of assessing and improving the capabilities of entities described in subsection (b) to prevent, prepare for, mitigate against, respond to, and recover from acts of terrorism.

(b) Covered entities

Entities to be assessed under the program shall include—

(1) Federal, State, and local agencies and tribal governments;

(2) public transportation agencies;

(3) governmental and nongovernmental emergency response providers and law enforcement personnel, including transit police; and

(4) any other organization or entity that the Secretary determines appropriate.

(c) Requirements

The Secretary shall ensure that the program—

(1) requires, for public transportation agencies which the Secretary deems appropriate, exercises to be conducted that are—

(A) scaled and tailored to the needs of specific public transportation systems, and include taking into account the needs of the elderly and individuals with disabilities;

(B) live;

(C) coordinated with appropriate officials;

(D) as realistic as practicable and based on current risk assessments, including credible threats, vulnerabilities, and consequences;

(E) inclusive, as appropriate, of frontline employees and managers; and

(F) consistent with the National Incident Management System, the National Response Plan, the National Infrastructure Protection Plan, the National Preparedness Guidance, the National Preparedness Goal, and other such national initiatives;

(2) provides that exercises described in paragraph (1) will be—

(A) evaluated by the Secretary against clear and consistent performance measures;

(B) assessed by the Secretary to learn best practices, which shall be shared with appropriate Federal, State, local, and tribal officials, governmental and nongovernmental emergency response providers, law enforcement personnel, including railroad and transit police, and appropriate stakeholders; and

(C) followed by remedial action by covered entities in response to lessons learned;

(3) involves individuals in neighborhoods around the infrastructure of a public transportation system; and

(4) assists State, local, and tribal governments and public transportation agencies in designing, implementing, and evaluating exercises that conform to the requirements of paragraph (2).

(d) National Exercise Program

The Secretary shall ensure that the exercise program developed under subsection (a) is a component of the National Exercise Program established under section 748 of this title.

(e) Ferry system exemption

This section does not apply to any ferry system for which drills are required to be conducted pursuant to section 70103 of title 46.

(Pub. L. 110–53, title XIV, §1407, Aug. 3, 2007, 121 Stat. 408.)

§1137. Public transportation security training program

(a) In general

Not later than 90 days after August 3, 2007, the Secretary shall develop and issue detailed interim final regulations, and not later than 1 year after August 3, 2007, the Secretary shall develop and issue detailed final regulations, for a public transportation security training program to prepare public transportation employees, including frontline employees, for potential security threats and conditions.

(b) Consultation

The Secretary shall develop the interim final and final regulations under subsection (a) in consultation with—

(1) appropriate law enforcement, fire service, security, and terrorism experts;

(2) representatives of public transportation agencies; and

(3) nonprofit employee labor organizations representing public transportation employees or emergency response personnel.

(c) Program elements

The interim final and final regulations developed under subsection (a) shall require security training programs to include, at a minimum, elements to address the following:

(1) Determination of the seriousness of any occurrence or threat.

(2) Crew and passenger communication and coordination.

(3) Appropriate responses to defend oneself, including using nonlethal defense devices.

(4) Use of personal protective devices and other protective equipment.

(5) Evacuation procedures for passengers and employees, including individuals with disabilities and the elderly.

(6) Training related to behavioral and psychological understanding of, and responses to, terrorist incidents, including the ability to cope with hijacker behavior, and passenger responses.

(7) Live situational training exercises regarding various threat conditions, including tunnel evacuation procedures.

(8) Recognition and reporting of dangerous substances and suspicious packages, persons, and situations.

(9) Understanding security incident procedures, including procedures for communicating with governmental and nongovernmental emergency response providers and for on scene interaction with such emergency response providers.

(10) Operation and maintenance of security equipment and systems.

(11) Other security training activities that the Secretary deems appropriate.

(d) Required programs

(1) Development and submission to Secretary

Not later than 90 days after a public transportation agency meets the requirements under subsection (e), each such public transportation agency shall develop a security training program in accordance with the regulations developed under subsection (a) and submit the program to the Secretary for approval.

(2) Approval

Not later than 60 days after receiving a security training program proposal under this subsection, the Secretary shall approve the program or require the public transportation agency that developed the program to make any revisions to the program that the Secretary determines necessary for the program to meet the requirements of the regulations. A public transportation agency shall respond to the Secretary's comments within 30 days after receiving them.

(3) Training

Not later than 1 year after the Secretary approves a security training program proposal in accordance with this subsection, the public transportation agency that developed the program shall complete the training of all employees covered under the program.

(4) Updates of regulations and program revisions

The Secretary shall periodically review and update, as appropriate, the training regulations issued under subsection (a) to reflect new or changing security threats. Each public transportation agency shall revise its training program accordingly and provide additional training as necessary to its workers within a reasonable time after the regulations are updated.

(e) Applicability

A public transportation agency that receives a grant award under this subchapter shall be required to develop and implement a security training program pursuant to this section.

(f) Long-term training requirement

Any public transportation agency required to develop a security training program pursuant to this section shall provide routine and ongoing training for employees covered under the program, regardless of whether the public transportation agency receives subsequent grant awards.

(g) National Training Program

The Secretary shall ensure that the training program developed under subsection (a) is a component of the National Training Program established under section 748 of this title.

(h) Ferry exemption

This section shall not apply to any ferry system for which training is required to be conducted pursuant to section 70103 of title 46.

(i) Report

Not later than 2 years after the date of issuance of the final regulation, the Comptroller General shall review implementation of the training program, including interviewing a representative sample of public transportation agencies and employees, and report to the appropriate congressional committees, on the number of reviews conducted and the results. The Comptroller General may submit the report in both classified and redacted formats as necessary.

(Pub. L. 110–53, title XIV, § 1408, Aug. 3, 2007, 121 Stat. 409.)

§ 1138. Public transportation research and development

(a) Establishment of research and development program

The Secretary shall carry out a research and development program through the Homeland Security Advanced Research Projects Agency in the Science and Technology Directorate and in consultation with the Transportation Security Administration and with the Federal Transit Administration, for the purpose of improving the security of public transportation systems.

(b) Grants and contracts authorized

The Secretary shall award grants or contracts to public or private entities to conduct research and demonstrate technologies and methods to reduce and deter terrorist threats or mitigate damages resulting from terrorist attacks against public transportation systems.

(c) Use of funds

Grants or contracts awarded under subsection (a)—

(1) shall be coordinated with activities of the Homeland Security Advanced Research Projects Agency; and

(2) may be used to—

(A) research chemical, biological, radiological, or explosive detection systems that do not significantly impede passenger access;

(B) research imaging technologies;

(C) conduct product evaluations and testing;

(D) improve security and redundancy for critical communications, electrical power, and computer and train control systems;

(E) develop technologies for securing tunnels, transit bridges and aerial structures;

(F) research technologies that mitigate damages in the event of a cyber attack; and

(G) research other technologies or methods for reducing or deterring terrorist attacks against public transportation systems, or mitigating damage from such attacks.

(d) Privacy and civil rights and civil liberties issues

(1) Consultation

In carrying out research and development projects under this section, the Secretary shall consult with the Chief Privacy Officer of the Department and the Officer for Civil Rights and Civil Liberties of the Department, as appropriate, and in accordance with section 142 of this title.

(2) Privacy impact assessments

In accordance with sections 142 and 345 of this title, the Chief Privacy Officer shall conduct privacy impact assessments and the Officer for Civil Rights and Civil Liberties shall conduct reviews, as appropriate, for research and development initiatives developed under this section.

(e) Reporting requirement

Each entity that is awarded a grant or contract under this section shall report annually to the Department on the use of grant or contract funds received under this section to ensure that the awards made are expended in accordance with the purposes of this subchapter and the priorities developed by the Secretary.

(f) Coordination

The Secretary shall ensure that the research is consistent with the priorities established in the National Strategy for Public Transportation Security and is coordinated, to the extent practicable, with other Federal, State, local, tribal, and private sector public transportation, railroad, commuter railroad, and over-the-road bus research initiatives to leverage resources and avoid unnecessary duplicative efforts.

(g) Return of misspent grant or contract funds

If the Secretary determines that a grantee or contractor used any portion of the grant or contract funds received under this section for a purpose other than the allowable uses specified under subsection (c), the grantee or contractor shall return any amount so used to the Treasury of the United States.

(h) Authorization of appropriations

There are authorized to be appropriated to the Secretary to make grants under this section—

(1) such sums as necessary for fiscal year 2007;

(2) $25,000,000 for fiscal year 2008;
(3) $25,000,000 for fiscal year 2009;
(4) $25,000,000 for fiscal year 2010; and
(5) $25,000,000 for fiscal year 2011.

(Pub. L. 110–53, title XIV, § 1409, Aug. 3, 2007, 121 Stat. 411.)

§ 1139. Information sharing

(a) Intelligence sharing

The Secretary shall ensure that the Department of Transportation receives appropriate and timely notification of all credible terrorist threats against public transportation assets in the United States.

(b) Information Sharing and Analysis Center

(1) Authorization

The Secretary shall provide for the reasonable costs of the Information Sharing and Analysis Center for Public Transportation (referred to in this subsection as the "ISAC").

(2) Participation

The Secretary—

(A) shall require public transportation agencies that the Secretary determines to be at high risk of terrorist attack to participate in the ISAC;

(B) shall encourage all other public transportation agencies to participate in the ISAC;

(C) shall encourage the participation of nonprofit employee labor organizations representing public transportation employees, as appropriate; and

(D) shall not charge a fee for participating in the ISAC.

(c) Report

The Comptroller General shall report, not less than 3 years after August 3, 2007, to the appropriate congressional committees, as to the value and efficacy of the ISAC along with any other public transportation information-sharing programs ongoing at the Department. The report shall include an analysis of the user satisfaction of public transportation agencies on the state of information-sharing and the value that each system provides the user, the costs and benefits of all centers and programs, the coordination among centers and programs, how each center or program contributes to implementing the information sharing plan under section 1203,[1] and analysis of the extent to which the ISAC is duplicative with the Department's information-sharing program.

(d) Authorization

(1) In general

There are authorized to be appropriated to the Secretary to carry out this section—

(A) $600,000 for fiscal year 2008;
(B) $600,000 for fiscal year 2009;
(C) $600,000 for fiscal year 2010; and
(D) such sums as may be necessary for 2011, provided the report required in subsection (c) of this section has been submitted to Congress.

(2) Availability of funds

Such sums shall remain available until expended.

(Pub. L. 110–53, title XIV, § 1410, Aug. 3, 2007, 121 Stat. 412.)

REFERENCES IN TEXT

Section 1203, referred to in subsec. (c), is section 1203 of title XII of Pub. L. 110–53, Aug. 3, 2007, 121 Stat. 383, which amended section 114 of Title 49, Transportation, and enacted provisions set out as a note under section 114 of Title 49.

§ 1140. Threat assessments

Not later than 1 year after August 3, 2007, the Secretary shall complete a name-based security background check against the consolidated terrorist watchlist and an immigration status check for all public transportation frontline employees, similar to the threat assessment screening program required for facility employees and longshoremen by the Commandant of the Coast Guard under Coast Guard Notice USCG–2006–24189 (71 Fed. Reg. 25066 (April 8, 2006)).

(Pub. L. 110–53, title XIV, § 1411, Aug. 3, 2007, 121 Stat. 413.)

§ 1141. Reporting requirements

(a) Annual report to Congress

(1) In general

Not later than March 31 of each year, the Secretary shall submit a report, containing the information described in paragraph (2), to the appropriate congressional committees.

(2) Contents

The report submitted under paragraph (1) shall include—

(A) a description of the implementation of the provisions of this subchapter;

(B) the amount of funds appropriated to carry out the provisions of this subchapter that have not been expended or obligated;

(C) the National Strategy for Public Transportation Security required under section 1133 of this title;

(D) an estimate of the cost to implement the National Strategy for Public Transportation Security which shall break out the aggregated total cost of needed capital and operational security improvements for fiscal years 2008–2018; and

(E) the state of public transportation security in the United States, which shall include detailing the status of security assessments, the progress being made around the country in developing prioritized lists of security improvements necessary to make public transportation facilities and passengers more secure, the progress being made by agencies in developing security plans and how those plans differ from the security assessments and a prioritized list of security improvements being compiled by other agencies, as well as a random sample of an equal number of large- and small-scale projects currently underway.

(3) Format

The Secretary may submit the report in both classified and redacted formats if the

[1] See References in Text note below.

Secretary determines that such action is appropriate or necessary.

(b) Annual report to Governors

(1) In general

Not later than March 31 of each year, the Secretary shall submit a report to the Governor of each State with a public transportation agency that has received a grant under this Act.

(2) Contents

The report submitted under paragraph (1) shall specify—

(A) the amount of grant funds distributed to each such public transportation agency; and

(B) the use of such grant funds.

(Pub. L. 110–53, title XIV, § 1412, Aug. 3, 2007, 121 Stat. 413.)

REFERENCES IN TEXT

This Act, referred to in subsec. (b)(1), is Pub. L. 110–53, Aug. 3, 2007, 121 Stat. 266, known as the Implementing Recommendations of the 9/11 Commission Act of 2007, which enacted this chapter and enacted and amended numerous other sections and notes in the Code. For complete classification of this Act to the Code, see Short Title of 2007 Amendment note set out under section 101 of this title and Tables.

§ 1142. Public transportation employee protections

(a) In general

A public transportation agency, a contractor or a subcontractor of such agency, or an officer or employee of such agency, shall not discharge, demote, suspend, reprimand, or in any other way discriminate against an employee if such discrimination is due, in whole or in part, to the employee's lawful, good faith act done, or perceived by the employer to have been done or about to be done—

(1) to provide information, directly cause information to be provided, or otherwise directly assist in any investigation regarding any conduct which the employee reasonably believes constitutes a violation of any Federal law, rule, or regulation relating to public transportation safety or security, or fraud, waste, or abuse of Federal grants or other public funds intended to be used for public transportation safety or security, if the information or assistance is provided to or an investigation stemming from the provided information is conducted by—

(A) a Federal, State, or local regulatory or law enforcement agency (including an office of the Inspector General under the Inspector General Act of 1978 (5 U.S.C. App.; Public Law 95–452);[1]

(B) any Member of Congress, any Committee of Congress, or the Government Accountability Office; or

(C) a person with supervisory authority over the employee or such other person who has the authority to investigate, discover, or terminate the misconduct;

(2) to refuse to violate or assist in the violation of any Federal law, rule, or regulation relating to public transportation safety or security;

(3) to file a complaint or directly cause to be brought a proceeding related to the enforcement of this section or to testify in that proceeding;

(4) to cooperate with a safety or security investigation by the Secretary of Transportation, the Secretary of Homeland Security, or the National Transportation Safety Board; or

(5) to furnish information to the Secretary of Transportation, the Secretary of Homeland Security, the National Transportation Safety Board, or any Federal, State, or local regulatory or law enforcement agency as to the facts relating to any accident or incident resulting in injury or death to an individual or damage to property occurring in connection with public transportation.

(b) Hazardous safety or security conditions

(1) A public transportation agency, or a contractor or a subcontractor of such agency, or an officer or employee of such agency, shall not discharge, demote, suspend, reprimand, or in any other way discriminate against an employee for—

(A) reporting a hazardous safety or security condition;

(B) refusing to work when confronted by a hazardous safety or security condition related to the performance of the employee's duties, if the conditions described in paragraph (2) exist; or

(C) refusing to authorize the use of any safety- or security-related equipment, track, or structures, if the employee is responsible for the inspection or repair of the equipment, track, or structures, when the employee believes that the equipment, track, or structures are in a hazardous safety or security condition, if the conditions described in paragraph (2) of this subsection exist.

(2) A refusal is protected under paragraph (1)(B) and (C) if—

(A) the refusal is made in good faith and no reasonable alternative to the refusal is available to the employee;

(B) a reasonable individual in the circumstances then confronting the employee would conclude that—

(i) the hazardous condition presents an imminent danger of death or serious injury; and

(ii) the urgency of the situation does not allow sufficient time to eliminate the danger without such refusal; and

(C) the employee, where possible, has notified the public transportation agency of the existence of the hazardous condition and the intention not to perform further work, or not to authorize the use of the hazardous equipment, track, or structures, unless the condition is corrected immediately or the equipment, track, or structures are repaired properly or replaced.

(3) In this subsection, only subsection (b)(1)(A) shall apply to security personnel, including

[1] So in original. The semicolon probably should be preceded by an additional closing parenthesis.

transit police, employed or utilized by a public transportation agency to protect riders, equipment, assets, or facilities.

(c) Enforcement action

(1) Filing and notification

A person who believes that he or she has been discharged or otherwise discriminated against by any person in violation of subsection (a) or (b) may, not later than 180 days after the date on which such violation occurs, file (or have any person file on his or her behalf) a complaint with the Secretary of Labor alleging such discharge or discrimination. Upon receipt of a complaint filed under this paragraph, the Secretary of Labor shall notify, in writing, the person named in the complaint and the person's employer of the filing of the complaint, of the allegations contained in the complaint, of the substance of evidence supporting the complaint, and of the opportunities that will be afforded to such person under paragraph (2).

(2) Investigation; preliminary order

(A) In general

Not later than 60 days after the date of receipt of a complaint filed under paragraph (1) and after affording the person named in the complaint an opportunity to submit to the Secretary of Labor a written response to the complaint and an opportunity to meet with a representative of the Secretary of Labor to present statements from witnesses, the Secretary of Labor shall conduct an investigation and determine whether there is reasonable cause to believe that the complaint has merit and notify, in writing, the complainant and the person alleged to have committed a violation of subsection (a) or (b) of the Secretary of Labor's findings. If the Secretary of Labor concludes that there is a reasonable cause to believe that a violation of subsection (a) or (b) has occurred, the Secretary of Labor shall accompany the Secretary of Labor's findings with a preliminary order providing the relief prescribed by paragraph (3)(B). Not later than 30 days after the date of notification of findings under this paragraph, either the person alleged to have committed the violation or the complainant may file objections to the findings or preliminary order, or both, and request a hearing on the record. The filing of such objections shall not operate to stay any reinstatement remedy contained in the preliminary order. Such hearings shall be conducted expeditiously. If a hearing is not requested in such 30-day period, the preliminary order shall be deemed a final order that is not subject to judicial review.

(B) Requirements

(i) Required showing by complainant

The Secretary of Labor shall dismiss a complaint filed under this subsection and shall not conduct an investigation otherwise required under subparagraph (A) unless the complainant makes a prima facie showing that any behavior described in subsection (a) or (b) was a contributing factor in the unfavorable personnel action alleged in the complaint.

(ii) Showing by employer

Notwithstanding a finding by the Secretary of Labor that the complainant has made the showing required under clause (i), no investigation otherwise required under paragraph (A) shall be conducted if the employer demonstrates, by clear and convincing evidence, that the employer would have taken the same unfavorable personnel action in the absence of that behavior.

(iii) Criteria for determination by Secretary of Labor

The Secretary of Labor may determine that a violation of subsection (a) or (b) has occurred only if the complainant demonstrates that any behavior described in subsection (a) or (b) was a contributing factor in the unfavorable personnel action alleged in the complaint.

(iv) Prohibition

Relief may not be ordered under paragraph (A) if the employer demonstrates by clear and convincing evidence that the employer would have taken the same unfavorable personnel action in the absence of that behavior.

(3) Final order

(A) Deadline for issuance; settlement agreements

Not later than 120 days after the date of conclusion of a hearing under paragraph (2), the Secretary of Labor shall issue a final order providing the relief prescribed by this paragraph or denying the complaint. At any time before issuance of a final order, a proceeding under this subsection may be terminated on the basis of a settlement agreement entered into by the Secretary of Labor, the complainant, and the person alleged to have committed the violation.

(B) Remedy

If, in response to a complaint filed under paragraph (1), the Secretary of Labor determines that a violation of subsection (a) or (b) has occurred, the Secretary of Labor shall order the person who committed such violation to—

(i) take affirmative action to abate the violation; and

(ii) provide the remedies described in subsection (d).

(C) Order

If an order is issued under subparagraph (B), the Secretary of Labor, at the request of the complainant, shall assess against the person against whom the order is issued a sum equal to the aggregate amount of all costs and expenses (including attorney and expert witness fees) reasonably incurred, as determined by the Secretary of Labor, by the complainant for, or in connection with, bringing the complaint upon which the order was issued.

(D) Frivolous complaints

If the Secretary of Labor finds that a complaint under paragraph (1) is frivolous or has been brought in bad faith, the Secretary of Labor may award to the prevailing employer reasonable attorney fees not exceeding $1,000.

(4) Review

(A) Appeal to Court of Appeals

Any person adversely affected or aggrieved by an order issued under paragraph (3) may obtain review of the order in the United States Court of Appeals for the circuit in which the violation, with respect to which the order was issued, allegedly occurred or the circuit in which the complainant resided on the date of such violation. The petition for review must be filed not later than 60 days after the date of the issuance of the final order of the Secretary of Labor. Review shall conform to chapter 7 of title 5. The commencement of proceedings under this subparagraph shall not, unless ordered by the court, operate as a stay of the order.

(B) Limitation on collateral attack

An order of the Secretary of Labor with respect to which review could have been obtained under subparagraph (A) shall not be subject to judicial review in any criminal or other civil proceeding.

(5) Enforcement of order by Secretary of Labor

Whenever any person has failed to comply with an order issued under paragraph (3), the Secretary of Labor may file a civil action in the United States district court for the district in which the violation was found to occur to enforce such order. In actions brought under this paragraph, the district courts shall have jurisdiction to grant all appropriate relief including, but not limited to, injunctive relief and compensatory damages.

(6) Enforcement of order by parties

(A) Commencement of action

A person on whose behalf an order was issued under paragraph (3) may commence a civil action against the person to whom such order was issued to require compliance with such order. The appropriate United States district court shall have jurisdiction, without regard to the amount in controversy or the citizenship of the parties, to enforce such order.

(B) Attorney fees

The court, in issuing any final order under this paragraph, may award costs of litigation (including reasonable attorney and expert witness fees) to any party whenever the court determines such award is appropriate.

(7) De novo review

With respect to a complaint under paragraph (1), if the Secretary of Labor has not issued a final decision within 210 days after the filing of the complaint and if the delay is not due to the bad faith of the employee, the employee may bring an original action at law or equity for de novo review in the appropriate district court of the United States, which shall have jurisdiction over such an action without regard to the amount in controversy, and which action shall, at the request of either party to such action, be tried by the court with a jury. The action shall be governed by the same legal burdens of proof specified in paragraph (2)(B) for review by the Secretary of Labor.

(d) Remedies

(1) In general

An employee prevailing in any action under subsection (c) shall be entitled to all relief necessary to make the employee whole.

(2) Damages

Relief in an action under subsection (c) (including an action described in (c)(7))[2] shall include—

(A) reinstatement with the same seniority status that the employee would have had, but for the discrimination;

(B) any backpay, with interest; and

(C) compensatory damages, including compensation for any special damages sustained as a result of the discrimination, including litigation costs, expert witness fees, and reasonable attorney fees.

(3) Possible relief

Relief in any action under subsection (c) may include punitive damages in an amount not to exceed $250,000.

(e) Election of remedies

An employee may not seek protection under both this section and another provision of law for the same allegedly unlawful act of the public transportation agency.

(f) No preemption

Nothing in this section preempts or diminishes any other safeguards against discrimination, demotion, discharge, suspension, threats, harassment, reprimand, retaliation, or any other manner of discrimination provided by Federal or State law.

(g) Rights retained by employee

Nothing in this section shall be construed to diminish the rights, privileges, or remedies of any employee under any Federal or State law or under any collective bargaining agreement. The rights and remedies in this section may not be waived by any agreement, policy, form, or condition of employment.

(h) Disclosure of identity

(1) Except as provided in paragraph (2) of this subsection, or with the written consent of the employee, the Secretary of Transportation or the Secretary of Homeland Security may not disclose the name of an employee who has provided information described in subsection (a)(1).

(2) The Secretary of Transportation or the Secretary of Homeland Security shall disclose to the Attorney General the name of an employee described in paragraph (1) of this subsection if the matter is referred to the Attorney General for enforcement. The Secretary making such disclosure shall provide reasonable advance

[2] So in original. Probably should be "subsection (c)(7))".

notice to the affected employee if disclosure of that person's identity or identifying information is to occur.

(i) Process for reporting security problems to the Department of Homeland Security

(1) Establishment of process

The Secretary shall establish through regulations after an opportunity for notice and comment, and provide information to the public regarding, a process by which any person may submit a report to the Secretary regarding public transportation security problems, deficiencies, or vulnerabilities.

(2) Acknowledgment of receipt

If a report submitted under paragraph (1) identifies the person making the report, the Secretary shall respond promptly to such person and acknowledge receipt of the report.

(3) Steps to address problem

The Secretary shall review and consider the information provided in any report submitted under paragraph (1) and shall take appropriate steps to address any problems or deficiencies identified.

(Pub. L. 110–53, title XIV, § 1413, Aug. 3, 2007, 121 Stat. 414.)

REFERENCES IN TEXT

The Inspector General Act of 1978, referred to in subsec. (a)(1)(A), is Pub. L. 95–452, Oct. 12, 1978, 92 Stat. 1101, which is set out in the Appendix to Title 5, Government Organization and Employees.

§ 1143. Security background checks of covered individuals for public transportation

(a) Definitions

In this section, the following definitions apply:

(1) Security background check

The term "security background check" means reviewing the following for the purpose of identifying individuals who may pose a threat to transportation security, national security, or of terrorism:

(A) Relevant criminal history databases.

(B) In the case of an alien (as defined in section 101 of the Immigration and Nationality Act (8 U.S.C. 1101(a)(3))), the relevant databases to determine the status of the alien under the immigration laws of the United States.

(C) Other relevant information or databases, as determined by the Secretary.

(2) Covered individual

The term "covered individual" means an employee of a public transportation agency or a contractor or subcontractor of a public transportation agency.

(b) Guidance

(1) Any guidance, recommendations, suggested action items, or any other widely disseminated voluntary action item issued by the Secretary to a public transportation agency or a contractor or subcontractor of a public transportation agency relating to performing a security background check of a covered individual shall contain recommendations on the appropriate scope and application of such a security background check, including the time period covered, the types of disqualifying offenses, and a redress process for adversely impacted covered individuals consistent with subsections (c) and (d) of this section.

(2) Not later than 60 days after August 3, 2007, any guidance, recommendations, suggested action items, or any other widely disseminated voluntary action item issued by the Secretary prior to August 3, 2007, to a public transportation agency or a contractor or subcontractor of a public transportation agency relating to performing a security background check of a covered individual shall be updated in compliance with paragraph (b)(1).

(3) If a public transportation agency or a contractor or subcontractor of a public transportation agency performs a security background check on a covered individual to fulfill guidance issued by the Secretary under paragraph (1) or (2), the Secretary shall not consider such guidance fulfilled unless an adequate redress process as described in subsection (d) is provided to covered individuals.

(c) Requirements

If the Secretary issues a rule, regulation or directive requiring a public transportation agency or contractor or subcontractor of a public transportation agency to perform a security background check of a covered individual, then the Secretary shall prohibit a public transportation agency or contractor or subcontractor of a public transportation agency from making an adverse employment decision, including removal or suspension of the employee, due to such rule, regulation, or directive with respect to a covered individual unless the public transportation agency or contractor or subcontractor of a public transportation agency determines that the covered individual—

(1) has been convicted of, has been found not guilty of by reason of insanity, or is under want, warrant, or indictment for a permanent disqualifying criminal offense listed in part 1572 of title 49, Code of Federal Regulations;

(2) was convicted of or found not guilty by reason of insanity of an interim disqualifying criminal offense listed in part 1572 of title 49, Code of Federal Regulations, within 7 years of the date that the public transportation agency or contractor or subcontractor of the public transportation agency performs the security background check; or

(3) was incarcerated for an interim disqualifying criminal offense listed in part 1572 of title 49, Code of Federal Regulations, and released from incarceration within 5 years of the date that the public transportation agency or contractor or subcontractor of a public transportation agency performs the security background check.

(d) Redress process

If the Secretary issues a rule, regulation, or directive requiring a public transportation agency or contractor or subcontractor of a public transportation agency to perform a security background check of a covered individual, the Secretary shall—

(1) provide an adequate redress process for a covered individual subjected to an adverse employment decision, including removal or suspension of the employee, due to such rule, regulation, or directive that is consistent with the appeals and waiver process established for applicants for commercial motor vehicle hazardous materials endorsements and transportation workers at ports, as required by section 70105(c) of title 49;[1] and

(2) have the authority to order an appropriate remedy, including reinstatement of the covered individual, should the Secretary determine that a public transportation agency or contractor or subcontractor of a public transportation agency wrongfully made an adverse employment decision regarding a covered individual pursuant to such rule, regulation, or directive.

(e) False statements

A public transportation agency or a contractor or subcontractor of a public transportation agency may not knowingly misrepresent to an employee or other relevant person, including an arbiter involved in a labor arbitration, the scope, application, or meaning of any rules, regulations, directives, or guidance issued by the Secretary related to security background check requirements for covered individuals when conducting a security background check. Not later than 1 year after August 3, 2007, the Secretary shall issue a regulation that prohibits a public transportation agency or a contractor or subcontractor of a public transportation agency from knowingly misrepresenting to an employee or other relevant person, including an arbiter involved in a labor arbitration, the scope, application, or meaning of any rules, regulations, directives, or guidance issued by the Secretary related to security background check requirements for covered individuals when conducting a security background check.

(f) Rights and responsibilities

Nothing in this section shall be construed to abridge a public transportation agency's or a contractor or subcontractor of a public transportation agency's rights or responsibilities to make adverse employment decisions permitted by other Federal, State, or local laws. Nothing in the section shall be construed to abridge rights and responsibilities of covered individuals, a public transportation agency, or a contractor or subcontractor of a public transportation agency under any other Federal, State, or local laws or collective bargaining agreement.

(g) No preemption of Federal or State law

Nothing in this section shall be construed to preempt a Federal, State, or local law that requires criminal history background checks, immigration status checks, or other background checks of covered individuals.

(h) Statutory construction

Nothing in this section shall be construed to affect the process for review established under section 70105(c) of title 46, including regulations issued pursuant to such section.

[1] So in original. Probably should be title "46;".

(Pub. L. 110–53, title XIV, §1414, Aug. 3, 2007, 121 Stat. 419.)

§1144. Limitation on fines and civil penalties

(a) Inspectors

Surface transportation inspectors shall be prohibited from issuing fines to public transportation agencies for violations of the Department's regulations or orders except through the process described in subsection (b).

(b) Civil penalties

The Secretary shall be prohibited from assessing civil penalties against public transportation agencies for violations of the Department's regulations or orders, except in accordance with the following:

(1) In the case of a public transportation agency that is found to be in violation of a regulation or order issued by the Secretary, the Secretary shall seek correction of the violation through a written notice to the public transportation agency and shall give the public transportation agency reasonable opportunity to correct the violation or propose an alternative means of compliance acceptable to the Secretary.

(2) If the public transportation agency does not correct the violation or propose an alternative means of compliance acceptable to the Secretary within a reasonable time period that is specified in the written notice, the Secretary may take any action authorized in section 114 of title 49.

(c) Limitation on Secretary

The Secretary shall not initiate civil enforcement actions for violations of administrative and procedural requirements pertaining to the application for and expenditure of funds awarded under transportation security grant programs under this subchapter.

(Pub. L. 110–53, title XIV, §1415, Aug. 3, 2007, 121 Stat. 422.)

SUBCHAPTER IV—SURFACE TRANSPORTATION SECURITY

PART A—GENERAL PROVISIONS

§1151. Definitions

In this subchapter, the following definitions apply:

(1) Appropriate congressional committees

The term "appropriate congressional committees" means the Committee on Commerce, Science, and Transportation and the Committee on Homeland Security and Governmental Affairs of the Senate and the Committee on Homeland Security and the Committee on Transportation and Infrastructure of the House of Representatives.

(2) Secretary

The term "Secretary" means the Secretary of Homeland Security.

(3) Department

The term "Department" means the Department of Homeland Security.

(4) Over-the-road bus

The term "over-the-road bus" means a bus characterized by an elevated passenger deck located over a baggage compartment.

(5) Over-the-road bus frontline employees

In this section,[1] the term "over-the-road bus frontline employees" means over-the-road bus drivers, security personnel, dispatchers, maintenance and maintenance support personnel, ticket agents, other terminal employees, and other employees of an over-the-road bus operator or terminal owner or operator that the Secretary determines should receive security training under this subchapter.

(6) Railroad frontline employees

In this section,[1] the term "railroad frontline employees" means security personnel, dispatchers, locomotive engineers, conductors, trainmen, other onboard employees, maintenance and maintenance support personnel, bridge tenders, and any other employees of railroad carriers that the Secretary determines should receive security training under this subchapter.

(7) Railroad

The term "railroad" has the meaning that term has in section 20102 of title 49.

(8) Railroad carrier

The term "railroad carrier" has the meaning that term has in section 20102 of title 49.

(9) State

The term "State" means any one of the 50 States, the District of Columbia, Puerto Rico, the Northern Mariana Islands, the Virgin Islands, Guam, American Samoa, and any other territory or possession of the United States.

(10) Terrorism

The term "terrorism" has the meaning that term has in section 101 of this title.

(11) Transportation

The term "transportation", as used with respect to an over-the-road bus, means the movement of passengers or property by an over-the-road bus—

(A) in the jurisdiction of the United States between a place in a State and a place outside the State (including a place outside the United States); or

(B) in a State that affects trade, traffic, and transportation described in subparagraph (A).

(12) United States

The term "United States" means the 50 States, the District of Columbia, Puerto Rico, the Northern Mariana Islands, the Virgin Islands, Guam, American Samoa, and any other territory or possession of the United States.

(13) Security-sensitive material

The term "security-sensitive material" means a material, or a group or class of material, in a particular amount and form that the Secretary, in consultation with the Secretary of Transportation, determines, through a rulemaking with opportunity for public comment, poses a significant risk to national security while being transported in commerce due to the potential use of the material in an act of terrorism. In making such a designation, the Secretary shall, at a minimum, consider the following:

(A) Class 7 radioactive materials.

(B) Division 1.1, 1.2, or 1.3 explosives.

(C) Materials poisonous or toxic by inhalation, including Division 2.3 gases and Division 6.1 materials.

(D) A select agent or toxin regulated by the Centers for Disease Control and Prevention under part 73 of title 42, Code of Federal Regulations.

(14) Disadvantaged business concerns

The term "disadvantaged business concerns" means small businesses that are owned and controlled by socially and economically disadvantaged individuals as defined in section 124,[2] of title 13, Code of Federal Regulations.

(15) Amtrak

The term "Amtrak" means the National Railroad Passenger Corporation.

(Pub. L. 110–53, title XV, § 1501, Aug. 3, 2007, 121 Stat. 422.)

REFERENCES IN TEXT

This subchapter, referred to in text, was in the original "this title", meaning title XV of Pub. L. 110–53, Aug. 3, 2007, 121 Stat. 422, which enacted this subchapter, amended section 1992 of Title 18, Crimes and Criminal Procedure, and sections 114, 5103a, 14504, 20106, 20109, 24301, 28101, and 31105 of Title 49, Transportation, enacted provisions set out as notes under sections 13908 and 14504 of Title 49, and amended provisions set out as a note under section 14504 of Title 49. For complete classification of title XV to the Code, see Tables.

§ 1152. Oversight and grant procedures

(a) Secretarial oversight

The Secretary, in coordination with[1] Secretary of Transportation for grants awarded to Amtrak, shall establish necessary procedures, including monitoring and audits, to ensure that grants made under this subchapter are expended in accordance with the purposes of this subchapter and the priorities and other criteria developed by the Secretary.

(b) Additional audits and reviews

The Secretary, and the Secretary of Transportation for grants awarded to Amtrak, may award contracts to undertake additional audits and reviews of the safety, security, procurement, management, and financial compliance of a recipient of amounts under this subchapter.

(c) Procedures for grant award

Not later than 180 days after August 3, 2007, the Secretary shall prescribe procedures and schedules for the awarding of grants under this subchapter, including application and qualification procedures, and a record of decision on applicant eligibility. The procedures shall include the execution of a grant agreement between the

[1] So in original. "In this section," probably should not appear.

[2] So in original. Probably should be "part 124,".

[1] So in original. The word "the" probably should appear.

grant recipient and the Secretary and shall be consistent, to the extent practicable, with the grant procedures established under section 70107(i) and (j) of title 46.

(d) Additional authority

(1) Issuance

The Secretary may issue non-binding letters of intent to recipients of a grant under this subchapter, to commit funding from future budget authority of an amount, not more than the Federal Government's share of the project's cost, for a capital improvement project.

(2) Schedule

The letter of intent under this subsection shall establish a schedule under which the Secretary will reimburse the recipient for the Government's share of the project's costs, as amounts become available, if the recipient, after the Secretary issues that letter, carries out the project without receiving amounts under a grant issued under this subchapter.

(3) Notice to Secretary

A recipient that has been issued a letter of intent under this section shall notify the Secretary of the recipient's intent to carry out a project before the project begins.

(4) Notice to Congress

The Secretary shall transmit to the appropriate congressional committees a written notification at least 5 days before the issuance of a letter of intent under this subsection.

(5) Limitations

A letter of intent issued under this subsection is not an obligation of the Federal Government under section 1501 of title 31, and the letter is not deemed to be an administrative commitment for financing. An obligation or administrative commitment may be made only as amounts are provided in authorization and appropriations laws.

(e) Return of misspent grant funds

As part of the grant agreement under subsection (c), the Secretary shall require grant applicants to return any misspent grant funds received under this subchapter that the Secretary considers to have been spent for a purpose other than those specified in the grant award. The Secretary shall take all necessary actions to recover such funds.

(f) Congressional notification

Not later than 5 days before the award of any grant is made under this subchapter, the Secretary shall notify the appropriate congressional committees of the intent to award such grant.

(g) Guidelines

The Secretary shall ensure, to the extent practicable, that grant recipients under this subchapter who use contractors or subcontractors use small, minority, women-owned, or disadvantaged business concerns as contractors or subcontractors when appropriate.

(Pub. L. 110–53, title XV, § 1502, Aug. 3, 2007, 121 Stat. 424.)

REFERENCES IN TEXT

This subchapter, referred to in text, was in the original "this title", meaning title XV of Pub. L. 110–53, which is classified principally to this subchapter. For complete classification of title XV to the Code, see References in Text note under section 1151 of this title and Tables.

§ 1153. Authorization of appropriations

There are authorized to be appropriated to the Secretary of Transportation to carry out section 1165 of this title—

(1) $38,000,000 for fiscal year 2008;
(2) $40,000,000 for fiscal year 2009;
(3) $55,000,000 for fiscal year 2010; and
(4) $70,000,000 for fiscal year 2011.

(Pub. L. 110–53, title XV, § 1503(b), Aug. 3, 2007, 121 Stat. 425.)

§ 1154. Public awareness

Not later than 180 days after August 3, 2007, the Secretary shall develop a national plan for railroad and over-the-road bus security public outreach and awareness. Such a plan shall be designed to increase awareness of measures that the general public, passengers, and employees of railroad carriers and over-the-road bus operators can take to increase the security of the national railroad and over-the-road bus transportation systems. Such a plan shall also provide outreach to railroad carriers and over-the-road bus operators and their employees to improve their awareness of available technologies, ongoing research and development efforts, and available Federal funding sources to improve security. Not later than 9 months after August 3, 2007, the Secretary shall implement the plan developed under this section.

(Pub. L. 110–53, title XV, § 1504, Aug. 3, 2007, 121 Stat. 425.)

PART B—RAILROAD SECURITY

§ 1161. Railroad transportation security risk assessment and National Strategy

(a) Risk assessment

The Secretary shall establish a Federal task force, including the Transportation Security Administration and other agencies within the Department, the Department of Transportation, and other appropriate Federal agencies, to complete, within 6 months of August 3, 2007, a nationwide risk assessment of a terrorist attack on railroad carriers. The assessment shall include—

(1) a methodology for conducting the risk assessment, including timelines, that addresses how the Department will work with the entities described in subsection (c) and make use of existing Federal expertise within the Department, the Department of Transportation, and other appropriate agencies;

(2) identification and evaluation of critical assets and infrastructure, including tunnels used by railroad carriers in high-threat urban areas;

(3) identification of risks to those assets and infrastructure;

(4) identification of risks that are specific to the transportation of hazardous materials via railroad;

(5) identification of risks to passenger and cargo security, transportation infrastructure protection systems, operations, communications systems, and any other area identified by the assessment;

(6) an assessment of employee training and emergency response planning;

(7) an assessment of public and private operational recovery plans, taking into account the plans for the maritime sector required under section 70103 of title 46, to expedite, to the maximum extent practicable, the return of an adversely affected railroad transportation system or facility to its normal performance level after a major terrorist attack or other security event on that system or facility; and

(8) an account of actions taken or planned by both public and private entities to address identified railroad security issues and an assessment of the effective integration of such actions.

(b) National Strategy

(1) Requirement

Not later than 9 months after August 3, 2007, and based upon the assessment conducted under subsection (a), the Secretary, consistent with and as required by section 114(t)[1] of title 49, shall develop and implement the modal plan for railroad transportation, entitled the "National Strategy for Railroad Transportation Security".

(2) Contents

The modal plan shall include prioritized goals, actions, objectives, policies, mechanisms, and schedules for, at a minimum—

(A) improving the security of railroad tunnels, railroad bridges, railroad switching and car storage areas, other railroad infrastructure and facilities, information systems, and other areas identified by the Secretary as posing significant railroad-related risks to public safety and the movement of interstate commerce, taking into account the impact that any proposed security measure might have on the provision of railroad service or on operations served or otherwise affected by railroad service;

(B) deploying equipment and personnel to detect security threats, including those posed by explosives and hazardous chemical, biological, and radioactive substances, and any appropriate countermeasures;

(C) consistent with section 1167 of this title, training railroad employees in terrorism prevention, preparedness, passenger evacuation, and response activities;

(D) conducting public outreach campaigns for railroads regarding security, including educational initiatives designed to inform the public on how to prevent, prepare for, respond to, and recover from a terrorist attack on railroad transportation;

(E) providing additional railroad security support for railroads at high or severe threat levels of alert;

(F) ensuring, in coordination with freight and intercity and commuter passenger railroads, the continued movement of freight and passengers in the event of an attack affecting the railroad system, including the possibility of rerouting traffic due to the loss of critical infrastructure, such as a bridge, tunnel, yard, or station;

(G) coordinating existing and planned railroad security initiatives undertaken by the public and private sectors;

(H) assessing—

(i) the usefulness of covert testing of railroad security systems;

(ii) the ability to integrate security into infrastructure design; and

(iii) the implementation of random searches of passengers and baggage; and

(I) identifying the immediate and long-term costs of measures that may be required to address those risks and public and private sector sources to fund such measures.

(3) Responsibilities

The Secretary shall include in the modal plan a description of the roles, responsibilities, and authorities of Federal, State, and local agencies, government-sponsored entities, tribal governments, and appropriate stakeholders described in subsection (c). The plan shall also include—

(A) the identification of, and a plan to address, gaps and unnecessary overlaps in the roles, responsibilities, and authorities described in this paragraph;

(B) a methodology for how the Department will work with the entities described in subsection (c), and make use of existing Federal expertise within the Department, the Department of Transportation, and other appropriate agencies;

(C) a process for facilitating security clearances for the purpose of intelligence and information sharing with the entities described in subsection (c), as appropriate;

(D) a strategy and timeline, coordinated with the research and development program established under section 1168 of this title, for the Department, the Department of Transportation, other appropriate Federal agencies and private entities to research and develop new technologies for securing railroad systems; and

(E) a process for coordinating existing or future security strategies and plans for railroad transportation, including the National Infrastructure Protection Plan required by Homeland Security Presidential Directive-7; Executive Order No. 13416: "Strengthening Surface Transportation Security" dated December 5, 2006; the Memorandum of Understanding between the Department and the Department of Transportation on Roles and Responsibilities dated September 28, 2004, and any and all subsequent annexes to this Memorandum of Understanding, and any other relevant agreements between the two Departments.

(c) Consultation with stakeholders

In developing the National Strategy required under this section, the Secretary shall consult with railroad management, nonprofit employee

[1] See References in Text note below.

organizations representing railroad employees, owners or lessors of railroad cars used to transport hazardous materials, emergency responders, offerors of security-sensitive materials, public safety officials, and other relevant parties.

(d) Adequacy of existing plans and strategies

In developing the risk assessment and National Strategy required under this section, the Secretary shall utilize relevant existing plans, strategies, and risk assessments developed by the Department or other Federal agencies, including those developed or implemented pursuant to section 114(t)[1] of title 49 or Homeland Security Presidential Directive–7, and, as appropriate, assessments developed by other public and private stakeholders.

(e) Report

(1) Contents

Not later than 1 year after August 3, 2007, the Secretary shall transmit to the appropriate congressional committees a report containing—

(A) the assessment and the National Strategy required by this section; and

(B) an estimate of the cost to implement the National Strategy.

(2) Format

The Secretary may submit the report in both classified and redacted formats if the Secretary determines that such action is appropriate or necessary.

(f) Annual updates

Consistent with the requirements of section 114(t)[1] of title 49, the Secretary shall update the assessment and National Strategy each year and transmit a report, which may be submitted in both classified and redacted formats, to the appropriate congressional committees containing the updated assessment and recommendations.

(g) Funding

Out of funds appropriated pursuant to section 114(w) of title 49, there shall be made available to the Secretary to carry out this section $5,000,000 for fiscal year 2008.

(Pub. L. 110–53, title XV, § 1511, Aug. 3, 2007, 121 Stat. 426.)

REFERENCES IN TEXT

Section 114(t) of title 49, referred to in subsecs. (b)(1), (d), and (f), was redesignated section 114(s) of title 49 by Pub. L. 110–161, div. E, title V, § 568(a), Dec. 26, 2007, 121 Stat. 2092.

Executive Order No. 13416, referred to in subsec. (b)(3)(E), is set out as a note under section 1101 of this title.

§ 1162. Railroad carrier assessments and plans

(a) In general

Not later than 12 months after August 3, 2007, the Secretary shall issue regulations that—

(1) require each railroad carrier assigned to a high-risk tier under this section to—

(A) conduct a vulnerability assessment in accordance with subsections (c) and (d); and

(B) to[1] prepare, submit to the Secretary for approval, and implement a security plan in accordance with this section that addresses security performance requirements; and

(2) establish standards and guidelines, based on and consistent with the risk assessment and National Strategy for Railroad Transportation Security developed under section 1161 of this title, for developing and implementing the vulnerability assessments and security plans for railroad carriers assigned to high-risk tiers.

(b) Non high-risk programs

The Secretary may establish a security program for railroad carriers not assigned to a high-risk tier, including—

(1) guidance for such carriers in conducting vulnerability assessments and preparing and implementing security plans, as determined appropriate by the Secretary; and

(2) a process to review and approve such assessments and plans, as appropriate.

(c) Deadline for submission

Not later than 9 months after the date of issuance of the regulations under subsection (a), the vulnerability assessments and security plans required by such regulations for railroad carriers assigned to a high-risk tier shall be completed and submitted to the Secretary for review and approval.

(d) Vulnerability assessments

(1) Requirements

The Secretary shall provide technical assistance and guidance to railroad carriers in conducting vulnerability assessments under this section and shall require that each vulnerability assessment of a railroad carrier assigned to a high-risk tier under this section, include, as applicable—

(A) identification and evaluation of critical railroad carrier assets and infrastructure, including platforms, stations, intermodal terminals, tunnels, bridges, switching and storage areas, and information systems as appropriate;

(B) identification of the vulnerabilities to those assets and infrastructure;

(C) identification of strengths and weaknesses in—

(i) physical security;

(ii) passenger and cargo security, including the security of security-sensitive materials being transported by railroad or stored on railroad property;

(iii) programmable electronic devices, computers, or other automated systems which are used in providing the transportation;

(iv) alarms, cameras, and other protection systems;

(v) communications systems and utilities needed for railroad security purposes, including dispatching and notification systems;

(vi) emergency response planning;

(vii) employee training; and

(viii) such other matters as the Secretary determines appropriate; and

(D) identification of redundant and backup systems required to ensure the continued op-

[1] So in original. The word "to" probably should not appear.

eration of critical elements of a railroad carrier's system in the event of an attack or other incident, including disruption of commercial electric power or communications network.

(2) Threat information

The Secretary shall provide in a timely manner to the appropriate employees of a railroad carrier, as designated by the railroad carrier, threat information that is relevant to the carrier when preparing and submitting a vulnerability assessment and security plan, including an assessment of the most likely methods that could be used by terrorists to exploit weaknesses in railroad security.

(e) Security plans

(1) Requirements

The Secretary shall provide technical assistance and guidance to railroad carriers in preparing and implementing security plans under this section, and shall require that each security plan of a railroad carrier assigned to a high-risk tier under this section include, as applicable—

(A) identification of a security coordinator having authority—

(i) to implement security actions under the plan;

(ii) to coordinate security improvements; and

(iii) to receive immediate communications from appropriate Federal officials regarding railroad security;

(B) a list of needed capital and operational improvements;

(C) procedures to be implemented or used by the railroad carrier in response to a terrorist attack, including evacuation and passenger communication plans that include individuals with disabilities as appropriate;

(D) identification of steps taken with State and local law enforcement agencies, emergency responders, and Federal officials to coordinate security measures and plans for response to a terrorist attack;

(E) a strategy and timeline for conducting training under section 1167 of this title;

(F) enhanced security measures to be taken by the railroad carrier when the Secretary declares a period of heightened security risk;

(G) plans for providing redundant and backup systems required to ensure the continued operation of critical elements of the railroad carrier's system in the event of a terrorist attack or other incident;

(H) a strategy for implementing enhanced security for shipments of security-sensitive materials, including plans for quickly locating and securing such shipments in the event of a terrorist attack or security incident; and

(I) such other actions or procedures as the Secretary determines are appropriate to address the security of railroad carriers.

(2) Security coordinator requirements

The Secretary shall require that the individual serving as the security coordinator identified in paragraph (1)(A) is a citizen of the United States. The Secretary may waive this requirement with respect to an individual if the Secretary determines that it is appropriate to do so based on a background check of the individual and a review of the consolidated terrorist watchlist.

(3) Consistency with other plans

The Secretary shall ensure that the security plans developed by railroad carriers under this section are consistent with the risk assessment and National Strategy for Railroad Transportation Security developed under section 1161 of this title.

(f) Deadline for review process

Not later than 6 months after receiving the assessments and plans required under this section, the Secretary shall—

(1) review each vulnerability assessment and security plan submitted to the Secretary in accordance with subsection (c);

(2) require amendments to any security plan that does not meet the requirements of this section; and

(3) approve any vulnerability assessment or security plan that meets the requirements of this section.

(g) Interim security measures

The Secretary may require railroad carriers, during the period before the deadline established under subsection (c), to submit a security plan under subsection (e) to implement any necessary interim security measures essential to providing adequate security of the railroad carrier's system. An interim plan required under this subsection will be superseded by a plan required under subsection (e).

(h) Tier assignment

Utilizing the risk assessment and National Strategy for Railroad Transportation Security required under section 1161 of this title, the Secretary shall assign each railroad carrier to a risk-based tier established by the Secretary:

(1) Provision of information

The Secretary may request, and a railroad carrier shall provide, information necessary for the Secretary to assign a railroad carrier to the appropriate tier under this subsection.

(2) Notification

Not later than 60 days after the date a railroad carrier is assigned to a tier under this subsection, the Secretary shall notify the railroad carrier of the tier to which it is assigned and the reasons for such assignment.

(3) High-risk tiers

At least one of the tiers established by the Secretary under this subsection shall be designated a tier for high-risk railroad carriers.

(4) Reassignment

The Secretary may reassign a railroad carrier to another tier, as appropriate, in response to changes in risk. The Secretary shall notify the railroad carrier not later than 60 days after such reassignment and provide the railroad carrier with the reasons for such reassignment.

(i) Nondisclosure of information

(1) Submission of information to Congress

Nothing in this section shall be construed as authorizing the withholding of any information from Congress.

(2) Disclosure of independently furnished information

Nothing in this section shall be construed as affecting any authority or obligation of a Federal agency to disclose any record or information that the Federal agency obtains from a railroad carrier under any other Federal law.

(j) Existing procedures, protocols and standards

(1) Determination

In response to a petition by a railroad carrier or at the discretion of the Secretary, the Secretary may determine that existing procedures, protocols, and standards meet all or part of the requirements of this section, including regulations issued under subsection (a), regarding vulnerability assessments and security plans.

(2) Election

Upon review and written determination by the Secretary that existing procedures, protocols, or standards of a railroad carrier satisfy the requirements of this section, the railroad carrier may elect to comply with those procedures, protocols, or standards instead of the requirements of this section.

(3) Partial approval

If the Secretary determines that the existing procedures, protocols, or standards of a railroad carrier satisfy only part of the requirements of this section, the Secretary may accept such submission, but shall require submission by the railroad carrier of any additional information relevant to the vulnerability assessment and security plan of the railroad carrier to ensure that the remaining requirements of this section are fulfilled.

(4) Notification

If the Secretary determines that particular existing procedures, protocols, or standards of a railroad carrier under this subsection do not satisfy the requirements of this section, the Secretary shall provide to the railroad carrier a written notification that includes an explanation of the determination.

(5) Review

Nothing in this subsection shall relieve the Secretary of the obligation—

(A) to review the vulnerability assessment and security plan submitted by a railroad carrier under this section; and

(B) to approve or disapprove each submission on an individual basis.

(k) Periodic evaluation by railroad carriers required

(1) Submission of evaluation

Not later than 3 years after the date on which a vulnerability assessment or security plan required to be submitted to the Secretary under subsection (c) is approved, and at least once every 5 years thereafter (or on such a schedule as the Secretary may establish by regulation), a railroad carrier who submitted a vulnerability assessment and security plan and who is still assigned to the high-risk tier must also submit to the Secretary an evaluation of the adequacy of the vulnerability assessment and security plan that includes a description of any material changes made to the vulnerability assessment or security plan.

(2) Review of evaluation

Not later than 180 days after the date on which an evaluation is submitted, the Secretary shall review the evaluation and notify the railroad carrier submitting the evaluation of the Secretary's approval or disapproval of the evaluation.

(*l*) Shared facilities

The Secretary may permit under this section the development and implementation of coordinated vulnerability assessments and security plans to the extent that a railroad carrier shares facilities with, or is colocated with, other transportation entities or providers that are required to develop vulnerability assessments and security plans under Federal law.

(m) Consultation

In carrying out this section, the Secretary shall consult with railroad carriers, nonprofit employee labor organizations representation railroad employees, and public safety and law enforcement officials.

(Pub. L. 110–53, title XV, § 1512, Aug. 3, 2007, 121 Stat. 429.)

§ 1163. Railroad security assistance

(a) Security improvement grants

(1) The Secretary, in consultation with the Administrator of the Transportation Security Administration and other appropriate agencies or officials, is authorized to make grants to railroad carriers, the Alaska Railroad, security-sensitive materials offerors who ship by railroad, owners of railroad cars used in the transportation of security-sensitive materials, State and local governments (for railroad passenger facilities and infrastructure not owned by Amtrak), and Amtrak for intercity passenger railroad and freight railroad security improvements described in subsection (b) as approved by the Secretary.

(2) A railroad carrier is eligible for a grant under this section if the carrier has completed a vulnerability assessment and developed a security plan that the Secretary has approved in accordance with section 1162 of this title.

(3) A recipient of a grant under this section may use grant funds only for permissible uses under subsection (b) to further a railroad security plan that meets the requirements of paragraph (2).

(4) Notwithstanding the requirement for eligibility and uses of funds in paragraphs (2) and (3), a railroad carrier is eligible for a grant under this section if the applicant uses the funds solely for the development of assessments or security plans under section 1162 of this title.

(5) Notwithstanding the requirements for eligibility and uses of funds in paragraphs (2) and

(3), prior to the earlier of 1 year after the date of issuance of final regulations requiring vulnerability assessments and security plans under section 1162 of this title or 3 years after August 3, 2007, the Secretary may award grants under this section for rail security improvements listed under subsection (b) based upon railroad carrier vulnerability assessments and security plans that the Secretary determines are sufficient for the purposes of this section but have not been approved by the Secretary in accordance with section 1162 of this title.

(b) Uses of funds

A recipient of a grant under this section shall use the grant funds for one or more of the following:

(1) Security and redundancy for critical communications, computer, and train control systems essential for secure railroad operations.

(2) Accommodation of railroad cargo or passenger security inspection facilities, related infrastructure, and operations at or near United States international borders or other ports of entry.

(3) The security of security-sensitive materials transportation by railroad.

(4) Chemical, biological, radiological, or explosive detection, including canine patrols for such detection.

(5) The security of intercity passenger railroad stations, trains, and infrastructure, including security capital improvement projects that the Secretary determines enhance railroad station security.

(6) Technologies to reduce the vulnerabilities of railroad cars, including structural modification of railroad cars transporting security-sensitive materials to improve their resistance to acts of terrorism.

(7) The sharing of intelligence and information about security threats.

(8) To obtain train tracking and communications equipment, including equipment that is interoperable with Federal, State, and local agencies and tribal governments.

(9) To hire, train, and employ police and security officers, including canine units, assigned to full-time security or counterterrorism duties related to railroad transportation.

(10) Overtime reimbursement, including reimbursement of State, local, and tribal governments for costs, for enhanced security personnel assigned to duties related to railroad security during periods of high or severe threat levels and National Special Security Events or other periods of heightened security as determined by the Secretary.

(11) Perimeter protection systems, including access control, installation of improved lighting, fencing, and barricades at railroad facilities.

(12) Tunnel protection systems.

(13) Passenger evacuation and evacuation-related capital improvements.

(14) Railroad security inspection technologies, including verified visual inspection technologies using hand-held readers.

(15) Surveillance equipment.

(16) Cargo or passenger screening equipment.

(17) Emergency response equipment, including fire suppression and decontamination equipment, personal protective equipment, and defibrillators.

(18) Operating and capital costs associated with security awareness, preparedness, and response training, including training under section 1167 of this title, and training developed by universities, institutions of higher education, and nonprofit employee labor organizations, for railroad employees, including frontline employees.

(19) Live or simulated exercises, including exercises described in section 1166 of this title.

(20) Public awareness campaigns for enhanced railroad security.

(21) Development of assessments or security plans under section 1162 of this title.

(22) Other security improvements—

(A) identified, required, or recommended under sections 1161 and 1162 of this title, including infrastructure, facilities, and equipment upgrades; or

(B) that the Secretary considers appropriate.

(c) Department of Homeland Security responsibilities

In carrying out the responsibilities under subsection (a), the Secretary shall—

(1) determine the requirements for recipients of grants;

(2) establish priorities for uses of funds for grant recipients;

(3) award the funds authorized by this section based on risk, as identified by the plans required under sections 1161 and 1162 of this title, or assessment or plan described in subsection (a)(5);

(4) take into account whether stations or facilities are used by commuter railroad passengers as well as intercity railroad passengers in reviewing grant applications;

(5) encourage non-Federal financial participation in projects funded by grants; and

(6) not later than 5 business days after awarding a grant to Amtrak under this section, transfer grant funds to the Secretary of Transportation to be disbursed to Amtrak.

(d) Multiyear awards

Grant funds awarded under this section may be awarded for projects that span multiple years.

(e) Limitation on uses of funds

A grant made under this section may not be used to make any State or local government cost-sharing contribution under any other Federal law.

(f) Annual reports

Each recipient of a grant under this section shall report annually to the Secretary on the use of grant funds.

(g) Non-Federal match study

Not later than 240 days after August 3, 2007, the Secretary shall provide a report to the appropriate congressional committees on the feasibility and appropriateness of requiring a non-Federal match for grants awarded to freight railroad carriers and other private entities under this section.

(h) Subject to certain standards

A recipient of a grant under this section and sections 1164 and 1165 of this title shall be required to comply with the standards of section 24312 of title 49, as in effect on January 1, 2007, with respect to the project in the same manner as Amtrak is required to comply with such standards for construction work financed under an agreement made under section 24308(a) of that title.

(i) Authorization of appropriations

(1) In general

Out of funds appropriated pursuant to section 114(w) of title 49, there shall be made available to the Secretary to carry out this section—

(A) $300,000,000 for fiscal year 2008;

(B) $300,000,000 for fiscal year 2009;

(C) $300,000,000 for fiscal year 2010; and

(D) $300,000,000 for fiscal year 2011.

(2) Period of availability

Sums appropriated to carry out this section shall remain available until expended.

(Pub. L. 110–53, title XV, § 1513, Aug. 3, 2007, 121 Stat. 433.)

§ 1164. Systemwide Amtrak security upgrades

(a) In general

(1) Grants

Subject to subsection (b), the Secretary, in consultation with the Administrator of the Transportation Security Administration, is authorized to make grants to Amtrak in accordance with the provisions of this section.

(2) General purposes

The Secretary may make such grants for the purposes of—

(A) protecting underwater and underground assets and systems;

(B) protecting high-risk and high-consequence assets identified through systemwide risk assessments;

(C) providing counterterrorism or security training;

(D) providing both visible and unpredictable deterrence; and

(E) conducting emergency preparedness drills and exercises.

(3) Specific projects

The Secretary shall make such grants—

(A) to secure major tunnel access points and ensure tunnel integrity in New York, New Jersey, Maryland, and Washington, DC;

(B) to secure Amtrak trains;

(C) to secure Amtrak stations;

(D) to obtain a watchlist identification system approved by the Secretary;

(E) to obtain train tracking and interoperable communications systems that are coordinated with Federal, State, and local agencies and tribal governments to the maximum extent possible;

(F) to hire, train, and employ police and security officers, including canine units, assigned to full-time security or counterterrorism duties related to railroad transportation;

(G) for operating and capital costs associated with security awareness, preparedness, and response training, including training under section 1167 of this title, and training developed by universities, institutions of higher education, and nonprofit employee labor organizations, for railroad employees, including frontline employees; and

(H) for live or simulated exercises, including exercises described in section 1166 of this title.

(b) Conditions

The Secretary shall award grants to Amtrak under this section for projects contained in a systemwide security plan approved by the Secretary developed pursuant to section 1162 of this title. Not later than 5 business days after awarding a grant to Amtrak under this section, the Secretary shall transfer the grant funds to the Secretary of Transportation to be disbursed to Amtrak.

(c) Equitable geographic allocation

The Secretary shall ensure that, subject to meeting the highest security needs on Amtrak's entire system and consistent with the risk assessment required under section 1161 of this title and Amtrak's vulnerability assessment and security plan developed under section 1162 of this title, stations and facilities located outside of the Northeast Corridor receive an equitable share of the security funds authorized by this section.

(d) Availability of funds

(1) In general

Out of funds appropriated pursuant to section 114(w) of title 49, there shall be made available to the Secretary and the Administrator of the Transportation Security Administration to carry out this section—

(A) $150,000,000 for fiscal year 2008;

(B) $150,000,000 for fiscal year 2009;

(C) $175,000,000 for fiscal year 2010; and

(D) $175,000,000 for fiscal year 2011.

(2) Availability of appropriated funds

Amounts appropriated pursuant to paragraph (1) shall remain available until expended.

(Pub. L. 110–53, title XV, § 1514, Aug. 3, 2007, 121 Stat. 435.)

§ 1165. Fire and life safety improvements

(a) Life-safety needs

There are authorized to be appropriated to the Secretary of Transportation for making grants to Amtrak for the purpose of carrying out projects to make fire and life safety improvements to Amtrak tunnels on the Northeast Corridor the following amounts:

(1) For the 6 New York and New Jersey tunnels to provide ventilation, electrical, and fire safety technology improvements, emergency communication and lighting systems, and emergency access and egress for passengers—

(A) $25,000,000 for fiscal year 2008;

(B) $30,000,000 for fiscal year 2009;
(C) $45,000,000 for fiscal year 2010; and
(D) $60,000,000 for fiscal year 2011.

(2) For the Baltimore Potomac Tunnel and the Union Tunnel, together, to provide adequate drainage and ventilation, communication, lighting, standpipe, and passenger egress improvements—

(A) $5,000,000 for fiscal year 2008;
(B) $5,000,000 for fiscal year 2009;
(C) $5,000,000 for fiscal year 2010; and
(D) $5,000,000 for fiscal year 2011.

(3) For the Union Station tunnels in the District of Columbia to improve ventilation, communication, lighting, and passenger egress improvements—

(A) $5,000,000 for fiscal year 2008;
(B) $5,000,000 for fiscal year 2009;
(C) $5,000,000 for fiscal year 2010; and
(D) $5,000,000 for fiscal year 2011.

(b) Infrastructure upgrades

Out of funds appropriated pursuant to section 1153 of this title, there shall be made available to the Secretary of Transportation for fiscal year 2008, $3,000,000 for the preliminary design of options for a new tunnel on a different alignment to augment the capacity of the existing Baltimore tunnels.

(c) Availability of amounts

Amounts appropriated pursuant to this section shall remain available until expended.

(d) Plans required

The Secretary of Transportation may not make amounts available to Amtrak for obligation or expenditure under subsection (a)—

(1) until Amtrak has submitted to the Secretary of Transportation, and the Secretary of Transportation has approved, an engineering and financial plan for such projects; and

(2) unless, for each project funded pursuant to this section, the Secretary of Transportation has approved a project management plan prepared by Amtrak.

(e) Review of plans

(1) In general

The Secretary of Transportation shall complete the review of a plan required under subsection (d) and approve or disapprove the plan within 45 days after the date on which each such plan is submitted by Amtrak.

(2) Incomplete or deficient plan

If the Secretary of Transportation determines that a plan is incomplete or deficient, the Secretary of Transportation shall notify Amtrak of the incomplete items or deficiencies and Amtrak shall, within 30 days after receiving the Secretary of Transportation's notification, submit a modified plan for the Secretary of Transportation's review.

(3) Approval of plan

Within 15 days after receiving additional information on items previously included in the plan, and within 45 days after receiving items newly included in a modified plan, the Secretary of Transportation shall either approve the modified plan, or if the Secretary of Transportation finds the plan is still incomplete or deficient, the Secretary of Transportation shall—

(A) identify in writing to the appropriate congressional committees the portions of the plan the Secretary finds incomplete or deficient;

(B) approve all other portions of the plan;

(C) obligate the funds associated with those portions; and

(D) execute an agreement with Amtrak within 15 days thereafter on a process for resolving the remaining portions of the plan.

(f) Financial contribution from other tunnel users

The Secretary of Transportation, taking into account the need for the timely completion of all portions of the tunnel projects described in subsection (a), shall—

(1) consider the extent to which railroad carriers other than Amtrak use or plan to use the tunnels;

(2) consider the feasibility of seeking a financial contribution from those other railroad carriers toward the costs of the projects; and

(3) obtain financial contributions or commitments from such other railroad carriers at levels reflecting the extent of their use or planned use of the tunnels, if feasible.

(Pub. L. 110–53, title XV, § 1515, Aug. 3, 2007, 121 Stat. 437.)

§ 1166. Railroad carrier exercises

(a) In general

The Secretary shall establish a program for conducting security exercises for railroad carriers for the purpose of assessing and improving the capabilities of entities described in subsection (b) to prevent, prepare for, mitigate, respond to, and recover from acts of terrorism.

(b) Covered entities

Entities to be assessed under the program shall include—

(1) Federal, State, and local agencies and tribal governments;

(2) railroad carriers;

(3) governmental and nongovernmental emergency response providers, law enforcement agencies, and railroad and transit police, as appropriate; and

(4) any other organization or entity that the Secretary determines appropriate.

(c) Requirements

The Secretary shall ensure that the program—

(1) consolidates existing security exercises for railroad carriers administered by the Department and the Department of Transportation, as jointly determined by the Secretary and the Secretary of Transportation, unless the Secretary waives this consolidation requirement as appropriate;

(2) consists of exercises that are—

(A) scaled and tailored to the needs of the carrier, including addressing the needs of the elderly and individuals with disabilities;

(B) live, in the case of the most at-risk facilities to a terrorist attack;

(C) coordinated with appropriate officials;

(D) as realistic as practicable and based on current risk assessments, including credible threats, vulnerabilities, and consequences;

(E) inclusive, as appropriate, of railroad frontline employees; and

(F) consistent with the National Incident Management System, the National Response Plan, the National Infrastructure Protection Plan, the National Preparedness Guidance, the National Preparedness Goal, and other such national initiatives;

(3) provides that exercises described in paragraph (2) will be—

(A) evaluated by the Secretary against clear and consistent performance measures;

(B) assessed by the Secretary to identify best practices, which shall be shared, as appropriate, with railroad carriers, nonprofit employee organizations that represent railroad carrier employees, Federal, State, local, and tribal officials, governmental and nongovernmental emergency response providers, law enforcement personnel, including railroad carrier and transit police, and other stakeholders; and

(C) used to develop recommendations, as appropriate, from the Secretary to railroad carriers on remedial action to be taken in response to lessons learned;

(4) allows for proper advanced notification of communities and local governments in which exercises are held, as appropriate; and

(5) assists State, local, and tribal governments and railroad carriers in designing, implementing, and evaluating additional exercises that conform to the requirements of paragraph (1).

(d) National Exercise Program

The Secretary shall ensure that the exercise program developed under subsection (c) is a component of the National Exercise Program established under section 748 of this title.

(Pub. L. 110–53, title XV, § 1516, Aug. 3, 2007, 121 Stat. 438.)

§ 1167. Railroad security training program

(a) In general

Not later than 6 months after August 3, 2007, the Secretary shall develop and issue regulations for a training program to prepare railroad frontline employees for potential security threats and conditions. The regulations shall take into consideration any current security training requirements or best practices.

(b) Consultation

The Secretary shall develop the regulations under subsection (a) in consultation with—

(1) appropriate law enforcement, fire service, emergency response, security, and terrorism experts;

(2) railroad carriers;

(3) railroad shippers; and

(4) nonprofit employee labor organizations representing railroad employees or emergency response personnel.

(c) Program elements

The regulations developed under subsection (a) shall require security training programs described in subsection (a) to include, at a minimum, elements to address the following, as applicable:

(1) Determination of the seriousness of any occurrence or threat.

(2) Crew and passenger communication and coordination.

(3) Appropriate responses to defend or protect oneself.

(4) Use of personal and other protective equipment.

(5) Evacuation procedures for passengers and railroad employees, including individuals with disabilities and the elderly.

(6) Psychology, behavior, and methods of terrorists, including observation and analysis.

(7) Training related to psychological responses to terrorist incidents, including the ability to cope with hijacker behavior and passenger responses.

(8) Live situational training exercises regarding various threat conditions, including tunnel evacuation procedures.

(9) Recognition and reporting of dangerous substances, suspicious packages, and situations.

(10) Understanding security incident procedures, including procedures for communicating with governmental and nongovernmental emergency response providers and for on-scene interaction with such emergency response providers.

(11) Operation and maintenance of security equipment and systems.

(12) Other security training activities that the Secretary considers appropriate.

(d) Required programs

(1) Development and submission to Secretary

Not later than 90 days after the Secretary issues regulations under subsection (a), each railroad carrier shall develop a security training program in accordance with this section and submit the program to the Secretary for approval.

(2) Approval or disapproval

Not later than 60 days after receiving a security training program proposal under this subsection, the Secretary shall approve the program or require the railroad carrier that developed the program to make any revisions to the program that the Secretary considers necessary for the program to meet the requirements of this section. A railroad carrier shall respond to the Secretary's comments within 30 days after receiving them.

(3) Training

Not later than 1 year after the Secretary approves a security training program in accordance with this subsection, the railroad carrier that developed the program shall complete the training of all railroad frontline employees who were hired by a carrier more than 30 days preceding such date. For such employees employed less than 30 days by a carrier preceding such date, training shall be completed within the first 60 days of employment.

(4) Updates of regulations and program revisions

The Secretary shall periodically review and update as appropriate the training regulations issued under subsection (a) to reflect new or changing security threats. Each railroad carrier shall revise its training program accordingly and provide additional training as necessary to its frontline employees within a reasonable time after the regulations are updated.

(e) National Training Program

The Secretary shall ensure that the training program developed under subsection (a) is a component of the National Training Program established under section 748 of this title.

(f) Reporting requirements

Not later than 2 years after the date of regulation issuance, the Secretary shall review implementation of the training program of a representative sample of railroad carriers and railroad frontline employees, and report to the appropriate congressional committees on the number of reviews conducted and the results of such reviews. The Secretary may submit the report in both classified and redacted formats as necessary.

(g) Other employees

The Secretary shall issue guidance and best practices for a railroad shipper employee security program containing the elements listed under subsection (c).

(Pub. L. 110–53, title XV, §1517, Aug. 3, 2007, 121 Stat. 439.)

§1168. Railroad security research and development

(a) Establishment of research and development program

The Secretary, acting through the Under Secretary for Science and Technology and the Administrator of the Transportation Security Administration, shall carry out a research and development program for the purpose of improving the security of railroad transportation systems.

(b) Eligible projects

The research and development program may include projects—

(1) to reduce the vulnerability of passenger trains, stations, and equipment to explosives and hazardous chemical, biological, and radioactive substances, including the development of technology to screen passengers in large numbers at peak commuting times with minimal interference and disruption;

(2) to test new emergency response and recovery techniques and technologies, including those used at international borders;

(3) to develop improved railroad security technologies, including—

(A) technologies for sealing or modifying railroad tank cars;

(B) automatic inspection of railroad cars;

(C) communication-based train control systems;

(D) emergency response training, including training in a tunnel environment;

(E) security and redundancy for critical communications, electrical power, computer, and train control systems; and

(F) technologies for securing bridges and tunnels;

(4) to test wayside detectors that can detect tampering;

(5) to support enhanced security for the transportation of security-sensitive materials by railroad;

(6) to mitigate damages in the event of a cyber attack; and

(7) to address other vulnerabilities and risks identified by the Secretary.

(c) Coordination with other research initiatives

The Secretary—

(1) shall ensure that the research and development program is consistent with the National Strategy for Railroad Transportation Security developed under section 1161 of this title and any other transportation security research and development programs required by this Act;

(2) shall, to the extent practicable, coordinate the research and development activities of the Department with other ongoing research and development security-related initiatives, including research being conducted by—

(A) the Department of Transportation, including University Transportation Centers and other institutes, centers, and simulators funded by the Department of Transportation;

(B) the National Academy of Sciences;

(C) the Technical Support Working Group;

(D) other Federal departments and agencies; and

(E) other Federal and private research laboratories, research entities, and universities and institutions of higher education, including Historically Black Colleges and Universities, Hispanic Serving Institutions, or Indian Tribally Controlled Colleges and Universities;

(3) shall carry out any research and development project authorized by this section through a reimbursable agreement with an appropriate Federal agency, if the agency—

(A) is currently sponsoring a research and development project in a similar area; or

(B) has a unique facility or capability that would be useful in carrying out the project;

(4) may award grants, or enter into cooperative agreements, contracts, other transactions, or reimbursable agreements to the entities described in paragraph (2) and the eligible grant recipients under section 1163 of this title; and

(5) shall make reasonable efforts to enter into memoranda of understanding, contracts, grants, cooperative agreements, or other transactions with railroad carriers willing to contribute both physical space and other resources.

(d) Privacy and civil rights and civil liberties issues

(1) Consultation

In carrying out research and development projects under this section, the Secretary shall consult with the Chief Privacy Officer of the Department and the Officer for Civil Rights and Civil Liberties of the Department as appropriate and in accordance with section 142 of this title.

(2) Privacy impact assessments

In accordance with sections 142 and 345 of this title, the Chief Privacy Officer shall conduct privacy impact assessments and the Officer for Civil Rights and Civil Liberties shall conduct reviews, as appropriate, for research and development initiatives developed under this section that the Secretary determines could have an impact on privacy, civil rights, or civil liberties.

(e) Authorization of appropriations

(1) In general

Out of funds appropriated pursuant to section 114(w) of title 49, there shall be made available to the Secretary to carry out this section—

(A) $33,000,000 for fiscal year 2008;
(B) $33,000,000 for fiscal year 2009;
(C) $33,000,000 for fiscal year 2010; and
(D) $33,000,000 for fiscal year 2011.

(2) Period of availability

Such sums shall remain available until expended.

(Pub. L. 110–53, title XV, § 1518, Aug. 3, 2007, 121 Stat. 441.)

REFERENCES IN TEXT

This Act, referred to in subsec. (c)(1), is Pub. L. 110–53, Aug. 3, 2007, 121 Stat. 266, known as the Implementing Recommendations of the 9/11 Commission Act of 2007, which enacted this chapter and enacted and amended numerous other sections and notes in the Code. For complete classification of this Act to the Code, see Short Title of 2007 Amendment note set out under section 101 of this title and Tables.

§ 1169. Railroad tank car security testing

(a) Railroad tank car vulnerability assessment

(1) Assessment

The Secretary shall assess the likely methods of a deliberate terrorist attack against a railroad tank car used to transport toxic-inhalation-hazard materials, and for each method assessed, the degree to which it may be successful in causing death, injury, or serious adverse effects to human health, the environment, critical infrastructure, national security, the national economy, or public welfare.

(2) Threats

In carrying out paragraph (1), the Secretary shall consider the most current threat information as to likely methods of a successful terrorist attack on a railroad tank car transporting toxic-inhalation-hazard materials, and may consider the following:

(A) Explosive devices placed along the tracks or attached to a railroad tank car.

(B) The use of missiles, grenades, rockets, mortars, or other high-caliber weapons against a railroad tank car.

(3) Physical testing

In developing the assessment required under paragraph (1), the Secretary shall conduct physical testing of the vulnerability of railroad tank cars used to transport toxic-inhalation-hazard materials to different methods of a deliberate attack, using technical information and criteria to evaluate the structural integrity of railroad tank cars.

(4) Report

Not later than 30 days after the completion of the assessment under paragraph (1), the Secretary shall provide to the appropriate congressional committees a report, in the appropriate format, on such assessment.

(b) Railroad tank car dispersion modeling

(1) In general

The Secretary, acting through the National Infrastructure Simulation and Analysis Center, shall conduct an air dispersion modeling analysis of release scenarios of toxic-inhalation-hazard materials resulting from a terrorist attack on a loaded railroad tank car carrying such materials in urban and rural environments.

(2) Considerations

The analysis under this subsection shall take into account the following considerations:

(A) The most likely means of attack and the resulting dispersal rate.

(B) Different times of day, to account for differences in cloud coverage and other atmospheric conditions in the environment being modeled.

(C) Differences in population size and density.

(D) Historically accurate wind speeds, temperatures, and wind directions.

(E) Differences in dispersal rates or other relevant factors related to whether a railroad tank car is in motion or stationary.

(F) Emergency response procedures by local officials.

(G) Any other considerations the Secretary believes would develop an accurate, plausible dispersion model for toxic-inhalation-hazard materials released from a railroad tank car as a result of a terrorist act.

(3) Consultation

In conducting the dispersion modeling under paragraph (1), the Secretary shall consult with the Secretary of Transportation, hazardous materials experts, railroad carriers, nonprofit employee labor organizations representing railroad employees, appropriate State, local, and tribal officials, and other Federal agencies, as appropriate.

(4) Information sharing

Upon completion of the analysis required under paragraph (1), the Secretary shall share the information developed with the appropriate stakeholders, given appropriate information protection provisions as may be required by the Secretary.

(5) Report

Not later than 30 days after completion of all dispersion analyses under paragraph (1), the Secretary shall submit to the appropriate congressional committees a report detailing the Secretary's conclusions and findings in an appropriate format.

(Pub. L. 110–53, title XV, § 1519, Aug. 3, 2007, 121 Stat. 443.)

§ 1170. Security background checks of covered individuals

(a) Definitions

In this section, the following definitions apply:

(1) Security background check

The term "security background check" means reviewing, for the purpose of identifying individuals who may pose a threat to transportation security or national security, or of terrorism—

(A) relevant criminal history databases;

(B) in the case of an alien (as defined in the Immigration and Nationality Act (8 U.S.C. 1101(a)(3)),[1] the relevant databases to determine the status of the alien under the immigration laws of the United States; and

(C) other relevant information or databases, as determined by the Secretary.

(2) Covered individual

The term "covered individual" means an employee of a railroad carrier or a contractor or subcontractor of a railroad carrier.

(b) Guidance

(1) Any guidance, recommendations, suggested action items, or any other widely disseminated voluntary action items issued by the Secretary to a railroad carrier or a contractor or subcontractor of a railroad carrier relating to performing a security background check of a covered individual shall contain recommendations on the appropriate scope and application of such a security background check, including the time period covered, the types of disqualifying offenses, and a redress process for adversely impacted covered individuals consistent with subsections (c) and (d) of this section.

(2) Within 60 days after August 3, 2007, any guidance, recommendations, suggested action items, or any other widely disseminated voluntary action item issued by the Secretary prior to August 3, 2007, to a railroad carrier or a contractor or subcontractor of a railroad carrier relating to performing a security background check of a covered individual shall be updated in compliance with paragraph (1).

(3) If a railroad carrier or a contractor or subcontractor of a railroad carrier performs a security background check on a covered individual to fulfill guidance issued by the Secretary under paragraph (1) or (2), the Secretary shall not consider such guidance fulfilled unless an adequate redress process as described in subsection (d) is provided to covered individuals.

(c) Requirements

If the Secretary issues a rule, regulation, or directive requiring a railroad carrier or contractor or subcontractor of a railroad carrier to perform a security background check of a covered individual, then the Secretary shall prohibit the railroad carrier or contractor or subcontractor of a railroad carrier from making an adverse employment decision, including removal or suspension of the covered individual, due to such rule, regulation, or directive with respect to a covered individual unless the railroad carrier or contractor or subcontractor of a railroad carrier determines that the covered individual—

(1) has been convicted of, has been found not guilty by reason of insanity, or is under want, warrant, or indictment for a permanent disqualifying criminal offense listed in part 1572 of title 49, Code of Federal Regulations;

(2) was convicted of or found not guilty by reason of insanity of an interim disqualifying criminal offense listed in part 1572 of title 49, Code of Federal Regulations, within 7 years of the date that the railroad carrier or contractor or subcontractor of a railroad carrier performs the security background check; or

(3) was incarcerated for an interim disqualifying criminal offense listed in part 1572 of title 49, Code of Federal Regulations, and released from incarceration within 5 years of the date that the railroad carrier or contractor or subcontractor of a railroad carrier performs the security background check.

(d) Redress process

If the Secretary issues a rule, regulation, or directive requiring a railroad carrier or contractor or subcontractor of a railroad carrier to perform a security background check of a covered individual, the Secretary shall—

(1) provide an adequate redress process for a covered individual subjected to an adverse employment decision, including removal or suspension of the employee, due to such rule, regulation, or directive that is consistent with the appeals and waiver process established for applicants for commercial motor vehicle hazardous materials endorsements and transportation employees at ports, as required by section 70105(c) of title 46; and

(2) have the authority to order an appropriate remedy, including reinstatement of the covered individual, should the Secretary determine that a railroad carrier or contractor or subcontractor of a railroad carrier wrongfully made an adverse employment decision regarding a covered individual pursuant to such rule, regulation, or directive.

(e) False statements

A railroad carrier or a contractor or subcontractor of a railroad carrier may not knowingly misrepresent to an employee or other relevant person, including an arbiter involved in a labor arbitration, the scope, application, or meaning of any rules, regulations, directives, or guidance issued by the Secretary related to security background check requirements for covered individuals when conducting a security background check. Not later than 1 year after August 3, 2007, the Secretary shall issue a regulation that prohibits a railroad carrier or a contractor or subcontractor of a railroad carrier from knowingly misrepresenting to an employee or other relevant person, including an arbiter involved in a labor arbitration, the scope, application, or meaning of any rules, regulations, directives, or guidance issued by the Secretary related to security background check requirements for covered individuals when conducting a security background check.

[1] So in original. Another closing parenthesis probably should precede the comma.

(f) Rights and responsibilities

Nothing in this section shall be construed to abridge a railroad carrier's or a contractor or subcontractor of a railroad carrier's rights or responsibilities to make adverse employment decisions permitted by other Federal, State, or local laws. Nothing in the section shall be construed to abridge rights and responsibilities of covered individuals, a railroad carrier, or a contractor or subcontractor of a railroad carrier, under any other Federal, State, or local laws or under any collective bargaining agreement.

(g) No preemption of Federal or State law

Nothing in this section shall be construed to preempt a Federal, State, or local law that requires criminal history background checks, immigration status checks, or other background checks, of covered individuals.

(h) Statutory construction

Nothing in this section shall be construed to affect the process for review established under section 70105(c) of title 46, including regulations issued pursuant to such section.

(Pub. L. 110–53, title XV, §1522, Aug. 3, 2007, 121 Stat. 448.)

REFERENCES IN TEXT

The Immigration and Nationality Act, referred to in subsec. (a)(1)(B), is act June 27, 1952, ch. 477, 66 Stat. 163, which is classified principally to chapter 12 (§1101 et seq.) of Title 8, Aliens and Nationality. The term "alien" is defined in section 101(a)(3) of the Act which is classified to section 1101(a)(3) of Title 8. For complete classification of this Act to the Code, see Short Title note set out under section 1101 of Title 8 and Tables.

§1171. International railroad security program

(a) In general

(1) The Secretary shall develop a system to detect both undeclared passengers and contraband, with a primary focus on the detection of nuclear and radiological materials entering the United States by railroad.

(2) SYSTEM REQUIREMENTS.—In developing the system under paragraph (1), the Secretary may, in consultation with the Domestic Nuclear Detection Office, Customs and Border Protection, and the Transportation Security Administration—

(A) deploy radiation detection equipment and nonintrusive imaging equipment at locations where railroad shipments cross an international border to enter the United States;

(B) consider the integration of radiation detection technologies with other nonintrusive inspection technologies where feasible;

(C) ensure appropriate training, operations, and response protocols are established for Federal, State, and local personnel;

(D) implement alternative procedures to check railroad shipments at locations where the deployment of nonintrusive inspection imaging equipment is determined to not be practicable;

(E) ensure, to the extent practicable, that such technologies deployed can detect terrorists or weapons, including weapons of mass destruction; and

(F) take other actions, as appropriate, to develop the system.

(b) Additional information

The Secretary shall—

(1) identify and seek the submission of additional data elements for improved high-risk targeting related to the movement of cargo through the international supply chain utilizing a railroad prior to importation into the United States;

(2) utilize data collected and maintained by the Secretary of Transportation in the targeting of high-risk cargo identified under paragraph (1); and

(3) analyze the data provided in this subsection to identify high-risk cargo for inspection.

(c) Report to Congress

Not later than September 30, 2008, the Secretary shall transmit to the appropriate congressional committees a report that describes the progress of the system being developed under subsection (a).

(d) Definitions

In this section:

(1) International supply chain

The term "international supply chain" means the end-to-end process for shipping goods to or from the United States, beginning at the point of origin (including manufacturer, supplier, or vendor) through a point of distribution to the destination.

(2) Radiation detection equipment

The term "radiation detection equipment" means any technology that is capable of detecting or identifying nuclear and radiological material or nuclear and radiological explosive devices.

(3) Inspection

The term "inspection" means the comprehensive process used by Customs and Border Protection to assess goods entering the United States to appraise them for duty purposes, to detect the presence of restricted or prohibited items, and to ensure compliance with all applicable laws.

(Pub. L. 110–53, title XV, §1524, Aug. 3, 2007, 121 Stat. 451.)

§1172. Railroad security enhancements; Model State legislation

Not later than November 2, 2007, the Secretary of Transportation shall develop and make available to States model legislation to address the problem of entities that claim to be railroad carriers in order to establish and run a police force when the entities do not in fact provide railroad transportation. In developing the model State legislation the Secretary shall solicit the input of the States, railroads carriers, and railroad carrier employees. The Secretary shall review and, if necessary, revise such model State legislation periodically.

(Pub. L. 110–53, title XV, §1526(b), Aug. 3, 2007, 121 Stat. 452.)

PART C—OVER-THE-ROAD BUS AND TRUCKING SECURITY

§1181. Over-the-road bus security assessments and plans

(a) In general

Not later than 18 months after August 3, 2007, the Secretary shall issue regulations that—

(1) require each over-the-road bus operator assigned to a high-risk tier under this section—

(A) to conduct a vulnerability assessment in accordance with subsections (c) and (d); and

(B) to prepare, submit to the Secretary for approval, and implement a security plan in accordance with subsection (e); and

(2) establish standards and guidelines for developing and implementing the vulnerability assessments and security plans for carriers assigned to high-risk tiers consistent with this section.

(b) Non high-risk programs

The Secretary may establish a security program for over-the-road bus operators not assigned to a high-risk tier, including—

(1) guidance for such operators in conducting vulnerability assessments and preparing and implementing security plans, as determined appropriate by the Secretary; and

(2) a process to review and approve such assessments and plans, as appropriate.

(c) Deadline for submission

Not later than 9 months after the date of issuance of the regulations under subsection (a), the vulnerability assessments and security plans required by such regulations for over the road bus operators assigned to a high-risk tier shall be completed and submitted to the Secretary for review and approval.

(d) Vulnerability assessments

(1) Requirements

The Secretary shall provide technical assistance and guidance to over-the-road bus operators in conducting vulnerability assessments under this section and shall require that each vulnerability assessment of an operator assigned to a high-risk tier under this section includes, as appropriate—

(A) identification and evaluation of critical assets and infrastructure, including platforms, stations, terminals, and information systems;

(B) identification of the vulnerabilities to those assets and infrastructure; and

(C) identification of weaknesses in—

(i) physical security;

(ii) passenger and cargo security;

(iii) the security of programmable electronic devices, computers, or other automated systems which are used in providing over-the-road bus transportation;

(iv) alarms, cameras, and other protection systems;

(v) communications systems and utilities needed for over-the-road bus security purposes, including dispatching systems;

(vi) emergency response planning;

(vii) employee training; and

(viii) such other matters as the Secretary determines appropriate.

(2) Threat information

The Secretary shall provide in a timely manner to the appropriate employees of an over-the-road bus operator, as designated by the over-the-road bus operator, threat information that is relevant to the operator when preparing and submitting a vulnerability assessment and security plan, including an assessment of the most likely methods that could be used by terrorists to exploit weaknesses in over-the-road bus security.

(e) Security plans

(1) Requirements

The Secretary shall provide technical assistance and guidance to over-the-road bus operators in preparing and implementing security plans under this section and shall require that each security plan of an over-the-road bus operator assigned to a high-risk tier under this section includes, as appropriate—

(A) the identification of a security coordinator having authority—

(i) to implement security actions under the plan;

(ii) to coordinate security improvements; and

(iii) to receive communications from appropriate Federal officials regarding over-the-road bus security;

(B) a list of needed capital and operational improvements;

(C) procedures to be implemented or used by the over-the-road bus operator in response to a terrorist attack, including evacuation and passenger communication plans that include individuals with disabilities, as appropriate;

(D) the identification of steps taken with State and local law enforcement agencies, emergency responders, and Federal officials to coordinate security measures and plans for response to a terrorist attack;

(E) a strategy and timeline for conducting training under section 1184 of this title;

(F) enhanced security measures to be taken by the over-the-road bus operator when the Secretary declares a period of heightened security risk;

(G) plans for providing redundant and backup systems required to ensure the continued operation of critical elements of the over-the-road bus operator's system in the event of a terrorist attack or other incident; and

(H) such other actions or procedures as the Secretary determines are appropriate to address the security of over-the-road bus operators.

(2) Security coordinator requirements

The Secretary shall require that the individual serving as the security coordinator identified in paragraph (1)(A) is a citizen of the United States. The Secretary may waive this requirement with respect to an individual if the Secretary determines that it is appropriate to do so based on a background check of the individual and a review of the consolidated terrorist watchlist.

(f) Deadline for review process

Not later than 6 months after receiving the assessments and plans required under this section, the Secretary shall—

(1) review each vulnerability assessment and security plan submitted to the Secretary in accordance with subsection (c);

(2) require amendments to any security plan that does not meet the requirements of this section; and

(3) approve any vulnerability assessment or security plan that meets the requirements of this section.

(g) Interim security measures

The Secretary may require over-the-road bus operators, during the period before the deadline established under subsection (c), to submit a security plan to implement any necessary interim security measures essential to providing adequate security of the over-the-road bus operator's system. An interim plan required under this subsection shall be superseded by a plan required under subsection (c).

(h) Tier assignment

The Secretary shall assign each over-the-road bus operator to a risk-based tier established by the Secretary:

(1) Provision of information

The Secretary may request, and an over-the-road bus operator shall provide, information necessary for the Secretary to assign an over-the-road bus operator to the appropriate tier under this subsection.

(2) Notification

Not later than 60 days after the date an over-the-road bus operator is assigned to a tier under this section, the Secretary shall notify the operator of the tier to which it is assigned and the reasons for such assignment.

(3) High-risk tiers

At least one of the tiers established by the Secretary under this section shall be a tier designated for high-risk over-the-road bus operators.

(4) Reassignment

The Secretary may reassign an over-the-road bus operator to another tier, as appropriate, in response to changes in risk and the Secretary shall notify the over-the-road bus operator within 60 days after such reassignment and provide the operator with the reasons for such reassignment.

(i) Existing procedures, protocols, and standards

(1) Determination

In response to a petition by an over-the-road bus operator or at the discretion of the Secretary, the Secretary may determine that existing procedures, protocols, and standards meet all or part of the requirements of this section regarding vulnerability assessments and security plans.

(2) Election

Upon review and written determination by the Secretary that existing procedures, protocols, or standards of an over-the-road bus operator satisfy the requirements of this section, the over-the-road bus operator may elect to comply with those procedures, protocols, or standards instead of the requirements of this section.

(3) Partial approval

If the Secretary determines that the existing procedures, protocols, or standards of an over-the-road bus operator satisfy only part of the requirements of this section, the Secretary may accept such submission, but shall require submission by the operator of any additional information relevant to the vulnerability assessment and security plan of the operator to ensure that the remaining requirements of this section are fulfilled.

(4) Notification

If the Secretary determines that particular existing procedures, protocols, or standards of an over-the-road bus operator under this subsection do not satisfy the requirements of this section, the Secretary shall provide to the operator a written notification that includes an explanation of the reasons for nonacceptance.

(5) Review

Nothing in this subsection shall relieve the Secretary of the obligation—

(A) to review the vulnerability assessment and security plan submitted by an over-the-road bus operator under this section; and

(B) to approve or disapprove each submission on an individual basis.

(j) Periodic evaluation by over-the-road bus provider required

(1) Submission of evaluation

Not later than 3 years after the date on which a vulnerability assessment or security plan required to be submitted to the Secretary under subsection (c) is approved, and at least once every 5 years thereafter (or on such a schedule as the Secretary may establish by regulation), an over-the-road bus operator who submitted a vulnerability assessment and security plan and who is still assigned to the high-risk tier shall also submit to the Secretary an evaluation of the adequacy of the vulnerability assessment and security plan that includes a description of any material changes made to the vulnerability assessment or security plan.

(2) Review of evaluation

Not later than 180 days after the date on which an evaluation is submitted, the Secretary shall review the evaluation and notify the over-the-road bus operator submitting the evaluation of the Secretary's approval or disapproval of the evaluation.

(k) Shared facilities

The Secretary may permit under this section the development and implementation of coordinated vulnerability assessments and security plans to the extent that an over-the-road bus operator shares facilities with, or is colocated with, other transportation entities or providers that are required to develop vulnerability assessments and security plans under Federal law.

(*l*) Nondisclosure of information

(1) Submission of information to Congress

Nothing in this section shall be construed as authorizing the withholding of any information from Congress.

(2) Disclosure of independently furnished information

Nothing in this section shall be construed as affecting any authority or obligation of a Federal agency to disclose any record or information that the Federal agency obtains from an over-the-road bus operator under any other Federal law.

(Pub. L. 110–53, title XV, § 1531, Aug. 3, 2007, 121 Stat. 454.)

§ 1182. Over-the-road bus security assistance

(a) In general

The Secretary shall establish a program for making grants to eligible private operators providing transportation by an over-the-road bus for security improvements described in subsection (b).

(b) Uses of funds

A recipient of a grant received under subsection (a) shall use the grant funds for one or more of the following:

(1) Constructing and modifying terminals, garages, and facilities, including terminals and other over-the-road bus facilities owned by State or local governments, to increase their security.

(2) Modifying over-the-road buses to increase their security.

(3) Protecting or isolating the driver of an over-the-road bus.

(4) Acquiring, upgrading, installing, or operating equipment, software, or accessorial services for collection, storage, or exchange of passenger and driver information through ticketing systems or other means and for information links with government agencies, for security purposes.

(5) Installing cameras and video surveillance equipment on over-the-road buses and at terminals, garages, and over-the-road bus facilities.

(6) Establishing and improving an emergency communications system linking drivers and over-the-road buses to the recipient's operations center or linking the operations center to law enforcement and emergency personnel.

(7) Implementing and operating passenger screening programs for weapons and explosives.

(8) Public awareness campaigns for enhanced over-the-road bus security.

(9) Operating and capital costs associated with over-the-road bus security awareness, preparedness, and response training, including training under section 1184 of this title and training developed by institutions of higher education and by nonprofit employee labor organizations, for over-the-road bus employees, including frontline employees.

(10) Chemical, biological, radiological, or explosive detection, including canine patrols for such detection.

(11) Overtime reimbursement, including reimbursement of State, local, and tribal governments for costs, for enhanced security personnel assigned to duties related to over-the-road bus security during periods of high or severe threat levels, National Special Security Events, or other periods of heightened security as determined by the Secretary.

(12) Live or simulated exercises, including those described in section 1183 of this title.

(13) Operational costs to hire, train, and employ police and security officers, including canine units, assigned to full-time security or counterterrorism duties related to over-the-road bus transportation, including reimbursement of State, local, and tribal government costs for such personnel.

(14) Development of assessments or security plans under section 1181 of this title.

(15) Such other improvements as the Secretary considers appropriate.

(c) Due consideration

In making grants under this section, the Secretary shall prioritize grant funding based on security risks to bus passengers and the ability of a project to reduce, or enhance response to, that risk, and shall not penalize private operators of over-the-road buses that have taken measures to enhance over-the-road bus transportation security prior to September 11, 2001.

(d) Department of Homeland Security responsibilities

In carrying out the responsibilities under subsection (a), the Secretary shall—

(1) determine the requirements for recipients of grants under this section, including application requirements;

(2) select grant recipients;

(3) award the funds authorized by this section based on risk, as identified by the plans required under section 1181 of this title or assessment or plan described in subsection (f)(2); and

(4) pursuant to subsection (c), establish priorities for the use of funds for grant recipients.

(e) Distribution of grants

Not later than 90 days after August 3, 2007, the Secretary and the Secretary of Transportation shall determine the most effective and efficient way to distribute grant funds to the recipients of grants determined by the Secretary under subsection (a). Subject to the determination made by the Secretaries, the Secretary may transfer funds to the Secretary of Transportation for the purposes of disbursing funds to the grant recipient.

(f) Eligibility

(1) A private operator providing transportation by an over-the-road bus is eligible for a grant under this section if the operator has completed a vulnerability assessment and developed a security plan that the Secretary has approved under section 1181 of this title. Grant funds may only be used for permissible uses under subsection (b) to further an over-the-road bus security plan.

(2) Notwithstanding the requirements for eligibility and uses in paragraph (1), prior to the

earlier of 1 year after the date of issuance of final regulations requiring vulnerability assessments and security plans under section 1181 of this title or 3 years after August 3, 2007, the Secretary may award grants under this section for over-the-road bus security improvements listed under subsection (b) based upon over-the-road bus vulnerability assessments and security plans that the Secretary deems are sufficient for the purposes of this section but have not been approved by the Secretary in accordance with section 1181 of this title.

(g) Subject to certain terms and conditions

Except as otherwise specifically provided in this section, a grant made under this section shall be subject to the terms and conditions applicable to subrecipients who provide over-the-road bus transportation under section 5311(f) of title 49 and such other terms and conditions as are determined necessary by the Secretary.

(h) Limitation on uses of funds

A grant made under this section may not be used to make any State or local government cost-sharing contribution under any other Federal law.

(i) Annual reports

Each recipient of a grant under this section shall report annually to the Secretary and on the use of such grant funds.

(j) Consultation

In carrying out this section, the Secretary shall consult with over-the-road bus operators and nonprofit employee labor organizations representing over-the-road bus employees, public safety and law enforcement officials.

(k) Authorization

(1) In general

From the amounts appropriated pursuant to section 114(w) of title 49, there shall be made available to the Secretary to make grants under this section—

(A) $12,000,000 for fiscal year 2008;

(B) $25,000,000 for fiscal year 2009;

(C) $25,000,000 for fiscal year 2010; and

(D) $25,000,000 for fiscal year 2011.

(2) Period of availability

Sums appropriated to carry out this section shall remain available until expended.

(Pub. L. 110–53, title XV, § 1532, Aug. 3, 2007, 121 Stat. 457.)

§ 1183. Over-the-road bus exercises

(a) In general

The Secretary shall establish a program for conducting security exercises for over-the-road bus transportation for the purpose of assessing and improving the capabilities of entities described in subsection (b) to prevent, prepare for, mitigate, respond to, and recover from acts of terrorism.

(b) Covered entities

Entities to be assessed under the program shall include—

(1) Federal, State, and local agencies and tribal governments;

(2) over-the-road bus operators and over-the-road bus terminal owners and operators;

(3) governmental and nongovernmental emergency response providers and law enforcement agencies; and

(4) any other organization or entity that the Secretary determines appropriate.

(c) Requirements

The Secretary shall ensure that the program—

(1) consolidates existing security exercises for over-the-road bus operators and terminals administered by the Department and the Department of Transportation, as jointly determined by the Secretary and the Secretary of Transportation, unless the Secretary waives this consolidation requirement, as appropriate;

(2) consists of exercises that are—

(A) scaled and tailored to the needs of the over-the-road bus operators and terminals, including addressing the needs of the elderly and individuals with disabilities;

(B) live, in the case of the most at-risk facilities to a terrorist attack;

(C) coordinated with appropriate officials;

(D) as realistic as practicable and based on current risk assessments, including credible threats, vulnerabilities, and consequences;

(E) inclusive, as appropriate, of over-the-road bus frontline employees; and

(F) consistent with the National Incident Management System, the National Response Plan, the National Infrastructure Protection Plan, the National Preparedness Guidance, the National Preparedness Goal, and other such national initiatives;

(3) provides that exercises described in paragraph (2) will be—

(A) evaluated by the Secretary against clear and consistent performance measures;

(B) assessed by the Secretary to identify best practices, which shall be shared, as appropriate, with operators providing over-the-road bus transportation, nonprofit employee organizations that represent over-the-road bus employees, Federal, State, local, and tribal officials, governmental and nongovernmental emergency response providers, and law enforcement personnel; and

(C) used to develop recommendations, as appropriate, provided to over-the-road bus operators and terminal owners and operators on remedial action to be taken in response to lessons learned;

(4) allows for proper advanced notification of communities and local governments in which exercises are held, as appropriate; and

(5) assists State, local, and tribal governments and over-the-road bus operators and terminal owners and operators in designing, implementing, and evaluating additional exercises that conform to the requirements of paragraph (2).

(d) National Exercise Program

The Secretary shall ensure that the exercise program developed under subsection (c) is consistent with the National Exercise Program established under section 748 of this title.

(Pub. L. 110–53, title XV, § 1533, Aug. 3, 2007, 121 Stat. 460.)

§1184. Over-the-road bus security training program

(a) In general

Not later than 6 months after August 3, 2007, the Secretary shall develop and issue regulations for an over-the-road bus training program to prepare over-the-road bus frontline employees for potential security threats and conditions. The regulations shall take into consideration any current security training requirements or best practices.

(b) Consultation

The Secretary shall develop regulations under subsection (a) in consultation with—

(1) appropriate law enforcement, fire service, emergency response, security, and terrorism experts;

(2) operators providing over-the-road bus transportation; and

(3) nonprofit employee labor organizations representing over-the-road bus employees and emergency response personnel.

(c) Program elements

The regulations developed under subsection (a) shall require security training programs, to include, at a minimum, elements to address the following, as applicable:

(1) Determination of the seriousness of any occurrence or threat.

(2) Driver and passenger communication and coordination.

(3) Appropriate responses to defend or protect oneself.

(4) Use of personal and other protective equipment.

(5) Evacuation procedures for passengers and over-the-road bus employees, including individuals with disabilities and the elderly.

(6) Psychology, behavior, and methods of terrorists, including observation and analysis.

(7) Training related to psychological responses to terrorist incidents, including the ability to cope with hijacker behavior and passenger responses.

(8) Live situational training exercises regarding various threat conditions, including tunnel evacuation procedures.

(9) Recognition and reporting of dangerous substances, suspicious packages, and situations.

(10) Understanding security incident procedures, including procedures for communicating with emergency response providers and for on-scene interaction with such emergency response providers.

(11) Operation and maintenance of security equipment and systems.

(12) Other security training activities that the Secretary considers appropriate.

(d) Required programs

(1) Development and submission to Secretary

Not later than 90 days after the Secretary issues the regulations under subsection (a), each over-the-road bus operator shall develop a security training program in accordance with such regulations and submit the program to the Secretary for approval.

(2) Approval

Not later than 60 days after receiving a security training program under this subsection, the Secretary shall approve the program or require the over-the-road bus operator that developed the program to make any revisions to the program that the Secretary considers necessary for the program to meet the requirements of the regulations. An over-the-road bus operator shall respond to the Secretary's comments not later than 30 days after receiving them.

(3) Training

Not later than 1 year after the Secretary approves a security training program in accordance with this subsection, the over-the-road bus operator that developed the program shall complete the training of all over-the-road bus frontline employees who were hired by the operator more than 30 days preceding such date. For such employees employed less than 30 days by an operator preceding such date, training shall be completed within the first 60 days of employment.

(4) Updates of regulations and program revisions

The Secretary shall periodically review and update, as appropriate, the training regulations issued under subsection (a) to reflect new or changing security threats. Each over-the-road bus operator shall revise its training program accordingly and provide additional training as necessary to its employees within a reasonable time after the regulations are updated.

(e) National Training Program

The Secretary shall ensure that the training program developed under subsection (a) is a component of the National Training Program established under section 748 of this title.

(f) Reporting requirements

Not later than 2 years after the date of regulation issuance, the Secretary shall review implementation of the training program of a representative sample of over-the-road bus operators and over-the-road bus frontline employees, and report to the appropriate congressional committees of such reviews. The Secretary may submit the report in both classified and redacted formats as necessary.

(Pub. L. 110–53, title XV, §1534, Aug. 3, 2007, 121 Stat. 461.)

§1185. Over-the-road bus security research and development

(a) Establishment of research and development program

The Secretary, acting through the Under Secretary for Science and Technology and the Administrator of the Transportation Security Administration, shall carry out a research and development program for the purpose of improving the security of over-the-road buses.

(b) Eligible projects

The research and development program may include projects—

(1) to reduce the vulnerability of over-the-road buses, stations, terminals, and equipment to explosives and hazardous chemical, biological, and radioactive substances, including the

development of technology to screen passengers in large numbers with minimal interference and disruption;

(2) to test new emergency response and recovery techniques and technologies, including those used at international borders;

(3) to develop improved technologies, including those for—

(A) emergency response training, including training in a tunnel environment, if appropriate; and

(B) security and redundancy for critical communications, electrical power, computer, and over-the-road bus control systems; and

(4) to address other vulnerabilities and risks identified by the Secretary.

(c) Coordination with other research initiatives

The Secretary—

(1) shall ensure that the research and development program is consistent with the other transportation security research and development programs required by this Act;

(2) shall, to the extent practicable, coordinate the research and development activities of the Department with other ongoing research and development security-related initiatives, including research being conducted by—

(A) the Department of Transportation, including University Transportation Centers and other institutes, centers, and simulators funded by the Department of Transportation;

(B) the National Academy of Sciences;

(C) the Technical Support Working Group;

(D) other Federal departments and agencies; and

(E) other Federal and private research laboratories, research entities, and institutions of higher education, including Historically Black Colleges and Universities, Hispanic Serving Institutions, and Indian Tribally Controlled Colleges and Universities;

(3) shall carry out any research and development project authorized by this section through a reimbursable agreement with an appropriate Federal agency, if the agency—

(A) is currently sponsoring a research and development project in a similar area; or

(B) has a unique facility or capability that would be useful in carrying out the project;

(4) may award grants and enter into cooperative agreements, contracts, other transactions, or reimbursable agreements to the entities described in paragraph (2) and eligible recipients under section 1182 of this title; and

(5) shall make reasonable efforts to enter into memoranda of understanding, contracts, grants, cooperative agreements, or other transactions with private operators providing over-the-road bus transportation willing to contribute assets, physical space, and other resources.

(d) Privacy and civil rights and civil liberties issues

(1) Consultation

In carrying out research and development projects under this section, the Secretary shall consult with the Chief Privacy Officer of the Department and the Officer for Civil Rights and Civil Liberties of the Department as appropriate and in accordance with section 142 of this title.

(2) Privacy impact assessments

In accordance with sections 142 and 345 of this title, the Chief Privacy Officer shall conduct privacy impact assessments and the Officer for Civil Rights and Civil Liberties shall conduct reviews, as appropriate, for research and development initiatives developed under this section that the Secretary determines could have an impact on privacy, civil rights, or civil liberties.

(e) Authorization of appropriations

(1) In general

From the amounts appropriated pursuant to section 114(w) of title 49, there shall be made available to the Secretary to carry out this section—

(A) $2,000,000 for fiscal year 2008;

(B) $2,000,000 for fiscal year 2009;

(C) $2,000,000 for fiscal year 2010; and

(D) $2,000,000 for fiscal year 2011.

(2) Period of availability

Such sums shall remain available until expended.

(Pub. L. 110–53, title XV, § 1535, Aug. 3, 2007, 121 Stat. 462.)

REFERENCES IN TEXT

This Act, referred to in subsec. (c)(1), is Pub. L. 110–53, Aug. 3, 2007, 121 Stat. 266, known as the Implementing Recommendations of the 9/11 Commission Act of 2007, which enacted this chapter and enacted and amended numerous other sections and notes in the Code. For complete classification of this Act to the Code, see Short Title of 2007 Amendment note set out under section 101 of this title and Tables.

§ 1186. Memorandum of Understanding annex

Not later than 1 year after August 3, 2007, the Secretary of Transportation and the Secretary shall execute and develop an annex to the Memorandum of Understanding between the two departments signed on September 28, 2004, governing the specific roles, delineations of responsibilities, resources, and commitments of the Department of Transportation and the Department of Homeland Security, respectively, in addressing motor carrier transportation security matters, including over-the-road bus security matters, and shall cover the processes the Departments will follow to promote communications, efficiency, and nonduplication of effort.

(Pub. L. 110–53, title XV, § 1541, Aug. 3, 2007, 121 Stat. 469.)

PART D—HAZARDOUS MATERIAL AND PIPELINE SECURITY

§ 1201. Railroad routing of security-sensitive materials

(a) In general

Not later than 9 months after August 3, 2007, the Secretary of Transportation, in consultation with the Secretary, shall publish a final rule based on the Pipeline and Hazardous Materials Safety Administration's Notice of Proposed Rulemaking published on December 21, 2006, entitled "Hazardous Materials: Enhancing Railroad Transportation Safety and Security for Hazardous Materials Shipments". The final rule shall incorporate the requirements of this section and, as appropriate, public comments received during the comment period of the rulemaking.

(b) Security-sensitive materials commodity data

The Secretary of Transportation shall ensure that the final rule requires each railroad carrier transporting security-sensitive materials in commerce to, no later than 90 days after the end of each calendar year, compile security-sensitive materials commodity data. Such data must be collected by route, line segment, or series of line segments, as aggregated by the railroad carrier. Within the railroad carrier selected route, the commodity data must identify the geographic location of the route and the total number of shipments by the United Nations identification number for the security-sensitive materials.

(c) Railroad transportation route analysis for security-sensitive materials

The Secretary of Transportation shall ensure that the final rule requires each railroad carrier transporting security-sensitive materials in commerce to, for each calendar year, provide a written analysis of the safety and security risks for the transportation routes identified in the security-sensitive materials commodity data collected as required by subsection (b). The safety and security risks present shall be analyzed for the route, railroad facilities, railroad storage facilities, and high-consequence targets along or in proximity to the route.

(d) Alternative route analysis for security-sensitive materials

The Secretary of Transportation shall ensure that the final rule requires each railroad carrier transporting security-sensitive materials in commerce to—

(1) for each calendar year—

(A) identify practicable alternative routes over which the railroad carrier has authority to operate as compared to the current route for such a shipment analyzed under subsection (c); and

(B) perform a safety and security risk assessment of the alternative route for comparison to the route analysis specified in subsection (c);

(2) ensure that the analysis under paragraph (1) includes—

(A) identification of safety and security risks for an alternative route;

(B) comparison of those risks identified under subparagraph (A) to the primary railroad transportation route, including the risk of a catastrophic release from a shipment traveling along the alternate route compared to the primary route;

(C) any remediation or mitigation measures implemented on the primary or alternative route; and

(D) potential economic effects of using an alternative route; and

(3) consider when determining the practicable alternative routes under paragraph (1)(A) the use of interchange agreements with other railroad carriers.

(e) Alternative route selection for security-sensitive materials

The Secretary of Transportation shall ensure that the final rule requires each railroad carrier transporting security-sensitive materials in commerce to use the analysis required by subsections (c) and (d) to select the safest and most secure route to be used in transporting security-sensitive materials.

(f) Review

The Secretary of Transportation shall ensure that the final rule requires each railroad carrier transporting security-sensitive materials in commerce to annually review and select the practicable route posing the least overall safety and security risk in accordance with this section. The railroad carrier must retain in writing all route review and selection decision documentation and restrict the distribution, disclosure, and availability of information contained in the route analysis to appropriate persons. This documentation should include, but is not limited to, comparative analyses, charts, graphics, or railroad system maps.

(g) Retrospective analysis

The Secretary of Transportation shall ensure that the final rule requires each railroad carrier transporting security-sensitive materials in commerce to, not less than once every 3 years, analyze the route selection determinations required under this section. Such an analysis shall include a comprehensive, systemwide review of all operational changes, infrastructure modifications, traffic adjustments, changes in the nature of high-consequence targets located along or in proximity to the route, or other changes affecting the safety and security of the movements of security-sensitive materials that were implemented since the previous analysis was completed.

(h) Consultation

In carrying out subsection (c), railroad carriers transporting security-sensitive materials in commerce shall seek relevant information from State, local, and tribal officials, as appropriate, regarding security risks to high-consequence targets along or in proximity to a route used by a railroad carrier to transport security-sensitive materials.

(i) Definitions

In this section:

(1) The term "route" includes storage facilities and trackage used by railroad cars in transportation in commerce.

(2) The term "high-consequence target" means a property, natural resource, location, area, or other target designated by the Secretary that is a viable terrorist target of national significance, which may include a facility or specific critical infrastructure, the attack of which by railroad could result in—

(A) catastrophic loss of life;

(B) significant damage to national security or defense capabilities; or

(C) national economic harm.

(Pub. L. 110–53, title XV, § 1551, Aug. 3, 2007, 121 Stat. 469.)

§ 1202. Railroad security-sensitive material tracking

(a) Communications

(1) In general

In conjunction with the research and development program established under section 1168 of this title and consistent with the results of research relating to wireless and other tracking technologies, the Secretary, in consultation with the Administrator of the Transportation Security Administration, shall develop a program that will encourage the equipping of railroad cars transporting security-sensitive materials, as defined in section 1151 of this title, with technology that provides—

(A) car position location and tracking capabilities; and

(B) notification of railroad car depressurization, breach, unsafe temperature, or release of hazardous materials, as appropriate.

(2) Coordination

In developing the program required by paragraph (1), the Secretary shall—

(A) consult with the Secretary of Transportation to coordinate the program with any ongoing or planned efforts for railroad car tracking at the Department of Transportation; and

(B) ensure that the program is consistent with recommendations and findings of the Department of Homeland Security's hazardous material railroad tank car tracking pilot programs.

(b) Funding

From the amounts appropriated pursuant to 114(w) of title 49, there shall be made available to the Secretary to carry out this section—

(1) $3,000,000 for fiscal year 2008;

(2) $3,000,000 for fiscal year 2009; and

(3) $3,000,000 for fiscal year 2010.

(Pub. L. 110–53, title XV, § 1552, Aug. 3, 2007, 121 Stat. 471.)

§ 1203. Hazardous materials highway routing

(a) Route plan guidance

Not later than 1 year after August 3, 2007, the Secretary of Transportation, in consultation with the Secretary, shall—

(1) document existing and proposed routes for the transportation of radioactive and nonradioactive hazardous materials by motor carrier, and develop a framework for using a geographic information system-based approach to characterize routes in the national hazardous materials route registry;

(2) assess and characterize existing and proposed routes for the transportation of radioactive and nonradioactive hazardous materials by motor carrier for the purpose of identifying measurable criteria for selecting routes based on safety and security concerns;

(3) analyze current route-related hazardous materials regulations in the United States, Canada, and Mexico to identify cross-border differences and conflicting regulations;

(4) document the safety and security concerns of the public, motor carriers, and State, local, territorial, and tribal governments about the highway routing of hazardous materials;

(5) prepare guidance materials for State officials to assist them in identifying and reducing both safety concerns and security risks when designating highway routes for hazardous materials consistent with the 13 safety-based nonradioactive materials routing criteria and radioactive materials routing criteria in subpart C part 397 of title 49, Code of Federal Regulations;

(6) develop a tool that will enable State officials to examine potential routes for the highway transportation of hazardous materials, assess specific security risks associated with each route, and explore alternative mitigation measures; and

(7) transmit to the appropriate congressional committees a report on the actions taken to fulfill paragraphs (1) through (6) and any recommended changes to the routing requirements for the highway transportation of hazardous materials in part 397 of title 49, Code of Federal Regulations.

(b) Route plans

(1) Assessment

Not later than 1 year after August 3, 2007, the Secretary of Transportation shall complete an assessment of the safety and national security benefits achieved under existing requirements for route plans, in written or electronic format, for explosives and radioactive materials. The assessment shall, at a minimum—

(A) compare the percentage of Department of Transportation recordable incidents and the severity of such incidents for shipments of explosives and radioactive materials for which such route plans are required with the percentage of recordable incidents and the severity of such incidents for shipments of explosives and radioactive materials not subject to such route plans; and

(B) quantify the security and safety benefits, feasibility, and costs of requiring each motor carrier that is required to have a hazardous material safety permit under part 385 of title 49, Code of Federal Regulations, to maintain, follow, and carry such a route plan that meets the requirements of section 397.101 of that title when transporting the type and quantity of hazardous materials described in section 385.403, taking into account the various segments of the motor carrier industry, including tank truck, truckload and less than truckload carriers.

(2) Report

Not later than 1 year after August 3, 2007, the Secretary of Transportation shall submit a report to the appropriate congressional committees containing the findings and conclusions of the assessment.

(c) Requirement

The Secretary shall require motor carriers that have a hazardous material safety permit under part 385 of title 49, Code of Federal Regulations, to maintain, follow, and carry a route plan, in written or electronic format, that meets the requirements of section 397.101 of that title when transporting the type and quantity of hazardous materials described in section 385.403 if the Secretary determines, under the assessment required in subsection (b), that such a requirement would enhance security and safety without imposing unreasonable costs or burdens upon motor carriers.

(Pub. L. 110–53, title XV, § 1553, Aug. 3, 2007, 121 Stat. 472.)

§ 1204. Motor carrier security-sensitive material tracking

(a) Communications

(1) In general

Not later than 6 months after August 3, 2007, consistent with the findings of the Transportation Security Administration's hazardous materials truck security pilot program, the Secretary, through the Administrator of the Transportation Security Administration and in consultation with the Secretary of Transportation, shall develop a program to facilitate the tracking of motor carrier shipments of security-sensitive materials and to equip vehicles used in such shipments with technology that provides—

(A) frequent or continuous communications;

(B) vehicle position location and tracking capabilities; and

(C) a feature that allows a driver of such vehicles to broadcast an emergency distress signal.

(2) Considerations

In developing the program required by paragraph (1), the Secretary shall—

(A) consult with the Secretary of Transportation to coordinate the program with any ongoing or planned efforts for motor carrier or security-sensitive materials tracking at the Department of Transportation;

(B) take into consideration the recommendations and findings of the report on the hazardous material safety and security operational field test released by the Federal Motor Carrier Safety Administration on November 11, 2004; and

(C) evaluate—

(i) any new information related to the costs and benefits of deploying, equipping, and utilizing tracking technology, including portable tracking technology, for motor carriers transporting security-sensitive materials not included in the hazardous material safety and security operational field test report released by the Federal Motor Carrier Safety Administration on November 11, 2004;

(ii) the ability of tracking technology to resist tampering and disabling;

(iii) the capability of tracking technology to collect, display, and store information regarding the movement of shipments of security-sensitive materials by commercial motor vehicles;

(iv) the appropriate range of contact intervals between the tracking technology and a commercial motor vehicle transporting security-sensitive materials;

(v) technology that allows the installation by a motor carrier of concealed electronic devices on commercial motor vehicles that can be activated by law enforcement authorities to disable the vehicle or alert emergency response resources to locate and recover security-sensitive materials in the event of loss or theft of such materials;

(vi) whether installation of the technology described in clause (v) should be incorporated into the program under paragraph (1);

(vii) the costs, benefits, and practicality of such technology described in clause (v) in the context of the overall benefit to national security, including commerce in transportation; and

(viii) other systems and information the Secretary determines appropriate.

(b) Funding

From the amounts appropriated pursuant to section 114(w) of title 49, there shall be made available to the Secretary to carry out this section—

(1) $7,000,000 for fiscal year 2008 of which $3,000,000 may be used for equipment;

(2) $7,000,000 for fiscal year 2009 of which $3,000,000 may be used for equipment; and

(3) $7,000,000 for fiscal year 2010 of which $3,000,000 may be used for equipment.

(c) Report

Not later than 1 year after the issuance of regulations under subsection (a), the Secretary shall issue a report to the appropriate congressional committees on the program developed and evaluation carried out under this section.

(d) Limitation

The Secretary may not mandate the installation or utilization of a technology described under this section without additional congressional authority provided after August 3, 2007.

(Pub. L. 110–53, title XV, § 1554, Aug. 3, 2007, 121 Stat. 473.)

§ 1205. Hazardous materials security inspections and study

(a) In general

The Secretary of Transportation shall consult with the Secretary to limit, to the extent practicable, duplicative reviews of the hazardous materials security plans required under part 172, title 49, Code of Federal Regulations.

(b) Transportation costs study

Within 1 year after August 3, 2007, the Secretary of Transportation, in conjunction with the Secretary, shall study to what extent the insurance, security, and safety costs borne by railroad carriers, motor carriers, pipeline carriers, air carriers, and maritime carriers associated with the transportation of hazardous materials are reflected in the rates paid by offerors of such commodities as compared to the costs and rates, respectively, for the transportation of non-hazardous materials.

(Pub. L. 110–53, title XV, §1555, Aug. 3, 2007, 121 Stat. 475.)

§1206. Use of transportation security card in hazmat licensing

(1) Background check

An individual who has a valid transportation employee identification card issued by the Secretary under section 70105 of title 46 shall be deemed to have met the background records check required under section 5103a of title 49.

(2) State review

Nothing in this section prevents or preempts a State from conducting a criminal records check of an individual that has applied for a license to operate a motor vehicle transporting in commerce a hazardous material.

(Pub. L. 110–53, title XV, §1556(b), Aug. 3, 2007, 121 Stat. 475.)

§1207. Pipeline security inspections and enforcement

(a) In general

Not later than 9 months after August 3, 2007, consistent with the Annex to the Memorandum of Understanding executed on August 9, 2006, between the Department of Transportation and the Department, the Secretary, in consultation with the Secretary of Transportation, shall establish a program for reviewing pipeline operator adoption of recommendations of the September 5, 2002, Department of Transportation Research and Special Programs Administration's Pipeline Security Information Circular, including the review of pipeline security plans and critical facility inspections.

(b) Review and inspection

Not later than 12 months after August 3, 2007, the Secretary and the Secretary of Transportation shall develop and implement a plan for reviewing the pipeline security plans and an inspection of the critical facilities of the 100 most critical pipeline operators covered by the September 5, 2002, circular, where such facilities have not been inspected for security purposes since September 5, 2002, by either the Department or the Department of Transportation.

(c) Compliance review methodology

In reviewing pipeline operator compliance under subsections (a) and (b), risk assessment methodologies shall be used to prioritize risks and to target inspection and enforcement actions to the highest risk pipeline assets.

(d) Regulations

Not later than 18 months after August 3, 2007, the Secretary and the Secretary of Transportation shall develop and transmit to pipeline operators security recommendations for natural gas and hazardous liquid pipelines and pipeline facilities. If the Secretary determines that regulations are appropriate, the Secretary shall consult with the Secretary of Transportation on the extent of risk and appropriate mitigation measures, and the Secretary or the Secretary of Transportation, consistent with the Annex to the Memorandum of Understanding executed on August 9, 2006, shall promulgate such regulations and carry out necessary inspection and enforcement actions. Any regulations shall incorporate the guidance provided to pipeline operators by the September 5, 2002, Department of Transportation Research and Special Programs Administration's Pipeline Security Information Circular and contain additional requirements as necessary based upon the results of the inspections performed under subsection (b). The regulations shall include the imposition of civil penalties for noncompliance.

(e) Funding

From the amounts appropriated pursuant to section 114(w) of title 49, there shall be made available to the Secretary to carry out this section—

(1) $2,000,000 for fiscal year 2008;

(2) $2,000,000 for fiscal year 2009; and

(3) $2,000,000 for fiscal year 2010.

(Pub. L. 110–53, title XV, §1557, Aug. 3, 2007, 121 Stat. 475.)

§1208. Pipeline security and incident recovery plan

(a) In general

The Secretary, in consultation with the Secretary of Transportation and the Administrator of the Pipeline and Hazardous Materials Safety Administration, and in accordance with the Annex to the Memorandum of Understanding executed on August 9, 2006, the National Strategy for Transportation Security, and Homeland Security Presidential Directive–7, shall develop a pipeline security and incident recovery protocols plan. The plan shall include—

(1) for the Government to provide increased security support to the most critical interstate and intrastate natural gas and hazardous liquid transmission pipeline infrastructure and operations as determined under section 1207 of this title when—

(A) under severe security threat levels of alert; or

(B) under specific security threat information relating to such pipeline infrastructure or operations exists; and

(2) an incident recovery protocol plan, developed in conjunction with interstate and intrastate transmission and distribution pipeline operators and terminals and facilities operators connected to pipelines, to develop protocols to ensure the continued transportation of natural gas and hazardous liquids to essential markets and for essential public health or national defense uses in the event of an incident affecting the interstate and intrastate natural gas and hazardous liquid transmission and distribution pipeline system, which shall include protocols for restoring essential services supporting pipelines and granting access to pipeline operators for pipeline infrastructure repair, replacement, or bypass following an incident.

(b) Existing private and public sector efforts

The plan shall take into account actions taken or planned by both private and public entities to address identified pipeline security issues and assess the effective integration of such actions.

(c) Consultation

In developing the plan under subsection (a), the Secretary shall consult with the Secretary of Transportation, interstate and intrastate transmission and distribution pipeline operators, nonprofit employee organizations representing pipeline employees, emergency responders, offerors, State pipeline safety agencies, public safety officials, and other relevant parties.

(d) Report

(1) Contents

Not later than 2 years after August 3, 2007, the Secretary shall transmit to the appropriate congressional committees a report containing the plan required by subsection (a), including an estimate of the private and public sector costs to implement any recommendations.

(2) Format

The Secretary may submit the report in both classified and redacted formats if the Secretary determines that such action is appropriate or necessary.

(Pub. L. 110–53, title XV, §1558, Aug. 3, 2007, 121 Stat. 476.)

CHAPTER 5—BORDER INFRASTRUCTURE AND TECHNOLOGY MODERNIZATION

§ 1401. Definitions

In this chapter:

(1) Commissioner

The term "Commissioner" means the Commissioner of U.S. Customs and Border Protection of the Department of Homeland Security.

(2) Maquiladora

The term "maquiladora" means an entity located in Mexico that assembles and produces goods from imported parts for export to the United States.

(3) Northern border

The term "northern border" means the international border between the United States and Canada.

(4) Secretary

The term "Secretary" means the Secretary of the Department of Homeland Security.

(5) Southern border

The term "southern border" means the international border between the United States and Mexico.

(Pub. L. 110–161, div. E, title VI, §602, Dec. 26, 2007, 121 Stat. 2094.)

SHORT TITLE

Pub. L. 110–161, div. E, title VI, §601, Dec. 26, 2007, 121 Stat. 2094, provided that: "This title [enacting this chapter] may be cited as the 'Border Infrastructure and Technology Modernization Act of 2007'."

§ 1402. Port of Entry Infrastructure Assessment Study

(a) Requirement to update

Not later than January 31 of every other year, the Commissioner, in consultation with the Administrator of General Services shall—

(1) review—

(A) the Port of Entry Infrastructure Assessment Study prepared by the United States Customs Service, the Immigration and Naturalization Service, and the General Services Administration in accordance with the matter relating to the ports of entry infrastructure assessment set forth in the joint explanatory statement on page 67 of conference report 106–319, accompanying Public Law 106–58; and

(B) the nationwide strategy to prioritize and address the infrastructure needs at the land ports of entry prepared by the Department of Homeland Security and the General Services Administration in accordance with the committee recommendations on page 22 of Senate report 108–86, accompanying Public Law 108–90;

(2) update the assessment of the infrastructure needs of all United States land ports of entry; and

(3) submit an updated assessment of land port of entry infrastructure needs to the Committees on Appropriations of the Senate and the House of Representatives, the Senate Committee on Environment and Public Works, the Senate Committee on Homeland Security and Governmental Affairs, the House Committee on Transportation and Infrastructure, and the House Committee on Homeland Security.

(b) Consultation

In preparing the updated studies required under subsection (a), the Commissioner and the Administrator of General Services shall consult with the Director of the Office of Management and Budget, the Secretary, and affected State and local agencies on the northern and southern borders of the United States.

(c) Content

Each updated study required in subsection (a) shall—

(1) identify port of entry infrastructure and technology improvement projects that would enhance border security and facilitate the flow of legitimate commerce if implemented;

(2) include the projects identified in the National Land Border Security Plan required by section 1403 of this title; and

(3) prioritize the projects described in paragraphs (1) and (2) based on the ability of a project—

(A) to enhance the ability of U.S. Customs and Border Protection to achieve its mission and to support operations;

(B) to fulfill security requirements; and

(C) facilitate trade across the borders of the United States.

(d) Project implementation

The Commissioner, as appropriate, shall—

(1) implement the infrastructure and technology improvement projects described in subsection (c) in the order of priority assigned to each project under subsection (c)(3); or

(2) forward the prioritized list of infrastructure and technology improvement projects to the Administrator of General Services for implementation in the order of priority assigned to each project under subsection (c)(3).

(e) Divergence from priorities

The Commissioner may diverge from the priority order if the Commissioner determines that significantly changed circumstances, including immediate security needs, changes in infrastructure in Mexico or Canada, or similar concerns, compellingly alter the need for a project in the United States.

(Pub. L. 110–161, div. E, title VI, § 603, Dec. 26, 2007, 121 Stat. 2094.)

REFERENCES IN TEXT

Public Law 106–58, referred to in subsec. (a)(1)(A), is Pub. L. 106–58, Sept. 29, 1999, 113 Stat. 430, known as the Treasury and General Government Appropriations Act, 2000. For complete classification of this Act to the Code, see Tables.

Public Law 108–90, referred to in subsec. (a)(1)(B), is Pub. L. 108–90, Oct. 1, 2003, 117 Stat. 1137, known as the Department of Homeland Security Appropriations Act, 2004. For complete classification of this Act to the Code, see Tables.

§ 1403. National Land Border Security Plan

(a) Requirement for plan

Not later than January 31 of every other year, the Secretary, acting through the Commissioner, shall prepare a National Land Border Security Plan and submit such plan to the Committees on Appropriations of the Senate and the House of Representatives, the Senate Committee on Environment and Public Works, the Senate Committee on Homeland Security and Governmental Affairs, the Senate Committee on the Judiciary, the House Committee on Transportation and Infrastructure, the House Committee on Homeland Security, and the House Committee on the Judiciary.

(b) Consultation

In preparing the plan required under subsection (a), the Commissioner shall consult with other appropriate Federal agencies, State and local law enforcement agencies, and private entities that are involved in international trade across the northern or southern border.

(c) Vulnerability assessment

(1) In general

The plan required under subsection (a) shall include a vulnerability, risk, and threat assessment of each port of entry located on the northern border or the southern border.

(2) Port security coordinators

The Secretary, acting through the Commissioner, may establish one or more port security coordinators at each port of entry located on the northern border or the southern border—

(A) to assist in conducting a vulnerability assessment at such port; and

(B) to provide other assistance with the preparation of the plan required under subsection (a).

(d) Coordination with the Secure Border Initiative

The plan required under subsection (a) shall include a description of activities undertaken during the previous year as part of the Secure Border Initiative and actions planned for the coming year as part of the Secure Border Initiative.

(Pub. L. 110–161, div. E, title VI, § 604, Dec. 26, 2007, 121 Stat. 2095.)

§ 1404. Port of entry technology demonstration program

(a) Establishment

The Secretary, acting through the Commissioner, shall carry out a technology demonstration program to test and evaluate new port of entry technologies, refine port of entry technologies and operational concepts, and train personnel under realistic conditions.

(b) Technology tested

Under the demonstration program, the Commissioner shall test technologies that enhance port of entry operations, including those related to inspections, communications, port tracking, identification of persons and cargo, sensory devices, personal detection, decision support, and the detection and identification of weapons of mass destruction.

(c) Demonstration sites

(1) Number

The Commissioner shall carry out the demonstration program at not less than three sites and not more than five sites.

(2) Location

Of the sites selected under subsection (c)—

(A) at least one shall be located on the northern border of the United States; and

(B) at least one shall be located on the southern border of the United States.

(3) Selection criteria

To ensure that one of the facilities selected as a port of entry demonstration site for the demonstration program has the most up-to-date design, contains sufficient space to conduct the demonstration program, has a traffic volume low enough to easily incorporate new technologies without interrupting normal processing activity, and can efficiently carry out demonstration and port of entry operations, one port of entry selected as a demonstration site may—

(A) have been established not more than 15 years before December 26, 2007;

(B) consist of not less than 65 acres, with the possibility of expansion onto not less than 25 adjacent acres; and

(C) have serviced an average of not more than 50,000 vehicles per month during the 12 months preceding December 26, 2007.

(d) Relationship with other agencies

The Secretary, acting through the Commissioner, shall permit personnel from appropriate

Federal agencies to utilize a demonstration site described in subsection (c) to test technologies that enhance port of entry operations, including those related to inspections, communications, port tracking, identification of persons and cargo, sensory devices, personal detection, decision support, and the detection and identification of weapons of mass destruction.

(e) Report

(1) Requirement

Not later than 1 year after December 26, 2007, and annually thereafter, the Secretary shall submit to the Committees on Appropriations of the Senate and the House of Representatives, the Senate Committee on Environment and Public Works, the Senate Committee on Homeland Security and Governmental Affairs, the House Committee on Transportation and Infrastructure, and the House Committee on Homeland Security a report on the activities carried out at each demonstration site under the technology demonstration program established under this section.

(2) Content

The report shall include an assessment by the Commissioner of the feasibility of incorporating any demonstrated technology for use throughout U.S. Customs and Border Protection.

(Pub. L. 110–161, div. E, title VI, § 605, Dec. 26, 2007, 121 Stat. 2096.)

§ 1405. Authorization of appropriations

(a) In general

In addition to any funds otherwise available, there are authorized to be appropriated such sums as may be necessary to carry out this chapter for fiscal years 2009 through 2013.

(b) International agreements

Funds authorized to be appropriated under this chapter may be used for the implementation of projects described in the Declaration on Embracing Technology and Cooperation to Promote the Secure and Efficient Flow of People and Commerce across our Shared Border between the United States and Mexico, agreed to March 22, 2002, Monterrey, Mexico (commonly known as the Border Partnership Action Plan) or the Smart Border Declaration between the United States and Canada, agreed to December 12, 2001, Ottawa, Canada that are consistent with the provisions of this chapter.

(Pub. L. 110–161, div. E, title VI, § 606, Dec. 26, 2007, 121 Stat. 2097.)

Made in the USA
Monee, IL
05 November 2026

67810975R00148